Lecture Notes in Computer Sc

Commenced Publication in 1973
Founding and Former Series Editors:
Gerhard Goos, Juris Hartmanis, and Jan van Leeuwen

Editorial Board

Lecture Notes in Computer Science

Liqun Chen   Moti Yung
Liehuang Zhu (Eds.)

Trusted Systems

Third International Conference
INTRUST 2011
Beijing, China, November 27-29, 2011
Revised Selected Papers

 Springer

Volume Editors

Liqun Chen
Hewlett-Packard Laboratories
Long Down Avenue, Stoke Gifford
Bristol, BS34 8QZ Bristol, UK
E-mail: liqun.chen@hp.com

Moti Yung
Columbia University
Computer Science Department
S.W. Mudd Building
New York, NY 10027, USA
E-mail: my123@columbia.edu

Liehuang Zhu
Beijing Institute of Technology
Beijing Key Lab of Intelligent
Information Technology
100081 Beijing, China
E-mail: liehuangz@bit.edu.cn

ISSN 0302-9743   e-ISSN 1611-3349
ISBN 978-3-642-32297-6   e-ISBN 978-3-642-32298-3
DOI 10.1007/978-3-642-32298-3

Springer Heidelberg Dordrecht London New York

Library of Congress Control Number: 2012943158

CR Subject Classification (1998): D.4.6, E.3, K.6.5, C.2, K.4.4, J.1, H.4

LNCS Sublibrary: SL 4 – Security and Cryptology

Typesetting: Camera-ready by author, data conversion by Scientific Publishing Services, Chennai, India

Printed on acid-free paper

Springer is part of Springer Science+Business Media (www.springer.com)

Preface

These proceedings contains the 21 papers presented at the INTRUST 2011 conference, held in Beijing, China, in November 2011. INTRUST 2011 was the third international conference on the theory, technologies, and applications of trusted systems. It was devoted to all aspects of trusted computing systems, including trusted modules, platforms, networks, services, and applications, from their fundamental features and functionalities to design principles, architecture and implementation technologies. The goal of the conference was to bring academic and industrial researchers, designers, and implementers together with end-users of trusted systems, in order to foster the exchange of ideas in this challenging and fruitful area.

INTRUST 2011 built on the successful INTRUST 2009 and INTRUST 2010 conferences, held in Beijing in December 2009 and December 2010, respectively. The proceedings of INTRUST 2009, containing 16 papers, were published in volume 6163 of the *Lecture Notes in Computer Science*. The proceedings of INTRUST 2010, containing 23 papers, were published in volume 6802 of the *Lecture Notes in Computer Science*.

Apart from the 21 contributed papers, the program of INTRUST 2011 also consisted of a workshop, titled "Asian Lounge on Trust, Security and Privacy." The workshop included six keynote speeches from Yanan Hu (Broadband Wireless IP Standard Group and China IWNCOMM Co., Ltd.), Wenbo Mao (Daoli Limited), Graeme Proudler (Hewlett-Packard Laboratories and TCG), Kouichi Sakurai (Kyushu University), Moti Yung (Columbia University and Google), and Huanguo Zhang (Wuhan University). Special thanks are due to these speakers.

The contributed papers were selected from 34 submissions from 18 countries. All submissions were blind-reviewed, i.e., the Program Committee members provided reviews on anonymous submissions. The refereeing process was rigorous, involving on average three (and mostly more) independent reports being prepared for each submission. The individual reviewing phase was followed by profound discussions about the papers, which contributed greatly to the quality of the final selection. A number of accepted papers were shepherded by some Program Committee members in order to make sure the review comments were addressed properly. We are very grateful to our hard-working and distinguished Program Committee for doing such an excellent job in a timely fashion.

For the proceedings the papers have been divided into seven main categories, namely, trusted services, mobile trusted systems, trusted networks, security analysis, cryptographic aspects, implementation, and anonymous direct attestation.

We also want to thank the conference Steering Committee organized by Yongfei Han, the conference General Chairs, Robert Deng, Heyan Huang and Chris Mitchell, the Organizing Chair Liehuang Zhu, and Publicity Chairs, Xuhua Ding, and Lejian Liao, for valuable guidance and assistance and for handling the arrangements in Beijing. Thanks are also due to EasyChair for providing the submission and review webserver and to Guoyong Cheng for maintaining the conference webpage.

On behalf of the conference organization and participants, we would like to express our appreciation to Beijing Institute of Technology, ONETS Wireless & Internet Security Company, Singapore Management University, and the Administrative Committee of Zhongguangcun Haidian Science Park for their generous sponsorship of this event.

We would also like to thank all the authors who submitted their papers to the INTRUST 2011 conference, all external referees, and all the attendees of the conference. Authors of accepted papers are thanked again for revising their papers according to the feedback from the conference participants. The revised versions were not checked by the Program Committee, so authors bear full responsibility for their contents. We thank the staff at Springer for their help with producing the proceedings.

February 2012   Liqun Chen
                                                                  Moti Yung
                                                               Liehuang Zhu

INTRUST 2011

The Third International Conference on Trusted Systems
Beijing, P.R. China
November 27–29, 2011

Sponsored by
Beijing Institute of Technology
ONETS Wireless & Internet Security Company
Singapore Management University
The Administrative Committee of Zhongguangcun Haidian Science Park

General Chairs

Robert Deng   Singapore Management University, Singapore
Heyan Huang   Beijing Institute of Technology, China
Chris Mitchell   Royal Holloway, University of London, UK

Program Chairs

Liqun Chen   Hewlett-Packard Laboratories, UK
Moti Yung   Columbia University and Google Inc., USA
Liehuang Zhu   Beijing Institute of Technology, China

Program Committee

Endre Bangerter   Bern University of Applied Sciences,
     Switzerland
Boris Balacheff   HP Laboratories, UK
Feng Bao   I2R, Singapore
Kefei Chen   Shanghai Jiaotong University, China
Haibo Chen   Fudan University, China
Zhen Chen   Tsinghua University, China
Zhong Chen   Peking University, China
Xuhua Ding   Singapore Management University, Singapore
Kurt Dietrich   Graz University of Technology, Austria
Loïc Duflot   SGDN, France
Dengguo Feng   Chinese Academy of Sciences, China
Dieter Gollmann   Hamburg University of Technology, Germany
David Grawrock   Intel, USA

Steering Committee

Organizing Chair

Liehuang Zhu   Beijing Institute of Technology, China

Publication Chairs

Xuhua Ding   Singapore Management University, Singapore
Lejian Liao   Beijing Institute of Technology, China

External Reviewers

Yuichi Asahiro   Yizhi Ren
Man Ho Au   Thomas Schneider
Andreas Fuchs   Jae Hong Seo
Wei Gao   Isamu Teranishi
Yun Huang   Yasuyuki Tsukada
Tingting Lin   Ronald Tögl
Yu Long   Christian Wachsmann
Yiyuan Luo   Liangliang Wang
Bart Mennink   Laiping Zhao
Mridul Nandi

Table of Contents

Trusted Services

Mobile Trusted Systems

Security Analysis

Cryptographic Aspects

Trusted Networks

Implementation

Direct Anonymous Attestation

A Flexible Software Development and Emulation Framework for ARM TrustZone

Johannes Winter, Paul Wiegele, Martin Pirker, and Ronald Tögl

Institute for Applied Information Processing and Communications
Graz University of Technology
Inffeldgasse 16a, 8010 Graz, Austria
{johannes.winter,martin.pirker,ronald.toegl}@iaik.tugraz.at,
wiegele@student.tugraz.at

Abstract. ARM TrustZone is a hardware isolation mechanism to improve software security. Despite its widespread availability in mobile and
embedded devices, development of software for it has been hampered by
a lack of openly available emulation and development frameworks. In this
paper we provide a comprehensive open-source software environment for
experiments with ARM TrustZone, based on the foundations of the well
known open-source QEMU platform emulator. Our software framework
is complemented by a prototype kernel running within a trusted environment. We validate our software environment with an application example
featuring a software based Trusted Platform Module hosted in a Trust-
Zone protected runtime environment and an Android operating system
accessing it through an high-level, industry-standard Trusted Computing
API.

1 Introduction

One of dominant processor architectures used in current and future mobile and
embedded devices is the ARM architecture. Current ARM-based processor design span a wide range of application fields ranging from tiny embedded devices
(e.g. ARM Cortex-M3) to powerful multi-core systems (e.g. ARM Cortex-A9
MPCore).

Threats, attacks and implementation challenges, which were previously known
only in the x86 desktop and server domain, are already moving on to mobile and
embedded devices. Especially the emerging scenario of highly-connected mobile
clients, interacting with countless remote software-as-a-service entities hosted
in the *Cloud* pose new challenges and threats. In the desktop and server area
Trusted Computing has been proposed as one possible way to improve security
with the help of additional hardware components.

However, on the mobile and embedded market resources are strictly limited
and any solutions requiring additional dedicated security hardware components
are eschewed. Integrated into the CPU core, ARM TrustZone is an emerging
technology to increase security without the need of extra hardware chips. On
the hardware-side TrustZone provides processor and platform extensions to partition the system in two isolated protection domains. This hardware isolation

L. Chen, M. Yung, and L. Zhu (Eds.): INTRUST 2011, LNCS 7222, pp. 1–15, 2012.

mechanism is accompanied by software components creating so called "secure-world" runtime environments bundled with but isolated from "normal world" software stacks (cf. [2]).

Although the introduction of TrustZone has stimulated mobile and embed-ded system security research and development activities, in academia as well as industry, there have been only few attempts of open-source development for ARM's TrustZone technology.

We assume that this apparent lack of interest by the community has two primary causes, which we try to address with this paper: First, there are no easily available general purpose open-source hardware and software platforms with adequate support for ARM TrustZone. In our experience it is quite difficult and costly to acquire suitable development platforms, which allow the developers to access and control *all* aspects of the platform.

Further, publication of technical implementation details, including complete and fully functional source code, often turns out to be rather difficult due to non-disclosure agreements on parts of the hardware platform documentation.

Within the remainder of this paper, especially in section 2, we assume that the reader is somewhat familiar with basic concepts of ARM TrustZone and of the ARM processor architecture in general. We refer to secondary literature, especially to [1], [2] and [3] for in-depth information on these topics.

Contribution. In this paper we address the lack of – up until now – an open-source TrustZone development environment which is suitable for use in academic research and education settings. We contribute a set of open-source software tools which enables experiments with ARM TrustZone, including system-level development of secure-world software, for a wide developer audience.

The core of our tool-chain is a modified version of the QEMU[8] emulator, which has been extended to support simulation of ARM TrustZone enabled processors and platforms. We demonstrate how TrustZone can be employed on this virtual TrustZone platform to partition software into *secure* and *non-secure* worlds. Part of our contribution is a small proof-of-concept secure-world kernel – or secure monitor – providing a runtime environment for secure-world software. With the platform simulator and secure monitor in place, we show how inter-action between the two TrustZone worlds can be implemented. We then extend our development framework to provide a trusted software security module to a managed, platform-independent and Trusted Computing standards-compliant application environment and its developers.

Outline. The remainder of this paper is structured into six major sections. Sec-tion 1 starts with a brief introduction of the main topics discussed in this paper, along with an overview of related work. Section 2 starts with the discussion of an open-source emulator framework for simulating ARM TrustZone enabled proces-sors. We then continue to present a simple secure-world kernel in section 3. Based upon these foundations we discuss a prototype realization of a virtual Android sys-tem featuring an ARM TrustZone protected software-implementation of a Trusted Platform Module (TPM) in section 4. Finally, section 5 concludes the paper.

1.1 Related Work

Several scientific publications deal with proposals for secure mobile and embedded system designs based on the ARM TrustZone security extensions. Use of ARM TrustZone hardware to securely manage and execute small programs ("credentials") were described in [19] and [11]. A similar runtime infrastructure was used by the authors of [12] to implement a mobile trusted platform module. Similarly [22] proposes a trusted runtime environment utilizing Microsoft's .NET Framework inside the TrustZone secure world. With the use of a managed runtime environment the authors try to benefit from the advantages of a high-level language combined with hardware security and isolation mechanisms provided by the underlaying platform.

A large number of publications deal with possible applications of ARM TrustZone to implement, for example, digital rights management [16], cryptographic protocols [25], mobile ticketing [15] or wireless sensor networks [29].

Possible applications of ARM TrustZone in mobile virtualization scenarios have been discussed in [13], [20] and [27]. The authors of [13] and [20] based the system design on the Fiasco L4 micro-kernel. Their system allows secure world L4 tasks to create and interact with normal world operating systems. Another approach based on a modified Linux kernel acting as secure world operating system has been discussed in [27]. Apart from the obvious difference in the operating system architecture both of these prototypes offer comparable functionality with regard to mobile virtualization.

Within this paper we concentrate on a system-level view and on system-level details of ARM TrustZone, which includes aspects that are typically of (too) little interest to high-level application developers. Therefore, we intend to show all levels of software involved to give the full picture of our architecture.

2 Simulating ARM TrustZone Systems with QEMU

QEMU[8] is a machine emulator capable of simulating a number of processor architectures such as ARM, x86, SPARC, MIPS, PowerPC, and many more. Dynamic translation between instruction sets provides for good performance. A range of devices and peripherals can be emulated to offer full software emulation of complex platforms such as servers or smart phones. QEMU is a robust technology and popular choice in industrial-grade deployments. Furthermore, it is free of cost and available to modifications and research as it is provided as open source software.

Support of the ARM instruction set covers large parts of the recent ARMv7 architecture. Yet, the main objective behind the ARM architecture support included in QEMU appears to have been the simulation of application-level code with system-level emulation mostly restricted to the needs of popular ARM Linux kernels. As a consequence, several advanced system-level features, including the ARM security extensions marketed as "TrustZone", are not available in common QEMU distributions.

At the time of this writing, the QEMU branch maintained by the Linaro project[1] contains only several minimal TrustZone support patches contributed by NOKIA employees, which add a very crude emulation of the Secure Monitor Call instruction. Their patch just adds minimal functionality for some specific cache-maintenance operations found on some OMAP3 system-on-chip platforms. We have independently developed a series of patches on top of that QEMU source tree which aim to add more complete support for ARM TrustZone. Our patch series, which is accompanying this paper, can be downloaded at [28] .

In the remainder of this section, after a brief introduction to the basics of the ARM architecture and QEMU's internals, we discuss the implementation challenges, details and current limitations of our TrustZone implementation for QEMU.

2.1   The ARM Programmer's Model, a Short Overview

ARM CPUs are a family of 32-bit/64-bit RISC processors developed by ARM Holdings. The ARM instruction set has a width of 32 bits to ease decoding and pipelining, while a second set, called Thumb, provides increased code density. ARM processors support different modes of execution, which can be divided into two classes, privileged and unprivileged. The ARMv7 core supports 8 modes of operation: Secure Monitor, Supervisor, Fast Interrupt, Interrupt Request, Abort, Undefined, System and User. The idea behind the variety of modes is to reflect the processor's current task. Transition between states are triggered by special instructions or internal or external events. Most of the time the processor will be executing code in user mode. Operational modes like Fast Interrupt and Interrupt Request are often used to handle real-time events. Abort or Undefined are used to recover from memory access violations or instructions fetching errors. Of special interest is Secure Monitor mode, which serves as a gatekeeper between the secure and non-secure world (see Section 2.3).

The ARMv7 processor has a total of 37 32-bit wide registers. Regardless of the current processor mode, 15 general purpose registers (r0, r1, ... r14) and the program counter (r15) are always visible. Depending on the mode of execution, registers are shared among different modes or restricted to particular modes (banked registers).

The Current Program Status Register (CPSR) holds information on the current mode of execution and condition code flags. The condition code flags are influenced by arithmetic and logical operations. These flags are heavily exploited by the ARM architecture to achieve conditional execution of instructions in order to decrease code size and increase speed. TrustZone adds a Secure Configuration Register (SCR) for system security state control.

2.2   Exploring QEMU's Internals

Bellard discussed the internal details of a previous version of QEMU in [8]. Since this publication a significant evolution of the QEMU source code has taken place.

---

[1] http://www.linaro.org/

Nevertheless the overall program structure discussed in Bellard's paper remains largely valid. We restrict our summary of QEMU to the details relevant to this paper and outline the differences to the older ([8]) version where appropriate.

Dynamic Translation. The design of QEMU's processor emulation is centered around a dynamic translation of binary code targeted at a specific processor model. This translator is responsible for decoding the emulated CPU's instruction stream and for rewriting the decoded instructions into translation blocks (TBs) containing functionally equivalent instruction sequences for the host CPU. In case of simple instructions, like register moves or arithmetics, the dynamic translator is often able to directly generate equivalent host CPU instructions that do not rely on any external functions. Complex instructions, including memory access or most co-processor operations, are translated into (slower) calls to processor architecture specific helper functions.

Current versions of QEMU include the *Tiny Code Generator (TCG)* library, which decouples the target processor specific binary translators from most details of the host processor architecture. The code generator library's set of micro-operation primitives for intermediate representation is interpreted by target specific translator front-ends. When building translation blocks the tiny code generator library performs a series of optimizations, like dead variable elimination, which are intended to boost emulation performance.

Caching of Translation Blocks. QEMU maintains a cache of the most recently translated blocks to curb the relatively high costs of binary translation. This translation block cache is indexed by the physical address of the target memory space. Self-modifying code requires special handling in order to maintain correctness of the translation blocks (see [8] for details).

Specifically to the ARM architecture, the binary translator needs to pay special attention to certain load and store instructions. Currently the ARM binary translator encodes the processor mode (kernel- vs. user-mode) directly as constant value into the generated translation blocks. If no precautions were taken, this could lead to unintended cache aliasing effects, causing invalid simulation results, if the same physical memory location were executed from both user- and kernel-mode code.

Memory Management Unit. All system emulation targets supported by QEMU share a common software MMU framework to implement virtual memory and to provide a generic MMU translation caching mechanism. Simulated memory load and store operations consider the MMU translation cache first and only fall-back to a target specific page table walk if no cached translation can be found[2].

This software MMU cache is organized as a two-level structure with indexing by i) MMU mode and ii) the virtual memory address. Conceptually, these

---

[2] In this sense QEMU's caching mechanism behaves like the Translation Look-aside Buffers (TLBs) found on ARM processors.

MMU modes are cached views of virtual memory translations, with the active view depending on the current processor state. Due to this mechanism it is not necessary to flush all cached MMU translations when changing the processor state – instead, it is sufficient to have all simulated load and store instructions use the proper MMU mode.

The default ARM target utilizes two MMU modes to represent the different virtual memory views for unprivileged modes (MMU_USER_IDX) and by privileged modes (MMU_KERNEL_IDX). All simulated standard load and store instructions use the currently active processor mode as indicated by the simulated CPSR register to select the correct MMU mode and translation cache. Special unprivileged load and store instructions[3] directly select the unprivileged MMU mode. This solution is sufficient to simulate ARM systems which do not support TrustZone or which only use one of the two worlds supported by the TrustZone architecture.

2.3   Secure and Normal World Memory

With ARM's TrustZone security extensions, the physical ARM processor can be thought of as a virtual dual-processor system containing a "secure" and a "non-secure" virtual processor core (cf. [26]). Both virtual processor cores support the full set of privileged and non-privileged processor modes defined for the ARM architecture. On the secure world side, Secure monitor mode has been introduced to allow proper interfacing between the two TrustZone worlds.

We recall from section 2.2 that the ARM MMU emulation found in the standard QEMU versions uses two MMU modes to maintain separate translation caches for privileged processor modes and unprivileged processor modes. If we want to provide support for ARM TrustZone systems we need to investigate how QEMU's current approach to virtual memory system emulation can be extended in a consistent and minimally intrusive manner. We initially considered not to change QEMU's virtual memory system emulation as well as the ARM binary translator at all. In order to make this approach viable it would be necessary to perform a full flush of all cached MMU translations whenever a switch between normal and secure world takes place. While this operation can be quite costly, there would be the advantage that only a small number of mutually isolated section in the emulator would have to be patched. In particular virtually no changes would be necessary to the relatively complex binary translator code.

We discarded this naive approach, when realizing that QEMU's way of handling MMU modes perfectly matches the TrustZone concept of a "four-quadrant" world partitioned into secure kernel-, secure user-, normal kernel- and normal-user space. We started by adding two new MMU modes representing non-secure privileged (MMU_NS_KERNEL_IDX) and unprivileged modes (MMU_NS_USER_IDX) to the existing ARM MMU emulation. We then extended the ARM architecture specific code for handling translation tables to reflect the current processor security state during translation table walks. It also proved to be necessary to slightly adapt the ARM binary translator to consider the processor security state and MMU modes.

---

[3] e.g. LDRT and STRT

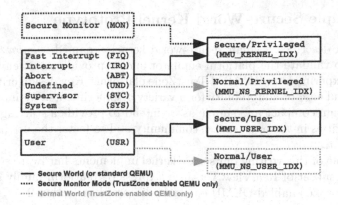

Fig. 1. Processor modes, security states and corresponding QEMU MMU modes

Figure 1 depicts the relationships between ARM processor modes, processor security states and the four MMU modes present in our implementation. Solid black lines indicate the interaction between secure-world and the secure-world MMU modes. These relations are identical to the standard QEMU version without TrustZone support. Dotted gray lines show the newly added relations between normal-world and the two new normal world MMU modes. Secure monitor mode is shown as a special case (dotted black lines) introduced on TrustZone-aware systems.

Simulating Memory Access Restrictions. The MMU emulation described above is sufficient to run simple well-behaved software that does not attempt to break the hardware-enforced memory isolation barriers introduced by TrustZone. In order to simulate properly enforced HW-based access restrictions to platform memory and peripherals it is necessary to augment the MMU with access checks. This is done in two fundamental building blocks of the TrustZone architecture, the Address Space Controller [6] and the TrustZone Protection Controller [5], which we add both as simplified models to our simulator.

Both of these peripherals allow partitioning of the platform memories and peripherals into a secure and a non-secure world domain. The TrustZone Protection Controller is conceptually the simpler device and allows a single memory region as well as peripherals to be marked as either exclusive secure world resources or as shared resources. The TrustZone Address Space controller provides a superset of this functionality by means of fine-grained and region-oriented access control to parts of the platform's physical address space.

We prototyped a common simulation framework for both of these devices based on the capabilities of the more powerful address space controller. Our implementation hooks into the QEMU's MMU helper routines and triggers an additional check against the TrustZone memory access restrictions after performing a normal MMU address translation. Using this mechanism we are able to model memory access restrictions accurately at the expense of slightly decreased simulation performance.

3   A Simple Secure-World Kernel Prototype

This section describes a small secure-world kernel – named *"umonitor"* – we developed to validate the platform emulator and to provide a test environment for further experiments with ARM TrustZone platforms. Key design criteria were simplicity and ease-of-adaptability for a variety of experiments. We intentionally keep the design compact and simple as we intend to provide a starting point for further activities in the open source community and to foster the use in research and education.

At the time of this writing our secure kernel implements hardware support for a functional subset of RealView Versatile Express [7] platform family simulated by the TrustZone enabled QEMU emulator discussed in section 2.

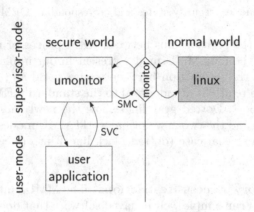

Fig. 2. Components of a typical "umonitor" based system

Figure 2 outlines the overall structure and the components of a prototype system based on the *umonitor* kernel. The two left quadrants represent kernel and user-space of the secure-world.

3.1   Handling Normal and Secure-World Interaction

A main task of a secure kernel in an ARM TrustZone system is to provide an efficient and effective interface for communication between secure-world and normal-world.

To switch between normal and secure-world in TrustZone architecture, it is possible to directly manipulate the *non-secure bit* of the secure configuration register within the secure privileged processor mode, or to trap external data abort exceptions to certain system memory areas. Finally, there is a "canonical" method to gracefully enter secure monitor mode from either secure-world or non-secure-world by means of the *secure monitor call* (SMC) processor instruction.

Our prototype uses this canonical approach to provide a system-call style interface for use by the secure as well as the non-secure-world. This convention enables us to perform all manipulations of the non-secure bit in only a small number of isolated places with well-defined call chains inside the secure kernel source code.

Still, handling secure monitor mode exceptions requires a number of special considerations. Secure monitor mode exception handlers, like that for the SMC, can be entered from either non-secure or secure world. When dispatching to a secure monitor mode exception handler, the ARM processor switches to secure monitor mode which in turn causes the system to enter a secure state[4].

Note that the non-secure bit (SCR.NS) of the secure configuration register is *not* automatically cleared upon entry to the exception handler as this bit serves a twofold purpose in secure monitor mode: First it allows exception handlers to distinguish invocations from secure and from non-secure-world. Second the SCR.NS controls the active system register bank which is manipulated by the MCR and MRC instructions used for co-processor and MMU access.

```
...
__msr_smc:
  SRSDB sp!, #MON_MODE
  STMFD sp!, {r0-r12}        // Save register context

  MRC   p15, 0, r0, c1, c1, 0  // Read SCR
  STMFD sp!, {r0}            // Save old SCR value
  TST   r0, #SCR_NS
  BICNE r0, r0, #SCR_NS      // Clear SCR.NS bit
  MCRNE p15, 0, r0, c1, c1, 0  // Write SCR

  MOV   r0, sp
  BL    monitor_smc_entry    // Call upper-level C handler

  LDMFD sp!, {r0}            // Read save value of SCR
  TST   r0, #SCR_NS
  MCRNE p15, 0, r0, c1, c1, 0  // Restore old SCR value

  LDMFD sp!, {r0-r12}        // Load register context
  RFEIA sp!                  // Return from exception
...
```

Fig. 3. Secure monitor call low-level exception handler

This behavior of the non-secure bit requires additional steps when a secure monitor mode exception handler decides to leave secure monitor mode. Clearing the non-secure bit ensures that we do not end up in a non-secure system state when switching away from secure monitor mode. Furthermore it might be necessary to preserve the values of the banked ARM core registers (like stack pointers and link register) for the "entry" world and to restore the corresponding registers of the "exit" world when the exception handler finishes execution.

Within our prototype secure kernel we attempted to keep handling of secure monitor mode events as simple as possible. The low-level assembly implementation of the secure monitor call exception handler is outlined in figure 3. Saving the ARM core registers r0-r12 and the current value of the secure configuration

---

[4] As a consequence the processor uses the secure banked system registers independent of the SCR.NS bit value.

register upon entry are the only steps performed by this low-level handler. Afterwards the low-level handler ensures that the secure-bit is cleared and invokes an upper-level handler routine called `monitor_smc_entry` which is implemented in C. At this point the CPU is still in secure monitor mode.

Within the upper-level handler we can now identify the calling world and the reason of the secure monitor call. Entering the low-level handler from normal world always triggers a switch to secure-world and invokes the required context save and context restore code needed to complete the world switch. When entering the low-level handler from secure-world we use register `r12` to mimic a system call number; we only switch to normal world if the appropriate call number and arguments are given.

3.2   Runtime Environment for Secure User-Space Applications

User-space applications need a facility to delegate operations to an authorized domain. These operations require elevated privileges not available within user-mode. In normal-world this facility would be a standard system call to the operating system kernel. Low-level details of system call interfaces, like parameter passing rules or the supported syscall numbers, are highly dependent on the operating system and are in general incompatible between different operating systems.

When designing the environment for secure-world user-space applications we faced the challenge to select a simple system call interface which ideally should be supported across different compiler tool-chains and C run-time libraries. We decided to settle with the interface used by ARM semihosting for reasons explained below.

ARM Semihosting. ARM semihosting [4] is a mechanism that is used during development of software for a bare-metal ARM target. At this early stage there is usually no operating system available to offer even basic console input/output capabilities or a filesystem.

Semihosting allows such bare-metal ARM targets to utilize basic operating system services without an actual operating system. The manual of the ARM compiler tool-chain [4] defines a basic system call interface to be exposed by a semihosting capable environment.

A typical ARM semihosting call is triggered by a supervisor call instruction with special immediate value (e.g. `SVC #0x123456`). A debug monitor residing on the platform or a JTAG-emulator hooked up to the platform intercepts these supervisor call instructions and inspects their immediate value. The debug monitor handles the call as a semihosting request, if the immediate value matches a magic value. Otherwise the supervisor call will be forwarded to the target application.

Compilers targeting bare-metal environments provide special run-time libraries which do not rely on any kind of operating system. Functions which require operating system support are typically either emulated using semihosting facilities or are provided as stub versions which always fail.

Bouncing Semihosting Calls to the Platform Simulator. QEMU implements basic support for ARM semihosting[5], which turned out to be very helpful during development of the *umonitor* kernel. In particular, QEMU only recognizes supervisor calls as semihosting calls if they are performed from within a privileged processor mode[6]. Semicalls triggered by user-mode are handled like any other normal SVC instruction.

We observe that this behavior can be used to trivially (and insecurely) provide a complete semihosting interface to secure-world user-space by simply reissuing – or bouncing – the supervisor calls within the kernel's supervisor call handler.

Therefore, within our framework, we are able to build non-trivial secure-world application software.

4   Experiment: A Trusted Mobile Application Development Framework

The security and privacy of mobile applications can be greatly improved by building upon hardware based roots-of-trust which help create resilience against software-based attacks. Yet, developers face a number of practical challenges when attempting to create a co-design of hardware and software. Hardware resources in terms of memory, CPU performance, power and even physical size and weight allowance are limited while the market dictates designs with minimal costs. Adding additional hardware security components is therefore hard to justify. Implementation and test of accessible, user-oriented Apps and services using security hardware tends to become a complex endeavor, as testing and debugging becomes more time consuming with security devices designed to hide their internal states and key materials. In our experience it is difficult and expensive to acquire ARM TrustZone development kits in the first place and academic discourse on implementation details and experimental results tends to be hampered by legal obstacles such as non-disclosure agreements on parts of the documentation.

A practically usable software development environment for ARM TrustZone should allow to implement and test security-enabled, yet platform independent applications in software; this frees developers of the need to design for a specific piece of hardware only, that is difficult to get hold of and equally difficult to talk about.

We now demonstrate how the TrustZone emulation introduced in sections 2 and 3 can act as the technological basis for a software development framework for trusted mobile applications.

We base our normal world environment on the popular Android [14] mobile platform, commonly used in modern smart-phones. Based on a Linux kernel, it offers a broad application library framework and the Dalvik virtual machine with

---

[5] See `arm-semi.c` in the QEMU source tree for details.

[6] The intrigued reader is referred to the source comments in QEMU's `target-arm/helper.c` for more details.

just-in-time compilation for code written in the Java language. The managed environments helps application developers to program in a platform-independent manner. It currently lacks integration and support for strong roots-of-trust, which are not available on most platforms anyway.

To overcome similar restrictions on desktop and server PCs, the Trusted Platform Module (TPM) [24] was introduced as an add-on device offering roots-of-trust for storage, reporting and identity with privacy protection [10,21] mechanisms. TrustZone enables us to offer similar services even without additional hardware elements. To this end, we run IBM's TPM [18] open source emulator in the secure world of our emulation framework. Cryptographic mechanisms are software implementations using the OpenSSL library, yet the code is is well isolated from the normal world. This architecture suggests a level of security comparable with dedicated security co-processors.

Communication between both worlds is provided by a simple Linux kernel driver that exposes a `/dev/tpm` style interface to the normal world user-space TCG core services. In the Android environment we need to assemble and parse TPM command structures, perform the necessary, but not security critical management of resources, and follow the authentication and integrity protecting protocols of the TPM. To this end, we have adapted IAIK's jTSS [17], which is a full Java implementation of the TCG Software Stack specification for the TPM. This setup already provides full TPM functionality, still, like any TSS-based technology, it comes with a complex API that requires substantial efforts of familiarization from implementors before it can be used in projects with agile and user-oriented development processes.

A novel high-level API and official Java industry standard aiming to overcome these limitations is Java Specification Request 321 (JSR321) [23]. It provides a simple interface for access to commonly used TPM functionality in a fully object-oriented manner that hides low-level details and provides the level of abstraction Java and Android developers expect. We therefore integrate IAIK's implementation[7] of JSR321 with our framework to provide a fully platform-independent abstraction of security services to software developers. In related work, experimental TPM-integration into normal world Android was previously demonstrated by [9] to simulate attestation services; our framework adds actual hardware security mechanism simulation and provides the more advanced JSR321 programming interface.

5   Conclusion

Our aim was to demonstrate that software development for ARM TrustZone platforms is feasible with open-source tools. To prove this statement we first introduced an open-source platform emulation tool, based on the well-known QEMU platform emulator, which is capable of simulating system-level details of ARM TrustZone platforms.

---

[7] `http://jsr321.java.net/`

Based on the open-source platform emulator we discussed a small experimental secure-world kernel which provides a basic C run-time environment as well as normal world interaction facilities for application running in secure-world userspace. This allows to construct and simulate complex software configurations, which include typical secure and normal world components found on a Trust-Zone platform. On the higher layers, our framework allows the development of modern, user-friendly Android applications which make use of well-established security mechanisms. Developing trusted applications is aided through the reliance on publicly available open source components and software debugging features. In addition, we offer a high-level, platform independent and standard-complying programming interface to provide an object-oriented API that hides low-level details and provides the level of abstraction Java and Android developers expect.

We hope that our open source framework will foster research and development of trusted mobile applications.

Acknowledgements. The authors thank the anonymous reviewers for their very helpful comments. This work has been supported in part by the European Commission through the FP7 programme under contract 257433 SEPIA.

References

1. Alves, T., Felton, D.: TrustZone: Integrated Hardware and Software Security - Enabling Trusted Computing in Embedded Systems (July 2004),
   http://www.arm.com/pdfs/TZ_Whitepaper.pdf
2. ARM Limited: ARM TrustZone API Specification, Version 3.0 (2009), ARM PRD29-USGC-000089 3.1
3. ARM Limited: ARM Architecture Reference Manual, ARMv7-A and ARMv7-R edition, Errata Markup (2010), ARM DDI 0406B_errata_2010_Q3
4. ARM Ltd.: ARM compiler toolchain,
   http://infocenter.arm.com/help/
   topic/com.arm.doc.dui0471c/DUI0471C_developing_for_arm_processors.pdf
5. ARM Ltd.: PrimeCell Infrastructure AMBA 3 TrustZone Protection Controller (BP147), Introduction online at:
   http://infocenter.arm.com/help/topic/com.arm.doc.dto0015a/
   DTO0015_primecell_infrastructure_amba3_tzpc_bp147_to.pdf
6. ARM Ltd.: TrustZone Address Space Controller (TZC-380), Introduction online at: http://infocenter.arm.com/help/topic/com.arm.doc.ddi0431b/
   DDI0431B_tzasc_tzc380_r0p0_trm.pdf
7. ARM Ltd.: Versatile Express Product Family (2011), Information online at:
   http://www.arm.com/products/tools/development-boards/
   versatile-express/index.php
8. Bellard, F.: QEMU, a fast and portable dynamic translator. In: Proceedings of the Annual Conference on USENIX Annual Technical Conference, ATEC 2005, p. 41. USENIX Association, Berkeley (2005),
   http://dl.acm.org/citation.cfm?id=1247360.1247401

9. Bente, I., Dreo, G., Hellmann, B., Heuser, S., Vieweg, J., von Helden, J., Westhuis, J.: Towards Permission-Based Attestation for the Android Platform - (Short Paper). In: McCune, J.M., Balacheff, B., Perrig, A., Sadeghi, A.-R., Sasse, A., Beres, Y. (eds.) Trust 2011. LNCS, vol. 6740, pp. 108–115. Springer, Heidelberg (2011), http://dx.doi.org/10.1007/978-3-642-21599-5_8

10. Brickell, E., Camenisch, J., Chen, L.: Direct anonymous attestation. In: Proceedings of the 11th ACM Conference on Computer and Communications Security, pp. 132–145. ACM, Washington DC (2004)

11. Ekberg, J.E., Asokan, N., Kostiainen, K., Rantala, A.: Scheduling execution of credentials in constrained secure environments. In: Proceedings of the 3rd ACM Workshop on Scalable Trusted Computing, STC 2008, pp. 61–70. ACM, New York (2008), http://doi.acm.org/10.1145/1456455.1456465

12. Ekberg, J.E., Bugiel, S.: Trust in a small package: minimized MRTM software implementation for mobile secure environments. In: Proceedings of the 2009 ACM Workshop on Scalable Trusted Computing, STC 2009, pp. 9–18. ACM, New York (2009), http://doi.acm.org/10.1145/1655108.1655111

13. Frenzel, T., Lackorzynski, A., Warg, A., Härtig, H.: ARM TrustZone as a Virtualization Technique in Embedded Systems. In: Twelfth Real-Time Linux Workshop (October 2010)

14. Google Inc.: Android OS (2011), http://www.android.com/

15. Hussin, W.H.W., Coulton, P., Edwards, R.: Mobile Ticketing System Employing TrustZone Technology. In: Proceedings of the International Conference on Mobile Business, pp. 651–654. IEEE Computer Society, Washington, DC (2005), http://dl.acm.org/citation.cfm?id=1084013.1084282

16. Hussin, W.H.W., Edwards, R., Coulton, P.: E-Pass Using DRM in Symbian v8 OS and TrustZone: Securing Vital Data on Mobile Devices. In: International Conference on Mobile Business, p. 14 (2006)

17. IAIK: Trusted Computing for the Java(tm) Platform (2011), http://trustedjava.sourceforge.net/

18. IBM: IBM's Software Trusted Platform Module, http://sourceforge.net/projects/ibmswtpm/

19. Kostiainen, K., Ekberg, J.E., Asokan, N., Rantala, A.: On-board credentials with open provisioning. In: Proceedings of the 4th International Symposium on Information, Computer, and Communications Security, ASIACCS 2009, pp. 104–115. ACM, New York (2009), http://doi.acm.org/10.1145/1533057.1533074

20. Lackorzynski, A., Frenzel, T., Roitzsch, M.: D2.6 First Initial Proof of Concept for Trust-Enhanced Virtualisation System (June 23, 2009), http://www.tecom-project.eu/downloads/deliverables2009/TECOM-D02.6-First-initial-proof-of-concept-for-trust-enhanced-virtualization-system.pdf

21. Pirker, M., Toegl, R., Hein, D., Danner, P.: A PrivacyCA for Anonymity and Trust. In: Chen, L., Mitchell, C.J., Martin, A. (eds.) Trust 2009. LNCS, vol. 5471, pp. 101–119. Springer, Heidelberg (2009)

22. Santos, N., Raj, H., Saroiu, S., Wolman, A.: Trusted Language Runtime (TLR): Enabling Trusted Applications on Smartphones (2011)

23. Toegl, R., Winkler, T., Nauman, M., Hong, T.W.: Specification and Standardization of a Java Trusted Computing API. Softw. Pract. Exper. (2011), http://dx.doi.org/10.1002/spe.1095

24. Trusted Computing Group: TCG TPM Specification Version 1.2 (2011), https://www.trustedcomputinggroup.org/developers/

25. Wachsmann, C., Chen, L., Dietrich, K., Löhr, H., Sadeghi, A.-R., Winter, J.: Lightweight Anonymous Authentication with TLS and DAA for Embedded Mobile Devices. In: Burmester, M., Tsudik, G., Magliveras, S., Ilić, I. (eds.) ISC 2010. LNCS, vol. 6531, pp. 84–98. Springer, Heidelberg (2011), http://dx.doi.org/10.1007/978-3-642-18178-8_8
26. Wilson, P., Frey, A., Mihm, T., Kershaw, D., Alves, T.: Implementing Embedded Security on Dual-Virtual-CPU Systems. IEEE Design and Test of Computers 24(6), 582–591 (2007)
27. Winter, J.: Trusted computing building blocks for embedded linux-based ARM trustzone platforms. In: Proceedings of the 3rd ACM Workshop on Scalable Trusted Computing, STC 2008, pp. 21–30. ACM, New York (2008), http://doi.acm.org/10.1145/1456455.1456460
28. Winter, J., Wiegele, P., Lipp, M., Niederl, A., et al.: Experimental version of QEMU with basic support for ARM TrustZone (source code repository) (July 28, 2011), Public GIT repository at: https://github.com/jowinter/qemu-trustzone
29. Yussoff, Y.M., Hashim, H.: Trusted Wireless Sensor Node Platform. In: Ao, S.I., Gelman, L., Hukins, D.W., Hunter, A., Korsunsky, A.M. (eds.) Proceedings of the World Congress on Engineering, WCE 2010, London, U.K., June 30-July 2. Lecture Notes in Engineering and Computer Science, vol. I, pp. 774–779. International Association of Engineers, Newswood Limited (2010)

Building General Purpose Security Services on Trusted Computing[*]

Chunhua Chen[1,**], Chris J. Mitchell[2], and Shaohua Tang[1,***]

[1] School of Computer Science and Engineering
South China University of Technology
Guangzhou 510640, China
chen.chunhua@mail.scut.edu.cn, csshtang@scut.edu.cn
[2] Information Security Group
Royal Holloway, University of London
Egham, Surrey TW20 0EX, UK
c.mitchell@rhul.ac.uk

Abstract. The Generic Authentication Architecture (GAA) is a standardised extension to the mobile telephony security infrastructures (including the Universal Mobile Telecommunications System (UMTS) authentication infrastructure) that supports the provision of generic security services to network applications. In this paper we propose one possible means for extending the widespread Trusted Computing security infrastructure using a GAA-like framework. This enables an existing security infrastructure to be used as the basis of a general-purpose authenticated key establishment service in a simple and uniform way, and also provides an opportunity for trusted computing aware third parties to provide novel security services. We also discuss trust issues and possible applications of GAA services.

Keywords: Generic Authentication Architecture, Trusted Computing, security service.

1 Introduction

Almost any large scale network security system requires the establishment of some kind of a security infrastructure. For example, if network authentication or authenticated key establishment is required, then the communicating parties typically need access to a shared secret key or certificates for each other's public keys.

---

[*] This work was partially sponsored by the Natural Science Foundation of Guangdong Province, China (No. 9351064101000003) and the Science and Technology Project of Guangzhou, China (No. 2011J4300028).

[**] The author is a PhD student at the South China University of Technology. This work was performed during a visit to the Information Security Group at Royal Holloway, University of London, sponsored by the Chinese Scholarship Council.

[***] The author is the corresponding author, and sponsored by the Guangdong Province Universities and Colleges Pearl River Scholar Funded Scheme (2011).

L. Chen, M. Yung, and L. Zhu (Eds.): INTRUST 2011, LNCS 7222, pp. 16–31, 2012.
© Springer-Verlag Berlin Heidelberg 2012

Setting up a new security infrastructure for a significant number of clients is by no means a trivial task. For example, establishing a public key infrastructure (PKI) for a large number of users involves setting up a secure certification authority (CA), getting every user to securely generate a key pair, securely registering every user and corresponding public key, and securely generating and distributing public key certificates. In addition, the ongoing management overhead is non-trivial, covering issues such as revocation and key update.

At the same time, there are a number of existing security infrastructures, in some cases with almost ubiquitous coverage. When deploying a new network security protocol it is therefore tempting to try to exploit one of these existing security infrastructures to avoid the need for the potentially costly roll-out of a new infrastructure.

This is by no means a new idea (see, for example, [9]). However, previous proposals have been application-specific. We instead propose the use of a general framework which enables almost any pre-existing infrastructure to be used as the basis for the provision of generic security services.

Of particular (and motivating) importance to our work is the Generic Authentication Architecture (GAA) [1]. This architecture has been designed to enable the Universal Mobile Telecommunications System (UMTS) authentication infrastructure to be exploited for the provision of security services. Building on previous work [4], we propose the adoption of the architecture used by UMTS GAA to enable a wide range of other pre-existing infrastructures to be similarly exploited. One security infrastructure of particular interest is the emerging Trusted Computing (TC) infrastructure, including the Trusted Platform Modules (TPMs) present in a significant proportion of all new Personal Computers (PCs).

We first generalise the concepts and procedures of GAA. We then consider how this generalised notion can be supported by the trusted computing security infrastructure. We refer to this combination as TC GAA. We also discuss related trust issues and consider possible applications of GAA services.

The remainder of this paper is organised as follows. In section 2 we introduce our generalised version of GAA, and also briefly describe the standardised version building on the UMTS authentication infrastructure. In section 3 we give details of TC GAA, building on a general Trusted Computing security infrastructure. This is followed by a description of an instantiation of TC GAA using TPMs in section 4. In section 5 we provide an informal security analysis. We discuss related trust issues and possible applications of GAA services in section 6. In section 7 we draw conclusions.

2   Generic Authentication Architecture

We start by describing our generalised version of the GAA architecture, introducing the main roles in the framework, the goals and rationales, and the two main procedures. This generalised GAA architecture was first described in [4]. We follow this by briefly describing the standardised implementations of GAA as supported by the UMTS authentication infrastructure.

2.1   Overview of GAA

As shown in Figure 1, the following entities play a role in the GAA architecture.

- The *Bootstrapping Server Function* (BSF) *server B* acts as a Trusted Third Party (TTP), and is assumed to have the means to access credentials belonging to a pre-existing security infrastructure. B uses the pre-established credentials to provide authenticated key establishment services to *GAA-enabled user platforms* and *GAA-aware application servers*.
- A *GAA-aware application server S* is assumed to have the means to establish a mutually authenticated and confidential secure channel with B, and an arrangement to access the security services provided by B. The means by which the secure channel between B and S is established is outside the scope of the GAA framework. In the GAA context, the functionality of a *GAA-aware application server* is also referred to as the *Network Application Function* (NAF) *server*. We use the terms application server and NAF server interchangeably throughout.
- A *GAA-enabled user platform P* is assumed to be equipped with credentials belonging to the pre-existing security infrastructure. P possesses a BSF client C_B, which uses the platform credentials to interact with B to provide authenticated key establishment services. P also possesses a NAF client C_S that accesses services provided by S. C_S interacts with C_B to obtain the cryptographic keys necessary to provide client-server security services.

The user platform and the BSF server need to interact with the pre-existing security infrastructure, whereas the application server does not (it only needs to interact with the BSF server and the user platform). Also, the user platform and the application server do not need to have a pre-existing security relationship.

GAA provides a general purpose key establishment service for user platforms and application servers. As described below, GAA uses a two-level key hierarchy, consisting of a master session key and server- and application-specific session keys. The master session key is established using the pre-existing security infrastructure, and is not used directly to secure GAA-based applications. Instead it is used to generate the server/application-specific session keys using a *key diversification* function. By choosing a function with appropriate properties, it can be arranged that knowledge of a server/application specific session key will not reveal any information about the master session key or any other server/application-specific keys.

2.2   GAA Procedures

As we now describe, GAA incorporates two main procedures: *GAA bootstrapping* and *Use of bootstrapped keys*.

GAA bootstrapping uses the pre-existing security infrastructure to set up a shared master key MK between P and B. Also established is a Bootstrapping Transaction Identifier *B-TID* for MK and the lifetime of this key. *B-TID* must

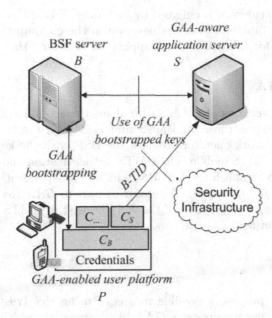

GAA-aware
application server

BSF server
B   S

Use of GAA
bootstrapped keys

GAA
bootstrapping   B-TID

Security
Infrastructure

C... C_S

C_B

Credentials

GAA-enabled user platform
P

Fig. 1. GAA framework

consist of a (statistically) unique value which can identify an instance of *GAA bootstrapping* as well as B's network domain name.

The *Use of bootstrapped keys* procedure establishes a server/application-specific session key SK between P and S, using the master key MK shared by P and B. The procedure operates in the following way. P first derives a session key SK as:

$$SK = \text{KDF}(MK, NAF\text{-}Id, \text{other values})$$

where KDF is a one-way *key diversification* function, and *NAF-Id* is an application-specific value consisting of the Fully Qualified Domain Name (FQDN) of S and the identifier of the underlying application protocol. Other values may be included in the key derivation computation depending on the nature of the underlying security infrastructure. P (strictly, C_S) then starts the application protocol by sending a request containing *B-TID* to S. S submits the received *B-TID* and its own identifier *NAF-Id* to B to request the session key SK. Note that *B-TID* contains B's network domain name, so S knows where to send the request. As stated above, we require that S and B have the means to establish a mutually authenticated and confidential secure channel, and hence B can verify S against its FQDN. If S is authorised, B derives SK from the MK identified by *B-TID*, and sends SK, its lifetime, and other relevant information to S via the secure channel. P and S now share SK, which they can use to secure application-specific messages.

Note that *key separation* is enforced by including *NAF-Id* as an input to the *key diversification* function. Other values used in the computation of *SK* could include identifiers for the GAA bootstrapping instance and the user platform.

2.3   UMTS GAA

The standardised versions of GAA [1] build on the mobile authentication infrastructures (including those for UMTS and GSM). In the UMTS version of GAA, a UMTS network operator provides the BSF with the key *MK*, and the user platform is a UMTS mobile. The UMTS authentication and key agreement protocol is used to establish the key *MK*, which is independently generated by the user platform and the network operator as part of *GAA bootstrapping*. The identifier *B-TID* is a combination of the *RAND* used in UMTS authentication and the BSF's identifier.

3   TC GAA

In this section we propose a possible means of using the Trusted Computing security infrastructure to support a GAA-like framework, which we refer to as TC GAA. We start by giving a high-level description of the Trusted Computing security infrastructure, without referring to any specific trusted computing technology. We then specify the operation of TC GAA as built on this general infrastructure. A specific instantiation of TC GAA using the features of a TCG-compliant TPM is described in the next section.

Note that a very brief sketch of a possible TC GAA implementation has previously been described [4]. By contrast, in this paper we give detailed descriptions of instantiations of TC GAA, and provide an analysis of its security properties.

3.1   Trusted Computing Security Infrastructure

A fundamental notion in Trusted Computing (TC) is the Trusted Platform (TP). According to Balacheff et al. [2]: "A trusted platform (TP) is defined as a computing platform that has a trusted component, which is used to create a foundation of trust for software processes". We refer to such a trusted component as a Trusted Module (TM). A TM encompasses all the platform functionalities and data areas within a TP that must be trusted, if the platform is to be trusted. Gallery [5] identifies a minimum set of trusted TM features. In practice, a trusted computing technology might make use of a range of mechanisms to meet these requirements.

Listed below (following Gallery [5]) are the features that a TM must possess in order to support our general instantiation of TC GAA.

– The TM is a self-contained processing module containing specialist capabilities, including random number generation, asymmetric key generation, digital signing, encryption/decryption and hashing.

- The TM contains shielded locations, data stored in which (e.g. TM-generated keys) is protected against interference or snooping and is only accessible to the specified capabilities.
- The TM is equipped with a unique asymmetric encryption key pair at the time of (or soon after) manufacture. The private decryption key is stored securely in the TM-shielded location and is never exported from the TM. A certificate for the associated public key, containing a general description of the TM and its security properties, is generated by a CA.
- The TM is capable of generating asymmetric signature key pairs. The TM can, by some means, obtain certificates for the public keys of such key pairs from a CA. The private signature keys are securely held by the TM.
- The TM is capable of generating asymmetric encryption key pairs. The TM can generate certificates for the public keys of these key pairs using the signature keys described above. The private decryption keys are securely held by the TM.

Note that information said to be held securely by the TM may actually be stored externally to the TM, encrypted using a key known only to the TM.

A TM will typically possess a range of other security-related features, not directly used by TC GAA. Some of these features could be used to enhance the trustworthiness of the TC GAA application software running on the TP. In particular, platform integrity measurement, storage and reporting services could be used to provide assurance regarding the software state of the platform.

Trusted Computing makes use of public key cryptography, and realising its full potential requires a supporting PKI. We use the term Trusted Computing security infrastructure to refer to the set of deployed TMs, the associated keys, and the supporting PKIs. Trusted computing technology can be implemented in a variety of computing platforms, including PCs (e.g. laptops) and mobile devices (e.g. mobile phones). In this paper we focus on PC-based TPs.

3.2   The TC GAA Architecture

As shown in Figure 2, the following Trusted Computing specific entities play a role in TC GAA.

- The supporting PKIs. We assume that all relevant certificates are obtainable by the entities involved.
- The *GAA-enabled user platform P* is a Trusted Platform containing a Trusted Module M, as defined in section 3.1. We assume that M has already generated a signature key pair, and has obtained a certificate Cert$_M$ for the public key of this key pair from a CA, where Cert$_M$ binds an identity of M (Id$_M$) to the public key (where M may have many such identities). The private signing key is available only to M (we assume it is stored externally to M, encrypted using a key known only to M). The BSF client, C_B, implements the authentication and key establishment protocol which forms part of the *TC GAA bootstrapping* procedure specified below.

– The BSF server B has a signature key pair and a certificate Cert$_B$ for the public key of this key pair. This key pair is used for entity authentication.

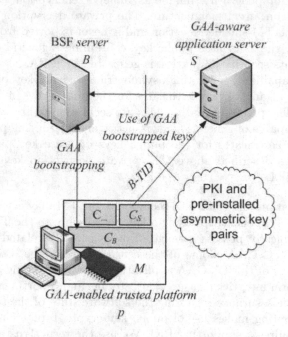

Fig. 2. TC GAA framework

In practice, M might be equipped with multiple certified signature key pairs. We assume that the certified signature key pair specified above is used for *TC GAA bootstrapping*, and is used for multiple instances of the protocol. Typically this involves M, in conjunction with C_B, obtaining such a key pair via a separate configuration procedure prior to the *TC GAA bootstrapping* procedure. Thus C_B knows which signature key pair is to be used in *TC GAA bootstrapping*.

3.3   The TC GAA Procedures

In this section we specify the *TC GAA bootstrapping* and the *TC GAA Use of bootstrapped keys* procedures, which use the general Trusted Computing security infrastructure defined in section 3.1. The authentication and key establishment protocol which forms part of *TC GAA bootstrapping* is motivated by the protocol defined in Gallery and Tomlinson [6]. Table 1 summarises the notation used in the remainder of this paper.

Table 1. Notation

P	a GAA-enabled trusted platform
M	a trusted module embedded in P
I	integrity metrics that reflect a certain state of P
B	a BSF server
C_B	a BSF client residing in P
S	a GAA-aware application server
CA	a Certification Authority trusted by all entities
Cert_X	a certificate for entity X's signature public key
Id_X	an identity of entity X
R_X	a random number issued by entity X
M_{pub}	a TM-generated temporary public encryption key
M_{pri}	a TM-generated temporary private decryption key corresponding to M_{pub}
$E_{M_{pub}}(Z)$	the result of the asymmetric encryption of data Z using the public key M_{pub}
H	a one-way hash function
$S_X(Z)$	the digital signature of data Z computed using entity X's private signature transformation
$X\|Y$	the concatenation of data items X and Y in that order

The TC GAA *bootstrapping* protocol involves the following sequence of steps, where $X \rightarrow Y : Z$ is used to indicate that message Z is sent by entity X to entity Y.

1. $C_B \rightarrow B$: request to bootstrap a master session key MK.
2. B: generates and caches a random value R_B.
3. $B \rightarrow C_B$: R_B.
4. $C_B \rightarrow M$: request to generate a random number.
5. $M \rightarrow C_B$: R_M.
6. $C_B \rightarrow M$: request to load M's private signature key.
   (Note that M's private signing key must be loaded into M before use because it is stored externally to M.)
7. M: loads M's private signing key.
8. $M \rightarrow C_B$: the handle of the loaded private signing key.
9. $C_B \rightarrow M$: request generation of an asymmetric encryption key pair (M_{pub}, M_{pri}), and association of M_{pri} with a specified protected environment state of P.
10. M: generates (M_{pub}, M_{pri}), where M_{pri} is bound to the specified protected environment state.
11. $M \rightarrow C_B$: (M_{pub}, M_{pri}), where M_{pri} is encrypted using a key available only to M.

12. $C_B \rightarrow M$: request to generate a certificate for M_{pub} in association with R_M, R_B, Id_B and I.

    (Id_B is B's network domain name. The integrity metrics I reflect both the state of the protected environment when the key pair (M_{pub}, M_{pri}) was generated and the state required for use of the newly generated M_{pri}.)

13. M: signs a data string including M_{pub}, R_M, R_B, Id_B and I using its private signing key to obtain: $S_M(R_M||R_B||Id_B||M_{pub}||I)$.

14. $M \rightarrow C_B$: $M_{pub}||I||S_M(R_M||R_B||Id_B||M_{pub}||I)$.

15. $C_B \rightarrow B$: $\text{Cert}_M||Id_M||R_M||R_B||Id_B||M_{pub}||I||S_M(R_M||R_B||Id_B||M_{pub}||I)$.

16. B: retrieves Cert_M and verifies it.

    B: verifies $S_M(R_M||R_B||Id_B||M_{pub}||I)$.

    B: verifies R_B to ensure that the message is fresh.

    B: verifies Id_B to ensure that the message is intended for it.

    B: verifies that I indicates that C_B is executing as expected, i.e. that it has not been tampered with.

17. Assuming that the signature from M verifies correctly, the value of R_B is fresh, the value of Id_B is as expected, and the integrity metrics I are acceptable, then

    B: generates a master session key MK, sets the lifetime of MK according to B's local policies, and generates an identifier B-TID for MK consisting of R_M, R_B and B's network domain name.

18. B: caches B-TID, MK, lifetime of MK, R_M, R_B, and Id_M.

19. $B \rightarrow C_B$: $\text{Cert}_B||B\text{-}TID||\text{lifetime of } MK||R_B||R_M||Id_M||E_{M_{pub}}(MK)|| S_B(R_B||R_M||Id_M||E_{M_{pub}}(MK))$.

20. C_B: retrieves Cert_B and verifies it.

    C_B: verifies $S_B(R_B||R_M||Id_M||E_{M_{pub}}(MK))$

    C_B: verifies R_M to ensure that the message is fresh.

    C_B: verifies Id_M to ensure that the message is intended for it.

21. Assuming that the signature from B verifies correctly, the value of R_M is fresh, and the value of Id_M is as expected, then:

    $C_B \rightarrow M$: request to load the encrypted key M_{pri}.

22. M: loads the encrypted key M_{pri}.

23. $M \rightarrow C_B$: the handle of the loaded M_{pri}.

24. $C_B \rightarrow M$: request to decrypt $E_{M_{pub}}(MK)$ using M_{pri}.

25. M: decrypts $E_{M_{pub}}(MK)$ and deletes M_{pri}.

26. $M \rightarrow C_B$: MK.

27. C_B: caches B-TID, MK, lifetime of MK, R_M, R_B, and Id_M.

28. C_B: deletes the part-encrypted key pair (M_{pub}, M_{pri}).

After successful execution of the above protocol, B and C_B share a new set of bootstrapped credentials, including random challenges R_M and R_B, M's identity Id_M, and a master session key MK together with its identifier B-TID and lifetime. We assume that these bootstrapped credentials are held securely by C_B by some means (e.g. encrypted and integrity protected by M).

Verifying the trustworthiness of P's software environment is not necessary in order to complete authenticated key establishment, which is, of course, the main goal of the *TC GAA bootstrapping* protocol. If B does not need to verify the trustworthiness of P's software environment at the time of protocol execution, a fresh encryption key pair (M_{pub}, M_{pri}) does not need to be generated for every instance of the bootstrap procedure. Instead M could generate a encryption key pair (without associating it with a specified protected environment state) in advance of the protocol, and use it multiple times. When bootstrapping, M would load the public key of this encryption key pair and use its private signing key to generate a certificate for this public key that includes the nonces for the current session (i.e. R_M and R_B).

In the *TC GAA use of bootstrapped keys* procedure, C_S and S follow the procedure defined in section 2.2 to establish a server/application-specific session key SK. The session key SK is derived as follows:

$$SK = \text{KDF}(MK, R_M, R_B, Id_M, NAF\text{-}Id).$$

4   Building TC GAA Using the TCG Specifications

The generic version of TC GAA described above could be implemented using a range of technologies, including a platform constructed in accordance with the specifications of the Trusted Computing Group (TCG). In this section we specify an instantiation using TPMs as defined in the version 2.1 of the Trusted Computing Group (TCG) specifications [11–13].

4.1   The TCG Specifications

A TCG-compliant TPM meets the requirements for the TM identified in section 3.1. Gallery [5] describes the TPM features. In this section we map the necessary features for a TM identified section 3.1 onto a TPM.

- The TPM is a secure module which contains protected capabilities and shielded locations. The protected capabilities include all the functionalities required for TC GAA, as well as other capabilities such as a SHA-1 engine, a HMAC engine, and a monotonic counter. When implemented as a hardware chip, the TPM must be inextricably bound to its host platform.
- The TPM is equipped with a unique Endorsement Key (EK) pair, an RSA encryption key pair, at the time of (or soon after) manufacture. The private decryption key is stored in a TPM-shielded location and is never exported from the TPM. An endorsement credential (a certificate for the public key of this EK key pair) is signed by a CA (as provided by a Trusted Platform Module Entity (TPME)). The endorsement credential, in conjunction with its associated conformance credential and platform credential, describes the security properties of the TPM and its host platform.
- The TPM is capable of generating Attestation Identity Keys (AIKs), which are RSA signature key pairs. A certificate Cert_{TPM} for the public key of an AIK key pair can be obtained in two ways: using a privacy CA, and using Direct Anonymous Attestation [3]. The associated private key is securely held by the TPM. The TPM can use an AIK to certify other TPM-generated keys.

- The TPM is capable of generating asymmetric encryption key pairs on demand, which can be migratable or non-migratable. For the purposes of TC GAA, we assume that non-migratable keys are used. The private key of a TPM-generated encryption key pair is securely held by the TPM. A certificate for the encryption public key can be generated by the TPM using an AIK.
- Integrity measurement, storage and reporting are supported. Measuring events on a platform is a two-stage process that begins with appending a hash of the event (e.g. the launch of an application) being measured to the content of one of a number of internal registers (known as Platform Configuration Registers (PCRs)). The hash of the resulting string is written back to the PCR concerned. The other part of the process involves recording details of the event in the Stored Measurement Log (SML) file. The values of the PCRs identify the current platform state. When a challenger wishes to verify a trusted platform's integrity, it requests (a portion) of the platform's SML, together with a TPM-generated signature (generated using an AIK) on a subset of PCR values that describe the desired portion of the platform's operating state.

4.2   TC GAA Procedures Using a TPM

A trusted platform which contains a TCG-compliant TPM M can play the role of the *GAA-enabled user platform P*. M must possess an AIK pair, which plays the role of the signature key pair used in the *TC GAA bootstrapping* protocol. A certificate Cert_M is required to bind an identity of M (Id_M) to the public key of the AIK. We suppose that the private signing key is stored externally to M, encrypted using a key available only to M.

We now describe a means of using the version 1.2 TCG TPM data structures [12] and command set [13] to implement the *TC GAA bootstrapping* protocol defined in section 3.3. The data structures involved include TPM_NONCE, TPM_KEY_HANDLE, TPM_KEY and TPM_CERTIFY_INFO. The TPM commands involved include TPM-CreateWrapKey, TPM_GetRandom, TPM_LoadKey, TPM-CertifyKey and TPM-UnBind.

During protocol execution, C_B calls the TPM_GetRandom command to request M to generate a random value R_M (step 4). M returns R_M in a TPM_NONCE data structure (step 5). C_B then calls the TPM_LoadKey command, requesting M to load a private signing key (step 6). M returns the handle of the loaded key in a TPM_KEY_HANDLE data structure (step 8). C_B next invokes the TPM-CreateWrapKey command, requesting M to generate an encryption key pair (M_{pub}, M_{pri}) (step 9). The TPM-CreateWrapKey command arguments include an unwrapped TPM_KEY data structure and a parent wrapping key. The unwrapped TPM_KEY specifies information about the key pair to be created, such as the key size (e.g. 1024 bits), the key usage (i.e. TPM_KEY_BIND), and the key flag (i.e. non-migratable); it also specifies the platform state at the time the key pair is created (referred to as digestAtCreation) and the platform state required for use of the generated private key (referred to as digestAtRelease).

M returns a wrapped TPM_KEY data structure (step 11). The wrapped TPM_KEY contains M_{pub}, the encrypted M_{pri} (encrypted using the parent wrapping key), a value indicating that the key pair is non-migratable, and a value indicating that the key pair can only be used for TPM-Bind and TPM-UnBind operations. The wrapped TPM_KEY also identifies the PCRs whose values are bound to M_{pri}, the PCR digests at the time of key pair creation, and the PCR digests required for M_{pri} use. The PCR data included in the wrapped TPM_KEY maps to the integrity metrics I in the generic protocol.

M is then requested to sign M_{pub} and I in conjunction with external data R_M, R_B and Id_B (step 12). This involves a call to the TPM-CertifyKey command, which takes arguments that include the public key of the TPM-generated key pair to be certified (i.e. a wrapped TPM_KEY) and a private signature key (i.e. M's private signing key). A hash of R_M, R_B and Id_B is also input as 160 bits of externally supplied data. In response, M returns a TPM_CERTIFY_INFO data structure and a signature on TPM_CERTIFY_INFO (step 14). The string TPM_CERTIFY_INFO contains (a description of) the public key that has been certified, the 160 bits of externally supplied data, a hash of the certified public key, and the PCR data in use.

B needs to encrypt MK so that it can be decrypted by M (step 19). B calls the Tspi_Data_Bind command ([10], p. 363), which takes a data block to be encrypted (i.e. MK) and a public encryption key (i.e. M_{pub}) as arguments and returns an encrypted MK (i.e. $E_{M_{pub}}(MK)$).

Assuming that the response from B is correct, C_B requests M to load the encrypted key M_{pri} (step 21), and then calls the TPM-UnBind command to decrypt $E_{M_{pub}}(MK)$ (step 24). M outputs the master key MK to C_B (step 26).

We now summarise the *TC GAA bootstrapping* protocol using the version 1.2 TCG TPM commands and data structures.

1. $C_B \rightarrow B$: request to bootstrap a master session key MK.
2. B: generates and caches a random value R_B.
3. $B \rightarrow C_B$: R_B.
4. $C_B \rightarrow M$: TPM_GetRandom.
5. $M \rightarrow C_B$: TPM_NONCE (containing R_M).
6. $C_B \rightarrow M$: TPM_LoadKey (M's private signing key).
7. M: loads M's private signing key.
8. $M \rightarrow C_B$: TPM_HANDLE (containing the handle of M's private signing key).
9. $C_B \rightarrow M$: TPM-CreateWrapKey (an unwrapped TPM_KEY, the handle of the loaded parent wrapping key).
10. M: generates (M_{pub}, M_{pri}), where M_{pri} is bound to a specified protected environment state.
11. $M \rightarrow C_B$: a wrapped TPM_KEY.
12. $C_B \rightarrow M$: TPM-CertifyKey (the wrapped TPM_KEY, $H(R_M\|R_B\|\mathrm{Id}_B)$). (Note that the PCR data included in TPM_KEY maps to the integrity metrics I).

13. M: generates TPM_CERTIFY_INFO data structure, and signs it.
14. $M \to C_B$: TPM_CERTIFY_INFO$||S_M(H(R_M||R_B||\mathrm{Id}_B)||H(M_{pub})||I)$.
    (We represent the signature on TPM_CERTIFY_INFO generated by M in simplified form as $S_M(H(R_M||R_B||\mathrm{Id}_B)||H(M_{pub})||I)$.)
15. $C_B \to B$: Cert$_M||\mathrm{Id}_M||R_M||R_B||\mathrm{Id}_B||TPM_Key||$SMLData
    TPM_Certify_Info$||$ $S_M(H(R_M||R_B||\mathrm{Id}_B)||H(M_{pub})||I)$.
16. B: verifies Cert$_M$, the received signature, R_B, Id$_B$ and I, as described in section 3.3.
    (B uses the SML data received in step 15 to recompute I for verification. If B does not want to verify the trustworthiness of P's software environment, the SML data does not need to be sent.)
17. Assuming that the signature from M verifies correctly, the values of R_B and Id$_B$ are as expected, and the integrity metrics I are acceptable, then:
    B: Generates a symmetric session key MK, sets the lifetime of MK according to B's local policies, and generates an identifier B-TID for MK consisting of R_{TPM}, R_{BSF} and B's network domain name.
18. B: caches B-TID, MK, lifetime of MK, R_M, R_B and Id$_M$.
19. $B \to C_B$: Cert$_B||B$-$TID||$lifetime of $MK||R_B||R_M||\mathrm{Id}_M||E_{M_{pub}}(MK)||$
    $S_B(R_B||R_M||\mathrm{Id}_M||E_{M_{pub}}(MK))$.
20. C_B: verifies Cert$_B$, the received signature, R_M and Id$_M$, as described in section 3.3.
21. Assuming that the signature from B verifies correctly, the value of R_M is fresh, and the value of Id$_M$ is as expected, then:
    $C_B \to M$: TPM_LoadKey (the encrypted key M_{pri}).
22. M: loads the encrypted key M_{pri}.
23. $M \to C_B$: KEY_HANDLE (containing the handle of M_{pri}).
24. $C_B \to M$: TPM-UnBind ($E_{M_{pub}}(MK)$, the handle of the loaded key M_{pri}).
25. M: decrypts $E_{M_{pub}}(MK)$ and deletes M_{pri}.
26. $M \to C_B$: MK.
27. C_B: caches B-TID, MK, lifetime of MK, R_M, R_B and Id$_m$.
28. C_B: deletes the part-encrypted key pair (M_{pub}, M_{pri}).

5   Informal Security Analysis

We now provide an informal security analysis of the authentication and key establishment protocol used by the *TC GAA bootstrapping* protocol in section 3.3 (including steps 3, 15 and 19). We consider a threat model in which an attacker $\mathcal{A}$ is able to observe and make arbitrary modifications to messages exchanged between B and P, including replaying and blocking messages as well as inserting completely spurious messages. This allows a trivial denial of service attack which cannot be prevented. Note that $\mathcal{A}$ is not allowed to compromise the implementations of B and P; such attacks on system integrity cannot be prevent by the key establishment process, and are thus not addressed by the schemes we propose.

1. *Entity authentication.* The protocol provides mutual authentication between B and M using digital signature techniques. B can verify the identity of the M (Id_M); that is, the signature of M on R_B and Id_B allows B to authenticate M (step 15). Similarly, M can authenticate B by verifying the signature of B on R_M and Id_M (step 19). Step 3, 15 and 19 of the protocol conform to the three pass unilateral authentication protocol mechanism described in clause 5.2.2 of ISO/IEC 9798-3:1998 [8], in which the values R_B and R_M, generated by B and M respectively, serve as the nonces.

2. *Confidentiality of the master session key MK.* The signature of M on M_{pub} allows B to verify that M generated the key pair (M_{pub}, M_{pri}) (step 15). MK is generated by B, and is encrypted using the TM-generated temporary public key M_{pub} before being sent to M (step 19). The corresponding private key M_{pri} is securely held by M, and is only useable when the protected platform is in a particular trusted state. Hence, $\mathcal{A}$ cannot access to MK under the assumed threat model.

3. *Origin authentication.* R_B, R_M, Id_B, Id_M, M_{pub} and $E_{M_{pub}}(MK)$ are signed by B and M (steps 15 and 19), and thus both parties can verify the origin of the received message. The signatures also provide integrity protection.

4. *Freshness.* R_B, generated by B, is included in the signed bundle sent to B in step 15; similarly R_M, generated by M, is included in the signed bundle sent to C_B in step 19. Hence, $\mathcal{A}$ cannot later replay the messages to either entity.

5. *Key confirmation.* Upon receipt of the message in step 19, C_B can be sure that B has generated the MK within the current session by verifying the signature of B on R_M, Id_M and $E_{M_{pub}}(MK)$. However, C_B does not confirm the receipt of MK to B. Note that $\mathcal{A}$ can block all the messages exchanged, and network errors might occur, and hence only C_B can be sure that it shares a fresh MK with B (until successful use of the key by P).

6. *Key control.* The protocol is an authentication and key transport protocol. B generates the master session key MK, and hence B has key control.

6   Using the GAA Framework

We now discuss trust issues and possible applications of the GAA services.

6.1   Trust Issues

The nature of the GAA architecture means that the end users implicitly trust the provider of the BSF service. This means that the entity providing this service needs to be selected with care, and it may also mean that the service may not be appropriate for every application. Nevertheless, in the non-electronic world, trusted third parties are relied on for a huge range of services, some very sensitive, and hence this does not appear to be a fundamental obstacle. In addition, if security sensitivity justifies the additional cost, multiple BSF services could be accessed simultaneously, thereby distributing the necessary trust.

6.2 Applications

A wide range of applications for UMTS GAA have been explored — see, for example, Holtmanns et al. [7]. Any other scheme providing a GAA service such as the system described here can support very similar applications.

In ongoing work we are examining ways in which a range of variants of the GAA service can be used to support one time passwords [4]. The schemes enable an *GAA enabled user platform* (e.g. a mobile phone or a trusted commodity computer) to act as a one-time password generator. If a user registers with an application server (establishing a *username* and *password*, a human-memorable weak secret), one-time passwords can be generated as a function of on-demand GAA bootstrapped application-specific keys and the shared password. A prototype of one of the schemes (*Ubipass*[1], which makes use of UMTS GAA services) has been developed in collaboration with the Nokia Research Center in Helsinki. We are currently studying its usability and performance. The same OTP generation protocol (the *OTP agreement* protocol in *Ubipass*) could also be built using the TC GAA service. *Ubipass* provides an Internet one-time password solution which could be deployed to enable the provision of ubiquitous one-time password services for a large class of users.

7 Conclusions

GAA is a framework that enables pre-existing security infrastructures to be used to provide general purpose security services, such as key establishment. We have shown how GAA services can be built on the Trusted Computing security infrastructure, complementing the previously standardised GAA schemes built on the mobile phone infrastructures. The solution described in section 3.3 has been designed to apply to a range of trusted computing technologies. We have also provided an instantiation of this solution as supported by the TCG specifications.

TC GAA provides a way of exploiting the now very widespread trusted computing infrastructure (as supported by PC-based trusted platforms) for the provision of fundamentally important generic security services. Of course, application-specific security protocols building on the infrastructure can be devised independently of any generic service and, indeed, there is a large and growing literature on such schemes. However, the definition of a standard GAA-based security service enables the trusted computing infrastructure to be exploited in a simple and uniform way, and it also provides an opportunity for trusted computing aware third parties to provide novel security services. This may help with providing the business case necessary for the emergence of the wide range of third party security services necessary to fully realise the goals of trusted computing.

References

1. 3rd Generation Partnership Project (3GPP): Technical Specification Group Services and Systems Aspects, Generic Authentication Architecture (GAA), Generic Bootstrapping Architecture, Technical Specification TS 33.220, Version 9.2.0 (2009)

---

[1] http://ubipass.research.isg.rhul.ac.uk/

2. Balacheff, B., Chen, L., Pearson, S., Plaquin, D., Proundler, G.: Trusted Computing Platforms: TCPA Technology in Context. Prentice Hall (2003)
3. Brickell, E.F., Camenisch, J., Chen, L.: Direct anonymous attestation. In: Atluri, V., Pfitzmann, B., McDaniel, P.D. (eds.) Proceedings of the 11th ACM Conference on Computer and Communications Security, CCS 2004, Washingtion, DC, USA, October 25-29, pp. 132–145. ACM (2004)
4. Chunhua, C., Mitchell, C., Shaohua, T.: Ubiquitous One-Time Password Service Using the Generic Authentication Architecture. Mobile Networks and Applications, http://rd.springer.com/article/10.1007/s11036-011-0329-z
5. Gallery, E.: An overview of trusted computing technology. In: Mitchell, C.J. (ed.) Trusted Computing, pp. 29–114. IEE (2005)
6. Gallery, E., Tomlinson, A.: Secure Delivery of Conditional Access Applications to Mobile Receivers. In: Mitchell, C.J. (ed.) Trusted Computing, pp. 195–237. IEE (2005)
7. Holtmanns, S., Niemi, V., Ginzboorg, P., Laitinen, P., Asokan, N.: Cellular Authentication for Mobile and Internet Services. John Wiley and Sons (2008)
8. International Organization for Standardization, Genève, Switzerland: ISO/IEC 9798-3:1998, Information technology—Security techniques—Entity authentication—Part 3: Mechanisms using Digital Signature Techniques (1998)
9. Pashalidis, A., Mitchell, C.J.: Single Sign-On Using Trusted Platforms. In: Boyd, C., Mao, W. (eds.) ISC 2003. LNCS, vol. 2851, pp. 54–68. Springer, Heidelberg (2003)
10. Trusted Computing Group: TCG Software Stack (TSS) Specification Part 1: Commands and Structures, Version 1.2 (2007)
11. Trusted Computing Group: TPM Main, Part 1 Design Principles, TCG Specification, Version 1.2, Revision 103 (2007)
12. Trusted Computing Group: TPM Main, Part 2 TPM Data Structures, TCG Specification, Version 1.2, Revision 103 (2007)
13. Trusted Computing Group: TPM Main, Part 3 Commands, TCG Specification, Version 1.2, Revision 103 (2007)

Enforcing Sticky Policies
with TPM and Virtualization

Gina Kounga[1] and Liqun Chen[2]

[1] EADS UK
Homeland Security and CNI Protection
Quadrant House, Celtic Springs, Coedkernew
Newport, NP10 8FZ, UK
gina.kounga@eads.com
[2] Hewlett-Packard Laboratories
Long Down Avenue, Stoke Gifford
Bristol, BS34 8QZ, UK
liqun.chen@hp.com

Abstract. For the proper provision of online services, service providers need to collect some personal data from their customers; for instance, an address is collected in order to deliver goods to the right customer. Here the service provider and customer are called data collector (DC) and data subject (DS) respectively. After receiving the personal data, the DC is free to use them as he likes: he may process them for purposes which are not consented by the DS, and even share them with third parties (TPs). Researchers have paid attention to this problem, but previously proposed solutions do not guarantee that, after they have been disclosed to DCs, personal data can only be used as specified by DSs. These solutions require good behaving DCs and assume that DCs' behavior is verifiable, but do not actually show what happens after DCs get the data. In this paper, we propose a solution that guarantees this by enforcing sticky policies along communication chains composed of a DS, a DC and one (or more) TPs. Our solution uses trusted platform modules (TPMs) and virtual machines (VMs).

Keywords: Sticky policies, TPM, Virtual machine, Privacy.

1 Introduction

In order to be properly provided specific online services, data subjects (DSs for short) – i.e., individuals to whom personal data relate [1] – are often required to provide their personal data items, such as names, addresses and dates of birth, to some service providers, such as banks. Some of these personal data can be necessary to the proper provision of these services (e.g. delivery of goods bought online). Therefore, the DSs do not have any other choice than disclosing their personal data to service providers, called data collectors (DCs for short). These DCs are then free to use the collected personal data as they wish. Besides this, for the purpose of their own businesses, the DCs can share the collected personal

L. Chen, M. Yung, and L. Zhu (Eds.): INTRUST 2011, LNCS 7222, pp. 32–47, 2012.

data items with their business partners (called the third parties (TPs)), such as
financial advisers or service evaluators, which are then also free to use these
personal data as they wish. Considering that a communication chain may be
composed of one DS, one DC and many TPs as represented in Figure 1, it can
be anticipated that a unique disclosure of personal data to a DC can lead to
serious loss of privacy.

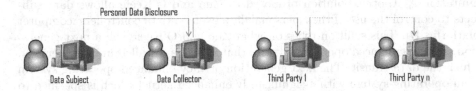

Fig. 1. A communication Chain

1.1 Related Work

A number of researchers have worked on this area in order to guarantee that
policies governing the access and management of personal data could always
be enforced wherever the personal data flow. For example, Karjoth et al. introduced the sticky policy paradigm [2]. This paradigm specifies the requirement
to guarantee that data subjects' preferences always flow with the personal data
that they have disclosed. However, in order to guarantee that these preferences
are always enforced, it must further be guaranteed that data are only accessed
under the conditions specified by the preferences. When data have been sent
to another entities' computing platform, the previous means that the platform
should be continuously monitored to allow the specific conditions in which the
data are accessed to be evaluated against the preferences. It is further required
to guarantee that, on that platform, only the applications that do allow the
preferences to be fulfilled can access the data. Other applications should not be
authorized to access them.

Many implementations of the sticky policy paradigm have been proposed in
the literature [2][3] [4][5]. However, Karjoth et al.'s solution does not avoid personal data and preferences to be separated. It therefore does not constrain access
requesters to verify the conditions expressed by the preferences in oder to access personal data. To avoid the previous, Tang [4] and Casassa Mont et al. [3][6]
study and propose the use of cryptographic means to bind data subjects' personal
data to their preferences. However, these solutions only secure the transmission
of personal data between the data subjects and the DCs. When the data reach a
DC, their solution does not make it possible to control that data are only used in
the conditions specified in the preferences. Cassasa Mont et al. further propose to
use a trusted platform module (TPM) located at a trusted authority (TA). The
TA uses its TPM to evaluate whether a data requester fulfills the data subjects'
preferences. If it is the case, the TA discloses the data to the data requester. This
approach guarantees that, when the data are sent to the data requester, the data

subject's preferences are fulfilled. However, after the data have been disclosed by the TA, the solution does not allow a continuous monitoring of the conditions in which data are accessed and do not isolate applications to guarantee that only those that fulfill the preferences can access to the data. It therefore does not allow to enforce the data subject's preferences after the data have been received by the data requester. Pearson et al. [5] use a similar approach relying on TAs, except that they do not use TPMs. Therefore, their solution has the same limitations. Another solution proposed by Zuo and O'Keefe allows data subjects to control the use of their personal data even on data controllers' computer platforms [7]. This solution relies on what Zuo and O'Keefe call a next generation privacy-enhanced operating system that must be installed in all systems on which the data transit. The next generation privacy-enhanced operating system is an operating system with a significantly enhanced kernel which is specified to provide a trustworthy platform for the operations performed by the entities exchanging personal data. The solution also requires existing computer hardware such as Network Interface Cards (NICs) to be modified and NICs driver files to be reprogrammed to provide some specific capabilities introduced by Zuo and O'Keefe. However this is a strong assumption that may require a very expensive modification on the current computer infrastructure.

1.2   Our Contribution

In this paper, we define a solution that allows DSs to control their personal data along communication chains as represented in Figure 1. This work can be seen as an extension to the solution proposed in [3][6]. The differentiation is that the previous work focuses on the communication between a DS and DC that allows data to be given to a good behaved DC and assumes the DC's behavior can be verified by the DS, but it does not show how to achieve such a good behaved DC. Here, we include their result but also show how to protect the data after giving them to the DC.

Our solution does not assume that principals' [8] – here, the DS(s), the DC(s) and the TP(s) – computing systems are equipped with specific operating systems or with hardware that must be modified. Instead, our solution is independent of the operating system and relies on TPMs [9], which are already part of more than 100 million computing systems that have been shipped to date [10], together with virtual machine technology, e.g. [11,12,13]. Virtual machine technology makes it possible to isolate applications running on a same computing platform. It therefore makes it possible to allow, on a same computing platform, the applications which fulfil DS's preferences to access personal data while others cannot access them. This is necessary to enforce sticky policies and it is not provided by previously proposed solutions. After the submission of this paper, we have been informed that Sandhu and Zhang [14] proposed a solution for access control, which like ours, relies on TPMs and virtual machine technologies. However, in Sandhu and Zhang's approach only the trusted reference monitor operates in isolation. Therefore, their approach cannot guarantee that only the specific applications which fulfil the DS's preferences can access the DS's personal data.

Besides this, their approach does not make it possible for the trusted reference monitor to verify the applications' capabilities as their solution does not rely on conformance certificates. As a consequence, it is not possible for the trusted reference monitor to know whether or not an application is able to fulfil the DS's preferences before sending that application the DS's personal data. The solution proposed by Han et al. [15], which extends Sandhu and Zhang's approach to a client/server context, has the same limitations. It additionally does not apply to communication chains has considered in this paper.

Here, we use TPMs' capabilities to cryptographically bind the access and use of a personal data item to the fulfillment of conditions specified by the DS this data item relates to. As TPMs are designed to be tamper-resistant, the previous cryptographic binding cannot be unbound. Hence, the data item cannot be used in other conditions than those defined by the DS. Contrary to most previously proposed solutions, we do not only use TPMs at one unique entity but at all the entities that need to receive some personal data. This makes it possible to continuously control the state of the platform on which DS's data seat and to guarantee that the data can only be accessed if DS's preferences are fulfilled. The concept of the personal data certificate (PDC) is introduced. A PDC is similar to a X.509 certificate [16] except that it binds some encrypted personal data items, disclosed by a DS bound to the TPM in the DS's platform, to:

- Some preferences that another(other) principal(s), bound to the TPM(s) in this(these) principal(s)'s platform(s), must fulfil;
- The secret key SK used to encrypt the personal data items to be disclosed.

Remark 1. Our solution might be compared to digital right management (DRM) solutions since, like a DRM, our solution makes it possible to control the access to some digital resources. However, while a DRM is designed to control the access to a specific type of resource by a specific application, our solution applies to any type of resource accessed by any type of application. It is also designed to both make it possible for individuals to protect their privacy by controlling the use of their personal data and make it easier for organizations to use and manage personal data in a user-centric privacy preserving way for their business interests.

1.3 Organisation of the Paper

This paper is organised as follows. In the next section, we present some technical background. Then, in Section 3 we present our approach at a high level before detailing our solution in Section 4. We illustrate how the solution can be integrated into an organisation's infrastructure in Section 5 and conclude the paper in Section 6.

2 Technical Background

Our solution is based on two existing technologies: virtual machine technology and trusted computing technology.

A virtual machine (VM) is an isolated operating system installation within a normal operating system, as discussed in [17]. Generally speaking, there are two major types of virtual machines: a system VM provides a complete system platform and supports the execution of a complete operating system (OS); a process VM, also called an application virtual machine, runs as a normal application inside a host OS and supports a single process. For our purpose, either of these two VMs can be used. For simplicity, we choose process VMs in our explanation. We assume that all the principals (DSs, DCs and TPs) involved in the above scenario are equipped with platforms on which applications have a degree of isolation that allow them to run in their own virtualised environment but also to establish some communication with each other. Solutions such as those proposed by Karger [11] and Cabuk et al. [12] can be used to achieve our goal. We propose to install a personal data manager (PDM), which is an isolated application, on each platform. The technical details of such PDMs will be given in Section 3.

Platforms are also equipped with TPMs which can be fully used by the isolated applications. Solutions such as those proposed by England and Loeser [13] or Garfinkel et al. [18] indeed permit to achieve the foregoing. England and Loeser particularly propose a solution that allows each operating system on which an isolated application runs to have an associated Platform Configuration Register (PCR) value [13]. Here, we use TPMs to securely perform some critical cryptographic operations and to avoid unauthorised entities to access personal data items.

In the trusted computing environment, a TPM is authenticated by any entity who either locally or remotely communicates with the TPM. TPM authentication is based on the TPM long-term endorsement key, which is an asymmetric key pair, created in the TPM manufacture line and usually certified by the manufacturer. However, for privacy reasons, the endorsement key is not used directly by end users; otherwise any authentic communication with the TPM will reveal the TPM identity and multiple authentic communications with the same TPM will be connected. This might bring some privacy concerns for the DS, who is also the owner of the TPM.

In order to achieve authentication while preserving user privacy, there are two cryptographic mechanisms recommended by the trusted computing group (TCG). The first is a privacy-CA solution, where a trusted third party named privacy-CA validates the TPM's long-term endorsement key and then certifies its short-term attestation identity key (AIK); the second one is a direct anonymous attestation (DAA) solution [19], where the TPM, after demonstrating its possession of the endorsement key, receives a DAA credential from a semi-trusted DAA issuer and then self-certifies its AIK using a DAA signature. The DAA signature is anonymous for both the signature verifier and DAA issuer. In this paper, we do not restrict our solution to use either of them. The choice is dependent on the applications and availability of the privacy-CA and DAA issuer.

3 An Overview of the Approach

The main technique in our solution is a personal data manager PDM, which is a special application and isolated from other applications, and is designed specifically to achieve personal data management on each computer platform. The PDM has a public/private key pair issued by a TPM embedded in the platform. In order to prove that this key pair is associated with a genuine PDM, a conformance authority able to check the authenticity of the PDM must sign the key pair. To allow this, the process detailed in Section 4.2 is run.

Any disclosure, collection and transfer of personal data is mediated by the PDM owned by the principal which sends or collects personal data items. The Figure 2 represents the communication between two instances of PDM running on two different platforms.

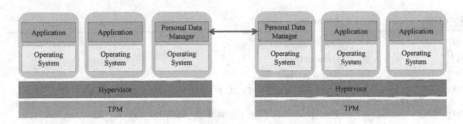

Fig. 2. Interactions between two PDMs located on two computing platforms

PDMs are responsible for enforcing DSs' privacy preferences. In other terms, they guarantee that locally stored personal data items can only be accessed by entities that fulfil the conditions specified by the DSs who disclosed these data items. For that, PDMs rely on TPMs' capabilities. Personal data items to be disclosed by a DS to a given principal are indeed encrypted in such a way that they can only be accessed by this principal's PDM after this PDM has requested the principal's TPM to perform a decryption operation. Such a request is only done by the principal's PDM after it has successfully verified that a requesting entity fulfills the condition defined by the DS. Therefore, our approach can guarantee that personal data are only accessed as specified by the DS, if the following requirements are fulfilled on each platform:

- Disclosure or transfer of personal data should only happen between genuine and *healthy* – i.e., untampered – PDM applications;
- Platforms on which these PDMs run should be genuine, that means the integrity of their configuration can be verified;
- No other entity than the genuine PDM running on a platform should be able to request the TPM to decrypt some data allowing the access to some personal data items;
- No entity that does not fulfil the conditions defined by the DSs with their preferences should access to personal data items;

– Entities that are not able to manage personal data as specified by the DSs should not access to any of these DSs' personal data.

4   Description of the Proposed Solution

In this section we describe the mechanisms that allow the data subject (DS) to control his personal data even after he has disclosed them.

4.1   Notation

In the remainder of this paper, we use the notation detailed in Table 1.

Table 1. Notation

Notation	Meaning
DS	Data subject.
DC	Data collector.
TP	Third party.
TPM_P	The principal P's TPM. $P = \{DS,\ DC,\ TP\}$.
$PrivAIK_P$	The principal P's attestation identity private key generated by TPM_P.
$PubAIK_P$	The principal P's attestation identity public key generated by TPM_P.
$CertAIK_P$	The principal P's attestation identity public key certificate issued by the Privacy-CA or self-certified by the TPM using DAA. It contains $PubAIK_P$.
PDM_P	The principal P's PDM application.
$PDM-ConfCert_P$	The conformance certificate of PDM_P issued by $PDM-Producer_P$ the trusted third party which produced PDM_P or which is able to verify the integrity of PDM_P. It contains $PDM-PubKey_P$.
$PDM-PrivKey_P$	The private key of PDM_P. It is securely stored by TPM_P.
$PDM-PubKey_P$	PDM_P's public key.
$PDM-Cert_P$	PDM_P's certificate. It is signed with $PrivAIK_P$ and contains $PDM-PubKey_P$.
$PDM-PCR_P$	The current PCR value issued by TPM_P for PDM_P.
$PDM-SML_P$	The current Stored Measurement Log for PDM_P.
$App-ConfCert_P$	The conformance certificate of P's application App.
$App-PrivKey_P$	The private key of P's application App. It is securely stored by the TPM.
$App-PubKey_P$	The public key of P's application App.
$App-Cert_P$	The certificate of P's application App. It contains $App-PubKey_P$ and is signed with $PrivAIK_P$.
$App-PCR_P$	The current Platform Configuration Registers (PCR) value issued by the TPM for P's application App.

Table 1. (*Continued*)

$App - SML_P$	The current Stored Measurement Log for P's application App.
SIG($prikey, msg$)	Signature generated with the private key $prikey$ on the message msg.
VER($pubkey, sig, msg$)	Verification of the signature sig generated on the message msg with the public key $pubkey$.
ENC(key, msg)	Encryption of the message msg with the key key.
DEC($key, cipher$)	Decryption of the encrypted message $cipher$ with the key key.

4.2   Issue of the Conformance Certificate

The conformance certificate is the credential that proves that an application fulfills specific requirements. It is issued by a conformance authority. The conformance authority only issues a conformance certificate to an application after it has successfully verified that the application is designed and implemented to fulfill the specific requirements. These requirements are specified on the certificate to be issued. The certificate further contains the application's public key. Finally, the application is signed by the conformance certificate to allow its integrity to be checked. In our solution, applications have public keys issued by TPMs which means that conformance certificates cannot be issued when the application is being produced. In this section, we explain how this is achieved. Here, the conformance authority which issues PDMs' conformance certificates is $PDM - Producer$, the entity which produced the PDM. The conformance authority can be any trusted entity. Here, we only consider that it is the producer of the PDM as an example.

The first time that PDM_{DS} has to be launched, a validation process is run. This validation process requires DS to enter PDM_{DS}'s license key which was provided to him. After that, the protocol represented in Figure 3 is run between PDM_{DS}, $PDM - Producer_{DS}$ and TPM_{DS}. It allows $PDM - Producer_{DS}$ to know whether PDM_{DS} is a genuine PDM and whether the TPM, which issued $PDM - PubKey_{DS}$ to PDM_{DS}, is genuine. If all the verifications are successful, $PDM - Producer_{DS}$ issues PDM_{DS} the conformance certificate $PDM - ConfCert_{DS}$ that contains $PDM - PubKey_{DS}$. Who is able to play the role of the $PDM - Producer_{DS}$ is dependent on usage models and applications.

4.3   Disclosure of Personal Data to the Data Collector

When DS wants to disclose some personal data items to DC, he runs PDM_{DS} and specifies: the personal data items he would like to disclose, the DC which the items should be disclosed to and his privacy preferences. After it has been done, PDM_{DS} verifies that the DC has the capabilities to properly manage the personal data items to be sent. For that, PDM_{DS} first generates an unpredictable nonce $Nonce_{DS}$. Then, PDM_{DS} and PDM_{DC} exchange the messages (1) to (3) represented in Figure 4 in order to mutually verify that they both: (a) run on platforms equipped with a genuine TPM whose security components

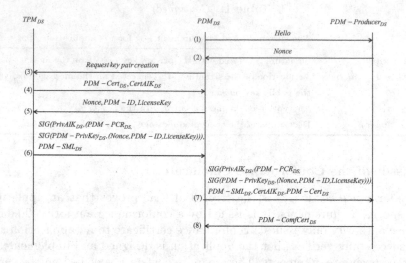

Fig. 3. Issue of the conformance certificate to the personal data manager

and properties are genuine, (b) are genuine and currently *healthy* PDMs able to manage personal data as specified by their DSs and (c) hold valid public keys certified by their respective TPMs.

After receiving the message (2), PDM_{DS} verifies the validity of $CertAIK_{DC}$. If it is valid, PDM_{DS} knows that $PubAIK_{DC}$, contained in $CertAIK_{DC}$, was generated by a genuine TPM whose security components and properties are genuine. PDM_{DS} can therefore use $PubAIK_{DC}$ to verify the validity of the signature contained in message (2). If the signature is valid, then PDM_{DS} has the insurance that the signature contained in message (2) has been generated by TPM_{DC} after the message (1) was sent. PDM_{DS} then verifies the validity of $PDM - Cert_{DC}$. If it is valid, it further verifies that $PDM - ConfCert_{DC}$ contained in message (2) is valid. If the verification is successful, PDM_{DS} knows that $PDM - PubKey_{DC}$ contained in $PDM - Cert_{DC}$ belongs to a genuine PDM whose corresponding private key is protected by a genuine TPM.

After it has been done, PDM_{DS} processes $PDM - SML_{DC}$ and recomputes the received PCR before comparing it to the received $PDM - PCR_{DC}$ [20]. If they match then PDM_{DS} knows that PDM_{DC} is currently in a healthy state. The same verifications are performed by PDM_{DC}. If all the previous verifications are successful, the exchange can continue. PDM_{DS} then generates a secret key SK and individually encrypts with it each of the personal data items to be sent to DC. PDM_{DS} further generates PDC_{DS} represented in Figure 5, which contains, among others: $DS - ID$ and $DC - ID$, i.e. DS's and DC's respective identifiers[1].

---

[1] Such identifiers should uniquely identify DS and DC. These may be distinguished name [21] as specified in [16] or email addresses. Using email addresses allows notification information to be sent back to DS. If required, email addresses that do not contain any identifiable information can be used.

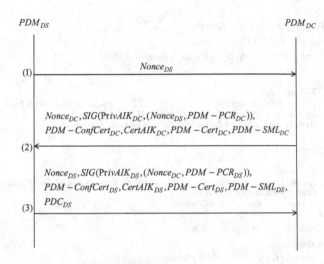

Fig. 4. Message exchanged between PDM_{DS} and PDM_{DC} when DS discloses some data to DC

The PDC further contains, for each personal data item to be disclosed:

- The type of the data item e.g., Name in Figure 5
- An index e.g., d_1 in Figure 5. It permits to differentiate data items of the same type contained in a PDC.
- The encrypted personal data items to be sent e.g., $ENC(SK, John)$ in Figure 5.

It also contains:

- The privacy preferences that apply to each personal data item or group of personal data items.
- The secret key SK used to encrypt the personal data items to be sent. SK is encrypted with $PDM - PubKey_{DC}$ the public key of PDM_{DC} included in $PDM - Cert_{DC}$ (see message (2) in Figure 4).
- The issue date of PDC_{DS}.
- The digital signature generated by DS on PDC_{DS} with $PrivAIK_{DS}$.

After generating PDC_{DS}, PDM_{DS} discloses DS's personal data by sending PDM_{DC} the message (3) of Figure 4[2]. As the personal data items within PDC_{DS} are encrypted with a secret itself encrypted with $PDM - PubKey_{DC}$, only TPM_{DC} can decrypt the personal data items. This, only after PDM_{DC} has requested it.

---

[2] After receiving messages (2) and (3) PDM_{DS} and PDM_{DC} can store the received certificates in their repositories for future interactions.

$DS - ID$
$DC - ID$
$Name,\ d_1,\ ENC(SK,\ John)$
$Surname,\ d_2,\ ENC(SK,\ Doe)$
$Date\ of\ birth,\ d_3,\ ENC(SK,\ 25\ November\ 1956)$
$Preferences1$

- $Target: d_1,\ d_2$
- $Authorised\ principal: DC,\ TP1,\ TP2,\ Applications\ certified$
  $by\ conformance\ authority\ ConfAuth1$
- $Access\ and\ use\ until: certificateissuedate + 3months$

$Preferences2$

- $Target:d_3$
- $Authorised\ principal:DC,\ TP1,$ Applications certified by conformance authority $ConfAuth2$
- $Access\ and\ use\ until:$unlimited

$ENC(PDM - PubKey_{DC},\ SK)$
Issue date
$SIG(PrivAIK_{DS},\ PDC_{DS}'s\ fields)$

Fig. 5. Fields composing PDC_{DS}

4.4   Management of Personal Data at the DC

Access Request from an Application

After receiving PDC_{DS}, PDM_{DC} verifies its authenticity with $PubAIK_{DS}$ – contained in $CertAIK_{DS}$ received in message (2) of Figure 4. If it is authentic, PDM_{DC} extracts the encrypted personal data items identified by d_1, d_2 and d_3 and stores them on DC's platform in a location that can be accessed by other applications. PDM_{DC} then stores the remaining fields of the PDC_{DS} in its local repository – only accessible by PDM_{DC}. It also maintains a link between these remaining fields and the location where are stored d_1, d_2 and d_3.

When an application $App1$ tries to access to d_1 and d_2, the access is intercepted by PDM_{DC}. PDM_{DC} then verifies that the conditions specified by the preferences associated to these data items are fulfilled. In the considered case (see Figure 5), PDM_{DC} verifies that, as specified in PDC_{DS}:

- $App1$ has a valid conformance certificate issued by $ConfAuth1$ which certifies that $App1$ does manage personal data as specified by their DSs.
- The access is made less than three months after PDC_{DS} was issued.

Besides this, PDM_{DC} further verifies that $App1$ is in an healthy state by checking $App1 - PCR_{DC}$ (see Section 4.3) . If all the verifications are successful, then PDM_{DC} knows that $App1$ is able to manage the accessed personal data items as specified by the preferences. Therefore, PDM_{DC} generates a secret key SK_{App1} and requests TPM_{DC} to decrypt a copy of $ENC(PDM - PubKey_{DC},\ SK)$

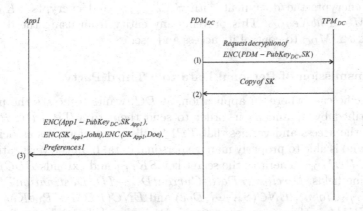

Fig. 6. Actions performed after $App1$ has tried to access d_1 and d_2 and PDM_{DC} has successfully verified that $App1$ can be authorised to access the data

as represented in Figure 6. For that, PDM_{DC} uses its authentication data $authDataManager_{DC}$ to prove to TPM_{DC} that it is authorised to request data to be decrypted with $PDM - PrivKey_{DC}$. After receiving the copy of SK from the TPM, PDM_{DC} re-encrypts d_1 an d_2 with SK_{App1} and encrypts SK_{App1} with $App1$'s public key $App1 - PubKey_{DC}$. PDM_{DC} then transmits $ENC(App1 - PubKey_{DC}, SK_{App1})$, $ENC(SK_{App1}, John)$ and $ENC(SK_{App1}, Doe)$ to $App1$ as well as the preferences associated to d_1 and d_2 (see message (3) in Figure 6) before destroying the copy of SK.

It is important to note that the access to the personal data items is fully controlled by PDM_{DC}. Therefore, no entity can access personal data items if PDM_{DC} has not authorised it. If the TPM_{DC} is configured in such a way that PDM_{DC} can only obtain the copy of SK in clear if PDM_{DC} is in an *healthy* state, then, the solution further guarantees that only applications that fulfil DS's preferences can access to DS's personal data.

Access to a Document Containing Some Personal Data

In order to control the access to personal data used in documents, PDM_{DC} requests DC to specify the preferences of each document that DC creates. After it has been done, PDM_{DC} stores, in its repository, a correspondence between each document and the associated document's preferences. PDM_{DC} further generates a secret key $SK_{document}$ that it securely stores encrypted with its public key. Another link is maintained between the document and the encrypted secret key $ENC(PDM - PubKey_{DC}, SK_{Document})$. Then, similar mechanisms are those described in the previous section are used to guarantee that personal data can only be used in the document if the document's preferences do not contradict these data 's preferences. Because of space limitation, we do not describe these mechanisms here. If personal data have been added to the document,

PDM_{DC} encrypts the document with $SK_{document}$ and encrypts $SK_{document}$ with $PDM - PubKey_{DC}$. This prevents any entity from using the document and allows PDM_{DC} to control its access and use.

4.5   Transmission of Personal Data to a Third Party

In the specific case where an application, at DC, wants to access the personal data identified by d_1 and d_2 in order to send them to a TP $TP1$, PDM_{DC} intercepts the access and verifies that $TP1$ fulfills the preferences associated to d_1 and d_2 and is able to properly manage personal data. If all the verifications are successful, PDM_{DC} generates the secret key SK_{TP1} and extends PDC_{DS} with the following fields: $DisclosureDate, CurrentDC - ID, DestinationTP - ID$, $ENC(SK_{TP1}, John), ENC(SK_{TP1}, Doe)$ and $ENC(PDM - PubKey_{TP1}, SK_{TP1})$. PDM_{DC} then generates a hash of the extended PDC_{DS} and requests TPM_{DC} to sign it with $PrivAIK_{DC}$. PDM_{DC} then adds the signed hash in the extended PDC_{DS} as an additional extension. The resulting $PDC_{DS}^{extended}$ is then sent to PDM_{TP1}. PDM_{DC} also stores locally $PDC_{DS}^{extended}$ and adds $TP1$ into the list of the principals to which it sent PDC_{DS}. PDM_{DC} further sends $PDC_{DS}^{extended}$ to PDM_{DS}. PDM_{DS} verifies the authenticity of the received $PDC_{DS}^{extended}$ and if it is authentic, it stores it as a proof that DC sent his personal data items to $TP1$. After receiving $PDC_{DS}^{extended}$, PDM_{TP1} verifies its authenticity. If it is authentic, $TP1$ uses it as described in Sections 4.

In the case where an application wants to send to $TP1$ the document containing d_1 and d_2, similar mechanisms as those previously described apply.

4.6   Enforcing Update of Preferences

DS may wish new preferences to be applied to the data items he disclosed in the past. In order to guarantee that this update is enforced by all the entities which received DS's data, DS uses PDM_{DS} to send PDM_{DC} an update request. The request specifies, among others: the preferences to be updated as well as the new preferences to be applied. After having received it, PDM_{DC} sends a copy of this statement to all the PDMs to which it previously sent the data. This is repeated by each PDM receiving the statement until the statement reaches the last PDM in the communication chain. This last PDM then enforces the updated preferences, as previously described, before sending to its predecessor within the chain a digitally signed message confirming that the update statement was received and enforced. Such a confirmation is cascaded until it reaches PDM_{DS}. A PDM only sends a confirmation message to its predecessor within the chain after that PDM has received a confirmation from all the PDMs to which it sent the data.

5   An Application of Our Solution

Let us consider the following situation. Alice, who is living in the United Kingdom, has a meeting with Bob, an investment advisor of her local bank, say

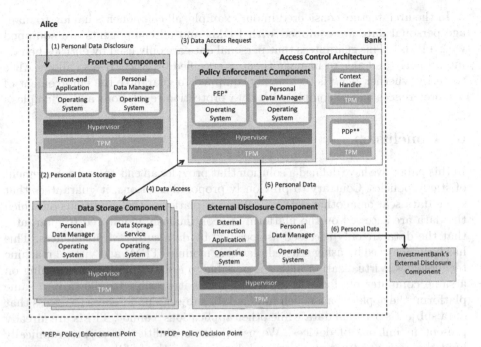

Fig. 7. Example of integration of the proposed solution into an organisation's infrastructure

Bank for short, in order to decide where to invest her savings. Bob advises Alice to invest in a project proposed by *InvestmentBank* in France, which is a business partner of *Bank*. Alice then contacts *InvestmentBank* via *Bank*, transmits to *InvestmentBank* the required data and also indicates that she was advised by someone of *Bank*. To do this, Alice discloses her data to *Bank* ((1)and (2) in Figure 7); this process is handled by her PDM, which sends *Bank* a statement specifying that the data required for the investment must only be sent to *InvestmentBank* and that her advisor is Bob. Later, *Bank*'s process managing investments verifies that the components composing the access control architecture are not tampered and, if it is the case, sends a request for the required data to be sent to *InvestmentBank* (3).

Similar verifications are made by all the components that need to interact in order to: evaluate the request, request the data to the storage components (4), send these data in an extended PDC to the external interaction application (4 and 5), i.e., the interface communicating with TPs without disclosing information about *Bank*'s internal architecture. If *InvestmentBank* has a PDM fulfilling the suitable requirements, the later application sends the PDC to that PDM (6). Later, Alice can use her PDM to send an update statement to *Bank* specifying that the data sent to *InvestmentBank* should not be used anymore. The update statement is then transmitted to *InvestmentBank*'s PDM which will enforce the new preferences.

In the architecture considered in our example, all components having to manage personal data are equipped with PDMs and all components are equipped with TPMs[3]. This guarantees that personal data are only used by entities behaving properly and able to manage them as specified by Alice. It also allows Alice to verify whether *Bank* is technically equipped to guarantee the enforcement of her preferences and to comply with data protection regulations and principles.

6 Conclusion

In this paper, we have defined a solution that provides an end-to-end enforcement of sticky policies. Contrary to previously proposed solutions, it guarantees that when data seat on another entity's computer platform, the conditions on which the data are accessed on the platform are continuously monitored to guarantee that the data are only accessed as specified by data subjects' preferences. This has been achieved by using trusted platform module (TPM) and virtual machine technologies. Virtualization makes it possible to isolate applications running on a same computer platform. It therefore makes it possible to allow, on a same platform, the applications which fulfil a data subject's preferences to access that data subject's personal data while other applications' cannot. TPMs are already present in millions of devices. We use their capabilities to cryptographically bind the access and use of a personal data item to the fulfillment of conditions specified by the data subject to which the data relate. As TPMs are designed to be tamper-resistant, the previous cryptographic binding cannot be unbound. Hence, the data item cannot be used in other conditions than those defined by the data subject. As TPMs are already embedded into many equipments composing organisations' information infrastructures, our solution can be used in realistic organisational settings to allow individuals to evaluate whether organisations are technically equipped to (1) manage their personal data as required and to (2) comply with data protection regulations and principles.

References

1. UK Parliament: Data Protection Act 1998 (1998)
2. Karjoth, G., Schunter, M., Waidner, M.: Platform for Enterprise Privacy Practices: Privacy-Enabled Management of Customer Data. In: Dingledine, R., Syverson, P.F. (eds.) PET 2002. LNCS, vol. 2482, pp. 69–84. Springer, Heidelberg (2003)
3. Casassa Mont, M., Pearson, S., Bramhall, P.: Towards accountable management of identity and privacy: Sticky policies and enforceable tracing services. In: DEXA Workshops, pp. 377–382 (2003)
4. Tang, Q.: On using encryption techniques to enhance sticky policies enforcement. Technical report, Enschede (2008)
5. Pearson, S., Casassa Mont, M., Kounga, G.: Enhancing accountability in the cloud via sticky policies. In: STAVE (2011)

---

[3] It is important to note that TPMs are already incorporated into many equipments (such as servers[9]).

6. Casassa Mont, M., Pearson, S., Bramhalll, P.: Towards Accountable Management of Identity and Privacy: Sticky Policies and Enforceable Tracing Services. Technical Report Marco Casassa Mont, Siani Pearson, Pete Bramhall (2003)
7. Zuo, Y., O'Keefe, T.: Post-release information privacy protection: A framework and next-generation privacy-enhanced operating system. Information Systems Frontiers 9(5), 451–467 (2007)
8. Bishop, M.: Computer Security: Art and Science. Addison–Wesley (2003)
9. Trusted Computing Group: Trusted Platform Module Specification Main page, http://www.trustedcomputinggroup.org/resources/tpm_main_specification
10. Trusted Computing Group: Enterprise Security: Putting the TPM to Work, http://www.trustedcomputinggroup.org/files/temp/4B52C159-1D09-3519-AD2F881556C29076/TPM/Applications/Whitepaper.pdf
11. Karger, P.A.: Multi-level security requirements for hypervisors. In: ACSAC 2005: Proceedings of the 21st Annual Computer Security Applications Conference, pp. 267–275. IEEE Computer Society, Washington, DC (2005)
12. Cabuk, S., Chen, L., Plaquin, D., Ryan, M.: Trusted Integrity Measurement and Reporting for Virtualized Platforms. In: Chen, L., Yung, M. (eds.) INTRUST 2009. LNCS, vol. 6163, pp. 180–196. Springer, Heidelberg (2010)
13. England, P., Loeser, J.: Para-Virtualized TPM Sharing. In: Lipp, P., Sadeghi, A.-R., Koch, K.-M. (eds.) Trust 2008. LNCS, vol. 4968, pp. 119–132. Springer, Heidelberg (2008)
14. Sandhu, R.S., Zhang, X.: Peer-to-peer access control architecture using trusted computing technology. In: SACMAT, pp. 147–158 (2005)
15. Han, W., Xu, M., Zhao, W., Li, G.: A trusted decentralized access control framework for the client/server architecture. J. Network and Computer Applications 33(2), 76–83 (2010)
16. Housley, R., Polk, W., Ford, W., Solo, D.: Internet X.509 Public Key Infrastructure Certificate and Certificate Revocation List (CRL) Profile. RFC 3280 (Proposed Standard) (April 2002); Obsoleted by RFC 5280, updated by RFCs 4325, 4630
17. Smith, J., Nair, R.: The architecture of virtual machines. Computer 38(5), 32–38 (2005)
18. Garfinkel, T., Pfaff, B., Chow, J., Rosenblum, M., Boneh, D.: Terra: a virtual machine-based platform for trusted computing. In: SOSP, pp. 193–206 (2003)
19. Brickell, E., Camenisch, J., Chen, L.: Direct anonymous attestation. In: CCS 2004: Proceedings of the 11th ACM Conference on Computer and Communications Security, pp. 132–145. ACM, New York (2004)
20. Stumpf, F., Fuchs, A., Katzenbeisser, S., Eckert, C.: Improving the scalability of platform attestation. In: STC 2008: Proceedings of the 3rd ACM Workshop on Scalable Trusted Computing, pp. 1–10. ACM, New York (2008)
21. Zeilenga, K.: Lightweight Directory Access Protocol version 3 (LDAPv3): All Operational Attributes. RFC 3673 (Proposed Standard) (December 2003)

Mass Transit Ticketing with NFC Mobile Phones

Jan-Erik Ekberg and Sandeep Tamrakar

Nokia Research Center, Helsinki
{Jan-Erik.Ekberg,Sandeep.Tamrakar}@nokia.com

Abstract. Mass transport ticketing with mobile phones is already deployed in many metropolitan areas, but current solutions and protocols are not secure, and they are limited to one-time or fixed-time ticketing in non-gated transport systems. The emergence of NFC-enabled phones with trusted execution environments makes it possible to not only integrate mobile phone ticketing with existing and future transport authority ticket readers, but also to construct secure protocols for non-gated travel eliminating many associated possibilities for ticketing fraud. This paper presents an architecture and implementation for such a system.

1 Introduction

In mobile handsets, the Near-Field Communication (NFC) radio standards [13] is by many seen as *the* user-friendly enabler for the implementation of payment, ticketing, access control tokens and other services typically existing in the user's wallet and key ring. Information gathered from a survey [26] predicts that 400 million mobile subscribers will use mobile ticketing on their devices by 2013. Such an uptake is not surprising considering the benefits of having a local "ticketing user interface" on the device. The interface can not only provide handy information like ticket expiry time, account balance and real-time traffic information but can also be used to purchase new tickets. Also, many people use their mobile device while waiting for and during transport for communication, browsing or reading. Thus the mobile phone is anyway present and ready to be used when a ticketing activity is required.

All over the world, transport ticketing has for years been implemented with wireless technologies, increasingly using the ISO / IEC 14443 [12] contact-less card standard. Common references to such technologies include the Felica®[1] system in Asia, the Oyster card[2] e.g. in London, and protocols like MiFare[3] developed by NXP semiconductors.

This paper presents a trial implementation of a ticketing architecture for mobile phones that implements a new take on how to bind the ticketed identity to the place and time when the journey begins and ends. With this feature we enable deployment of complex fare and discount calculations, e.g. distance-based

---

[1] Felicity Card - www.sony.net/Products/felica
[2] https://oyster.tfl.gov.uk/oyster/entry.do
[3] http://mifare.net

L. Chen, M. Yung, and L. Zhu (Eds.): INTRUST 2011, LNCS 7222, pp. 48–65, 2012.
© Springer-Verlag Berlin Heidelberg 2012

ticket pricing. Earlier, this has been practical only in gated transport systems, but not in systems with non-gated parts. Central to our approach is the use of the trusted execution environment in the phone not only for securing digital signature generation but also for local protocol state enforcement. To meet the very tight timing constraints for contact-less ticketing especially in gated transport, we streamline all NFC interaction and revisit the ticketing credential, where we leverage the message recovery property of RSA signatures not only to achieve size-efficiency but also as a privacy-implementing primitive.

We begin in Section 2 by listing related work. Section 3 outlines processes in ticketing systems and Section 4 lists functional and security requirements. Our system architecture is introduced in Section 5. Section 6 outlines our ticketing credentials. Sections 7 and 8 present the ticketing protocols in gated and non-gated systems. We discuss implementation in Section 9, and requirements analysis in Section 10.

2   Related Work and Background Technologies

NFC ticketing [11] — a project by RFID Lab of the University of Rome "Sapienza" provides a public transport NFC ticketing prototype for usability research. Their system is implemented as a Java application, and provisions data over SMS.

A thesis work by Kooman [17] presents a cryptographic model for using NFC enabled mobile phones for public transport payment. Strong privacy is achieved by selective blinded attribute verification between the phone and a validating device. These protocols are not size-efficient, and no implementation was presented in the thesis.

Since 2001, public transport ticketing using Short Message Service (SMS) has been deployed in various cities around the world e.g. Helsinki, Prague and Rome. Current systems are open to ticket copying attacks [20].

2.1   Trusted Hardware

For electronic ticketing, the default hardware element is the smart card, typically adhering to the ISO / IEC 7816 [16] interface primitives and to ISO / IEC 14443 [12] for the wireless interface. Smart card security confirms to the GlobalPlatform Card Specification standard [24], which defines key management and provisioning. Applications for smart cards are developed with the the JavaCard programming environment.

During the last decade, trusted execution environments (TEE)s have emerged based on the general-purpose secure hardware. These have been incorporated into mobile phones, and are widely deployed. Designs like Mobile Trusted Modules (MTM) [7], M-Shield [25] and ARM TrustZone [3] are available.

The user device TEE chosen for this work is the On-board Credentials (ObC) architecture [18], deployed in all Nokia Symbian ∧3 phones to date. ObC uses ARM TrustZone on a processor manufactured by Texas Instruments. ObC relies on the underlying hardware to isolate credentials from the operating system.

Additionally, it provides a provisioning system and a byte-code interpreter with an extensive cryptographic Application Programming Interface (API) for the implementation of credential algorithms (ObC programs).

2.2   NFC

NFC is a wireless Radio Frequency Identification (RFID) technology standardized in ISO / IEC 18092 [13] and ISO / IEC 21481 [14]. An industry consortium, the NFC forum [4], provides compliance-testing and additional standards for NFC use. NFC encompasses three different types (A, B and Felica) of radio communication, with theoretical speeds ranging from 106 to 424 kbps. Many NFC readers readily available in Europe are limited to 106 kbps.

The lower layers of NFC include no communication security primitives. It is also well known that NFC technology is susceptible to e.g. both eavesdropping and man-in-the middle attacks [6], despite the fact that NFC is a short-range radio technology. To date, some 20 phone models from different manufacturers support NFC[5]. Only a handful of models embed a secure element or TEE that can be used for securing a ticketing transaction.

3   On Transport Ticketing

In recent years, new approaches [22,4] to electronic transport ticketing has emerged, stimulated by the ongoing mass deployment of EMV (EuroPay, MasterCard and Visa) contact-less credit cards [9] in many countries. From the perspective of the public transport authority, it has been identified that the cost of fare collection, i.e. operating the ticketing system and collecting the money from users is significant [19]. Thus, one option is to outsource this function to e.g. credit card companies, telecom operators, or any other stake-holder that is prepared to take on such a responsibility. The outsourcing option does not however apply to *fare calculation*, i.e. determining the price of a given trip, since it is intimately tied to the transport function itself.

In currently deployed non-gated ticketing systems, it is often hard to accurately determine journey length or duration, since it is impractical to collect data about the journey endpoint. When the end event cannot be collected, a typical solution is to define so called transport zones and to assume that the user buys an appropriate ticket for his travel under the threat of randomly applied ticket inspection. These mechanisms are coarse-grained, and often difficult to resolve for users traveling along unfamiliar routes. Another common shortcoming is that the incompatibilities between the ticketing principles (zones, validity time, gated vs. non-gated) and the deployed ticketing technologies of local transport within a single metropolitan area (e.g. between underground, buses and local trains) often makes combination ticketing difficult.

---

[4] www.nfc-forum.org

[5] http://en.wikipedia.org/wiki/Near_field_communication

Our work further develops the approach taken with e.g. credit-card ticketing. In this context, a transport user fundamentally is represented by a ticketing identity, or in credit card terminology by his Primary Account Number (PAN) [15]. The identity is presented to the transport authority at system entry (and exit), where the PAN is bound to the time and location of those respective events. A proper ticketing system also allows the ticket to be inspected during the journey of the user.

We construct a system where the PAN can be securely bound to the place and time of the ticketing "tap", where the mobile device touches a gate or bus stop touch point. If the resulting transaction evidence can be moved reliably to a back-end computing system, then the fare calculation for a specific journey, undertaken by a user / PAN is trivially achievable. We will need security-enabled protocols, since the transport user has a clear incentive to cheat. We also need to arrange for the transfer of transaction evidence to back-end systems in a manner that is cost-effective not only in metro stations with tens of thousands of users passing each day, but also at bus stops with, say only 10 people boarding a bus every workday morning.

4   Requirements

Many important requirements for a transport system are functional. In gated mass transport, rapid people throughput is a paramount consideration, and the Smart Card Alliance sets the unofficial maximum transaction time to 300 ms per gate entry [1]. This time constraint in practice eliminates the possibility of on-line verification supported by a back-end. Since a tap-and-hold transaction, say 700ms, is significantly more difficult for the user, speedy tap transaction times are also advantageous in a non-gated system. Additionally, in contemporary NFC ticket readers, hardware acceleration support is often available only for RSA, ruling out the use of more size-efficient cryptographic primitives like elliptic-curve cryptography.

In non-gated systems, the tapped "terminals" are located e.g at bus stops, train stations and the like. A user is required to tap a terminal prior to vehicle entry and after he or she finishes the journey. For cost saving reasons, such terminals shall not require electricity or back-end connectivity. Deploying tamper-resistant processor chips with NFC antennas (contact-less smartcards) for this purpose is one cost-efficient solution. Protocols and processes shall also be designed to minimize operating and maintenance cost of such terminals.

The security requirements for public transport ticketing stem from countering fraud and maintaining user privacy. Mayes et. al. [21] provide a good topical introduction to ticketing and fraud control. In terms of revenue loss, the main system fraud are individuals that enter and exit the system without paying. Thus, it is not surprising that the biggest reduction in public transport fraud to date happened with the introduction of reliable gates and machine-readable tickets or physical tokens, since this eliminates traveling without a ticket or with a cheaper minimal distance ticket in the gated systems. A similar paradigm shift has not yet occurred in the non-gated systems. We set our target to implement a ticketing system that enables distance-based fare calculation also for the non-gated travel, and the main security requirements for such a system can be formulated as:

R1. The identity of the traveler must be determined off-line and cryptographic evidence must be produced during the transaction to provide non-repudiation.

R2. Eavesdropping and replay attacks shall not provide an attacker the possibility to impersonate another user.

R3. It shall not be possible to produce starting point (or ending point) evidence without being present at that location at the given time. Users shall not be able to tap in only when they see a ticket inspector.

R4. It shall not be possible to withhold evidence and hinder it from eventually reaching the back-end fare calculation engine

R5. It shall not be feasible to confuse the ticketing system by replacing / adding fake bus and train stop passive tapping terminals. These are placed in locations that cannot be assumed to be well guarded.

R6. Ticketing credentials shall be protected against modification. Since the identity is traveler-specific, credential migration needs to be controlled.

Additionally user privacy shall be maintained. In a ticketing system using a radio channel (NFC), the main privacy threat is eavesdroppers performing *device tracking*, to determine the movements of particular users. We assume that the back-end systems adhere to standard privacy norms and legislation in terms of handling user data, and back-end data privacy issues are not considered further in this paper.

5   Architecture

In this section, we briefly present a generalized architecture for a PAN-based ticket scheme as outlined in Figure 1. The *transport authority* operates the vehicles and also provides an integrated network for its gated ticket readers. The gated NFC readers are assumed to be connected to a back-end system. Therefore, these readers can receive information like certificate revocation lists (CRL)s which they refer to during user verification. All the information exchanged during such verification is collected as transaction evidence and forwarded to a back-end processing unit, e.g. a fare calculation engine. This database can e.g. be maintained by the transport authority.

The transport authority is also responsible for distributing and maintaining the terminals (i.e. smart cards) for non-gated travel. We assume that these smart cards are physically and firmly attached to their location, and also that these smart cards are tamper-resistant.

The *accounting authority* is responsible for fare collection from the users. A transport authority can simultaneously be connected to several accounting authorities. All users have a relationship with one accounting authority, in the form of a prepaid or credit-based user account. Exactly how user invoices are

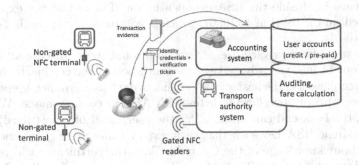

Fig. 1. Overall architecture

cleared by the accounting system is not relevant here, although it will affect e.g. the logic for black-listing users.

The accounting authority is also responsible for generating ticketing credentials and provisioning secrets to the TEE in user devices. In our system, we use the proprietary ObC provisioning system [18] for this activity, but e.g. GlobalPlatform compliant data and program provisioning [24] can also be used. The cryptographic validation of transport evidence and user backlisting are also likely to be the reponsibility of the accounting function.

Although the distinction between accounting authority and transport authority includes security-relevant interactions, e.g. related to user device blacklisting and auditing, these are not further explored in this paper. We use the term "back-end" as a collective term for all back-end operations.

6   Ticketing Credentials

It is typical not to use X.509 certificates in ticketing and payment systems, e.g. EMV [8] specifies its own size-optimized identity certificate. We go one step further in the minimization effort, and exploit the message recovery property in RSA signatures. In this way, the user identity and the public key of the user device can be extracted from the signature itself, thereby avoiding the need to transfer the device public key separately. Additionally we add a flavor of privacy protection to the construction.

The certificate outline is shown in Figure 2. A standard RSA signature consists of a private key exponentiation of an algorithm identifier and a 20 byte hash (SHA1) as payload, padded according to PKCS#1.5. In our ticketing credetials, we concatenate as much certificate payload to the hash as we can (inside the RSA exponentiation) to minimize the the overall certificate length. The shortest possible PKCS#1.5 padding is 11 bytes, so e.g. for a 1024 bit key we can save around 90 bytes with this approach. Like in the EMV standard, the certificate carries only a bare minimum of attributes. We include only the expiry time, the public key modulus of the client RSA key, and the user's identity, i.e. his primary account number (PAN) [15]. A truncated SHA-256 hash is put first so that it always fits inside the RSA exponentiation. The public key exponent is not included and is fixed at 0x10001, which is compatible with both TCG and EMV standards.

To achieve address privacy, we add an additional twist. In case all certified data does not fit into the private key exponentiation of the certificate authority (CA) signature, we use the hash of the certificate data as a symmetric encryption key, and encrypt any overflowing bytes with AES in counter mode. With this packaging, the back-end can produce, for the user, a set of (short lived) certificates for a single RSA key such that their expiry times are e.g. set one second apart. Without knowledge of the CA public key, the certificates will reveal no plaintext data, and two certificates from the same set cannot be linked.

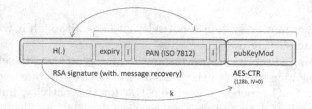

Fig. 2. Certificate with message recovery

This approach requires that the ticketing system treats the CA "public" key for user credentails as a secret. This is possible, since it will only be distributed to gated ticket terminals and ticket inspector devices. In both of these device categories, the CA key can with a high likelihood be remotely provisioned in a secure manner and locally be treated as a secret.

In our system, we use a CA key of 1408 bits, which is the current estimate for the minimum RSA key length accepted by EMV standards from 2013 onwards. The short-lived ticketing signature keys are 1024 bits to keep the certificate size small. With these parameters and assuming a PAN number length of 16 digits (typical credit card number), we end up with a certificate size of 176 bytes.

7 Gated Ticketing Protocol

The use of the ticketing credential is visible in the ticketing protocol at a gated system entry or exit. Figure 3 shows this very standard procedure for identity verification. As preconditions we assume that

1. The phone generates an RSA key pair, a transport key, inside its TEE. The phone sends the public component to the back-end, which generates a set, say 50, short-term transport "ticketing credentials" (with e.g. a one-week expiry time) for that public key component and the user's PAN.
2. The user's debit / credit rating is in order, and the device / user has not been blacklisted by the back-end since the credential was issued. The gated readers are updated with the latest CRLs.

3. For the transaction, the user's device always selects a ticketing credential that has not been presented to any ticket reader before.
4. The gated reader, being connected to the back-end, will eventually send any transaction evidence with timestamps and other context information to the backend for further processing and fare calculation.

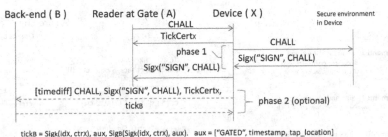

tickB = Sigk(idx, ctrx), aux, SigB(Sigk(idx, ctrx), aux).   aux = ["GATED", timestamp, tap_location]

Fig. 3. Gated tap protocol

The operation proceeds as follows. The user touches the gate. Within the NFC transaction, the reader A sends a challenge to the device X. The challenge contains at least a nonce and a reader / station Id. The client immediately responds with the selected ticketing credential, and in parallel or subsequently signs the challenge with the current transport key. Once computed the signature is then returned to the reader. Since the ticket reader knows the CA public key, it can validate the credential. With the recovered device public key, in can further verify the signature on the challenge. On successful verification the gate is opened.

With an optional handshake between the user device and the back-end servers the user device can receive a ticket inspection token signed by the back-end, in return for the uploaded transaction evidence.

8   Non-gated Ticketing

The non-gated PAN-based ticketing variant uses the same basic building blocks as gated ticketing, i.e. signatures and certificates. Minimizing NFC transaction time is still of importance, thus we will not add the cost of mutual authentication over NFC. The off-line communication overhead for such authentication is at least two times the public key modulus size (i.e. optimized certificate + signature) which adds an extra 300 ms, see Section 9.

Compared to the gated protocol variant, the main new property that we add for non-gated operation is a device-specific counter that can be attested by a signature. Such a primitive is trivially implementable with ObC or an embedded secure element with JavaCard^{TM}. Even with TPMv1.2, which is not programmable, such a primitive can be constructed by attesting to a repeatedly extended PCR [23]. We believe this section will show the usefulness of this simple TEE construction.

8.1   TEE Operation

Figure 4 summarizes the TEE operation. The *sign challenge* is the basic signature primitive, used in gated ticketing. This operation signs an incoming challenge with the transport key x. All signatures generated with x contain a four-byte prefix that identifies the signature context, i.e. the invoked TEE command.

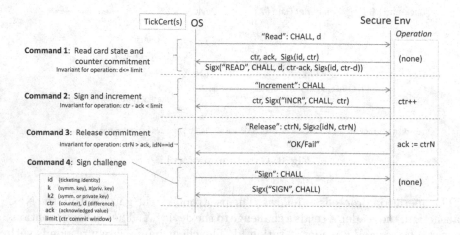

Fig. 4. TEE operations

The *sign and increment* is the augmented signature primitive, that signs a challenge, but also includes a counter value in the signature. The command primitive updates the monotonically increasing counter at every use. The TEE program state includes a counter window, i.e. the amount of *sign and increment* signatures are limited by the current size of that window. Only an external release, implemented by the *release commitment* command and secured by signature key $k2$, can open up that window and allow more counter-bound signatures to be made. This will be one incentive for user devices to report ticket evidence in non-gated operation. We use a symmetric, AES-based MAC for the signature with $k2$, since ObC-enabled devices on the market do not support public-key RSA operations inside the TEE.

The *read card state and counter commitment* is used for ticket inspection and for retrieving a counter value commitment, $Sig_k(id, ctr)$. This attribute uses a symmetric signature primitive with a key k that is shared between the device and the back-end and possibly ticket inspectors. Key k can e.g. be derived from a master secret with a key diversification algorithm: $k = KDIV(master, id)$. Using the d input parameter, a commitment for the current, or any past counter value can be requested. The difference between the current counter value and the counter indicated by the commitment value is visible in an additional asymmetric signature used with ticket inspection. That signature also binds the number of counter values used, but not yet released by a back-end server. For the device's benefit the command also returns the current counter value and the last value acknowledged by the back-end server.

8.2   Non-gated Protocol

The non-gated ticketing operation is presented in Figure 5. The user device X taps a *terminal* R (labeled "Bus Stop Card" for clarity), and then performs an internal operation eventually followed by a reporting activity towards the accounting authority. We will look at these different stages in order:

In *phase 0*, which can be done inside the device at any time preparing for the next ticketing event, the device X invokes the *read card state and counter commitment* command with $d = 0$, i.e. it retrieves the commitment $Sig_k(id_X, ctr_X)$ for its latest counter value. The rest of the data returned by the TEE command is not used at this point.

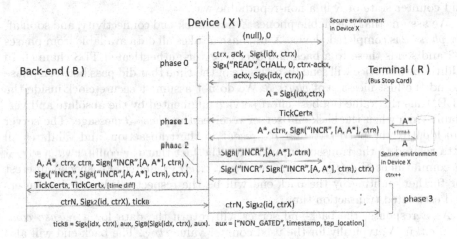

tickB = Sigk(idx, ctrx), aux, SigB(Sigk(idx, ctrx), aux).   aux = ["NON_GATED", timestamp, tap_location]

Fig. 5. Non-gated tap protocol

The tap on the terminal R, i.e. *phase 1*, is more or less exactly the gated protocol, run by device X as the challenger. As a result, the terminal R will return its device certificate $TickCert_R$ to X as well as a signature with counter binding for the terminal's counter ctr_R over the user device challenge which was its counter commitment $Sig_k(id_X, ctr_X)$. Note that the terminal R also adds to the signed response some auxiliary data $A*$, which we will discuss later. For now it suffices to note that $A*$ will have to be transported along with the terminal signature Sig_R towards the back-end in order for that signature to be verifiable.

The TEE logic in terminals R can be equivalent to the one in user devices X. However, for this protocol, the counter limit in terminals is not really used, and neither is the read operation, so in essence only the *sign and increment* operation is necessary on terminals B.

As $Sig_k(id_X, ctr_X)$ cannot be resolved by entities without knowledge of k, and since ctr_X is always a fresh value, we can deduce that the user device X maintains unlinkability when transmitting $Sig_k(id_X, ctr_X)$. On the contrary, terminal R has no privacy requirement, thus $TickCert_R$, which is of the format described in Section 6, can be signed by a CA key whose public component is truly public, e.g. known by device X. Based on R's ticketing certificate and signature, X can determine the identity and validity of R - an important protection against a specific denial-of-service attack (requirement R5). As we can adjust the lengths of A, $A*$ and ctr_R to be roughly of the same size as the challenge in the gated operation, we will see that the tap time is composed of the transmission cost (250ms) and the speed of the RSA exponentiation in a legacy smart card which unfortunately can be 400ms or higher [2,22].

In *phase 2*, device X re-invokes its own TEE, and issues the *sign and increment* command, with the *phase 1* protocol response received from R as the challenge. This operation binds the current identity and counter state of X to the identity and counter state of R in a non-repudiable way.

We assume that the mobile phones X have back-end connectivity, and soon after *phase 2* is completed, device X in *phase 3* takes all data available from phases 0-2 and sends these to a back-end over a server-authenticated TLS channel. In addition, the device will send its estimate of the time that did pass between phase 1, and the first message of *phase 3*. We do not assume a secure clock inside the TEE, thus this value is a best-effort service augmented by the absolute and verifiable time when the back-end server receives the *phase 3* message. The server can identify the parties X and R present in the transaction, and validates all data related to the transaction, including the fact that the counter values ctr_X in commitment $Sig_k(id_X, ctr_X)$ and $Sig_x(\ldots, ctr_X)$ match. Of special interest for further auditing by the back-end will be the respective identities, counters and estimated transaction time.

As a response, the back-end server will return the data for a *release commitment* in X, typically for the used counter value ctr_X. The back-end will also return some information to X for ticket inspection. With respect to the evidence collected, a back-end auditing function will execute a process for dealing with "lost" counter values, i.e. counter values of X that are never reported back to the system.

We see that if X consistently suppresses the *phase 3*, transaction will eventually cause the TEE to "lock up" due to window-size exhaustion. This is the main enforcement for reporting evidence. Nevertheless, we did not want to put the immediate availability of the back-end communication channel from X in the critical path for ticket inspection and neither did we want to only rely on local window enforcement to suppress last-minute tap reporting. We return to these issues in the next two subsections.

8.3   Non-gated Ticket Inspection

In a PAN-based system, ticket inspection takes a different role than it typically has today. What the inspector will determine is that the device has tapped on a terminal R that is consistent (in time and place) with the ongoing user journey. By default, not much can be determined about the final destination of the transport user, if that information is not provided as an add-on commitment by the user's device X. Such information should not be necessary, though.

The default inspection protocol is outlined in Figure 6, and relies on the inspection data $tick_B$. In essence, $tick_B$ is a statement, signed by the back-end, that includes the counter commitment for X, i.e. $Sig_k(id_X, ctr_X)$, as well as auxiliary information containing e.g. the estimated time of the transaction and the tap location (identity of terminal R). The ticket validation device V will challenge the device X. The difference between the current counter value and the counter value at the time of the tap is represented as d. Typically this value is 1, if we validate the last tap. The device invokes the *read card state and counter commitment* TEE command for that d, and returns the signed response Sig_x to the validator along with $TickCert_X$ and the values d and $ctr - ack$, since they are required for signature validation. From this information the validator device can determine that $Sig_k(id_X, ctr_X)$ has been emitted from this specific device X, and it can hence trust the time and location information present in $tick_B$ and use those values to determine whether the user being present in this vehicle is consistent with the provided evidence.

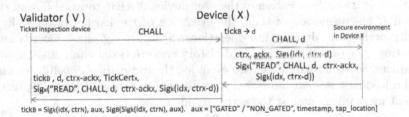

Fig. 6. Ticket inspection

Ticket inspection in the default scenario is mostly resistant against device tracking. The commitment will be visible, thus an eavesdropped message exchange during the tap can be matched with the exchange during inspection. Also the difference between the current counter value and the ticketed counter value (d), as well as the available counter window in X are visible, however the resolution of these values are too low to be useful for tracking. Ticket inspection can also be conducted before X has contacted the back-end. This is described in Appendix A.

8.4 Transaction Evidence Feedback

To identify devices X whose TEE has been broken (especially the counter window feature), and to provide a way to generally audit non-reporting devices, the stand-alone smart cards terminals R collect a log of past transactions, containing terminal R's counter value at the time of the transaction (4 bytes), the challenge from a device X (20 bytes) and the number of times this record has been reported (1B). E.g. 100 KB of card storage can accommodate a ring buffer of 4000 such records. These logs are assumed to be available for an evidence collector, e.g. ticket validation devices, but the protocol for that information retrieval is not considered here. However, for each ticketing tap, the card will at random select several (at least 2) of these past transactions into a tuple set $A*$ and bind that data to the return message signature, forcing the tapping device to convey $A*$, along with its own evidence A, back to the back-end. If the length of $A*$ is two records, then in normal (non-attacked) operation, the back-end will typically receive each tap challenge three times even without explicit evidence collection from terminals R.

The challenge commitments $Sig_k(id_X, ctr_X)$ of all participating devices can be calculated a-priori by the back-end server, since it knows the key k and the last used counter value. If such future commitment values are put in a database, the back-end can resolve identities from the $A*$ commitments even if the device X that generated a tap does not immediately report it. The main benefit of this system is to catch devices that repeatedly use the same non-reported commitment as well as devices where the counter window is broken, thereby allowing them to forward the counter and related commitments without being forced to report any evidence to the back-end.

As there is no authentication of the user device X that touches R, and since terminal R has no notion of time, the event log of the card is erasable by repeatedly performing dummy tap operations. Still, for e.g. 4000 records and a transaction time of 300-600ms, a card history erasure takes a full 20-40 minutes to complete. So even though the card event log theoretically is erasable, we claim that the feedback system motivates its existence in terms of being a practical deterrent mechanism against the active fraudster.

9   Implementation and Measurements

This paper reports on ongoing work for building a ticketing system for trialing the presented concepts in a real environment. At the time of writing, the gated protocol implementation is fully functional. Our terminal (smart card) implementation is also ready, but for non-gated operation our phone client is still under development. Thus, non-gated measurements are done between a PC and the smart card, whereas all other values are measured between a Symbian phone and its respective counterparts.

We have implemented the ticketing application on a Nokia C7 phone, which includes necessary hardware and software support for both the TEE and NFC capabilities. The terminal is a NXP SmartMX card, produced in 2009. The TEE application for the terminal is written in JavaCard 2.2.1, and the one for the phone in ObC bytecode. The NFC channel is operating at 106 kbps. Our reference terminal/reader is a Linux PC, running Ubuntu Maverick with an NFC reader (ACR 122U) connected to it. The open-source project *libnfc* provides the Linux NFC stack, whereas a "gate application" controls the protocol flow.

In gated operation the NFC communication runs in peer-to-peer mode [10], whereas in non-gated the phone operates as a card reader. Back-end reference servers, e.g. for transaction evidence collection and certificate provisioning, are traditional LAMP setups, but those interfaces are not time-critical and therefore not measured.

Table 1. Time taken for each ticketing protocol execution

Protocol	Target discovery	Message 1	NFC Hand Over	Message 2	Process 1	Message 3	Process 2	Total
Gated	36 ms	24 ms	18 ms	94 ms	[~60 ms]	74 ms	10 ms	256 ms
Non-gated	36 ms	14 ms	[18 ms]	~ 50 ms	≥ 297 ms	~ 102 ms	—	~ 499 ms
Ticket Inspection	36 ms	14 ms	18 ms	290 ms	20 ms	—	—	378 ms

Table 1 presents the time taken by different events in each NFC transaction to complete. Messages 1, 2 and 3 represent PDUs that are exchanged in each protocol. For instance, in the gated protocol these represent $CHALL$, $TickCert_x$ and Sig_x, respectively. Similarly Process 1 and 2 represent the TEE cryptographic operations. For some protocols, the TEE can be consulted in parallel with transmission which eliminates those timings from the critical path in the protocol.

The main insight from the measurements is that for now, the TEE invocation cost (60-70 ms in ObC) in legacy devices is insignificant compared to the cost caused by very poor NFC throughput (only around 1 byte/ms).

10 Requirements Analysis

We are likely to fulfill the main functional arguments. For gated transactions we already know that the implementation meets the 300ms transaction time goal. The non-gated protocol shows that we can implement passive terminals with contact-less smart card technology, and we believe that the transaction time for tapping the terminals can be kept acceptable.

For security, the **isolation** of credential secrets and all operations on them, i.e. the RSA private key, its use as well as counter management is for user devices X guaranteed by the TEE and the ObC, as is outlined in [18], and for terminals by the smart cards which are integrated components with tamper-protection. The same reasoning holds for the confidentiality and integrity of credential data provisioning, say for the secret k. In ObC this is guaranteed by its own provisioning protocol [18], and for smart cards the use GlobalPlatform protocols [24] ascertain the same properties.

The security requirements are met as follows: The identity of the traveler can at any time be proven based on a signature-based challenge-response protocol and a ticketing credential for the used key. This can be done off-line (R1). Impersonation is not possible due to the interactiveness of all protocols involving the user device (R2). In the current implementation the ticketing identity is bound to the TEE and non-migratable. The ticketing credentials are signed by the CA, thus their integrity is assured (R6).

We acknowledge the potential cryptographic danger of using PKCS#1.5 padded RSA signatures with recovery for our certificates[5]. We still chose the approach, since we need to target both privacy and size requirements. With more bytes to spare in our protocols, our preferred solution is to use that additional transmission budget for mutual authentication, which can solve the privacy issue more reliably than by applying a safer (and bigger) signature primitive with message recovery.

The tap location evidence is bound in time by the counter of terminal R. For very remote locations with little traffic, an interactive relay attack to the terminal may be successful. Not reporting an executed tap is very likely to be caught by auditing based on the terminal feedback channel $A*$ through other devices. (R3). The TEE will only cooperate within a limited window if evidence is withheld, thereby suppressing the release commitments from the backend (R4). The terminals are authenticated by the user devices tapping them, so impersonation attacks on terminals is not feasible (R5).

For privacy, our user-device to back-end connections are run over server-authenticated TLS. For the NFC transactions, the client is given many "anonymized" certificates that are valid simultaneously. We also assume that the system is set up with two CAs, one for certifying users' devices, which is kept secret as outlined in Section 6, and a public CA key used for certifying terminal cards. With these preconditions, if the client devices vary the certificates they use, an eavesdropper cannot bind the NFC ticketing transactions to any given PAN or user — there is no plaintext data visible in the certificate nor in the challenge - response protocols. The Nokia C7 phone that we use also randomizes the NFC radio identity, eliminating the address tracking threat also on lower protocols levels. Also ticket inspection, in the presence of $tick_B$, will reveal no user data on the NFC radio.

11   Future Work and Conclusions

This paper provides a protocol framework for combining gated and non-gated ticketing into one coherent system. Some parts of the architecture are already implemented, and we are working on the rest of the system to get it ready for trialing. Especially the non-gated protocols leverage the TEE present in mobile phones to securely bind the ticket system state of the phone to the one present in the terminal. In combination with the TEE-enforced transaction window limit we can reliably use the phone as a reporting channel. To our knowledge, we are also the first to report on a RSA-based system that deploys full identity verification (with certificate and signature) for NFC ticketing within 300ms using keys of acceptable length. Our system additionally provides protection against device tracking, also a first in this context.

References

1. Smart Card Alliance. Transit and contactless financial payments: New opportunities for collaboration and convergence. A Smart Card Alliance Transportation Council White Paper (October 2006), http://www.smartcardalliance.org/resources/lib/Transit_Retail_Pmt_Report.pdf (accessed: August 2011)
2. Anderson, R., Bond, M., Choudary, O., Murdoch, S.J., Stajano, F.: Might Financial Cryptography Kill Financial Innovation? – The Curious Case of EMV. In: Danezis, G. (ed.) FC 2011. LNCS, vol. 7035, pp. 220–234. Springer, Heidelberg (2012)
3. ARM. Technical reference manual: Arm 1176jzf-s (trustzone-enabled processor), http://www.arm.com/pdfs/DDI0301D_arm1176jzfs_r0p2_trm.pdf
4. Brakewood, C.E.: Contactless prepaid and bankcards in transit fare collection systems. Master's thesis, Massachusetts Institute of Technology (2010), http://hdl.handle.net/1721.1/60796
5. Coron, J.-S., Naccache, D., Stern, J.: On the Security of RSA Padding. In: Wiener, M. (ed.) CRYPTO 1999. LNCS, vol. 1666, pp. 1–18. Springer, Heidelberg (1999)
6. de Koning Gans, G., Hoepman, J.-H., Garcia, F.: A Practical Attack on the MIFARE Classic. In: Grimaud, G., Standaert, F.-X. (eds.) CARDIS 2008. LNCS, vol. 5189, pp. 267–282. Springer, Heidelberg (2008), 10.1007/978-3-540-85893-5_20
7. Ekberg, J.-E., Kylanpaa, M.: Mobile trusted module. Technical Report NRC-TR-2007-015, Nokia Research Center (November 2007), http://research.nokia.com/files/NRCTR2007015.pdf
8. EMV. Integrated Circuit Card Specifications for Payment System. Version 4.2, EMVCo (2008)
9. EMV. Contactless Specifications for Payment System. Version 2.1, EMVCo (2011)
10. NFC Forum. Logical Link Control Protocol. NFCForum-TS-LLCP_1.0, Technical Specification (2000)
11. Ghiron, S.L., Sposato, S., Medaglia, C.M., Moroni, A.: Nfc ticketing: A prototype and usability test of an nfc-based virtual ticketing application. In: First International Workshop on Near Field Communication, NFC 2009, pp. 45–50 (February 2009)
12. ISO/IEC 14443. Identification cards – Contactless integrated circuit cards – Proximity cards. ISO, Geneva, Switzerland (2008)
13. ISO/IEC 18092:2004. Information technology – Telecommunications and information exchange between systems – Near Field Communication – Interface and Protocol (NFCIP-1), 1st edn., ISO, Geneva, Switzerland (2004)
14. ISO/IEC 21481:2005. Information technology – Telecommunications and information exchange between systems – Near Field Communication Interface and Protocol -2 (NFCIP-2), 1st edn., Geneva (2005)
15. ISO/IEC 7812-1:2006. Identification Cards - Idnetification of issuers - Part 1: Numbering system, 3rd edn., ISO, Geneva (2006)
16. ISO/IEC 7816-4:2005. Identification cards - Integrated circuit cards - Part 4: Organization, security and commands for interchange, 2nd edn., ISO, Geneva, Switzerland (2005)
17. KooMan, F.: Using mobile phones for public transport payment. Master's thesis, Radboud University Nijmegen (2009)
18. Kostiainen, K., Ekberg, J.-E., Asokan, N., Rantala, A.: On-board credentials with open provisioning. In: ASIACCS 2009: Proceedings of the 4th International Symposium on Information, Computer, and Communications Security, pp. 104–115. ACM, New York (2009)

19. Lau, P.S.C.: Developing a contactless bankcard fare engine for transport for london. Master's thesis, Massachusetts Institute of Technology (2009), http://hdl.handle.net/1721.1/55337
20. Luptak, P.: Public transport sms ticket hacking. Presented in Hacking at Random (2009), https://har2009.org/program/events/89.en.html
21. Mayes, K.E., Markantonakis, K., Hancke, G.: Transport ticketing security and fraud controls. Information Security Technical Report 14(2), 87–95 (2009); Smart Card Applications and Security
22. Mehta, S.: Analysis of future ticketing scenarios for transport for london. Master's thesis, Massachusetts Institute of Technology (June 2006), http://hdl.handle.net/1721.1/34592
23. Parno, P., Lorch, J., Douceur, J., Mickens, J., McCune, J.: Memoir: Practical state continuity for protected modules. In: IEEE Symposium on Research in Security and Privacy (2011)
24. Global platform. Globalplatform card specification v2.2.1 (2011), http://www.globalplatform.org/specificationscard.asp
25. Srage, J., Azema, J.: M-Shield mobile security technology. TI White paper (2005), http://focus.ti.com/pdfs/wtbu/ti_mshield_whitepaper.pdf
26. Wilcox, H.: Mobile ticketing: Transport, sport, entertainment event 2008-2013. Technical report, Juniper Research (October 2008), http://www.juniperresearch.com/reports.php?id=155 (accessed: July 2011)

Appendix A: Ticket Inspection w.o. Back-End Confirmation

If the *phase 3* of the ticketing protocol has not yet been conducted by device X, ticket inspection can be done based on the complete tap transaction evidence and an additional device identification signature as shown in Figure 7. For non-gated transactions this amounts to 600-700 bytes, and will take around 1s to transfer over NFC. The validation device will not be able to reliably determine the tap time, so in this sense the protocol is weaker than the default validation. However, if the user consistently uses old tap evidence, the inspection transaction is enough to catch him. Even as the validation device may not have an exact time for the tap, it can have a list of terminal counters from e.g. a day back, since the back-end will get this information and can periodically distribute it to validation devices. Since the terminal R counter values will be visible in this validation protocol option, also the counters of legitimately tapping users traveling on a given route (e.g. in the same bus) will provide current counter ranges for the bus stop cards relevant for this vehicle. Furthermore, the ticket inspection devices can also be assumed to eventually report their validation evidence back to the back-end, which has more accurate terminal R counter vs time information. In combination, all of these mechanisms makes it very hard for an active fraudster to not be caught by ticket inspection, espcially as his TEE identity will be unconditionally mapped to the inspection.

A privacy drawback of the ticket inspection without back-end confirmation is that it exposes the exact counter values of device X to an eavesdropper. Those values may be enough to track a single user.

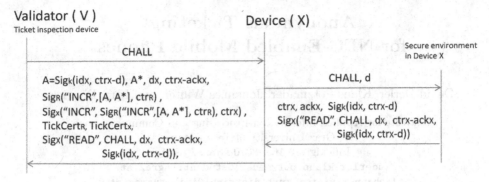

Fig. 7. Ticket inspection before phase 3

Appendix B: Back-End Data Auditing

In our ticketing system, the taps that are received either for gated or non-gated travel can be collected and indexed for a given user PAN. The taps form a series of waypoints in place and time for the fare calculation system to determine the applicable user charges. The system allowes charging based on fixed monthly, regionalized fees, hourly fees or any other schemes in use today. The main advantage of the approach is however that it does open up the possibility for much more flexible charging options where the user is charged with much finer granularity than today, e.g. based on travelled distance, time-of-day, volume discounts etc.

It is also relevant to perform some data mining on the received data, to identify fraud attempts and anomalies of various kinds. The input data is structurally simple - terminals R and gates represent locations, for gates the transaction time for each entry or exit of devices X is trivially logged, in non-gated operation, the monotonic counter value of the terminals R is a representation of time. The back-end receives time estimates for those values from devices X, and a hard bound for the time, based on the time of reporting. Thus, for each counter increment in R a statistically accurate mapping can be made for most terminals R, even in the absence of some reported evidence. Combined with the identification provided by the commitments returned in the $A*$ data elements, the back-end server should be able to patch together a fairly accurate picture of who tapped what and when, and evidence for all of these events should eventually flow back to the back-end. Based on the data, information about fraud attempts as well as malfunctioning or non-reporting devices can be mined from the data. With this information the appropriate user can be notified, and if necessary, extra invoicing, device black-listing or even legal penalties can be applied.

We believe that both the fare calculation and security auditing processes are good research problems in their own right, and constitute excellent further work when the system is deployed in a live test or field trial.

Anonymous Ticketing
for NFC-Enabled Mobile Phones

David Derler, Klaus Potzmader, Johannes Winter, and Kurt Dietrich

Institute for Applied Information Processing and Communications
Graz University of Technology
Inffeldgasse 16a, 8010 Graz, Austria
{dderler,klaus.potzmader}@student.tugraz.at,
{johannes.winter,kurt.dietrich}@iaik.tugraz.at

Abstract. Modern smart-phones are equipped with various interfaces
such as NFC, allowing a versatile use of the device for many different
applications. However, every transaction of the phone especially via its
NFC interface can be recorded and stored for further analysis, bearing
a threat to the privacy of the device and its user. In this paper, we
propose and analyze the efficiency of a mobile ticketing system that is
designed for privacy protection. In our investigation, we lay focus on
the specific algorithms which are based on selective disclosure protocols
and Brands' one-time show credential system. Our proof-of-concept prototype includes client- and terminal side implementations for detailed
analysis. Moreover, we propose algorithm improvements to increase the
performance and efficiency of the NFC transactions on the client side in
our system.

1 Introduction

The broad availability of NFC (Near-Field-Communication)-capable mobile devices is an essential enabler for contact-less applications. Different applications
have been developed and deployed taking advantage of this new technology, e.g.
mobile payment, mobile ticketing. Although all these applications allow the user
to ease his life, they pose a threat to its privacy. For instance, having your tickets
for public transport ready on your mobile enables you to easily use the tickets
without fiddling with ticket vending machines or old-fashioned paper tickets.
However, the actual use of the electronic ticket may enable operators to track
the owner of the ticket while passing checkpoints, entering a train or verifying
the ticket by a conductor. Combing all these checkpoints in combination with
information about the time allows to reproduce the daily route of an individual.
The use of mobile-phones and Near Field Communication further pushes this
threat of mobile ticketing as modern devices have permanent Internet access allowing operators of readily available services much insight into their customers
and their behavior. Consequently, privacy-preserving methods are required in
order to use the advantages of easing one's life without being a threat to one's
privacy.

L. Chen, M. Yung, and L. Zhu (Eds.): INTRUST 2011, LNCS 7222, pp. 66–83, 2012.
© Springer-Verlag Berlin Heidelberg 2012

Modern smart-phones do not only own a rich set of interfaces such as NFC, but are are also equipped with security enhancing features like Secure elements or the ARMs TrustZone CPU Extension [1]. Such security features are a requirement for protecting sensitive data from the mobile's owner as well as from any other adversary trying to get access to the sensitive information.

Hence, the question arises how these security features can be used in electronic ticketing scenarios and further, how can they be used in a way that service operators may not link a customer to a certain ticket, whilst still being able to ensure that the ticket is valid. In addition, the identity of the ticket owner has to remain anonymous. Unfortunately, most of the existing NFC enabled applications completely neglect privacy protection. For this reason, we investigated the requirements for a privacy protecting mobile ticketing application. In this article, a DSA-based protocol is illustrated, and pros and cons regarding its implementation on devices with limited computational power are discussed. As a result, detailed timing measurements are presented.

1.1 Related Work

The first approach for anonymity protection based on zero-knowledge proofs was introduced by Chaum [8], which has been extended and adapted multiple times since. Brands [4] and Camenisch and Lysyanskaya [7] proposed schemes for private credential protocols, of which we use a version of Brands' DSA-based private credential protocol as summarized in [11].

Bichsel [2] implemented a prototype using the K-show credential protocol by Camenisch et al. [6], resulting in computation times of about 9 minutes for issuing and 7 minutes for showing credentials. Tews and Jacobs [22] analyzed the performance of the RSA-based Brands protocols on Java Cards and concluded that they perform rather badly and that elliptic curve cryptography would not improve performance due to the crypto coprocessor lacking support for point additions. The runtime mentioned for a verification session with four attributes was about 9 seconds. Bichsel et al.[3] implemented a prototype using the Camenisch and Lysyanskaya scheme on a standard JavaCard with regard to fully exploiting the crypto coprocessor and transient memory. They stated that those protocols seem unsuited for a JavaCard implementation due to the long execution time. Nevertheless, partial solutions to the performance problematics and thus delivering vital insight on how to speed up modular arithmetic on JavaCards were offered. Dietrich introduced a Direct Anonymous Attestation [5] based scheme using a similar approach with regard to utilizing the secure element for computing and storing sensitive parts of the operation [9]. Madlmayr et al. [18] implemented a mobile ticketing system using public key cryptography and utilizing near field communication to issue and verify tickets, although not in an anonymous manner.

1.2 Our Contribution

In this paper, we analyze the efficiency of selective disclosure protocols on modern mobile phones with respect to available security components i.e. secure elements and ARM TrustZone. As the efficiency of such protocols is crucial for their acceptance by users, we focus on optimized implementations of the *issue-* and *showing-protocol.* High efficiency is important as the single user will hardly accept a long waiting time when showing his electronic ticket. Moreover, the efficiency of the used algorithms and the overall system must allow a certain number of clients to pass a checkpoint in order to provide sufficient handling of larger groups of ticket holders.

In detail, we analyze the efficiency of a mobile ticketing application based on Brands' private credential protocol as defined in [11]. For our investigations. we used a NFC-enabled Nokia 6131 mobile phone that provides a secure computing environment and a NFC interface in order to gain measurement results. In our e-ticketing application, the tickets are stored on the device's security component rather than on the back-end service. Moreover, we propose optimizations of the protocol for implementation on Secure elements and the ARM TrustZone security extension. We selected a one-time show protocol for our ticketing system because these kinds of systems are much more simpler than k- or *multi*-show credential systems and it is sufficient for the requirements of our system.

2   Background

2.1   Near Field Communication

Near Field Communication is a wireless communication technology allowing NFC-enabled devices to exchange data if their antennas are within range (usually 5-10 centimeters). In contrast to bluetooth, no pairing is required which makes it a very interesting technology for many applications. In other words, there is no need for initial configuration in order to establish a connection. ISO14443 [13] defines standards for NFC communication with smart cards while ISO18092 [14] mainly defines standards for device to device communication. Since many NFC readers are only capable of communicating according to ISO14443, we opt for a direct connection between the reader and the secure element. NFC operates at a carrier frequency of 13.56 MHz with data rates of up to 424kBit/s.

2.2   Selective Disclosure Protocols

Selective disclosure protocols provide methods for blinding parts of a certain set of credentials. Signatures over credentials are jointly computed during the issuing phase involving a trusted certification authority that ensures the authenticity of a signed credential. The person in possession of the credential is able to hide certain attributes of such a credential while still being able to prove validity. Due to this setup, operators of ticketing systems based on such kinds of protocols are not able to track their customers because they lack knowledge of who used a certain ticket.

In this paper, we used the DSA-based protocol proposed by Glenn et al. [11].

3   Protocol

3.1   Preliminaries

The whole protocol proposed by Glenn et al. is based on the discrete logarithm problem which is considered to be a hard mathematical problem [11]. In this section, we want to discuss the mathematical background of the protocol mentioned before. For our explanations, we assume to have four private credentials denoted as x_1, x_2, x_3, x_4.

In order to prove the possession of the credentials without disclosing all attributes, some kind of selective disclosure mechanism is needed. Therefore, a discrete logarithm representation as stated in equation 1 is introduced.

$$h = g_1^{x_1} \cdot g_2^{x_2} \cdot g_3^{x_3} \cdot g_4^{x_4} \tag{1}$$

From now on, let

- $\mathbb{Z}_q$ be the set $\{0, 1, \ldots q\text{-}1\}$ for a prime q
- $\mathbb{Z}_p$ be the set $\{0, 1, \ldots p\text{-}1\}$ for a prime p

If one now wants to prove knowledge of the discrete logarithm representation he randomly chooses $w_1, \ldots, w_4$ in $\mathbb{Z}_q$ and computes

$$a = SHA1(g_1^{w_1} \cdot g_2^{w_2} \cdot g_3^{w_3} \cdot g_4^{w_4}) \tag{2}$$

$$c = SHA1(a\|M) \tag{3}$$

with M being a message known to both parties containing a nonce to ensure the freshness of c. Furthermore, he computes $r_1, \ldots, r_4$ according to equation 4:

$$r_i = c \cdot x_i + w_i \tag{4}$$

Afterwards, the prover transmits (a, r_1, r_2, r_3, r_4) to the verifier who can now compute c as in equation 3 and verify that:

$$a \stackrel{!}{=} SHA1((g_1^{r_1} \cdot g_2^{r_2} \cdot g_3^{r_3} \cdot g_4^{r_4}) \cdot h^{-c}) \tag{5}$$

As mentioned before, the protocol we used is a slightly modified version of Glenn et al. [11], which in turn is based on the work of Brands [4]. Since the single steps of the protocol have been rearranged, the protocol is listed in detail in the following subsections, although the computations remain the same as in the referred paper. The protocol requires an agreement upon the DSA parameters. In our prototype. we used ps ranging from 768 to 1984 bits and a q with 160 bit length. The generator g is the same length as p. As the whole protocol relies on the ability to prove knowledge of a discrete logarithm representation, there is need for a CA to publish the generators $g_1, \ldots, g_4$ and h_0 required for the discrete logarithm function stated in equation 8. The generators are numbers in $\mathbb{Z}_p$ and are calculated by taking the DSA Generator g to the powers of n randomly generated values $y_0, ..., y_{n-1}$ in $\mathbb{Z}_q$:

$$h_0 = g^{y_0} \bmod p \tag{6}$$

$$g_i = g^{y_i} \bmod p \text{ with } 1 \leq i \leq n-1 \tag{7}$$

$$f(x_1, x_2, x_3, ...x_n, \alpha) := (g_1^{x_1} \cdot g_2^{x_2} \cdot g_3^{x_3} \cdot .... \cdot g_n^{x_n} \cdot h_0)^{\alpha} \bmod p \tag{8}$$

In the equation above $x_1, ..., x_n$ represent the credentials to be blinded. They are assumed to be in $\mathbb{Z}_q$.

3.2   Issuing

In the issuing phase, the client obtains a ticket from a terminal that is connected to the certification authority. Figure 1 shows the basic process of issuing a ticket and the algorithms below describe the individual steps required on terminal- and client-side in order to gain a jointly computed ticket.

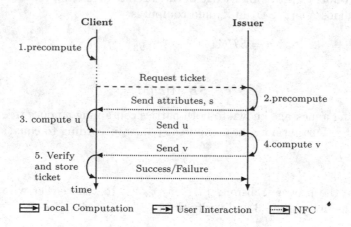

Fig. 1. Issuing Protocol

Algorithm 1 shows the precomputation phase, where the secret alphas are randomly generated for future use, and the modulo inverse of alpha is computed beforehand. As soon as the client chooses a ticket using the user interface on terminal side and moves the mobile phone towards the NFC reader, the issuing process starts. Issuing uses the precomputed alphas in case there are values present, otherwise the precomputation phase is started initially.

On the terminal side, a random nonce k is generated and the blinded k, called s, is computed as shown in algorithm 2 and sent over to the secure element. In contrast to the original protocol the attributes encoded within the chosen ticket

---

Algorithm 1. Step 1 - Precomputation Client side

1: Pick random values in $\mathbb{Z}_q$ for α, α_2, α_3
2: Compute $\alpha^{-1} \bmod q$
3: Pick a random value w_l of length q for verification purposes

---

Algorithm 2. Step 2 - Precomputation Terminal side

1: Pick a random value k in $\mathbb{Z}_q$
2: Compute blinded k: $s \leftarrow g^k \bmod p$

(expiration date, ...) are sent over. The terminal is expected to have enough computational power to carry out the operations within acceptable time limits.

Step 3 computes the first part of the signature over the credentials (u') as in algorithm 3 and sends u, which represents the blinded u', back to the terminal.

Algorithm 3. Step 3 - Computation of u

1: $h \leftarrow g_1^{x_1} \cdot \ldots \cdot g_n^{x_n}$
2: $h' \leftarrow (h_0 \cdot h)^\alpha \bmod p$
3: $\beta \leftarrow g^{\alpha_2} \cdot (h_0 \cdot h)^{\alpha_3} \bmod p$
4: $\gamma \leftarrow \beta \cdot s \bmod p$
5: $u' \leftarrow \text{SHA1}(h' \| \gamma) \bmod q$
6: $u \leftarrow u' - \alpha_2 \bmod q$

As shown in algorithm 4, the terminal then computes t and v and sends v over to the client.

As a last step, the client computes the remaining part of the signature over the attributes and verifies whether the u' calculated using the signature is the same as computed above (see algorithm 5). If this is the case, a valid ticket consisting of

$$h', u', v', x_1, ..., x_n, \alpha^{-1} \bmod q$$

has been issued and is kept within the secure element.

3.3 Verification

The verification procedure is the same as the one proposed by Glenn et al. [11]. In this phase, the client shows that he is in possession of a valid ticket by proving knowledge of the discrete logarithm representation of the credentials. This is done by splitting the discrete logarithm representation up in a show- and a hide-product where the hide-product is computed with blinded values of the credentials as shown in algorithms 6 and 7.

Algorithm 4. Step 4 - Computation of t and v

1: $t \leftarrow (y_0 + x_1 y_1 + ... + x_n y_n)^{-1} \bmod q$
2: $v \leftarrow (k - u)t \bmod q$

Algorithm 5. Step 5 - Validation of ticket

1: $v' \leftarrow (v + \alpha_3)\alpha^{-1} \bmod q$
2: **if** $u' = \mathrm{SHA1}(h' \| (g^{u'} h'{}^{v'}) \bmod p) \bmod q$ **then**
3:     Keep Ticket
4:     **return** Success
5: **else**
6:     **return** Failure
7: **end if**

After the verification phase, the operator knows whether the shown ticket is valid or not. Figure 2 provides an overview of how the showing process is executed, detailed information about what is computed in each step during verification is given in the following algorithms.

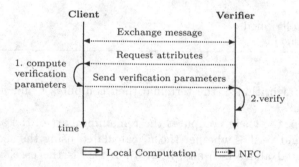

Fig. 2. Verification Protocol

As shown in algorithm 1 ,the random generation of w_l is already invoked in the precomputation phase in order to be prepared for the first showing process. If w_l was used once, a new random value has to be assigned to it. This approach decreases the showing time in case of outsourcing the random generation after each showing procedure to a service running in the background.

Algorithm 6 shows the computations performed on the client side. In step 2 a, a proof for knowing the credentials is computed. The rs in steps 4 to 7 are blinding values for the attributes whose values should remain secret. As we already assign a random value to w_l in the precomputation phase, we have to make sure that a new value is generated after step 7.

Algorithm 6. Step 1 - Compute verification parameters

1: Pick random values in $\mathbb{Z}_q$ for w_i where $i \in$ hide
2: $a \leftarrow SHA1\left(\left(\left(\prod_{i \in \text{hide}} g_i^{w_i}\right) \cdot h'^{\,w_l}\right) \bmod p\right)$
3: $c \leftarrow SHA1(a\|M) \bmod q$
4: **for all** $i \in hide$ **do**
5: $\quad r_i = (c \cdot x_i + w_i) \bmod q$
6: **end for**
7: $r_l \leftarrow \left(-c \cdot \alpha^{-1} + w_l\right) \bmod q$
8: regenerate w_l

Once the client has finished his computations he sends

$$a, h', u', v', \{x_i\}_{i \in show}, \{r_i\}_{i \in hide}, r_l$$

over to the operator. The operator then verifies the signature over the discrete logarithm representation and checks if the proof for possession of the credentials is correct. The exact steps are described in algorithm 7.

Algorithm 7. Step 2 - Verify

1: **if** $u \neq SHA1(h'\|((g^{u'} \cdot h'^{\,v'}) \bmod p)) \bmod q$ **then**
2: $\quad$ **return** Failure (Signature incorrect)
3: **end if**
4: $c \leftarrow SHA1(a\|M) \bmod q$
5: $e \leftarrow \left(\left(\prod_{i \in show} g_i^{x_i}\right) \cdot h_0\right)^c \bmod p$
6: **if** $a = SHA1\left(\left(\left(\prod_{i \in hide} g_i^{r_i}\right) \cdot h'^{\,r_l} \cdot e\right) \bmod p\right)$ **then**
7: $\quad$ **return** Success (Verification succeeded)
8: **else**
9: $\quad$ **return** Failure (Verification failed)
10: **end if**

4 Implementation Aspects

This section outlines the key decisions in implementing a mobile ticketing system based on the private credential protocol [11] and using Near Field Communication as transportation technology. As we figured that the used hardware is of importance, the following subsection lists what we work with.

4.1 Test Environment

The hardware setup for this prototype consists of the following parts:

- NFC-supporting off-the-shelf mobile device Nokia 6131 NFC with an embedded G&D Sm@rtCafe Expert 3.1 Javacard
- SDM SDI010 NFC Reader on the host side

The whole prototype is implemented in Java without any custom third party libraries, utilizing JavaME on the mobile device, Javacard on the secure element and JavaSE on the host side. Up to now, no mobile device that supports NFC and additionally has an ECC-capable secure element embedded exists. Due to that circumstance, an ECC-based protocol was not an option, despite the promising aspect of smaller key lengths and, therefore, expectedly faster computation times.

4.2 Long Integer Operations on Javacard

Implementing DSA-based selective disclosure protocols requires modular arithmetic operations on large integer numbers. The Javacard API does not provide this functionality out of the box, as is the case for Java SE which ships `java.math.BigInteger` (further referenced to as BigInteger). Therefore, we implemented a class `BigInt` that supports the operations we need. This particularly adheres to *addition/subtraction, modulo, modular multiplication, modular exponentiation, modular inversion, left shift* and *right shift*. Whereas addition, subtraction, modulo and shift operations are implemented in software, the crypto coprocessor is utilized for exponentiation and multiplication as described in [3][9][20]. Due to the fact that we only use prime moduli, we are also able to compute the modular inverse of a number with crypto coprocessor support. This is done by one subtraction and one exponentiation using the Euler Fermat theorem as shown in [19]. One might also think that the modulo operation could be computed by modular exponentiation but this is not possible as the RSA cipher does not accept an exponent of one.

An important design decision regarding our BigInt implementation was that its representation is compatible to Java SE's BigInteger `byte[]` representation as retrieved using `BigInteger. toByteArray()`. Java's BigInteger internally uses an `int[]`-representation, which is not available on a standard Javacard due to its 16-bit nature. Therefore, we decided to use a `byte[]` as our internal data container. Nevertheless, with the byte array representation being compatible, a BigInteger can be reconstructed from a BigInt value using its byte array constructor. Furthermore, it eases comprehension and ensures the re-usability of this implementation.

Our BigInt uses temporary, transient byte arrays to store intermediate results whose lengths are defined by the key length used. Details about memory management are given in section 4.4. The BigInt class itself is stateless and provides all operations as static methods, thus saving memory resources.

4.3 Architecture

Our architectural model consists of five fundamental components as shown in figure 3. The idea is a distributed environment with a single certification authority ran by the operator, which publishes the DSA parameters as well as the generators used by the issuing and verification terminals. The number of terminals and clients is not limited to one. Although possible, a terminal who verifies certain tickets is assumed to be not the same as the one who issued the ticket.

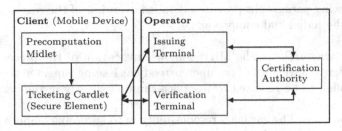

Fig. 3. Architectural model

Figure 4 digs a little deeper into the placement of the individual components within the terminal and mobile hardware. The left stack displays the terminal side, with the PCP[1] library built upon the standard JVM. It is up to the hardware's purpose whether a verification or issuing applet is being run. The stack to the right displays the inner components of the mobile device, combining the secure element running the cardlet implementation with the Java ME runtime where the MIDlet is built atop.

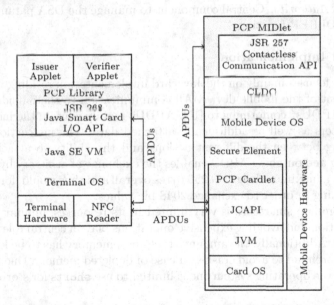

Fig. 4. Componentized view of terminal and mobile device

Prototype applets have been written in order to provide means for specifying the attributes, both for issuing and showing purposes. The reason why we decided to use applets is that for larger scenarios, these applets may be signed in order to gain local access to the NFC reader and can then be centrally deployed. Talking back to the CA in order to retrieve the published generators is not a problem with this approach either.

---

[1] Private Credential Prototype.

The following paragraphs provide a detailed overview of the roles and responsibilites of the individual components.

Precomputation MIDlet. The MIDlet allows invocation of the precomputation phase in order to have a set of parameters ready at issuing time. On the long run, this is intended to be replaced by a service running silently in the background.

Ticketing Cardlet. The cardlet's responsibility is to securely compute and store the ticket's information. The joint computations are directly carried out between the issuer/verifier and the secure element over NFC.

Issuing Terminal. Acts as the opposite party for the (slightly modified) issuing process defined above. This component can be seen as an arbitrary terminal with an embedded NFC reader to communicate with the mobile device.

Verification Device. Responsible for verifying tickets using the show protocol as defined beforehand.

Certification Authority. Central component to manage the DSA parameters and publish the DLREP function.

4.4 Client Implementation

This chapter focuses mainly on the Javacard implementation residing within the secure element of the mobile device. All communication to the outside world is done using APDUs[2] conforming to [15]. APDUs mainly contain the instructions and parameters as well as additionally attached data. The instructions enable distinguishing between the different actions and the ability to attach data to any incoming and outgoing APDU enables the exchange of arbitrary byte arrays. APDUs have a maximum length of 256 bytes overall and thus would, for instance, require chaining in order to exchange 2048 bit values.

Since a common smartcard is very limited in its resources, minimizing memory consumption and avoiding expensive operations plays a central role in cardlet development. Additionally, the amount of required memory has to be known and allocated beforehand to avoid crashes in case of depleted memory. Due to the 16-bit nature of the operating system one is limited to use `shorts` for storing integer values.

The sample prototype supports up to four showable attributes and is capable of storing one ticket at a time. However, we do not expect problems when increasing these amounts within reasonable constraints.

Structure. As figure 5 shall clarify, our implementation consists of the three major parts `PCP`, `BigInt` and `MemManager` as well as additional classes to encapsulate stored parameters. PCP extends `javacard.framework.Applet` and is, therefore, the main entry point that gets instantiated at installation time. The overridden

---

[2] Application Protocol Data Unit.

method process() allows handling of incoming APDUs and delegates the requested tasks to private submethods. The requested actions as identified by predefined instructions and parameters are carried out within the PCP class using both the memory manager and the BigInt class. Within BigInt, the individual calculations are carried out, whereas in PCP the protocol steps are executed.

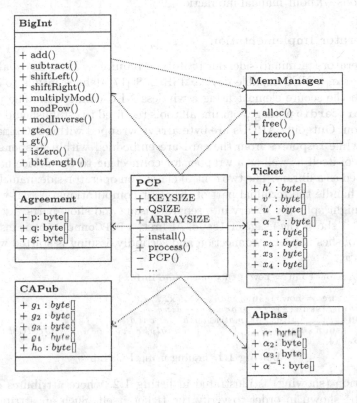

Fig. 5. A structural view of the cardlet implementation

Memory organization. The memory manager provides methods for allocating and deallocating memory while ensuring that a block of memory is zeroed out before reuse. A total of seven transient byte arrays to store intermediate results is sufficient for computing all steps of the protocol. Those general purpose byte arrays are allocated at installation time with their length being defined by the desired key length (the parameter p of the DSA setup). PCP stores any intermediate results needed across multiple protocol steps, Alphas encapsulates precomputable αs and the modular inverse, and Ticket saves the resulting values that form a ticket, namely $h', u', v', \alpha^{-1} \mod q, x_i$. In the prototype, the agreed-upon DSA parameters p, q, g are stored in Agreement and the public CA-values in CAPub. The modular inverse of alpha is stored in Alphas if precomputed and moved to Ticket if finished, which allows another precomputation without invalidating an existing ticket.

MIDlet. A MIDlet was written in order to trigger the precomputation phase. Since the MIDlet is kept very simple and basically has just the ability to send a precompute instruction to the secure element by means of JSR 257 [16], further details are omitted. Although, in the long run the MIDlet can also be implemented as a task running silently in the background and executing the computations without manual interaction.

4.5   Operator Implementation

On the operator (terminal) side, our prototype requires a Java SE-capable host, and, of course, a NFC-capable device. JSR 268 [17] defines means to communicate with the secure element using a wireless NFC-connection. The provided `javax.smartcardio` package contains all tools required to establish and use such a connection. Outgoing APDUs are byte arrays wrapped within a `CommandAPDU` instance, while responses from the card are embedded within `ResponseAPDUs`. The protocol itself as well as a wrapper for connecting to the device have been implemented as a library. The two central classes on operator-side, namely `Issue` and `Show`, handle the terminal part of the joint computations. A real-world application might split the library into separate issue and show parts.

Listing 1.1 shows the usage of `Issue`. At first, a `PCPConnection` is instatiated which establishes the NFC connection and secondly, issuing is started with four credentials x_i.

```
1  PCPConnection conn = new PCPConnection(index);
2  try{
3    Issue issue = new Issue(conn, x1, x2, x3, x4);
4    if(!issue.issue()) // process issuing
5      // error, u' did not match hash on card
6  } catch(IssueException e) {  /* probably cardlet not installed */ }
7  conn.close();
```
Listing 1.1. Issuing using PCPLib

Verification (showing) is illustrated in listing 1.2, where attributes one and two shall be shown in order to verify the ticket itself. Such an attribute may encode, for instance, an expiration date of the ticket which can then be easily verified by the host in a second step.

```
1  PCPConnection conn = new PCPConnection(index);
2  try{
3    // we request attributes 1 and 2
4    byte[] toShow = new byte[0x1, 0x1, 0x0, 0x0];
5
6    Show show = new Show(conn, toShow);
7    ShowResultSet rs = show.show();
8
9    byte[] x1 = rs.getShowedCredentials()[0];
10   byte[] x2 = rs.getShowedCredentials()[1];
11
12   if(rs.getVerificationSuccess()) // verification successful
13
14   /* check here whether attributes match required criteria */
15  } catch(ShowException e) { /* probably no ticket issued, ...*/ }
16  conn.close();
```
Listing 1.2. Showing using PCPLib

4.6   Moving to Next Generation Smart-Phone Platforms

Many next generation smart-phone platforms, which are based on the ARM microprocessor, include powerful built-in security features which can be leveraged to eliminate the need for a dedicated smart card chip. ARM's TrustZone security extensions[1],[23] provide a powerful dual-virtual CPU mechanism which allows a separation between secure software components and normal less-trusted software.

To study the feasibility of realizing the smartcard component of our mobile ticketing system as virtual software smartcard we reimplemented a minimal subset of the JavaCard 2.2.1 framework on top of the K Virtual Machine [21]. Additionally, we adapted the K Virtual Machine to function as secure world operating system on an simulated ARM TrustZone system [24]. Cryptography support within this prototype implementation is based on a well-known java-only J2ME cryptography library. The overall binary size, including all Java classes, of our prototype virtual JavaCard environment lies in the range of 540-590 kilobytes when compiled with a GNU Newlib based compiler toolchain[3]. We estimate that this size figures can be easily reduced by at least 100 kilobytes just by removing unused features like ASN1 encoding and X509 certificates from the abovementioned J2ME cryptography library.

5   Performance Evaluation

This chapter gives an overview of our implementation's computation times. We try to give a clear insight into the timing issues of Javacard-based selective disclosure protocols by providing a detailed table containing our actual computation times, see table 1. These timings have been averaged over a hundred iterations. The tested key sizes range from 768 to 1984 bits for p, while q is fixed at 160 bit as FIP186-3 [10] does not define key sizes between 1024 and 2048 bit and we do not expect much impact on the computation time when interpolating the size of q between 160 and 224 bit. Larger key sizes have been omitted for various reasons: First of all, issuing one attribute with precomputed alphas using a key length of 1984 bit is already taking about 20 seconds, which is considered too long to be usable. Another reason is that sending larger numbers from terminal to card or vice versa exceeds the maximum APDU size of 256 bytes and thus requires chaining. Finally, we require up to seven general-purpose arrays in order to store various intermediate values; using larger key sizes leads to maxing out the available transient memory and requires using EEPROM as intermediate storage. Since EEPROM is much slower and chaining APDUs leads to additional overhead, the results are not comparable anymore. In fact, the results for a key length of 1984 bit displayed below were already determined with the least used one of seven general purpose arrays located in EEPROM. Figure 6 shows the impact very clearly. There is a trick introduced by [3], who used the incoming APDU buffer as additional transient memory. This approach would help to avoid

---

[3] http://www.codesourcery.com/sgpp/lite/arm

placing a general-purpose array in EEPROM for 1984 bit but with increasing
key length the transient memory will not suffice. Our results regarding basic
multiplication and exponentiation correspond to those presented in [22].

Table 1. Protocol computation Times

Mode\ Key Length [bit]	p = 768 q = 160	p = 1024 q = 160	p = 1280 q = 160	p = 1536 q = 160	p = 1792 q = 160	p = 1984 q = 160
Issuing						
w/o precomputation						
one attribute	6642ms	7341ms	9638ms	11583ms	12937ms	22052ms
two attributes	6937ms	7649ms	9823ms	11559ms	14070ms	26066ms
three attributes	7111ms	7740ms	9770ms	11682ms	14233ms	26268ms
four attributes	7014ms	7954ms	9968ms	11928ms	14501ms	26510ms
w precomputation						
one attribute	5484ms	6716ms	8571ms	9932ms	11609ms	20763ms
two attributes	5636ms	7005ms	8507ms	9782ms	12346ms	24784ms
three attributes	5914ms	7047ms	8435ms	10022ms	12556ms	25120ms
four attributes	5852ms	7242ms	8752ms	10062ms	13023ms	25288ms
Showing						
one attribute	7717ms	9518ms	11541ms	13293ms	15923ms	16747ms
two attributes	5935ms	7239ms	8833ms	10267ms	12092ms	12675ms
three attributes	3974ms	4970ms	6048ms	7047ms	8300ms	8562ms
four attributes	2015ms	2804ms	3158ms	3747ms	4437ms	4539ms
Precomputation	1235ms	725ms	1100ms	1639ms	1308ms	1345ms

Depending on the key length, issuing lasts about 5-13 seconds with precomputed alphas. Issuing tasks without precomputation, but with crypto co-processor
supported inversion take from 6 to 14 seconds. Note that issuing without precomputation using a modular inversion as introduced by [12] carried out in software
takes about one to two minutes (depending on the key length), so the speedup
gained by using hardware support is immense. The show-processing time depends
on the key length and the number of plain text attributes as this influences the
number of random numbers and modular multi-powers to compute. Showing is
done within 2-15 seconds.

As stated before, the last column showing the times for p being 1984 Bits
long is not quite comparable to the other entries since we have used EEPROM
instead of transient memory at some point. Nevertheless, we mention it here in
order to give a preview for larger key lengths where this seems unavoidable.

Note the diverging timings for the precomputation step, for instance between
768 and 1024 bit key length. The precomputation timings depend on whether
the generated random values are within $\mathbb{Z}_q$ or need extra modulation. Therefore,
those timings may vary strongly, depending on q.

Figure 6 shows the evolution of computation times with growing key sizes. In general, computation times seem to roughly increase in a linear manner. While computation times are within acceptable limits for key lengths up to 1024 bit, larger key lengths tend to render the system unusable.

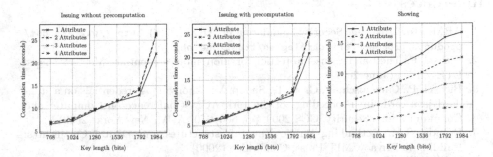

Fig. 6. Computation times in relation to key lengths

To summarize our measurements, we conclude that the processing time is acceptable up to a key length of 1024 bit, with both issuing and showing times of about seven seconds. Using the precomputation mechanism, a speedup of about one second can be achieved.

6   Conclusion and Future Work

In this paper, we discuss an efficient implementation of the selective disclosure protocol defined by [11] on a standard Javacard. The problems that arise when trying to implement such a protocol on a smart card alongside partial solutions to these are shown. In order to compute the complex operations required by this protocol within acceptable time constraints, a Javacard-compatible long integer class that utilizes the inherent crypto coprocessor is presented. Additionally, detailed performance measurements are shown. To summarize our timing results, key lengths of up to 1024 bit seem to be within acceptable limits while larger key sizes lead to inconveniently large computation times. A possible solution to the performance limitations may be ARM's TrustZone approach, where the full computational power can be exploited within a secure execution environment [1]. The feasibility of an ARM TrustZone based realization of our framework, based on a virtual JavaCard, has been demonstrated in section 4.6. For JavaCard approaches utilizing a dedicated smartcard, ECC-based systems seem to be better suited, although current off-the-shelf smart cards lack the required functionality. With JavaCard 3.0 Connected, a seemingly useful class, BigNumber, was introduced. It contains the whole `java.math.BigInteger` functionality. Evaluating the speed of those operations on a Javacard 3.0 smart card would be of interest to determine whether there is any speedup regarding additions and/or multiplications. Additionally, further support for elliptic curve cryptography on Javacard platforms is needed in order to be able to realize an ECC-based prototype on a smart card.

An analysis regarding power consumption when computing an issue- or show-operation to derive a tamper-proof version of the protocols is desirable.

References

1. ARM, Ltd. TrustZone Security Foundation by ARM (2011), http://www.arm.com/products/processors/technologies/trustzone.php
2. Bichsel, P.: Theft and misuse protection for anonymous credentials. Master's thesis, ETH Zurich (June 2007)
3. Bichsel, P., Camenisch, J., Groß, T., Shoup, V.: Anonymous credentials on a standard java card. In: Proceedings of the 16th ACM Conference on Computer and Communications Security, CCS 2009, pp. 600–610. ACM, New York (2009)
4. Brands, S.A.: Rethinking Public Key Infrastructures and Digital Certificates: Building in Privacy. MIT Press, Cambridge (2000)
5. Brickell, E., Camenisch, J., Chen, L.: Direct Anonymous Attestation. In: Proceedings of the 11th ACM Conference on Computer and Communications Security, CCS 2004, pp. 132–145. ACM, New York (2004)
6. Camenisch, J., Hohenberger, S., Kohlweiss, M., Lysyanskaya, A., Meyerovich, M.: How to win the clonewars: efficient periodic n-times anonymous authentication. In: Proceedings of the 13th ACM Conference on Computer and Communications Security, CCS 2006, pp. 201–210. ACM, New York (2006)
7. Camenisch, J., Lysyanskaya, A.: An Efficient System for Non-transferable Anonymous Credentials with Optional Anonymity Revocation. In: Pfitzmann, B. (ed.) EUROCRYPT 2001. LNCS, vol. 2045, pp. 93–118. Springer, Heidelberg (2001)
8. Chaum, D.: Security without identification: transaction systems to make big brother obsolete. Commun. ACM 28, 1030–1044 (1985)
9. Dietrich, K.: Anonymous RFID Authentication Using Trusted Computing Technologies. In: Ors Yalcin, S.B. (ed.) RFIDSec 2010. LNCS, vol. 6370, pp. 91–102. Springer, Heidelberg (2010)
10. Federal Information Processing Standards. FIPS: 186-3 Digital Signature Standard, DSS (2009)
11. Glenn, A., Goldberg, I., Légaré, F., Stiglic, A.: A description of protocols for private credentials (2001), http://crypto.cs.mcgill.ca/~stiglic/Papers/brands.pdf
12. Hars, L.: Modular inverse algorithms without multiplications for cryptographic applications. EURASIP J. Embedded Syst., 2 (January 2006)
13. International Organization for Standardization. ISO/IEC 14443 Identification cards - Contactless integrated circuit(s) cards - Proximity cards (2000)
14. International Organization for Standardization. ISO/IEC 18092 - Information technology – Telecommunications and information exchange between systems – Near Field Communication – Interface and Protocol, NFCIP-1 (2004)
15. International Organization for Standardization. ISO/IEC 7816-4 Identification cards - Integrated circuit cards - Cryptographic information application (2005)
16. Java Community Process. Contactless Communication API (JSR 257) (October 17, 2006), http://jcp.org/aboutJava/communityprocess/final/jsr257/index.html
17. Java Community Process. Java Smart Card I/O API (JSR 268) (December 11, 2006), http://jcp.org/aboutJava/communityprocess/final/jsr268/index.html

18. Madlmayr, G., Kleebauer, P., Langer, J., Scharinger, J.: Secure Communication between Web Browsers and NFC Targets by the Example of an e-Ticketing System. In: Psaila, G., Wagner, R. (eds.) EC-Web 2008. LNCS, vol. 5183, pp. 1–10. Springer, Heidelberg (2008)

19. Paar, C., Pelzl, J.: Understanding Cryptography: A Textbook for Students and Practitioners. Springer (2010)

20. Sterckx, M., Gierlichs, B., Preneel, B., Verbauwhede, I.: Efficient implementation of anonymous credentials on java card smart cards. In: 1st IEEE International Workshop on Information Forensics and Security (WIFS 2009), pp. 106–110. IEEE, London (2009)

21. Sun Microsystems Inc. J2ME Building Blocks for Mobile Devices (May 19, 2000), http://java.sun.com/products/kvm/wp/KVMwp.pdf

22. Tews, H., Jacobs, B.: Performance Issues of Selective Disclosure and Blinded Issuing Protocols on Java Card. In: Markowitch, O., Bilas, A., Hoepman, J.-H., Mitchell, C.J., Quisquater, J.-J. (eds.) WISTP 2009. LNCS, vol. 5746, pp. 95–111. Springer, Heidelberg (2009)

23. Wilson, P., Frey, A., Mihm, T., Kershaw, D., Alves, T.: Implementing Embedded Security on Dual-Virtual-CPU Systems. IEEE Design and Test of Computers 24(6), 582–591 (2007)

24. Winter, J., Wiegele, P., Lipp, M., Niederl, A., et al.: Experimental version of QEMU with basic support for ARM TrustZone (source code repository) (July 28, 2011), Public GIT repository at: https://github.com/jowinter/qemu-trustzone

Some Improvements to the Cost-Based Framework for Analyzing Denial of Service Attacks

Qinggang Yue[1,2], Feng Liu[1], and Rui Xue[1]

[1] The State Key Laboratory of Information Security,
Institute of Software, Chinese Academy of Sciences, Beijing 100190, China
[2] Graduate University of the Chinese Academy of Sciences, Beijing 100190, China
{yueqinggang,liufeng,rxue}@is.iscas.ac.cn

Abstract. Recently, people are paying more attention to formalizing and analyzing Denial of Service (DoS) attacks, but the known analysis models are either not precise enough or not readily used in an automatic way. In this paper, we make some improvements to the cost-based framework proposed by Meadows that aims to formalize DoS attacks. After improvement, the framework models intruders and protocols faithfully in CoreASM, and in a more accurate way in specification. Besides, the analysis can be performed automatically. In the improvements, a more flexible tolerance relation is defined so that the analysis result is in a broad form rather than merely binary as in previous works. Also, concrete values are used for representing the operational costs so as to make cost functions more precise and flexible in analysis.

In this paper, the JFKi protocol is automatically analyzed as an indication of the advantages of the improvements. It explores the vulnerability that was previously found manually. The discussion on the JFKi protocol shows some difficulties in designing and analyzing DoS-resistent protocols.

Keywords: Denial of Service, Formal modeling, Cost-based framework, JFKi protocol.

1 Introduction

In Denial of Service (DoS) attacks, the intruder uses any possible way to prevent legitimate participants from completing protocols or getting the corresponding service. The attack may target to the server side, the network infrastructure (routers, domain name servers, etc.) or specific client systems [15]. Colin Boyd et al. [2] divides DoS attacks into connection depletion attacks and resource depletion attacks, which try to exhaust the allowed number of connections and the computation or memory resources of the server respectively. In fact, it is impossible to prevent DoS attacks completely, since, with a certain connection request, the server should either allocate a connection or expend some resources to establish it as illegitimate. The SYN attack on TCP/IP [7] is a classic example, in which the intruder initiates excessive instances of the protocol without

L. Chen, M. Yung, and L. Zhu (Eds.): INTRUST 2011, LNCS 7222, pp. 84–101, 2012.

completing them, and exhausts the server's resources. So what we can do is just to reduce its impact. In this paper, we mainly focus on resource depletion attacks on the server side which is supposed to interact with many clients.

Resource depletion attacks are classified into flooding attacks and logical attacks (non-flooding) [19]. In the flooding attacks, the intruder initiates excessive requests for the service of a server in order to exhaust its resources, thereby preventing legitimate access to the service. To launch flooding attacks, the intruder needs to expend some resources, so the success of the attack depends on the unbalanced resource expenditure (the cost of the server is beyond its limitation while the cost of the intruder is acceptable, otherwise the intruder will exhaust its own resources before the server collapses). In logical attacks, the intruder should have a deep understanding of the protocol so as to utilize its weakness and this can reduce the cost to successfully launch a DoS attack. In this paper, we only consider the case where the intruder launches flooding attacks by generating bogus instances of a protocol repetitively.

In recent years, more and more papers appeared in the evaluation of protocols' DoS-resistance property. Both provable security methods and formal methods are proposed. D. Stebila et al. [20] put forward a security model based on the extend Canetti-Krawczyk (eCK) model proposed in [12] and gave a DoS-resistent protocol under their model. However, the model is very rough and has not been proved to be useful in analyzing other protocols. In contrast, formal methods can model the protocol and the environment more faithfully to reality, and are also proved to be effective in analyzing protocols. For example, the JFKi protocol [1] was once considered being DoS-resistent. But J.Smith et al. [18] analyzed the protocol using the formal method given by [13] and found two possible attacks. That shows the advantage of formal methods. Another advantage of formal methods comparing with provable security methods is that they can be easily adapted to perform analysis with the assistance of computers and automatically analyze.

The first work in this direction was that by Meadows in 1999 [14], where a cost-based framework was proposed by modifying the fail-stop model in [9]. A protocol is fail-stop if whenever an intruder interferes with a message and this is detected by the receiver, it will stop executing the protocol immediately. In the cost-based framework, the protocol analyzer assigns costs to all possible actions that intruders and participants may take during the execution, and also gives some tolerance relations which describe how much effort the server can take in face of an intruder of a given ability. At any accessible point of the protocol execution, the cost of the intruder and the cost of the server should fall into the defined tolerance relations, otherwise the protocol is vulnerable to DoS attacks.

Later on, Ramachandran [17] applied the cost-based framework to the JFKi protocol [1] and some other protocol fragments, and showed that JFKi is DoS-resistant if bogus messages are handled in an appropriate way. However, in 2006, J.Smith et al. [18] analyzed the JFKi protocol carefully within Meadows's framework, found some attacks. All of them were done totally by hand.

Recently, B.Groza et al.[10] formalized the tolerance relation into rules which describe protocols as state transition systems, and implemented automatic analysis. They analyzed the modified JFKi protocol in [18] and found an attack to the initiator due to the puzzle's property [3].

There exist some common weaknesses in the above works [10, 17, 18]. First, the cost of the actions taken by the principals is coarsely represented by 'cheap', 'medium' or 'expensive'. But in practice, it may be difficult to decide the cost of some actions. For example, the cost of hashing is believed to be 'cheap', but it is difficult to decide whether the cost of solving one hash-based puzzle of some difficulty level should be 'medium' or 'expensive'. Also, in different scenarios, the same operation should be given different values. For example, it may be easy to do an encryption operation on a PC, but it is an expensive operation for a mobile phone.

What is more, the sum of costs is roughly modeled as the maximum one. However, the accurate total cost of the participants is sometimes very important for analyzing protocols in detail. S.Tritilanunt[21] assigned each action a concrete value to represent the cost, analyzed the HIP protocol and showed some limitations of Meadows's framework. But the tool there supports only integers, and thus some rounding of the costs into integers are necessary to adapt to the tool. Furthermore, S.Tritilanunt's work is based on simulation which can be seen as an occurrence sequence consisting of markings that are reached and steps [21], and it does not model the specific execution of protocols.

In the automatic analysis [10] aspects, the model of intruders and protocols is not faithful enough to reality: the participants are only allowed to dispose messages that are specified by the protocol. However, in the reality, semi-bogus messages, which do not fully satisfy the condition and take participants some computational resources to detect this, are also necessarily dealt with. J.Smith et al.[18] modeled this, but it was done only manually. To judge whether the protocol is vulnerable to DoS attacks, S.Tritilanunt [21] and B.Groza et al.[10] give the following tolerance relations separately: at a particular state during the execution, the cost of the server should be smaller than that of the intruder, or the difference between them should be smaller than some given threshold.

However, they just consider some particular scenarios or just some particular aspects of the problem, and in many other scenarios the tolerance relations are too strong or too weak. For example, some scenarios allow the server to expend more resources than intruder in a session to some extent. And, in some other scenarios, they should consider not only the difference, but also the specific cost of each side. Up to now, the known analysis result is only binary: DoS-resistent or not. However, the result may be quite different depending on various scenarios.

Motivated by the vulnerabilities as above, we make some improvements to the cost-based framework to formalize DoS attacks. Specifically, the main contributions are:

- To use more precise values (supporting rational numbers) to evaluate the action costs during the executions. That allows a more precise model of costs and cost functions so that the analysis could be more flexible;

- To model intruders to be able to, among others, forge semi-bogus messages, and meanwhile the server to be able to dispose them so that the execution of the protocol is more faithfully described;
- A tolerance relation defined to be that r (defined as the ratio of the cost of servers to that of intruders) should be smaller than a prescribed threshold t, which allows flexible adjusting by the analyzer according to different scenarios. In this way, it enables the evaluation of vulnerabilities of a protocol in different scenarios rather than only to give a binary result of yes or no;
- As an application, we realize an automatic analysis of the JFKi protocol within the improved framework. The experiment explores the attack indicated in [18]. We stress that this attack, however, is explored there totally by hand.

We also make a discussion on the JFKi protocol, and point out the difficulties of designing and analyzing DoS-resistent protocols. The improvements will be illustrated and compared with some well-known works in detail in Section 3.

In this paper, we employ CoreASM to model the protocol, and ASM-SPV to analyze it automatically (see more details in Section 2.3). The tolerance relations defined in [10, 21] are also tested in our experiment, and ASM-SPV outputs another attack. Details indicate that to successfully launch such an attack, the intruder needs to expend nearly the same amount of resources as the server does. Thus, the intruder collapses before the server is exhausted, and the attack should not be viewed as effective in practice. That shows the advantage of the improvements.

The rest of the paper is organized as follows: In Section 2, we give some background knowledge for this work. In Section 3, we show the improvements to Meadows's cost-based framework. In Section 4, we model and analyze the JFKi protocol within the improved framework, and give some discussions. The paper is concluded in Section 5.

2   Preliminary

In this section, we introduce Meadows's cost-based framework, the JFKi protocol, and the Abstract State Machines-Security Protocol Verifier (ASM-SPV) employed in this paper.

2.1   Meadows's Cost-Based Framework

Meadows's work [14] is the first to formalize DoS attacks and a lot of subsequent work, including ours, is based on it. Here we show the basic definitions of the framework from [13].

Protocol Specification. Protocols in the framework are specified by the annotated Alice-and-Bob language, the following definition gives the specification:

Definition 1. *An annotated Alice-and-Bob specification P is a sequence of statements of the form* $L_i : A \rightarrow B : T_1, ..., T_m \parallel M \parallel O_1, ..., O_n$ *where:*

1. L_i *denotes the ith line in the specification*
2. *M represents the message sent from A to B*
3. T_j *is the operation performed by A,* $T_1, ..., T_m$ *refer to the ordered steps taken by A to produce M*
4. O_k *is the operation performed by B,* $O_1, ..., O_n$ *refer to the ordered steps taken by B to process and verify M*

The operations in the protocol specification are classified into three types of events:

Definition 2. *Let* $L = A \rightarrow B : T_1, ..., T_m \parallel M \parallel O_1, ..., O_n$ *be a line in an annotated Alice-and-Bob specification, we say that X is an event occurring in L if:*

1. *X is one of* T_i *or* O_j, *or;*
2. *X is 'A sends M to B' or 'B receives M from A'.*

We say that the events $T_1, ..., T_m$ *and 'A sends M to B' occur at A and the events* $O_1, ..., O_n$ *and 'B receives M from A' occur at B. There are three types of events:*

1. *Normal events, include the send and receive events and computation events such as exponentiation, and they always succeed*
2. *Verification events, may succeed or fail and only occur at the receiver side of a message*
3. *Accept event, is always the last operation on the line,* O_n, *and means that after the processing of M, B accepts it.*

Cost Sets and Cost Functions. The following definitions show the requirements that costs and cost functions should satisfy.

Definition 3. *A cost set C is a monoid with monoid operation* $+$ *and partial order* $\geq$ *such that* $x + y \geq x$ *and* $x + y \geq y$, $\forall x, y \in C$

Definition 4. *The event cost function* δ *maps events defined in an annotated Alice-and-Bob P to a cost set C and is 0 on accept events.*

Definition 5. *Let P be an annotated Alice-and-Bob protocol, C be a cost set, and* δ *be the event cost function defined on P and C. We define the message processing cost function associated with* δ *to be the function* δ' *on verifying events following the receipt of a message as follows:* $\delta'(V_j) = \delta(V_1) + ... + \delta(V_j)$

Definition 6. *We define the protocol engagement cost function associated with* δ *to be the function* Δ *defined on the accept events as follows:*
If the line $A \rightarrow B : T_1, ..., T_m \parallel M \parallel V_1, ..., V_n$ *appears in the protocol, where* V_n *is the accept event, then:*

1. *If there is no line $B \to X : O'_1, ... O'_k \parallel M' \parallel V'_1, ..., V'_n$, then $\Delta(V_n)$ is all the costs of all operations occur to B up to the accept event V_n*
2. *If there is a line $B \to X : O'_1, ... O'_k \parallel M' \parallel V'_1, ..., V'_n$, then $\Delta(V_n)$ is all the costs of all operations occur to B up to the accept event V_n, plus the sum of the costs of the O'_i*

Intruder and Intruder Cost Functions. In the framework, the Intruder controls the network. The following cost function is used to compute the cost of the intruder for interfering with a protocol:

Definition 7. *We define an intruder action to be an event engaged in by an intruder that affects messages received by legitimate participants in a protocol. Let C be a cost set. We define ϕ to be a function from the intruder actions to C. We extend ϕ to a function Φ from an intruder capability to C by defining $\Phi(x_1, ..., x_n) = \phi(x_1) + ... + \phi(x_n)$. We call Φ an intruder cost function.*

Fail-Stop Protocols and Assessing DoS-Resistance. A fail-stop protocol stops whenever participants of the protocol detect the execution deviating from protocol specification. The following definitions give details of fail-stop protocols and how to assess protocols' DoS-resistance property:

Definition 8. *Let Θ be a function from the set of events defined by an annotated Alice-and-Bob specification P to a cost set C. We refer to Θ as the attack cost function. We say that P is fail-stop with respect to Θ if, for each event E in the system, if the intruder interferes with any message that should arrive before or at E, then no events that should occur after E will occur, unless the cost expended by the intruder to interfere with the message is at least $\Theta(E)$.*

A question is which Θ the analyst should use, the next definition gives a criteria to evaluate whether this Θ is reasonable:

Definition 9. *Let C be a server cost set, and G be an intruder cost set. We define a tolerance relation to be the set of $C \times G$ consisting all pairs (c, g) such that the protocol designer is willing to tolerate a situation in which an intruder cannot force a server to expend resources of cost c or greater without revealing its identity or expending resources of cost g or greater. We say (c', g') is within the tolerance relation if there is a (c, g) such that $c' \leq c$ and $g' \geq g$*

Next, we show how to evaluate the protocol's DoS-resistance property under the framework:

step 1. Determine the intruder ability and the cost functions
step 2. Determine the tolerance relation τ
step 3. Determine the minimal attack cost functions with respect to which the protocol is fail-stop
step 4. For each attack cost function Θ defined in step 3, verify that:
    (a) for every event E_1 immediately preceding a verification event E_2, $(\delta'(E_2), \Theta(E_1)) \subset \tau$
    (b) if event E is an accept event, then $(\Delta(E), \Theta(E)) \subset \tau$

2.2 The Just Fast Keying Protocol (JFKi)

The JFK protocol, a key agreement protocol, an alternative to IKE [11], was developed by Aiello et al. [1]. It provides identity protection, and uses several techniques to withstand DoS attacks. The message components are given in Table 1, and the version of the protocol that implements identity protection for the initiator (JFKi) is presented in Table 2 (specified by annotated Alice-and-Bob language). The session key they establish is K_{ir}.

Table 1. Just Fast Keying (JFKi) Message Components

$H_k(M)$	Keyed hash of M with key k
$M_{K_a}^{K_e}$	Encryption of M using symmetric key K_e, followed by MAC authentication over the resultant cipher with symmetric key K_a
$S_x[M]$	Digital signature of message M with the private key belonging to principal x
$H(M)$	Unkeyed hash of message M
IP_I	Initiator's network address
g	Generator of a multiplicative group of order q
r, i	Integers between 1 and q chosen at random by R and I
g^i, g^r	Initiator and responder's respective current exponential, $(mod\ p)$
N_I, N_R	Nonces chosen by the initiator and responder
ID_I, ID_R	Initiator and responder's certificates
$ID_{R'}$	An indication by the initiator to the responder as to what authentication information the later should use
HK_R	A transient hash key private to the responder
sa	Cryptographic and service properties of the security association (SA) that the initiator wants to establish
sa'	SA information the responder may need to give to the initiator
$grpinfo_R$	Groups supported by the responder, algorithms to protect Message (3) and (4) of the protocol, and the hash function for key generation

2.3 ASM-SPV Protocol Verifier

In this paper, we employ ASM-SPV to automatically analyze the protocol. ASM-SPV accepts protocol and intruder models specified by CoreASM, and attack conditions described by Computation Tree Logic (CTL) formula.

CoreASM language [8] is an extension of ASM (Abstract State Machines) which was developed as a generalized machine to model any algorithm faithfully. It uses classic mathematical structures to describe states precisely and allows for the use of functions which can describe the operations in security protocols easily.

CTL [4] was developed by E. Clark and E. A. Emerson in 1981. This logic can be used to describe all possible ways from the beginning by modeling time into a tree. CTL provides two branching operators (A and E), and five temporal operators (X, F, G, W and U) to define properties of the computation tree.

ASM-SPV [16] is designed to analyze various properties of security protocols. It uses the on-the-fly technique to verify whether the protocol satisfies the goals required, if not, attack routes will be provided. Also, details of the attack can be got from an interface ASM-SPV supplies.

Table 2. Annotated Alice-and-Bob Specification of JFKi

$L_1.\ I \to R:$	$computenonce_1(N_I), N_I' = hash_1(N_I), createexp_1(g^i)\ \|$ $N_I', g^i, ID_{R'}\ \|$ $verifygroup(g^i), accept_1$
$L_2.\ R \to I:$	$computenonce_2(N_R), token = generatemac_1(HK_R, \{g^r, N_R, N_I', IP_I\})\ \|$ $N_I', N_R, g^r, groupinfo_R, ID_R, S_R\{g^r, groupinfo_R\}, token\ \|$ $verifysig_1, accept_2$
$L_3.\ I \to R:$	$generatedh_1(g^{ir}), K_e = generatekeys(N_I', N_R, "1", g^{ir}),$ $K_a = generatekeys(N_I', N_R, "2", g^{ir}),$ $T = generatesig_1(N_I', N_R, g^i, g^r, ID_R, sa)$ $C = encrypt_1(K_e, \{ID_I, sa, T\}), C' = generatemac_2(Ka, C),$ $K_{ir} = generatekeys(N_I', N_R, "0", g^{ir})\ \|$ $N_I, N_R, g^i, g^r, token, C, C'\ \|$ $verify(N_I' = hash_2(N_I)),$ $verify_2(tokcn = generatemac_3(HK_R, \{g^r, N_R, N_I', IP_I\})),$ $generatedh_2(g^{ir}), K_a = generatekeys(N_I', N_R, "2", g^{ir}),$ $verify_3(C' = generatemac_4(Ka, C)),$ $K_e = generatekeys(N_I', N_R, "1", g^{ir}),$ $D = decrypt(K_e, C), verify_4(D), verifysig_2(T),$ $K_{ir} = generatekeys(N_I', N_R, "0", g^{ir}), accept3$
$L_4.\ R \to I:$	$W = generatesig_3(N_I', N_n, g^i, g^r, ID_I, sa, sa'),$ $E = encrypt_2(K_e, \{W, sa'\}), E' = generatemac_5(K_a, E)\ \|$ $E, E'\ \|$ $verify(E' = generatemac_6(K_a, E), decrypt_2(K_e, E)),$ $verifysig_3(W), accept_4$

ASM-SPV accepts models with concrete values, and calculation of them, thus we can use concrete values to represent costs. This is one reason why we can model DoS attacks more precisely and analyze protocols' DoS-resistance property more in detail. In contrast, former analysis [10] using OFMC and other analysis tools whose models use symbolic variables to represent the cost can only give binary results.

3   Improvements to Meadows's Cost-Based Framework

In this section, we show the improvements to the framework in detail and compare them with some well-known work.

3.1   Improved Cost Function

In the work done by Meadows [13] and others [10, 17, 18], because of the modeling language or the analyzing tools they use, costs are roughly represented by three symbols: 'cheap', 'medium', and 'expensive'. As we have analyzed in Section 1, modeling costs in such a way prevents us from analyzing protocols accurately. Therefore, as done in [21], we use concrete values which show the amount of resources required by different algorithms to represent the cost of each action. Thus costs are more precise and cost functions can be accurately computed. Although the values vary a lot according to different computing environments, it is still reasonable to use the data got from some typical environment to make comparisons.

To estimate the cost, we use the cryptographic protocol benchmarks of Wei Dai 2009 [5], which include tested results of most commonly used cryptographic algorithms from Crypto++ version 5.6. The algorithms are coded in C++ and compiled with Microsoft Visual C++ 2005 SP1, and ran on an Intel Core 2 1.83 GHz processor under Windows Vista in 32-bit mode. Table 3 shows results for some specific algorithms available for the JFKi protocol.

With the results and the parameter specification, we are able to estimate the CPU usage of actions taken in the protocol. The costs of engaging in the protocol, generating or disposing messages can be computed through summing all the costs of actions taken to do that mathematically. Since ASM-SPV supports all rational numbers, we do not need to round the values into integers, however, this is required by [21]. In Section 4.1, we will show how to compute the cost function with an example of the JFKi protocol.

Table 3. Computational Cost of CPU for Specific Algorithms

Algorithm	cycle/Byte	Operation	cycle/Operation
SHA-512	17.7	RSA 1024 Signature	2.71×10^6
HMAC(SHA-1)	11.9	RSA 1024 Verification	0.13×10^6
AES/CBC (256-bit key)	21.7	DH 1024 Key-Pair Generation	0.82×10^6

3.2 Improved Tolerance Relation

Defining the tolerance relations in Meadows's framework can be a very difficult work, and carelessly defined relations may omit flaws of protocols, as discussed in [13]. The tolerance relation defined in [10] is

$$\tau = \{less(Server's\ Cost, Intruder's\ Cost)\}$$

which means that, at the same state, the server's cost should be smaller than the intruder's cost. Apparently, it is very rough, not considering resources of both sides concretely. Since, in some scenarios, it may be allowed that, in one instance of the protocol execution, the intruder expends fewer resources than the server to some extent.

The tolerance relation defined in [21] is not very precise either. It aims to examine whether the intruder can mount DoS attacks with cheap operations to cause the server to engage in expensive operations such as digital signature generation and verification, etc.. The tolerance relation defined is as follows:

$$\tau = \{(Server's\ Cost - Intruder's\ Cost) < Thres\}$$

where *Thres* is an acceptable threshold defined as the computational cost of digital signature verification.

After careful analysis, we see that the relation only reflects the difference between the cost of the intruder and that of the server, and it says nothing about the cost of the intruder and the cause of the difference. It may be the case that the cost of the intruder is also very large because of some expensive operations. It can also be the case that the difference is the accumulation of costs of some simple operations rather than an expensive one. In Section 4, we will show limitations of these definitions through experimental results.

Our tolerance relation is defined as :

$$\tau = \{Server's\ Cost / Intruder's\ Cost < t\}$$

where t is a threshold defined by the analyzer according to their estimation of the situation where the protocol is used and the resources of the server. For example, if the sever has quite a lot of resources, t can be assigned a big value, however if the server is only a common PC, or even equipments with few resources such as sensors, mobile phones, the value should be quite small.

For different values of t, we may get some or no attack routes on the protocol from ASM-SPV. This means that, in such scenarios, the protocol is vulnerable or less vulnerable to DoS attacks. If we define ratio of the cost of the server to that of the intruder in a particular state to be r, then in the same scenario, for a particular state, the bigger the value r is, the more vulnerable the protocol is to DoS attacks. Because, to get the same effect (consuming certain amount of resources of the server), the intruder needs to expend fewer resources or a smaller portion of the resources expended by the server. Thus, the analysis result is no longer binary as in [10, 18, 21], and it shows protocols' vulnerability to DoS attacks.

We have to point out that, in reality, DoS attack is related with many factors, such as, the bandwidth, the resources of the server, the tactics the intruder deploys, the mechanisms taken by the server to deal with abnormal situations etc.. We just estimate the vulnerability of protocols in a particular perspective.

3.3   Improved Protocol Specification and Intruder Model

In the real environment, messages are transmitted in form of 0 or 1 bits. To verify whether a message is of some form (such as an encryption of a particular value), some computation should be done first and then analyze the results (first decrypt the message and then verify the result). This means that no matter the message satisfies the condition or not, some computation must be done. However, in symbolic protocol verifiers, messages are modeled into symbols, their form determines whether they will be accepted or not. If we only model the protocol as specified, then only messages that fully satisfy the specification will be disposed. But, in DoS attacks, the intruder often forges semi-bogus messages to waste the server's resources. Here, we use the word "semi-bogus"to emphasize that messages that do not fully satisfy the condition are disposed in reality until their illegitimacy is detected. J.Smith et al. [18] modeled the intruder's ability of forging semi-bogus messages. However, it was done manually, and did not specify them formally.

In our work, we propose a method to formalize this into a model that could be checked automatically. The main idea is that we use "cipher"to represent messages completely not satisfying the condition (which can be seen as a random value). For example, for a message of the form $\{sig_I(M), N\}_k$ (which denotes an encryption of a signature (M signed with the private key of agent I) and N with the key k), we can use $\{cipher, N\}_k$ (which denotes an encryption of a random value rather than the correct signature and N with the key k) to represent one semi-bogus message of it (getting such a message, the receiver should first decrypt the message, verify that the second part of the message is N, and then verify the first part of the message, it discards the message on detecting that its first part is not the signature of M). Like this, we can model all the possible semi-bogus messages that would be generated and disposed.

Meadows's framework did not give specific definition of the intruder. Usually, when we analyze protocols, the intruder is modeled according to the Dolev-Yao intruder model [6], who controls the whole network, and can eavesdrop, divert and memorize messages, encrypt and decrypt messages as long as it has the corresponding key. But, in this framework, we do not allow the intruder to be able to do arbitrary work, it can only execute protocols as honest participants, as well as forge semi-bogus messages mentioned above. What's more, we require that the intruder has limited resources.

In the protocol specification,we model the participants to act as the protocol specifies when receiving legitimate messages, and to stop executing when receiving semi-bogus ones. And we model the intruder to be able to execute as honest participants and forge semi-bogus messages as well. Thus, protocols and intruders are modeled faithfully. To the best of our knowledge, former automatic methods only model participants disposing messages specified by the protocol, and this is the first time to model the protocol faithfully for automatic analysis.

4   Formal Modeling and Analyzing the JFKi Protocol

In this section, we show details of modeling and analyzing the JFKi protocol within the improved framework. We also display and analyze the experimental results, and give some comments on the protocol.

4.1   Cost Function and Tolerance Relations

In our work, we only analyze participants' computation resource cost (memory resource cost can be modeled in a similar way). The cost of each action is represented by the amount of resources used executing the action on a common type of processor. According to the specification of the JFKi protocol and specific cost of each algorithm, we calculate and assign each action a cost value. According to the annotated Alice-and-Bob specification for JFKi presented in Table 2 and costs of actions we get, we can compute costs of engaging in the protocol, generating and disposing messages (including semi-bogus ones), through summing up all the costs of actions taken to do that.

As we have analyzed, and according to the specification of the JFKi protocol and the specific algorithms we use, costs of actions taken in the protocol execution are defined below (the unit is kcycles per operation):

- *computenonce*: generate a nonce, since the cost is small, $\delta(computenonce) = 0$
- *createxp*: generate an exponential, since it is precomputed, $\delta(createxp) = 0$
- *hash*: hash a nonce, $\delta(hash) = 1.13$
- *generatekeys*: generate the encryption and authentication keys through a keyed hash function, $\delta(generatekeys) = 3.05$
- *generatemac*: generate a message authentication code, basing on a keyed hash function, $\delta(generatemac) = 3.05$
- *generatesig/verifysig*: generate/verify a signature, using "hash and sign" paradigm, $\delta(generatesig) = 2720.2$, $\delta(verifysig) - 140.2$
- *generatedh*: generate a Diffe-Hellman ephemeral key, $\delta(generatedh) = 820$
- *encrypt/decrypt*: encrypt/decrypt a message, $\delta(encrypt/decrypt) = 6.95$

Note: In our experiment, according to the protocol specification [1], we use the specific algorithms as shown in Table 3 to replace the corresponding function symbols. The nonce is assumed to be 512 bits, the exponent to be 1024 bits, and SA to be 1024 bits. Then according to Table 3, we can get the above cost function. For example, since the nonce is 512 bits and the cost of hashing a value of a byte is 17.7 cycles, thus, $\delta(hash) = 17.7 \times (512 \div 8) \div 1000 = 1.13$ *kcycles*.

Since the JFKi protocol is designed as an internet key agreement protocol, we assume the server has many resources and it allows some kind of unbalanced resource expenditure. In the experiment, we intend to set t in the tolerance relation to be 100, in this scenario, the server tolerates expending as much as 100 times the cost of the initiator in a protocol execution. In fact, as we have explained in Section 3.2, to define the value of t is an empirical work. Given a smaller t, we may get more attacks, a larger one, we get fewer. Since, for a particular state, if r is larger than t, it is sure to be larger than a value smaller than t, but it may not be larger than a value bigger than t. If the situation is more stringent, to get a more detailed analysis of the protocol, t can be assigned a smaller value, such as 10 or even smaller.

4.2   Modeling JFKi with CoreASM

In the real environment, the participant processes the received message, if the message is legitimate, it acts as the protocol specifies; otherwise it stops executing the protocol. Since, we have given the annotated Alice-and-Bob specification of JFKi, we have a good understanding of the protocol execution and know what kind of messages are illegal or semi-bogus. In our model, we assume that the intruder only attacks the server, and that the server is honest (it executes as specified). Thus, the initiator only deals with legitimate messages, and the server should dispose both legitimate and semi-bogus ones.

In the CoreASM model, participants are modeled into a subroutine, which describes what messages they can receive and the corresponding actions they should take. So we model participants to deal with messages, if the messages are established to be legal, participants act as specified, otherwise stop executing the protocol. The costs of engaging in the protocol will be updated as the execution progresses. After every step of the server, we verify whether the cost of the intruder and that of the server satisfy the defined tolerance relation. If not, we set the variable $ATTACK$ to be true (this will be explained in Section 4.3).

In the model of the JFKi protocol, to reduce the cost of the intruder, we assume that it does not verify the signature of message 2 from the server. So, we do not model the group information and the signature into message 2 as specified. For convenience, we model the intruder sending the hash of the initially generated nonce in the first message rather than the nonce itself (which is specified by the protocol) as the first component of message 3, but, to ensure the correctness of the cost, we will add the cost of hashing a nonce to the intruder's cost.

4.3   Intruder Model and Attack Condition

As mentioned in Section 3.3, the intruder in our model can only execute as honest participants as well as forge semi-bogus messages. In the CoreASM model, the intruder is also modeled into a subroutine, which describes its ability to act as honest participants and forge messages from its knowledge. Intruder cost functions are defined as those for the honest participants in Section 4.1. The cost of the intruder's engaging in the protocol will be updated after every taken step.

The attack condition for the JFKi protocol written in CTL is: $AG!ATTACK$. In the formula, we use the boolean variable $ATTACK$ (initialized as false) to denote whether the current state is an attack state, and it is set to be true whenever the protocol reaches a state where the tolerance relation is violated. The formula means that in the future the value of $ATTACK$ will always be false. Whenever the value of $ATTACK$ is true at some state, the verifier regards it as an attack state and will show the route from the initial state of the protocol execution to that state. And this occurs when $r \geqslant 100$ (r is as defined in Section 3.2).

4.4   Experimental Results and Discussions

In this subsection, we first show and analyze the experimental results, and then discuss the JFKi protocol.

Experimental Results. Getting the protocol and intruder model and the attack condition, we use ASM-SPV to verify it. When we set $t = 100$, ASM-SPV gives the attack in Table 4. The attack was also found by J.Smith et al. [18], but it was totally by hand.

Table 4. Attack route 1

$Intruder \rightarrow Bob : 1\ [NONCE285, EXP310, Bob]$
$Bob \rightarrow Intruder : 2\ [NONCE285, NONCE698, EXP709, TOKEN721]$
$Intruder \rightarrow Bob : 3\ [NONCE285, NONCE698, EXP310, EXP709, TOKEN721,$ $cipher, cipher]$

Note: In Table 4, NONCE285, EXP310 represent the nonce, and exponent the Intruder generates, and Token721 is the cookie Bob creates for the session with Intruder. "cipher" represents a random value with no meaning. Other symbols are defined in the same way.

Details show that, when the intruder and Bob arrive at this state, the cost of Bob is 833.33, while the cost of the intruder is 1.13, the ratio between them is 737.46, which is much larger than 100. Thus, the intruder can consume great amount of resources with little cost.

However, When we use the tolerance relations defined in [10, 21] (as discussed in Section 3.2), besides the attack in Table 4, ASM-SPV shows another attack described in Table 5. At this state, the cost of Bob is 3716.78, the cost of the intruder is 3557.43, and the ratio is 1.04, very near to 1. To get this state, the intruder expends nearly the same amount of resources as the server does. Since, we assume that the intruder have fewer resources than the server does, thus, the intruder collapses before it exhausts the server's resources, so this should not be regarded as an effective attack.

Table 5. Attack route 2

$Intruder \rightarrow Bob : 1\ [NONCE396, EXP420, Bob]$
$Bob \rightarrow Intruder : 2\ [NONCE396, NONCE924, EXP935, TOKEN946]$
$Intruder \rightarrow Bob : 3\ [NONCE396, NONCE924, EXP420, EXP935, TOKEN946,$ [Intruder, [NONCE396, NONCE924, EXP420, EXP935,   PRIVATEKEY115, signature], KEY1523, encrypt], [[Intruder,   [NONCE396, NONCE924, EXP420, EXP935, PRIVATEKEY115,   signature], KEY1523, encrypt], KEY1541, hash]]
$Bob \rightarrow Intruder :$ message 4

Note:

1. In Table 5, symbols with prefixes of NONCE, TOKEN, EXP are defined as in Table 4, PRIVATEKEY115 represents the private key of the intruder, KEY1523, KEY1541 represent the keys generated for hash and encryption respectively. In CoreASM, $\{m_1, m_2\}_k$ (the encryption of m_1, m_2 with the key k) is expressed as the list $[m_1, m_2, k, encrypt]$. If the last component is changed into "signature" or "hash", then it means the signature or hash of m_1, m_2 with the key k.

2. In our model, to reduce the cost of the intruder, we do not model the intruder dealing with the last message from Bob, but after receiving the correct message 3, Bob is supposed to send message 4. So we don't formally model message 4, just add the cost of producing message 4 to the cost of Bob and use "message 4" to represent the message transmitted.

Table 6. Modified JFKi

$1. I \rightarrow R : N_I', g^i, ID_{R'}$
$2. R \rightarrow I : N_I', N_R, g^r, grpinfo_R, ID_R, S_R[g^r, grpinfo_R], token, \mathbf{k}$
$3. I \rightarrow R : N_I, N_R, g^i, g^r, H_{HK_R}(g^r, N_R, N_I', IP_I),$
$\qquad \{ID_I, sa, S_I[N_I', N_R, g^i, g^r, ID_R, sa]\}_{K_a}^{K_e}, \mathbf{sol}$
$4. R \rightarrow I : \{S_R[N_I', N_R, g^i, g^r, ID_I, sa, sa'], sa'\}_{K_a}^{K_e}$

where $N_I' = H(N_I)$
$\qquad token = H_{HK_R}(g^r, N_R, N_I', IP_I)$
$\qquad K_e = H_{g^{ir}}(N_I', N_R, "1")$
$\qquad K_a = H_{g^{ir}}(N_I', N_R, "2")$
$\qquad K_{ir} = H_{g^{ir}}(N_I', N_R, "0")$
$\qquad$ **challenge** $= token$
$\qquad$ **sol** such that H(**challenge** $\parallel$ **sol**) produces an output with **k** leading zeros

---

Discussions about JFKi. The attack in Table 4 was also found in [18]. They introduced a puzzle [3] to balance the cost as shown in Table 6.

Bogdan et al.[10] analyzed the modified protocol and found an attack on the initiator. For legibility, we modify it to the form shown in Table 7. In the attack, the intruder just intercepts the first message of the protocol from a to b, and then forwards it to b with identity of i. When the intruder gets the puzzle from b, it passes the puzzle on to a. The intruder intercepts the solution from a for other use.

After analysis, we find that the main reason that causes the attack on the initiator is the absence of authentication of the puzzle: the initiator cannot verify that the puzzle is really from the server to it and that the puzzle has not been tampered. However, authenticating such a puzzle may cause other DoS attacks.

Since, up to now, the main known authentication tools contain: signatures, MACs, encryption systems. It is apparent that signatures and public encryption systems shouldn't be used in our scheme, since the computational cost is heavy and the intruder can just repetitively initiate sessions inducing the server to produce puzzles with authentication and exhaust its resources. To use MACs or symmetric encryption systems, some private information between the two is needed. Since, they do not share a key before the conversation, they need to negotiate one. But, the cost of agreeing a key is very heavy and this gives the intruder another chance to launch DoS attacks on the server because it should compute the key first. This reflects difficulties of designing and analyzing DoS-resistent protocols.

Table 7. Attack to modified JFKi

$a \rightarrow i : N'_a, g^{x_a}, Idb1$
$i \rightarrow b : N'_a, g^{x_a}, Idb1$
$b \rightarrow i : N'_a, N_b, g^{x_b}, Idb, sig_b g^{x_b}, token, k$
$i \rightarrow a : N'_a, N_b, g^{x_b}, Idb, sig_b g^{x_b}, token, k$
$a \rightarrow i : N_a, N_b, g^{x_a}, g^{x_b}, token, \{Ida, sa, sig_a[N'_a, N_b, g^{x_a}, g^{x_b}, idb, sa]\}^{k_e}_{k_a}, \text{sol}(token)$
   where $N'_a = h(N_a)$
        $k_e = h_{g^{x_a x_b}}(N'_a, N_b, "1")$
        $k_a = h_{g^{x_a x_b}}(N'_a, N_b, "2")$
        $token = h_{hkb}(g^{x_b}, N_b, N'_a)$

5 Conclusions and Future Work

In this paper, we analyzed Meadows's cost-based framework and some other well-known work, and made some improvements to the framework. The improvements include: A more precise cost function; A more flexible tolerance relation, thus a more reasonable analysis result; Modeling intruders and protocols more precisely. From modeling and analyzing the JFKi protocol, we showed advantages of the improvements. During our study, we found the following possible directions for future work:

1. From the analysis, we can see that before the automatic analysis, much work need to be done manually, and this may be error-prone. Finding a way to model the protocol automatically will greatly reduce the manual work and the possibility of errors, and quicken the analysis work.
2. To reduce the vulnerability to DoS attacks, resource-consuming work is often done in advance, and can be reused. However, it also induces the problem that some information the intruder gets through computation can be reused too. Also, the intruder may ignore some resource-consuming work. How to evade this by preventing the intruder getting some essential information without paying some cost should be considered.
3. Up to now, the known ways to balance costs between participants (such as puzzles) mainly aim to protect the server from DoS attacks. And this may give the intruder a chance to attack the initiator (the attack in Table 7 can be seen as an example). How to protect the initiator form DoS attacks is another problem that should be taken into consideration.

Acknowledgements. The authors are grateful for helpful suggestions from anonymous referees. This work was supported by NSFC grants No. 60873260, No. 60903210 and No.61170280, China national 863 program No.2009AA01Z414 and China national 973 program No.2007CB311202.

References

1. Aiello, W., Bellovin, S.M., Blaze, M., Canetti, R., Ioannidis, J., Keromytis, A.D., Reingold, O.: Just fast keying: key agreement in a hostile network. ACM Transactions on Information and System Security 7(2), 242–273 (2004)
2. Boyd, C., Mathuria, A.: Protocols for Authentication and Key Establishment. Springer (2003)
3. Chen, L., Morrissey, P., Smart, N.P., Warinschi, B.: Security Notions and Generic Constructions for Client Puzzles. In: Matsui, M. (ed.) ASIACRYPT 2009. LNCS, vol. 5912, pp. 505–523. Springer, Heidelberg (2009)
4. Clarke, E.M., Emerson, E.A.: Design and Synthesis of Synchronization Skeletons Using Branching-Time Temporal Logic. In: Engeler, E. (ed.) Logic of Programs 1979. LNCS, vol. 125, pp. 52–71. Springer, Heidelberg (1981)
5. Dai, W.: Crypto++ 5.2.1 benchmarks. Technical report (2009), http://www.cryptopp.com/benchmarks.html
6. Dolev, D., Yao, A.: On the security of public key protocols. IEEE Transactions on Information Theory 29(2), 198–208 (1983)
7. Eddy, W.: TCP SYN Flooding Attacks and Common Mitigations. Request for Comments: 4987 (2007), http://tools.ietf.org/html/rfc4987
8. Farahbod, R.: CoreASM language user manual. Technical report (2006), http://www.coreasm.org
9. Gong, L., Syverson, P.: Fail-stop protocols: an approach to designing secure protocols. In: Iyer, R.K., Morganti, M., Fuchs, W.K., Gligor, V. (eds.) Dependable Computing for Critical Applications 5, pp. 79–99. IEEE Computer Society (1998)
10. Groza, B., Minea, M.: Formal modelling and automatic detection of resource exhaustion attacks. In: Proceedings of the 6th ACM Symposium on Information, Computer and Communications Security (ASIACCS), pp. 326–333 (2011)
11. Harkins, D., Carrel, D.: The Internet Key Exchange (IKE). Request for comments (proposed standard) 2409, Internet Engineering Task Force (1998)
12. LaMacchia, B., Lauter, K., Mityagin, A.: Stronger Security of Authenticated Key Exchange. In: Susilo, W., Liu, J.K., Mu, Y. (eds.) ProvSec 2007. LNCS, vol. 4784, pp. 1–16. Springer, Heidelberg (2007)
13. Meadows, C.: A cost-based framework for analysis of denial of service in networks. Journal of Computer Security 9(1/2), 143–164 (2001)
14. Meadows, C.: A formal framework and evaluation method for network denial of service. In: Proceedings of the 12th IEEE Computer Security Foundations Workshop, pp. 4–13. Computer Society Press (June 1999)
15. Needham, R.M.: Denial of Service. In: The 1st ACM Conference on Computer and Communications Security, Fairfax, VA, pp. 151–153 (1993)
16. Peng, J., Liu, F., Zhao, Z., Huang, D., Xue, R.: ASM-SPV: a model checker for security protocols. In: 2010 Sixth International Conference on Intelligent Information Hiding and Multimedia Signal Processing, pp. 458–461 (2010)
17. Ramachandran, V.: Analyzing DoS-resistance of protocols using a cost-based framework. Technical Report DCS/TR-1239, Yale University (2002)
18. Smith, J., González Nieto, J.M., Boyd, C.: Modelling denial of service attacks on JFK with Meadows's cost-based framework. In: 4th Australasian Information Security Workshop, pp. 125–134 (2006)
19. Smith, J., Tritilanunt, S., Boyd, C., Nieto, J.M.G., Foo, E.: Denial-of-Service resistance in key establishment. In: Wireless and Mobile Computing, vol. 2, pp. 59–71 (2007)

20. Stebila, D., Ustaoglu, B.: Towards Denial-of-Service-Resilient Key Agreement Protocols. In: Boyd, C., González Nieto, J. (eds.) ACISP 2009. LNCS, vol. 5594, pp. 389–406. Springer, Heidelberg (2009)
21. Tritilanunt, S.: Protocol engineering for protection against Denial-of-Service attacks. PhD thesis, Information Security Institute Queensland University of Technology (2009)

Fault Detection of the MacGuffin Cipher against Differential Fault Attack

Wei Li[1,2,*], Dawu Gu[3], Zhiqiang Liu[3], Ya Liu[3], and Xiaohu Huang[1]

[1] School of Computer Science and Technology, Donghua University,
Shanghai 201620, China
[2] Shanghai Key Laboratory of Integrate Administration Technologies for Information
Security, Shanghai 200240, China
[3] Department of Computer Science and Engineering, Shanghai Jiao Tong University,
Shanghai 200240, China

Abstract. Since the early work of Biham and Shamir on differential
fault attack against block ciphers at CRYPTO 1997, much work has
been devoted to reducing the number of faults and to improving the
time complexity of this attack. This attack is very efficient when a single
fault is injected on the last several rounds, and it allows to recover the
whole secret key. Thus, it is an open question whether detecting the
faults injected into a block cipher against this attack with low overhead
of space and time tolerance. The MacGuffin cipher, a representative of
the Unbalanced Feistel Network(UFN) structure, is vulnerable to fault
attack at the last four rounds. In this paper, we give an answer to this
problem by presenting a fault detection of the MacGuffin block cipher.
Our result in this study could detect the faults with negligible cost when
faults are injected into the last four rounds.

1 Introduction

During the last years a new class of attacks against cryptographic devices has
become public. These attacks exploit easily accessible information like power consumption, running time, input–output behavior under malfunctions, and can be
mounted by anyone only using low–cost equipment. These side–channel attacks
amplify and evaluate leaked information with the help of statistical methods,
and are often much more powerful than classical cryptanalysis. Examples show
that a very small amount of side–channel information is enough to completely
break a cryptosystem. While many previously–known cryptanalytic attacks can
be analyzed by studying algorithms, the vulnerabilities of side–channel attacks
result from electrical behavior of transistors and circuits of an implementation.
This ultimately compromises cryptography, and shifts the top priority in cryptography from the further improvement of algorithms to the prevention of such
attacks by reducing variations in timing, power and radiation from the hardware,
reduction of observability of system behavior after fault injection. Therefore, it

---

* Corresponding author.

L. Chen, M. Yung, and L. Zhu (Eds.): INTRUST 2011, LNCS 7222, pp. 102–112, 2012.

extends theoretically the current mathematical models of cryptography to the physical setting which takes into consideration side–channel attacks.

As one type of side–channel attacks, differential fault analysis (DFA) was proposed by Biham and Shamir as an attack on DES in 1997 [1]. The similar attacks have been applied to other block ciphers [2–6]. The DFA attack is based on deriving information about the secret key by examining the differences between a cipher resulting from a correct operation and a cipher of the same initial message resulting from a faulty operation.

MacGuffin is a block cipher which was proposed by Blaze and Schneier [7]. Its fundamental structure is the contracting Unbalanced Feistel Network, and supports 64–bit block size and 128–bit key size. Up to now, some literature is available on the security of MacGuffin against the classical cryptanalysis, such as differential attack, and linear attack [8]. MacGuffin is vulnerable to Differential Fault Analysis(DFA)[9]. The secret key of MacGuffin could be obtained by inducing faults into the computation of the last four rounds. This method requires 355 and 165 faulty ciphertexts in two byte–oriented fault models, respectively.

In this paper, we focus on the security application of MacGuffin against the fault analysis. In the literature, countermeasures against fault attacks could help a cryptographic algorithm to avoid, detect or correct faults. In practice, many proposed schemes are based on fault detection, including code–based technique and redundancy–based technique [10–18].

Code based detections are divided into coding method and error detection code (EDC). Coding method means encoding message before encryption and checking errors after decryption. Its overhead depends on encoding and decoding progress to translate plaintexts and ciphertexts into codes. Its time redundancy also depends on the code processes. As for block ciphers, the EDC approach is often used in each rounds' inner parts with the implementation of parity–based EDC. The parity of linear layers is easy to implement since permutations do not change the parity. More consideration should be given to the nonlinear layers. Whether the parity of input joins in encryption determines how the parity constructs. Approximately, 10%~20% overhead is required, and so does time tolerance.

The redundancy–based solution for implementing fault detection in the encryption module is to perform a test decryption immediately after the encryption, and then check whether the original data block is obtained. If a decryption module is already present in the implementation, the hardware overhead reduces to the cost of a comparator for two data blocks of 128 bits. Otherwise, the overhead is close to 100 percent since the decryption module is very similar to the encryption one. The overall time penalty in either of these two cases is the time required to decrypt a data block, plus the time required for the comparison. This technique is independent of the adopted fault model.

The above techniques of fault detection seem to ensure a high level of security. However, only checking the correctness of the computed encryption result may not be enough to prevent fault analysis since an attacker may destroy the detector.

In order to resist the differential fault analysis with low cost, we propose a fault detection technique to protect MacGuffin against the previous attacks. Our work not only helps to detect the errors with low overhead of space and time tolerance, but also can be applied in all kinds of software implementation. The idea of this attack and the related countermeasure are naturally suitable for other block ciphers.

The rest of this paper is organized as follows. Section 2 briefly introduces the MacGuffin cryptosystem. The next section shows the previous differential fault analysis on MacGuffin. Then section 4 presents our fault detection on MacGuffin. Finally section 5 concludes the paper.

2   Description of MacGuffin

MacGuffin is a 64–bit block cipher, which supports 128–bit key lengths [7]. It has 32–round unbalanced Feistel structure. The input of MacGuffin is partitioned into four registers from left to right (See Figure 1). Every register is composed of double bytes. In every round, the three rightmost registers comprise the control block and are bitwise exclusive–ORed with 48 bits derived from the subkey. These 48 bits are split eight branches to provide input to eight functions of six bits (the S–boxes), and then output two bits for every S–box. The 16–bit S–boxes output are then XORed with the bits in the leftmost register. Finally, the leftmost register is rotated into the rightmost register. Figure 1 shows the block diagram of the MacGuffin cipher.

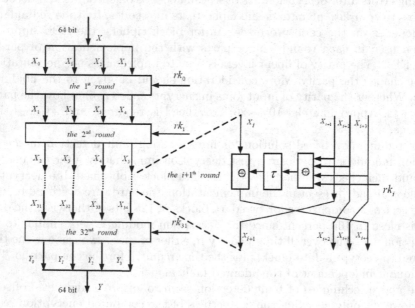

Fig. 1. The MacGuffin cipher

2.1 Encryption Process

Let $X = (X_0, X_1, X_2, X_3) \in (\{0,1\}^{16})^4$ be the plaintext and $Y = (Y_0, Y_1, Y_2, Y_3)$ $\in (\{0,1\}^{16})^4$ be the ciphertext. Let $rk_i \in (\{0,1\}^{16})^3$ denote the i-th subkey, $(X_i, X_{i+1}, X_{i+2}, X_{i+3})$ denote the $i + 1$-th round inputs, and R_i denote the $i+1$-th round $(i = 0, 1, \cdots, 31)$. Then the MacGuffin scheme can be written as

$$X_{i+4} = F(X_i, X_{i+1}, X_{i+2}, X_{i+3}, rk_i),$$

$$(Y_0, Y_1, Y_2, Y_3) = (X_{32}, X_{33}, X_{34}, X_{35}),$$

where $i \in \{0, 1, \cdots, 31\}$, F is the i–th round function defined below:

$$F(X_i, X_{i+1}, X_{i+2}, X_{i+3}, rk_i) = X_i \oplus \tau(X_{i+1} \oplus X_{i+2} \oplus X_{i+3} \oplus rk_i).$$

Here τ are defined as follows.

τ–function is a nonlinear transformation layer with 8 parallel 6×2 S-boxes, which are specified in [7]. That is,

$$\tau : (\{0,1\}^6)^8 \to (\{0,1\}^2)^8.$$

2.2 Decryption Process

The decryption procedure of MacGuffin can be done in the same way as the encryption procedure by reversing the order of the subkeys.

2.3 Key Schedule

In the MacGuffin cryptosystem, the key schedule generates a total of 32 subkeys $(rk_0, rk_1, \cdots, rk_{31})$. Each round of the cipher uses the secret key parameter to perturb the S–boxes by bitwise XOR against the S–box inputs. Each round thus requires 48 key bits. To covert the 128–bit secret key to a sequence of 48–bit values for each round, MacGuffin uses an iterated version of its own block encryption function. In our fault detection, all errors are injected in the encryption procedure. Thus, we could omit the structure of the key schedule.

3   The Previous Differential Fault Analysis on MacGuffin

The previous differential fault analysis on the security of MacGuffin adopts two basic assumptions as follows:

(1) The attacker can induce a single byte error to a 16–bit register. However, the location of this byte in this register and the value of the error are both unknown.
(2) The attacker has the capability to obtain the right and the corresponding faulty ciphertexts when encrypting one plaintext with the same secret key.

On the above basic assumptions, they induce a random error in the last four rounds at the beginning of the attack, and thus obtain a faulty ciphertext. By differential fault analysis, part or all bytes of the subkeys in the last round can be recovered. The location of fault injection may be not the location of subkeys which will be recovered. For example, to recover the subkeys in the last round, they induce errors in the penultimate round. This kind of fault injection could derive multiple bytes of one subkey and avoids decreasing the efficiency of fault injection. Repeat this procedure until the subkey is obtained. Then they decrypt the right ciphertext to obtain the input of the last round, which is the output of the penultimate round. Repeat the above procedure until the secret key is obtained by the key schedule.

4   Our Proposed Fault Detection of MacGuffin

Our objective is to develop fault detection techniques which will be independent of the particular hardware implementation. To this end, we make the following assumptions:

(1) The MacGuffin algorithm is partitioned into three basic modules: encryption, decryption, and key schedule.
(2) All the modules have in common the same basic operations; hence, only the encryption module is examined in detail since most conclusions will hold for the remaining modules as well.

Thus, a fault injected into the first round is comparable to encoding a different input. The injection of a fault in one of the inner rounds is more complicated and it is necessary to follow the errors as they propagate along the execution path.

Every round of MacGuffin consists of the round function, which is composed of two transformations: subkey addition(SA), S–boxes. Different from the other block ciphers, MacGuffin has no linear transformation. The propagation of a single fault is influenced by the execution of the round components. The result can be classified into only one cases: the fault affects only one byte in the output. The situation includes the S–boxes and SA transformations, where the error is only moved within a byte, respectively. When using a specific input and injecting lots of a single–byte fault into every different round, the average number of erroneous bytes in the ciphertext has the following characteristic (See Fig. 2):

(1) If there are less than 8 nonzero erroneous bytes, the fault must occur in the last four rounds. The average number of erroneous bytes is 7.75, 6, 4.25 and 3.25, respectively.
(2) If all bytes are erroneous, most faults may occur before the last four rounds.

To date, little research has been done on the related attacking method when the faults are induced before the four rounds. Thus, MacGuffin is secure even if the errors have been induced before the four rounds. We put emphasis on the

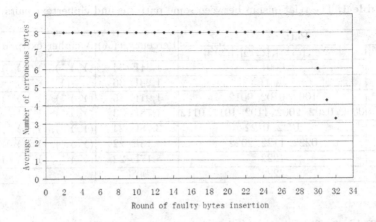

Fig. 2. Erroneous bytes in the ciphertext of MacGuffin

research of the errors induced into the last four rounds. In the DFA analysis, the attacker must capture at least two ciphertexts, including one right ciphertext and one faulty ciphertext. On the basis of this assumption, we propose a pattern–based technique to infer whether the attacker induce faults into the encryption module.

For MacGuffin, let Y, Y^*, $\triangle Y$ be the correct ciphertext, the faulty ciphertext, and ciphertext difference. Let $|\triangle Y|$, $|\triangle Y_0|$, $|\triangle Y_1|$, $|\triangle Y_2|$ and $|\triangle Y_3|$ be the number of erroneous bytes in $\triangle Y$, $\triangle Y_0$, $\triangle Y_1$, $\triangle Y_2$ and $\triangle Y_3$. The pattern is defined within the bounds of remote possibility as the result of the XOR operation between two right ciphertexts (See Table 1). If the distribution of a ciphertext difference satisfies these patterns, then we could derive that the attacker has induced faults into the encryption module and at least one ciphertext is faulty. In other words, if the ciphertext difference satisfies the distribution of some patterns in Table 1, it shows that the error has been induced into the encryption module. Otherwise, it is not feasible for DFA to derive the secret key of MacGuffin. In Table 1, the pattern 0001 denotes $\triangle Y$ has one nonzero byte, which locates in the register Y_3. The ciphertext pair with this pattern could be one correct ciphertext and one faulty ciphertext, or two faulty ciphertext, since the two correct ciphertexts with the pattern has the remote probability of 1.31E–34%.

Depending on the pattern of the ciphertext difference between one correct ciphertext and one faulty ciphertext, we could detect the fault location as Table 2 shows. For example, if the pattern is 0001, the fault must be injected in the register X_{31} of the 32nd round.

When some patterns are within the bounds of average possibility as the result of the XOR operation of one correct ciphertext and one faulty ciphertext. For example, when an error is injected into the last four round, the ratio of 1, 2, 3, 4, 5, 6, 7, and 8 erroneous bytes occur at 6.25%, 0%, 25&, 6.25%, 18.75%, 12.5%, 12.5%, and 18.75%, respectively(See Figure 3).

Table 1. The relationship between some patterns and ciphertext pairs

$|\triangle Y|$	Pattern $|\triangle Y_0|, |\triangle Y_1|, |\triangle Y_2|, |\triangle Y_3|$	Percentage(%)	A ciphertext pair
1	0001	1.31E–34	$(Y, Y^*), (Y^*, Y^*)$
2	0002	1.23E–36	(Y^*, Y^*)
3	1002, 0102, 0012	1.91E–25	$(Y, Y^*), (Y^*, Y^*)$
4	0022, 0202, 2002, 1102, 1012, 0112	1.78E–23	$(Y, Y^*), (Y^*, Y^*)$
5	1022, 0122	3.78E–24	$(Y, Y^*), (Y^*, Y^*)$
6	0222, 1122, 2022	4.15E–22	$(Y, Y^*), (Y^*, Y^*)$
7	1222	5.17E–22	$(Y, Y^*), (Y^*, Y^*)$
8	2222	99%	

Table 2. The relationship between the pattern and fault locations

$|\triangle Y|$	Pattern $|\triangle Y_0|, |\triangle Y_1|, |\triangle Y_2|, |\triangle Y_3|$	R_{32}	R_{31}	R_{30}	R_{29}
1	0001	X_{31}	/	/	/
3	1002	X_{32}	/	/	/
	0102	X_{33}	/	/	/
	0012	X_{34}	X_{30}	/	/
4	0022	/	X_{31}	/	/
5	1022	/	X_{32}	/	/
	0122	/	X_{33}	X_{29}	/
6	0222	/	/	X_{30}, X_{31}	/
7	1222	/	/	X_{32}	X_{28}
8	2222	/	/	/	X_{29}, X_{30}, X_{31}

In real application, one correct ciphertext and one faulty ciphertext as a ciphertext pair is ideal. However, there exist two faulty ciphertexts as Table 1 shows. On the basis of Table 2, we build up the pattern of ciphertext difference between two faulty ciphertexts(See Table 3). Thus, we derive the relationship between the pattern of two faulty ciphertext and the fault locations in Table 4.

When two error are injected independently into the last four round, the ratio of 1, 2, 3, 4, 5, 6, 7, and 8 erroneous bytes occurs at 0.20%, 0.20%, 5.08%, 6.84%, 16.21%, 19.53%, and 26.95%, respectively(See Figure 4).

If the distribution of a ciphertext difference satisfies these above patterns, then the attacker has induced faults into the encryption module and at least one ciphertext is faulty. It is helpful for the MacGuffin cipher to be secure against the differential fault analysis. In other words, if the ciphertext difference satisfies the distribution of some patterns in Table 1, it shows that the error has been induced into the encryption module. Otherwise, it is not feasible for DFA to derive the secret key of MacGuffin.

For example, if the ciphertext difference has 2 nonzero bytes, there are only one pattern which is 0002. It shows that the attacker injects two faults, whose

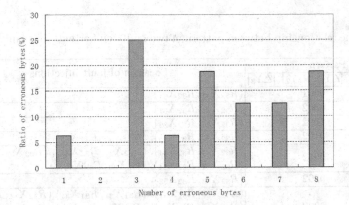

Fig. 3. Ratio of Erroneous bytes in one correct ciphertext and one faulty ciphertext in the last four rounds

Table 3. Patterns of two faulty ciphertexts

	0001	1002	0102	0012	0022	1022	0122	0222	1222	2222
0001	0001,0002	1002	0102	0012	0022	1022	0122	0222	1222	2222
1002	1002	2002	1102	1012	1022	1022,2022	1122	1222	1222,2222	2222
0102	0102	1102	0102,0202	0112	0122	1122	1122	0222	1222	2222
0012	0012	1012	0112	0012,0022	0022	1022	0122	0222	1222	2222
0022	0022	1022	0122	0022	0022	1022	0122	0222	1222	2222
1022	1022	1022,2022	1122	1022	1022	1022,2022	1122	1222	1222,2222	2222
0122	0122	1122	1122	0122	0122	1122	0122,0222	0122	1222	2222
0222	0222	1222	0222	0222	0222	1222	0122	0222	1222	2222
1222	1222	1222,2222	1222	1222	1222	1222,2222	1222	1222	1222,2222	2222
2222	2222	2222	2222	2222	2222	2222	2222	2222	2222	2222

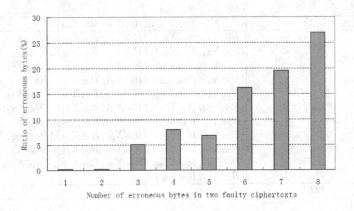

Fig. 4. Ratio of Erroneous bytes of two faulty ciphertexts in the last four rounds

Table 4. The relationship between pattern of two faulty ciphertexts and fault injection

	Pattern	Location of fault injections
$|\triangle Y|$	$|\triangle Y_0|, |\triangle Y_1|, |\triangle Y_2|, |\triangle Y_3|$	
1	0001	$(R_{32}X_{31}, R_{32}X_{31})$
2	0002	$(R_{32}X_{31}, R_{32}X_{31})$
3	1002	$(R_{32}X_{31}, R_{32}X_{32})$
	0102	$(R_{32}X_{31}, R_{32}X_{33}), (R_{32}X_{33}, R_{32}X_{33})$
	0012	$(R_{32}X_{31}, R_{32}X_{34}), (R_{32}X_{31}, R_{32}X_{30}), (R_{32}X_{34}, R_{32}X_{30})$ $(R_{32}X_{34}, R_{32}X_{34}), (R_{32}X_{30}, R_{32}X_{30})$
4	0202	$(R_{32}X_{33}, R_{32}X_{33})$
	0022	$(R_{32}X_{31}, R_{31}X_{31}), (R_{31}X_{31}, R_{31}X_{31}), (R_{32}X_{34}, R_{32}X_{34}),$ $(R_{32}X_{34}, R_{31}X_{31}), (R_{32}X_{30}, R_{31}X_{31}), (R_{32}X_{30}, R_{32}X_{30}),$ $(R_{32}X_{34}, R_{32}X_{30})$
	2002	$(R_{32}X_{32}, R_{32}X_{32})$
	1102	$(R_{32}X_{32}, R_{32}X_{33})$
	1012	$(R_{32}X_{32}, R_{32}X_{34}), (R_{32}X_{32}, R_{32}X_{30})$
	0112	$(R_{32}X_{33}, R_{32}X_{34}), (R_{32}X_{33}, R_{32}X_{30})$
5	1022	$(R_{32}X_{31}, R_{31}X_{32}), (R_{32}X_{32}, R_{31}X_{31}), (R_{31}X_{31}, R_{32}X_{32}),$ $(R_{32}X_{34}, R_{31}X_{31}), (R_{32}X_{30}, R_{31}X_{31}), (R_{31}X_{32}, R_{31}X_{32}),$ $(R_{32}X_{32}, R_{31}X_{32})$
	0122	$(R_{32}X_{31}, R_{31}X_{33}), (R_{32}X_{31}, R_{30}X_{29}), (R_{30}X_{29}, R_{31}X_{31}),$ $(R_{32}X_{33}, R_{31}X_{31}), (R_{31}X_{33}, R_{31}X_{31}), (R_{32}X_{34}, R_{31}X_{32}),$ $(R_{32}X_{30}, R_{31}X_{32}), (R_{32}X_{34}, R_{30}X_{29}), (R_{32}X_{31}, R_{32}X_{31})$
6	0222	$(R_{32}X_{31}, R_{30}X_{30}), (R_{32}X_{31}, R_{30}X_{31}), (R_{30}X_{29}, R_{30}X_{29})$ $(R_{32}X_{33}, R_{30}X_{30}), (R_{32}X_{33}, R_{30}X_{31}), (R_{30}X_{31}, R_{32}X_{34}),$ $(R_{30}X_{30}, R_{32}X_{34}), (R_{30}X_{30}, R_{32}X_{30}), (R_{30}X_{31}, R_{32}X_{30})$ $(R_{30}X_{30}, R_{31}X_{31}), (R_{30}X_{31}, R_{31}X_{31}), (R_{30}X_{30}, R_{30}X_{31}),$ $(R_{30}X_{30}, R_{30}X_{30}), (R_{30}X_{31}, R_{30}X_{31}), (R_{31}X_{33}, R_{30}X_{29})$ $(R_{31}X_{33}, R_{31}X_{33})$
	1122	$(R_{32}X_{33}, R_{31}X_{32}), (R_{32}X_{32}, R_{31}X_{33}), (R_{32}X_{32}, R_{30}X_{29}),$ $(R_{32}X_{32}, R_{30}X_{29}), (R_{31}X_{32}, R_{31}X_{33}), (R_{32}X_{33}, R_{31}X_{33})$ $(R_{30}X_{29}, R_{31}X_{32})$
	2022	$(R_{32}X_{32}, R_{31}X_{32}), (R_{31}X_{32}, R_{31}X_{32})$
7	1222	$(R_{32}X_{31}, R_{30}X_{32}), (R_{32}X_{31}, R_{29}X_{28}), (R_{32}X_{32}, R_{30}X_{32}),$ $(R_{32}X_{32}, R_{30}X_{30}), (R_{32}X_{32}, R_{30}X_{31}), (R_{32}X_{32}, R_{29}X_{28}$ $(R_{32}X_{33}, R_{30}X_{32}), (R_{32}X_{33}, R_{29}X_{28}), (R_{32}X_{34}, R_{30}X_{32}),$ $(R_{32}X_{31}, R_{30}X_{32}), (R_{32}X_{31}, R_{29}X_{28}), (R_{32}X_{30}, R_{29}X_{28})$ $(R_{32}X_{30}, R_{30}X_{32}), (R_{32}X_{34}, R_{29}X_{28}), (R_{31}X_{31}, R_{30}X_{32})$ $(R_{30}X_{30}, R_{31}X_{32}), (R_{30}X_{31}, R_{31}X_{32}), (R_{31}X_{31}, R_{29}X_{28})$ $(R_{31}X_{32}, R_{30}X_{32}), (R_{31}X_{32}, R_{29}X_{28}), (R_{30}X_{29}, R_{30}X_{32}),$ $(R_{31}X_{33}, R_{30}X_{32}), (R_{30}X_{29}, R_{29}X_{28}), (R_{31}X_{33}, R_{29}X_{28})$ $(R_{30}X_{30}, R_{30}X_{32}), (R_{30}X_{31}, R_{29}X_{28}), (R_{30}X_{32}, R_{30}X_{32})$ $(R_{30}X_{31}, R_{30}X_{32}), (R_{30}X_{30}, R_{29}X_{28}), (R_{29}X_{28}, R_{29}X_{28})$ $(R_{29}X_{28}, R_{30}X_{32})$
8	2222	

locations are both in the register X_{31} of the 31st round. If the ciphertext difference has 3 nonzero bytes and its pattern is 1002, the attacker might inject one or two faults. The locations might be in the register X_{31} of the 32nd round and the register X_{32} of the 32nd round.

We implemented the experiment on a PC using Visual C++ on a 1.60 GHz centrino with 2GB memory. The fault induction was simulated by computer software. In this situation, we ran the attacking algorithm to 1000 encryption unit with different random generated keys. And then we could detect about 77.15% errors into the last four rounds of MacGuffin. Unless the errors' pattern is 2222, we could detect 100% errors.

Compared with the previous techniques, the overhead and time tolerance of required for the comparison in our method is negligible (see Table 5). As one countermeasure of MacGuffin against DFA, the pattern–based technique could not only help to detect the errors with low overhead of space and time tolerance, but also be applied in hardware or software implementation.

Table 5. Comparison of overhead and tolerance

Approaches	Overhead	Time tolerance
Duplication	100%	100%
Coding method	Encoding dependent	Encoding dependent
EDC method	10-20%	Parity dependent
Proposed method	Negligible	Negligible

5   Conclusion

In this study, we present a fault injection of MacGuffin in software implementation. This method adopts the special pattern of ciphertext pairs in the attacking assumption and procedure of differential fault analysis. It is simple to detect errors in real applications and provides a practical approach for fault detection on block ciphers.

Future analysis should be able to detect differential fault analysis when the faults are injected into deeper rounds and the ciphertext difference has no special patterns. For the hardware situation, we will leave it for the future research.

Acknowledgment. This work is supported by the National Natural Science Foundation of China under Grant No. 61003278, the Opening Project of Shanghai Key Laboratory of Integrate Administration Technologies for Information Security, and the Fundamental Research Funds for the Central Universities. The authors wish to acknowledge the anonymous referees for helpful suggestions.

References

[1]   Biham, E., Shamir, A.: Differential Fault Analysis of Secret Key Cryptosystems. In: Kaliski Jr., B.S. (ed.) CRYPTO 1997. LNCS, vol. 1294, pp. 513–525. Springer, Heidelberg (1997)

[2] Moradi, A., Manzuri Shalmani, M.T., Salmasizadeh, M.: A Generalized Method of Differential Fault Attack Against AES Cryptosystem. In: Goubin, L., Matsui, M. (eds.) CHES 2006. LNCS, vol. 4249, pp. 91–100. Springer, Heidelberg (2006)

[3] Hemme, L.: A Differential Fault Attack Against Early Rounds of (Triple-)DES. In: Joye, M., Quisquater, J.-J. (eds.) CHES 2004. LNCS, vol. 3156, pp. 254–267. Springer, Heidelberg (2004)

[4] Clavier, C., Gierlichs, B., Verbauwhede, I.: Fault Analysis Study of IDEA. In: Malkin, T. (ed.) CT-RSA 2008. LNCS, vol. 4964, pp. 274–287. Springer, Heidelberg (2008)

[5] Li, W., Gu, D., Li, J.: Differential fault analysis on the ARIA algorithm. Information Sciences 178(19), 3727–3737 (2008)

[6] Li, W., Gu, D., Li, J., Liu, Z., Liu, Y.: Differential fault analysis on Camellia. Journal of Systems and Software 83, 844–851 (2010)

[7] Blaze, M., Schneier, B.: The MacGuffin Block Cipher Algorithm. In: Preneel, B. (ed.) FSE 1994. LNCS, vol. 1008, pp. 97–100. Springer, Heidelberg (1995)

[8] Rijmen, V., Preneel, B.: Cryptanalysis of MacGuffin. In: Preneel, B. (ed.) FSE 1994. LNCS, vol. 1008, pp. 353–358. Springer, Heidelberg (1995)

[9] Li, W., Gu, D., Wang, Y.: Differential Fault Analysis on the Contracting UFN Structure, with Application to SMS4 and MacGuffin. Journal of Systems and Software 82(2), 346–354 (2009)

[10] Karpovsky, M., Kulikowski, K.J., Taubin, A.: Differential fault analysis attack resistant architectures for the Advanced Encryption Standard. In: International Conference on Smart Card Research and Advanced Applications – CARDIS 2004, pp. 177–192. IEEE Computer Society (2004)

[11] Karri, R., Wu, K., Mishra, P., Kim, Y.: Concurrent error detection schemes for fault–based side–channel cryptanalysis of symmetric block ciphers. IEEE Transactions on Computer–Aided Design 21(12), 1509–1517 (2002)

[12] Karpovsky, M., Kulikowski, K.J., Taubin, A.: Robust protection against fault injection attacks on smart cards implementing the Advanced Encryption Standard. In: International Conference on Dependable Systems and Networks–DSN 2004, pp. 93–101. IEEE Computer Society (2004)

[13] Malkin, T.G., Standaert, F.-X., Yung, M.: A Comparative Cost/Security Analysis of Fault Attack Countermeasures. In: Breveglieri, L., Koren, I., Naccache, D., Seifert, J.-P. (eds.) FDTC 2006. LNCS, vol. 4236, pp. 159–172. Springer, Heidelberg (2006)

[14] Wu, K., Karri, R., Kuznetsov, G., Goessel, M.: Low cost error detection for the Advanced Encryption Standard. In: International Test Conference–ITC 2004, pp. 1242–1248. IEEE Computer Society (2004)

[15] Knudsen, L.: Truncated and Higher Order Differentials. In: Nyberg, K., Heys, H.M. (eds.) SAC 2002. LNCS, vol. 2595, pp. 196–211. Springer, Heidelberg (2003)

[16] Karri, R., Gössel, M.: Parity–based concurrent error detection in symmetric block ciphers. In: International Test Conference–ITC 2003, pp. 919–926. IEEE Computer Society (2003)

[17] Joshi, N., Wu, K., Karri, R.: Concurrent Error Detection Schemes for Involution Ciphers. In: Joye, M., Quisquater, J.-J. (eds.) CHES 2004. LNCS, vol. 3156, pp. 400–412. Springer, Heidelberg (2004)

[18] Karri, R., Kuznetsov, G., Gössel, M.: Parity-Based Concurrent Error Detection of Substitution-Permutation Network Block Ciphers. In: Walter, C.D., Koç, Ç.K., Paar, C. (eds.) CHES 2003. LNCS, vol. 2779, pp. 113–124. Springer, Heidelberg (2003)

Computationally Sound Symbolic Analysis
of EAP-TNC Protocol

Zijian Zhang[1], Liehuang Zhu[1,*], Feng Wang[2],
Lejian Liao[1], Cong Guo[1], and Hongyuan Wang[1]

[1] Beijing Key Lab of Intelligent Information Technology,
Beijing Institute of Technology, Beijing, China
{zhangzijian,liehuangz,liaolj,guocong,wanghongyuan}@bit.edu.cn
[2] Naval Academy of Armament, Beijing, 100161
lionkingwf@hotmail.com

Abstract. The Trusted Computing Group has proposed Trusted Network Connection (TNC) Architecture and a series of interface specifications, such as IF-T and IF-TNCCS, to solve the interoperability of network access control. In particular, IF-T describes the mapping of IF-TNCCS messages to a standard TNC Extensible Authentication Protocol (EAP) method. It includes specification of the standard EAP method called EAP-TNC. Since EAP-TNC is important to encapsulate TNCCS messages so that they can be carried over tunneled EAP methods, this paper proposes a computationally sound symbolic analysis of EAP-TNC protocol to prove composable security property.

Keywords: Computationally Sound; EAP-TNC; Trusted Network Connection; Trusted Computing.

1 Introduction

Computational analysis and symbolic analysis are two different approaches to analyze the security of cryptographic protocols. Computational approach is computational sound, because the security of cryptographic protocols is reduced to some cryptographic hardness assumptions [1]. However, it is hard to realize automation. That is, it needs human intervention. In comparison, symbolic approach is amenable to automation. There are a lot of automated tools, such as ProVerif [2], SMV, and Isabelle to analyze cryptographic protocols effectively. However, it is criticized since its computational soundness is not clear.

Since symbolic analysis is more effective than computational analysis, researchers have focused on its computational soundness for many years. Abadi and Rogaway [3] first bridged the gap between computational analysis and symbolic analysis of formal encryption scheme. Recently, Canetti [4] has proposed universally composable symbolic analysis (UCSA) of mutual authentication and key exchange protocols to prove composable security property. Such properties

---

* Corresponding author.

L. Chen, M. Yung, and L. Zhu (Eds.): INTRUST 2011, LNCS 7222, pp. 113–128, 2012.

are defined for individual protocol sessions but remain valid even when the analyzed session is composed with an unbounded number of other sessions [4]. As a result, we can only analyze a single session and still deduce security properties of the overall system [4]. Furthermore, they have proved that symbolic analysis is computationally sound in UC model. Canetti and Gajek [5] extended UCSA to analyze key exchange protocol based on Diffie-Hellman. Zhang and Zhu [6,7] extended UCSA to analyze Burmester-Desmedt protocol with three parties, and group key exchange protocols based on bilinear pairings. However, UCSA does not consider cryptographic protocols in the area of trusted computing.

Since any tiny system vulnerability may bring critical social problems, such as the leakage of personal privacy or the use of illegal copyright software, trusted computing has been proposed to enhance the security of computing environment in disparate computer platforms. Consequently, the Trusted Computing Group (TCG) has provided the specifications of Trusted Network Connection (TNC) Architecture [8] and a series of interface specifications, such as IF-T [9] and IF-TNCCS [10] to solve the interoperability of network access control. In particular, IF-T describes the mapping of IF-TNCCS messages to a standard TNC Extensible Authentication Protocol (EAP) method. It includes specification of the standard EAP method called EAP-TNC. Since EAP-TNC is important to encapsulate TNCCS messages so that they can be carried over tunneled EAP methods, it is necessary to analyze its security.

We extend UCSA approach to analyze EAP-TNC protocol that use Diffie-Hellman Pre-Negotiation (D-H PN), hash function and digital signature. It is tricky to analyze cryptographic protocols that use Diffie-Hellman pre-negotiation, hash function and digital signature simultaneously in symbolic model, because how to establish the appropriate rules for adversary to derive messages is not explicit for the complex protocols. Furthermore, The mapping from computational model to symbolic model is complicated. We solve these problems by symbolic adversary strategy, mapping theorem and computational soundness theorem, based on that D-H PN satisfies computational Diffie-Hellman (CDH) assumption, hash function is collision resistant, and digital signature scheme is existentially unforgeable. The specific steps are as follow:

1. Model symbolic analysis. More specially, we define symbolic algebra, symbolic protocol, symbolic adversary, symbolic trace occurred in the execution of symbolic protocol;
2. Model computational analysis. More specially, we define computational trace occurred in the execution of computational protocol, and ideal functionality of EAP-TNC protocol;
3. Define the syntax, symbolic semantics, and computational semantics of EAP-TNC protocol that has clear symbolic forms;
4. Define a mapping algorithm from computational traces to symbolic traces, based on the syntax and semantics of EAP-TNC protocol. Furthermore, prove that the mapping algorithm is always valid except with a negligible probability;
5. Prove that the symbolic analysis of EAP-TNC protocol is computationally sound in computational model, based on the valid mapping algorithm;

6. Define symbolic security criterion, and analyze security of EAP-TNC protocol via ProVerif in symbolic model.

2   EAP-TNC Protocol with Diffie-Hellman Pre-Negotiation

In this section, we first recall the location and description of EAP-TNC protocol with D-H DN in IF-T. First, the location of EAP-TNC protocol in TNC Architecture [8] is as in Fig 1, and the specific description of EAP-TNC protocol with D-H PN in IF-T [9] is as in Fig 2.

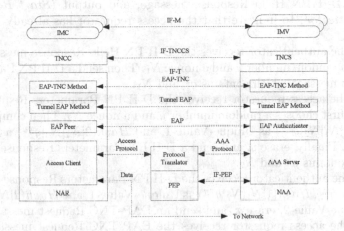

Fig. 1. The Location of EAP-TNC Protocol

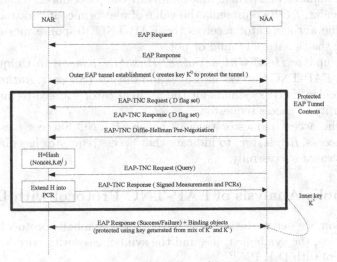

Fig. 2. The Specific Description of EAP-TNC Protocol

Next we recall the description of EAP-TNC protocol with D-H PN [9] as follow:

1. The authenticator first sends an EAP-TNC Request message at the start.
2. When the access requestor receives the EAP-TNC Request message, send an EAP-TNC Response message.
3. When the authenticator receives the EAP-TNC Response message, send a D-H PN Hello Request message to carry out D-H PN protocol, and output $(Start, Authenticator, Requestor)$. In particular, $Start$ indicates that the authenticator has been initialized, $Authenticator$ represents the identity of authenticator, while $Requestor$ represents the identity of access requestor.
4. When the access requestor receives the D-H PN Hello Request message, send a D-H PN Hello Response message, and output $(Start, Requestor, Authenticator)$ to indicate that the access requestor has already been initialized.
5. When the authenticator receives the D-H PN Hello Response message, first choose a random number x and a nonce N_1. Then send a D-H PN Parameters Request message which contains g^x and N_1.
6. When the access requestor receives the D-H PN Parameters Request message, it first chooses a random number y and a nonce N_2. Then compute g^{xy}, $Hash(1|N_1|N_2|g^{xy})$ as Unique-Value-1, and $Hash(2|N_1|N_2|g^{xy})$ as Unique-Value-2. Finally, erase y, and send a D-H PN Parameters Response message which contains g^y and N_2.
7. When the authenticator receives the D-H PN Parameters Response message, compute g^{xy}, $Hash(1|N_1|N_2|g^{xy})$ as Unique-Value-1, and $Hash(2|N_1|N_2|g^{xy})$ as Unique-Value-2, erase x, and send an EAP-TNC Request message.
8. When the access requestor receives the EAP-TNC Request message, send an EAP-TNC Response message:
   $(PCRs, UniqueValue1, Sig_{sk}(PCRs|UniqueValue1))$, and update $Hash(UniqueValue2|Hash(Response))$ to Unique-Value-2.
   In particular, $PCRs$ represents the value of platform configuration registers.
9. When the authenticator receives the EAP-TNC Response message, verify whether the signature is valid or not.
   If valid, update $Hash(UniqueValue2|Hash(Response))$ to Unique-Value-2 send an EAP-TNC Success message, and output $(Success, Authenticator)$. In particular, $Success$ stands for the authenticator succeed to authenticate the identity of access requestor.
10. When the access requestor receives the EAP-TNC Success message, output $(Success, Requestor)$ to indicate that access requestor has already been authenticated successfully.

3   Symbolic Analysis of EAP-TNC Protocol with D-H PN

In this section, we define the symbolic algebra, the symbolic protocol, the symbolic adversary, the symbolic trace, and the symbolic security criterion of EAP-TNC protocol with D-H PN.[1]

---

[1] The definitions from section 3 to section 6 are extended from [4,5].

3.1 Symbolic Algebra and Symbolic Protocol

Definition 1 (Symbolic Algebra A). *First, eight necessary types of atomic messages for EAP-TNC protocol with D-H PN are defined as follow:*

1. *Group. We denote G as a group with a prime order q, and g is a generator of G.*
2. *Participant Identity. Each participant identity is denoted by pid, and the set of the whole participant identities is denoted by PID.*
3. *Private Key. The private key of each participant is denoted by sk. The set of the private keys is denoted by SK.*
4. *Public Key. The public key of each participant is denoted by pk. The set of the public keys is denoted by PK. In addition, assume that the public key can be computed by the private key.*
5. *Random Number. The random number is denoted by $r, (r \in_R Z_q^*)$. It is used to keep the freshness of a message, and represent the internal state of an honest participant.*
6. *Message Digest. They are denoted by MD and used to represent the message digest of the messages.*
7. *Output. Each output is denoted by o, and the set of the outputs is denoted by O. There are two kinds of output: $(Start, pid, pid')$ is at the start of the protocol; $(Success, pid)$ is at the end of the protocol.*
8. *Evaluation. The evaluation is denoted by E. If the result of an evaluation is valid, it is denoted by $\top$, Otherwise, it is denoted by $\bot$. The execution of the protocol will continue, if the result is $\top$. Otherwise, it will terminate immediately.*

Next nine operations for EAP-TNC protocol with D-H PN are defined as follow:

1. *Get Public Key Operation. This operation is denoted by $GPK(sk) : SK \rightarrow PK$, and used to get the public key of a honest participant via sk.*
2. *Modular Exponentiation Operation. This operation is denoted by $ME(r) : R \rightarrow G$, and used to modular multiply g by r times, where g is the generator of G and r is a random element of Z_q^*.*
3. *Modular Multiplication Operation. This operation is denoted by $MM(r, s) : R \times G \rightarrow G$, and used to modular multiply s by r times. This operation contains two parameters: r is used to count the times, and it is a random element of Z_q^*; s is the result of the modular exponentiation operation.*
   For example, $MM(r_1, ME(r_2))$ means that modular multiply $ME(r_2)$ by r_1 times. Moreover, this operation satisfies the commutative law, and the result of this operation is still an element of G.
4. *Hash Operation. This operation is denoted by $Hash(x) : A \rightarrow MD$, and used to compute the message digest of a message $x, (x \in A)$.*
5. *Signature Operation. This operation is denoted by $Sig(z, x) : sk \times A \rightarrow A$, and used to sign a message x via the private key z, where $z \in SK, x \in A$.*
6. *Verification of Signature Operation. This operation is denoted by $VerSig(z, x, y) : pk \times A \times A \rightarrow E$, and used to verify the signature y of message x via public key z, where $z \in PK, x \in A, y \in A$.*

7. *Pair Operation.* This operation is denoted as $Pair(m_0, m_1) : A \times A \to A$, and used to represent the concatenation of two messages in A. In particular, we write $m_0|m_1$ for short.

8. *Extract Left Operation.* This operation is denoted by $Ex\_l(m) : A \to A$, and used to extract the left half of m. In addition, if m is not the form of $m_0|m_1$, the result is $\perp$.

9. *Extract Right Operation.* This operation is denoted by $Ex\_r(m) : A \to A$, and used to extract the right half of m. In addition, if m is not the form of $m_0|m_1$, the result is $\perp$.

Definition 2 (Symbolic Protocol). *The symbolic expression of EAP-TNC protocol with D-H PN $\overline{\pi}$ is a mapping from (1) the set PID of participant identities, (2) the set $S = (A)^*$ of states, and (3) the set of the algebra A which represents the possible incoming messages of the participants, to (1) the set E of evaluation, or (2) the set of ("message" $\times A$) which represents the possible outgoing messages of the participants, or (3) the set of ("output" $\times O$) which describes the possible outputs of the participants, (4) the set of ("erase", R) which indicates that the honest participants erase the internal states. (5) and the set $S = (A)^*$ of the new states. Formally, $\overline{\pi} : PID \times S \times A \to E \cup ("message" \times A) \cup ("output" \times O) \times \cup("erase", R) \times S$.*

3.2 Symbolic Adversary and Symbolic Trace

Definition 3 (Initial Knowledge of Symbolic Adversary). *The initial knowledge of symbolic adversary in EAP-TNC protocol with D-H PN is defined as a set, including (1) the prime order q of G and the generator g, (2) all the participant identities PID, (3) all the public key PK, and (4) the random elements of Z_q^* generated by the adversary itself.*

Definition 4 (Analysis Closure of Symbolic Adversary). *Let $R_{adv}(R_{adv} \subset Z_q^*)$ denotes the subset of Z_q^* generated by the adversary. Let A_{adv} denotes the set of messages which can be received from honest participants, when EAP-TNC protocol with D-H PN is executed. Then the analysis closure $C[A_{adv}]$ of the adversary is defined recursively as the smallest subset of A, such that:*

$A_{adv} \subseteq C[A_{adv}]$;
$R_{adv} \subseteq C[A_{adv}]$;
if $sk \in C[A_{adv}]$, then $GPK(sk) \in C[A_{adv}]$;
if $r \in C[A_{adv}]$, then $ME(r) \in C[A_{adv}]$;
if $r, s \in C[A_{adv}]$, then $MM(r, s) \in C[A_{adv}]$;
if $x \in C[A_{adv}]$, then $Hash(x) \in C[A_{adv}]$;
if $z, x \in C[A_{adv}]$, then $Sig(z, x) \in C[A_{adv}]$;
if $z, x, y \in C[A_{adv}]$, then $VerSig(z, x, y) \in C[A_{adv}]$;
if $m_0, m_1 \in C[A_{adv}]$, then $m_0|m_1 \in C[A_{adv}]$;
if $m_0|m_1 \in C[A_{adv}]$, then $m_0, m_1 \in C[A_{adv}]$.

Definition 5 (Symbolic Trace). *The symbolic trace $\overline{t}$ is a sequence of events $H_0, H_1, \ldots, H_n$, each H_i is one of the triple:*

1. *Initialization Event*
   ["*init*", $pid, pid', S_{i,init}$] *represents the input for participant pid with initial state S_{init}, and partner pid'.*
2. *Honest Participant Event*

   - ["*message*", m] *represents that a participant sends a message m.*
   - ["*output*", o] *represents that a participant generates an output o.*
   - ["*erase*, r] *represents that a participant erase its internal state r.*

3. *Adversary Event*

   - ["*name*", pid] *represents that symbolic adversary generates a participant identity pid, where $pid \in C[A_{adv}]$.*
   - ["*sk*", sk] *represents that symbolic adversary generates a private key sk, where $sk \in C[A_{adv}]$.*
   - ["*random*", r] *represents that symbolic adversary generates a random number r, where $r \in R_{adv}$.*
   - ["*GPK*", sk] *represents that symbolic adversary computes $GKE(sk)$, where $sk \in C[A_{adv}]$.*
   - ["*ME*", r] *represents that symbolic adversary computes $ME(r)$, where $r \in R_{adv}$.*
   - ["*MM*", r, s] *represents that symbolic adversary computes $MM(r, s)$, where $r, s \in C[A_{adv}]$.*
   - ["*MD*", x] *represents that symbolic adversary computes $Hash(x)$, where $x \in C[A_{adv}]$.*
   - ["*SIG*", z, x] *represents that symbolic adversary computes $Sig(z, x)$, where $z, x, y \in C[A_{adv}]$.*
   - ["*VERSIG*", z, x, y] *represents that symbolic adversary computes $VerSig(z, x, y)$, where $z, x, y \in C[A_{adv}]$.*
   - ["*PAIR*", m_0, m_1] *represents that symbolic adversary computes $Pair(m_0, m_1)$, where $m_0, m_1 \in C[A_{adv}]$.*
   - ["*SEP*", m] *represents that symbolic adversary computes $Ex\_l(m)$ and $Ex\_r(m)$, where $m \in C[A_{adv}]$.*
   - ["*deliver*", m, pid] *represents that symbolic adversary delivers a message m to the participant pid.*

Furthermore, if there exists a message in $\bar{t}$ which does not belong to any kind of the triple above, we regard $\bar{t}$ as an invalid symbolic trace.

Definition 6 (Adversary Strategy). *With the execution of EAP-TNC protocol with D-H PN $\bar{\pi}$, adversary strategy Ψ is a sequence of adversary instructions $I_0, I_1, \ldots, I_n$, each I_i is either:*

["*receive*", m],	["*name*", pid],	["*sk*", sk],	["*random*", r],
["*GPK*", sk],	["*ME*", r],	["*MM*", r, s],	["*MD*", x],
["*SIG*", z, x],	["*VERSIG*", z, x, y],	["*PAIR*", m_0, m_1],	["*SEP*", m],
["*deliver*", m, pid].			

The adversary strategy Ψ produces the following symbolic trace $\Psi(\bar{\pi})$:

For each form of ["receive", m] instruction, if the participant pid is just activated by D-H PN Hello Request message or EAP-TNC Response message,
["output", (Start, pid, pid')] is added to the symbolic trace.

If the participant pid is just activated and sent a message m, ["message", m]
is added to the symbolic trace.

If the authenticator is activated and sent the EAP-TNC Success message or
the access requestor pid is activated by the EAP-TNC Success message,
["output", (Success, pid)] is added to the symbolic trace.

If the internal state r is erased, ["erase", r] is added to the symbolic trace.
Otherwise, output ⊥ for failure.

For any other instructions, add the corresponding adversary events to the
symbolic trace. If anyone of the event results in an invalid symbolic trace, output
⊥.

4   Computational Analysis of EAP-TNC Protocol with D-H PN

In this section, we define the computational trace and functionality of EAP-TNC
protocol with D-H PN.

Definition 7 (Computational Trace). Let $TRACE_{\pi,S,Z}(k, z)$ denote the trace
of EAP-TNC protocol with D-H PN, where the protocol is denoted by π, the computational adversary is denoted by S, the environment is denoted by Z, security
parameter is denoted by k, and the input is denoted by z. The computational
trace is the sequence of events $H_1, H_2, \ldots, H_n$, each of which is one of the triple:

1. Initialization Event
   The initialization event of ["init", pid, pid'] represents that the participant
   pid starts to execute π with its partner pid'.
2. Adversary Event
   The adversary event of ["adversary", m, pid] represents that the adversary
   sends a message m to the participant pid.
3. Honest Participant Event
   The honest participant event of ["message", m], ["output", o], ["erase", r].
   The first indicates that a participant sends a message m on adversarial incoming communication tape. The second represents that a participant generates outputs o on its local output tape. The third expresses that a participant
   erases its internal state r.

The ensemble $\{TRACE_{\pi,S,Z}(k, z)\}_{k \in N, z \in \{0,1\}^*}$ is denoted by $EXEC_{\pi,S,Z}$.

Definition 8 (Authentication Functionality $\mathcal{F}_{AF}$). $\mathcal{F}_{AF}$ proceeds   as
follows, when parameterized with security parameter k, an ideal adversary S:

1. Initially, set a variable **Finished** to false.
2. Upon receiving an input (pid, pid') from some participant pid, do:

– If there is no record for (pid, pid'), then record (pid, pid'), and send (pid, pid') to the adversary.

– If (pid', pid) has already been recorded, then set **Finished** to true.

3. Upon receiving from the adversary a request (Success,pid"), if pid" is either pid or pid', and **Finished** is true, send (Success,pid") to pid".

5   Syntax and Semantics of EAP-TNC Protocol with D-H PN

In this section, we first define the syntax of EAP-TNC protocol with D-H PN.

Definition 9 (The Syntax of Simple Protocol). *EAP-TNC protocol with D-H PN π is a pair of programs $\pi = (\pi_0, \pi_1)$, each of which is given by the grammar as follow:*

$PROGRAM ::= init(pid, pid'); COMMAND$
$COMMAND ::= COMMAND; COMMAND|done$
$|receive(v); |send(vc); |output(vc); |GPK(vc, v); |ME(vc, v); |MM(vc_0, vc_1, v);$
$|Hash(vc, v); |Sig(vc_0, vc_1, v); |VerSig(vc_0, vc_1, vc_2, v); |newrandom(v);$
$|Pair(vc_0, vc_1, v); |Sep(vc, v_0, v_1); |erase(vc);$

Here vc, vc_0, vc_1, vc_2 stand for constants and v, v_0, v_1 stand for variables.

Next we define the symbolic and computational semantics of EAP-TNC protocol with D-H PN.

Definition 10 (Symbolic Semantics). *Let $\pi = (\pi_1, \pi_2)$ be a simple protocol. Let $\overline{\pi}$ be the symbolic protocol of π where the set of states S consist of a program counter Γ that indicates the next command to execute, and a store command Δ that maps variables in π to the corresponding symbols in the algebra A. For all $(\Gamma, \Delta) \in S, m \in A, p \in PID$, the mapping $\overline{\pi}$ is defined on the commands in $\pi = (\pi_1, \pi_2)$ as follow:*

1. If Γ points to send(vc), then $\overline{\pi}(s, p, (\Gamma, \Delta), m) \rightarrow ("message", \Delta(vc), (\Gamma', \Delta))$, Γ' points to the next command.
2. If Γ points to erase(vc), then $\overline{\pi}(s, p, (\Gamma, \Delta), m) \rightarrow ("erase", \Delta(vc), (\Gamma', \Delta))$, Γ' points to the next command.
3. If Γ points to output(vc), then $\overline{\pi}(s, p, (\Gamma, \Delta), m) \rightarrow ("output", \Delta(vc), (\Gamma', \Delta))$, Γ' points to the next command.
4. If Γ points to one of the following commands, then $\overline{\pi}(p, (\Gamma, \Delta), m) \rightarrow (p, (\Gamma', \Delta'), m)$, where Γ' points to the next command and Δ' is equal to Δ, except that:
   – receive(v) : $\Delta'(v) = m$.
   – GKE(vc, v) : $\Delta'(v) = GPK(vc)$.
   – ME(vc, v) : $\Delta'(v) = ME(vc)$.
   – $MM(vc_0, vc_1, v) : \Delta'(v) = MM(vc_0, vc_1)$.

- $Hash(vc, v) : \Delta'(v) = Hash(vc)$.
- $Sig(vc_0, vc_1, v) : \Delta'(v) = Sig(vc_0, vc_1)$.
- $VerSig(vc_0, vc_1, vc_2, v) : \Delta'(v) = VerSig(vc_0, vc_1, vc_2)$.
- $newrandom(v) : \Delta'(v)$ is the first element of R that is not in the range of Δ.
- $Pair(vc_1, vc_2, v) : \Delta'(v) = Pair(\Delta(vc_1), \Delta(vc_1))$.
- $Sep(vc, v_1, v_2) :$ If $\Delta(vc) = Pair(\Delta(vc_1), \Delta(vc_2)), \Delta'(v_1) = Ex\_l(\Delta(vc))$, $\Delta'(v_2) = Ex\_r(\Delta(vc))$. Otherwise, $\Delta'(v) = \perp$.

Definition 11 (Computational Semantics). *Let a PPT ITM $\pi = (\pi_1, \pi_2)$ be a simple protocol. The state set S_M consists of $\{$ "init" $\} \cup S_1 \cup S_2$, where "init" represents the initial state of M_π, and each state $S_i = (pid_i, \Delta_i, \Gamma_i), (i \in \{1, 2\})$ represents the protocol program with a participant pid_i, a store command Δ_i which maps from variable names in pid_i to locations on the work tape, and a program counter Γ_i which indicates the current command of pid_i. To encode the execution of each pid_i, the transition function is defined over S_M as follow:*

1. *If M_π is in the initial state "init", it will first read the security parameter k, two participant identities pid_1, pid_2. Then M_π initializes the storage and writes ["init", $Start, pid_1, pid_2$]. Finally, it sets the program counter Γ_i to the next command and executes it.*
2. *After initialization, the transition function will continue to execute the command of π_i by program counter Γ_i:*
   - *$receive(v)$: If the command has already been executed in this activation, M_π waits to be reactivated. Otherwise, it reads the message from its incoming communication tape and stores it in v, instructs Γ_i to next command and executes it.*
   - *$send(vc)$: M_π writes vc to adversarial incoming communication tape, instructs Γ_i to next command and executes it.*
   - *$output(vc)$: M_π writes vc to its local output tape, instructs Γ_i to next command and executes it.*
   - *$GPK(vc, v)$: M_π stores ["gpk", vc] in v, instructs Γ_i to next command and executes it.*
   - *$ME(vc, v)$: M_π stores ["me", vc] in v, instructs Γ_i to next command and executes it.*
   - *$MM(vc_0, vc_1, v)$: M_π stores ["mm", vc_0, vc_1] in v, instructs Γ_i to next command and executes it.*
   - *$Hash(vc, v)$: M_π stores ["hash", vc] in v, instructs Γ_i to next command and executes it.*
   - *$Sig(vc_0, vc_1, v)$: M_π stores ["sig", vc_0, vc_1] in v, instructs Γ_i to next command and executes it.*
   - *$VerSig(vc_0, vc_1, vc_2, v)$: M_π stores ["versig", vc_0, vc_1, vc_2] in v, instructs Γ_i to next command and executes it.*
   - *$newrandom(v)$: M_π generates a random number $r \leftarrow \{0, 1\}^k$, stores ["random", r] in v, instructs Γ_i to next command and executes it.*
   - *$pair(vc_1, vc_2, v)$: M_π stores ["pair", vc_0, vc_1] in v, instructs Γ_i to next command and executes it.*

- *erase(vc)*: M_π *deletes the value of vc from its work tape, instructs Γ_i to next command and executes it.*
- *sep(vc, v_1, v_2)*: M_π *compute Ex_l(vc) and Ex_r(vc), stores Ex_l(vc) in v_1, Ex_r(vc) in v_2, instructs Γ_i to next command and executes it.*

6   Mapping Algorithm and Mapping Theorem of EAP-TNC Protocol with D-H PN

In this section, we first define the mapping algorithm for EAP-TNC protocol with D-H PN.

Definition 12 (Mapping Algorithm). *Assume that the computational trace of π is denoted by $TRACE_{\pi,S,Z}(k,z)$, the computational adversary is denoted by S, the environment is denoted by Z, the security parameter is denoted by k, and the input is denoted by z. In addition, assume that $\overline{\pi}$ is the correspondent symbolic protocol for π, $\overline{t}$ is the symbolic trace of $\overline{\pi}$, and the symbolic adversary is $\overline{S}$. The mapping algorithm δ from $TRACE_{\pi,S,Z}(k,z)$ to $\overline{t}$ be defined as follow:*

First, read all the trace $TRACE_{\pi,S,Z}(k,z)$ character by character to build the mapping from bit-strings to the elements of the symbolic algebra A. That is $\delta : \{0,1\}^* \to A$, according to the cases below:

1. *When parsing a pattern ["name", pid], set $\delta(\text{"name"}, pid) = pid$.*
2. *When parsing a pattern ["sk", sk], set $\delta(\text{"sk"}, sk) = sk$.*
3. *When parsing a pattern ["random", r], set $\delta(\text{"random"}, r) = r$.*
4. *When parsing a pattern ["gpk", sk], set $\delta(\text{"gpk"}, sk) = GPK(\delta(sk))$.*
5. *When parsing a pattern ["me", r], set $\delta(\text{"me"}, r) = ME(\delta(r))$.*
6. *When parsing a pattern ["mm", r, s], set $\delta(\text{"mm"}, r, s) = MM(\delta(r), \delta(s))$.*
7. *When parsing a pattern ["hash", x], set $\delta(\text{"hash"}, x) = Hash(\delta(x))$.*
8. *When parsing a pattern ["sig", z, x, y], set $\delta(\text{"sig"}, z, x) = Sig(\delta(z), \delta(x))$.*
9. *When parsing a pattern ["versig", z, x, y], set $\delta(\text{"versig"}, z, x, y)$ $= VerSig(\delta(z), \delta(x), \delta(y))$.*
10. *When parsing a pattern ["pair", a, b], set $\delta(\text{"pair"}, a, b) = \delta(a)|\delta(b)$.*

In addition, all the other bit-strings, such as $\top$ and $\bot$, are the same on both sides.

After that, construct the symbolic trace. Assume that $H_1, H_2, \ldots, H_n$ is the events of a computational trace, the corresponding symbolic trace is produced as follow:

1. *If $H = [\text{"init"}, pid, pid']$, then generate the event $[\text{"init"}, \delta(\text{"name"}, pid), \delta(\text{"name"}, pid'), S_{init}]$.*
2. *If $H = [\text{"adversary"}, m]$, map it to $[\text{"deliver"}, \delta(m), \delta(pid)]$, which indicates to send message m to participant pid. In particular, pid is obtained from the message m.*
3. *If $H = [\text{"message"}, m]$, then the event maps to $[\text{"message"}, \delta(m)]$.*
4. *If $H = [\text{"output"}, o]$, then the event maps to $[\text{"output"}, \delta(o)]$.*
5. *If $H = [\text{"erase"}, r]$, then the event maps to $[\text{"erase"}, \delta(r)]$.*

Next we prove the validity of Definition 12 as follow:

Theorem 1 (Mapping Theorem). *Let δ be the mapping algorithm from the computational trace $TRACE_{\pi,S,Z}(k,z)$ to the symbolic trace $\bar{t}$. If D-H PN satisfies CDH assumption, Sig is a secure digital signature scheme, and Hash is collision resistant, then we have:*

$$Pr[t \leftarrow EXEC_{\pi,S,Z}] : \bar{t} \text{ is not valid}] \leq negl(k).$$

Proof. The initialization event and the honest participant event are always valid by Definition 5. Therefore, we just need to prove that it is negligible that the adversary event is invalid. In other words, it is negligible that there is a message M_* which can be generated by the computational adversary but not be generated by the symbolic adversary. Therefore, some of the parameters used to compute M_* need not be known by the symbolic adversary.

Assume that m_t^* represents all the messages previous to m_*. There are four kinds of possibilities:

First, M_* is a random number. Since the honest participants choose it randomly from Z_q^*, the probability that M_* equals the nonce generated by some honest participants is negligible in probabilistic polynomial time (PPT).

Second, M_* is a value of $MM(r_1, ME(r_2))$. Based on computational Diffie-Hellman assumption, if $r_1 \notin C[m_t^*]$ or $r_2 \notin C[m_t^*]$, the probability that M_* is equal to the value of $MM(r_1, ME(r_2))$ generated by some honest participants is also negligible in PPT.

Third, M_* is a value of $Hash((1, r_1, r_2, MM(y, ME(x))))$ or $Hash((2, r_1, r_2, MM(y, ME(x))))$. Since Hash function is collision resistant, the probability is negligible in PPT that M_* generates r_1', r_2', y', x', such that $Hash(1, r_1', r_2', y', ME(x')) = Hash((1, r_1, r_2, MM(y, ME(x))))$ or $Hash(2, r_1', r_2', y', ME(x')) = Hash((2, r_1, r_2, MM(y, ME(x))))$.

Fourth, M_* is a value of $Sig(GPK(sk), (PCRs, hash\_value\_1))$. Since Sig is a secure digital signature scheme, the probability that M_* forges a valid signature is also negligible in PPT.

Above all, the probability that $\bar{t}$ is not valid is negligible.

We complete the proof.

7   Security Analysis of EAP-TNC Protocol with D-H PN

In this section, we first prove computational soundness of DYSA.

Theorem 2 (Computational Soundness). *For any adversary strategy Ψ, if EAP-TNC protocol with D-H PN π has a mapping from computational traces to symbolic traces, then π securely realizes $\mathcal{F}_{AF}$, if $\overline{\pi}$ satisfies DYSA.*

Proof. We prove if we can distinguish the real protocol π and real adversary from the ideal functionality $\mathcal{F}_{AF}$ and ideal adversary, $\overline{\pi}$ does not satisfy DYSA.

We first construct a simulator (i.e., an ideal adversary) to show how to simulate π and the real adversary via $\mathcal{F}_{AF}$ and the simulator. The simulator proceeds as follow:

The simulator simulates the participants $'pid,'\,pid'$, but neither of these simulated participants are running.

When the simulator receives a message (pid, pid') from $\mathcal{F}_{AF}$, the simulator activates the simulated participant $'pid$ by the input $("init", Start,'\,pid,'\,pid')$.

When the simulator receives a message sent by the environment to the participant pid, forward it to the simulated participant $'pid$.

When the simulated participant $'pid$ sends a message on its communication tape, send it to the environment.

When the simulated participant $'pid$ produces an output $(Success, pid)$, send it to $\mathcal{F}_{AF}$.

Then, if the environment can distinguish the real protocol π and real adversary from the ideal functionality $\mathcal{F}_{AF}$ and the simulator, there must exist a symbolic adversary strategy, such that $(Success, pid)$ or $(Success, pid')$ has been occurred, before (pid, pid') or (pid', pid) for $\mathcal{F}_{AF}$. This implies that $("output", (Success, pid))$ or $("output", (Success, pid'))$ has been occurred, before $("output", (Start, pid, pid'))$ or $("output", (Start, pid', pid))$ in a computational trace t. If t can be mapped to a valid symbolic trace $\bar{t}$, π does not satisfy DYSA.

We complete the proof.

Next we provide the criterion of symbolic secure authentication, and discuss the security of EAP-TNC protocol with D-H PN in symbolic model. In particular, we only need to analyze a single session but remain valid when the analyzed session is composed with an unbounded number of other sessions, based on the work of [4].

Definition 13 (Criterion of Dolev-Yao Secure Authentication). *The symbolic protocol fulfills Dolev-Yao secure authentication (DYSA), if participant pid generates an output $(Success, pid)$ imply that participant pid generates an output $(Start, pid, pid')$, and its partner pid' generates an output $(Start, pid', pid)$.*

Theorem 3 (DYSA of EAP-TNC Protocol). *EAP-TNC protocol with D-H PN is DYSA.*

We analyze EAP-TNC protocol via an automated tool ProVerif. The specific implementation is enumerated in Fig 3, and the analysis result is enumerated in Fig 4.

```
free c. data EAP_TNC_Request/0. data EAP_TNC_Response/0.
data DH_PN_Hello_Request/0. data DH_PN_Hello_Response/0.
data EAP_TNC_Success/0. fun GPK/1. fun ME/1. fun MM/2.
fun Hash/1. fun Sig/2. fun erase/1. data one/0. data two/0. data true/0.
equation MM(y,ME(x)) = MM(x,ME(y)).
reduc VerSig(GPK(z), x, Sig(z,x)) = true.
query ev:endARParam(x1,x2) ==> ev:beginARParam(x1,x2).
query ev:endARFull(x1,x2,x3) ==> ev:beginARFull(x1,x2,x3).
let AR = in (c, m1);
let (=EAP_TNC_Request) = m1 in
out (c, EAP_TNC_Response); in (c, m2);
let (=DH_PN_Hello_Request) = m2 in
out (c, DH_PN_Hello_Response); in (c, m3);
let (gx,n1) = m3 in new y; new N2; out(c, (ME(y),N2));
event beginARParam(ME(y),N2); in (c, m4);
let (=EAP_TNC_Request) = m4 in
let hash_value_1 = Hash((one,n1,N2,MM(y,gx))) in
let hash_value_2 = Hash((two,n1,N2,MM(y,gx))) in out(c,erase(y));
out(c,(PCRs, hash_value_1, Sig(sk_AR,(PCRs,hash_value_1))));
event beginARFull(PCRs, hash_value_1, Sig(sk_AR,(PCRs,hash_value_1)));
let hash_value_2 = Hash((hash_value_2,(PCRs, hash_value_1, Sig(sk_AR,(PCRs,
hash_value_1))))) in in (c, m5);
let (=EAP_TNC_Success) = m5 in 0.
let AA = out(c,EAP_TNC_Request); in (c, m1);
let (=EAP_TNC_Response) = m1 in
out (c, DH_PN_Hello_Request); in (c, m2);
let (=EAP_TNC_Hello_Response) = m2 in
new x; new N1; out (c, (ME(x),N1)); in (c, m3);
let (gy,n2) = m3 in
let hash_value_1 = Hash((one,N1,n2,MM(x,gy))) in
let hash_value_2 = Hash((two,N1,n2,MM(x,gy))) in out(c,erase(x));
out(c, EAP_TNC_Request); in (c, m4);
let (m4_1,m4_2,m4_3) = m4 in
let (=hash_value_1) = m4_3 in
if VerSig(pk_AR, (m4_1,m4_2), m4_3) = true then
let hash_value_2 = Hash((hash_value_2, (PCRs, hash_value_1, Sig(sk_AR,(PCRs,
hash_value_1))))) in
out(c, EAP_TNC_Success);
event endARParam(gy,n2);
event endARFull(m4_1,m4_2,m4_3).
process new sk_AR;
let pk_AR = GPK(sk_AR) in (AA | AR)
```

Fig. 3. The symbolic analysis of EAP-TNC protocol with D-H PN

```
– Query ev:endARFull(x1_48,x2_49,x3_50)
==> ev:beginARFull(x1_48,x2_49,x3_50)
Completing...
Starting query ev:endARFull(x1_48,x2_49,x3_50)
==> ev:beginARFull(x1_48,x2_49,x3_50)
RESULT ev:endARFull(x1_48,x2_49,x3_50)
==> ev:beginARFull(x1_48,x2_49,x3_50) is true.
– Query ev:endARParam(x1_463,x2_464)
==> ev:beginARParam(x1_463,x2_464)
Completing...
Starting query ev:endARParam(x1_463,x2_464)
==> ev:beginARParam(x1_463,x2_464)
RESULT ev:endARParam(x1_463,x2_464)
==> ev:beginARParam(x1_463,x2_464) is true.
```

Fig. 4. The result of the specific implementation

Fig 4 shows that the endARFull event of authenticator imply that the beginARFull event of access requestor. In other words, the output EAP-TNC-Success of authenticator indicates that the access requestor has sent the EAP-TNC-Response message. Therefore, according to the order of protocol execution, $(Start, Requestor, Authenticator)$ and $(Start, Authenticator, Requestor)$ must occur, before $(Success, Requestor)$ and $(Success, Authenticator)$, respectively. Otherwise, symbolic adversary must fake EAP-TNC-Response message. $(PCRs, UniqueValue1, Sig_{sk}(PCRs|UniqueValue1))$ by itself successfully. It is negligible because the digital signature scheme is existentially unforgeable.

Above all, based on Theorem 1, 2, 3, EAP-TNC protocol with D-H PN securely realizes $\mathcal{F}_{AF}$, since EAP-TNC protocol with D-H PN satisfies DYSA.

8   Conclusion

We try to analyze the security of EAP-TNC protocol with D-H PN in the extension of UCSA. Our approach could prove composable security property of protocols in the area of trusted computing by computationally sound and fully automated symbolic analysis. Our work laid the root for analyzing the other protocols in TNC Architecture automatically, without sacrificing computational soundness of cryptography.

In this paper, the ideal functionality is basic. Researchers can modify it for more complex target and more powerful adversary. In that case, researchers can also modify EAP-TNC protocol to improve its security property.

Acknowledgment. Corresponding Author: Liehuang Zhu. This paper is supported by National Natural Science Foundation of China No.61003262, and National Natural Science Foundation of China No.60873237.

References

1. Canetti, R.: Universally composable security: A new paradigm for cryptographic protocols. In: 42nd Annual Symposium on Foundations of Computer Science, pp. 136–145. IEEE Computer Society (2001)
2. Blanchet, B.: Automatic verification of correspondences for security protocols. Journal of Computer Security 17(4), 363–434 (2009)
3. Abadi, M., Rogaway, P.: Reconciling two views of cryptography (the computational soundness of formal encryption). Journal of Cryptology 15(2), 103–127 (2002)
4. Canetti, R., Herzog, J.: Universally Composable Symbolic Analysis of Mutual Authentication and Key-Exchange Protocols. In: Halevi, S., Rabin, T. (eds.) TCC 2006. LNCS, vol. 3876, pp. 380–403. Springer, Heidelberg (2006)
5. Canetti, R., Gajek, S.: Universally composable symbolic analysis of Diffie-Hellman based key exchange, http://eprint.iacr.org/2010/303.pdf
6. Zhang, Z.J., Zhu, L.H., Liao, L.J.: Universally composable symbolic analysis of group key exchange protocol. China Communications 8(2), 59–65 (2011)
7. Zhang, Z.J., Zhu, L.H., Liao, L.J., Wang, M.Z.: Computationally Sound Symbolic Security Reduction Analysis of the Group Key Exchange Protocol using Bilinear Pairings. Information Sciences (2012), doi:
   http://dx.doi.org/10.1016/j.ins.2012.04.029
8. Trusted Computing Group, TNC Architecture for Interoperability, Specification Version 1.4, Revision 4 (2009),
   https://www.trustedcomputinggroup.org/specs/TNC
9. Trusted Computing Group, TNC IF-T: Protocol Bindings for Tunneled EAP Methods Specification Version 1.1, Revision 10 (2007),
   https://www.trustedcomputinggroup.org/specs/TNC
10. Trusted Computing Group, TCG Trusted network connect TNC IF-TNCCS Specification Version 1.1, Revision 10 (2007),
    https://www.trustedcomputinggroup.org/specs/TNC

A Technique for Remote Detection
of Certain Virtual Machine Monitors

Christopher Jämthagen, Martin Hell, and Ben Smeets

Department of Electrical and Information Technology,
Lund University, P.O. Box 118, 221 00 Lund, Sweden
{christopher,martin,ben}@eit.lth.se

Abstract. The ability to detect a virtualized environment has both malicious and non-malicious uses. This paper reveals a new exploit and technique that can be used to remotely detect VMware Workstation, VMware Player and VirtualBox. The detection based on this technique can be done completely passively in that there is no need to have access to the remote machine and no network connections are initiated by the verifier. Using only information in the IP packet together with information sent in the user-agent string in an HTTP request, it is shown how to detect that the traffic originates from a guest in VMware Workstation, VMware Player or VirtualBox client. The limitation is that NAT has to be turned on and that the host and guest need to run different operating system families, e.g., Windows/Linux.

1 Introduction

Virtualization can be applied as a solution to various kinds of problems. One common motivation for deploying virtualization is to improve utilization of server farm hardware resources and thus cutting down on investment and energy costs. Virtualization is also useful from a security point of view. One particular usecase in this aspect is malware analysis. Here virtualization makes it easy for the analyst to restore the operating system, in which the analysis took place, to an earlier non-infected state. With virtualization the analyst can avoid reinstalling the operating system between each sample analysis and become more efficient.

In some circumstances, detecting the presence of a virtual environment is important. Some examples include detecting virtual machine based rootkits (VM-BRs), honeypots and preventing trial software that is time-limited to be reused. Detection is possible when a discrepancy in execution in, or communication from, a virtual machine can be detected. Because of the hypervisor's involvement, discrepancies are a natural consequence of virtualization and it can often be difficult, or even impossible, to avoid them. Several VMM detection techniques have been proposed, one notable being the red pill [16] which, even if it is not practically useful anymore, is a good example of how discrepancies facilitate VMM detection.

In this paper we exploit a peculiar behaviour of the NAT implementation in the popular client virtualization tools VMware Workstation/Player and VirtualBox. We explain how the described behaviour can be used for malicious

L. Chen, M. Yung, and L. Zhu (Eds.): INTRUST 2011, LNCS 7222, pp. 129–137, 2012.

purposes. Our proposed technique is remote and optionally passive. As opposed to active techniques, our technique does not require the external verifier to run benchmarking code on the target host or probe the target for open ports. In our proposed technique, neither of this is necessary as it is solely based on network traffic initiated by and sent from the target itself. In our proof-of-concept implementation we only require that the target connects to a web server that we control. This will (under some reasonable circumstances) allow us to determine if the client is run as a guest in VMware Workstation/Player or VirtualBox. In the sequel, for simplicity, we only refer to VMware/VirtualBox, when we mean all three products.

If the target is being used as a server, with ports open for probing, the technique can be easily modified to perform active detection. It would then be possible to check any computer if a service is running in a virtual machine using VMware/VirtualBox. However, server virtualization typically do not use the mentioned virtual machine monitors, as they are primarily client virtualization products.

The paper is outlined as follows: In Section 2 we motivate why VMM detection is an interesting research area. In Section 3 we present related work. Section 4 provides the prerequisites needed and gives a detailed description of the different parts used in our new detection technique. Section 5 gives an overview of the proof-of-concept implementation and the paper is concluded in Section 6.

2   Motivation

As mentioned above, there are several reasons, both malicious and non-malicious, for why detecting the presence of a virtualized environment is interesting. One malicious motivation for VMM detection is similar to OS and service detection; namely to find vulnerable systems. If an attacker is aware of a vulnerability in the target virtualization product and has an accompanying exploit, detection will allow him to exploit vulnerable systems only. As opposed to trying to exploit non-vulnerable systems which may cause the vulnerability to be detected and patched by the vendor sooner than necessary, effectively decreasing the value of the exploit. There have been several vulnerabilities in VMware's virtualization products over the last couple of years, including vulnerabilities allowing an attacker to execute code on the host from a guest [4,11,13,18]. In this case, the malware will execute malicious code if a virtual machine is detected.

It is well-known that many anti-virus vendors use virtualization in their analysis of potential malware [12]. Virtualization allows the analyst to revert the system to a previously non-infected state, and thus avoiding the hassle of reinstalling the entire system to be sure of removing any possible infection. VMM detection techniques can be used by malware to delay, and perhaps even avoid detection all together. If the malware is obfuscated or encrypted before execution, and it detects that it is in a virtual machine at the moment of execution, it could do several things:

- By refusing to decrypt itself, the analyst is forced to spend more time analyzing the sample.
- The malware can decrypt itself into a piece of harmless code. This could allow the malware to go undetected all together because the analyst may not realize that there is any malicious code in the sample.

If the malware does not detect any virtualization, it can execute the malicious code, causing the target machine to become infected. There is known malware that utilizes VMM detection, e.g., the conficker worm [1]. In this case, the malware will *not* execute malicious code if a virtual machine is detected.

Passive remote detection of a virtual machine can be considered more powerful than the active or local attacks. In the passive case, no code has to be executed on the local machine. One motivating scenario is a remote variant of the malware described above, where malicious code is not executed if a virtual machine is detected. Instead of locally detecting if it is running in a virtual machine, consider the case with a server hosting malicious code. The code exploits a vulnerability in e.g., the web browser. At the same time, an analyst checks the content of the web server by sending HTTP requests from a virtual machine. If malicious code is returned, the webpage is considered harmful and users are warned from visiting that URL. If the returned content is non-malicious, the webpage is considered benign. In order to avoid being detected by the analyst, the webpage can return benign code if the requests are sent from a virtual machine, and return malicious code otherwise.

VMM detection can however be used against attackers as well. There has been research over the years on hypervisor based malware. The main idea here is that hypervisor technology is used to put the user in a guest OS, while the attacker has control of the host OS and can monitor the user in a very stealthy way. Examples of proof-of-concept hypervisor rootkits are the blue pill [15] and SubVirt [17].

The use of VMM detection can also be used for and against attackers when considering honeypot technologies. On one hand it can help gather statistics about the attackers and their use of virtualization technology, and on the other hand it can aid attackers to stay away from honeypots, as it is not unusual that honeypots are based on virtualization technology.

3   Related Work

Several methods to detect virtual machines have been proposed. Redpill [16] is a detection technique for VMware Workstation and Microsoft's Virtual PC, that reads the location of the Interrupt Descriptor Table (IDT). If the location is one of those known to be used by the virtualization product, virtualization is detected. Since this address is returned by the hypervisor itself, it is easy to protect against this technique. Red pill is also interesting due to the fact that unprivileged users could retrieve the IDT location. Blue pill [15] and SubVirt [17] are examples of VMBRs. These VMMs show why detection techniques are important in order to detect malicious use of virtualization. Remote detection of VMMs were proposed in [8]. However, root access to at least one VM was required in order to execute the benchmarking code with highest privilege level and interrupts turned off. Our technique does not require any access to the remote machine at all. Only a TCP connection is required. Our technique is similar to OS detection, where differences in the implementation of the IP stack can be used to detect which operating system is used. One example of an implementation is NMAP [2] which sends TCP and UDP packets to remote hosts and analyses the TCP/IP header fields of the responses. Using a database with known characteristics of operating systems, an informed guess can be made as to which OS is used on the remote machine. Our technique is based on similar characteristics, but is completely passive and is thus very difficult to detect.

One characteristic that we use in the detection is the algorithm used to generate the IP identification (IP ID) value in the IP header. The IP ID has been used in [5] to gain information about the number of hosts behind a NAT. The IP ID field of packets leaving the NAT was used to count the number of hosts. A fictional story based on incrementing IP ID values is given in [9]. In this story the character abuses the fact that the IP ID is incremented by one for each outgoing packet. Over time he can see patterns in the traffic to different organizations and correlate the increment in the IP ID and how much the stock of that company has gone up or down. Based on these observations, it was possible to get a better idea of whether or not to invest in the future. Even though this is only a fictional story, it is an interesting idea, similar to the idea in [10], where tracking spam could give leverage on the stock market. Finally, steganography software exists which hides data within the IP ID field [19].

4   VMware/VirtualBox NAT Device

The proposed technique is based on the fact that the NAT device used in VMware/VirtualBox heavily interferes with the network traffic. A NAT device is used to allow a user with a limited amount of global IP addresses (usually just one) to connect several internal machines to the Internet by having the NAT supply a number of local IP addresses for the internal network. Typically, a NAT only changes the source IP address and source TCP/UDP port in outgoing packets and destination IP address and destination TCP/UDP port in incoming packets. Additional changes are made by the VMware/VirtualBox virtual NAT device as these NAT engines receive the network traffic and resend it using their own TCP/IP stack, basically recreating all packet headers. This behaviour is documented in VirtualBox user manual [6, Ch. 6], but we have not found it in any VMware documentation.

We have identified three additional changes, which give rise to anomalies, allowing us to distinguish these NAT implementations from other NATs. Each anomaly is presented in detail in this section. Other NATs that have been considered, and which do not have any of these anomalies, include the NATs in the competing virtualization products Xen and Virtual PC, IP tables and the dd-wrt firmware used in many home routers. Note that we consider default installations as e.g., in IP tables it is possible to configure the TTL value in outgoing packets. While our list of tested NATs is not exhaustive, and it cannot be due to the large number of proprietary implementatons, the fact that only the VMware/VirtualBox NATs show this behaviour indicates that the probability for false positives are low.

4.1 Prerequisites

The proposed technique for detecting VMware/VirtualBox is based on anomalies in the NAT implementations. The detection is partly facilitated by differences between how Windows and Linux sets the TTL and IP ID fields in the IP header and thus, we need the following prerequisites:

- The target must enable the VMware/Virtualbox NAT device.
- The target's guest and host operating system must provide different initial TTL values and/or different IP ID generation methods. Examples of operating systems that differ in these aspects are Windows and Linux, which are both supported by VMware and VirtualBox.

Using bridged networking and/or the same operating system family for both guest and host would result in a false negative.

4.2 TTL

The purpose of the 8-bit time to live (TTL) value in the IP header is to avoid having a packet circulating infinitely on the Internet in e.g., a routing loop. It is decremented by one for each router hop. The initial value of the TTL in outgoing packets is implementation specific. In Windows, the initial value is 128, while a typical Linux system sets it to 64. While a NAT can modify the TTL before sending a packet out on the network, to the best of our knowledge it has no particular reason to do so. However, the value of the TTL is changed when using the VMware/VirtualBox virtual NAT device. Due to the fact that the host operating systems TCP/IP stack is used to rebuild outgoing packets, the TTL is always changed to the default value used by the host. A Windows guest running on a Linux host will create IP packets with a TTL of 128, but it is changed to 64 before sending the packet out on the network. A corresponding behaviour can be seen for a Linux guest on a Windows host, i.e., the TTL is changed from 64 to 128 when passing the NAT. This modification of the TTL value has an effect on tools that rely on the TTL. As an example, `traceroute` relies on incrementing the TTL for each new packet in order to determine the route taken for a packet to a given destination. Using traceroute in a guest running on VMware/VirtualBox does not give the expected behaviour as the TTL is rewritten in the NAT to the initial value set by the host OS.

4.3   IP ID

The main purpose of the IP ID value is to reassemble fragmented packets. The exact value of the IP ID value is irrelevant, instead it is important that all packets from one host that is currently on the network have different IP ID values. Otherwise, the reassembling of fragmented packets would be ambigous. The generation algorithm of IP ID values is implementation specific. RFC 4413 [14] specifies three distinct ways for generating the IP ID value:

- **Sequential Jump:** One *global counter* is used. All outgoing packets receives an IP ID value from this counter and the counter is incremented by one for each outgoing packet. This generation method is used by e.g., the Windows operating systems.
- **Sequential:** Each outgoing packet stream has its *own counter* which is incremented by one for each outgoing packet in the stream. This generation method is e.g., used by Linux operating systems.
- **Random:** Each outgoing packet is assigned a random value generated from a Pseudo Random Number Generator (PRNG). This method is e.g., used in the OpenBSD operating system.

Similar to the initial TTL value, the Windows and Linux operating systems differ in the way that the IP ID in the IP header is treated. Again, similar to the initial TTL value, the VMware/VirtualBox virtual NAT device changes the IP ID value, by using the algorithm which is default for the host operating system. While we have not found any other NAT implementation that changes the IP ID for outgoing packets using a different algorithm than that of the originating OS, there are apparent benefits of having the NAT control the IP ID. With several guests running on one host, or alternatively, several computers behind one NAT, one guest (or computer) has no information about the IP ID values generated by other guests (or computers). Thus, the probability of collisions in IP ID values leaving the NAT increases. If the NAT is allowed to control this value, collisions can be avoided. The fact that this control is implemented by the VMware/VirtualBox NAT is clear when examining packets originating from a Linux guest on a Windows host. The IP ID of these packets are generated by the same sequential jump algorithm as packets originating from the host itself.

It should be noted that packets from two different connections are needed in order to reliably distinguish the generation algorithms used by Windows and Linux operating systems. It is possible to use only one connection, but that assumes that the guest is also using other connections and that packets are examined and compared before and after packets are sent on other connections.

4.4   TCP Control Flags

While the TTL and IP ID fields are located in the IP header, the third anomaly we have found is in the TCP header. More specifically, in the TCP control flags. A connection can be terminated either by sending a FIN packet or a RST packet, i.e., a packet with either the FIN or the RST control flag set. When a guest terminates a connection by sending an RST packet, VMware/VirtualBox translates this, in some cases, to a FIN packet. This can be seen as creating a graceful shutdown of the connection instead of tearing it down with a connection reset. An interesting fact is that this behaviour is more prominent when the guest and host use different operating system families, i.e., Linux host and Windows guest or Windows host and Linux guest. It does however happen in some cases when the host and guest are using the same OS.

5 Implementation

A small detection deamon has been implemented as a proof of concept. It uses the anomalies in the TTL and IP ID fields in the IP header to detect if HTTP packets originates from a VMware/VirtualBox guest. The implementation uses a web server, in our case an Apache server [3] on a Linux system. On the server, a small custom packet sniffing daemon is run, collecting IP ID and TTL values from connecting clients. The daemon utilizes the libpcap packet capture library. The daemon also analyze and writes the IP address of a detected virtual machine to a file *detected.txt*.

The TTL gives information about the client operating system or, in the case of VMware/VirtualBox, the host operating system. In order to also use the information provided by the IP ID generation algorithm, two connections are needed. When a user connects to the default HTTP port (80) on the web server, it is immediately redirected to another port, 8080 in our case. Comparing the IP ID values in packets to different ports will allow us to make an informed guess about the generation algorithm. We compare the IP ID value of the last packet from the connection to port 80 and the IP ID value of the first packet from the second connection. If the difference between those two values are below a certain threshold value, we conclude that the sequential jump generation method, i.e., Windows is used. The server queries the file *detected.txt* and can determine the contents of the returned web page based on the result.

However, the information given by the TTL and IP ID is not enough. It can tell us that the client uses e.g., Linux, but it can not distinguish between a plain Linux computer, Xen or Virtual PC with Linux guest or VMware/VirtualBox with Linux host and Windows guest. However, looking at the *user-agent* string found in the HTTP request header, we can get information about the operating system used for the original IP packet. The user-agent string will often contain a substring of the base operating system, and this will not be changed by the NAT. As the VMware/VirtualBox NAT is the only NAT that translate TTL and IP ID, as far as we are concerned, we can distinguish this from other NAT implementations and also packets not passing through a NAT.

In Fig. 1 a flow diagram is given, showing the communication between server and client when the server attempts to gain information about the clients usage of virtualization.

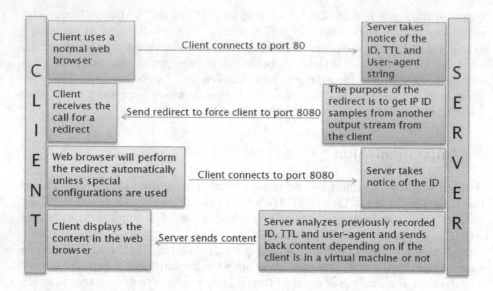

Fig. 1. Flow diagram of communication between client and server

6   Conclusions

We have proposed a new passive remote detection technique for VMware Work-station, VMware Player and VirtualBox. It is based on the fact that the NAT used in these VMMs rewrites information before it is sent out on the network. The fact that this behaviour has not been found in other common NAT implementations, together with the assumption that different TTL default values and IP ID generation algorithms are used in the guest and host machines, will allow us to determine that one of these VMMs is used and that the traffic originates from a guest in this VMM. If the TTL and IP ID generation algorithm is changed on the network and the TCP RST control flag is replaced by a FIN, then our detection will receive false positives. It is an open problem to determine under which other circumstances, if any, that false positives occur. Possible applications could be e.g., anonymity solutions such as Tor [7], web proxies and VPNs.

Users who consider this possibility for remote detection to be a threat should use bridged networking for their guests. If VMware inc. or Oracle consider this a security problem, they could consider a redesign of their NAT implementation so that this information leakage is prevented.

References

1. Conficker's virtual machine detection,
   http://nakedsecurity.sophos.com/2009/03/27/confickers-virtual-machine-detection/

2. Nmap, http://nmap.org/ (last accessed on June 22, 2011)
3. Official website of the apache http server, http://httpd.apache.org/
4. Path traversal vulnerability in vmware's shared folders implementation, http://www.immunityinc.com/documentation/cloudburst-vista.html
5. Bellovin, S.: A technique for counting natted hosts, pp. 267–272. ACM, New York (2002)
6. Oracle Corporation. Oracle vm virtualbox, user manual, http://www.virtualbox.org/manual/
7. Dingledine, R., Mathewson, N., Syverson, P.: The second-generation onion router. In: Proceedings of the 13th USENIX Security Symposium (2004)
8. Franklin, J., Luk, M., McCune, J.M., Seshadri, A., Perrig, A., van Doorn, L.: Remote detection of virtual machine monitors with fuzzy benchmarking. SIGOPS Oper. Syst. Rev. 42, 83–92 (2008)
9. Fyodor. Return on investment, http://insecure.org/stc/
10. Jordan, G.: Stealing profits from stock market spammers (2009), http://www.defcon.org/images/defcon-17/dc-17-presentations/defcon-17-grant_jordan-stock_market_spam.pdft
11. Kortchinsky, K.: Cloudburst vista - vmware vulnerability, http://www.immunityinc.com/documentation/cloudburst-vista.html
12. Lau, B., Svajcer, V.: Measuring virtual machine detection in malware using dsd tracer. Journal in Computer Virology 6, 181–195 (2008)
13. MacManus, G.: Vmware workstation shared folders directory traversal vulnerability, http://www.immunityinc.com/documentation/cloudburst-vista.html
14. West, M., McCann, S.: Tcp/ip field behavior (2006), http://www.ietf.org/rfc/rfc4413.txt
15. Rutkowska, J.: Introducing blue pill, http://theinvisiblethings.blogspot.com/2000/00/introducing blue pill.htmll
16. Rutkowska, J.: Red pill... or how to detect vmm using (almost) one cpu instruction, http://invisiblethings.org/papers/redpill.html
17. Wang, Y.-M., Verbowski, C., Wang, H.J., King, S.T., Chen, P.M., Lorch, J.R.: SubVirt: implementing malware with virtual machines. In: Proceedings of the IEEE Symposium on Security and Privacy (May 2006)
18. Wojtczvk, R.: Cve-2007-4496 - vmware vulnerability, http://www.immunityinc.com/documentation/cloudburst-vista.html
19. Xu, B., Wang, J., Peng, D.: Practical protocol steganography: Hiding data in ip header. In: Asia International Conference on Modelling & Simulation, pp. 584–588 (2007)

Indifferentiability of Domain Extension Modes for Hash Functions

Yiyuan Luo[1,*], Xuejia Lai[1,*], and Zheng Gong[2,**]

[1] Department of Computer Science and Engineering,
Shanghai Jiao Tong University, China
luoyiyuan@sjtu.edu.cn
[2] School of Computer Science,
South China Normal University, China

Abstract. In this paper, we show that four domain extension modes for hash functions: pfMD, chopMD, NMAC and HMAC have different indifferentiable security levels. Our synthetic analysis shows the chopMD, NMAC and HMAC modes can sustain more weaknesses of the compression function than the pfMD mode. For the pfMD mode, there exist 12 out of 20 collision resistant PGV hash functions which are indifferentiable from a random oracle. This is an improvement on the result of Chang et al. For the chopMD, NMAC and HMAC modes, all the 20 PGV compression functions are indifferentiable from a random oracle. The chopMD mode has better indifferentiable security bound but lower output size than the pfMD, NMAC and HMAC mode; and the HMAC mode can be implemented easier than NMAC. We also show that there exist flaws in the indifferentiability proofs by Coron et al., Chang et al. and Gong et al.

1 Introduction

Cryptographic hash function, which is defined as an admissible algorithm that uniformly maps arbitrary length inputs to fixed length outputs, is widely used as a pivotal primitive for ensuring the integrity of information. A hash function usually consists of iteration of a compression function with fixed input and output length. One first designs a fixed domain compression function and then extend the domain to an arbitrary domain by iterating the compression function several times. This type of hash function is called an iterated hash function.

The most popular method for iterating a hash function is known as Merkle-Damgård (MD) construction [13,25]. In recent years, the hash community starts to argue that the traditional MD construction is not a good design viewed as a random oracle [10]. Since the well-known length extension attack allows one to take a value $H(x)$ for x, and then computes the value $H(x, |x|, y)$, where $|x|$

* The first two authors are supported by NSFC 60773092,61073149 and RFDP 20090073110027.
** This author is supported by NSFC 61100201 and Foundation for Distinguished Young Talents in Higher Education of Guangdong (LYM11053), China.

is the length of x and y is an arbitrary suffix. However, this extension property is not allowed for any truly random oracle. Even if the underlying compression function f is assumed to be a fixed-length random oracle, any hash function H^f under MD construction will unlikely to be indifferentiable with a random oracle. For this reason, a rich literature analyzed the security of hash functions obtaining variable-input-length (VIL) from an ideal fixed-input-length (FIL) compression function[1,2,3,10,18,5,19].

In *TCC'04*, Maurer *et al.* introduced a strong security notion called as indifferentiability [23] which is an extension of the classical indistinguishability security notion. Later, in *Crypto'05*, Coron *et al.* first implemented the indifferentiability in analysis of hash functions and provide four domain extension modes[10], which are the pfMD, chopMD, NMAC and HMAC to meet the indifferentiable security notion. The compression function is viewed as a fixed-length random oracle or built from an ideal block cipher with Davies-Meyer scheme. Following that, several works have investigated the indifferentiability of a hash construction [2,3,4,8,14,15].

At *Asiacrypt'06*, Chang *et al.* present a unified way to prove the indifferentiability for pfMD [8]. They found that, in the pfMD mode, there are 16 out of 20 collision resistant PGV functions will be indifferentiable from a random oracle and other 4 are differentiable from a random oracle in the ideal cipher model. Then in [16], Gong *et al.* provided a synthetic indifferentiability analysis of some *block-cipher-based* hash functions and claimed that all 20 PGV compression functions are indifferentiable from a random oracle in the four modes, which contradicts Chang *et al.*'s results. In *FSE'08*, Chang and Nandi presented an improved indifferentiable security bound for the chopMD mode [9]. The improved bound is beyond the birthday complexity.

Since it seems that there are many choices of modes for iterating a hash function, an interesting question raised, i.e, do these four modes pfMD, chopMD, NMAC and HMAC have the same indifferentiable security levels? It is worth to know that which one is the strongest even there exist some weaknesses in the compression function and which one is the best choice for designing a hash function in practice.

Our Contributions. We show that four domain extension modes for hash functions: pfMD, chopMD, NMAC and HMAC have different indifferentiable security levels. We give an indifferentiability classification of these four modes based on PGV compression functions. The results are listed in Table 4.1. The chopMD, NMAC and HMAC modes can sustain more weaknesses of the compression function than the pfMD mode. In the pfMD mode, there are 12 out of 20 PGV compression functions are indifferentiable from a random oracle. In the chopMD, NMAC and HMAC mode, all the 20 PGV compression functions are indifferentiable from a random oracle.

We also give a simpler proof of the indifferentiability bound for chopMD than that of Chang *et al.* The bound is also beyond the birthday complexity. The chopMD has better indifferentiable security bound than pfMD and NMAC/HMAC;

the security bound is beyond the birthday complexity. Since the chopMD mode has lower output size and the HMAC mode is simpler than NMAC, we recommend HMAC instead of pfMD, chopMD, NMAC for practical use.

We find a new attack on 4 out of 16 PGV compression functions in the pfMD mode, which is an improvement on the result of Chang et al. We also show that there exist flaws in the indifferentiability proofs of Coron et al., Chang et al. and Gong et al.

Organization. The organization of this paper is as follows. In Section 2, we give some definitions and results which will be used. In Section 3, we present our new attacks and point out some flaws in previous works. Then, based on the result in Section 3, we show the main results and give a classification of the four modes in Section 4. Section 5 concludes this paper.

2   Preliminaries

Ideal Cipher Model and Random Oracle Model. Ideal cipher model, which is called black box model as well, is a formal model for the security analysis of block-cipher-based hash functions. An ideal cipher is an ideal primitive that models a random block-cipher $E : \{0,1\}^\kappa \times \{0,1\}^n \mapsto \{0,1\}^n$. Each key $k \in \{0,1\}^\kappa$ defines a random permutation $E_k = E(k, \cdot)$ on $\{0,1\}^n$. An adversary is given forward or inverse queries to oracles E, when he makes a forward query to E with $(+, k, p)$, it returns the point c such that $E_k(p) = c$, when he makes an inverse query to E with $(-, k, c)$, it returns the point p such that $E_k(p) = c$.

As the ideal cipher model, the random oracle model(ROM) is also a method of developing provably secure cryptosystems. Simply says, A random oracle (RO) is an ideal primitive which provides a random output for each new query. Identical input queries are given the same answer.

PGV Hash Functions. Preneel, Govaerts and Vandewalle (PGV) [26] proposed a synthetic approach to design single block length hash function based on block ciphers. They considered the method of turning a block cipher $E : \{0,1\}^n \times \{0,1\}^n \to \{0,1\}^n$ into a hash function $H : \{0,1\}^* \to \{0,1\}^n$ using a compression function $f : \{0,1\}^n \times \{0,1\}^n \to \{0,1\}^n$ derived from E. For a fixed n-bit constant v, PGV considered all 64 compression functions f of the form $f(h_{i-1}, m_i) = E_k(p) \oplus a$ where $k, p, a \in \{h_{i-1}, m_i, w_i, v\}$, where $w_i = h_{i-1} \oplus m_i$. The hash function $H(m_1, \ldots, m_l)$ can subsequently be described as follows:

$$h_i = f(h_{i-1}, m_i), i = 1, 2, \ldots, l$$

Here f is the underlying compression function, h_0 is equal to a fixed initial value IV, $|m_i| = n$ for each $i \in [1 \cdots l]$ and h_l is the hashcode. Of the 64 such schemes, PGV regard 12 schemes as secure in the sense of both the preimage resistance and the collision resistance. Black et al. [6] revisited all the 64 PGV compression functions in the ideal cipher model. They proved that the 12 compression functions that PGV had singled out can build a collision resistant hash

Table 1. 20 PGV compression functions which can be built collision resistant PGV hash functions in [6]. $w_i = h_{i-1} \oplus m_i$.

Group-1 schemes					
Case	PGV	Case	PGV	Case	PGV
1	$E_{h_{i-1}}(m_i) \oplus m_i$	5	$E_{m_i}(h_{i-1}) \oplus h_{i-1}$	9	$E_{w_i}(m_i) \oplus m_i$
2	$E_{h_{i-1}}(w_i) \oplus w_i$	6	$E_{m_i}(w_i) \oplus w_i$	10	$E_{w_i}(h_{i-1}) \oplus h_{i-1}$
3	$E_{h_{i-1}}(m_i) \oplus w_i$	7	$E_{m_i}(h_{i-1}) \oplus w_i$	11	$E_{w_i}(m_i) \oplus h_{i-1}$
4	$E_{h_{i-1}}(w_i) \oplus m_i$	8	$E_{m_i}(w_i) \oplus h_{i-1}$	12	$E_{w_i}(h_{i-1}) \oplus m_i$
Group-2 schemes					
Case	PGV	Case	PGV	Case	PGV
13	$E_{w_i}(m_i) \oplus v$	16	$E_{w_i}(h_{i-1}) \oplus v$	19	$E_{m_i}(w_i) \oplus v$
14	$E_{w_i}(m_i) \oplus w_i$	17	$E_{m_i}(h_{i-1}) \oplus m_i$	20	$E_{m_i}(w_i) \oplus m_i$
15	$E_{m_i}(h_{i-1}) \oplus v$	18	$E_{w_i}(h_{i-1}) \oplus w_i$		

function in the black-box analysis. They denoted these 12 compression functions as the Group-1 schemes. Additionally, there are 8 compression functions can also build a collision resistant but not preimage resistant hash function. They denoted these 8 compression functions as the Group-2 schemes. The 20 PGV compression functions are listed in Table 1.

Four Domaim Extension Modes for Hash Functions. In [10], Coron *et al.* proposed four domain extension modes such that the arbitrary length hash function H must behave as a random oracle when the fixed-length building block is viewed as a random oracle or an ideal block cipher, namely, the pfMD, the chopMD and the NMAC/HMAC. In this paper only PGV compression functions are considered. The four modes are described in Table 2.

In the pfMD mode, message $(m_1, \ldots, m_l)$ are guaranteed to be prefix-free. This is because prefix-free encoding enables to eliminate the length extension attack on hash functions. In fact, the chopMD and NMAC/HMAC mode are the same as pfMD in order to avoid the length extension attack. There are different prefix-free encoding functions. In this paper, we adopt Coron *et al.*'s prefix-free encoding function $g(M) : \{0,1\}^* \to \{0,1\}^n$: first write M as $(m_1, \ldots, m_l)$ where for all $0 < i \leq l$, $|m_i| = n - 1$, then returns $(0|m_1, \ldots, 0|m_{l-1}, 1|m_l)$.

Indifferentiability. In the following part, we recall the definition for indifferentiability [10,23]. This definition is a slightly modified version[9] of the original definition[23,11], where the condition that the maximum number of message blocks queried by a distinguisher is σ is not described.

Definition 1. *A Turing machine H with oracle access to an ideal primitive E is said to be $(t_D, t_S, q, \sigma, \epsilon)$-indifferentiable from an ideal primitive $\mathcal{F}$ if there exists a simulator S with oracle access to $\mathcal{F}$ and running in time at most t_S, such that for any distinguisher D it holds that:*

$$Adv(D) = |Pr[D^{H,E} = 1] - Pr[D^{\mathcal{F},S} = 1]| < \epsilon$$

The distinguisher runs in time at most t_D and makes at most q queries. The total message blocks queried by the distinguisher is at most σ.

Table 2. Definitions of the four domain extension modes[10]. g is the prefix-free encoding function. $f, f' : \{0,1\}^{2n} \to \{0,1\}^n$ are independent PGV compression functions, s is the number of chopped bits. IV is the initial value. IV_1, IV_2 are two different initial values.

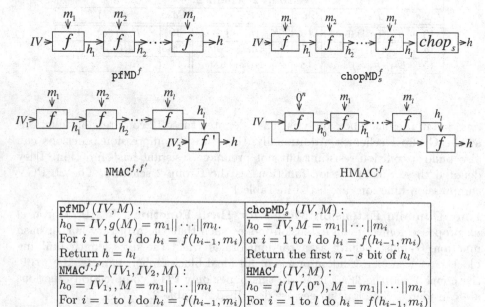

pfMD^f (IV, M) :	chopMD$_s^f$ (IV, M) :
$h_0 = IV, g(M) = m_1 \|\| \cdots \|\| m_l$.	$h_0 = IV, M = m_1 \|\| \cdots \|\| m_i$
For $i = 1$ to l do $h_i = f(h_{i-1}, m_i)$	or $i = 1$ to l do $h_i = f(h_{i-1}, m_i)$
Return $h = h_l$	Return the first $n - s$ bit of h_l
NMAC$^{f,f'}$ (IV_1, IV_2, M) :	HMAC^f (IV, M) :
$h_0 = IV_1,, M = m_1 \|\| \cdots \|\| m_l$	$h_0 = f(IV, 0^n), M = m_1 \|\| \cdots \|\| m_l$
For $i = 1$ to l do $h_i = f(h_{i-1}, m_i)$	For $i = 1$ to l do $h_i = f(h_{i-1}, m_i)$
Return $h = f'(IV_2, h_l)$	Return $h = f(IV, h_l)$

In this paper, E is an ideal cipher, H will represent the construction of an iterative hash function based on E. $\mathcal{F}$ is a random oracle with the same domain and range as H. The task of the simulator S is to simulate E. The distinguisher is interacting with the cryptosystem $(\mathcal{O}_1, \mathcal{O}_2)$, where either $(\mathcal{O}_1, \mathcal{O}_2) = (H, E)$ or $(\mathcal{O}_1, \mathcal{O}_2) = (\mathcal{F}, S)$. The distinguisher's goal is to distinguish which scenario it is after queries to $(\mathcal{O}_1, \mathcal{O}_2)$.

In [11], Coron *et al.* stated the indifferentiability of the four modes when the compression function is built on Davies-Meyer scheme, the theorem is as follows.

Theorem 1. *The four domain extension modes pfMD^f, chopMD$_s^f$, NMAC$^{f,f'}$ and HMAC^f are $(t_D, t_S, q, \sigma, \epsilon)$-indifferentiable from a random oracle in the ideal cipher model when the compression function is built on Davies-Meyer scheme. For any t_D, with $t_S = \mathcal{O}(\sigma^2)$, with $\epsilon = 2^{-n} \cdot \mathcal{O}(\sigma^2)$ for pfMD, $\epsilon = 2^{-s} \cdot \mathcal{O}(\sigma^2)$ for chopMD, $\epsilon = 2^{-n} \cdot \mathcal{O}(\sigma^2)$ for NMAC and HMAC.*

It was observed that Coron *et al.*'s bound of chopMD is not tight. In [9], Chang and Nandi presented an improved indifferentiable security bound for chopMD and stated the following theorem:

Theorem 2. *The chopMD$_s^f$ construction is $(t_D, t_S, q, \sigma, \epsilon)$-indifferentiable from a random oracle, in the random oracle model for the compression function, for any t_D, with $t_S = O(\sigma^2)$ and $\epsilon = O(\frac{(3(n-s)+1)q}{2^s} + \frac{q}{2^{n-s-1}} + \frac{\sigma^2}{2^{n+1}})$, where q is the total number of queries , σ is the total number of queried message blocks and s is the number of chopped bits.*

3 Improved Indifferentiability Analysis of pfMD Based on PGV Schemes

In this section, we analyze the indifferentiability of pfMD based on PGV compression functions. Our result is an improvement on that of Chang *et al.* and Gong *et al.*. In the pfMD mode, there are only 12 PGV compression functions are indifferentiable from a random oracle. We present a new distinguishing attack on 4 PGV compression functions in the pfMD mode. We also describe flaws in Coron *et al.*'s, Chang *et al.*'s and Gong *et al.*'s work.

3.1 Distinguishing Attack on 4 PGV Compression Functions in the pfMD Mode

At *Asiacrypt'06*, Chang *et al.* presented an indifferentiable security analysis of 20 PGV compression functions in the pfMD mode. They proved there are 16 out of 20 are indifferentiable from a random oracle. The other 4 PGV compression functions (PGV 1, 2, 3, 4) are differentiable from a random oracle in the pfMD mode.

Here we find that in the remaining 16 PGV compression functions, there are 4 can be differentiable from a random oracle in the pfMD mode.[1] The 4 compression functions are PGV 15, 17, 19, 20. First we give a distinguish attack on PGV-15: $f(h_{i-1}, m_i) = E_{m_i}(h_{i-1}) \oplus v$ in the pfMD mode. We have the following distinguisher.

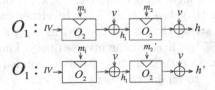

Fig 3.1 Distinguishing attack on PGV-15 in the pfMD mode

---

[1] We found the attack in February, 2009, wrote a paper on March, 4th and submitted it to Asiacrypt'09 on May 24th and eprint on June 5th[22]. Recently, Kuwakado *et al.* present a similar attack on these 4 PGV compression functions [21]. Note that their paper was submitted on May 27th, so these works are independent.

Distinguisher D can access to oracles $(\mathcal{O}_1, \mathcal{O}_2)$ where $(\mathcal{O}_1, \mathcal{O}_2)$ is (H, E) or $(\mathcal{F}, S)$.

1. D selects two messages M, M' such that $g(M) = (m_1 \parallel m_2)$ and $g(M') = (m_1 \parallel m_2')$ where $m_2 \neq m_2'$ and $|m_1| = |m_2| = |m_2'| = n$, then makes the query M to $\mathcal{O}_1$ and receives h and the query M' to $\mathcal{O}_1$ and receives h'.
2. D makes an inverse query $(-, m_2, h \oplus v)$ to $\mathcal{O}_2$ and receives h_1, then makes an inverse query $(-, m_2', h' \oplus v)$ to $\mathcal{O}_2$ and receives h_1'.
3. If $h_1 = h_1'$, D outputs 1, otherwise outputs 0.

If $h_1 = h_1'$, then $(\mathcal{O}_1, \mathcal{O}_2)$ is (H, E), otherwise $(\mathcal{O}_1, \mathcal{O}_2)$ is $(\mathcal{F}, S)$. Since the simulator doesn't know whether two inverse queries $(-, m_2, h \oplus v)$ and $(-, m_2', h' \oplus v)$ will lead to a same intermediate value. The simulator S can output the right response with a negligible probability 2^{-n},

$$Adv(D) = |Pr[D^{H,E} = 1] - Pr[D^{\mathcal{F},S} = 1]| = 1 - 2^{-n} \approx 1$$

So PGV 15 is differentiable from a random oracle in the pfMD mode. Similarly, we can give distinguishing attacks on PGV 17, 19, 20.

These 4 compression functions have the same weakness, that is, h_{i-1} can be deduced from (h_i, m_i). Take PGV 15 as example, we can write $h_{i-1} = E_{m_i}^{-1}(h_i \oplus v)$. If a PGV compression function has such a weakness, then it must be differentiable from a random oracle in the pfMD mode.

3.2   Flaws in Previous Indifferentiability Proofs

In [11], Coron et al. presented the detailed proof of the indifferentiability of the Davies-Meyer compression function in the pfMD, chopMD and NMAC/HMAC modes. Chang et al. also proposed a proof of the Davies-Meyer compression function in the pfMD mode. Here we point out some flaws in Coron et al.'s proofs of pfMD and NMAC, and Chang et al.'s proof of pfMD when the compression function is built on Davies-Meyer scheme.

In [11], page 22, Coron et al. gave a proof of the indifferentiability of Davies-Meyer compression function in the pfMD mode. In their proof, the simulator S accepts either forward ideal cipher queries, $(+, k, p)$, or inverse ideal cipher queries, $(-, k, c)$, such that $k, p, c \in \{0, 1\}^n$. In either case, the simulator S responds with a n-bit string that is interpreted as $E_k(p)$ in case of a forward query $(+, k, p)$ and as $E_k^{-1}(c)$ in case of an inverse query. The simulator maintains a table $\mathcal{T}$ of triples (k, p, c), such that it either responded with c to a forward query $(+, k, p)$ or with p to an inverse query $(-, k, c)$.

It is easy to verify that on getting a forward query $(+, k, p)$, Coron et al.'s simulator works fine. The problem is how to respond an inverse query. In their proof, On receiving an inverse query $(-, k, c)$, the simulator S searches its table $\mathcal{T}$ for a triple (k, p, c) for any p. If it finds such a triple, then it outputs p as its response. If it does not find such a triple, it choose a random n-bit string p and responds with p. It then stores the triple (k, p, c) into its table $\mathcal{T}$.

In case of Coron et $al.$'s simulator, we can easily build a distinguisher D. D first makes a query M to $\mathcal{O}_1$ where $g(M) = m$ and $|m| = n$, and gets respond h. Then D makes an inverse query $(-, m, h \oplus IV)$ to $\mathcal{O}_2$ and gets respond IV^*. If $IV = IV^*$, then D knows $(\mathcal{O}_1, \mathcal{O}_2)$ is (H, E), otherwise $(\mathcal{O}_1, \mathcal{O}_2)$ is $(\mathcal{F}, S)$. In such a case, the simulator S fails. This is because S responds a new inverse query randomly. Here a new query means it is not a repetition query.

Fortunately, Coron et $al.$'s simulator can be corrected easily. On receiving an new inverse query $(-, k, c)$, S cannot respond randomly. S first searches table $\mathcal{T}$ for a sequence of triples $(k_1, p_1, c_1) \dots (k_i, p_i, c_i)$ such that:

- The bit string $k_1 \| \dots \| k_i \| k$ is an valid encoding of message M under the prefix-free encoding g.
- $p_j = c_{j-1} \oplus p_{j-1}$ for $j = 2 \dots i$ and $p_1 = IV$.
- S queries M to $\mathcal{O}_1$ and receives h.
- If $p_i \oplus c_i = h \oplus c$, then S returns $p = p_i \oplus c_i$, else returns a random n-bit string p. It then stores the triple (k, p, c) into its table $\mathcal{T}$.

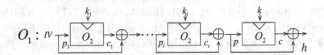

Fig. 4.1 Correction of Coron et $al.$'s simulator in the pfMD mode

Note that for an empty sequence of triples, i.e. when just considering the block k from the current query, we additionally require that $p_1 = IV$ in this case.

Chang et $al.$ may observe Coron et $al.$'s flaw since their simulator was different from Coron et $al.$'s. But they neglected the case of an empty sequence. Their simulator had avoid attacks which involve queries which the length are at least two blocks. But they didn't consider the scenario that an attack which applied in only one block length and the distinguisher's goal is to receive the initial value IV.

Moreover, one can verify there is a problem in the inequation in section 3 of Chang et al.'s paper[8], which denotes the maximum advantage of the distinguisher. The inequation (1) can not be deduced from previous equation. So the results in that paper should be revised.

As pfMD, Coron et $al.$'s indifferentiability proof of Davies-Meyer compression function in the NMAC mode has the same flaw. One can correct their proof easily.

In [16], Gong et $al.$ also provided an indifferentiability analysis of 20 PGV compression functions in the pfMD mode and claimed that all 20 are indifferentiable from a random oracle. There is an obvious error in their simulators that the simulators needed to record the distinguisher's queries to the random oracle $\mathcal{F}$. In fact, the simulator never have the record of the distinguisher's queries to $\mathcal{F}$, which can be derived from the definition of indifferentiability.

3.3 Indifferentiability of 12 PGV Compression Functions in the pfMD Mode

By combining our and Chang *et al.*'s results, it is known in the pfMD mode, PGV 1, 2, 3, 4 and PGV 15, 17, 19, 20 are differentiable from a random oracle in the ideal cipher mode. The Davies-Meyer scheme has been shown to be indifferentiable from random oracle in the pfMD mode[10,8]. For the other 11 cases, we can give a similar analysis. We prove that, all the 12 PGV schemes are indifferentiable from a random oracle in the pfMD mode.

Theorem 3. *The 12 PGV compression functions, which are PGV 5-14, 16, 18 are $(t_D, t_S, q, \sigma, \epsilon)$ indifferentiable from a random oracle in the pfMD mode. For any t_D, with $t_S = O(\sigma^2)$, with $\epsilon = 2^{-n} \cdot O(\sigma^2)$, where σ is the total number of maximum message blocks queried by the distinguisher D.*

Proof. We can define a general simulator for these 12 PGV compression functions. Since a repetition query doesn't help anything in the view of the distinguisher, we assume that there is no repetition query.

The simulator S accepts either forward ideal cipher queries, $(+, k, p)$, or inverse ideal cipher queries, $(-, k, c)$, such that $k, p, c \in \{0, 1\}^n$. In either case, the simulator S responds with a n-bit string that is interpreted as $E_k(p)$ in case of a forward query $(+, k, p)$ and as $E_k^{-1}(c)$ in case of an inverse query. The simulator maintains a table $\mathcal{T}$ of triples (k, p, c) and (h_{i-1}, m_i, h_i), where (h_{i-1}, m_i, h_i) is the input-output value of the corresponding PGV compression function deduced from (k, p, c). Take PGV 5 $(f(h_{i-1}, m_i) = E_{m_i}(h_{i-1}) \oplus h_{i-1})$ as example, $(h_{i-1}, m_i, h_i) = (p, k, p \oplus c)$.

1. On getting a new forward query $(+, k, p)$, S deduces h_{i-1} and m_i from (k, p), where h_{i-1} and m_i is the input value of the corresponding PGV compression function, and then searches its table $\mathcal{T}$ for a sequence of triples $\{(h_0 = IV, m_1, h_1), (h_1, m_2, h_2) \ldots (h_{j-1}, m_j, h_j)\} \cup \{(\emptyset, \emptyset, IV)\}$ where $(\emptyset, \emptyset, IV)$ is the empty sequence (i.e. h_{j-1}, m_j are empty strings and $h_j = IV$) :
   - The bit string $m_1 \| \ldots \| m_j \| m_i$ is an valid encoding of message M under the prefix-free encoding g.
   - $h_{i-1} = h_j$.
   If S finds such a sequence of triples, then it needs to give a response that is consistent with the random oracle output on M. Thus, S runs $\mathcal{F}(M)$ and receives h_i. If S does not find such a sequence of triples, it outputs a random response c, otherwise it deduces c from (h_{i-1}, m_i, h_i) and stores the triple (k, p, c) and (h_{i-1}, m_i, h_i) into its table $\mathcal{T}$.
2. On receiving a new inverse query $(-, k, c)$, the simulator S searches its table $\mathcal{T}$ for all the sequence of triples $\{(IV, m_1, h_1), (h_1, m_2, h_2),$
   $\ldots, (h_{i-2}, m_{i-1}, h_{i-1})\} \cup \{(\emptyset, \emptyset, IV)\}$ where $(\emptyset, \emptyset, IV)$ is the empty sequence (i.e, h_{j-1}, m_j are empty strings and $h_j = IV$) :
   - For every such sequence, S deduces m_i from (h_{i-1}, k_i). If the bit string $m_1 \| \ldots \| m_{i-1} \| m_i$ is an valid encoding of message M under the prefix-free encoding g, S runs $\mathcal{F}(M)$ and receives h_i'. Then S deduces (p, h_i) from (h_{i-1}, m_i, c_i) for the corresponding PGV compression function.

– If there exists any sequence such that $h_i = h'_i$, S returns p, else S returns a random p. In either case, S updates its table $\mathcal{T}$.

It follows the running time of the simulator is $t_S = l \cdot O(\sigma^2)$. The simulator will fail if there are two sequences $(IV, m_1, h_1), (h_1, m_2, h_2) \ldots (h_{i-2}, m_{i-1}, h)$ and $(IV, m'_1, h'_1), (h_1, m'_2, h'_2) \ldots (h_{j-2}, m'_{j-1}, h)$ which begin with IV and end in the same value h. This event can be divided into the following situations:

– For the ith response to a forward query, the simulator calculates (h_{i-1}, m_i, h_i).
 B1. It is the case $h_i = IV$.
 B2. There is a triple (h_{j-1}, m_j, h_j) such that $h_i = h_j$.
 B3. There is a triple (h_{j-1}, m_j, h_j) such that $h_i = h_{j-1}$.
– For the ith response to a inverse query, the simulator calculates (h_{i-1}, m_i, h_i).
 C1. It is the case $h_{i-1} = IV$ or $h_i = IV$.
 C2. There is a triple (h_{j-1}, m_j, h_j) such that $h_i = h_j$.
 C3. There is a triple (h_{j-1}, m_j, h_j) such that $h_i = h_{j-1}$.

We call the above events "bad", since if these events happens, the simulator may not work.

Now we will estimate the occurrence probability for each of the above bad events. Since the number of maximum message blocks queried is σ, the number of maximum queries to ideal cipher and random oracle is at most σ. The occurrence probability of event B1 is:

$$Pr[B1] = 1 - (1 - \frac{1}{2^n})^\sigma \leq \frac{\sigma}{2^n}.$$

We can bound the occurrence probability of condition B2 by the birthday bound. Let $Collision_i$ be the event that the collision occurs in the ith query but there are no collisions in the previous $i - 1$ th queries. The occurrence probability of event B2 is:

$$Pr[B2] = \sum_{i=1}^{\sigma} Pr[Collision_i] \leq \sum_{i=2}^{n} \frac{i}{2^n} \leq \frac{\sigma(\sigma + 1)}{2^{n+1}}$$

Similarly, the occurrence probability of event B3 is $Pr[B3] \leq \frac{\sigma(\sigma+1)}{2^{n+1}}$. The probability bound for the event C1, C2, C3 can be estimated in the same way.

Next we estimate the advantage of the distinguisher via a hybrid games. We need to prove that the distinguisher cannot tell apart the two scenarios (H, E) and $(\mathcal{F}, S)$.

Game 1. The distinguisher is interacting with $(\mathcal{F}, S^{\mathcal{F}})$. Let G_1 denote the event that D outputs 1 after interacting with $\mathcal{F}$ and S. Thus,

$$Pr[G_1] = Pr[D^{\mathcal{F},S} = 1].$$

Game 2. The distinguisher is interacting with $(H^S, S^{\mathcal{F}})$. In this game, we replace $\mathcal{F}$ with H, which computes pfMD using $S^{\mathcal{F}}$ as its compression function. Let G_2 denote the event that D outputs 1 after interacting with $(H^S, S^{\mathcal{F}})$. Thus,

$$Pr[G_2] = Pr[D^{(H^S, S^{\mathcal{F}})} = 1].$$

If no bad events occur, then Game 1 and Game 2 are perfectly indistinguishable. The view of the distinguisher of the distinguisher remains unchanged from Game 1 to Game 2 if the simulator S does not fail in either of the two games in the pfMD mode.

$$|Pr[G_1] - Pr[G_2]| \leq Pr[\text{S fails in Game 1}]$$
$$+ Pr[\text{S fails in Game 2}]$$
$$\leq \mathcal{O}(\frac{\sigma^2}{2^n})$$

Game 3. The distinguisher is interacting with (H^E, E). Game 3 and Game 2 are indistinguishable whenever no bad events above occurs or S fails to simulate the ideal cipher in Game 2. S fails to simulate an ideal cipher if it outputs an input/output collision for the same ideal cipher key. The probability of this event is easily seen to be at most the birthday bound. Let G_3 denote the event that D outputs 1 after interacting with (H, E). Thus, $Pr[G_3] = Pr[D^{(H,E)} = 1]$. Then we can deduce that

$$|Pr[G_3] - Pr[G_2]| \leq Pr[\text{S fails in Game 2}]$$
$$= \mathcal{O}(\frac{\sigma^2}{2^n})$$

Now we can complete our proof of pfMD by combining Game 1 to 3, and observing that Game 1 is same as the random oracle model while Game 3 is same as the ideal cipher model. Hence we can deduce that

$$\epsilon = |Pr[G_3] - Pr[G_1]|$$
$$\leq |Pr[G_3] - Pr[G_2]| + |Pr[G_2] - Pr[G_1]|$$
$$= \mathcal{O}(\frac{\sigma^2}{2^n})$$

Thus the theorem follows.   □

4   Indifferentiability of chopMD and NMAC/HMAC Based on PGV Schemes

We have analyzed the indifferentiability of pfMD based on PGV schemes. It is worth to know whether the other modes chopMD, NMAC and HMAC have the same indifferentiable security as pfMD. And which is strongest among the four domain extension modes even there exist some weaknesses in the compression function? In this part we analyze the indifferentiability of chopMD and NMAC/HMAC based on 20 PGV compression functions. Since HMAC is a special case of NMAC, the security bound of NMAC can be extended to HMAC. We give a classification of the four domain extension modes based on 64 PGV compression functions.

In the above analysis, there are only 12 of the 20 PGV compression functions are indifferentiable from a random oracle in the pfMD mode. In this following part we will show the chopMD and NMAC/HMAC are stronger such that they can sustain more weaknesses of the compression function. That is, all 20 PGV compression functions are indifferentiable from a random oracle in the chopMD and NMAC/HMAC mode.

Table 3. A classification of four domain extension modes based on 64 PGV schemes with the corresponding security bounds (the maximum advantage of a distinguisher). CR^H and PR^H denote the collision-resistance bound and preimage-resistance bound of the PGV compression function iterated with MD Strengthening respectively.

PGV Case	CR^H	PR^H	pfMD^f	chopMD$_s^f$	NMAC$^{f,f'}$
$1-4$	$\mathcal{O}(\frac{\sigma^2}{2^n})$	$\mathcal{O}(\frac{\sigma}{2^n})$	1	$\begin{cases} \mathcal{O}(\frac{\sigma^2}{2^n} + \frac{\sigma}{2^s} - \frac{\sigma}{2^{n-s}}),\ s < \frac{n}{2} \\ \mathcal{O}(\frac{\sigma}{2^n}),\ \qquad\qquad s \geq \frac{n}{2} \end{cases}$	$\mathcal{O}(\frac{\sigma^2}{2^n})$
$5-12$	$\mathcal{O}(\frac{\sigma^2}{2^n})$	$\mathcal{O}(\frac{\sigma}{2^n})$	$\mathcal{O}(\frac{\sigma^2}{2^n})$	$\begin{cases} \mathcal{O}(\frac{\sigma^2}{2^n} + \frac{\sigma}{2^s} - \frac{\sigma}{2^{n-s}}),\ s < \frac{n}{2} \\ \mathcal{O}(\frac{\sigma^2}{2^n}),\ \qquad\qquad s \geq \frac{n}{2} \end{cases}$	$\mathcal{O}(\frac{\sigma^2}{2^n})$
$13, 14, 16, 18$	$\mathcal{O}(\frac{\sigma^2}{2^n})$	$\mathcal{O}(\frac{\sigma^2}{2^n})$	$\mathcal{O}(\frac{\sigma^2}{2^n})$	$\begin{cases} \mathcal{O}(\frac{\sigma^2}{2^n} + \frac{\sigma}{2^s} - \frac{\sigma}{2^{n-s}}),\ s < \frac{n}{2} \\ \mathcal{O}(\frac{\sigma^2}{2^n}),\ \qquad\qquad s \geq \frac{n}{2} \end{cases}$	$\mathcal{O}(\frac{\sigma^2}{2^n})$
$15, 17, 19, 20$	$\mathcal{O}(\frac{\sigma^2}{2^n})$	$\mathcal{O}(\frac{\sigma^2}{2^n})$	1	$\begin{cases} \mathcal{O}(\frac{\sigma^2}{2^n} + \frac{\sigma}{2^s} - \frac{\sigma}{2^{n-s}}),\ s < \frac{n}{2} \\ \mathcal{O}(\frac{\sigma^2}{2^n}),\ \qquad\qquad s \geq \frac{n}{2} \end{cases}$	$\mathcal{O}(\frac{\sigma^2}{2^n})$
$21-64$	1	1	1	1	1

It is easy to see the distinguishing attack on PGV 1-4 and PGV 15, 17, 19, 20 in the pfMD cannot be applied in the chopMD mode directly. The Davies-Meyer scheme has been shown to be indifferentiable from random oracle in the chopMD mode. However, Coron *et al.*'s bound of chopMD is not tight. In [9], Chang and Nandi present an improved indifferentiable security bound for chopMD. Their improved indifferentiable security bound is proved when one looks the compression function as a random oracle and the proof is complicated. Here we give a more clear proof in the ideal cipher model. Our result shows that the indifferentiable security bound of chopMD is $\mathcal{O}((\frac{\sigma}{2^s})^2)$ when $n = 2s$, which is also beyond the birthday complexity.

Theorem 4. *The 20 PGV compression functions are $(t_D, t_S, q, \sigma, \epsilon)$ indifferentiable from a random oracle in the chopMD$_s^f$ mode, in the ideal cipher model for any t_D, with $t_S = \mathcal{O}(\sigma^2)$, $\epsilon = \mathcal{O}(\frac{\sigma^2}{2^n} + \frac{\sigma}{2^s} - \frac{\sigma}{2^{n-s}})$ when $s < n/2$ and $\epsilon = \mathcal{O}(\frac{\sigma^2}{2^n})$ when $s \geq n/2$, where σ is the total number of message blocks queried.*

Proof. We can define a general simulator for these 20 PGV compression functions in the chopMD mode. Since a repetition query doesn't help anything in the view of the distinguisher, we assume that there is no repetition query.

The simulator S accepts either forward ideal cipher queries, $(+, k, p)$, or inverse ideal cipher queries, $(-, k, c)$, such that $k, p, c \in \{0,1\}^n$. In either case, the simulator S responds with a n-bit string that is interpreted as $E_k(p)$ in case of a forward query $(+, k, p)$ and as $E_k^{-1}(c)$ in case of an inverse query. The simulator maintains a table $\mathcal{T}$ of triples (k, p, c) and (h_{i-1}, m_i, h_i), where (h_{i-1}, m_i, h_i) is the input-output value of the corresponding PGV compression function deduced from (k, p, c).

1. On getting a new forward query $(+, k, p)$, S deduces h_{i-1} and m_i from (k, p), where h_{i-1} and m_i is the input value of the corresponding PGV compression function, and then searches its table $\mathcal{T}$ for a sequence of triples $\{(\emptyset, \emptyset, IV)\} \cup \{(IV, m_1, h_1), (h_1, m_2, h_2) \ldots (h_{j-1}, m_j, h_j)\}$ such that $h_{i-1} = h_j$.

   If S finds such a sequence of triples, then it needs to give a response that is consistent with the random oracle output on $M = (m_1, \ldots, m_j, m_i)$. Thus, S runs $\mathcal{F}(M)$ and receives h_i. If S does not find such a sequence of triples, it chooses a random response h_i. Here the bit length of h_i is $n - s$. In either case, it samples a uniformly random s-bit string h' and responses $h_i \parallel h'$ deduces c from $(h_{i-1}, m_i, h_i \parallel h')$ and stores the triple (k, p, c) and $(h_{i-1}, m_i, h_i \parallel h')$ into its table $\mathcal{T}$.

2. On receiving a new inverse query $(-, k, c)$, the simulator S returns a random $p \in \{0, 1\}^n$. It then deduces (h_{i-1}, m_i, h_i) from (k, p, c) and updates its table $\mathcal{T}$.

It follows the running time of the simulator is $t_S = O(\sigma^2)$. The simulator will fail if there are two sequences $(IV, m_1, h_1), (h_1, m_2, h_2) \ldots (h_{i-2}, m_{i-1}, h)$ and $(IV, m_1', h_1'), (h_1, m_2', h_2') \ldots (h_{j-2}, m_{j-1}', h)$ which begin with IV and end in the same value h. This event can be divided into the following situations:

– For the ith response to a forward query, the simulator calculates (h_{i-1}, m_i, h_i).
  B1. It is the case $h_i = IV$.
  B2. There is a triple (h_{j-1}, m_j, h_j) such that $h_i = h_j$.
  B3. There is a triple (h_{j-1}, m_j, h_j) such that $h_i = h_{j-1}$.
– For the ith response to a inverse query, the simulator calculates (h_{i-1}, m_i, h_i).
  C1. It is the case $h_{i-1} = IV$ or $h_i = IV$.
  C2. There is a triple (h_{j-1}, m_j, h_j) such that $h_i = h_j$.
  C3. There is a triple (h_{j-1}, m_j, h_j) such that $h_i = h_{j-1}$.

We call the above events "bad", since if these events happens, the simulator may not work.

Now we will estimate the occurrence probability for each of the above bad events. Since the number of maximum message blocks queried is σ, the number of maximum queries to ideal cipher and random oracle is at most σ. The occurrence probability of event B1 is:

$$Pr[B1] = 1 - (1 - \frac{1}{2^n})^\sigma \le \frac{\sigma}{2^n}.$$

We can bound the occurrence probability of condition B2 by the birthday bound. Let $Collision_i$ be the event that the collision occurs in the ith query but there are no collisions in the previous $i - 1$ th queries. The occurrence probability of event B2 is:

$$Pr[B2] = \sum_{i=1}^{\sigma} Pr[Collision_i] \leq \sum_{i=2}^{n} \frac{i}{2^n} \leq \frac{\sigma(\sigma + 1)}{2^{n+1}}$$

In order to bound the occurrence probability of bad event B3, we note that the simulator first choose s random and independent bits in its response, then the other $n - s$ bits are either random chosen later by the simulator or it is forced to make the remaining $n - s$ bits consistent with the random oracle. Since the outputs of the random oracle for two different queries are random and independent, the simulator always returns uniformly random responses. The occurrence probability of event B3 is $Pr[B3] \leq \frac{\sigma(\sigma+1)}{2^{n+1}}$.

The probability bound for the event C1,C2,C3 can be estimated in the same way.

Next we estimate the advantage of the distinguisher via a hybrid games. We need to prove that the distinguisher cannot tell apart the two scenarios (H, E) and $(\mathcal{F}, S)$.

Game 1. The distinguisher is interacting with $(\mathcal{F}, S^{\mathcal{F}})$. Let G_1 denote the event that D outputs 1 after interacting with $\mathcal{F}$ and S. Thus,

$$Pr[G_1] = Pr[D^{\mathcal{F},S} = 1].$$

Game 2. The distinguisher is interacting with $(H^S, S^{\mathcal{F}})$. In this game, we replace $\mathcal{F}$ with H, which computes pfMD using $S^{\mathcal{F}}$ as its compression function. Let G_2 denote the event that D outputs 1 after interacting with $(H^S, S^{\mathcal{F}})$. Thus,

$$Pr[G_2] = Pr[D^{(H^S, S^{\mathcal{F}})} = 1].$$

For PGV 5-14, 16, 18, if no bad events occur, the view of the distinguisher D remains unchanged from Game 1 to Game 2 except for the following situation:

1. D is interacting $(\mathcal{O}_1, \mathcal{O}_2)$, where either $(\mathcal{O}_1, \mathcal{O}_2)$ is $(H^S, S^{\mathcal{F}})$ or $(\mathcal{O}_1, \mathcal{O}_2)$ is $(\mathcal{F}, S)$.
2. D selects a message $M = (m_1, m_2)$ and queries M to $\mathcal{O}_1$ and receives h. D queries m_1 to $\mathcal{O}_1$ and receives h_1. Here h and h_1 are s bits.
3. For a random $n - s$ bits h_1', D deduces (k, p) from $(h_1 \| h_1', m_2)$ according to the corresponding PGV compression function, makes a forward query $(+, k, p)$ to S and gets c, then deduce h' from (k, p, c).
4. If the first $n - s$ bit of h' is equal to h, then D stops; otherwise repeats step 3 at most σ times.
5. If D succeed in finding an h' such that the first $n - s$ bit equals to h, then D outputs 1; otherwise D outputs 0.

If D is interacting with $(H^S, S^{\mathcal{F}})$, the probability of D outputs 1 is

$$Pr[D^{H^S, S^{\mathcal{F}}} = 1] \approx \begin{cases} \frac{\sigma}{2^s}, & s < \frac{n}{2} \\ \frac{\sigma}{2^{n-s}}, & s \geq \frac{n}{2} \end{cases}$$

And if D is interacting with $(\mathcal{F}, S)$, the probability of D outputs 1 is $Pr[D^{\mathcal{F},S} = 1] \approx \frac{\sigma}{2^{n-s}}$. So the probability of D distinguish these two scenarios through the above method is:

$$Adv'(D) = |Pr[D^{H^S,S^{\mathcal{F}}} = 1] - Pr[D^{\mathcal{F},S} = 1]|$$

$$\approx \begin{cases} \frac{\sigma}{2^s} - \frac{\sigma}{2^{n-s}}, & s < \frac{n}{2} \\ 0, & s \geq \frac{n}{2} \end{cases}$$

For PGV 1-4, 15, 17, 19, 20, the distinguisher can exploit the weakness of the compression function to distinguish Game 1 from Game 2. However, one can easily verify the advantage of that type of distinguishing is no more than $Adv'(D)$.

So the advantage of the distinguisher from Game 1 to Game 2 is

$$|Pr[G_1] - Pr[G_2]| \leq Pr[\text{S fails in Game 1}]$$

$$+ Pr[\text{S fails in Game 2}] + Adv'$$

$$\leq \begin{cases} \mathcal{O}(\frac{\sigma^2}{2^n} + \frac{\sigma}{2^s} - \frac{\sigma}{2^{n-s}}), & s < \frac{n}{2} \\ \mathcal{O}(\frac{\sigma^2}{2^n}), & s \geq \frac{n}{2} \end{cases}$$

Game 3. The distinguisher is interacting with (H^E, E). Game 3 and Game 2 are indistinguishable whenever no bad events occur or S fails to simulate the ideal cipher in Game 2. S fails to simulate an ideal cipher if it outputs an input/output collision for the same ideal cipher key. The probability of this event is easily seen to be at most the birthday bound. Let G_3 denote the event that D outputs 1 after interacting with (H, E). Thus, $Pr[G_3] = Pr[D^{(H,E)} = 1]$. Then we can deduce that

$$|Pr[G_3] - Pr[G_2]| \leq Pr[\text{S fails in Game 2}]$$

$$= \mathcal{O}(\frac{\sigma^2}{2^n})$$

Now we can complete our proof of `chopMD` by combining Game 1 to 3, and observing that Game 1 is same as the random oracle model while Game 3 is same as the ideal cipher model. Hence we can deduce that

$$\epsilon = |Pr[G_3] - Pr[G_1]|$$

$$\leq |Pr[G_3] - Pr[G_2]| + |Pr[G_2] - Pr[G_1]|$$

$$= \begin{cases} \mathcal{O}(\frac{\sigma^2}{2^n} + \frac{\sigma}{2^s} - \frac{\sigma}{2^{n-s}}), & s < \frac{n}{2} \\ \mathcal{O}(\frac{\sigma^2}{2^n}), & s \geq \frac{n}{2} \end{cases}$$

$\square$

This theorem says that to have an indifferentiability attack the distinguisher needs at least 2^s query complexity when $n = 2s$. This result implies the `chopMD` hash function is almost optimally secure with respect to second preimage and multicollision attack[8]. Note that it doesn't improve the security bound for the collision attack to `chopMD`, but does improve the security bound for distinguishing the `chopMD` hash function from a random oracle in the ideal model.

The proof of the following theorem is similar as the proof in the pfMD mode, thus we omit the proof here.

Theorem 5. *The 20 PGV compression functions are (t_D, t_S, q, ϵ) indifferentiable from a random oracle in the $NMAC^{f,f'}$ and $HMAC^f$ mode. For any t_D, with $t_S = O(\sigma^2)$ and $\epsilon = 2^{-n} \cdot O(\sigma^2)$, where σ is the total number of maximum message blocks queried by the distinguisher D.*

Thus we give a classification of the four domain extension modes. We show that chopMD and NMAC/HMAC can sustain more weaknesses of the compression functions. The indifferentiability bound of chopMD is beyond the birthday complexity, but the output size of chopMD is lower than NMAC/HMAC. HMAC is simpler than NMAC: it needs one initial value and one compression function. In [2], Bellare and Ristenpart discuss the notion of a multi-property preserving construction. In particular, such a construction is an indifferentiable random oracle construction as well as a domain extender for pseudorandom functions and collision-resistant hash functions. We note that if the length of message is appended to the input before applying the HMAC construction, then the modified construction is an indifferentiable random oracle as well as collision-resistant hash functions. Thus, we suggest HMAC (with a length padding) instead of pfMD, chopMD, NMAC in practical use.

5   Conclusion

In this paper, we have examined the indifferentiability of the pfMD, chopMD, NMAC and HMAC modes based on PGV compression functions. Our results show that the four domain extension modes have different indifferentiable security levels. The later three modes are better than pfMD since they can sustain more weaknesses of a compression function. The chopMD mode has lower output range and the NMAC mode needs two initial values and two independent compression functions. The HMAC would be a better choice for practical use. Our results also show that one should take care of the proof of the indifferentiability of a construction, since many flaws have been found in previous proofs.

References

1. Andreeva, E., Neven, G., Preneel, B., Shrimpton, T.: Seven-Property-Preserving Iterated Hashing: ROX. In: Kurosawa, K. (ed.) ASIACRYPT 2007. LNCS, vol. 4833, pp. 130–146. Springer, Heidelberg (2007)
2. Bellare, M., Ristenpart, T.: Multi-Property-Preserving Hash Domain Extension and the EMD Transform. In: Lai, X., Chen, K. (eds.) ASIACRYPT 2006. LNCS, vol. 4284, pp. 299–314. Springer, Heidelberg (2006)
3. Bellare, M., Ristenpart, T.: Hash Functions in the Dedicated-Key Setting: Design Choices and MPP Transforms. In: Arge, L., Cachin, C., Jurdziński, T., Tarlecki, A. (eds.) ICALP 2007. LNCS, vol. 4596, pp. 399–410. Springer, Heidelberg (2007)

4. Bertoni, G., Daemen, J., Peeters, M., Van Assche, G.: On the Indifferentiability of the Sponge Construction. In: Smart, N.P. (ed.) EUROCRYPT 2008. LNCS, vol. 4965, pp. 181–197. Springer, Heidelberg (2008)

5. Bhattacharyya, R., Mandal, A., Nandi, M.: Indifferentiability Characterization of Hash Functions and Optimal Bounds of Popular Domain Extensions. In: Roy, B., Sendrier, N. (eds.) INDOCRYPT 2009. LNCS, vol. 5922, pp. 199–218. Springer, Heidelberg (2009)

6. Black, J., Rogaway, P., Shrimpton, T.: Black-Box Analysis of the Block-Cipher-Based Hash-Function Constructions from PGV. In: Yung, M. (ed.) CRYPTO 2002. LNCS, vol. 2442, pp. 320–335. Springer, Heidelberg (2002)

7. Brachtl, B.O., Coppersmith, D., Hyden, M.M., Matyas, S.M., Meyer, C.H., Oseas, J., Pilpel, S., Schilling, M.: Data Authentication Using Modification Detection Codes Based on a Public One Way Encryption Function. U.S. Patent Number 4,908,861, March 13 (1990)

8. Chang, D.H., Lee, S.J., Nandi, M., Yung, M.: Indifferentiable Security Analysis of Popular Hash Functions with Prefix-Free Padding. In: Lai, X., Chen, K. (eds.) ASIACRYPT 2006. LNCS, vol. 4284, pp. 283–298. Springer, Heidelberg (2006)

9. Chang, D., Nandi, M.: Improved Indifferentiability Security Analysis of chopMD Hash Function. In: Nyberg, K. (ed.) FSE 2008. LNCS, vol. 5086, pp. 429–443. Springer, Heidelberg (2008)

10. Coron, J.-S., Dodis, Y., Malinaud, C., Puniya, P.: Merkle-Damgård Revisited: How to Construct a Hash Function. In: Shoup, V. (ed.) CRYPTO 2005. LNCS, vol. 3621, pp. 430–448. Springer, Heidelberg (2005)

11. Coron, J.S., Dodis, Y., Malinaud, C., Puniya, P.: Merkle-Damgard Revisited: How to Construct a Hash Function (Full Version) (2007), http://people.csail.mit.edu/dodis/ps/merkle.ps; A preliminary version was accepted by CRYPTO 2005. LNCS, vol. 3621, pp. 430–448 (2005)

12. Coron, J.-S., Patarin, J., Seurin, Y.: The Random Oracle Model and the Ideal Cipher Model Are Equivalent. In: Wagner, D. (ed.) CRYPTO 2008. LNCS, vol. 5157, pp. 1–20. Springer, Heidelberg (2008)

13. Damgård, I.B.: A Design Principle for Hash Functions. In: Brassard, G. (ed.) CRYPTO 1989. LNCS, vol. 435, pp. 416–427. Springer, Heidelberg (1990)

14. Dodis, Y., Reyzin, L., Rivest, R.L., Shen, E.: Indifferentiability of Permutation-Based Compression Functions and Tree-Based Modes of Operation, with Applications to MD6. In: Dunkelman, O. (ed.) FSE 2009. LNCS, vol. 5665, pp. 104–121. Springer, Heidelberg (2009)

15. Dodis, Y., Ristenpart, T., Shrimpton, T.: Salvaging Merkle-Damgård for Practical Applications. In: Joux, A. (ed.) EUROCRYPT 2009. LNCS, vol. 5479, pp. 371–388. Springer, Heidelberg (2009)

16. Gong, Z., Lai, X., Chen, K.: A Synthetic Indifferentiability Analysis of Some Block-Cipher-Based Hash Functions. Designs, Codes and Cryptography 48(3) (September 2008)

17. Hirose, S.: Some Plausible Constructions of Double-Block-Length Hash Functions. In: Robshaw, M. (ed.) FSE 2006. LNCS, vol. 4047, pp. 210–225. Springer, Heidelberg (2006)

18. Hirose, S., Park, J.H., Yun, A.: A Simple Variant of the Merkle-Damgård Scheme with a Permutation. In: Kurosawa, K. (ed.) ASIACRYPT 2007. LNCS, vol. 4833, pp. 113–129. Springer, Heidelberg (2007)

19. Hirose, S., Park, J., Yun, A.: A Simple Variant of the Merkle-Damgard Scheme with a Permutation. Journal of Cryptology (online first), doi:10.1007/s00145-010-9095-5

20. Kuwakado, H., Morii, M.: Indifferentiability of single-block-length and rate-1 compression functions. IEICE Trans. Fundamentals e90-A, 2301–2308 (2007)
21. Kuwakado, H., Hirose, S.: Differentiability of four prefix-free PGV hash functions. IEICE Electronics Express 6(13), 955–958 (2009)
22. Luo, Y., Gong, Z., Duan, M., Zhu, B., Lai, X.: Revisiting the Indifferentiability of PGV Hash Functions. Cryptology ePrint Archive: Report 2009/265
23. Maurer, U., Renner, R., Holenstein, C.: Indifferentiability, Impossibility Results on Reductions, and Applications to the Random Oracle Methodology. In: Naor, M. (ed.) TCC 2004. LNCS, vol. 2951, pp. 21–39. Springer, Heidelberg (2004)
24. Maurer, U., Tessaro, S.: Domain Extension of Public Random Functions: Beyond the Birthday Barrier. In: Menezes, A. (ed.) CRYPTO 2007. LNCS, vol. 4622, pp. 187–204. Springer, Heidelberg (2007)
25. Merkle, R.C.: One Way Hash Functions and DES. In: Brassard, G. (ed.) CRYPTO 1989. LNCS, vol. 435, pp. 428–446. Springer, Heidelberg (1990)
26. Preneel, B., Govaerts, R., Vandewalle, J.: Hash Functions Based on Block Ciphers: A Synthetic Approach. In: Stinson, D.R. (ed.) CRYPTO 1993. LNCS, vol. 773, pp. 368–378. Springer, Heidelberg (1994)
27. Winternitz, R.: A secure one-way hash function built from DES. In: Proceedings of the IEEE Symposium on Information Security and Privacy, pp. 88–90 (1984)

Multicollisions and Graph-Based Hash Functions

Kimmo Halunen

Oulu University Secure Programming Group
Department of Computer Science and Engineering
P.O. Box 4500
90014 University of Oulu
ouspg@ee.oulu.fi

Abstract. In this paper, we present some generalisations of previous multicollision finding methods and apply these against a new type of tree-based hash functions. We also show that the very general class of hash functions first presented by Nandi and Stinson can be understood as graph-based hash functions and a graph theoretical approach can be utilised in studying their properties. Previously, an efficient multicollision attack has been found against the basic iterated hash function construction. This method has been applied to the generalised iterated hash functions and binary tree-based hash functions. We show that similar methods can be utilised also against t-ary tree-based hash functions, simplify some definitions and conjecture a similar result for multicollisions against graph-based hash functions.

Keywords: hash functions, multicollisions, graphs.

1 Introduction

Hash functions are a basic building block in many cryptographic protocols. A *hash function* computes a fixed length value, known as the *hash value*, for any message of arbitrary length. If the hash function satisfies some security properties, the hash function can be utilised in cryptographic protocols. This in turn then enables more efficient cryptographic protocols.

Three main properties for cryptographic hash functions are *preimage resistance, second preimage resistance* and *collision resistance*. Assume that h is a hash function. Preimage resistance means that given a hash value x it should be hard to find a message y for which $h(y) = x$. For second preimage resistance it is required that given a message y and the hash value $h(y) = x$ it should be hard to find $y' \neq y$ such that $h(y) = h(y')$. Collision resistance means that it should be hard to find any two distinct messages y and y' such that $h(y) = h(y')$.

The basic construction method for hash functions has been the iterated method proposed by Merkle [16] and Damgård [4]. The idea is to use a compression function that takes messages of a fixed length to values of shorter length and apply this function to the message of an arbitrary length by inputting the message in blocks to the compression function and defining the final output as the hash value of the message. This construction preserves the collision resistance of the

L. Chen, M. Yung, and L. Zhu (Eds.): INTRUST 2011, LNCS 7222, pp. 156–167, 2012.
© Springer-Verlag Berlin Heidelberg 2012

compression function, when the messages are padded to full block length and the length of the message is included as a separate message block (or if a prefix-free encoding is used for the messages) [4].

However, the iterated construction has some flaws. In [9] Joux shows a method for constructing *multicollisions* against iterated hash functions more easily than for an ideal hash function. A multicollision is a set of messages such that all the messages have the same hash value. The method of Joux is very simple and it has been used to disprove some "folklore" on hash functions [9]. It has also become a useful tool in generating some second preimage attacks against iterated hash functions [10,1]. There is also a slight improvement of Joux's method in [13].

There have been several methods proposed to tackle the attack of Joux e.g. [14,6]. One idea is to use the message blocks several times and in permuted order. This idea was first presented by Nandi & Stinson [17]. They also give a result that shows the weakness of these generalised iterated hash functions against multicollisions in a limited case. Hoch & Shamir [8] improve this result and their method has been sharpened by Kortelainen *et al.* [7,11]. The results of [17] and [8] also show that similar approach works for an even more generalised class of hash functions, *tree-based* hash functions. However, they restrict their analysis to the case of binary tree-based hash functions.

More general treatment of tree-based hash functions can be found in [3]. There a very general class of tree-based hash functions is proved indistinguishable from a random oracle (an ideal hash function). The ideas of tree-based hash functions have been used in some of the SHA-3 competition candidates, e.g., MD6 [18] and ESSENCE [15].

In this paper, we show that the earlier methods proposed in [17] and [8] can also be applied to t-ary trees instead of just binary trees. Furthermore, we show that the extremely general class of hash functions defined by Nandi & Stinson in [17] can be expressed as a more general form of graph-based hash functions and argue that the previous multicollision finding methods also generalise to these hash functions. We also discuss the feasibility of both the graph-based hash functions and the multicollision attacks against them.

This paper is organised in the following way. The next section contains basic definitions and results used in our paper. The third section presents previous work on the subject of multicollisions and generalised iterated hash functions. The fourth section presents our findings on the multicollision attacks against t-ary tree-based and graph-based hash functions. The final sections contain discussion and conclusions from our research.

2   Definitions and Basics

The definitions of our work adapt the definitions from [17,8] and [11]. First we define a hash function to be any function $h : \{0,1\}^* \to \{0,1\}^n$, with $n \in \mathbb{N}_+$. A compression function is defined as $f : \{0,1\}^n \times \{0,1\}^m \to \{0,1\}^n$ such that $m, n \in \mathbb{N}_+$. Here n is the length of the hash or compression function and m is the block length of the compression function.

A *graph* $G = (V, E)$ consists of a finite set of *vertices* V and the set $E \subseteq V \times V$ of *edges* between vertices. A *path* between two vertices u and v is a sequence of vertices with an edge from each of the vertices to the next vertex in the sequence starting from u and ending with v. A path from v to v is called a *cycle*. A graph is *connected* if for each pair of vertices u, v there exists a path between them. A graph G is a *tree* if it is connected and has no cycles.

In the following, we consider only directed graphs (digraphs for short). In a digraph the *indegree* of a vertex v is the number of edges that have v as an endpoint and the *outdegree* of v is the number of edges that have v as a starting point. A *source* of a digraph is any vertex that has indegree equal to zero and a *sink* is a vertex with outdegree equal to zero. In a tree, sources are called *leaves* and sinks are called *roots* of the tree.

A t-ary tree G is a tree for which all vertices have indegree t or 0, outdegree equal to one and there is a unique sink r called the root of G. All non-leaf, non-root vertices are known as intermediate vertices. A 2-ary tree is also called a *binary* tree. For a more thorough presentation on graphs and their properties see for example [5].

Let $G = (V, E)$ be a digraph. For any vertex v in G we define $u \to v$ iff $(u, v) \in E$. Furthermore, we denote by $u \Rightarrow v$ if there exists a directed path from u to v or if $u = v$. If $u \Rightarrow v$, we say that v is *reachable* from u. Let $v \in V$. We denote by $G[v] = (V[v], E[v])$ the subgraph of G such that $V[v] = \{u \in V : u \Rightarrow v\}$ and $E[v] = \{(u, v) \in E : u, v \in V[v]\}$. Finally, we denote by $L(G)$ the set of sources of G and $L(v) := L(G[v])$ for any $v \in V$.

Let f be a compression function of length n and block length m. We define $M = m_1 m_2 \cdots m_l$ to be a binary message with l blocks. Let $\Omega = \{\omega_1, \omega_2, \ldots, \omega_d\}$ be a set of $d \in \mathbb{N}$ initial values (i.e. binary strings of length n) and $B_l = \{m_1, m_2, \ldots, m_l\}$ be the set of message blocks of length m corresponding to the message M. As in [17] and [8] we define ρ to be the initial assignment function of G. We adopt the definition from [17]: $\rho : L(G) \to \Omega \cup B_l$ and require that the image of ρ contains B_l as a subset. We define $\mathcal{G}$ to be an indexed family of pairs (G_l, ρ_l) with the property that for all $l \in \mathbb{N}$ we have that ρ_l is an initial assignment function from $L(G_l)$ to $B_l \cup \Omega$ and that $G_l = (V_l, E_l)$ is a directed graph for all $l \in \mathbb{N}$.

Let $v \in V_l \setminus L(G_l)$. We define the intermediate values of the graph-based hash function h at vertex v as $h(v) = f(z_1 z_2 \cdots z_t)$ where z_i is the intermediate value assigned to the vertex u_i with the property $u_i \to v$ for all $1 \le i \le t$. For all $v \in L(G_l)$ the intermediate value is the value $\rho_l(v)$. The value $h(M)$ is defined as the value assigned to the unique sink of G_l. Furthermore, we define $\Gamma(X)$ as the multiset of all the images of the elements of X under ρ_l. Let $x \in B_l$. Now $\mathrm{freq}(x, G_l)$ is the multiplicity of x in $\Gamma(L(G_l))$. We set $\mathrm{freq}(G_l) = \max\{\mathrm{freq}(x, G_l) : x \in B_l\}$. Finally, we define $S(v) = |\{x \in B_l : \mathrm{freq}(x, G[v]) \ge 1\}|$.

Remark 1. Notice that for graph-based hash functions the set of initial values can be empty. Because the computation of the hash is defined by the graph structure, there is no need to specify any initial values. We will return to this property in the discussion section of this paper.

We also adopt the definition of independent message blocks from [17]. For a digraph to be useful in the computation of a hash function, we require that it has a unique sink (a root) even if it is not a tree.

Definition 1. *Let $l \in \mathbb{N}$ and $(G_l, \rho_l) \in \mathcal{G}$. A sequence $(x_1, x_2, \ldots, x_k), k \in \mathbb{N}_+$ of message blocks is independent if there exist vertices $v_1, v_2, \ldots, v_k$ of G_l such that*

1. *All occurrences of x_i are in $\rho_l(L[v_i])$ for all $1 \leq i \leq k$*
2. *$x_i \notin \rho_l(L[v_j])$ for all $i > j$*
3. *v_k is the root of G_l.*

In the above definition, the value k is the length of the independent sequence. We denote by $I(G)$ the maximum value for k such that there exists an independent sequence of length k in the digraph G. Notice that the order of the message blocks is relevant in the definition. Furthermore, we observe that if G is a tree and $(x_1, x_2, \ldots, x_k)$ is an independent sequence in G (with vertices v_i numbered accordingly), then $(x_2, x_3, \ldots, x_k)$ is an independent sequence in $G - G[v_1]$ i.e. the subtree of G not containing $G[v_1]$ (see [17, Lemma 6]).

If G is a tree and there exist vertices $v_1, v_2, \ldots, v_d$ such that $S(G[v_i]) = S(G), i \in \{1, 2, \ldots, d\}$ and $I(G[v_i] - (\bigcup_{j<i} G[v_j])) = S(G)$, the tree G is said to have d independent subtrees. This definition corresponds to the "successive permutations" case in [8].

Let $X \subseteq B_l$ and ρ an initial assignment function for the digraph G. We define $G|_X = (V', F')$ as the subgraph of G such that $V' = \{v \in V : u \in L(G), x \subseteq X, \rho(u) = x, u \Rightarrow v\}$ and $F' = \{(u, v) \in F : u, v \in V'\}$. We call $G|_X$ the X reachable subgraph of G. The definition of $G|_X$ is equivalent with Definition 13 of [8]. Notice that if G is a tree, then the X-reachable subgraph of G is also a tree.

3   Previous Work

Multicollisions for iterated hash functions were shown to be fairly easy to construct by Joux [9]. The method is very simple, yet quite ingenious. Assume that h is an iterated hash function, with f as the underlying compression function. Let h_0 be the initial value of the hash function. Now, by basic birthday attack or any other, faster collision finding method, one may find two message blocks x_1 and y_1 with $f(h_0, x_1) = f(h_0, y_1) := h_1$. Now applying a second birthday attack, we may find x_2 and y_2 such that $f(h_1, x_2) = f(h_1, y_2) := h_2$. We can continue in this way and in the end obtain a 2^k-collision with only k collision attacks. This multicollision is also a multicollision for h as all the messages have the same length and yield the same value after the final iteration. Thus the complexity for this multicollision attack is in $O(k2^{\frac{n}{2}})$ instead of being in $O(2^k! 2^{\frac{(2^k-1)n}{2^k}})$ as would be the case for an ideal hash function (see [19] for details).

Nandi & Stinson proposed a very general class of hash functions in [17], which we will describe as graph-based hash functions. This class has two subclasses, namely generalised iterated hash functions and binary tree-based hash functions (which contains the former as a special case). For both of these classes Nandi & Stinson were able to prove that an efficient method for finding multicollisions exists, when the number of appearances of each message block is restricted to $q = 2$ [17].

Hoch & Shamir generalise the above results to the case where $q \in \mathbb{N}_+$ [8]. Their method was further examined and sharpened by Kortelainen et al. [7,11]. These results show that when q is treated as a constant, an efficient method for multicollisions can be found. However, in [11] it is stated that if q is treated as a variable, the complexity with respect to q is hugely exponential. Thus the efficiency of these methods is very much depended on how one views the parameter q. There are some results that lower this complexity in q is presented in [12].

The ideas of tree-based hash functions have been generalised by Bertoni et al. [3], where the authors present a very general class of tree-based hash functions that allows even for different compression functions to be applied at different vertices of the graph. They show that these type of hash functions are secure up to the birthday bound when the compression functions and graphs satisfy certain conditions.

Tree-based constructions have been used in MD6 [18] and ESSENCE [15] both of which were candidates for the SHA-3 standard. Thus the research on the theoretical limits of tree- and graph-based hash functions could have some practical impact on the design of hash functions.

4   Multicollisions and Graph-Based Hash Functions

In this section, we show how the previous multicollision finding methods generalise to the graph-based hash functions. We start by showing a very straightforward generalisation of the multicollision attack against binary tree-based hash functions to arbitrary t-ary tree-based hash functions, $t \in \mathbb{N}_+$. In all of the following we assume that the number of times a message block can appear in the computation of the hash function is bounded by a constant $q \in \mathbb{N}_+$.

4.1 t-Ary Tree-Based Hash Functions

Assume that $t \in \mathbb{N}_+, t > 1$ and $(G, \rho) \in \mathcal{G}$ such that G is a t-ary tree. The following lemmas are direct generalisations of lemmas from [17] and [8].

Lemma 1 (Lemma 6 from [17]). *Let $(G, \rho) \in \mathcal{G}$, G a directed t-ary tree and r be the root of G with $S(r) \geq tN$. Then there exists a vertex $v \in V$ such that $N \leq S(v) \leq tN$.*

Proof. Let v be a vertex with $u_i \rightarrow v, 1 \leq i \leq t$. Now we observe that $S(v) \geq S(u_i)$ for all i. Furthermore, $S(v) \leq S(u_1) + S(u_2) + \cdots + S(u_t)$. Now, assume $v = r$. Thus, $tN \leq S(r) \leq S(u_1) + S(u_2) + \cdots + S(u_t)$ and by the pigeonhole principle there exists at least one u_j with $S(u_j) \geq N$. If $S(u_j) \leq tN$, then we are ready. If not, we apply the same reasoning to u_j as to r. Because in the end we will reach the leaves of G, the process must end at some point with a vertex v which has the desired property.   □

Lemma 2 (Lemma 6 from [8]). *Let $(G, \rho) \in \mathcal{G}$ such that G is a directed t-ary tree with $S(G) \geq tMN$ and $M, N \in \mathbb{N}_+$ and $freq(G) \leq q$. Then at least one of the following conditions holds:*

1. $I(G) \geq M$ *or;*
2. *there exists a vertex v and $X \subseteq \rho(L(G))$ such that $freq(G[v]|_X) \leq q - 1$ and $S(G[v]|_X) \geq N$.*

Proof. The proof is exactly as in [8] with the constant 2 replaced by t. We present the proof for the completeness of our presentation. The proof is an induction on $l = S(G)$. Notice that when $M = 1$, we always have $I(G) \geq 1$. Now assume that the claim holds for all values less than l.

Now $S(G) \geq tMN \geq tN$ and by Lemma 1 we have that there exists a vertex v in G with $N \leq S(v) \leq tN$. If we now have $freq(G[v]) \leq q - 1$, we may choose $X = \rho(L(G))$ and have $S(G[v]|_X) \geq N$ and $freq(G[v]|_X) \leq q - 1$ and the proof is complete.

If the above is not the case, then we have a message block x_1 such that $freq(G[v], x_1) = q$. We set $G' = G - G[v]$ and X to be the set of message blocks appearing in $\rho(L(G'))$. Now $S(G') \geq tMN - tN = t(M - 1)N$ and thus we may apply the induction hypothesis. Now either $I(G') \geq M - 1$ or there exists v' and X' such that $S(G'[v']|_{X'}) \geq N$ and $freq(G'[v']|_{X'}) \leq q - 1$. In the latter case we are done and in the former case we note that we have an independent sequence of message blocks $x_2, \ldots, x_M$ and because x_1 does not appear in $\rho(L(G'))$ we may add x_1 as to the independent sequence and obtain $I(G) \geq M$.   □

Finally we extend one more lemma to our case.

Lemma 3 (Lemma 7 from [8]). *Let $(G, \rho) \in \mathcal{G}$ such that G is a directed t-ary tree with $S(G) \geq (tk - 1)x$ and $freq(G) = 1$. Then there exist k distinct vertices $v_1, \ldots, v_k$ such that $L(G[v_i]) \nsubseteq L(G[v_j])$ when $i > j$ and $S(G[v_i] - \bigcup_{j<i} G[v_j]) \geq x$.*

Proof. Again the proof is a straightforward adaptation from the original. We start the induction on k by observing that if $k = 1$ then for any G with $S(G) \geq (t-1)x \geq x$ we may set v_1 as the root of G and the claim holds. Thus assume, that the claim holds for all positive integers strictly less than k. Let G be a directed t-ary tree with $S(G) \geq (tk - 1)x \geq tx$. By Lemma 1 there is a vertex v in G such that $x \leq S(G[v]) \leq tx$. Let $G' = G - G[v]$. Now $S(G') \geq t(k-1)x - tx = (t(k - 1) - 1)x$ and by applying the induction hypothesis we get $k - 1$ vertices $v_2, \ldots, v_k$ that satisfy the claim of the lemma. Now adding $v = v_1$ we have the required k vertices as v does not appear in G' and $S(G[v]) \geq x$.   □

After these results it is fairly straightforward to use the theorems from [8] and [11] to get a multicollision method for t-ary tree based hash functions. However, it is shown in [11] that the complexity results in [8] are incorrect. Thus the resulting complexity is greater also in our case. First we present the t-ary version of Theorem 3 in [8] with the correct bound for $S(G_l)$ from [11].

Theorem 1. *Let h be tree-based hash function based on $\mathcal{G}$, with each G_l being a directed, t-ary tree and let G_l be in the form of q independent subtrees. Then finding a 2^k-collision for h requires $S(G_l) \geq t^{\frac{q(q-1)}{2}} k^{2q-3} n^{(q-1)^2}$.*

As stated in [8, Lemma 9], we can always find this independent subtrees representation for a suitable set $X \subseteq \rho(L(G_l))$, when l is chosen to be large enough. This structure induces a sequential structure to the message blocks that label the leaves of the tree. Thus the methods from the generalised iterated hash functions can be directly applied to the tree-based hash functions as well.

The value of l is dependent on the value q, which is the upper bound for the number of occurrences of any message block. These values are even more drastically exponential in q than the first value in the previous theorem [11]. However, by treating q as a constant, this value disappears in the O-notation. Of course, in real applications this huge constant is a very significant factor.

4.2   Graph-Based Hash Functions

In [17] Nandi & Stinson propose a general class of hash functions $\mathcal{D}$ that contains the generalised iterated and tree-based hash functions as special cases. Recall that if $M = m_1 m_2 \cdots m_l$ is a binary message with l blocks we have $B_l = \{m_1, m_2, \ldots, m_l\}$ and $\Omega = \{\omega_1, \omega_2, \ldots, \omega_d\}$ is a set of $d \in \mathbb{N}$ initial values. Let $s \in \mathbb{N}_+$. We define the set of precursors of an intermediate hash value y_i as $P_i = \{y_1, y_2, \ldots, y_{i-1}\}$ and the set of all intermediate values $P = \{y_1, y_2, \ldots, y_s\}$. The hash functions in the class $\mathcal{D}$ have the following properties. The computation of such a hash function is characterised by a list of triples

$$L = \{(h_i, x_i, y_i) : 1 \leq s, s \in \mathbb{N}_+\}$$

which satisfy for all $i \in \{1, 2, \ldots, s\}$:

$$f(h_i, x_i) = y_i$$
$$h_i = h_{(i,1)} h_{(i,2)} \cdots h_{(i,c)}$$
$$h_{(i,j)} \in \Omega \cup P_i$$
$$x_i = x_{(i,1)} x_{(i,2)} \cdots x_{(i,b)}$$
$$x_{(i,j)} \in B_l,$$

where $f : \{0,1\}^N \to \{0,1\}^n$ is a compression function. If the length of the message blocks is m and the length of the initial values n, we have that $cn + bm = N$ for all i. In the above, all y_i are called intermediate hash values and the value y_s is the hash value of M [17].

We give an alternate and more concise definition of $\mathcal{D}$ in the following.

Definition 2. *Let n, N and $s \in \mathbb{N}_+$, $n < N$ and M be a binary message of l blocks. Let $f : \{0,1\}^N \to \{0,1\}^n$ be a compression function. A hash function $h_{s,f}$ from the family $\mathcal{D}$ is defined as follows. Let $u_i \in \{0,1\}^N$, $u_i = v_1 v_2 \cdots v_{d_i}$ with $v_j \in \Omega \cup B_l \cup P_i$ for all $1 \leq j \leq d_i$ and $i \in \{1, 2, \ldots, s\}$. Now $y_i = f(u_i)$ for all $1 \leq i \leq s$ and $h_{s,f}(M) = y_s$.*

It should be noticed from the above definition that the word u_i should be identified by its factors and not just as a binary string over $\{0,1\}^N$. It is also worth mentioning that although no restriction on the number of steps s is given in the definition, it should be efficient to compute the hash value from any given message and thus the number of steps should be polynomial in the length of the message.

The representatives of the class $\mathcal{D}$ can also be described as graphs. These graphs turn out to be graphs that have somewhat more general structure than the t-ary trees described previously. However, some of the results also apply to these graphs.

There are two ways to approach these hash functions. First we describe the members of the class $\mathcal{D}$ as the generalisations of the tree-based hash functions. This method relies on the idea that the graph which the computation is based on is given and the labeling function sets the message blocks and initial values on the sources of the graph. The other way to approach these hash functions is to look at the definition of $\mathcal{D}$ and to build the graphs from there.

Let $(G_l, \rho_l) \in \mathcal{G}$ with $l \in \mathbb{N}$. The *computation graph* G_l of $h_{s,f} \in \mathcal{D}$ is an acyclic digraph, with the following properties. The maximum outdegree of sources that have labels from B is q and the minimum is 1. There is a unique sink r and $h_{s,f}(M) = h(r)$. For all vertices of G_l which are not sources, the indegree is $p = c+b$, where $c, b \in \mathbb{N}$, $cn+bm = N$ and $p \geq 2$ and there are s of these vertices. Each of these vertices corresponds to a step in the computation of the hash value of the message M and these are ordered by the number $i \in \{1, 2, \ldots, s\}$ with r having the number s. There may not be an edge from an intermediate vertex to another intermediate vertex of a higher order.

Let γ be the maximum indegree of the vertices in G_l. Then the maximum number of edges in the graph G_l is γs. The maximum number of vertices in the graph G_l is $s + ql + wd$ where w is the maximum number that a given inital value can appear in the computation of the hash value.

Lemma 1 can be generalised to the computation graphs of graph-based hash functions.

Lemma 4. *Let $(G_l, \rho_l) \in \mathcal{G}$ with $l \in \mathbb{N}_+$ and r be the root vertex of G_l. Furthermore, let G_l be a computation graph of a hash function $h_{s,f} \in \mathcal{D}$. Let γ be the maximum indegree of the vertices in G_l and $S(r) \geq \gamma N$. Then there exists a vertex $v \in G_l$ such that $N \leq S(v) \leq \gamma N$.*

The proof of Lemma 4 is exactly the same as the proof of Lemma 1 with t replaced by γ. The arguments about the indegrees of the vertices are still valid although the graph is not exactly a tree and thus the claim holds.

Unfortunately, Lemmas 2 and 3 do not directly generalise to the computation graphs of hash functions from $\mathcal{D}$. However, because of the fact that the indegree of all intermediate vertices is bound by γ and the total number of edges is bound by γs we make the following conjecture.

Conjecture 1. Let $h \in \mathcal{D}$ and $(G_l, \rho_l) \in \mathcal{G}$. Let $q \in \mathbb{N}_+$ with $\text{freq}(G) \leq q$. By choosing l to be large enough, $l \in O(\text{poly}(n,k)2^{\frac{n}{2}})$, we may find a 2^k-collision for h.

The basis of the conjecture is in the fact that we may grow l to be arbitrarily large and thus we may group the leaf vertices suitably, even in the most pathological cases where $\gamma = N$. Because this case means that either message blocks are the length of one bit or the length of the hash function is one bit, it could be possible to impose some reasonable practical limits for γ and then prove the necessary limits. However, proving the exact limits for both the restricted and unrestricted case has been difficult without having the suitable lemmas as in the t-ary trees case.

Another way to study these hash functions and their properties is to build a graph from the different dependencies that the computation induces between different message blocks, initial values and intermediate values.

Definition 3. *Let $h_{s,f}$ be a hash function from the family $\mathcal{D}$ as in Definition 2. The dependency graph of $h_{s,f}$ is a graph $G = (V, E)$ with $V = \Omega \cup B_l \cup P$ and $(a, b) \in E$ iff $a, b \in V$, $b = f(u_i)$ and $a \in \{v_1, v_2, \ldots, v_{d_i}\}$.*

The dependency graph shows how the different message blocks, initial values and intermediate values interact when the hash value of a message of a given block length is computed. There are some restrictions on the graph that arise from the definition of the hash function. The constant q is an upper bound for the outdegree of all the vertices from B_l. Let β be the maximum indegree of all the vertices of the dependency graph G. The maximum amount of edges in G is then βs. The maximum amount of vertices in the dependency graph is $d + l + s$.

5   Discussion

The results and conjecture presented in this paper show that even generalising the mode of combining the message blocks to use a graph representation does not bring suitable protection against the multicollision attacks presented before. The graph-based hash functions suffer also from a similar drawback as the generalised iterated hash functions as for each message length there needs to be a graph representing the computation of the hash value for the messages of this length. Thus the representations of these graphs have to be effectively encoded and this might lead to more predictable behaviour of the hash function, which would further weaken the construction. In the design of MD6 [18] the requirement of effective encoding led to the decision of having an option where the graph structure is replaced by sequential structure. This could then be used in some resource constrained devices. Of course this property could be used by attackers if this sequential structure is seen as less secure.

As stated in Remark 1, graph-based hash functions do not necessarily require any initial values for computation. This distinguishes them from sequential hash functions, where an initial value must be given in order to compute the hash function. In graph-based hash functions there is also a possibility to use more than one initial value, but there is very little use in that as it increases the amount on computation without introducing uncertainty. Of course these initial values may be necessary to complete the graph, if the graph needs some predefined structure that cannot be provided with just the message blocks and intermediate values. In any case, the most effective way to utilise the graph-based hashes would be to not use any initial values.

In one respect the graph-based hash functions are more effective than sequential ones. With the sequential structure, one can not compute the hash value until the next message block is available. In graph-based hash functions some amount of parallelisation can be utilised and the hash values for each vertex v can be computed as soon as the values for all vertices $u \to v$ have been determined. This could make them more attractive from a practical point of view as this property might allow some form of streaming computation of the hash value, which is possible for traditional iterated hash functions. In the MD6 design the graphical structure together with parallelisation led to the fairly efficient computation of the hash function.

One possibility to further generalise the hash functions from the class $\mathcal{D}$ would be to allow even more general graphs as the form of computation. For example removing the requirement for a single root vertex, would be a remarkable generalisation. However, this would also mean that the hash value would no longer be uniquely determined by the graph and this would undermine the usefulness of the construction. Then one would need to somehow specify the value of the hash function for the graph outside the definition of the graph. Thus it is fairly safe to say that the class $\mathcal{D}$ of hash functions grasps the main essence of hash functions based on the repeated use of a single compression function.

However, the generalisations presented in [3] also show a possibility of constructing secure hash functions with several different compression functions used during the computation and the class $\mathcal{D}$ does not contain this possibility. In a more general setting, these several compression functions could be taken into account. It is our opinion that the graphical structure and the restrictions imposed by that still enable efficient multicollision attacks. This is due to the fact that the results of [17,8] and this paper do no rely on any specific weakness of the underlying compression function. Thus using many different compression functions does not necessarily provide much added protection against these methods. There are also some other methods such as the sponge-like constructions [2] that might lie outside the scope of $\mathcal{D}$.

6 Conclusion

In this paper, we have demonstrated that multicollisions can be formed for a more general class of tree-based hash functions, the t-ary tree-based hash functions. The methods follow from previous methods that have been proposed to the subclasses of these hash functions. Furthermore, we conjecture that the more general class of graph-based hash functions is susceptible to similar attack due to the limitations imposed by the hash function computation on the structure of the graph. Thus by studying the graph theoretic properties of the hash functions we might gain some insight on the overall security of hash functions.

It is noteworthy that the class of hash functions $\mathcal{D}$ defined by Nandi & Stinson is very general and the simplified description given in this paper shows that the main idea behind this very general class of hash functions is fairly simple. Thus there might be a possibility to devise more complicated hashing methods that are more secure against multicollisions. However, the efficiency and applicability of such constructions should also be studied carefully.

Although the methods show some promise, it is worthwhile to notice that realising the hash functions from $\mathcal{D}$ is a very difficult task. Furthermore, there are only a few concrete proposals where the message blocks would be used many times. This comes from the fact that using such methods is fairly costly and as shown by our research and previous results, it provides little added security. Also the hash functions MD6 and ESSENCE that have employed the graphical structure have not been selected as finalists in the SHA-3 competition

References

1. Andreeva, E., Bouillaguet, C., Fouque, P.-A., Hoch, J.J., Kelsey, J., Shamir, A., Zimmer, S.: Second Preimage Attacks on Dithered Hash Functions. In: Smart, N.P. (ed.) EUROCRYPT 2008. LNCS, vol. 4965, pp. 270–288. Springer, Heidelberg (2008)
2. Bertoni, G., Daemen, J., Peeters, M., Van Assche, G.: Sponge functions. Sponge Functions website (2007), http://sponge.noekeon.org/SpongeFunctions.pdf
3. Bertoni, G., Daemen, J., Peeters, M., Van Assche, G.: Sufficient conditions for sound tree and sequential hashing modes. Cryptology ePrint Archive, Report 2009/210 (2009), http://eprint.iacr.org/
4. Damgård, I.B.: A Design Principle for Hash Functions. In: Brassard, G. (ed.) CRYPTO 1989. LNCS, vol. 435, pp. 416–427. Springer, Heidelberg (1990)
5. Diestel, R.: Graph Theory. Graduate Texts in Mathematics. Springer (2006)
6. Gauravaram, P., Millan, W., Dawson, E., Viswanathan, K.: Constructing Secure Hash Functions by Enhancing Merkle-Damgård Construction. In: Batten, L.M., Safavi-Naini, R. (eds.) ACISP 2006. LNCS, vol. 4058, pp. 407–420. Springer, Heidelberg (2006)
7. Halunen, K., Kortelainen, J., Kortelainen, T.: Combinatorial multicollision attacks on generalized iterated hash functions. In: Boyd, C., Susilo, W. (eds.) Eighth Australasian Information Security Conference (AISC 2010). CRPIT, vol. 105, pp. 86–93. ACS, Brisbane (2010)
8. Hoch, J.J., Shamir, A.: Breaking the ICE - Finding Multicollisions in Iterated Concatenated and Expanded (ICE) Hash Functions. In: Robshaw, M.J.B. (ed.) FSE 2006. LNCS, vol. 4047, pp. 179–194. Springer, Heidelberg (2006)
9. Joux, A.: Multicollisions in Iterated Hash Functions. Application to Cascaded Constructions. In: Franklin, M. (ed.) CRYPTO 2004. LNCS, vol. 3152, pp. 306–316. Springer, Heidelberg (2004)
10. Kelsey, J., Kohno, T.: Herding Hash Functions and the Nostradamus Attack. In: Vaudenay, S. (ed.) EUROCRYPT 2006. LNCS, vol. 4004, pp. 183–200. Springer, Heidelberg (2006)

11. Kortelainen, J., Halunen, K., Kortelainen, T.: Multicollision attacks and generalized iterated hash functions. Journal of Mathematical Cryptology 4 (2010)
12. Kortelainen, J., Kortelainen, T., Vesanen, A.: Unavoidable Regularities in Long Words with Bounded Number of Symbol Occurrences. In: Fu, B., Du, D.-Z. (eds.) COCOON 2011. LNCS, vol. 6842, pp. 519–530. Springer, Heidelberg (2011)
13. Kortelainen, T., Kortelainen, J., Halunen, K.: Variants of Multicollision Attacks on Iterated Hash Functions. In: Lai, X., Yung, M., Lin, D. (eds.) Inscrypt 2010. LNCS, vol. 6584, pp. 139–154. Springer, Heidelberg (2011)
14. Lucks, S.: A Failure-Friendly Design Principle for Hash Functions. In: Roy, B. (ed.) ASIACRYPT 2005. LNCS, vol. 3788, pp. 474–494. Springer, Heidelberg (2005)
15. Martin, J.W.: ESSENCE: A candidate hashing algorithm for the NIST competition. Submission to NIST (2008), http://www.math.jmu.edu/~martin/essence/Supporting_Documentation/essence_NIST.pdf
16. Merkle, R.C.: One Way Hash Functions and DES. In: Brassard, G. (ed.) CRYPTO 1989. LNCS, vol. 435, pp. 428–446. Springer, Heidelberg (1990)
17. Nandi, M., Stinson, D.R.: Multicollision attacks on generalized hash functions. Cryptology ePrint Archive, Report 2004/330 (2004), http://eprint.iacr.org/
18. Rivest, R.L.: The MD6 hash function – a proposal to NIST for SHA-3. Submission to NIST (2008),
http://groups.csail.mit.edu/cis/md6/submitted-2008-10-27/Supporting_Documentation/md6_report.pdf
19. Suzuki, K., Tonien, D., Kurosawa, K., Toyota, K.: Birthday paradox for multicollisions. IEICE Transactions 91-A(1), 39–45 (2008)

A General, Flexible and Efficient Proof of Inclusion and Exclusion

Kun Peng

Institute for Infocomm Research, Singapore
dr.kun.peng@gmail.com

Abstract. Inclusion proof shows that a secret committed message is in a finite group of messages, while exclusion proof shows that a secret committed message is not in a finite group of messages. A general, flexible and efficient solution to inclusion proof and exclusion proof is proposed in this paper. It overcomes the drawbacks of the existing solutions to inclusion proof and exclusion proof. It achieves all the desired security properties in inclusion proof and exclusion proof. It is the most efficient general solution to inclusion proof and exclusion proof and only costs $O(\sqrt{n})$ for any inclusion proof and exclusion proof regarding any finite group of n messages.

1 Introduction

In cryptographic secure protocols, sometimes a party chooses a message from a finite set $S = \{s_1, s_2, \ldots, s_n\}$ and then commits to it. He keeps the message secret and publishes the commitment. He needs to prove that the message in the commitment is indeed in S, but cannot reveal the secret message. Such a proof is called inclusion proof in this paper. For example, in e-auction [18,20,21,25] and e-voting [19,22,23,24,26], very often a bidder or voter has to prove that his secret bid or vote is chosen from a list of candidates. As explained in [5], inclusion proof is also useful in applications like e-cash systems and anonymous credential systems. In some cryptographic applications, it is needed for a party to prove that a committed secret message m is not in a finite set $S = \{s_1, s_2, \ldots, s_n\}$ without revealing it. For example, as explained in [14], a financial institute may ask a loan applier to prove that he is not in a black list, while the applier does not want to reveal his identity before the application goes to next step. This proof is called nonmembership proof in [14] and called exclusion proof in this paper.

According to [10], any secret knowledge can be proved without revealing it if there is no critical requirement on efficiency. There are some general zero knowldge proof techniques [10,9,13,12], which handles various proofs including inclusion proof and exclusion proof by reducing them to a standard form and then giving an all-purpose proof. We are not very interested in those techniques as we focus on high efficiency. Obviously, proof techniques specially designed for inclusion proof and exclusion proof have an advantage in efficiency improvement

L. Chen, M. Yung, and L. Zhu (Eds.): INTRUST 2011, LNCS 7222, pp. 168–183, 2012.
© Springer-Verlag Berlin Heidelberg 2012

of the two proofs over the general all-purposed proof techniques as the former does not need to consider any other proof. So we focus on proof techniques to handle only inclusion proof and exclusion proof in this paper.

Apart from the straightforward solution to inclusion proof through ZK (zero knowledge) proof of partial knowledge [7] and the brute-force solution to exclusion proof by proving that the committed integer is unequal to every integer in the set, there are several more efficient inclusion and exclusion proof schemes [3,14,5]. However, they have their drawbacks as will be detailed in Section 2. Inclusion proof in [3] is strictly limited by a few conditions and so lacks generality and flexibility. Exclusion proof in [14] is a variant of [3], so has the same drawback. Inclusion proof in [5] lacks public verifiability, must be interactive and is inefficient when there are many verifiers.

In this paper, new inclusion proof and new exclusion proof are proposed. They employ the same strategy: reducing a proof regarding a large set to multiple proofs regarding smaller sets and then reducing each proof regarding a smaller set to a proof regarding a single integer. In this way, a complex task is divided into multiple simpler tasks and high efficiency is achieved. After that a calculation-optimising method is designed to further improve efficiency. The new proof technique overcomes the drawbacks in [3,14,5] and are very efficient. It is more efficient than the existing general solutions to inclusion proof and exclusion proof including the straightforward simple solutions and [5], while [3,14] are special solutions strictly limited to special applications. When the size of S is n, it only costs $O(\sqrt{n})$ exponentiations in computation and transfers $O(\sqrt{n})$ integers in communication, no matter what messages are in S and committed.

2   Security Requirements and the Existing Solutions

The following security properties are usually desired in inclusion proof and exclusion proof.

- Completeness: in an inclusion proof protocol, if the committed integer is in the set and the prover strictly follows the inclusion proof protocol, he can pass the verification in the protocol; in an exclusion proof protocol, if the committed integer is not in the set and the prover strictly follows the exclusion proof protocol, he can pass the verification in the protocol.
- Soundness: in an inclusion proof protocol, if the committed integer is not in the set, the probability that the prover passes the verification in the protocol is negligible; in an exclusion proof protocol, if the committed integer is in the set, the probability that the prover passes the verification in the protocol is negligible.
- Zero knowledge: in an inclusion proof protocol, no information about the committed message is revealed except that it is in the set; in an exclusion proof protocol, no information about the committed message is revealed except that it is not in the set. More precisely, in both inclusion proof and exclusion proof, the proof transcript can be simulated without any difference by a party without any knowledge of any secret.

- Public verifiability: validity of all the operations can be publicly verified by any verifier and independent observer, in both inclusion proof and exclusion proof.
- Generality and flexibility: format of the committed integer and the set is not limited in any way. More precisely, in any application of inclusion proof or exclusion proof, just choose a large enough message space for the commitment algorithm to cover any possible committed integer and the set, then inclusion proof and exclusion proof can always work.
- Non-interaction: when necessary, inclusion proof and exclusion proof can be non-interactive.

The simplest solution to inclusion proof is ZK proof of partial knowledge [7], which proves that the committed message may be every message in the set one by one and then link the multiple proofs with OR logic. This solution is called simple inclusion proof in this paper. Similarly, exclusion proof can be implemented by proving that the committed message is unequal to each message in the set one by one and then linking the multiple proofs with AND logic. Inequality of two secret integers can be proved using techniques like ZK proof of inequality of discrete logarithm in [4]. This solution is called simple exclusion proof in this paper. The advantage of these two simple solutions is generality and versatility. They can prove inclusion and exclusion regarding any committed integer and any set. They can achieve all the desired security properties including public verifiability and flexibility. Their drawback is low efficiency. In communication, they have to to transfer $O(n)$ integers. In computation, they cost both the prover and the verifier $O(n)$ exponentiations.

A more efficient inclusion proof is proposed by Camenisch et al. [5]. In [5], a verifier signs every message in S using his own private key and sends all the signatures to the prover, who then proves that he knows the signature on the message in the commitment. In this method, the computational cost of a prover becomes constant and thus much more efficient although efficiency improvement in communication and on the verifier's side is not evident. This inclusion proof has several drawbacks. Its main drawback is lack of public verifiability. The signatures sent to the prover are not public. Except for the prover and the verifier generating them, the other parties including other verifiers do not know whether any signature of other messages is sent to the prover. So it is a two-party private proof between a prover and a certain verifier and it has to be separately and repeatedly run between the prover and every verifier. Therefore, when there are many verifiers, the overhead for the prover is very high. Moreover, Fiat-Shamir heuristic cannot be employed to achieve non-interaction and every verifier must interactively run the inclusion proof protocol with the prover. In addition, this proof technique cannot handle exclusion proof.

The most efficient inclusion proof is proposed by Camenisch et al. [3]. In [3] to show that a secret message committed in c is in S, knowledge of integers m and ϵ is proved such that m is committed in c and $\epsilon^m = g^{\prod_{i=1}^n s_i}$ where g is a generator of a cyclic multiplication group with a composite multiplication modulus difficult to factorize. Obviously, if $m = s_j$, the prover can use $\epsilon = g^{\prod_{i=1}^{j-1} s_i \prod_{i=j+1}^n s_i}$ to give the proof and pass the verification. The main drawback of this solution is lack of generality and flexibility. It is strictly limited by a few conditions. Firstly, the messages in the set must be positive prime integers in a certain interval range. Secondly, the committed message must be proved to be in the interval range to guarantee that the prover does not commit to the product of some integers in the set. This limitation implies that additional range proof is needed. Thirdly, a co-called strong RSA assumption is necessary for security of the inclusion proof in [3]. Apart from depending on an unusual computational hard problem, the assumption implies that the set must be chosen independent of the prover so that it appears random to him. Application of [3] to inclusion is so strictly limited that its own author Camenisch only suggests to use it in special applications like anonymous credential. For general purpose inclusion proof, Camenisch *et al.* later propose the inclusion proof technique in [5], which we have discussed.

The inclusion proof technique in [3] is extended to exclusion proof by Li *et al.* [14]. The key technique in [14] is an accumulator-based proof system, which can provide a witness for each integer in a special set but not in S to show its exclusion from S. It is more efficient than the simple exclusion proof, but like the inclusion proof technique in [3] it is strictly limited in application. It is subject to three conditions. Firstly, all the messages in S and the committed message must be prime integers. Secondly, all the messages in S and the committed message must be non-negative integers smaller than 2^{ι} where ι is a security parameter denoted as l in [14]. Thirdly, a necessary condition satisfied in [3] is ignored in [14]: no integer in the set can be larger than the product of any other integers in the set. Moreover, dependence on the strong RSA assumption implies another condition in [14]: the set must be chosen independent of the prover so that it appears random to him.

Although mapping all the the messages in the set and all the messages possible to commit to into the special supported set may improve applicability of [3] and [14], this method does not always work simply and effectively. Instead, its applicability and complexity depend on the application environment as explained in the following.

- Any two different messages in the set and out of the set respectively cannot share the same image in the mapping so that the mapping always distinguishes the messages in the set and the messages out of the set. Moreover, sometimes the committed message will be recovered and used later. So the mapping function needs to be invertible and some simple functions (like mapping an integer to the prime nearest to it) cannot work.
- Some invertible mapping functions need a large memory to store, especially when the message space is large.
- In some applications the committed message must be processed in the form of commitment (e.g. in multi-party secure computation or e-voting where the commitment function is in the form of an encryption algorithm). Such applications usually exploit homomorphism of the commitment algorithm to implement computation of commitments, so the original messages in them cannot be changed in any way.

There are some even more special proof schemes [1,15,11], which prove that a secret committed integer lies in a finite interval range. They are the so called "range proof" schemes and are incomparable to our work. Moroever, as stated in Section 1, unpublished and rejected proposals with problems and limitations are incomparable to our work.

3   New Inclusion Proof and Exclusion Proof

The main idea of the new design is to divide the set S into multiple subsets, so that inclusion of a message in S is reduced to its inclusion in one of the subsets and exclusion of a message from S is reduced to its exclusion from all of the subsets. In this way, an inclusion proof or exclusion proof is reduced to multiple inclusion proofs or multiple exclusion proofs in a smaller scale. Then each smaller-scale inclusion proof is reduced to proof of commitment and each smaller-scale exclusion proof is reduced to proof of uncommitment where the former proves that a message is committed in a commitment and the latter proves that a message is not committed in a commitment. To be consistent with the existing inclusion proof and exclusion proof schemes and make a fair comparison, the following commitment function is employed.

- p and q are large primes such that $q|p-1$ and $q > s_i$ for $i = 1, 2, \ldots, n$. G is the cyclic subgroup with order q of Z_p^*. Integers g and h are generators of G such that $\log_g h$ is unknown.
- From now on in this paper, all the computations involving the integers in any matrix and vector is carried out modulo q.
- A prover randomly chooses r from Z_q and commits to a secret integer m in $c = g^m h^r \bmod p$.

3.1   Reducing Inclusion Proof and Exclusion Proof to Simpler Proofs

The simplifying reduction from inclusion proof and exclusion proof to commitment proof and uncommitment proof is as follows.

1. For simplicity of description, suppose S can be divided into t subsets $S_1, S_2, \ldots, S_t$ and each S_l contains k integers $s_{l,1}, s_{l,2}, \ldots, s_{l,k}$.
2. The prover randomly chooses an integer s in Z_q and calculates for each S_l integers $b_{l,i}$ for $i = 1, 2, \ldots, k$ in Z_q to satisfy

$$\sum_{i=1}^{k} b_{l,i} s_{l,\rho}^i = s \bmod q \text{ for } \rho = 1, 2, \ldots, k. \tag{1}$$

More precisely, integers $b_{l,i}$ for $l = 1, 2, \ldots, t$ and $i = 1, 2, \ldots, k$ must satisfy

$$\begin{pmatrix} s_{l,1} & s_{l,1}^2 & \cdots & s_{l,1}^k \\ s_{l,2} & s_{l,2}^2 & \cdots & s_{l,2}^k \\ \cdots & \cdots & \cdots & \cdots \\ \cdots & \cdots & \cdots & \cdots \\ s_{l,k} & s_{l,k}^2 & \cdots & s_{l,k}^k \end{pmatrix} \begin{pmatrix} b_{l,1} \\ b_{l,2} \\ \cdots \\ \cdots \\ b_{l,k} \end{pmatrix} = \begin{pmatrix} s \\ s \\ \cdots \\ \cdots \\ s \end{pmatrix}$$

for $l = 1, 2, \ldots, t$. As $s_{l,i} < q$ for $l = 1, 2, \ldots, t$ and $i = 1, 2, \ldots, k$ and they are different integers,

$$M_l = \begin{pmatrix} s_{l,1} & s_{l,1}^2 & \cdots & s_{l,1}^k \\ s_{l,2} & s_{l,2}^2 & \cdots & s_{l,2}^k \\ \cdots & \cdots & \cdots & \cdots \\ \cdots & \cdots & \cdots & \cdots \\ s_{l,k} & s_{l,k}^2 & \cdots & s_{l,k}^k \end{pmatrix}$$

is a non-singular matrix for $l = 1, 2, \ldots, t$ and there is a unique solution for $b_{l,1}, b_{l,2}, \ldots, b_{l,k}$:

$$\begin{pmatrix} b_{l,1} \\ b_{l,2} \\ \cdots \\ \cdots \\ b_{l,k} \end{pmatrix} = M_l^{-1} \begin{pmatrix} s \\ s \\ \cdots \\ \cdots \\ s \end{pmatrix}$$

for $l = 1, 2, \ldots, t$. Therefore, functions $F_l(x) = \sum_{i=1}^{k} b_{l,i} x^i \bmod q$ for $l = 1, 2, \ldots, t$ are obtained, each to satisfy

$$F_l(s_{l,i}) = s \text{ for } i = 1, 2, \ldots, k. \tag{2}$$

The prover publishes s. Note that $F_l()$ is actually the unique polynomial with degree at most k to satisfy (2) and $F_l(0) = 0$. Readers with basic knowledge in linear algebra should know a few efficient methods, which do not cost any exponentiation, to calculate $F_l()$ from $s_{l,i}$ for $i = 1, 2, \ldots, k$. Our presentation of $F_l()$ through matrix calculations is only one of them, which seems formal and straightforward. Also note that if necessary calculation of $F_l()$ can be performed beforehand once S is published such that it is already available when the inclusion proof or exclusion proof starts.

3. The prover calculates $e_i = e_{i-1}^m h^{\gamma_i} \bmod p$ for $i = 1, 2, \ldots, k - 1$ where $e_0 = c$ and γ_i is randomly chosen from Z_q. The prover proves validity of $e_1, e_2, \ldots, e_{k-1}$ using a zero knowledge proof that he knows m, r and γ_i for $i = 1, 2, \ldots, k - 1$ such that $c = g^m h^r \bmod p$ and $e_i = e_{i-1}^m h^{\gamma_i} \bmod p$ for $i = 1, 2, \ldots, k - 1$, which can be implemented through a simple combination of ZK proof of knowledge of discrete logarithm [27] and ZK proof of equality of discrete logarithms [6].

4. A verifier
   (a) calculates $b_{l,i}$ for $l = 1, 2, \ldots, t$ and $i = 1, 2, \ldots, k$ to satisfy (1) like the prover does where s is provided by the prover;
   (b) verifies the prover's proof of validity of $e_1, e_2, \ldots, e_{k-1}$.

He accepts the reduction iff the prover's proof is passed and $e_1, e_2, \ldots, e_{k-1}$ are valid.

The operations above have reduced inclusion proof and exclusion proof to commitment proof and uncommitment proof respectively. More precisely,

- Inclusion of m in S is reduced to inclusion of m in S_1 or S_2 or ...... or S_t. As $s = F_l(m)$ if $m \in S_l$, inclusion of m in S_l is reduced to commitment of s in ω_l where

$$\omega_l = C(F_l(m)) = C(\textstyle\sum_{i=1}^{k} b_{l,i}x^i) = \prod_{i=0}^{k-1} e_i^{b_{l,i+1}} \bmod p.$$

and $C()$ denotes the commitment function to commit a message m' in $C(m') = g^{m'} h^\eta \bmod p$ using a random integer η in Z_q.

- Exclusion of m from S is reduced to exclusion of m from S_1 and S_2 and ...... and S_t, while exclusion of m from S_l is reduced to uncommitment of s from ω_l.

3.2   Specification of the Two Simpler Proofs

The reduction work above is the same for inclusion proof and exclusion proof. After that, the left work is different for inclusion proof and exclusion proof. In an inclusion proof, the prover has to prove that s is committed to by him in ω_1 or ω_2 or ...... or ω_t. More precisely, he has to prove that he knows $\log_h \omega_1/g^s$ or $\log_h \omega_2/g^s$ or ...... or $\log_h \omega_t/g^s$ as follows.

1. ω_l can be publicly calculated by any verifier in the form

$$\omega_l = \prod_{i=0}^{k-1} e_i^{b_{l,i+1}} \bmod p.$$

2. If needed the prover himself can secretly calculate ω_l/g^s more efficiently:

$$\omega_l/g^s = \begin{cases} h^{\sum_{i=0}^{k-1} b_{l,i+1}\Gamma_{i+1}} \bmod p & \text{if } m \in S_l \\ g^{(\sum_{i=0}^{k-1} b_{l,i+1}m^{i+1})-s} h^{\sum_{i=0}^{k-1} b_{l,i+1}\Gamma_{i+1}} \bmod p & \text{if } m \notin S_l \end{cases}$$

where $\Gamma_i = m\Gamma_{i-1} + \gamma_{i-1} \bmod q$ for $i = 2, 3, \ldots, k$, $\Gamma_1 = r$ and $m^2, m^3, \ldots, m^k$ can be calculated using $k-1$ multiplications and reused in calculation of $\omega_1, \omega_2, \ldots, \omega_t$.

3. The prover runs ZK proof of partial knowledge [7] to implement the proof that he knows one of t discrete logarithms $\log_h \omega_1/g^s$, $\log_h \omega_2/g^s$, ..., $\log_h \omega_t/g^s$.

4. Any verifier can publicly verify the prover's proof of knowledge of one of t discrete logarithms. He accepts the inclusion proof iff the prover's proof is successfully verified.

In an exclusion proof, the prover has to prove s is not committed in any of ω_1, ω_2, ..., ω_t. Proof that s is not committed in ω_l is as follows where the prover and the verifier can calculate ω_l respectively like in the inclusion proof and the prover knows $M_l = F_l(m) = \sum_{i=1}^{k} b_{l,i}m^i \bmod q$, which is committed in ω_l.

1. The prover randomly chooses a positive integer T in Z_q and publishes $y = g^{T(s-M_l)} \bmod p$.

2. He proves knowledge of secret integer $x = T(s - M_l)$ such that $y = g^x \bmod p$ using zero knowledge proof of knowledge of discrete logarithm [27].
3. He proves knowledge of secret integers T and r' such that $(g^s)^T h^{r'} = \omega_l^T y \bmod p$ where $r' = T \sum_{i=1}^{k}(b_{l,i} \Gamma_i) \bmod q$, $\Gamma_i = m\Gamma_{i-1} + \gamma_{i-1} \bmod q$ for $i = 2, 3, \ldots, k$ and $\Gamma_1 = r$ using zero knowledge proof of knowledge of discrete logarithm [27] and knowledge proof of equality of discrete logarithms [6].
4. Any verifier can verify $y > 1$ and the two zero knowledge proofs. He accepts the uncommitment claim if and only if all the three conditions are satisfied in his check.

This proof is called uncommitment proof. The prover repeats it for each l in $\{1, 2, \ldots, t\}$ and any verifier can verify the prover's proof. The verifier accepts the exclusion proof iff the all the t instances of proof are successfully verified. Note that $m^2, m^3, \ldots, m^k$ can be calculated using $k - 1$ multiplications and reused in calculation of $M_1, M_2, \ldots, M_t$ by the prover.

4   Security Analysis

Completeness of the new inclusion proof and exclusion proof is obvious. Any reader can follow the running of the two proof protocols step by step to verify that an honest prover can strictly follow them to pass their verifications. If the challenges in the employed zero knowledge proof primitives are generated by a pseudo-random function, no interactive verifier is needed and the new inclusion proof and exclusion proof can be non-interactive in the random oracle model. Moreover, public verifiability is achieved in the two proofs as every detail of them can be publicly verified by any one. Other security properties of them are proved in Theorems 1, 2 and 3.

Theorem 1. *Both the new inclusion proof protocol and the new exclusion proof protocol achieve honest-verifier zero knowledge.*

Proof: Both the new inclusion proof protocol and the new exclusion proof protocol only employ three zero knowledge proof primitives: zero knowledge proof of knowledge of discrete logarithm [27], zero knowledge proof of equality of discrete logarithms [6] and zero knowledge proof of partial knowledge [7]. Honest-verifier zero knowledge of these three proof primitives is formally proved when they are proposed. More precisely, the proof transcripts of the three primitives with an honest verifier can be simulated without any difference by a party without any secret knowledge.

Besides the three zero knowledge proof primitives, the two proofs only reveal s, e_1, e_2, ..., e_{k-1}. As s is randomly chosen from Z_q, the distribution of s is uniform in Z_q. As $e_i = e_{i-1}^m h^{\gamma_i} \bmod p$ for $i = 1, 2, \ldots, k - 1$ and γ_i is randomly chosen from Z_q, each e_i is uniformly distributed in G. So anybody can simulate s, e_1, e_2, ..., e_{k-1} without any difference by randomly choosing s in Z_q and every e_i in G.

Other integers used in the proof like $b_{l,i}$ and ω_l are deterministic public functions of $s_1, s_2, \ldots, s_n, s, c, e_1, e_2, \ldots, e_{k-1}$. So they are not independent variables affecting zero knowledge of the two proof primitives.

Since the whole proof transcripts of the two proof protocols with an honest verifier can be simulated without any difference by a party without any secret knowledge, they achieve honest-verifier zero knowledge.   □

Theorem 2. *The new inclusion proof is sound. More precisely, if a polynomial prover can extract an opening (m, r) of c such that $m \neq s_i \bmod q$ for $i = 1, 2, \ldots, n$, then the probability that the prover can pass the verification in the new inclusion proof is negligible.*

Proof: If the prover extracts m, r and passes the verification in the new inclusion proof with a non-negligible probability while $c = g^m h^r \bmod p$ and $m \neq s_i \bmod q$ for $i = 1, 2, \ldots, n$, a contradiction can be found as follows. As he passes the verification in the new inclusion proof with a non-negligible probability, he must have successfully proved validity of $e_1, e_2, \ldots, e_{k-1}$ with a non-negligible probability. As proof of validity of $e_1, e_2, \ldots, e_{k-1}$ is based on proof of knowledge of discrete logarithm in [27] and proof of equality of discrete logarithms in [6], whose soundness is formally proved when they are proposed, it is guaranteed with a non-negligible probability that the prover can calculate integers m, r and γ_i for $i = 1, 2, \ldots, k - 1$ in polynomial time such that

$$c = g^m h^r \bmod p \tag{3}$$
$$e_i = e_{i-1}^m h^{\gamma_i} \bmod p \text{ for } i = 1, 2, \ldots, k - 1 \tag{4}$$

where $e_0 = c$.

As he passes the verification in the new inclusion proof with a non-negligible probability, the prover also must have successfully passed the zero knowledge proof of knowledge of one out of t discrete logarithms [7] with a non-negligible probability. As soundness of zero knowledge proof of partial knowledge [7] is formally proved when it is proposed, it is guaranteed that for some l in $\{1, 2, \ldots, t\}$ the prover can calculate integers s and R in polynomial time such that

$$g^s h^R = \prod_{i=0}^{k-1} e_i^{b_{l,i+1}} \bmod p \tag{5}$$

with a non-negligible probability where $e_0 = c$.

(3), (4) and (5) imply that the prover can calculate integers s, R, $\sum_{i=0}^{k-1} b_{l,i+1} m^{i+1}$ and $\sum_{i=0}^{k-1} b_{l,i+1} \Gamma_{i+1}$ in polynomial time with a non-negligible probability such that

$$g^s h^R = \prod_{i=0}^{k-1} g^{b_{l,i+1} m^{i+1}} h^{b_{l,i+1} \Gamma_{i+1}} = g^{\sum_{i=0}^{k-1} b_{l,i+1} m^{i+1}} h^{\sum_{i=0}^{k-1} b_{l,i+1} \Gamma_{i+1}} \bmod p$$

where

$$\Gamma_i = m \Gamma_{i-1} + \gamma_{i-1} \bmod q \text{ for } i = 2, 3, \ldots, k$$

and $\Gamma_1 = r$. So

$$s = \sum_{i=0}^{k-1} b_{l,i+1} m^{i+1} = \sum_{i=1}^{k} b_{l,i} m^i \bmod q$$

with a non-negligible probability. Otherwise, with a non-negligible probability the prover can calculate non-zero (modulo q) integers $\alpha = s - \sum_{i=0}^{k-1} b_{l,i+1} m^{i+1}$ and $\beta = R - \sum_{i=0}^{k-1} b_{l,i+1} \Gamma_{i+1}$ in polynomial time to satisfy $g^\alpha h^\beta = 1$ and thus can calculate $\log_g h$ in polynomial time, which is a contradiction.

Note that $b_{l,1}, b_{l,2}, \ldots, b_{l,k}$ are generated through

$$\sum_{i=1}^{k} b_{l,i} s_{l,\rho}^i = s \bmod q \text{ for } \rho = 1, 2, \ldots, k.$$

So with a non-negligible probability

$$
\begin{pmatrix}
s_{l,1} & s_{l,1}^2 & \cdots & s_{l,1}^k \\
s_{l,2} & s_{l,2}^2 & \cdots & s_{l,2}^k \\
\cdots & \cdots & \cdots & \cdots \\
\cdots & \cdots & \cdots & \cdots \\
s_{l,k} & s_{l,k}^2 & \cdots & s_{l,k}^k \\
m & m^2 & \cdots, & m^k
\end{pmatrix}
\begin{pmatrix}
b_{l,1} \\
b_{l,2} \\
\cdots \\
\cdots \\
b_{l,k}
\end{pmatrix}
=
\begin{pmatrix}
s \\
s \\
\cdots \\
\cdots \\
s \\
s
\end{pmatrix}
\tag{6}
$$

However, as $m \neq s_i \bmod q$ for $i = 1, 2, \ldots, n$ and all the calculations in the matrix is performed modulo q, $\begin{pmatrix} s_{l,1} & s_{l,1}^2 & \cdots & s_{l,1}^k & s \\ s_{l,2} & s_{l,2}^2 & \cdots & s_{l,2}^k & s \\ \cdots & \cdots & \cdots & \cdots & \cdots \\ \cdots & \cdots & \cdots & \cdots & \cdots \\ s_{l,k} & s_{l,k}^2 & \cdots & s_{l,k}^k & s \\ m & m^2 & \cdots, & m^k & s \end{pmatrix}$ is a non-singular matrix and thus (6) absolutely and always fails. Therefore, a contradiction is found and the probability that a prover can pass the new inclusion proof is negligible if the integer he commits to in c is not in S. $\qquad\Box$

Theorem 3. *The new exclusion proof is sound and the probability that a prover can pass its verification is negligible if he can extract an opening (m, r) of c such that $m \in S$.*

Before Theorem 3 is proved, a lemma is proved first.

Lemma 1. *The uncommitment proof is sound. More precisely, if the prover passes its verification, then with an overwhelmingly large probability $s \neq M_l$.*

Proof: Note that the uncommitment proof is a simple combination of two instances of proof of knowledge of discrete logarithm [27] and one instance of proof of equality of discrete logarithms [6], whose soundness is formally proved when they are proposed. So it is guaranteed with an overwhelmingly large probability that the prover can calculate secret integers x, T and r' in polynomial time to satisfy
$$y = g^x \bmod p$$

$$(g^s)^T h^{r'} = \omega_l^T y \bmod p.$$

So with an overwhelmingly large probability

$$(g^s)^T h^{r'} = \omega_l^T g^x \bmod p. \tag{7}$$

As M_l is the message the prover commits to in ω_l, the prover can calculate integers M_l and R in polynomial time such that

$$\omega_l = g^{M_l} h^R \bmod p$$

and thus (7) implies that with an overwhelmingly large probability the prover can calculate x, T, r', M_l and R in polynomial time such that

$$(g^s)^T h^{r'} = (g^{M_l} h^R)^T g^x \bmod p.$$

So with an overwhelmingly large probability the prover can calculate $T(s-M_l)-x$ and $r'-TR$ in polynomial time such that

$$g^{T(s-M_l)-x} h^{r'-TR} = 1 \bmod p.$$

So with an overwhelmingly large probability

$$T(s-M_l)-x = 0 \bmod q$$

Otherwise, with an overwhelmingly large probability the prover can calculate $\log_g h = (TR-r')/(T(s-M_l)-x) \bmod q$ in polynomial time, which is a contradiction. As $y > 1$, $x \neq 0 \bmod q$ and so with an overwhelmingly large probability $s - M_l \neq 0 \bmod q$. Therefore, with an overwhelmingly large probability $s \neq M_l \bmod q$.   □

Proof of Theorem 3: If the prover passes the verification in the new exclusion proof with a non-negligible probability while $m \in S$ and $c = g^m h^r \bmod p$, a contradiction can be found as follows. As the prover passes the verification in the new exclusion proof with a non-negligible probability, he must have successfully proved validity of $e_1, e_2, \ldots, e_{k-1}$ with a non-negligible probability. As proof of validity of $e_1, e_2, \ldots, e_{k-1}$ is based on proof of knowledge of discrete logarithm in [27] and proof of equality of discrete logarithms in [6], whose soundness is formally proved when they are proposed, it is guaranteed with a non-negligible probability that the prover can calculate integers m, r and γ_i for $i = 1, 2, \ldots, k-1$ in polynomial time such that

$$c = g^m h^r \bmod p \tag{8}$$

$$e_i = e_{i-1}^m h^{\gamma_i} \bmod p \text{ for } i = 1, 2, \ldots, k-1 \tag{9}$$

where $e_0 = c$.

(8) and (9) imply that with a non-negligible probability

$$\prod_{i=0}^{k-1} e_i^{b_{l,i+1}} = \prod_{i=0}^{k-1} g^{b_{l,i+1} m^{i+1}} h^{b_{l,i+1} \Gamma_{i+1}}$$
$$= g^{\sum_{i=0}^{k-1} b_{l,i+1} m^{i+1}} h^{\sum_{i=0}^{k-1} b_{l,i+1} \Gamma_{i+1}} \bmod p \tag{10}$$

As $m \in S$, there must exist $l \in \{1, 2, \ldots, t\}$ such that $m \in S_l$. As

$$\begin{pmatrix} s_{l,1} & s_{l,1}^2 & \cdots & s_{l,1}^k \\ s_{l,2} & s_{l,2}^2 & \cdots & s_{l,2}^k \\ \cdots & \cdots & \cdots & \cdots \\ \cdots & \cdots & \cdots & \cdots \\ s_{l,k} & s_{l,k}^2 & \cdots & s_{l,k}^k \end{pmatrix} \begin{pmatrix} b_{l,1} \\ b_{l,2} \\ \cdots \\ \cdots \\ b_{l,k} \end{pmatrix} = \begin{pmatrix} s \\ s \\ \cdots \\ \cdots \\ s \end{pmatrix}$$

and $S_l = \{s_{l,1}, s_{l,2}, \ldots, s_{l,k}\}$, m satisfies

$$\sum_{i=1}^{k} b_{l,i} m^i = s \bmod q. \tag{11}$$

As $\omega_l = \prod_{i=0}^{k-1} e_i^{b_{l,i+1}}$, (10) and (11) imply that with a non-negligible probability

$$\omega_l = g^s h^{\sum_{i=0}^{k-1} b_{l,i+1} \Gamma_{i+1}} \bmod p$$

and thus s is committed to by the prover in ω_l with a non-negligible probability.

As the prover passes the verification in the new exclusion proof with a non-negligible probability, he must have successfully passed the t instances of proof of uncommitment with a non-negligible probability, say P_1. So according to Lemma 1, it is guaranteed with a probability $P_1 P_2$ that s is not committed to by the prover in ω_l for any l in $\{1, 2, \ldots, t\}$ where P_2 is an overwhelmingly large probability. As $P_1 P_2$ is non-negligible, it is guaranteed with an non-negligible probability that s is not committed to by the prover in ω_l for any l in $\{1, 2, \ldots, t\}$. So a contradiction is found. Therefore, the probability that a prover can pass the exclusion proof is negligible if $m \in S$.   □

5   Efficiency Optimisation

The cost of the new inclusion proof and exclusion proof includes communicational cost and computational cost. In communication, $3k + 3t + 2$ integers are transfered in the new inclusion proof and $3k + 6t + 2$ integers are transfered in the new exclusion proof. Their computational cost is measured in terms of the number of exponentiations. When estimating their computational cost, we have an observation: exponentiations with small (in comparison with q) exponents like s_ρ^i with $1 \leq i \leq k$ is much less costly than an exponentiation with an exponent chosen from Z_q. Actually, the $k - 1$ exponentiations $s_\rho^2, s_\rho^3, \ldots, s_\rho^k$ can be calculated in a batch using $k - 1$ multiplications. So, in efficiency analysis of cryptographic protocols (e.g. threshold secret sharing [17,28]), an exponentiation used in Lagrange Interpolation is usually not counted like an exponentiation with a full-length exponent as its exponent is usually much smaller. So the number of exponentiations needed in the new inclusion proof is $3k + 4t - 3$ for the prover and $4k + n + 2t$ for a verifier, while the number of exponentiations needed in the new exclusion proof is $3k + 6t - 3$ for the prover and $3k + n + 6t$ for a verifier.

Efficiency of general inclusion proof and exclusion proof has been greatly improved in our work as $O(k) + O(t)$ is actually $O(\sqrt{n})$. For the first time, communicational cost of general inclusion proof and general exclusion proof in a set with cardinality n is reduced to $O(\sqrt{n})$. Computational cost of the prover is $O(\sqrt{n})$ exponentiations as well, the most efficient in publicly verifiable general solutions to inclusion proof and exclusion proof. However, computational cost of a verifier still includes n exponentiations, which are needed to calculate $\omega_l = \prod_{i=0}^{k-1} e_i^{b_{l,i+1}}$ for $l = 1, 2, \ldots, t$. Those n exponentiations is the bottleneck in efficiency of the new inclusion proof and exclusion proof technique.

To overcome this bottleneck, we exploit a special phenomenon in the new inclusion proof and the new exclusion proof, which does not happen in the existing solutions to inclusion proof or exclusion proof. That is in the t instances of calculation of ω_l the same k bases $e_0, e_1, \ldots, e_{k-1}$ are used. Although directly calculating $\omega_1, \omega_2, \ldots, \omega_t$ is costly for a verifier, verification of validity of them can be efficient if someone else knows (e.g. using some other more efficient method) and publishes them. In the the new inclusion proof and the new exclusion proof the prover can calculate each ω_l using no more than 2 exponentiations. So if he publishes $\omega_1, \omega_2, \ldots, \omega_t$ a verifier only needs to verify validity of them. Therefore, calculation of $\omega_1, \omega_2, \ldots, \omega_t$ by a verifier in the new inclusion proof and the new exclusion proof can be optimised as follows.

1. The prover calculates and publishes for $l = 1, 2, \ldots, t$

$$\omega_l = \begin{cases} g^s h^{\sum_{i=1}^{k} b_{l,i} \Gamma_i} \bmod p & \text{if } m \in S_l \\ g^{\sum_{i=1}^{k} b_{l,i} m^i} h^{\sum_{i=1}^{k} b_{l,i} \Gamma_i} \bmod p & \text{if } m \notin S_l \end{cases}$$

2. A verifier randomly chooses integers $\theta_1, \theta_2, \ldots, \theta_t$ from Z_τ where τ is a security parameter smaller than q.
3. The verifier checks

$$\prod_{l=1}^{t} \omega_l^{\theta_l} = \prod_{i=0}^{k-1} e_i^{\sum_{l=1}^{t} \theta_l b_{l,i+1}} \bmod p. \tag{12}$$

He accepts validity of $\omega_1, \omega_2, \ldots, \omega_t$ iff (12) holds.

This method only transfers t integers and costs $t + k$ exponentiations, while as illustrated in Theorem 4, ω_l is guaranteed to be $\prod_{i=0}^{k-1} e_i^{b_{l,i+1}}$ for $l = 1, 2, \ldots, t$ if (12) is satisfied with a non-negligible probability.

Theorem 4. *If (12) is satisfied with a probability larger than $1/\tau$, then it is guaranteed that $\omega_l = \prod_{i=0}^{k-1} e_i^{b_{l,i+1}}$ for $l = 1, 2, \ldots, t$.*

Proof: For any integer L in $\{1, 2, \ldots, t\}$ there must exist integers $\theta_1, \theta_2, \ldots, \theta_{L-1}, \theta_{L+1}, \ldots, \theta_t$ in z_τ and two different integers θ_L and $\hat{\theta}_L$ in Z_τ such that

$$\prod_{l=1}^{t} \omega_l^{\theta_l} = \prod_{i=0}^{k-1} e_i^{\sum_{l=1}^{t} \theta_l b_{l,i+1}} \bmod p \tag{13}$$

$$(\prod_{l=1}^{L-1} \omega_l^{\theta_l}) \omega_L^{\hat{\theta}_L} \prod_{l=L+1}^{t} \omega_l^{\theta_l} \tag{14}$$

$$= \prod_{i=0}^{k-1} e_i^{(\sum_{l=1}^{L-1} \theta_l b_{l,i+1}) + \hat{\theta}_L b_{L,i+1} + \sum_{l=L+1}^{t} \theta_l b_{l,i+1}} \bmod p$$

Otherwise, with this L for any combination of $\theta_1, \theta_2, \ldots, \theta_{L-1}, \theta_{L+1}, \ldots, \theta_t$ there is at most one θ_L to satisfy (12) among the τ possible choices of θ_L, which leads to a contradiction: the probability that (12) is satisfied is no larger than $1/\tau$. (13)/(14) yields

$$\omega_L^{\theta_L - \hat{\theta}_L} = \prod_{i=0}^{k-1} e_i^{(\theta_L - \hat{\theta}_L) b_{L,i+1}} \bmod p$$

As θ_L, $\hat{\theta}_L < \tau < q$ and q is prime, $(\theta_L - \hat{\theta}_L)^{-1} \bmod q$ exists. So

$$\omega_L = \prod_{i=0}^{k-1} e_i^{b_{L,i+1}} \bmod p$$

Note that L can be any integer in $\{1, 2, \dots, t\}$. Therefore,

$$\omega_l = \prod_{i=0}^{k-1} e_i^{b_{l,i+1}} \text{ for } l = 1, 2, \dots, t.$$

□

6   Comparison and Conclusion

The new inclusion proof protocol and the new exclusion protocol are compared with the existing solutions to inclusion proof and exclusion proof in Table 1, which clearly demonstrates the advantages of the new scheme in both security and efficiency. As stated in Section 1, we focus on proof techniques to especially designed to handle inclusion proof and exclusion proof in this paper. Communicational cost is estimated in terms of the number of transferred integers. Computational cost is estimated in terms of the number of exponentiations with bases in G (or similar large cyclic groups) and exponents in Z_q (or a similar large range as wide as the order of a large cyclic group). The simple exclusion proof is assumed to employ ZK proof of inequality of discrete logarithm in [4]. Our new solution costs $O(\sqrt{n})$ and is more efficient than all the existing general solutions including the simple inclusion proof, the simple exclusion proof and the inclusion proof protocol in [5], while the inclusion proof protocol and exclusion proof protocols in [3,14] are only special solutions working under strict conditions. Moreover, our new technique overcomes the drawbacks of the existing solutions.

Table 1. Comparison of inclusion proof and exclusion proof schemes

scheme	type	public verifiability	generality & flexibility	non--interaction	communi--cation	computation prover	verifier
simple proof	inclusion	achieved	achieved	yes	$3n$	$2n - 1$	$2n$
simple proof	exclusion	achieved	achieved	yes	$6n$	$6n$	$6n$
[3]	inclusion	achieved	no and strictly limited	yes	54	46	56
[14]	exclusion	achieved	no and strictly limited	yes	68	56	67
[5]	inclusion	no	achieved	no	$n + 6$ for every verifier	7 for every verifier	$n + 9$
new proof	inclusion	achieved	achieved	yes	$3k + 4t + 2$	$3k + 4t - 3$	$4k + 3t$
new proof	exclusion	achieved	achieved	yes	$3k + 7t + 2$	$3k + 6t - 3$	$4k + 7t$

References

1. Boudot, F.: Efficient Proofs that a Committed Number Lies in an Interval. In: Preneel, B. (ed.) EUROCRYPT 2000. LNCS, vol. 1807, pp. 431–444. Springer, Heidelberg (2000)
2. Brickell, E.F., Gordon, D.M., McCurley, K.S., Wilson, D.B.: Fast Exponentiation with Precomputation. In: Rueppel, R.A. (ed.) EUROCRYPT 1992. LNCS, vol. 658, pp. 200–207. Springer, Heidelberg (1993)
3. Camenisch, J., Lysyanskaya, A.: Dynamic Accumulators and Application to Efficient Revocation of Anonymous Credentials. In: Yung, M. (ed.) CRYPTO 2002. LNCS, vol. 2442, pp. 61–76. Springer, Heidelberg (2002)
4. Camenisch, J., Shoup, V.: Practical Verifiable Encryption and Decryption of Discrete Logarithms. In: Boneh, D. (ed.) CRYPTO 2003. LNCS, vol. 2729, pp. 126–144. Springer, Heidelberg (2003)
5. Camenisch, J., Chaabouni, R., Shelat, A.: Efficient Protocols for Set Membership and Range Proofs. In: Pieprzyk, J. (ed.) ASIACRYPT 2008. LNCS, vol. 5350, pp. 234–252. Springer, Heidelberg (2008)
6. Chaum, D., Pedersen, T.P.: Wallet Databases with Observers (Extended Abstract). In: Brickell, E.F. (ed.) CRYPTO 1992. LNCS, vol. 740, pp. 89–105. Springer, Heidelberg (1993)
7. Cramer, R., Damgård, I., Schoenmakers, B.: Proof of Partial Knowledge and Simplified Design of Witness Hiding Protocols. In: Desmedt, Y.G. (ed.) CRYPTO 1994. LNCS, vol. 839, pp. 174–187. Springer, Heidelberg (1994)
8. Fujisaki, E., Okamoto, T.: Statistical Zero Knowledge Protocols to Prove Modular Polynomial Relations. In: Kaliski Jr., B.S. (ed.) CRYPTO 1997. LNCS, vol. 1294, pp. 16–30. Springer, Heidelberg (1997)
9. Goldreich, O., Micali, S., Wigderson, A.: Proofs that yield nothing but their validity and a methodology of cryptographic protocol design. In: FOCS 1986, pp. 174–187 (1986)
10. Goldwasser, S., Micali, S., Rackoff, C.: The knowledge complexity of interactive proof systems. SIAM J. Computer 18, 186–208 (1985)
11. Groth, J.: Non-interactive Zero-Knowledge Arguments for Voting. In: Ioannidis, J., Keromytis, A.D., Yung, M. (eds.) ACNS 2005. LNCS, vol. 3531, pp. 467–482. Springer, Heidelberg (2005)
12. Groth, J.: Linear Algebra with Sub-linear Zero-Knowledge Arguments. In: Halevi, S. (ed.) CRYPTO 2009. LNCS, vol. 5677, pp. 192–208. Springer, Heidelberg (2009)
13. Kilian, J., Petrank, E., Tardos, G.: Probabilistically checkable proofs with zero knowledge. In: STOC 1997, pp. 496–505 (1997)
14. Li, J., Li, N., Xue, R.: Universal Accumulators with Efficient Nonmembership Proofs. In: Katz, J., Yung, M. (eds.) ACNS 2007. LNCS, vol. 4521, pp. 253–269. Springer, Heidelberg (2007)
15. Lipmaa, H.: On Diophantine Complexity and Statistical Zero-Knowledge Arguments. In: Laih, C.-S. (ed.) ASIACRYPT 2003. LNCS, vol. 2894, pp. 398–415. Springer, Heidelberg (2003)
16. Micali, S., Rabin, M., Kilian, J.: Zero-knowledge sets. In: IEEE FOCS 2003, p. 80 (2003)
17. Pedersen, T.: Distributed Provers with Applications to Undeniable Signatures. In: Davies, D.W. (ed.) EUROCRYPT 1991. LNCS, vol. 547, pp. 221–242. Springer, Heidelberg (1991)

18. Peng, K., Boyd, C., Dawson, E., Viswanathan, K.: Robust, Privacy Protecting and Publicly Verifiable Sealed-Bid Auction. In: Deng, R.H., Qing, S., Bao, F., Zhou, J. (eds.) ICICS 2002. LNCS, vol. 2513, pp. 147–159. Springer, Heidelberg (2002)
19. Peng, K., Aditya, R., Boyd, C., Dawson, E., Lee, B.: Multiplicative Homomorphic E-Voting. In: Canteaut, A., Viswanathan, K. (eds.) INDOCRYPT 2004. LNCS, vol. 3348, pp. 61–72. Springer, Heidelberg (2004)
20. Peng, K., Boyd, C., Dawson, E.: Batch Verification of Validity of Bids in Homomorphic E-auction. Computer Communications 29, 2798–2805 (2006)
21. Peng, K., Dawson, E.: Efficient Bid Validity Check in ElGamal-Based Sealed-Bid E-Auction. In: Dawson, E., Wong, D.S. (eds.) ISPEC 2007. LNCS, vol. 4464, pp. 209–224. Springer, Heidelberg (2007)
22. Peng, K., Bao, F.: Efficient Vote Validity Check in Homomorphic Electronic Voting. In: Lee, P.J., Cheon, J.H. (eds.) ICISC 2008. LNCS, vol. 5461, pp. 202–217. Springer, Heidelberg (2009)
23. Peng, K.: A Hybrid E-Voting Scheme. In: Bao, F., Li, H., Wang, G. (eds.) ISPEC 2009. LNCS, vol. 5451, pp. 195–206. Springer, Heidelberg (2009)
24. Peng, K., Bao, F.: A Design of Secure Preferential E-Voting. In: Ryan, P.Y.A., Schoenmakers, B. (eds.) VOTE-ID 2009. LNCS, vol. 5767, pp. 141–156. Springer, Heidelberg (2009)
25. Peng, K., Bao, F.: Efficiency Improvement of Homomorphic E-Auction. In: Katsikas, S., Lopez, J., Soriano, M. (eds.) TrustBus 2010. LNCS, vol. 6264, pp. 238–249. Springer, Heidelberg (2010)
26. Peng, K., Bao, F.: Efficient Proof of Validity of Votes in Homomorphic E-Voting. In: NSS 2010, pp. 17–23 (2010)
27. Schnorr, C.: Efficient signature generation by smart cards. Journal of Cryptology 4, 161–174 (1991)
28. Schoenmakers, B.: A Simple Publicly Verifiable Secret Sharing Scheme and Its Application to Electronic Voting. In: Wiener, M. (ed.) CRYPTO 1999. LNCS, vol. 1666, pp. 148–164. Springer, Heidelberg (1999)

MQQ-SIG

An Ultra-Fast and Provably CMA Resistant Digital Signature Scheme

Danilo Gligoroski[1], Rune Steinsmo Ødegård[2], Rune Erlend Jensen[2],
Ludovic Perret[3], Jean-Charles Faugère[3],
Svein Johan Knapskog[2], and Smile Markovski[4]

[1] Department of Telematics,
The Norwegian University of Science and Technology (NTNU),
O.S. Bragstads plass 2E, N-7491 Trondheim, Norway
danilog@item.ntnu.no
[2] Centre for Quantifiable Quality of Service in Communication Systems, NTNU,
O.S. Bragstads plass 2E, N-7491 Trondheim, Norway
knapskog@Q2S.ntnu.no, rune.odegard@q2s.ntnu.no, runeerle@stud.ntnu.no
[3] INRIA, Paris-Rocquencourt Center, SALSA Project
UPMC Univ. Paris 06, UMR 7606, LIP6, F-75005, Paris, France
CNRS, UMR 7606, LIP6, F-75005, Paris, France
jean-charles.faugere@inria.fr, ludovic.perret@lip6.fr
[4] "Ss Cyril and Methodius" University,
Faculty of Natural Sciences and Mathematics, Institute of Informatics,
P.O. Box 162, 1000 Skopje, Macedonia
smile@ii.edu.mk

Abstract. We present MQQ-SIG, a signature scheme based on *"Multivariate Quadratic Quasigroups"*. The MQQ-SIG signature scheme has a public key consisting of $\frac{n}{2}$ quadratic polynomials in n variables where $n = 160, 192, 224$ or 256. Under the assumption that solving systems of $\frac{n}{2}$ MQQ's equations in n variables is as hard as solving systems of random quadratic equations, we prove that in the random oracle model our signature scheme is CMA (Chosen-Message Attack) resistant.

From efficiency point of view, the signing and verification processes of MQQ-SIG are three orders of magnitude faster than RSA or ECDSA. Compared with other MQ signing schemes, MQQ-SIG has both advantages and disadvantages. Advantages are that it has more than three times smaller private keys (from 401 to 593 bytes), and the signing process is an order of magnitude faster than other MQ schemes. That makes it very suitable for implementation in smart cards and other embedded systems. However, MQQ-SIG has a big public key (from 125 to 512 Kb) and it is not suitable for systems where the size of the public key has to be small.

Keywords: Public Key Cryptography, Ultra-Fast Public Key Cryptography, Multivariate Quadratic Polynomials, Quasigroup String Transformations, Multivariate Quadratic Quasigroup.

L. Chen, M. Yung, and L. Zhu (Eds.): INTRUST 2011, LNCS 7222, pp. 184–203, 2012.
© Springer-Verlag Berlin Heidelberg 2012

1   Introduction

Multivariate quadratic schemes (MQ schemes) are an active research area since their introduction more than 26 years ago in the papers of Matsumoto and Imai [25,31]. They have a lot of performance advantages over classical public key schemes based on integer factorization (RSA) and on the discrete logarithm problem in the additive group of points defined by elliptic curves over finite fields (ECC), but they have also one additional advantage: there are no known quantum algorithms that would break MQ schemes faster than generic brute force attacks.

We can say that MQ schemes can be generally divided in five types of schemes that conceptually differ in the construction of the nonlinear quadratic part of the scheme. There is a nice (but a little bit older survey from 2005) [49] that covers the first four classes of multivariate quadratic public key cryptosystems: MIA [25], STS [44,33,23], HFE [36] and UOV [28].

The fifth scheme MQQ was introduced in [21,22] in 2008. MQQ is based on the theory of quasigroups and quasigroup string transformations. Since it had interesting performance characteristics, it immediately attracted the attention of cryptographers trying to attack it. It was first successfully cryptanalysed independently by Perret [39] using Gröbner basis approach, and Mohamed et al. using MutantXL [35]. Later, improved cryptanalysis by Faugère et al. in [17] explained exactly why the MQQ systems are so easy to solve in practice.

In this paper we describe a digital signature variant of MQQ (called MQQ-SIG). To thwart previous successful attacks, we propose to use the *minus modifier*, i.e. to remove some equations of the public key. More specifically, we remove $\frac{1}{2}$ of the public equations of the original MQQ public key algorithm. We also present numerical (experimental) evidence that gives us arguments to believe that Gröbner bases approach (and having in mind that MutantXL approach is equivalent) is ineffective in solving the remaining known equations.

Thus, based on the assumption that solving $\frac{n}{2}$ quadratic MQQ's equations with n variables is as hard as solving systems of random quadratic equations, we show that in the random oracle model our signature scheme is provably CMA resistant.

The properties of MQQ-SIG digital signature scheme can be briefly summarized as:

- In the random oracle model it is provably CMA resistant under the assumption that solving $\frac{n}{2}$ MQQ's quadratic equations with n variables is as hard as solving systems of random equations;
- Its conjectured security level is at least $2^{\frac{n}{2}}$;
- The length of the signature is $2n$ bits where ($n = 160, 192, 224$ or 256);
- The size of the private key is between 401 and 593 bytes.
- The size of the public key is between 125 and 512 Kb.
- In software, its signing speed is in the range of 300–3,500 times faster than the most popular public key schemes, and 5 to 20 times faster than other multivariate quadratic schemes with equivalent security parameters;
- Its verification speed is comparable to the speed of other multivariate quadratic PKCs;

- In hardware, its signing or verification speed can be more than 10,000 times faster than the most popular public key schemes;
- In 8-bit MCUs, smart cards and RFIDs, it is hundreds or thousands times faster than the most popular public key signature schemes;

2   Preliminaries - Quasigroups and Multivariate Quadratic Quasigroups

Here we give a brief overview of quasigroups and quasigroup string transformations. A more detailed explanation can be found in [5,12,47].

Definition 1. *A quasigroup* $(Q, *)$ *is a groupoid satisfying the law*

$$(\forall u, v \in Q)(\exists! x, y \in Q) \quad u * x = v \ \& \ y * u = v. \tag{1}$$

This implies the cancelation laws $x*y = x*z \implies y = z$, $y*x = z*x \implies y = z$. Note also that the equations $a * x = b$, $y * a = b$ have unique solutions x, y for each $a, b \in Q$. Given a quasigroup $(Q, *)$ five so called "*parastrophes*" (or "*conjugate operations*") can be adjoint to $*$. Here, we use only two of them – denoted by $\backslash$ and $/$, – defined by

$$x * y = z \iff y = x \backslash z \iff x = z/y \tag{2}$$

Then $(Q, \backslash)$ and $(Q, /)$ are quasigroups too and the algebra $(Q, *, \backslash, /)$ satisfies the identities

$$x \backslash (x * y) = y, \quad (x * y)/y = x, \quad x * (x \backslash y) = y, \quad (x/y) * y = x \tag{3}$$

Conversely, if an algebra $(Q, *, \backslash, /)$ with three binary operations satisfies the identities (3), then $(Q, *)$, $(Q, \backslash)$, $(Q, /)$ are quasigroups and (2) holds.

In what follows we will work with finite quasigroups of order 2^d i.e. where $|Q| = 2^d$. To define a multivariate quadratic PKC for our purpose, we will use the following result.

Lemma 1 ([21,22]). *For every quasigroup* $(Q, *)$ *of order* 2^d *and for each bijection* $Q \to \{0, 1 \ldots, 2^d - 1\}$ *there are a uniquely determined vector valued Boolean functions* $*_{vv}$ *and d uniquely determined 2d-ary Boolean functions* $f_1, f_2, \ldots, f_d$ *such that for each* $a, b, c \in Q$ *the operation* $a * b = c$ *is represented by*

$$*_{vv}(x_1, \ldots, x_d, y_1, \ldots, y_d) = \big(f_1(x_1, \ldots, x_d, y_1, \ldots, y_d), \ldots, f_d(x_1, \ldots, x_d, y_1, \ldots, y_d)\big). \tag{4}$$

Recall that each k-ary Boolean function $f(x_1, \ldots, x_k)$ can be represented in a unique way by its algebraic normal form (ANF), i.e., as a sum of products $\text{ANF}(f) = \alpha_0 + \sum_{i=1}^{k} \alpha_i x_i + \sum_{1 \le i < j \le k} \alpha_{i,j} x_i x_j + \sum_{1 \le i < j < s \le k} \alpha_{i,j,s} x_i x_j x_s + \ldots,$ where the coefficients $\alpha_0, \alpha_i, \alpha_{i,j}, \ldots$ are in the set $\{0, 1\}$ and the addition and multiplication are in the field $GF(2)$.

The ANFs of the functions f_i defined in Lemma 1 give us information about the complexity of the quasigroup $(Q, *)$ via the degrees of the Boolean functions f_i. In general, for a randomly generated quasigroup of order 2^d, $d \ge 4$, the degrees are higher than 2. Such quasigroups are not quadratic and thus are not suitable for our construction of multivariate quadratic PKC.

Definition 2. *A quasigroup* $(Q, *)$ *of order* 2^d *is called Multivariate Quadratic Quasigroup (MQQ) of type* $Quad_{d-k}Lin_k$ *if exactly* $d - k$ *of the polynomials* f_i *are of degree 2 (i.e., are quadratic) and* k *of them are of degree 1 (i.e., are linear), where* $0 \leq k < d$.

In [21,22] the authors give sufficient conditions a quasigroup to be a MQQ as well as an algorithm for finding MQQs up to the order of 2^5. That work was later extended in [10] for constructing MQQs of order 2^d for any d. The common characteristic of the MQQs produced by those two methods is that the quasigroups are bilinear. Namely, the equations (4) describing a multivariate quadratic quasigroup $(Q, *)$ can be expressed in the following form:

$$\mathbf{A_1} \cdot (y_1, \ldots, y_d)^T + \mathbf{b_1} \equiv \mathbf{A_2} \cdot (x_1, \ldots, x_d)^T + \mathbf{b_2} \tag{5}$$

where $\mathbf{A_1} = [f_{ij}]_{d \times d}$ is a $d \times d$ matrix and $\mathbf{b_1} = [u_i]_{d \times 1}$ is a $d \times 1$ vector of linear Boolean expressions of the variables $x_1, \ldots, x_d$, while $\mathbf{A_2} = [g_{ij}]_{d \times d}$ is a $d \times d$ matrix and $\mathbf{b_2} = [v_i]_{d \times 1}$ is a $d \times 1$ vector of linear Boolean expressions of the variables $y_1, \ldots, y_d$.

A Multivariate Quadratic Quasigroup (MQQ) $*$ of order 2^d used in MQQ-SIG can be described shortly by the following expression:

$$\mathbf{x} * \mathbf{y} = \mathbf{B} \cdot \mathbf{U}(\mathbf{x}) \cdot \mathbf{A_2} \cdot \mathbf{y} + \mathbf{B} \cdot \mathbf{A_1} \cdot \mathbf{x} + \mathbf{c} \tag{6}$$

where $\mathbf{x} = (x_1, \ldots, x_d)$, $\mathbf{y} = (y_1, \ldots, y_d)$, the matrices $\mathbf{A_1}$, $\mathbf{A_2}$ and $\mathbf{B}$ are nonsingular of size $d \times d$ in $GF(2)$, the vector $\mathbf{c}$ is a random d-dimensional vector with elements in $GF(2)$ and all of them are generated by a uniformly random process. The matrix $\mathbf{U}(\mathbf{x})$ is an upper triangular matrix with all diagonal elements equal to 1, and the elements above the main diagonal are linear expressions of the variables of $\mathbf{x} = (x_1, \ldots, x_d)$. It is computed by the following expression:

$$\mathbf{U}(\mathbf{x}) = I + \sum_{i=1}^{d-1} \mathbf{U}_i \cdot \mathbf{A_1} \cdot \mathbf{x}, \tag{7}$$

where the matrices $\mathbf{U}_i$ have all elements 0 except the elements in the rows from $\{1, \ldots, i\}$ that are strictly above the main diagonal. Those elements can be either 0 or 1 generated by a uniformly random process.

Additionally, we require the quasigroups to satisfy the following two conditions:

$$\forall i \in \{1, \ldots, d\}, Rank(\mathbf{B}_{f_i}) \geq 2d - 4, \tag{8a}$$

$$\exists j \in \{1, \ldots, d\}, Rank(\mathbf{B}_{f_j}) = 2d - 2 \tag{8b}$$

where the matrices $\mathbf{B}_{f_i}$ are $2d \times 2d$ Boolean matrices defined from the expressions f_i as

$$\mathbf{B}_{f_i} = [b_{j,k}], \ b_{j,d+k} = b_{d+k,j} = 1, \text{ iff } x_j y_k \text{ is a term in } f_i. \tag{9}$$

The reasons why we need the additional conditions (8a) and (8b) will be explained in the beginning of the Section 5.

Proposition 1. *For* $d = 8$, *a multivariate quadratic quasigroup that satisfies the conditions (6), ..., (9) can be encoded in a unique way with 81 bytes.* $\square$

3   Description of the MQQ-SIG Digital Signature Scheme

Our scheme can be expressed as a $(\frac{1}{2})$ truncation of a typical multivariate quadratic system:

$$\mathbf{S} \circ P' \circ \mathbf{S}' : \{0,1\}^n \to \{0,1\}^n,$$

where $\mathbf{S}' = \mathbf{S} \cdot \mathbf{x} + \mathbf{v}$ (i.e. $\mathbf{S}'$ is a bijective affine transformation), $\mathbf{S}$ is a nonsingular linear transformation, and $P' : \{0,1\}^n \to \{0,1\}^n$ is a central bijective multivariate quadratic mapping defined in Table 1. It is graphically presented in Fig. 1.

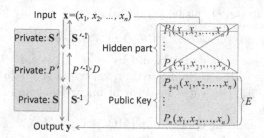

Fig. 1. A graphical presentation of our MQ "minus" scheme

The graphical presentation of the construction of the central mapping P' using the quasigroup operation $*$ is shown in Fig. 2, and its inverse P'^{-1} constructed with the parastrophe operations $\backslash$ and $/$ is shown in Fig. 3.

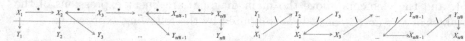

Fig. 2. A graphical presentation of the construction of the central bijective multivariate quadratic mapping P'

Fig. 3. A graphical presentation of the construction of the inverse central mapping P'^{-1} with parastrophe operations

The generation of the public and private key is defined in Table 2.

Let us denote by $D(\mathbf{y})$ the composition of inverse operations $\mathbf{S}^{-1}$, P'^{-1} and $\mathbf{S}'^{-1}$ on vector $\mathbf{y}$ i.e. $D(\mathbf{y}) \equiv \mathbf{S}^{-1}(P'^{-1}(\mathbf{S}'^{-1}(\mathbf{y})))$. Also, let us denote by $E(\mathbf{x})$ the mapping of a vector $\mathbf{x}$ with the public polynomials $P_i(x_1, \ldots, x_n)$ $i = 1 + \frac{n}{2}, \ldots, n$. Both signing and verification for MQQ-SIG are graphically presented on Fig. 4 while the algorithmic steps for the signing procedure are presented in details in Table 3, and the verification steps in Table 4.

4   Design Rationale

4.1   Nonsingular Boolean Matrices in MQQ-SIG

The nonsingular Boolean matrices that are used in MQQ-SIG are generated in a specific way. In general, we need n^2 bits to store a randomly generated

Table 1. Definition of the central bijective multivariate quadratic mapping P' : $\{0,1\}^n \to \{0,1\}^n$

The central Bijective multivariate quadratic mapping $P'(\mathbf{x})$
Input. A vector $\mathbf{x} = (f_1, \ldots, f_n)$ of n linear Boolean functions of n variables. We implicitly suppose that a multivariate quadratic quasigroup $*$ is previously defined, and that $n = 32 \times k$, with $k \in \{5, 6, 7, 8\}$ already fixed.
Output. 8 linear expressions $P_i'(x_1, \ldots, x_n), i = 1, \ldots, 8$ and $n - 8$ multivariate quadratic polynomials $P_i'(x_1, \ldots, x_n), i = 9, \ldots, n$
1. Represent a vector $\mathbf{x} = (f_1, \ldots, f_n)$ of n linear Boolean functions of n variables $x_1, \ldots, x_n$, as a string $\mathbf{x} = X_1 \ldots X_{\frac{n}{8}}$ where X_i are vectors of dimension 8;   2. Compute $\mathbf{y} = Y_1 \ldots Y_{\frac{n}{8}}$ where: $Y_1 = X_1$, $Y_{j+1} = X_j * X_{j+1}$, for even $j = 2, 4, \ldots$, and $Y_{j+1} = X_{j+1} * X_j$, for odd $j = 3, 5, \ldots$ 3. Output: $\mathbf{y}$.

Table 2. Generation of the public and the private key

Generation of the public and the private key for MQQ-SIG scheme.
Input. Integer n, where $n = 32 \times k$ and $k \in \{5, 6, 7, 8\}$.
Output. A public key $\mathbf{P}$ given by $\frac{n}{2}$ multivariate quadratic polynomials $P_i(x_1, \ldots, x_n)$, $i = 1 + \frac{n}{2}, \ldots, n$, and a private key given by two permutations σ_0^0 and σ_0^1 on $\{1, \ldots, n\}$, and 81 bytes for encoding a quasigroup $*$.
1. Generate an MQQ $*$ according to equations (6) ... (9).   2. Generate a nonsingular $n \times n$ Boolean matrix $\mathbf{S}$ and affine transformation $\mathbf{S}'$ according to equations (10), ..., (13).   3. Compute $\mathbf{y} = \mathbf{S}(P'(\mathbf{S}'(\mathbf{x})))$, where $\mathbf{x} = (x_1, \ldots, x_n)$.   4. Output: The public key is $\mathbf{y}$ as $\frac{n}{2}$ multivariate quadratic polynomials $P_i(x_1, \ldots, x_n)$ $i = 1 + \frac{n}{2}, \ldots, n$, and the private key is the tuple $(\sigma_0^0, \sigma_0^1, *)$.

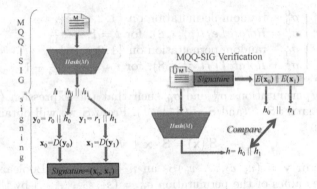

Fig. 4. A graphical presentation of the signing and verification process with MQQ-SIG

nonsingular Boolean matrix of size $n \times n$. In our case we need to store $\mathbf{S}^{-1}$ because we need it in the process of signing. With our proposed sizes for $n = 160, 192, 224, 256$, storing $\mathbf{S}^{-1}$ would require between 3.125 and 8.0 Kbytes.

The idea of reducing the size of the keys in MQ schemes by using circulant matrices has been applied previously in several works [51,46,40]. Instead of using one circulant matrix, we use two. The rationale why and how we construct the private linear (affine) transformations from them is given in what follows.

In order to compress the private information for the linear and affine transformations we define nonsingular matrices $\mathbf{S}$ by the following expression:

$$\mathbf{S}^{-1} = \bigoplus_{i=0}^{\frac{n}{16}} I_{\sigma_i^0} \oplus \bigoplus_{i=0}^{\frac{n}{16}+3} I_{\sigma_i^1}, \tag{10}$$

Table 3. Digital signing

Signing with a private key $(\sigma_0^0, \sigma_0^1, *)$
Input. A document M to be signed.
Output. A signature $\mathbf{sig} = (\mathbf{x}_0, \mathbf{x}_1)$.
1. Compute the pair $h = h_0 \| h_1 \leftarrow Hash(M)$, where $Hash()$ is the standardized hash function. Here we assume that the output of the hash function is n bits, and that h_0 and h_1 are $\frac{n}{2}$ bits long.
2. Set $\mathbf{y}_0 = r_0 \| h_0$ and $\mathbf{y}_1 = r_1 \| h_1$, where the values r_0 and r_1 are $\frac{n}{2}$-bit values chosen uniformly at random.
3. Compute $\mathbf{x}_0 = D(\mathbf{y}_0)$ and $\mathbf{x}_1 = D(\mathbf{y}_1)$.
4. The MQQ-SIG digital signature of the document M is the pair $\mathbf{sig} = (\mathbf{x}_0, \mathbf{x}_1)$.

Table 4. Digital verification

Signature verification with a public key $\mathbf{P} = \{P_i(x_1, \ldots, x_n) \mid i = 1 + \frac{n}{2}, \ldots, n\}$
Input. A document M and its signature $\mathbf{sig} = (\mathbf{x}_0, \mathbf{x}_1)$.
Output. TRUE or FALSE.
1. Compute $h = h_0 \| h_1 = Hash(M)$, where M is the signed message, and $Hash()$ is the standardized hash function.
2. Compute $\mathbf{z}_0 = E(\mathbf{x}_0)$ and $\mathbf{z}_1 = E(\mathbf{x}_1)$.
3. If $\mathbf{z}_0 = h_0$ and $\mathbf{z}_1 = h_1$ then return TRUE, else return FALSE.

where $I_{\sigma_i^0}, i = \{0, 1, 2, \ldots, \frac{n}{16}\}$ and $I_{\sigma_i^1}, i = \{0, 1, 2, \ldots, \frac{n}{16} + 1\}$ are permutation matrices of size n, the operation $\oplus$ is a "bitwise exclusive or" of the elements in the permutation matrices and permutations σ_i^0 and σ_i^1 are permutations on n elements. They are defined by the following expressions:

$$\begin{cases} \sigma_0^0 - \text{random permutation on } \{1, 2, \ldots n\}, \\ \sigma_i^0 = RotateLeft(\sigma_{i-1}^0, 8), \text{ for } i = 1, \ldots, \frac{n}{16}, \\ \sigma_0^1 - \text{random permutation on } \{1, 2, \ldots n\}, \\ \sigma_i^1 = RotateLeft(\sigma_{i-1}^1, 8), \text{ for } i = 1, \ldots, \frac{n}{16} + 1, \end{cases} \tag{11}$$

We chose the permutations σ_0^0 and σ_0^1 such that the expression (10) gives a non-singular matrix $\mathbf{S}^{-1}$ (and $\mathbf{S} = (\mathbf{S}^{-1})^{-1}$). From $\mathbf{S}$ we will obtain the affine transformation

$$\mathbf{S}'(\mathbf{x}) = \mathbf{S} \cdot \mathbf{x} + \mathbf{v}, \tag{12}$$

where the vector $\mathbf{v} = (v_1, v_2, \ldots, v_n)$ is an n–dimensional Boolean vector defined from the values of the permutation $\sigma_0^1 = (s_1, s_2, \ldots, s_n)$ by the following expression:

$$v_i = \left(\left(\frac{\left(\left(s_{1 + \lfloor \frac{i-1}{8} \rfloor} \right) \bmod 16 \right) \times 16}{2^{(8-i) \bmod 8}} \right) + \left(\frac{s_{65 + \lfloor \frac{i-1}{8} \rfloor}}{2^{(8-i) \bmod 8}} \right) \right) \bmod 2. \tag{13}$$

In words: we construct the bits of the vector $\mathbf{v}$ by constructing two arrays. The first array is constructed by taking the four least significant bits of the values $s_1, \ldots, s_{\frac{n}{8}}$ and each of them is shifted by four positions to the left. The second array is just simple extraction of the values $s_{65}, \ldots, s_{65 + \frac{n}{8}}$. Finally we XOR respectively those two arrays of values in order to produce the vector $\mathbf{v}$ of n bits. *Although the expression (13) looks complex, it is chosen specifically to be very fast in software and hardware.*

Proposition 2. *The linear transformation* $\mathbf{S}^{-1}$ *can be encoded in a unique way with $2n$ bytes.*   □

The reasons why we decided to use two permutations σ_0^0 and σ_0^1 in order to define the matrix $\mathbf{S}^{-1}$ as in (10) are due to the fact that the inverse matrix of any circulant matrix is again circulant [11]. Thus, if we would use a circulant matrix $\mathbf{S}^{-1}$, its inverse $\mathbf{S}$ that is used in the production of the public key would be also circulant. From a cryptographic point of view, we wanted to avoid the circular property of $\mathbf{S}$ since its strong regularity. This strong regularity might affect the randomness of the multivariate quadratic expressions in the public key. We have made a tradeoff between the totaly non-circulant matrix $\mathbf{S}$ generated completely by a uniformly distributed random process which will cost a lot in terms of space, and the regular circulant matrices, by using two circulant matrices that are combined as it is described in the expression (10). The obtained $\mathbf{S}$ from $\mathbf{S}^{-1}$ is without the circulant regularity, and still we can store it in just $2n$ bytes.

To illustrate our technique for producing non-circulant matrices $\mathbf{S}^{-1}$ and $\mathbf{S}$ we give the following baby example with $n = 16$ and where rotations to the left are performed by 2 positions.

Let $\sigma_0^0 = \left(\begin{smallmatrix} 0 & 1 & 2 & 3 & 4 & 5 & 6 & 7 & 8 & 9 & 10 & 11 & 12 & 13 & 14 & 15 \\ 0 & 6 & 2 & 5 & 15 & 8 & 11 & 12 & 1 & 9 & 14 & 3 & 10 & 7 & 4 & 13 \end{smallmatrix}\right)$ and $\sigma_0^1 = \left(\begin{smallmatrix} 0 & 1 & 2 & 3 & 4 & 5 & 6 & 7 & 8 & 9 & 10 & 11 & 12 & 13 & 14 & 15 \\ 12 & 5 & 14 & 2 & 6 & 7 & 9 & 0 & 10 & 11 & 8 & 4 & 1 & 15 & 13 & 3 \end{smallmatrix}\right)$.

Since this is a baby example, we have to adopt the expression (10) for this smaller value of n. The adopted expression is: $\mathbf{S}^{-1} = \bigoplus_{i=0}^{2} I_{\sigma_i^0} \oplus \bigoplus_{i=0}^{3} I_{\sigma_i^1}$ and we get

$$\mathbf{S}^{-1} = \begin{pmatrix} 1 & 0 & 1 & 0 & 0 & 0 & 1 & 0 & 0 & 1 & 0 & 0 & 1 & 0 & 1 & 1 \\ 1 & 0 & 1 & 0 & 0 & 0 & 1 & 1 & 1 & 0 & 0 & 0 & 0 & 0 & 0 & 0 \\ 0 & 0 & 1 & 0 & 0 & 0 & 1 & 0 & 0 & 1 & 1 & 1 & 0 & 0 & 1 & 1 \\ 1 & 0 & 1 & 0 & 0 & 1 & 0 & 1 & 1 & 0 & 0 & 1 & 0 & 0 & 0 & 0 \\ 0 & 1 & 0 & 0 & 0 & 0 & 1 & 0 & 1 & 1 & 1 & 1 & 0 & 0 & 0 & 1 \\ 1 & 0 & 0 & 0 & 1 & 0 & 0 & 1 & 1 & 1 & 0 & 1 & 1 & 0 & 0 & 0 \\ 0 & 0 & 0 & 0 & 0 & 0 & 0 & 1 & 1 & 1 & 1 & 0 & 0 & 1 & 0 \\ 1 & 0 & 0 & 1 & 1 & 0 & 0 & 0 & 0 & 1 & 0 & 1 & 1 & 0 & 0 & 1 \\ 0 & 0 & 0 & 0 & 0 & 0 & 0 & 1 & 0 & 0 & 0 & 1 & 1 & 0 \\ 0 & 0 & 0 & 0 & 1 & 0 & 0 & 1 & 0 & 1 & 0 & 1 & 0 & 0 & 0 & 1 \\ 0 & 1 & 0 & 0 & 1 & 0 & 0 & 0 & 1 & 0 & 1 & 0 & 1 & 1 & 1 & 0 \\ 0 & 0 & 0 & 0 & 1 & 1 & 0 & 1 & 0 & 0 & 0 & 0 & 0 & 1 & 0 & 1 \\ 1 & 1 & 0 & 0 & 1 & 0 & 0 & 0 & 0 & 1 & 0 & 1 & 1 & 1 & 0 \\ 0 & 0 & 1 & 1 & 0 & 1 & 1 & 1 & 0 & 0 & 0 & 0 & 0 & 1 & 0 & 1 \\ 1 & 0 & 1 & 0 & 1 & 0 & 1 & 0 & 0 & 0 & 0 & 0 & 1 & 1 & 1 & 0 \\ 0 & 0 & 1 & 1 & 0 & 0 & 1 & 1 & 0 & 0 & 0 & 0 & 0 & 1 & 0 & 0 \end{pmatrix} \quad \text{and} \quad \mathbf{S} = \begin{pmatrix} 1 & 0 & 0 & 1 & 1 & 1 & 0 & 0 & 0 & 1 & 1 & 1 & 0 & 0 & 0 & 0 \\ 1 & 0 & 1 & 1 & 1 & 1 & 0 & 0 & 1 & 0 & 0 & 0 & 0 & 1 & 1 & 1 \\ 1 & 0 & 1 & 1 & 0 & 0 & 1 & 1 & 0 & 0 & 0 & 0 & 1 & 1 & 0 \\ 0 & 1 & 1 & 0 & 0 & 1 & 1 & 1 & 0 & 0 & 1 & 0 & 1 & 0 & 0 & 0 \\ 1 & 0 & 1 & 1 & 1 & 0 & 1 & 0 & 1 & 0 & 0 & 1 & 1 & 0 & 1 & 0 \\ 0 & 1 & 1 & 0 & 0 & 0 & 1 & 1 & 1 & 1 & 1 & 1 & 0 & 1 & 1 \\ 0 & 1 & 1 & 0 & 1 & 1 & 1 & 0 & 1 & 0 & 1 & 0 & 0 & 0 & 0 \\ 1 & 0 & 0 & 1 & 1 & 1 & 0 & 1 & 1 & 0 & 0 & 0 & 1 & 1 & 0 \\ 1 & 0 & 0 & 1 & 1 & 1 & 0 & 0 & 0 & 1 & 0 & 1 & 1 & 0 & 0 & 0 \\ 0 & 1 & 1 & 1 & 1 & 1 & 1 & 0 & 0 & 1 & 1 & 0 & 0 & 1 & 1 & 1 \\ 0 & 1 & 1 & 0 & 0 & 0 & 0 & 1 & 0 & 0 & 1 & 0 & 1 & 0 & 1 & 1 \\ 0 & 0 & 1 & 1 & 1 & 0 & 1 & 0 & 1 & 1 & 0 & 0 & 1 & 1 & 0 & 1 \\ 0 & 1 & 1 & 0 & 0 & 1 & 1 & 1 & 1 & 0 & 0 & 1 & 0 & 1 & 1 & 0 \\ 0 & 0 & 1 & 0 & 0 & 1 & 1 & 1 & 0 & 0 & 0 & 0 & 0 & 0 & 0 \\ 1 & 0 & 1 & 1 & 0 & 1 & 1 & 1 & 0 & 1 & 1 & 0 & 0 & 1 \\ 0 & 1 & 1 & 0 & 0 & 0 & 1 & 1 & 1 & 1 & 1 & 1 & 1 & 1 & 0 \end{pmatrix}.$$

Note that $\mathbf{S}$ is not a circulant matrix.

4.2   Choosing the Order and Characteristics of Quasigroups

In the original MQQ proposal [21,22], the authors used several different multi-variate quasigroups of order 2^5. That design decision was mainly done because the authors did not know how to construct MQ quasigroups of bigger order.

In the meantime, Chen et al., in [10] and Samardjiska et al., in [42] have found ways how to construct MQQs of arbitrary order 2^d. Thus, we have decided to use quasigroups of order 2^8. That decision was made in order to match the byte size of 8 bits. This enables efficient implementations of MQQ-SIG even on tiny industrial 8-bit MCUs, as well as on high end systems (PCs or workstations). The left and right parastrophes can be pre-computed each taking 64KBytes. These pre-computed parastrophes can speedup the signing phase at least 10 times, but using pre-computed parastrophes of size 2^d where $d > 8$ simply becomes too costly.

Without going into details of the different characteristics of MQQs produced by methods described in [10] and [42] we can say that for encoding MQQs as described in [42] we need 256 bytes, while for MQQs from [10] we need just 81 bytes (see Proposition 1). This is due to the fact that MQQs in [10] have bi-linear nature, while MQQs constructed in [42] are based on T-functions and generally are not bi-linear.

We have performed experiments with both types of MQQs and after removing $\frac{n}{2}$ MQQ's expressions from the public key, we have not observed any security consequences of using the bi-linear MQQs from [10]. That fact combined with the fact that the knowledge of MQQ is a part of the private key, and that the encoding of MQQs from [10] needs just 81 bytes (versus 256 bytes for MQQs from [42]), was the decisive argument in favor of MQQs defined in [10].

In our design we use affine transformation S' instead of the linear one S, and we also use a non-zero vector c in the quasigroup construction. The reasons for this is that without S' our scheme would have the zeroth vector as a fixed point and the same is true for a quasigroup that has $c = 0$. We consider that these properties are unnecessary and easily avoidable weaknesses.

5   Security Analysis of the Algorithm

In this section we will describe all the security analysis we have performed during the design of MQQ-SIG. First we want to emphasize that MQQ-SIG similarly as the original MQQ is still resistant against the well know attacks such as: Patarin's chosen plaintext attack on MIA scheme [37], the attacks with differential cryptanalysis that were proposed by Fouque, Granboulan and Stern in [19], solving the isomorphism of polynomials with one secret done by Perret and others in [38,18,9] and MinRank attacks. For the resistance against MinRank attacks we want to note that the minimal rank r of the matrices $\mathbf{B}_{f_i}$ for the nonlinear part of our scheme have to fulfil the conditions (8a, 8b), thus at least one of the ranks is 14 and all of the ranks are at least 12. Additionally, it is not known how to extend the MinRank attack to our scheme, since some equations of the public-key have been removed. In [8], it has been proved that the attack can be extended when 1 equation is removed in HFE. However, the attack can not be applied in our context when $\frac{n}{2}$ equations are removed.

We suggest the reader to see [21,22] for the arguments why MQQ-SIG is resistant against these attacks.

5.1   Experiments with Gröbner Bases

The public key encryption algorithm MQQ introduced in [21,22] was quickly shown to be weak against algebraic cryptanalysis. It was broken both by Perret [39] using Gröbner basis approach, and by Emam Mohamed et al [35] using MutantXL. Later Faugère et al [17] explained why the MQQ systems are so easy to solve in practice. To understand their results we must first introduce to concept of degree of regularity.

As explained in [17], the complexity of computing a Gröbner basis of an ideal depends on the maximum degree of the polynomials appearing during the computation. This degree, called *degree of regularity*, is the key parameter for understanding the complexity of a Gröbner basis computation [3]. Indeed, the complexity of the computation is polynomial in the degree of regularity D_{reg}, more precisely the complexity is:

$$\mathcal{O}(n^{\omega D_{reg}}), \tag{14}$$

which basically correspond to the complexity of reducing a matrix of size $\approx n^{D_{reg}}$. Here $2 < \omega \leq 3$ is the "linear algebra constant", and n the number of variables of the system. Note that D_{reg} is a function of n and also of the number of equations m. The relation between D_{reg}, n and m depends on the specific system of equations. This relation is well understood for regular (and semi-regular) systems of equations [1,2,3,4]. However, as soon as the system has some kind of structure, this degree is much more difficult to predict.

In [17], the authors showed that the degree of regularity of the original public key algorithm MQQ was bounded from above by a small constant. Having in mind the successful and very efficient way how Gröbner bases and XL methods are solving the full systems of MQQ equations, we want to ensure that MQQ-SIG does not have a similar small bound on the degree of regularity. A classical way to avoid this is to remove some equations of the system. Indeed, an under-defined system of equations ($n > m$) will have an exponential number of solutions. This is an issue since the complexity of Gröbner bases is also related to the number of solutions [15]. To circumvent this problem, a solution is to fix $n - m$ variables (or more [7]). However, as soon as sufficiently many variables were fixed, we observed that the new system behaved as a "random" system of equations of the same size. This has been also observed and used in the hybrid approach [7].

To confirm this behavior in our context, we have performed experiments on MQQ-SIG equations systems of reduced sizes. The observed degree of regularity is compared to the expected degree of regularity for a random multivariate system of the same size. The strategy for choosing S has changed during the course of our experiments. The experiments where performed with random Boolean matrices. However, from a security against Gröbner bases attack point of view, the most important feature is that we ensure that the 8 linear expressions are removed from the equations set. Below is our experimental strategy for small-scale version of MQQ-SIG equation systems in n variables:

1. Repeat:
2. Generate a bijective multivariate quadratic mapping $P_i'(x_1, \ldots, x_n), i = 1, \ldots, n$
3. Remove the 8 linear expressions $P_i'(x_1, \ldots, x_n), i = 1, \ldots, 8$
4. Multiply with random nonsingular Boolean matrices S_R and T_R, $\mathbf{P} = \mathbf{S_R} \circ P' \circ \mathbf{T_R}$.
5. For $j = 8$ to $j = \frac{n}{2}$ do:
   (a) Remove the last $8 - j$ equations from $\mathbf{P}$.
   (b) Set a random Boolean vector $(x_{n-j+1}, \ldots, x_n) \in \{0, 1\}^j$
   (c) Obtain a system $\mathbf{P_1} = \{P_i(x_1, \ldots, x_{n-j}) \mid i = 1, \ldots, n - j\}$ of $n - j$ equations with $n - j$ variables $(x_1, \ldots, x_{n-j})$
   (d) Call $F_4(\mathbf{P_1})$ algorithm from Magma, to find a Gröbner basis for the system $\mathbf{P_1}$, and measure the degree of regularity.
6. Compute the average degree of regularity.

Table 5. The average degree of regularity for a MQQ signature system in V variables with R equations removed. In parentheses, the expected degree of regularity for a random system of size $V - R$.

R/V	16	24	32	40	48	56	64
8	**3,00(3)**	3,33 (5)	3,75 (6)	4,15 (6)	4,30 (7)	5 (8)	6 (9)
9		3,09 (4)	3,97 (5)	4,05 (6)	4,10 (7)	4 (8)	4 (9)
10		3,74 (4)	4,00 (5)	4,04 (6)	4,30 (7)	4 (8)	5 (9)
11		3,87 (4)	4,01 (5)	4,56 (6)	4,90 (7)	5 (8)	5 (9)
12		**3,93(4)**	4,06 (5)	5,00 (6)	5,00 (7)	5 (8)	5 (9)
13			4,33 (5)	5,00 (6)	5,00 (7)	5 (8)	· (9)
14			4,48 (5)	5,00 (6)	5,50 (7)	6 (8)	· (9)
15			4,46 (5)	5,00 (6)	5,60 (7)	6 (8)	· (8)
16			**4,21(5)**	5,00 (6)	5,60 (6)	6 (7)	· (8)
17				5,00 (5)	5,90 (6)	· (7)	· (8)
18				5,00 (5)	5,90 (6)	· (7)	· (8)
19				5,00 (5)	6,00 (6)	· (7)	· (8)
20				**5,00(5)**	6,00 (6)	· (7)	· (8)
21					6,00 (6)	· (7)	· (8)
22					6,00 (6)	· (7)	· (8)
23					6,00 (6)	· (7)	· (8)
24					**6,00(6)**	6 (6)	· (7)
25						6 (6)	· (7)
26						6 (6)	· (7)
27						6 (6)	· (7)
28						**6(6)**	· (7)
29							· (7)
30							· (7)
31							· (7)
32							**6(6)**

We have performed 100 experiments for $16, 24, 32$ and 40 variables. Due to the complexity, the experiments have only been repeated 10 times for 48 variables and just once for 56 and 64 variables. For 56 and 64 variables many of the instances either required more than the 1TB RAM our system has, or did not finish after about 1 month of computation. These instances are marked with a · in the table. We also experienced that 72 variables with 36 equations removed did not finish after about a month of computation. The experiments were done with Magma 2.17-3's implementation [30] of the F_4[16] algorithm on a workstation with 32 cores based on Intel Xeon 2.27GHz, with 1TB of RAM memory. The results of these experiments are listed in Table 5. In the table the expected degree of regularity for a random system of equations over $GF(2)$ in $V - R$ variables are also listed in parentheses. These numbers have been calculated using the formula provided in [2]. From the table we see that the bigger percentage of equations we remove from the system, the closer the measured degree of regularity is to a random system of equations. The reason for this is that we are removing crucial relations among terms, thus rendering the remaining sets of equations as random sets of multivariate equations. It is then natural to formulate the following conjecture:

Conjecture 1. For every full set of public key equations produced by MQQ as defined in steps 1–3 in Table 2, removing $\frac{n}{2}$ of the equations, makes the remaining set of $\frac{n}{2}$ multivariate quadratic equations to act as a set of $\frac{n}{2}$ random multivariate quadratic equations with $\frac{n}{2}$ variables in $GF(2)$.

5.2   The Size of the Pool of MQQs of Order 2^8

It is very important to address the question of the size of the set of MQQs of order 2^8 that we use in our MQQ-SIG scheme. In [10], Chen et al., gave a lower bound on the number of MQQs of order 2^8. That number is projected to 2^{273}. However, we are using additional conditions (8). By a heuristical measuring we have obtained that approximately one in 2^7 randomly generated MQQs of order 2^8 complies with the conditions (8). That means that the lower bound of the size of the pool of MQQs of order 2^8 is 2^{266}.

5.3   Secret Key Leakage Scenarios

Originally this attack was presented to us by an anonymous reviewer of an earlier variant of our scheme submitted to WCC 2011. We would like to express *big acknowledgement* to that anonymous reviewer.

In a previous version of our scheme instead of $\mathbf{y} = r_0 || h_0$, the value $\mathbf{y} = h$ obtained as the output of the hashing procedure is n bits long, and the signature part is $\mathbf{x} = D(\mathbf{y})$. The following Chosen Message Attack could then be launched. An attacker asks for signatures of $1 + n + \binom{n}{2} + O(1)$ messages i.e. he will have the triplets $(M_i, \mathbf{x}_i, \mathbf{y}_i \equiv Hash(M_i))$. He will then attempt to recover the missing $\frac{n}{2}$ equations in the public key. Given the missing equations he can successfully launch an efficient Gröbner bases attack.

Consider the extraction of the first missing equation $y_1 = P_1(x_1, \ldots, x_n)$, which can be expressed in a general form as:

$$y_1 = d_0 + d_1 x_1 + d_2 x_2 + \ldots + d_n x_n + d_{n+1} x_1 x_2 + \ldots + d_{2n+1} x_2 x_3 + \ldots + d_{1+n+\binom{n}{2}} x_{n-1} x_n.$$

$$(15)$$

Since the attacker knows the values of $1 + n + \binom{n}{2} + O(1)$ triplets $(M_i, \mathbf{x}_i, \mathbf{y}_i)$, from the equation (15), with high probability, he can obtain a full rank linear system of equations with $1 + n + \binom{n}{2}$ unknown variables d_j. Additionally and most importantly he knows the corresponding values $y_1^{(i)}$ for every of the values $\mathbf{y}_i = (y_1^{(i)}, \ldots, y_n^{(i)})$. Thus, by solving the obtained linear system of equations he can recover the values of the coefficients d_j i.e. he can recover the first missing equation. The extraction of other hidden equations is similar.

This attack is easily mitigated by our strategy to construct the values $\mathbf{y}_0 = r_0 || h_0$ and $\mathbf{y}_1 = r_1 || h_1$ where r_0 and r_1 are strings of $\frac{n}{2}$ randomly generated bits with every signing invocation, and $h = h_0 || h_1$ is the hash output that is digesting the message M.

We formulate the previous discussion about the leakage of the private key in the non-randomized MQQ-SIG and its prevention by the following two lemmas:

Lemma 2. *For any MQQ signature scheme with K expressions removed, if the signatures for the messages M are obtained as $\mathbf{x} = D(\mathbf{y})$, where $\mathbf{y} = Hash(M)$, the extraction of the removed part has complexity of $O(Kn^2)$.* $\square$

Lemma 3. *For the MQQ-SIG signature scheme as defined in steps 1–3 in Table 2, by removing $\frac{n}{2}$ of the expressions, an attack for extraction of the removed part as in Lemma 2 has complexity of $O(2^{n^3})$.*

Proof. Since the signature for a message M has two parts $\mathbf{x}_0$ and $\mathbf{x}_1$ that are computed as $\mathbf{x}_0 = D(r_0||h_0)$ and $\mathbf{x}_1 = D(r_1||h_1)$ where $h = h_0||h_1 = Hash(M)$, and the values r_0 and r_1 are $\frac{n}{2}$-bit values chosen uniformly at random for every particular procedure of signing, the extraction technique from Lemma 2 can give the correct extraction of the hidden part if and only if for all $O(n^2)$ queries, the random values r_0 and r_1 are known to the attacker. Having in mind that for every produced signature the values r_0 and r_1 are unknown, fresh, uniformly distributed random values, the probability of guessing their values is $2^{-\frac{n}{2}} \times 2^{-\frac{n}{2}} = 2^{-n}$. For all $O(n^2)$ queries this gives us a total probability of $(2^{-n})^{n^2} = 2^{-n^3}$, i.e. the complexity for extracting the hidden part is $O(2^{n^3})$.   □

5.4   MQQ-SIG Is Provably CMA Resistant

We will use the following definition of security against chosen message attack [27]:

Definition 3. *Signature scheme (Gen, Sign, Vrfy) is **existentially unforgeable under a chosen-message attack** if for all probabilistic, polynomial-time adversaries A, the success probability of A in the following experiment is negligible (as a function of k):*

1. *The key-generation algorithm $Gen(1^k)$ is run to obtain a pair of keys (pk, sk)*
2. *A is given pk and allowed to interact with a signing oracle $Sign_{sk}(\cdot)$, requesting signatures on as many messages as it likes. Let M denote the set of messages queried to the signing oracle by A.*
3. *Eventually, A outputs (m, σ)*
4. *A **succeeds** if $Vrfy_{pk}(m, \sigma) = 1$ and $m \notin M$*

It is well known that solving multivariate quadratic polynomials is an NP-complete problem (see for instance [20]). This theorem is repeated below.

Theorem 1 ([20]). *Let $P_i(x_1, \ldots, x_n), 1 \leq i \leq m$ be a collection of polynomials over $GF[2]$. The problem of finding $u_1, \ldots, u_n$ such that $P_i(u_1, \ldots, u_n) = 0$ for $1 \leq i \leq m$ remains NP-complete even if none of the polynomials has a term involving more than two variables or if there is just one polynomial.*

Theorem 2. *MQQ-SIG is CMA resistant in the random oracle model under the assumptions that solving $\frac{n}{2}$ MQQ equations with n variables is as hard as solving systems of $\frac{n}{2}$ random multivariate quadratic equations.*

In what follows we give a sketch of the proof and the ideas how to use the fact that the verification of the MQQ-SIG signatures depends on the values h_0 and h_1 that are each $\frac{n}{2}$ bits long. This fact implies that a chosen message attack on MQQ-SIG would need either at least $2^{\frac{n}{2}}$ pairs of messages in order to find a collision of the used hash function or to solve the system of $\frac{n}{2}$ random multivariate quadratic equations with n variables. A formal proof showing the strict reduction from the CMA-resistance of the scheme to the assumption that solving $\frac{n}{2}$ MQQ equations with n variables is as hard as solving systems of $\frac{n}{2}$ random multivariate quadratic equations with n variables will be given in the extended version of this paper.

Proof. (sketch) The security parameter input to the generating algorithm is $k = \frac{n}{2}$, which controls the number of equations over $GF(2)$ and is directly connected with the value n: the output size of the hash function.

Given the assumption that solving $\frac{n}{2}$ MQQ equations with n variables is as hard as solving systems of $\frac{n}{2}$ random multivariate quadratic equations, there are no structural weaknesses of the MQQ equations that can be exploited to solve the system faster then solving $\frac{n}{2}$ random multivariate quadratic equations. This means the adversary has basically three strategies of breaking MQQ-SIG:

1. To find a collision in the hash digest $(h_0||h_1)$ of length $n = 2k$.
2. To solve two systems of $\frac{n}{2}$ MQ equations with n Boolean variables.
3. Some combination of the two above.

Strategy 1: Breaking with the strategy 1 means finding a collision for a random oracle with a $n = 2k$ bit output. Interacting with the signing oracle will not help the adversary for this instance, since he is only interested in the output of the random oracle. By the generic birthday attack the adversary needs $O(2^k)$ queries to the random oracle to find a collision for the whole digest. The probability for a polynomial time adversary to break the signature scheme by finding a collision in the digest is therefore negligible in k.

Strategy 2: Under the assumption that solving the $\frac{n}{2}$ MQQ equations in n variables is as hard as solving k MQ equations in k variables, we know by Theorem 1 that the probability the adversary solves either of the equations with the strategy 2 is negligible in k. However, to prove that the signature scheme is CMA, we must also show that querying the signing oracle gives the adversary no significant advantage in solving the equations. There are two ways the signing oracle might leak information.

(a) Signing leaks information about the hidden equations:
    In Lemma 3 we proved that extracting information about the removed part has complexity $O(2^{n^3})$. With our security parameter of $k = \frac{n}{2}$ this is out of reach for a polynomially bound adversary.
(b) Signing leaks some other information that can help solve the equation system:
    Consider the following game where the adversary does not have access to the random oracle. The adversary asks for a signature for a chosen message M. The signing oracle then flips a coin.
    I If the coin land on heads the signing oracle outputs the digest $H(M) = (h_0||h_1)$, and the corresponding signature (x_0, x_1).

II If the coin lands on tails the signing oracle outputs the evaluation of the encryption function in some random numbers $(E(r_0), E(r_1))$, and the corresponding random numbers (r_0, r_1).

The adversary is then asked if the coin is heads or tails.

Since by the definition of random oracles the output of $H(M)$ is independent of M, it should be clear that the adversary has no way of winning the game above. This illustrates that from the adversary point of view, there is no difference between querying the signing oracle and evaluating the known equations on random inputs. The fact that the adversary actually has access to the random oracle does not change this conclusion because the adversary has no control over the output of the random oracle.

To summarize this means that signing reveals no information about the hidden equations, and leaks no other information that can be used to solve the equations. The signature scheme is therefore CMA with respect to the strategy number 2.

Strategy 3: First note that finding a $k - l$, $1 \leq l \leq k$, bit collision in, for instance h_0, will not help computing the corresponding $\mathbf{x}_0$. The reason for this is the nature of the random MQ equations, where the solution to the system will drastically change by just flipping one output bit. Namely, each output bit depends on average on $\frac{k(k-1)}{2}$ combination of all pairs of variables. This means that the best for the adversary in strategy attack number 3 is to find a collision in either h_0 or h_1, and to solve the equation system for the part that a solution is not known. This requires "just" $O(2^{\frac{k}{2}-1})$ calls to the random oracle. However, the adversary still needs to solve a system of k equations in $2k$ variables, proven to be CMA resistant by the arguments under the attack strategy number 2. $\square$

5.5   Non-applicability of Successful Attacks against STS on MQQ-SIG

An anonymous reviewer for IMACC 2011 (to whom we express *big acknowledgement*) has pointed out an interesting comment that MQQ-SIG scheme looks similar as STS schemes and thus the successful attacks that have broken STS schemes may also break MQQ-SIG. Here we explain the crucial and essential differences between STS and MQQ-SIG schemes and the non-applicability of successful attacks against STS on MQQ-SIG.

The Stepwise Triangular Scheme was introduced by Wolf et al., [48] as a generalization of earlier multivariate quadratic schemes, such as [45,34,24,26]. The main purpose of the generalization in [48] was to show how all these schemes, and the whole STS family in general, is either insecure or impractical. The general attacks presented exploit the chain of kernels introduced by the triangular structure of the hidden polynomials.

There are at least two important reasons why this attack is not applicable on MQQ-SIG. First, even tough the kernel of two adjacent sub-blocks share half of each others variables, the triangular structure of the hidden polynomials does not result in a chain of kernels. The production of the public key in MQQ-SIG is essentially parallel and chained for the whole n-dimensional space, while the production of the public key in STS is essentially sequential with increasingly larger embedded subspaces. It is this structure that the attacks on STS exploit.

The second reason is that the attacks linearly combine the public key expressions in order to get ranks within certain values. Non-applicability of these attacks against MQQ-SIG is due to the fact that half of the public key expressions are removed, and linearly combining the remaining half in order to obtain low ranks does not necessarily produce vectors from the kernel of the transformation T^{-1}.

6   Operating Characteristics

In this section we discuss the sizes of the private and public key as well as the number of operations for verification and signing.

Table 6. Comparison between RSA, ECDSA, and several MQ schemes: MQQ-SIG, Rainbow, TTS and 3ICP. Operations have been performed in 64-bit mode of operation on Intel Core i7 920X machine running at 2 GHz.

Security level (power of 2)	Algorithm	KeyGen	Sign 59 bytes (CPU cycles)	Verify (CPU cycles)	Private key size (bytes)	Public key size (bytes)	Signature size (bytes)
80	RSA1024	102,869,553	2,213,112	60,084	1024	128	128
	ECDSA160	1,201,188	944,364	1,083,060	60	40	40
	MQQSIG160	799,501,482	6,534	92,232	401	137,408	40
	RainbowBinary256181212	30,311,648	38,784	43,800	23,408	30,240	42
96	RSA1536	322,324,721	5,452,076	87,516	1536	192	192
	ECDSA192	1,799,284	1,390,560	1,662,664	72	48	48
	MQQSIG192	800,724,006	7,038	138,072	405	222,300	48
112	RSA2048	786,466,598	11,020,696	125,776	2048	256	256
	ECDSA224	2,022,896	1,555,740	1,821,348	84	56	56
	MQQSIG224	1,107,486,126	9,492	184,392	529	352,828	56
128	RSA3072	2,719,353,538	31,941,760	230,536	3072	384	384
	ECDSA256	2,296,976	1,780,524	2,085,588	96	64	64
	MQQSIG256	1,501,955,022	9,138	218,700	593	526,368	64
	TTS6440	60,827,704	84,892	76,224	16,608	57,600	43
	3ICP	15,520,100	1,641,032	60,856	12,768	35,712	36

6.1   The Size of the Public and the Private Key

Since the public key consists of $\frac{n}{2}$ randomly generated multivariate quadratic equations, the size of the public key follows the rules given in [49]. So, for n bit blocks the size of the public key is $0.5 \times n \times (1 + \frac{n(n+1)}{2})$ bits. The private key of our scheme is the tuple $(\sigma_0^0, \sigma_0^1, *)$. The corresponding memory size needed for storage of the private key is $2n + 81$ bytes.

In Table 6, there are two columns for the size of the private and public key and as we can see for MQQ-SIG the size of the public key for $n \in \{160, 192, 224, 256\}$ is in the range from 125 up to 521 KBytes.

We want to emphasize that recently Samardjiska and Chen in [43] have proposed extension of their algorithms for construction of MQQs over arbitrary finite fields and that by their construction it is possible to reduce the huge public key size of MQQ-SIG to be in the range 2.3 – 8.8 Kbytes.

6.2   Performance of the Software Implementation of the MQQ-SIG Algorithm

We have implemented MQQ-SIG in C for the SUPERCOP benchmarking system [6] and tested it together with the corresponding RSA [41] and ECC [32,29] (actually ECDSA) and several other multivariate quadratic systems such as: Rainbow [14], enhanced TTS [50] and 3ICP [13]. In Table 6 we give the comparison of the mentioned signatures schemes where the measurements were performed in 64-bit mode of operation on Intel Core i7 920X machine running at 2 GHz. Although, our C code is not yet optimized for the key generation part, we expect that the performance of key generation part to be the most time consuming part of our algorithm.

From the Table 6 it is clear that in signing of 59 bytes MQQ-SIG is faster than RSA in the range from 300 up to 3500 times, and is faster than ECDSA in the range from 140 up to 200 times. If we exclude the time for hashing the messages, signing operations in MQQ-SIG in Table 6 take from 2,500 up to 5,000 cycles. MQQ-SIG is also significantly faster than other multivariate methods such as Rainbow, TTS or 3ICP and that performance advantage in the signing procedure is in the range from 5 to 20 times.

The verification speed in our code is not optimized so far. We expect the optimized verification speed of MQQ-SIG to be in the range of Rainbow, TTS and 3ICP.

7   Conclusions

We have constructed a multivariate quadratic digital signature scheme MQQ-SIG based on multivariate quadratic quasigroups.

By learning about the weaknesses of the previous attempt to design a multivariate quadratic scheme based on quasigroups - MQQ, by analyzing the successful attacks on all existing MQ schemas, and by our experimentally supported assumption that solving $\frac{n}{2}$ quadratic polynomials with n variables is as hard as solving random systems of equations, we have designed a digital signature scheme that in the random oracle model is provably CMA resistant and that we believe is strong enough to attract the attention of the cryptographic community.

The efficiency of producing digital signatures of our scheme outperforms all the existing signature schemes (RSA, ECDSA and other MQ schemes) in the range from 5 up to 3,500 times. The speed of verification of our scheme is similar to the other MQ schemes. However the MQQ-SIG scheme that was described in this paper has an unpractically big public key. The ongoing research efforts are in this direction and soon we can expect MQQ-SIG variants with significantly smaller public keys.

We believe that its superior performance will allow an employment of strong and fast authentication protocols based on the paradigm of the public key cryptography in many new areas of our modern society.

Acknowledgements. We would like to thank anonymous reviewers of the IN-TRUST 2011 conference for their useful comments that improved the text of the paper. The work described in this paper has been supported by the Commission of the European Communities through the ICT program under contract ICT-2007-216676 (ECRYPT-II). J.-C. Faugère and L. Perret are also supported by the French ANR under the Computer Algebra and Cryptography (CAC) project (ANR-09-JCJCJ-0064-01).

References

1. Bardet, M.: Étude des systèmes algébriques surdéterminés. Applications aux codes correcteurs et à la cryptographie. PhD thesis, Université de Paris VI (2004)
2. Bardet, M., Faugère, J.-C., Salvy, B.: Complexity study of Gröbner basis computation. Technical report, INRIA (2002), http://www.inria.fr/rrrt/rr-5049.html
3. Bardet, M., Faugère, J.-C., Salvy, B.: On the complexity of Gröbner basis computation of semi-regular overdetermined algebraic equations. In: Proc. International Conference on Polynomial System Solving (ICPSS), pp. 71–75 (2004)
4. Bardet, M., Faugère, J.-C., Salvy, B., Yang, B.-Y.: Asymptotic behaviour of the degree of regularity of semi-regular polynomial systems. In: Proc. of MEGA 2005, Eighth International Symposium on Effective Methods in Algebraic Geometry (2005)
5. Belousov, V.D.: Osnovi teorii kvazigrup i lup, Nauka, Moscow (1967) (in russian)
6. Bernstein, D.J., Lange, T. (eds.): eBACS: ECRYPT benchmarking of cryptographic systems (accessed January 12, 2011)
7. Bettale, L., Faugère, J.-C., Perret, L.: Hybrid approach for solving multivariate systems over finite fields. Journal of Mathematical Cryptology 3(3), 177–197 (2009)
8. Bettale, L., Faugère, J.-C., Perret, L.: Cryptanalysis of Multivariate and Odd-Characteristic HFE Variants. In: Catalano, D., Fazio, N., Gennaro, R., Nicolosi, A. (eds.) PKC 2011. LNCS, vol. 6571, pp. 441–458. Springer, Heidelberg (2011)
9. Bouillaguet, C., Faugère, J.-C., Fouque, P.-A., Perret, L.: Practical Cryptanalysis of the Identification Scheme Based on the Isomorphism of Polynomial with One Secret Problem. In: Catalano, D., Fazio, N., Gennaro, R., Nicolosi, A. (eds.) PKC 2011. LNCS, vol. 6571, pp. 473–493. Springer, Heidelberg (2011)
10. Chen, Y., Knapskog, S.J., Gligoroski, D.: Multivariate quadratic quasigroups (MQQs): Construction, bounds and complexity. In: Inscrypt, 6th International Conference on Information Security and Cryptology. Science Press of China (October 2010)
11. Davis, P.J.: CirculantMatrices. AMS Chelsea Publishing (1994)
12. Denes, J., Keedwell, A.D.: Latin squares and their applications. Academic Press, New York (1974)
13. Ding, J., Wolf, C., Yang, B.-Y.: -Invertible Cycles for Ultivariate Uadratic (q) Public Key Cryptography. In: Okamoto, T., Wang, X. (eds.) PKC 2007. LNCS, vol. 4450, pp. 266–281. Springer, Heidelberg (2007)

14. Ding, J., Yang, B.-Y., Chen, C.-H.O., Chen, M.-S., Cheng, C.-M.: New Differential-Algebraic Attacks and Reparametrization of Rainbow. In: Bellovin, S.M., Gennaro, R., Keromytis, A.D., Yung, M. (eds.) ACNS 2008. LNCS, vol. 5037, pp. 242–257. Springer, Heidelberg (2008)
15. Faugère, J.C., Gianni, P., Lazard, D., Mora, T.: Efficient computation of zero-dimensional Gröbner bases by change of ordering. J. Symb. Comput. 16, 329–344 (1993)
16. Faugere, J.-C.: A new efficient algorithm for computing Gröbner basis, F4 (2000), http://citeseer.ist.psu.edu/faugere00new.html
17. Faugère, J.-C., Ødegård, R.S., Perret, L., Gligoroski, D.: Analysis of the MQQ Public Key Cryptosystem. In: Heng, S.-H., Wright, R.N., Goi, B.-M. (eds.) CANS 2010. LNCS, vol. 6467, pp. 169–183. Springer, Heidelberg (2010)
18. Faugère, J.-C., Perret, L.: Polynomial Equivalence Problems: Algorithmic and Theoretical Aspects. In: Vaudenay, S. (ed.) EUROCRYPT 2006. LNCS, vol. 4004, pp. 30–47. Springer, Heidelberg (2006)
19. Fouque, P.-A., Granboulan, L., Stern, J.: Differential Cryptanalysis for Multivariate Schemes. In: Cramer, R. (ed.) EUROCRYPT 2005. LNCS, vol. 3494, pp. 341–353. Springer, Heidelberg (2005)
20. Garey, M.R., Johnson, D.S.: Computers and Intractability. A guide to the theory of NP-Completeness. Bell Telephone Laboratories, Incoperated (1979)
21. Gligoroski, D., Markovski, S., Knapskog, S.J.: Public key block cipher based on multivariate quadratic quasigroups. Cryptology ePrint Archive, Report 2008/320
22. Gligoroski, D., Markovski, S., Knapskog, S.J.: Multivariate quadratic trapdoor functions based on multivariate quadratic quasigroups. In: MATH 2008: Proceedings of the American Conference on Applied Mathematics, pp. 44–49. World Scientific and Engineering Academy and Society (WSEAS), Stevens Point (2008)
23. Goubin, L., Courtois, N.T.: Cryptanalysis of the TTM Cryptosystem. In: Okamoto, T. (ed.) ASIACRYPT 2000. LNCS, vol. 1976, pp. 44–57. Springer, Heidelberg (2000)
24. Goubin, L., Courtois, N.T., Schlumbergersema, C.: Cryptanalysis of the TTM Cryptosystem. In: Okamoto, T. (ed.) ASIACRYPT 2000. LNCS, vol. 1976, pp. 44–57. Springer, Heidelberg (2000)
25. Imai, H., Matsumoto, T.: Algebraic Methods for Constructing Asymmetric Cryptosystems. In: Calmet, J. (ed.) AAECC-3. LNCS, vol. 229, pp. 108–119. Springer, Heidelberg (1986)
26. Kasahara, M., Sakai, R.: A construction of public key cryptosystem for realizing ciphertext of size 100 bit and digital signature scheme. IEICE Transactions 87-A(1), 102–109 (2004)
27. Katz, J.: Digital Signatures. Springer (2010)
28. Kipnis, A., Shamir, A.: Cryptanalysis of the HFE Public Key Cryptosystem by Relinearization. In: Wiener, M. (ed.) CRYPTO 1999. LNCS, vol. 1666, pp. 19–30. Springer, Heidelberg (1999)
29. Koblitz, N.: Elliptic Curve Cryptosystems. Mathematics of Computation 48(177), 203–209 (1987)
30. MAGMA. High performance software for algebra, number theory, and geometry — a large commercial software package, http://magma.maths.usyd.edu.au
31. Matsumoto, T., Imai, H.: Public Quadratic Polynomial-Tuples for Efficient Signature-Verification and Message-Encryption. In: Günther, C.G. (ed.) EUROCRYPT 1988. LNCS, vol. 330, pp. 419–453. Springer, Heidelberg (1988)
32. Miller, V.S.: Use of Elliptic Curves in Cryptography. In: Williams, H.C. (ed.) CRYPTO 1985. LNCS, vol. 218, pp. 417–426. Springer, Heidelberg (1986)

33. Moh, T.: A public key system with signature and master key functions. Communications in Algebra (1999)
34. Moh, T.: A public key system with signature and master key functions (1999)
35. Mohamed, M.S.E., Ding, J., Buchmann, J., Werner, F.: Algebraic Attack on the MQQ Public Key Cryptosystem. In: Garay, J.A., Miyaji, A., Otsuka, A. (eds.) CANS 2009. LNCS, vol. 5888, pp. 392–401. Springer, Heidelberg (2009)
36. Patarin, J.: Hidden Fields Equations (HFE) and Isomorphisms of Polynomials (IP): Two New Families of Asymmetric Algorithms. In: Maurer, U.M. (ed.) EUROCRYPT 1996. LNCS, vol. 1070, pp. 33–48. Springer, Heidelberg (1996)
37. Patarin, J.: Cryptanalysis of the Matsumoto and Imai public key scheme of Eurocrypt 98. Des. Codes Cryptography 20, 175–209 (2000)
38. Perret, L.: A Fast Cryptanalysis of the Isomorphism of Polynomials with One Secret Problem. In: Cramer, R. (ed.) EUROCRYPT 2005. LNCS, vol. 3494, pp. 354–370. Springer, Heidelberg (2005)
39. Perret, L.: Personal e-mail communication with Danilo Gligoroski (2008)
40. Petzoldt, A., Bulygin, S., Buchmann, J.: Cyclicrainbow - a multivariate signature scheme with a partially cyclic public key based on rainbow. Cryptology ePrint Archive, Report 2010/424 (2010), http://eprint.iacr.org/
41. Rivest, R.L., Shamir, A., Adleman, L.: A method for obtaining digital signatures and public-key cryptosystems. Communications of the ACM 21, 120–126 (1978)
42. Samardjiska, S., Markovski, S., Gligoroski, D.: Multivariate quasigroups defined by t-functions. In: Proceedings of SCC 2010 - The 2nd International Conference on Symbolic Computation and Cryptography (2010)
43. Samardjiska, S., Chen, Y., Gligoroski, D.: Construction of multivariate quadratic quasigroups (mqqs) in arbitrary galois fields. In: Proceedings of the International Conference on Information Assurance and Security (IAS) 2011, Malacca, Malaysia (2011)
44. Shamir, A.: Efficient Signature Schemes Based on Birational Permutations. In: Stinson, D.R. (ed.) CRYPTO 1993. LNCS, vol. 773, pp. 1–12. Springer, Heidelberg (1994)
45. Shamir, A.: Efficient Signature Schemes Based on Birational Permutations. In: Stinson, D.R. (ed.) CRYPTO 1993. LNCS, vol. 773, pp. 1–12. Springer, Heidelberg (1994)
46. Singh, R.P., Sarma, B.K., Saikia, A.: Public key cryptography using permutation p-polynomials over finite fields. Cryptology ePrint Archive, Report 2009/208 (2009), http://eprint.iacr.org/
47. Smith, J.D.H.: An introduction to quasigroups and their representations. Chapman & Hall/CRC (2007)
48. Wolf, C., Braeken, A., Preneel, B.: On the security of stepwise triangular systems. Des. Codes Cryptography 40, 285–302 (2006)
49. Wolf, C., Preneel, B.: Taxonomy of public key schemes based on the problem of multivariate quadratic equations. Cryptology ePrint Archive, Report 2005/077 (2005)
50. Yang, B.-Y., Chen, J.-M.: Building Secure Tame-like Multivariate Public-Key Cryptosystems: The New TTS. In: Boyd, C., González Nieto, J.M. (eds.) ACISP 2005. LNCS, vol. 3574, pp. 518–531. Springer, Heidelberg (2005)
51. Yang, B.-Y., Cheng, C.-M., Chen, B.-R., Chen, J.-M.: Implementing Minimized Multivariate PKC on Low-Resource Embedded Systems. In: Clark, J.A., Paige, R.F., Polack, F.A.C., Brooke, P.J. (eds.) SPC 2006. LNCS, vol. 3934, pp. 73–88. Springer, Heidelberg (2006)

Multifactor Authenticated Key Renewal

Shin'ichiro Matsuo[1], Daisuke Moriyama[1], and Moti Yung[2,3]

[1] National Institute of Information and Communications Technology (NICT), Japan
[2] Columbia University
[3] Google Inc.

Abstract. Establishing secure channels is one of the most important and fundamental trust issues in information security. It is of high important not only for servers and users computers but also for global connectivity among any kind of network devices. Most existing technologies for establishing secure channels are based on asymmetric cryptography which requires heavy computations, large memory and complicated supporting mechanism such as PKI. In this paper, we consider the setting of authentication with small devices possibly held by humans and possibly embedded in a semi secure environment. We propose a authenticated key renewal protocol which uses only symmetric cryptography. The protocol takes into account other factors important for embedded and human held network devices: It covers multi-factor authentication to take advantage of secrets possessed by the secure device as well as the memorable password of the device owner. The protocol can, further, allow partial leakage of stored secret from a secure device. The protocol's considerations are a good demonstration of designing "trusted procedure" in the highly constrained environment of mobile and embedded small devices which is expected to be prevalent in the coming years.

Keywords: Key exchange, Multi-factor authentication, and Leakage resilience.

1 Introduction

1.1 Background

Staring with Diffie-Hellman key exchange [4], establishing secure channels is one of the most fundamental issues in information security. Establishing such a channel among communicating entities, has two important trust requirements: authentication and session key secrecy. That is, when the session key is shared the counterpart of sharing must be correctly authenticated and the shared session encryption/decryption key must be kept secret against unauthorized entities.

Many types of authenticated key sharing protocol exist, for example SSL/TLS [5], IPSec [10] and SSH [18], are proposed and used in today's Internet. Most of these protocols are based on asymmetric key cryptography, because their basic mechanism of key sharing is based on the DH key exchange protocol. We consider here the setting of small low-power devices such as smartphones,

L. Chen, M. Yung, and L. Zhu (Eds.): INTRUST 2011, LNCS 7222, pp. 204–220, 2012.

sensors, and RFID-tags. When considering this setting, computing modular exponentiation is costly. Moreover, when we use asymmetric key cryptography for authentication, we need PKI, which is costly as well, and may not be accessible at a device level (i.e., CA identity not accessible for establishing root of trust). It is much easier to initiate a device (at manufacturing) with symmetric key capability.

Currently, the typical computing environment is a network with many mobile devices (such as iPad and Android devices). Whereas trusted module like TPM chips ensure many security functionalities required in computing devices in regular computers [17], in our setting it is hard to assume the devices will have modular exponentiation capability (even if some have, we want interoperability), and it is interesting to consider what is doable based on symmetric cryptography alone. Furthermore, in embedding devices the authentication is based on possession of a secure token. This means the authentication (and the key exchange) is based on ownership of the device. Then the authentication is slightly different from "entity" authentication (the entity may be embedded in another entity, and may be possessed by a human operator/ owner). In this direction, PAKE protocol realizes authentication function by using password, which is based on human memory and tightly related to the entity itself [3,8]. However in PAKE, the security parameter is limited by human capability. Long password is not suitable for PAKE, therefore it is not strong in cryptographic sense. To increase the accuracy of the authentication, it is good desirable to include multifactor into the authentication protocol. Examples of the factors are memory, ownership, biometric, device keys, etc. Also, small devices may operate in an environment which is leaky and this has to be taken into account as well.

1.2 Contribution of This Paper

In this paper, we propose a system model and a protocol for multifactor authenticated key establishment, named "Multifactor Authenticated Key Renewal (MAKeR) protocol". It aims to establish a random session key using multi-factor information.

MAKeR protocol uses symmetric cryptography only to realize authenticated key sharing, that is, uses only hash/pseudorandom function and pseudorandom generator. Though this protocol is not secure against online dictionary attack due to the limitation of symmetric cryptography techniques, it still present the best properties achievable under symmetric cryptography only conditions. Thus, this research goal is implementing better security mechanisms to low-power devices such as the smartphones, smart-cards, sensors, and RFID-tags.

Our proposal includes shared secret stored in trusted device (the device key), and password or other information as authentication factors. The former helps realization of both authentication factor of "what one possesses" and "secrecy" of session key. The latter is used for authentication by "human-related information" ("what one knows").

1.3   Related Works

As mentioned above, key sharing (exchange) protocols are extensively researched and many secure protocols have been proposed. Basic type of authenticated key exchange protocol is combination of entity authentication and Diffie-Hellman like key exchange protocol. Entity authentication protocols consist of asymmetric key based protocol and symmetric cryptography based protocol. However, Diffie-Hellman key exchange protocol needs asymmetric cryptographic calculation. As a user-friendly authenticated key exchange protocol, "Password-based Authenticated Key Exchange (PAKE)" protocols are widely studied. This protocol uses pre-shard (short) password as a factor of authentication. Most PAKE protocols include data from password into Diffie-Hellmann key exchange protocol, they still need asymmetric cryptographic calculation.

For low-power devices, many entity authentication protocol for RFID tags are proposed [1,11,2,12,16]. Most of these protocols are based on symmetric cryptography such as block cipher, stream cipher, hash function and so on. Our proposal is based on the existing authentication protocol for RFID-tags.

The other works related to this paper are about multi-factor authentication. Klesnikov and Rackoff proposed a multi-factor authenticated key exchange protocol [9]. In this paper, they use three factors: password, secret keys for symmetric key cryptography and asymmetric key cryptography. Pointcheval et al. proposed security model and authenticated key exchange protocol which uses biometrics as well as secret information as authentication factors [15]. However, the protocol is based on asymmetric cryptography.

This paper also deals with leakage of secret information from a device, which is realized by side-channel attacks or cold-boot attacks. This is a very current area of research. In ordinary cryptographic research, the security model does not consider leakage of secret information. In the symmetric world, Petit et al. [14] proposed a leakage-resilient pseudo-random generator from ideal ciphers. Dziembowski et al. [6] proposed a leakage-resilient stream cipher based on pseudo-random generator in the standard model. Then Pietrzak [13] proposed simplified leakage-resilient stream cipher from wPRF. We will use the same model of leakage as [6,13] in this paper.

2   System Model

The MAKeR protocol consists of two entity, Alice and Bob. Alice can be treated as client of some service. Alice has one device DEV_A connected to the Internet. An application program $PROG_A$ runs on the device and accepts multiple inputs from Alice such as password and other authentication factors. The device also havs some trusted module/ token TPM_A attached to it. TPM_A stores secret information sec_A, and conducts some (symmetric) cryptographic operations. TPM_A may be implemented into DEV_A (by the manufacturer, say) or is attached using a card slot and so on. TPM_A communicates with $PROG_A$.

Bob can be treated as a server. It is realized as a device DEV_B and also connected to the Internet. An application program $PROG_B$ executes authenticated

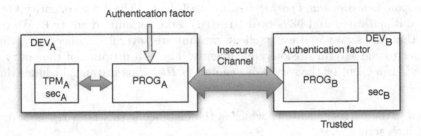

Fig. 1. System model of multi-factor authenticated key renewal

key renewal protocol. Some secret information sec_B and other multiple authentication factors shared with each client are stored in DEV_B, and $PROG_B$ accesses them in the execution of the protocol. We assume that DEV_B and $PROG_B$ is trusted. That is, the malicious adversary $\mathcal{A}$ against this protocol cannot corrupt DEV_B and $PROG_B$. Thus, $\mathcal{A}$ cannot obtain sec_B and any internal state of DEV_B and $PROG_B$.

DEV_A and DEV_B communicates over the Internet, which can be treated as insecure channel. That is $\mathcal{A}$ can eavesdrop, alter, intercept all communication data and send arbitrary message to Alice and Bob.

When Alice would like to establish a secure channel with Bob, she inputs required authentication information (which is shared) to $PROG_A$ through user interface of DEV_A. In the protocol execution, $PROG_A$ calculates protocol messages with help of TPM_A. $PROG_A$ and $PROG_B$ execute session key renewal protocol, then share the session key key at the end of the protocol.

This system model is shown in Fig.1.

3   Security Model

The goal of the protocol is establishing a session key from multi-factor secrets. The basic security for multi-factor key renewal protocol is that even if a malicious adversary $\mathcal{A}$ interacts with clients and the server, the communication messages leak no information about the session key computed by the server. Additionally, the protocol must guarantee secrecy of the future session key, and privacy for the past session key even if an attack is attempted (namely, it must be based on fresh randomness and be forward secure).

The device DEV_A stores secret value sec_A. We firstly consider the basic case that the device DEV_A as tamper-free, next we consider the several types of secret information leakage.

The formal security definition in the basic case (without any key leakage from DEV_A) is as follows.

3.1   Security Definition without Corruption

The basic security model is similar to that of multi-factor authentication proposed by Pointcheval et al. [15].

Participants, sessions and partnering. Let $\mathtt{DEV_A}$ be a client device of entity $\mathtt{Alice}$ to be authenticated and $\mathtt{DEV_B}$ be a (trusted) server organized entity $\mathtt{B}$. We consider that the server and every client can initiate several instances at a time, in order to run several sessions concurrently. The i-th instance of the entity U, where U is a client or the server, is denoted as Π_U^i. This instance includes three variables:

- pid_U^i: the partner identifier which is the instance with whom Π_U^i believes it is interacting,
- sid_U^i: the unique session identifier, in practice it can be the transcript seen by Π_U^i (concatenation of the received/sent flows, excepted the last one).
- acc_U^i: a boolean variable which is determined at the end of the session and denotes whether the instance Π_U^i goes in an accepted ($a_U^i = 1$) state or not ($acc_U^i = 0$).

The two instances Π_U^i and $\Pi_{U'}^j$ are said to be partners if the following conditions are fulfilled:

1. $pid_U^i = \Pi_{U'}^j$ and $pid_{U'}^j = \Pi_U^i$;
2. $sid_U^i = sid_{U'}^j \neq null$;
3. $acc_U^i = acc_{U'}^j = 1$.

Adversarial capabilities and goals. The semantic security of the key is modeled using the Real-or-Random paradigm. At the beginning of the game, the challenger chooses a random bit b which determines its behavior when answering $\mathtt{Test}$-query during the game (it provides either real session key or random to the adversary). The adversary may interact with protocol instances through several oracles, and at the end of the game, she outputs a bit b. If $b = b'$, she wins, otherwise, she looses. The available queries are as follows:

- $\mathtt{Send}(m, \Pi_U^i)$: this query allows the adversary to play with the instances, by intercepting, forwarding, modifying or creating messages. The output of this query is the answer generated by instance Π_U^i to the message m.
- $\mathtt{Reveal}(\Pi_U^i)$: this query models the leakage of information about the session key agreed on by the parties. For example, if it is misused afterward. Therefore, if no session key is defined for this instance, or if the instance (or its partner) has been tested (see below), then the output is $\perp$. Otherwise, the oracle outputs the session key computed by the instance Π_U^i.

To model the semantic security with respect to client authentication formally, the adversary can ask $\mathtt{Test}$-query, but to the server S only: we are interested in the privacy of the key established with the real server only. We only consider the adversary whose goal is to impersonate a client to the server. Of course, to achieve this goal, the adversary may try to impersonate the server to the client in order to learn some information about the internal state $\mathtt{sec_A}$ of $\mathtt{TPM_A}$ or other multiple authentication factors. But only a client impersonation will be considered as a successful attack:

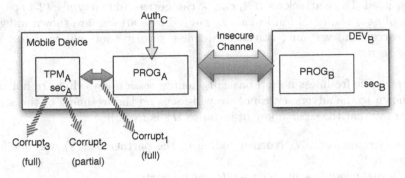

Fig. 2. Corruption model of multi-factor authenticated key renewal

- Test(Π_S^i): The oracle responds
  - the session key of instance (Π_S^i) (that is $Reveal(\Pi_S^i)$), if $b = 1$ - the real case;
  - a random key from the same domain, if $b = 0$ - the random case.

Semantic Security. Let denote by $Succ$ the event that the adversary $\mathcal{A}$ correctly guesses the bit b used by the challenger during the above attack game. We require that the test session where adversary issues the test query must be fresh (see below). The *maker-advantage* $adv_P^{maker}(\mathcal{A})$ and the advantage function of the protocol P are respectively:

$$adv_P^{maker}(\mathcal{A}) = |2 \cdot Pr[Succ] - 1|, adv_P^{maker}(t, Q) = \max_{\mathcal{A}}\{adv_P^{maker}(\mathcal{A})\}$$

where the maximum is over all the attackers with time-complexity at most t and number of queries at most Q.

Client authentication. We also usually model an attack against the unilateral authentication of the client to the server by considering sessions where the server accepts, but without any client-partner. Let denote by $Succ$ the event that a server instance accepts with no partner instance of the client (with the same partial transcript).

The *auth-success* $Succ_P^{auth}(\mathcal{A})$ and the success function of the protocol P are respectively:

$$Succ_P^{auth}(\mathcal{A}) = Pr[Succ], Succ_P^{auth}(t, Q) = \max_{\mathcal{A}}\{Succ_P^{auth}(\mathcal{A})\}$$

where the maximum is over all the attackers with time-complexity at most t and number of queries at most Q.

3.2 Considering Corruption of Client Device

Here, we think about corruption of client device DEV_A. We consider the following three types of attacks; (1) communication channel between TPM_A and $PROG_A$ and

(2) TPM_A itself. These attack on TPM_A can be categorized in two types; (2-1) partial leakage of sec_A and (2-2) full leakage of sec_A. These attacks are shown in fig. 2.

For corruption, we must consider two new security notions, *freshness* and *forward secrecy*.

Freshness. The freshness notion basically defines session keys that are not trivially known to the adversary. Since we will focus on the freshness of the server only, we say that the session key of instance Π_S^i is fresh if:

- upon acceptance, DEV_A (corresponding to the partner of Π_S^i) was not fully corrupted.
- no Reveal-query is sent to either Π_S^i or its partner.

Backward and forward-Secrecy. Backward-secrecy mean that after the time of corruption, the session keys in any following session remains secret against the adversary. In order to capture this security, the model must allow the adversary to perform Test-queries, which we will define after, on sessions occurred after the corruption. Forward-secrecy means that as soon as a session key is securely generated (semantically secure), it will remain secure even after corruption. In order to capture this security, the model must allow the adversary to perform Test-queries, on sessions completed before the corruption.

From here, we consider the cases which the adversary obtains leaked information. Note that in the following, we will restrict to non-adaptive corruptions: no corruption can be performed during a session, but before a new session starts.

Full Leakage in Communication Channel between TPM_A and $PROG_A$. This leakage models interception of full information between TMP_A and $PROG_A$. This type of attack is most easiest among three types of corruption, because this channel is not tamper-resistant in general. Moreover the TPM_A is a device which may be attached to DEV_A, the interception is quite easy. The adversary can acquire all communication data between TPM_A and $PROG_A$ by this attack.

To model this attack, we introduce $CORRUPT_1$ oracle.

$CORRUPT_1(DEV_A)$: Upon asking this query, the adversary can acquire all communication between TPM_A and $PROG_A$.

Partial Leakage of Internal Key. This attack is difficult because it need much expertise to do it. However, recent extensive researches on side-channel attacks, such attacks help the adversary to obtain internal secret information against tamper resistant mechanisms of TPM_A itself.

To model this attack, we introduce following $CORRUPT_2$ oracle.

$CORRUPT_2(DEV_A, \lambda)$: Upon asking this query, the adversary can acquire partial information of secret sec_A stored in TPM_A. The output of this oracle is $\lambda(sec_A)$, where $\lambda(\cdot)$ is a leakage function which models this partial leakage.

Full Leakage of Internal Key. Here we consider full corruption of internal secret sec_A of TPM_A. To conduct this attack, it takes much time. However, it is considered in the existing researches on key sharing protocols.

To model this attack, we introduce following $CORRUPT_3$ oracle.

$CORRUPT_3(DEV_A)$: Upon asking this query, the adversary can acquire sec_A stored in TPM_A.

Why Consider Both Partial and Full Leakage from TPM? As described above, in forward secrecy, we allow the adversary to obtain the full internal state of the device, denoted as "full leakage of internal key". Surely, we must consider this type of attack as the worst case. It is worth noting that, in the real usage of mobile devices, it apparently takes quite much time and effort to conduct attacks leading to full leakage of internal key (For example, the adversary steals the tag and brings it to his laboratory to obtain the internal state.) However, the adversary certainly has no chance to give the device to the original owner again.

In this paper, we additionally consider an attack scenario which we call "multi-time partial leakage". Namely, in the life time of a device, its internal state may be partially leaked in a gradual way. It is obvious that partial leakage is more likely to occur than full leakage, because the adversary can conduct such attacks in a shorter time, with cheap and small-size devices. Furthermore, the adversary has enough time to bring back the TPM/device to the original owner. Therefore, it is practical to consider the multi-time partial-leakage scenarios.

The partial leakage allows the adversary to conduct further key renewal. However, when full leakage occurred, the original user notice the attack and he could revoke the mobile device for key renewal. Thus, we consider only partial leakage for key indistinguishability against random and consider full leakage for forward secrecy.

4   Protocol Description

4.1   Basic Protocol

At first, we show the basic protocol which is secure against an adversary without corruption. Next, we will show the protocol which is secure against all types of corruptions.

The proposed protocol is combination of lightweight authentication scheme studied for RFID-tag and PRF (Pseudo Random Function).

Both the client (the person) DEV_A and the server DEV_B have fixed secret information for authentication. They consist of password, and so on. We represent it as $Auth_C = (pw_A, \ldots)$. TPM_A also has a pseudo-random generator implemented in TPM_A. It outputs a tuple of pseudorandom value $(k_i, k_i', k_i'', k_i''')$ for i-th authenticated key renewal.

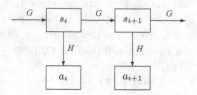

Fig. 3. Hash chain of OSK protocol

In the basic protocol, the pseudo-random generator is constructed from a kind of hash chain. OSK protocol [12], which is one of the most popular RFID authentication protocol, uses the hash chain. This hash chain is shown in Fig. 3.

In the basic protocol, $a_i = (k_i, k'_i, k''_i, k'''_i)$ are computed as three consecutive outputs of OSK hash chain. That is,

$$k_i = S_{4i-3}, k'_i = S_{4i-2}, k''_i = S_{4i-1}, k'''_i = S_{4i}$$

The server DEV$_B$ also has the same pseudo-random generator, which outputs same tuple of pseudorandom value for each authenticated key renewal.

The authenticated key renewal consists of authentication part and key establishment part.

Authentication Part

Step1. Client DEV$_A$ generates a random value r_A. Then DEV$_A$ sends r_A and identity A to the server DEV$_B$.

Step2. The server DEV$_B$ calculates message authentication code as follows:

$$Auth_B = MAC_{k'_i}(F_{k_i}(r_A \| r_B) \oplus Auth_C),$$

where $MAC_k(m)$ is a message authentication code of message m using key k, $F_K(\cdot)$ is pseudo random function with key K (for example, a block cipher like AES), $F_K(\cdot)$ is a message authentication code with key K and $\|$ represents concatenation of two data. Then, DEV$_B$ generates a random number r_B and sends $Auth_B, r_B, r_A$ and identity B to DEV$_A$.

Step3. The client DEV$_A$ verifies the message authentication code as follows:

$$Auth_B \stackrel{?}{=} MAC.Verify_{k'_i}((F_{k_i}(r_A \| r_B) \oplus Auth_C))$$

where $MAC.Verify_k(m)$ is verification algorithm of message authentication code of message m using key k. Then, DEV$_A$ calculates message authentication code as follows:

$$Auth_A = MAC_{k''_i}(F_{k_i}(r_B) \oplus Auth_C),$$

and send $Auth_A$ to the server.

Step4. The server DEV$_B$ verifies the message authentication code as follows:

$$Auth_A \stackrel{?}{=} MAC.Verify_{k''_i}((F_{k_i}(r_B) \oplus Auth_C))$$

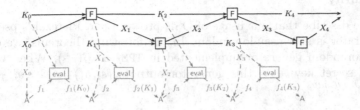

Fig. 4. Leakage resilient pseudorandom generator by Pietrzak et al.

Key Establishment Part: Both the server S and the client C calculates the session key as follows.

$$key_i = F_{k_i'''}(r_A) \oplus F_{k_i'''}(r_B) \oplus Auth_C$$

4.2 Protocol with Leakage Resilience

Next we move to the protocol with leakage resilience. To make the protocol with leakage resilience, we use Pietrzak's pseudorandom generator [13] for the physical pseudorandom generator. This pseudorandom generator has two sequences of random internal states and outputs one random value a_i for each authenticated key exchange. The Pietrzak's pseudorandom generator is shown in Fig.4.

As same as basic protocol we use three consecutive outputs of this pseudorandom generator. That is

$$a_i = (k_i = X_{5i-4}, k_i' = X_{5i-3}, k_i'' = X_{5i-2}, k_i''' = X_{5i-1}),$$

which are derived from $(K_{5i-5}, K_{5i-4}, X_{5i-5})$. a_i is transmitted to the PROG$_A$, then the same protocol as the basic protocol is executed.

5 Security Evaluation

5.1 Completeness

Theorem 1 (Completeness). *The DEV$_A$ and DEV$_B$ who have same internal secret and Auth$_C$ can authenticate each other and compute the same session key.*

Proof. DEV$_A$ can confirm the correctness of DEV$_B$ in the step 3, because she knows $k_i, k_i', r_A, Auth_C$. Similarly, DEV$_B$ can confirm the correctness of DEV$_A$ in the step 4, because she knows $k_i, k_i'', r_B, Auth_C$. Both DEV$_A$ and DEV$_A$ can calculate same session key key_i, because they knows k_i''', r_A, r_B and $Auth_C$. □

5.2   Security

At first we describe that our usage of OSK-protocol and Pietezak's pseudorandom generator is still pseudo-random. In the following theorems, we consider
the pseudorandom generator implemented in TPM$_A$ as $\mathcal{G}(i, \cdot)$. When we input
the latest secret key s_{i-1}, this generator outputs $(s_i, a_i) = \mathcal{G}(i, s_{i-1})$ where
$a_i = (k_i, k_i', k_i'', k_i''')$.

Theorem 2 (Security of underlying pseudorandom generator). *Output
of our usage of OSK protocol is still pseudo-random without leakage of internal state. And output of our usage of Pietrzak's pseudo-random generator is
still pseudo-random against the adversary who try to partial leakage allowed in
Pietrzak's mode-of-operation.*

Proof. This security of this theorem is distinguishing $(k_i, k_i', k_i'', k_i''')$ from random using $(k_{i-1}, k_{i-1}', k_{i-1}'', k_{i-1}''')$. Let the success probability of distinguishing k_i from random using k_{i-1}''' be $Pr[Succ(\mathcal{A}_{PRG})]$ and success probability
of distinguishing $(k_i, k_i', k_i'', k_i''')$ from random using $(k_{i-1}, k_{i-1}', k_{i-1}'', k_{i-1}''')$ be
$Pr[Succ(\mathcal{A}_{4PRG})]$.

Then

$$
\begin{aligned}
|1 - 2 \cdot Pr[Succ(\mathcal{A}_{4PRG})]| \leq |1 - 2 \cdot (& (Pr[Succ(\mathcal{A}_{PRG})])^4 \\
& + 4/2^{|k|} \times (Pr[Succ(\mathcal{A}_{PRG})])^3 \\
& + 6/2^{2|k|} \times (Pr[Succ(\mathcal{A}_{PRG})])^2 \\
& + 4/2^{3|k|} \times (Pr[Succ(\mathcal{A}_{PRG})]) \\
& + 1/2^{4|k|})|
\end{aligned}
$$

Theorem in [12] shows that $Pr[Succ(\mathcal{A}_{PRG})]$ is negligible without corruption.
Similarly, theorem in [13] shows that $Pr[Succ(\mathcal{A}_{PRG})]$ is negligible with partial
leakage. Thus, $Pr[Succ(\mathcal{A}_{4PRG})]$ is negligible.   □

Theorem 3 (Key security without any corruption). *The proposed protocols (both basic and leakage-resilient versions) have semantic security of renewal
session key against any adversary who observe protocol messages. This means
the adversary cannot obtain no information about further session keys.*

Proof. We proceed in games, starting with Game 0 which is the original security
game between a challenger and adversary in the proposed protocol. The challenger simulates all party's registration and the response to the oracle queries
that $\mathcal{A}$ issues. Let $Succ_f(\mathcal{B})$ be the event that an probabilistic algorithm $\mathcal{B}$ breaks
the security property of the function f.

In each Game i, we define adv_i as the advantage that the adversary wins the
game. We consider the following games:

Game 0. This is the original security game with adversary $\mathcal{A}$ so that $\mathsf{adv}_0 = adv_P^{maker}(t, Q)$.

Game 1. We proceed as Game 0 but add the following abort rule. The challenger proceeds as Game 0 but aborts the game if it does not correctly guess the test session.

Game 2. We transform Game 1 to Game 2 by changing the secret key $(k_i, k_i', k_i'', k_i''')$ used in the test session to random strings.

Game 3. We modify Game 2 by changing pseudorandom function $F_{k_i}(\cdot)$ to truly random function RF used at the test session.

Game 4. We proceed as Game 3 but add the following rule. If the adversary changes the communication message at the test session and the verification of the MAC function is accepted, the challenger aborts the security game in Game 4.

Game 5. We modify Game 4 by changing pseudorandom function $F_{k_i'''}(\cdot)$ to truly random function RF used at the test session.

Game 6. We modify Game 5 to Game 6 by changing the session key at the test session to the truly random string.

We evaluate the relations between the game transformation with the following claims.

Claim 1. We have $\mathsf{adv}_0 \leq Q/2 \cdot \mathsf{adv}_1$.

Proof. From the definition of the security model, the upper bound of the oracle queries issued by the adversary $\mathcal{A}$ is at most Q. To establish a server's accepted session, $\mathcal{A}$ must issue two send queries from the specification of the proposed protocol and the server executes at most $Q/2$ sessions in the security game. When the challenger uniformly selects i from $1, \ldots, q$ such that server's i-th session will be chosen as the test session. Then the probability that the challenger correctly guesses the test session is at least $2/Q$. Therefore, $\mathsf{adv}_0 \leq Q/2 \cdot \mathsf{adv}_1$.

Claim 2. We have $|\mathsf{adv}_1 - \mathsf{adv}_2| \leq \Pr[Succ_{\mathcal{G}}(\mathcal{B}'_{4PRG})]$.

Proof. If the adversary $\mathcal{A}$ can distinguish Game 2 from Game 1 with non-negligible probability, there exists an probabilistic algorithm $\mathcal{B}'_{4PRG}$ that can break the security of pseudorandom generator $\mathcal{G}(i, \cdot)$.

For a given instance $(k_i, k_i', k_i'', k_i''')$, $\mathcal{B}'_{PRG}$ proceeds as Game 1 except that $(k_i, k_i', k_i'', k_i''')$ is assigned as the secret key for the i-th server's session. When the adversary output a guess bit b' for the test session, $\mathcal{B}'_{4PRG}$ outputs the same bit b'. If the tuple is computed by pseudorandom generator, this game is equivalent to Game 1. Otherwise, $\mathcal{B}'_{4PRG}$ simulates Game 2 from the view point of the adversary. Therefore, it is clear that if the adversary can distinguishes Game 2 from Game 1 with probability ϵ_1, $\mathcal{B}'_{4PRG}$ can distinguishes $(k_i, k_i', k_i'', k_i''')$ with the same probability. However, Theorem 2 showed that this probability is already negligible.

Claim 3. We have $|\mathsf{adv}_2 - \mathsf{adv}_3| \leq \Pr[Succ_F(\mathcal{B}_{PRF})]$.

Proof. If the adversary $\mathcal{A}$ can distinguish Game 3 from Game 2 with non-negligible probability, there exists an probabilistic algorithm $\mathcal{B}_{PRF}$ that can break the security of pseudorandom function.

Consider that $\mathcal{B}_{PRF}$ interacts with pseudo-random function $F_{k_i}(\cdot)$ or truly random function RF. $\mathcal{B}_{PRF}$ proceeds as Game 2 and simulates all the oracle queries except the test session. We assume that the adversary sends $(r'_A, \cdot)$ to the server and $(r'_B, \cdot)$ to the client at the test session. $\mathcal{B}_{PRF}$ issues $r_A \| r'_B$ and $r'_A \| r_B$ to the oracle query where (r_A, r_B) is chosen by $\mathcal{B}_{PRF}$ and $\mathcal{B}_{PRF}$ computes $(Auth_B, Auth_A)$ using the response from the challenger. When the adversary output a guess bit b' for the test session, $\mathcal{B}_{PRF}$ outputs the same bit b'. From the security proof of the previous claim, each secret key input to the pseudorandom function is chosen by uniformly random. So if the adversary can distinguish these games, $\mathcal{B}_{PRF}$ can break the security of PRF with the same probability.

Claim 4. We have $|\mathsf{adv}_3 - \mathsf{adv}_4| \leq \Pr[Succ_{MAC}(\mathcal{B}_{MAC})] + 2/2^{l_F}$ where l_F is the output length of the pseudorandom function $F_{k_i}(\cdot)$.

Proof. It is clear that these games are equivalent if the adversary does not output the modification message such that the party accepts it. We show that if the adversary succeeds in outputting such a valid message with non-negligible probability, there exists an probabilistic algorithm $\mathcal{B}_{MAC}$ that can break the existential unforgeability of the MAC function.

Consider that the adversary sends $(r'_A, \cdot)$ to the server, $(r'_B, Auth'_B)$ to the client and $Auth'_A$ to the server at each round of the test session. If $r'_A \neq r_A$ or $r'_B \neq r_B$, the client and the server input different variables to the pseudorandom function $F_{k_i}(\cdot)$ and its outputs are completely independent from the previous claim. Thus, $m_B = F_{k'_i}(r'_A \| r_B) \oplus Auth_C$ computed by the server and $m_A = F_{k'_i}(r_A \| r'_B) \oplus Auth_C$ computed by the client are different messages except the negligible probability $1/2^F$. If $Auth'_B$ is accepted by the client, we can construct $\mathcal{B}_{MAC}$ who simulates the game as Game 3 and outputs $(m_A, Auth'_B)$ as a forgery. $\mathcal{B}_{MAC}$ issues m_B to the MAC oracle but $m_A = m_B$ happens with probability $1/2^{l_F}$. The same argument holds for the MAC value $Auth'_A$ if we assume that $r'_B \neq r_B$. So the probability that server accepts with modified message is also negligible. Therefore, we have $\|\mathsf{adv}_3 - \mathsf{adv}_4\| \leq \Pr[Succ_{MAC}(\mathcal{B}_{MAC})] + 2/2^{l_F}$.

Claim 5. We have $|\mathsf{adv}_4 - \mathsf{adv}_5| \leq \Pr[Succ_F(\mathcal{B}_{PRF})]$.

Proof. We can show the proof of this claim as previous claim for the difference between Game 2 and 3. In this case, $\mathcal{B}_{PRF}$ interacts with pseudo-random function $F_{k'''_i}$ or truly random function RF and issues (r_A, r_B) to the oracle query. So if the adversary can distinguishes these games, $\mathcal{B}_{PRF}$ can break the security of PRF with the same probability.

Claim 6. We have $|\mathsf{adv}_5 - \mathsf{adv}_6| = 0$.

Proof. The session key at the test session is already randomized since $F_{k'''_i}(r_B)$ is replaced by uniformly random string and it is effectively a one-time pad. Therefore, this change is purely conceptual and we obtain $|\mathsf{adv}_5 - \mathsf{adv}_6| = 0$.

It is obvious that $adv_6 = 0$, and we obtain

$$adv_P^{maker}(t, Q) \leq Q/2 \cdot (\Pr[Succ_{\mathcal{G}}(\mathcal{B}'_{4PRG})] + 2 \cdot \Pr[Succ_F(\mathcal{B}_{PRF})]$$
$$+ \Pr[Succ_{MAC}(\mathcal{B}_{MAC})] + 2/2^{l_F})$$

and conclude the proof of Theorem 3. $\qquad\square$

We remark that $Sucv_P^{auth}(t, Q)$ is also negligible from Claim 4.

Theorem 4 (Key security with CORRUPT$_1$). *The proposed protocols (both basic and leakage-resilient versions) have semantic security of renewal session key against any adversary who observe protocol messages and obtain output from* TPM$_A$. *This means the adversary cannot obtain no information about further session keys.*

Proof. The security proof of this theorem is derived from Theorem 2 and 3. The difference between Theorem 3 and 4 is that the adversary can obtain $\{(k_j, k'_j, k''_j, k'''_j)\}$ for $j = 1, \ldots, i-1$ whose variables are used as the secret key before the test session. Nonetheless, Theorem 2 shows that pseudorandom generator $\mathcal{G}(i, \cdot)$ still holds the security and $(k_i, k'_i, k''_i, k'''_i)$ is independent from these keys. Then we can easily construct the security proof based on Theorem 3. Therefore,

$$adv_P^{maker}(t, Q) \leq Q/2 \cdot (\Pr[Succ_{\mathcal{G}}(\mathcal{B}_{4PRG})] + 2 \cdot \Pr[Succ_F(\mathcal{B}_{PRF})]$$
$$+ \Pr[Succ_{MAC}(\mathcal{B}_{MAC})] + 2/2^{l_F})$$

and $\mathcal{B}_{4PRG}$ is negligible from Theorem 2.

Theorem 5 (Key security with CORRUPT$_1$ and CORRUPT$_2$). *The proposed protocols (only leakage-resilient versions) have for key security of renewal session key against any adversary who observe protocol messages and obtain output and partial internal information from* TPM$_A$. *This means the adversary cannot obtain no information about further session keys.*

Proof. In addition to Theorem 4, this type of adversary can issue leakage oracle and obtain $\lambda(a_i)$, where $\lambda(\cdot)$ is leakage function chosen by the adversary. When we consider the hash chain likes OSK protocol or traditional pseudorandom generator, the security is no more ensured. However, if we use the leakage resilient pseudorandom generator proposed by Pietrzak et al., our protocol also satisfies the leakage resilience and we can describe the security proof as in the Theorem 4. Therefore, we have

$$adv_P^{maker}(t, Q) \leq Q/2 \cdot (\Pr[Succ_{\mathcal{G}}(\mathcal{B}''_{4PRG})] + 2 \cdot \Pr[Succ_F(\mathcal{B}_{PRF})]$$
$$+ \Pr[Succ_{MAC}(\mathcal{B}_{MAC})] + 2/2^{l_F})$$

and we can show that $\Pr[Succ_{\mathcal{G}}(\mathcal{B}''_{4PRG})]$ is negligible from the theorem in Pietrzak et al. $\qquad\square$

Theorem 6 (Forward secrecy with CORRUPT₁ and CORRUPT₃). *The proposed protocols (both basic and leakage-resilient versions) have forward secrecy of re-newal session key against any adversary who observe protocol messages and obtain output and full internal information from* TPM$_A$. *This means the adversary cannot obtain no information about previous session keys.*

Proof. This type of adversary can obtain all the internal secret used after the test session, in addition to the adversary described in Theorem 3.

When we consider the OSK-type hash chain pseudorandom generator $\mathcal{G}$, the adversary can receive $(i + 1)$-th session's internal secret $s_{i+1} = G(H^{-1}(k_i'''))$ with CORRUPT₃ query. Note that the other secret keys are derived from this value. In this case, we can easily show the independence of the secret key of the test session. When we set as $t = H^{-1}(k_i''')$, we have $s_{i+1} = G(t)$ and $k_i''' = H(t)$. Since the each pseudorandom generator G and H implemented in the TPM$_A$ is independently chosen in our protocol, s_{i+1} does not affect the pseudorandomness of k_i'''. Of course, we can say that the pseudo-randomness of k_i'', k_i' and k_i also holds recursively.

In the case of leakage resilient pseudorandom generator $\mathcal{G}$, the output from the TPM$_A$ at the test session is $a_i = (k_i, k_i', k_i'', k_i''') = (X_{5i-4}, X_{5i-3}, X_{5i-2}, X_{5i-1})$. When the adversary issues CORRUPT₃ query to the $(i + 1)$-th session, he can receive $s_{i+1} = (K_{5i}, K_{5i+1}, X_{5i})$. Note that $(K_{5i}, X_{5i-1}) = \mathsf{F}(k_{5i-2}, X_{5i-2})$ and $(K_{5i+1}, X_{5i}) = \mathsf{F}(k_{5i-1}, X_{5i-1})$ where F is iterated pseudorandom generator used in $\mathcal{G}$. Thus s_{i+1} does not affect the pseudo-randomness of a_i.

Therefore, the corruptions after the test session does not affect the security proof and

$$adv_P^{maker}(t, Q) \leq Q/2 \cdot (\Pr[Succ_{\mathcal{G}}(\mathcal{B}'_{4PRG})] + 2 \cdot \Pr[Succ_F(\mathcal{B}_{PRF})]$$
$$+ \Pr[Succ_{\mathsf{MAC}}(\mathcal{B}_{MAC})] + 2/2^{l_F}).$$

We can evaluate the security reduction as Theorem 3.   □

5.3   Discussion

From the above security evaluation, we can see that security of one side of multi-factor $Auth_C$ cannot be guaranteed after any corruption (by only CORRUPT₁). This is because the adversary can obtain $r_A, r_B, Auth_A, Auth_B$ and its encryption key, then the security of $Auth_C$ is not guaranteed by definition of pseudorandom functions. This is the so, as is the fact that this protocol is not secure against online dictionary attack. However this is due to inherent limitations of using symmetric key cryptography, which is pointed out by Halevi et al [7]. The only countermeasure for this is slow-downing of calculation of inverses of pseudo-random function by using multiple PRFs.

However, generally $Auth_C$ contains a password, which can be changeable at any time (and is changed according to systems rules every so often). Even if CORRUPT₁ or CORRUPT₃ are made, the security of $Auth_C$ part revives after changing password. This is a different characteristics than that of internal secret (keys).

Internal secrets cannot be changed after corruption, thus it should be protected by hash chain or Pietrzak's mode. However, password can be easily changed, thus, the current setting is still effective in practice.

6   Conclusion

This paper proposed multifactor authenticated key renewal protocol, which realizes authenticated key establishment from symmetric (shared) key cryptography only. The authentication part of this protocol deals with both authentication from device's secret and human related authenticator like memorable password. The system model of this protocol is suitable for the situation of current mobile computing and other devices. In practice, all functions in this protocol are realized by the standard AES function or other secure light-weight block cipher. Thus, this is efficient enough for smartphone, mobile devices and smartcards. The proposed protocol deals with many types of attacks, such as data interception between TPM and application program, and side channel attacks on the TPM. This protocol assures session key secrecy and forward secrecy against the above attacks.

Acknowledgement. This work was supported by KAKENHI, Grant-in-Aid for Young Scientists (B) (22760287).

References

1. Avoine, G., Oechslin, P.: A scalable and provably secure hash-based RFID protocol. In: Proc. of the PerCom 2005 Workshops (2005)
2. Juels, A., Pappu, R.: Squealing Euros: Privacy Protection in RFID-Enabled Banknotes. In: Wright, R.N. (ed.) FC 2003. LNCS, vol. 2742, pp. 103–121. Springer, Heidelberg (2003)
3. Bellare, M., Pointcheval, D., Rogaway, P.: Authenticated Key Exchange Secure against Dictionary Attacks. In: Preneel, B. (ed.) EUROCRYPT 2000. LNCS, vol. 1807, pp. 139–155. Springer, Heidelberg (2000)
4. Diffie, W., Hellman, M.: New directions in cryptography. IEEE Transactions on Information Theory IT-22(6), 644–654 (1976)
5. Dierks, T., Rescorla, E.: The Transport Layer Security (TLS) Protocol Version 1.2. Internet Draft, RFC 5246 (2008)
6. Dziembowski, S., Pietrzak, K.: Leakage-resilient cryptography. In: Proc. FOCS, October 25-28, pp. 293–302 (2008)
7. Halevi, S., Krawczyk, H.: Public-key cryptography and password protocols. ACM Transactions on Information and System Security (TISSEC) 2(3), 230–268 (1999)
8. Katz, J., Ostrovsky, R., Yung, M.: Forward Secrecy in Password-Only Key Exchange Protocols. In: Cimato, S., Galdi, C., Persiano, G. (eds.) SCN 2002. LNCS, vol. 2576, pp. 29–44. Springer, Heidelberg (2003)
9. Kolesnikov, V., Rackoff, C.: Key Exchange Using Passwords and Long Keys. In: Halevi, S., Rabin, T. (eds.) TCC 2006. LNCS, vol. 3876, pp. 100–119. Springer, Heidelberg (2006)

10. Kent, S., Seo, K.: Security Architecture for the Internet Protocol. Internet Draft, RFC 4301 (2005)
11. Matsuo, S., Phong, L.T., Ohkubo, M., Yung, M.: Leakage-Resilient RFID Authentication with Forward-Privacy. In: Ors Yalcin, S.B. (ed.) RFIDSec 2010. LNCS, vol. 6370, pp. 176–188. Springer, Heidelberg (2010)
12. Ohkubo, M., Suzuki, K., Kinoshita, S.: Cryptographic Approach to "Privacy-Friendly" Tags. In: RFID Privacy Workshop. MIT, USA (2003)
13. Pietrzak, K.: A Leakage-Resilient Mode of Operation. In: Joux, A. (ed.) EURO-CRYPT 2009. LNCS, vol. 5479, pp. 462–482. Springer, Heidelberg (2009)
14. Petit, C., Standaert, F.-X., Pereira, O., Malkin, T., Yung, M.: A Block Cipher based Pseudo Random Number Generator Secure against Side-channel Key Recovery. In: Proc. of ASIACCS 2008, pp. 56–65 (2008)
15. Pointcheval, D., Zimmer, S.: Multi-factor Authenticated Key Exchange. In: Bellovin, S.M., Gennaro, R., Keromytis, A.D., Yung, M. (eds.) ACNS 2008. LNCS, vol. 5037, pp. 277–295. Springer, Heidelberg (2008)
16. Sarma, S.E., Weis, S.A., Engels, D.W.: RFID Systems and Security and Privacy Implications. In: Kaliski Jr., B.S., Koç, Ç.K., Paar, C. (eds.) CHES 2002. LNCS, vol. 2523, pp. 454–469. Springer, Heidelberg (2003)
17. Trusted Computing Group, http://www.trustedcomputinggroup.org/
18. Ylonen, T., Lonvick, C.: The Secure Shell (SSH) Protocol Architecture. Internet Draft, RFC 4541 (2006)

Restricted Identification Scheme and Diffie-Hellman Linking Problem*

Mirosław Kutyłowski, Łukasz Krzywiecki, Przemysław Kubiak, and Michał Koza

Faculty of Fundamental Problems of Technology,
Wrocław University of Technology
{miroslaw.kutylowski,lukasz.krzywiecki,
przemyslaw.kubiak,michal.koza}@pwr.wroc.pl

Abstract. We concern schemes designed for user authentication in different systems (called sectors) with a single private key so that activities of the same person in different sectors are not linkable. In particular, we consider Restricted Identification scheme implemented on personal identity cards (*neuer Personalausweis*) issued by German authorities. The schemes we concern are devoted for practical application on personal identity cards where limitations of memory size is a critical issue.

Unlinkability for German Restricted Identification is silently based on random oracle model. We prove that the construction can be simplified by eliminating hiding certain values with hash functions: we show that unlinkability can be based on a problem that we call *Linking Diffie-Hellman Problem (LDHP)*. We prove that LDHP is as hard as Decisional DHP. Thereby we justify unlinkability in the standard model.

We also introduce and analyze a variant of German Restricted Identification providing active authentication. This protocol is intended for application areas where the right to access a sector is not by default (as for German Restricted Identification) and can be both granted and blocked. It is intended to serve as anonymous identity for sectors such as access to medical data and law enforcement, where prevention of Sybil attacks is a fundamental requirement.

Keywords: anonymous identifier, unlinkability, ephemeral-static Diffie-Hellman authentication.

1 Introduction

In many countries (including European Community), decisions have been made to replace traditional personal identity cards with cards with a chip (e-ID). Primarily, this enables cryptographic protection against forgery of ID documents issued by the state. The second goal is to provide a trusted cryptographic platform for e-government applications. In some countries (e.g., Germany and Estonia) this platform has been really used. In some other cases no applications have been developed so far despite technical feasibility.

---
* The paper was partially supported by Polish Ministry of Science and Higher Education, grant N N206 1842 33. Later it was supported by Fundation for Polish Science, Programme "MISTRZ".

L. Chen, M. Yung, and L. Zhu (Eds.): INTRUST 2011, LNCS 7222, pp. 221–238, 2012.
© Springer-Verlag Berlin Heidelberg 2012

User Authentication with eID Card. One of primary goals of eID cards is to perform strong authentication of card holder for granting access to data and/or services. It is silently assumed that only the owner of an ID card can use it and therefore an eID card may serve as a secure token for authenticating a user in remote systems.

Using personal ID cards as a platform for electronic identity functions has many practical advantages:

- The citizens are well trained to protect the cards from the use by third parties: the citizens have learnt not to borrow or leave them unattended, they protect the ID cards against physical damage, lost or stolen cards are usually immediately reported to the authorities, ...
- The citizens carry personal ID cards for other reasons: e.g., as travel documents in Schengen countries, as identity documents when driving a car, for authentication when renting a city bike, ... Therefore authentication with an eID card is user friendly – the citizen need not to carry any *additional* card or authentication token.
- Since issuing personal identity cards is usually under strict control of a state, it applies also to authentication and supports accountability of user's behavior.
- Certain basic mechanisms have to be implemented on eID cards anyway; authentication protocols can reuse them at no additional implementation cost.

Data Protection Issues. Quite a frequent tendency is to design an authentication procedure consisting of identification of the user and presenting an access request digitally signed by the user or his personal device. However, such a signed request may be presented to a third party as a strong proof that a given person wanted to get access to the system. Consequently, the data created during execution of the authentication protocol must be strictly protected in order to fulfil the personal data protection law in most countries. This creates substantial risks and costs for system development and administration. So if there is no legal reason for storing an evidence that a request has occurred, it would be advantageous to build an authentication protocol based on a Zero Knowledge Proof. In such a case, by definition, a transcript of a protocol has no real value for a third party, as it could be created by a simulator from the definition of Zero Knowledge Proofs.

In many cases full identity of a user is not really necessary – a pseudonym is enough. Using an anonymous identity facilitates data protection issues – indeed, protection of personal data is limited to data that concerns a person that *can be identified*.

Idea of Sectors. One of the ideas to facilitate personal data protection is to divide the activity areas into disjoint *sectors* and to provide authentication/identity mechanisms for the sectors so that activities of the same person in different sectors cannot be linked (except for well defined situations). Sectors encompass different areas of activities of a citizen, which should be in any interaction. Some of these sectors are sensitive: let us mention health care services (e.g., psychiatry), employment related chores, and law enforcement (e.g., anonymous witness). Lack of a strict separation between the sectors may lead to severe problems like merging databases from different sectors and selling them. Of course, there are less sensitive sectors like auction services. However, even then a service provider might be forced to fulfill very high standards of personal data protection: according to European legislation every data (also non-sensitive) concerning an identifiable person must be protected against unauthorized access.

The idea of sectors is that:

- each user is given a different identity (and authorization possibilities) for each sector,
- the identities cannot be linked between the sectors,
- a person may be granted *only one identity in a sector*, a Sybil attack (returning to the sector under a different identity) must be impossible.

Protection against Sybil attacks should be based on technical limitations rather than organizational countermeasures.

Application Examples. In order to make the motivation for sectors more intuitive, we provide a couple of simple examples. Let us discuss a few sectors:

Law Enforcement. Cooperation between police and citizens is often complicated by lack of trust: a citizen informing the police about crimes, which they are witnessing, may fear revealing his identity to criminals and consequently a personal revenge. The situation would be much different, if the citizen could contact police using a pseudonym (and authentication mechanism linked to this pseudonym) so that the identity of the informant remains hidden even for the police unless there are extraordinary circumstances.

Such a channel for contacts with police must fulfill the following properties:

- A single person should have no real possibility to appear under different pseudonyms within the scope of the contacts with the police – otherwise a single person could generate hundreds of complaints under different pseudonyms thus preventing proper recognition of the scale of the reported problem. (This is why anonymous credential protocols are not well suited for this kind of applications.)
- Each pseudonym should correspond to a single person. Therefore all actions under a given pseudonym can be considered as coming from the same but unknown person. This is crucial for evaluating the information and credibility of its source based on the past experience.
- The identity used for contacts with police should not be used for different purposes. Indeed, otherwise a combination of activities under the same pseudonym may lead to a quick elimination of potential candidates and leave only the holder of the pseudonym as matching these activities.

Work Conditions Safety. Safety conditions rules on workplace may be violated by companies in order to increase the profits. Unfortunately, situations of this kind have been revealed for example after accidents in coal mines. Even if there are authorities responsible for monitoring safety, they often lack necessary information. On the other hand, an employee having knowledge of the violations may be reluctant to report anything in order to preserve his job. An anonymous channel between the whistle-blower and the inspection authority would solve the problem.

Again, it is not only necessary to provide pseudonyms, but also make sure that there is 1-to-1 correspondence between the employees and the pseudonyms: a report that comes from many sources is more reliable than the one coming from a single whistle-blower. There should be unlinkability guarantees, especially because different *sectors* may exist within the same organization. For instance, another pseudonyms may be used for voting during elections of representatives of employees (in some countries it is compulsory to make such elections). If in these sectors the employee uses the same cryptographic material, there is a danger of linking pseudonyms. For instance, if the employer can conclude that given whistle-blower has not participated in past elections of the board mentioned above, it could mean that he or she was hired *after* the last elections. This would substantially reduce the anonymity set of the whistle-blower. Note that the dishonest employer need not to identify exactly the whistle-blower: if the anonymity set is sufficiently small, all employees from this anonymity set might be fired (in order to avoid accusations some extra people not belonging to this anonymity set could be fired as well).

Access to Anonymized Medical Data. Online access to medical records is regarded as necessity for keeping patients aware of their own records. Personal data protection requires that the patient has access only to own health records – so a strong authentication is required. On the other hand, a patient may be forced to show his medical record, e.g. by his potential employer. Alone for this reason the data records should be anonymized (another reason is that the system might be penetrated and the data can be leaked outside). However, sheer anonymization does not suffice: it should be impossible to create a transcript of a session showing both the patients identity during authentication and the medical records. Note that it should be guaranteed that a single person has exactly one anonymous identity in the system and this identity is maintained for a long time.

Intersection Attack. As mentioned above linking different pseudonyms may lead to disclosure of identity of users. First observe that for a given sector the attacker might be able to provide an anonymity set of a pseudonym together with full identities of the members of the anonymity set. For instance, if a pseudonym is used in local elections, then this set is the set of the voters in a given district. Even if this list is not public, it is accessible to many people. Similarly, pseudonyms used in special social group (e.g. students in Austria and elections of student representatives) correspond to the members of that group. By their nature, the anonymity sets in different sectors are in some sense independent. Therefore intersecting them reduces significantly their size. As reduction of size is roughly exponential in the number of intersections, this technique may lead to a full disclosure of identity or at least leave a very small anonymity set for a given pseudonym. Of course, the attack does not work if we cannot link the pseudonyms from different sectors.

Electronic ID and Sectors. Introducing electronic identity card equipped with strong cryptography brings an opportunity to implement idea of unlinkable authentication in sectors.

A naïve way to implement this idea is to assign a separate and independently generated key pair for each (sector,user) pair. This approach is clean in a theoretical sense (obvious unlinkability between sector IDs), but in practice it leads to substantial problems. First, in certain situations it might be necessary to reveal that a holder of two public keys is the same person. For instance, this might happen in case of misuse of services such as eBay: identity of a misbehaving user should be revealed in case of criminal or civil procedures. If the public keys are really independent, the link between the keys is not guaranteed on a cryptographic level.

The second reason why the naïve solution does not work is purely technical. The number of sectors is potentially unlimited, while the memory size is probably the most important limitation of smart cards. First, a substantial part of memory must be reserved for personal data (such as face image), operating system and other applications. Second, the unit cost of a smart card is crucial: due to budget limitations the states are forced to optimize memory usage as the price grows substantially with the memory size.

In the situation described it would be desirable to re-use the same cryptographic secret material on an eID card for authentication in different sectors. This is not un-problematic, since for verification different (and unlinkable) public keys must be used.

Other Anonymization Techniques. Many anonymization techniques have been proposed in the literature. Usually they are addressing quite different requirements, so let us explain differences between them and our application scenario.

Group signatures protect anonymity of a signer while at the same time they provide a strong proof that the signer belongs to a given group. This is not anonymization that we focus on – in our scenario activities of an anonymous user within a sector must be assignable to a single anonymous person. Group signatures do exactly the opposite (which makes sense in the target application of group signatures – signatures created in name of an organization, where the identity of a organization representative is hidden).

Ring signatures provide unconditional anonymity, where anonymity set can be created arbitrarily without consent of ring members as long as their public keys are available. But again, we cannot link the documents signed by the same anonymous person – which is our basic requirement. While ring signatures are perfect tools for whistle-blowers, they cannot be used in scenarios described above.

Anonymous credentials is another major invention for privacy protection (see e.g. [1], [2]), also supported by some major vendors. Anonymous credentials enable a user to authenticate himself (and his rights) without revealing his identity. More specifically, a user obtains credentials stating his rights to access systems satisfying criteria stated in the credentials. Afterwards the user can use credentials to authenticate himself in systems matching the credentials at any later point. In fact, the credential systems even guarantee that the interactions involving the same user remain unlinkable. Thereby, anonymous credentials fulfil the first two conditions of sector authentication, but are not designed to fulfill the third one. Only if the user starts misbehaving, her/his identity is revealed. So anonymous credentials are designed for applications such as making online transactions where we do not wish to build a profile of a client.

1.1 Deployed Systems

Austrian Bürgerkarte and a Aymmetric Solution. The idea of sectors appeared in Austria many years ago. The Austrian solution was based on symmetric cryptography and unique numbers for each person (either a physical or a legal one) stored in a central registry. The system is very closely related to the PIN mechanism: for each sector the

Bürgerkarte of a user is generating a unique password which is checked centrally like it happens for PIN numbers for ATM machines. The main disadvantage is that the password for a sector is static, so if a document is authenticated with the password, then its recipient may later perform a replay attack and impersonate the author of the document by providing the same password (of course, this works only for the same sector). Nevertheless, the Austrian solution addresses the problem of a growing number of logins and passwords that we have to keep in memory for different e-government systems. However, the main motivation is to separate different public administration sectors in order to simplify personal data protection.

German Restricted Identification. Technical Guideline [3] defines a mechanism, called Restricted Identification, for generating passwords in different sectors from a single private key. The protocol has been designed for the new e-ID (*neuer Personalausweis*) issued in Germany since November 2010. During authentication a terminal checks that it talks with an e-ID, a secure channel is built between the e-ID and the terminal, and finally the password is generated. Password generation is based on ephemeral-static Diffie-Hellman protocol.

German Restricted Identification is based on the black list approach: a holder of an e-ID can use a password to authenticate himself, as long as it is not on a blacklist obtained by the sector concerned.

Due to the black list approach and strong focus on privacy, the protocol is intended for specific applications, such as login at e-Bay. It does not work for applications such as anonymous witness in criminal court procedures or identity cards for health care, as after breaking into an e-ID one can create new identities that cannot be blacklisted.

1.2 Our Contribution

We consider rigorously unlinkability issues that arise when the lists of public keys from different sectors are compared (this concerns black lists of not-hashed values as well as white lists). The problem is that the adversary might have some advantage due to the fact that he might know the users for each sector. This problem was alluded in [3] by hashing the entries, however this leads to security guarantees based on pseudo-randomness of hash functions in the random oracle model.

For restricted identification systems based on Discrete Logarithm Problem we develop a framework based on difficulty of so called *Linking Diffie-Hellman Problem* (LDHP). In simple words, LDHP is the simplest task that the adversary might be faced: it concerns two users and a list of two public keys. The adversary has to link which key belongs to whom. This is quite a different question than Decisional DHP, where with probability $\frac{1}{2}$ the input is a random triple. In Sect. 2 we will show that despite subtle but intuitively substantial advantage for the adversary, LDHP is not weaker than Decisional DH Problem.

In Sect. 3 we show the consequences of hardness of LDHP for German Restricted Identification. A good message is that the protocol can be slightly simplified and there are unlinkability guarantees in the standard model. It does not necessarily mean that the German protocol should be simplified – now there are two anonymity guarantees: one based on LDHP and the other based on properties of hash function. Since the second mechanism is cheap, there is not clear reason why not to use it.

In Sect. 4 we propose a simple restricted identification scheme based on white lists. It reuses many components of German Restricted Identification, however it is intended for different class of applications: namely the ones where the users are not admitted to all sectors by default. For this scheme we provide a security proof.

2 Linking Diffie-Hellman Problem

There are many variations of the original Diffie-Hellman problem, see for example [4], [5] [6], [7], [8], [9], [10]. with subtle differences in their definitions. For the purpose of the security proof of Restricted Identification we introduce here *Linking Diffie-Hellman Problem* (LDHP) and prove that its difficulty is equivalent with Decisional Diffie-Hellman Problem (DDHP). Let $x \leftarrow_\$ X$ mean that x is sampled uniformly at random from finite set X. First we recall the basic DDHP and then formulate LDHP:

Definition 1 (DDHP Assumption). *Let $\langle \tilde{g} \rangle$ be a cyclic group generated by element $\tilde{g}$ of order $\mathrm{ord}\tilde{g} = q'$. There is no probabilistic polynomial-time algorithm $\mathcal{A}_{\mathrm{DDHP}}$ that distinguishes with non-negligible probability between distributions $D_0 = (\tilde{g}, \tilde{g}^a, \tilde{g}^b, \tilde{g}^c)$ and $D_1 = (\tilde{g}, \tilde{g}^a, \tilde{g}^b, \tilde{g}^{ab})$, where a, b, c are chosen at random from $\mathbb{Z}_{\mathrm{ord}\tilde{g}}$. That is, for any probabilistic polynomial-time algorithm $\mathcal{A}_{\mathrm{DDHP}}$ the advantage of $\mathcal{A}_{\mathrm{DDHP}}$*

$$\mathbf{Adv}(\mathcal{A}_{\mathrm{DDHP}}) = \Pr[\mathcal{A}_{\mathrm{DDHP}}(D_1) = 1] - \Pr[\mathcal{A}_{\mathrm{DDHP}}(D_0) = 1]$$

is negligible, i.e., $\mathbf{Adv}(\mathcal{A}_{\mathrm{DDHP}}) \leq \epsilon_{\mathrm{DDHP}}$ for negligibly small ϵ_{DDHP}.

Definition 2 (LDHP). *Let $\langle g \rangle$ be a cyclic group generated by element g of a prime order $\mathrm{ord}g = q$. Let $\mathcal{A}_{\mathrm{LDHP}}$ be a probabilistic polynomial-time algorithm that takes an input that comes from distribution $D_0 = (g, g^a, g^b, g^r, g^{ra}, g^{rb})$ with probability $\frac{1}{2}$ and otherwise from distribution $D_1 = (g, g^a, g^b, g^r, g^{rb}, g^{ra})$, where $a, b, r \in \mathbb{Z}_{\mathrm{ord}g}$, and outputs 1 or 0. We define*

$$\mathbf{Adv}(\mathcal{A}_{\mathrm{LDHP}}) = |\Pr[d \leftarrow_\$ \{0,1\} : \mathcal{A}_{\mathrm{LDHP}}(D_d) = d] - \tfrac{1}{2}|$$

as the advantage of $\mathcal{A}_{\mathrm{LDHP}}$ in distinguishing between distributions D_0 and D_1 in $\langle g \rangle$. The LDHP is broken if $\mathbf{Adv}(\mathcal{A}_{\mathrm{LDHP}})$ is non negligible.

Note that the input of LDHP consists of two DH pairs and we are *only* asked to determine the ordering of the last two arguments (g^{ra}, g^{rb}) which are given in a random order. Note that there is some similarity in formulation of LDHP and Group DHP [5], and especially between LDHP and Twin DHP [10].

Clearly, if we can solve Decisional DHP, then we immediately can solve LDHP. However, it is not immediately clear if the converse is true. The input data for LDHP are in a very specific form and one may hope to find a clever algebraic procedure that is based on this properties. However we show that LDHP is not easier than DDHP:

Theorem 1. *If DDHP Assumption holds in $\langle g \rangle$, then the advantage of any algorithm $\mathcal{A}_{\mathrm{LDHP}}$ breaking the LDHP in $\langle g \rangle$ is negligible: $\mathbf{Adv}(\mathcal{A}_{\mathrm{LDHP}}) \leq \epsilon_{\mathrm{DDHP}} + 1/q$, where ϵ_{DDHP} is advantage of the adversary breaking DHP and q is the order of g.*

Proof. According to the framework of security games [11], we construct a sequence of games for adversary algorithm $\mathcal{A} := \mathcal{A}_{\text{LDHP}}$, where Game 0 represents the original attack.

Game 0. We define Game 0 as the attack game against $\mathcal{A}$ as follows:

$$x_0, x_1 \leftarrow_\$ \mathbb{Z}_q$$
$$b \leftarrow_\$ \mathbb{Z}_q$$
$$d \leftarrow_\$ \{0,1\}$$
$$\hat{d} \leftarrow \mathcal{A}(g, g^{x_0}, g^{x_1}, g^b, g^{bx_d}, g^{bx_{1-d}})$$

Let S_0 be the event that $d = \hat{d}$ in Game 0. Thus the advantage of $\mathcal{A}$ is $|\Pr[S_0] - \frac{1}{2}|$.

Game 1. This game is basically the same as Game 0. In this transitions we restate x_0, x_1 as computed in an equivalent way $\alpha_0 a + \beta_0, \alpha_1 a + \beta_1$ respectively, for randomly chosen $a, \alpha_0, \alpha_1, \beta_0, \beta_1 \in \mathbb{Z}_q$:

$$a, \alpha_0, \alpha_1, \beta_0, \beta_1 \leftarrow_\$ \mathbb{Z}_q$$
$$x_0 \leftarrow \alpha_0 a + \beta_0$$
$$x_1 \leftarrow \alpha_1 a + \beta_1$$
$$b \leftarrow_\$ \mathbb{Z}_q$$
$$d \leftarrow_\$ \{0,1\}$$
$$\hat{d} \leftarrow \mathcal{A}(g, g^{x_0}, g^{x_1}, g^b, g^{\alpha_d ab + \beta_d b}, g^{\alpha_{1-d} ab + \beta_{1-d} b})$$

Notice that since q is a prime and $\alpha_0, \alpha_1, \beta_0, \beta_1$ are pairwise stochastically independent, x_0 and x_1 are stochastically independent, too. As the ensamble $(g, g^{x_0}, g^{x_1}, g^b, g^{\alpha_d ab + \beta_d b}, g^{\alpha_{1-d} ab + \beta_{1-d} b})$ has the same probability distribution as the ensamble $(g, g^{x_0}, g^{x_1}, g^b, g^{bx_d}, g^{bx_{1-d}})$, $\mathcal{A}$ has the inputs with the same probability distributions in Games 0 and 1. Let S_1 be the event that $d = \hat{d}$ in Game 1. We conclude that $\Pr[S_0] = \Pr[S_1]$.

Game 2. Now in computations of exponents we replace all occurrences of ab by a random number c:

$$a, \alpha_0, \alpha_1, \beta_0, \beta_1 \leftarrow_\$ \mathbb{Z}_q$$
$$x_0 \leftarrow \alpha_0 a + \beta_0$$
$$x_1 \leftarrow \alpha_1 a + \beta_1$$
$$b \leftarrow_\$ \mathbb{Z}_q$$
$$c \leftarrow_\$ \mathbb{Z}_q$$
$$d \leftarrow_\$ \{0,1\}$$
$$\hat{d} \leftarrow \mathcal{A}(g, g^{x_0}, g^{x_1}, g^b, g^{\alpha_d c + \beta_d b}, g^{\alpha_{1-d} c + \beta_{1-d} b})$$

Let S_2 be the event that $d = \hat{d}$ in Game 2.

Claim 1. $|\Pr[S_1] - \Pr[S_2]| \leq \epsilon_{\text{DDHP}}$, where ϵ_{DDHP} is the advantage of some efficient algorithm solving DDH Problem (so ϵ_{DDHP} negligible under DDH Assumption).

The proof of Claim 1 is essentially the observation that in Game 1 the arguments g^{x_d}, g^b, g^{bx_d} for $\mathcal{A}$ are in the form $(g^a)^{\alpha_d} g^{\beta_d}, g^b, (g^{ab})^{\alpha_d} g^{\beta_d b}$ $(= ((g^a)^{\alpha_d} g^{\beta_d})^b)$ (which is a DH triple) while in Game 2 they are of the form $(g^a)^{\alpha_d} g^{\beta_d}, g^b, (g^c)^{\alpha_d} g^{\beta_d b}$ (which is a random triple). So we build a distinguisher $\mathcal{D}$ for DDH Problem for group $\langle g \rangle$:

Algorithm $\mathcal{D}(g^a, g^b, g^c)$
    $\alpha_0, \alpha_1, \beta_0, \beta_1 \leftarrow_\$ \mathbb{Z}_q$
    $d \leftarrow_\$ \{0, 1\}$
    $\hat{d} \leftarrow \mathcal{A}(g, (g^a)^{\alpha_0} g^{\beta_0}, (g^a)^{\alpha_1} g^{\beta_1}, g^b, (g^c)^{\alpha_d} g^{\beta_d b}, (g^c)^{\alpha_{1-d}} g^{\beta_{1-d} b})$
    if $(d = \hat{d})$
        then return 1
        else return 0

If the input to $\mathcal{D}$ is of the form (g^a, g^b, g^{ab}), for random a, b, then $\mathcal{A}$ receives the inputs with the same probability distribution as in Game 1, and therefore

$$\Pr[a, b \leftarrow_\$ \mathbb{Z}_q : \mathcal{D}(g^a, g^b, g^{ab}) = 1] = \Pr[S_1].$$

If the input to $\mathcal{D}$ is of the form (g^a, g^b, g^c), then computation proceeds just as in Game 2, and therefore

$$\Pr[a, b, c \leftarrow_\$ \mathbb{Z}_q : \mathcal{D}(g^a, g^b, g^c) = 1] = \Pr[S_2].$$

It follows that the DDH-advantage of $\mathcal{D}$ is equal to $|\Pr[S_1] - \Pr[S_2]|$.   □ Claim 1

Claim 2. $|\Pr[S_2] - \frac{1}{2}| \leq 1/q$.

The idea is that in Game 2, g^c serves as a one-time pad, and thus the adversary's output $\hat{d}$ is independent of the hidden bit d. To set up attention, let us assume that parameters a, b, c are fixed. Now let $y_1 = g^{\alpha_0 a + \beta_0}$, $y_2 = g^{\alpha_1 a + \beta_1}$, $y_3 = g^{\alpha_0 c + \beta_0 b}$, $y_4 = g^{\alpha_1 c + \beta_1 b}$, where as arguments of $\mathcal{A}$ in Game 2 values y_1, y_2, y_3, y_4 occur in the order (y_1, y_2, y_3, y_4) or (y_1, y_2, y_4, y_3). Let e_1, e_2, e_3, e_4 denote the discrete logarithms of y_1, y_2, y_3, y_4. Observe that for any fixed a, b, c we obtain the following linear equations:

$$\begin{cases} e_1 = \alpha_0 a + \beta_0 \\ e_3 = \alpha_0 c + \beta_0 b \end{cases}, \quad \begin{cases} e_2 = \alpha_1 a + \beta_1 \\ e_4 = \alpha_1 c + \beta_1 b \end{cases}. \tag{1}$$

Thereby, y_1, y_3 depend on α_0, β_0, and y_2, y_4 depend on α_1, β_1. Observe that if $c \neq ab \bmod q$, then the linear equations in each of the systems mentioned above are linearly independent. In such a case for each pair of values (y_1, y_3) there is exactly one setting for values (α_0, β_0). So y_1, y_3 are uniformly and independently distributed. Similarly, if $c \neq ab \bmod q$ variables y_2, y_4 are uniformly and independently distributed. Since y_2, y_4 depend on α_1, β_1 and they are independent from α_0, β_0, variables y_2, y_4 are independent from y_1, y_3. Let the event F that $c = ab \bmod q$ be treated as a fault event according to the framework of [11]. Then of course $\Pr[F] = \frac{1}{q}$. From now on assume that fault event F does not occur.

Let us fix a, b, c parameters and y_1, y_2, y_3, y_4 for further discussion. Each input sequence (y_1, y_2, y_3, y_4) to algorithm $\mathcal{A}$ can be obtained from two alternatives:

- When the bit d equals to 0, the input comes from a sequence (y_1, y_2, y_3, y_4) for exponents e_1, e_2, e_3, e_4 and unique parameters $\alpha_0, \beta_0, \alpha_1, \beta_1$.

- When the bit d equals to 1, the input comes from a sequence $(y_1', y_2', y_3', y_4') = (y_1, y_2, y_4, y_3)$ for different exponents e_1', e_2', e_3', e_4' and different (but again unique) parameters $\alpha_0', \beta_0', \alpha_1', \beta_1'$.

Consequently, for each sequence of values $(a, b, c, \tilde{y}_1, \tilde{y}_2, \tilde{y}_3, \tilde{y}_4)$ such that $c \neq ab \bmod q$ we have for each d exactly one system of α's and β's solving equations (1) defined by sequence of exponents $(\tilde{e}_1, \tilde{e}_2, \tilde{e}_3, \tilde{e}_4)$. That is,

$$\Pr[(d = 0, \alpha_0, \beta_0, \alpha_1, \beta_1) \text{ defines } (\tilde{y}_1, \tilde{y}_2, \tilde{y}_3, \tilde{y}_4))] =$$
$$= \Pr[(d = 1, \alpha_0', \beta_0', \alpha_1', \beta_1') \text{ defines } (\tilde{y}_1, \tilde{y}_2, \tilde{y}_3, \tilde{y}_4)].$$

Note that this means that for any fixed a, b, c such that $c \neq ab \bmod q$ we have the same probabilities of occurrences of the tuples $(d = 0, \tilde{y}_1, \tilde{y}_2, \tilde{y}_3, \tilde{y}_4)$, $(d = 1, \tilde{y}_1, \tilde{y}_2, \tilde{y}_3, \tilde{y}_4)$. Now, let

$$\Pr[\mathcal{A}(g, \tilde{y}_1, \tilde{y}_2, g^b, \tilde{y}_3, \tilde{y}_4) = 0] = p, \quad \Pr[\mathcal{A}(g, \tilde{y}_1, \tilde{y}_2, g^b, \tilde{y}_3, \tilde{y}_4) = 1] = 1 - p,$$

for certain p. Obviously those outputs are independent of whatever the parameters $(d = 0, \alpha_0, \beta_0, \alpha_1, \beta_1)$ or $(d = 1, \alpha_0', \beta_0', \alpha_1', \beta_1')$ defined the input $\tilde{y}_1, \tilde{y}_2, \tilde{y}_3, \tilde{y}_4$. Thus, for each sequence of values $(a, b, c, \tilde{y}_1, \tilde{y}_2, \tilde{y}_3, \tilde{y}_4)$ such that $c \neq ab \bmod q$:

$$\Pr[\mathcal{A}(g, \tilde{y}_1, \tilde{y}_2, g^b, \tilde{y}_3, \tilde{y}_4) = d] =$$
$$= \Pr[((d = 0, \alpha_0, \beta_0, \alpha_1, \beta_1) \text{ defines } (\tilde{y}_1, \tilde{y}_2, \tilde{y}_3, \tilde{y}_4)) \wedge \mathcal{A}(g, \tilde{y}_1, \tilde{y}_2, g^b, \tilde{y}_3, \tilde{y}_4) = 0]$$
$$+ \Pr[((d = 1, \alpha_0', \beta_0', \alpha_1', \beta_1') \text{ defines } (\tilde{y}_1, \tilde{y}_2, \tilde{y}_3, \tilde{y}_4)) \wedge \mathcal{A}(g, \tilde{y}_1, \tilde{y}_2, g^b, \tilde{y}_3, \tilde{y}_4) = 1]$$
$$= \Pr[(d = 0, \alpha_0, \beta_0, \alpha_1, \beta_1) \text{ defines } (\tilde{y}_1, \tilde{y}_2, \tilde{y}_3, \tilde{y}_4)] \cdot \Pr[\mathcal{A}(g, \tilde{y}_1, \tilde{y}_2, g^b, \tilde{y}_3, \tilde{y}_4) = 0]$$
$$+ \Pr[(d = 1, \alpha_0', \beta_0', \alpha_1', \beta_1') \text{ defines } (\tilde{y}_1, \tilde{y}_2, \tilde{y}_3, \tilde{y}_4)] \cdot \Pr[\mathcal{A}(g, \tilde{y}_1, \tilde{y}_2, g^b, \tilde{y}_3, \tilde{y}_4) = 1]$$
$$= \tfrac{1}{2} \cdot p + \tfrac{1}{2} \cdot (1 - p) = \tfrac{1}{2}.$$

Thus taking into account fault event F, we have $|\Pr[S_2] - 1/2| \leq 1/q$ Claim 2 $\Box$

Combining Claims 1 and 2, we see that $|\Pr[S_0] - \tfrac{1}{2}| \leq \epsilon_{\text{DDHP}} + 1/q$. This concludes the proof of Theorem 1. $\Box$

3   German Restricted Identification

In this section we recall German Restricted Identification scheme and apply to it the results from the previous section. As the system is already deployed in practice on a large scale, this is not an academic discussion, but an analysis of a real system.

There are the following actors in the scheme (cf. 4.5 in [3]): CA holding its private and public revocation key α, g^α, respectively, sector authorities S_j holding secret keys R_j, and the users U_i holding private and public keys respectively x_i and g^{x_i}. Key g^{x_i} is a *global* public key (*global* in contrary to *local* public keys of that user used in sectors).

The following protocol is run for authenticating user U_i in sector S_j:

1. In order to initiate the core procedure, terminal authentication and chip authentication procedures are executed at first; the latter procedure implies that the chip *must* possess some secret key, the key *must* be shared by many identity cards in order to guarantee anonymity within a large group of people.

2. Public key $g^{\alpha R_j}$ of the sector S_j is transferred to the e-ID of user U_i.
3. The e-ID calculates $\text{ID}_{i,j} = H((g^{\alpha R_j})^{x_i})$, the user's U_i identifier in sector S_j, and sends it to the sector terminal (H is a hash function).
4. If $\text{ID}_{i,j}$ is not on the black-list of S_j, the access to S_j is granted for the user U_i.

The black-lists hold the results of the revocation protocol. The revocation procedure is very efficient: in order to revoke user U_i from sector S_j his public key g^{x_i} is sent to CA. CA calculates $g^{x_i \alpha}$. Then the value $g^{x_i \alpha}$ is sent to the sector S_j, which computes $g^{(x_i \alpha) R_j}$. Finally, the value $H(g^{x_i \alpha R_j})$ is placed on the black-list of the sector S_j.

Since Restricted Identification procedure from [3] might only be executed *after* terminal authentication and chip authentication procedures (cf. Section 2.1.5 and 4.5.1 in [3]), the terminal learns the identity of the *group key* of the chip. Moreover, the chip transmits the sector-ID through the terminal, so the terminal learns the sector- identifier of the chip (this is the reason why terminal authentication must be executed first). An interesting feature of the above authentication protocol is that the terminal does not check validity of the received sector ID (cf. Table 4.1 in [3] and the protocol in Section 4.5 of [3]), it only checks if that ID has not been revoked. Hence, if a terminal is malicious and leaks the restricted ID of one chip, then the leaked ID might be used by another chip in communication with another terminal of the same sector.

If chip authentication is performed with a key shared by many identity cards, then so called anonymity set is large and privacy leakage is negligible. On the other hand, it requires very high security level for the chip cards: deriving such a key from a single chip would make it possible to go through Restricted Identification with a fake ID (which would not appear on the black lists). This is not very dangerous, if Restricted Identification is used for applications like age authentication on vending machines selling cigarettes. On the other hand, the situation becomes problematic since an adversary becomes a fully anonymous "account" in a really important sector (like e-health services, law enforcement, ...) and in case of criminal behavior we cannot use the fake ID(s) of the adversary to trace back the trouble maker. So the German solution must not be used in sensitive application areas unless the smart cards are ideally tamper resistant. However, German Restricted Identification is intended to be used for private systems with more focus on personal data protection than on preventing fake identities.

Note that if $\text{ID}_{i,j}$ would be calculated as $g^{x_i \alpha R_j}$ instead as $H(g^{x_i \alpha R_j})$, then the user U_i could prove that he is in possession of the private key x_i. The implicit proof of possession, quite similar to chip authentication procedure from [3], is utilized in Sect. 4. In fact in the sectors of restricted identification the protocol from Sect. 4 is intended to be used instead of the chip authentication procedure.

The main unlinkability question concerning the German solution is how to prove that different sectors cannot link the identifiers of the same user in different black lists. Recall that the identifiers of a user holding private key x_i in sectors S_j and $S_{j'}$ have the form $H(g^{x_i \alpha R_j})$ and $H(g^{x_i \alpha R_{j'}})$. Function H has to blind the identifiers and make it hard to link them with the public key g^{x_i} of the owner, and make it hard to show that the same private key has been used. We are not aware of any formal argument published before for unlinkability of $H(g^{x_i \alpha R_j})$ and $H(g^{x_{i'} \alpha R_{j'}})$ whenever $i = i'$. Usage of H shows reliance on pseudorandomness of hash functions (and "wiping out" all algebraic relationships) that can be modeled in the random oracle model.

With the result on LDHP we see that there is strong unlinkability for the black lists even for the case when H is not used. Obviously, usage of H does not weaken the system, since an adversary holding the "plain" black list could apply H on them and perform attack on the "hashed" version. (So in particular, there is no necessity to modify the protocol at this point.)

4   Restricted Identification with White Lists

In this section we first present a modified version of German Restricted Identification from [3]. Our target are applications like the ones mentioned in Sect. 1:

- explicit registration is necessary in order to become a user in a given sector,
- real identity of a misbehaving user in a sector may be revealed if an ID authority and the sector authority cooperate.

The restricted identification protocol described below includes (as a part) a kind of terminal authentication procedure. The protocol establishes some session key dependent on user's unique secret key stored on his smart card. The session key is used to protect communication between the card and the terminal. Consequently, for this protocol no chip authentication procedure (even with group key) is executed.

4.1   Algorithm Description

There are the following actors of the protocol: *ID Authority* – a central authority that maintains a database of all users together with their public keys, *sector authorities* - in each sector there is a single authority granting access to sector resources, *users* – each user holds a private key and authenticates himself against arbitrary sector authorities.

The protocol uses a group $\langle g \rangle$ of a prime order, where DDH Problem is hard.

Setup of Keys. The following keys are held by the protocol participants:

ID Authority holds a secret key r_j for each sector S_j, chosen at random by ID Authority. Additionally, it holds some keys to protect communication with sector authorities as well some key for signing certificates.
the authority of a sector S_j is assigned the following keys:
  - a pair of keys for encrypting messages to be sent to S_j, where the public key is called K_j. We assume that these are known to everybody or there is a reliable system confirming them, e.g. a system of digital certificates issued by trustworthy authorities, The encryption scheme E to be used has to be CPA secure.
  - a secret key (exponent) R_j chosen at random by S_j,
  - a public key $Y_j = g^{R_j \cdot r_j}$. The key Y_j is publicly known, an appropriate certificate issued by ID Authority confirms that it is the public key of S_j. (Note that S_j does not know the discrete logarithm of its public key.)
a user U_i holds a secret key x_i chosen by his card at random. His master public key is $y_i = g^{x_i}$.

There are the following lists of public keys maintained by the system:

main list of users maintained by ID Authority: it contains entries of the form (U_i, y_i),
public list of sectors maintained by ID Authority: It contains entries of the form
(S_j, Y_j, K_j). The list is signed by ID Authority in a standard way.
sector user lists: there is a separate white list W_j for each sector S_j. It contains public
keys of users entitled to log in S_j. The list W_j contains only public keys of the users
(without their ID's). The public key for user U_i in sector S_j equals $y_{i,j} = Y_j^{x_i}$.

Creating the List of Sectors. The key Y_j is generated by ID Authority and S_j as follows:
ID Authority chooses r_j at random, computes $z_j := g^{r_j}$, and sends it to S_j. Sector
authority of S_j computes R_j at random, computes $Y_j := z_j^{R_j}$ and shows Y_j to ID
Authority. Finally, ID Authority includes (S_j, Y_j, K_j) in the list of sectors and issues
appropriate certificate linking S_j with Y_j. Note that ID Authority operates on some
server and may utilize some secure environment like a *Hardware Security Module*. Thus
it is realistic to assume that ID Authority is capable to securely store even thousands of
sector exponents r_j.

Creating User's Public Keys for a Sector. We assume that there is some standard procedure for implementing the key pairs (x_i, y_i) of the users. Now we show how the keys
$y_{i,j}$ are generated. First, ID Authority checks the right of U_i to use sector S_j and computes $y_i' = y_i^{r_j}$. Then the authority of sector S_j obtains y_i' and computes $(y_i')^{R_j}$ (which
equals $(y_i^{r_j})^{R_j} = g^{x_i \cdot r_j \cdot R_j} = (g^{r_j \cdot R_j})^{x_i} = Y_j^{x_i} = y_{i,j}$).
Computed public keys can be placed on a white list or on the black list, depending
on the intended action. They can be transmitted in bulks, or just as single entries. One
can use a direct secure link between ID Authority and sector authority to transmit y_i',
or, alternatively, a user can carry it. In the last case, the user gets a signed ciphertext
of y_i' so that it cannot be manipulated by the user. We leave further details of possible
architectures for technical documents.

Authentication Against a Sector. When a user U_i wishes to access sector S_j, then the
ephemeral-static Diffie-Hellman protocol is executed between U_i and S_j:

1. U_i receives sector's S_j certificate containing key Y_j.
2. U_i computes his public key for sector S_j by computing $y_{i,j} = (Y_j)^{x_i}$. (Of course,
   U_i can compute $y_{i,j}$ just once and store it for a later use.)
3. U_i chooses a random challenge v, and encrypts v with the key K_j obtaining $e = E_{K_j}(v)$. Then U_i sends e to S_j together with an access request and together with
   ciphertext $E_{K_j}(y_{i,j}^v)$.
4. S_j decrypts the ciphertexts and checks, if $y_{i,j} = (y_{i,j}^v)^{v^{-1} \bmod \text{ord} g}$ appears on the
   white list W_i. If not, then the request is refused.
5. S_j generates exponents u_1, u_2 at random, computes $h_1 = Y_j^{u_1}$, $h_2 = Y_j^{u_2}$ and
   sends them to U_i together with a non-interactive Proof of Knowledge of discrete
   logarithm of h_2 with respect to Y_j. Simultaneously, S_j computes the session key
   $K = (y_{i,j}^{u_1})^v$ and a one-time token $S = (y_{i,j}^{u_2})^v$.
6. U_i computes the session key K as $(h_1^{x_i})^v$, and the token $S = (h_2^{x_i})^v$.

7. All further communication between U_i and S_j during this session is encrypted with the key K, authentication is implicit by correct encryption. Additionally, in the first message U_i transmits the token S. S_j checks the token against its value computed locally. Finally S_j replies with u_2 and U_i checks that $h_2 = Y_j^{u_2}$.

Since $h_1^{x_i} = (Y_j^{u_1})^{x_i} = (Y_j^{x_i})^{u_1} = y_{i,j}^{u_1}$, the key K is computed correctly on both sides. The same concerns the token S. The last step revealing u_2 prevents using the protocol as a oracle for computing a^{x_i} for arbitrary a. Indeed, notice that if h_2 is of the given form, then the answer of U_i does not bring a new knowledge to S_j, as S_j can compute it itself.

Simplified Version. In the above protocol the number of exponentiations is higher than in German Restricted Identification. This is not a major problem as the calculations can be performed within the practical time limit (for a user the computation time does not matter as long as it does not exceeds, say, a single second). Nevertheless, it is possible to simplify the protocol and remove creation of the token S. In this case the protocol should be appended by a proof of knowledge of the key K by both S_j and U_i. This solution might be more efficient, but may depend on other assumptions than DH Problem.

Prosecution. If a user with the sector public key $y'_{i,j}$ behaves so that his identity has to be revealed (e.g., in case of a fraud), then S_j raises $y'_{i,j}$ to power $R_j^{-1} \bmod \mathrm{ord}g$ and sends the result to ID Authority. After examining the legal situation, ID authority computes the public key of this user, by raising the element obtained to power $r_j^{-1} \bmod \mathrm{ord}g$. The result is the public key of the user concerned. A lookup in the list of users reveals identity of the owner of y'_i.

4.2   Security Analysis

In this section we consider verious attacks, each time giving the adversary all information apart from the secrets sought by the user or the secrets of the party that the adversary tries to impersonate.

Definition 3 (Attack Model 1). *The adversary $\mathcal{A}_1$ controls all parties except for U_i. The information available for $\mathcal{A}_1$ is a transcript of any number of messages exchanged according to the scheme (including the plaintexts corresponding to the ciphertexts exchanged between the users and sector authorities) the private keys of all parties but U_i, and all public keys. The goal of $\mathcal{A}_1$ is to obtain the private key x_i of U_i.*

Proposition 1. *If $\mathcal{A}_1$ can succeed with probability p_1 when U_i chooses x_i at random, then Discrete Logarithm Problem for a random element from $\langle g \rangle$ can be solved in base g with probability p_1 with a comparable computational effort.*

Proof. We construct an algorithm $\mathcal{B}$ that for a given $y \in \langle g \rangle$ looks for x such that $y = g^x$. Assume that $\mathcal{C}$ is an algorithm used by $\mathcal{A}_1$ that succeeds with probability p_1. From an input of $\mathcal{B}$ we can easily construct an input for $\mathcal{C}$. Namely, we choose at random the private and public keys for all protocol participants except for U_i, who gets the public key y. Note that the public key of U_i for sector S_j can be obtained as

$y^{r_j \cdot R_j}$. Then we generate a transcript of communication exchanged in the system. This is possible, since during key establishment between U_i and, say S_j, the session key and the one-time token can be computed by S_j. For so prepared data we run $\mathcal{C}$ in order to derive the private key of U_i, that is, the discrete logarithm of y. $\square$

We may consider a similar attack against S_j aiming to gain R_j. We skip the considerations concerning interaction between ID authority and S_j as we assume that ID Authority is honest.

Definition 4 (Attack Model 1'). *The adversary $\mathcal{A}'_1$ controls all parties except for S_j. The information available for $\mathcal{A}'_1$ is a transcript of any number of messages exchanged according to the scheme (including the plaintexts corresponding to the ciphertexts exchanged between the users and sector authorities), the private keys of all parties but S_j, and all public keys. The goal of $\mathcal{A}'_1$ is to obtain the key R_j of S_j.*

Proposition 2. *If $\mathcal{A}'_1$ can succeed with probability p_1 when S_j chooses R_j at random, then Discrete Logarithm Problem for a random element from $\langle g \rangle$ can be solved in base g with probability p_1 with a comparable computational effort.*

Proof. One can easily see that the whole transcript of communication between S_j and U_i may be created by a simulator, so an attack can be played offline without interaction with S_j. Then it can be directly used for computing discrete logarithm of a given β with respect to g^{r_j}, where we seek for R_j such that $\beta = (g^{r_j})^{R_j}$. The sought discrete logarithm can be finally computed as $r_j \cdot R_j$. $\square$

Note that in Attack Model 1 it does not make sense to impersonate U_i, since all sectors S_j are controlled by the adversary. This problem is considered by the next model:

Definition 5 (Attack Model 2). *The adversary $\mathcal{A}_2$ controls all parties except for U_i and S_j. $\mathcal{A}_2$ has access to a transcript of any number of messages exchanged according to the scheme (including the plaintexts of the ciphertexts exchanged by the users U_i and S_j), all public keys, the private keys of all parties except for x_i and the decryption key of S_j. The goal of $\mathcal{A}_2$ is to impersonate U_i against S_j in a single authentication session.*

Proposition 3. *If $\mathcal{A}_2$ can succeed with probability p_2 when U_i and S_j choose their private keys at random, then Computational DH Problem for a random input can be solved with probability p_2 with a comparable computational effort.*

Proof. For clarity we follow the framework of security games according to [11]. Since most details are straightforward, we omit detailed listing of the games.

The game G_0 describes the attack performed by $\mathcal{A}_2$. Game G_1 differs from G_0 in that there are no users other than U_i. The adversary from game G_1 can emulate any number of users by choosing their private keys, computing public keys for all sectors according to the protocol, and generating communication transcripts with these users. So if there is an attack with advantage ϵ_0 for G_0, then the adversary of G_1 can prepare the input for G_0 from the input of G_1. So the advantage ε_1 of G_1 satisfies $\varepsilon_1 \geq \varepsilon_0$.

Game G_2 differs from G_1 in that it eliminates all previous communication sessions of U_i. The advantage ε_2 of game G_2 satisfies $\varepsilon_2 \geq \varepsilon_1$, since the adversary of G_2 may emulate any previous sessions of U_i and use this as input for the adversary of G_1. Indeed, the adversary of G_2 can create session keys from previous sessions without knowing the key x_i and therefore create transcript of all previous sessions.

Note that game G_2 essentially works with the keys $y_i = g^{x_i}$, $Y_j = g^{r_j \cdot R_j}$, and $y_{i,j} = Y_j^{x_i}$. In game G_3 we reveal r_j, R_j to the adversary. Then the parameter y_i can be eliminated, since it can be computed by the adversary from $y_{i,j}$. Obviously, the advantage ε_3 of G_3 satisfies $\varepsilon_3 \geq \varepsilon_2$. However, in an attack of game G_3 the adversary has to create ciphertexts encrypted with the key $K = Y_j^{x_i \cdot u_1 \cdot v}$ and present the token $S = Y_j^{x_i \cdot u_2 \cdot v}$ given $Y_j, Y_j^{x_i}, Y_j^{u_1}, Y_j^{u_2}$ and v.

Game G_3 can be used to solve Computational DHP in $\langle g \rangle$ with advantage at least ε_3 as the adversary can apply the following strategy: Given input A, B, C for Computational DHP in $\langle g \rangle$ prepare an input for G_3 by setting $(Y_j, Y_j^{x_i}, Y_j^{u_2}) = (A, B, C)$ and $Y_j^{u_1} = C^r$ (so assuming $u_1 = r \cdot u_2 \bmod \mathrm{ord} g$ for some r). Then run the adversary from the game G_3. The adversary presents S, so in particular can derive $S^{v^{-1}}$ which equals $Y_j^{x_i \cdot u_2}$ thereby solving the CDHP for B, C and base A. □

Now we consider a dual situation when an adversary is trying to impersonate S_j:

Definition 6 (Attack Model 3). *Adversary $\mathcal{A}_3$ controls all parties except for U_i and S_j. $\mathcal{A}_3$ has access to a transcript of any number of messages exchanged according to the scheme (including the plaintexts of the ciphertexts exchanged by the users U_i and S_j), the private keys of all parties but U_i and S_j and all public keys. The goal of $\mathcal{A}_3$ is to impersonate S_j against U_i in a single authentication session.*

Proposition 4. *If $\mathcal{A}_3$ can succeed with probability p_3, then the encryption scheme E is not semantically secure, i.e. there is an adversary that succeeds with probability p_3.*

Proof. We construct an attack for a security game GE describing semantic security of E. Recall that the scheme E is asymmetric with public key K_j. During GE, two messages v_0, v_1 are chosen at random. Then a bit b is chosen at random and v_b is encrypted with key K_j, yielding a ciphertext $C = E_{K_j}(v_b)$. In the next step the adversary has to guess b based on C, v_0, v_1 and K_j (of course E should be a probabilistic scheme).

An adversary from game GE can adopt the following strategy: generate all private keys of all participants except for S_j. Then generate a transcript of some number of sessions. Finally, generate a session in which U_i transmits C as the ciphertext of parameter v during Step 3 of the protocol. In this session the adversary $\mathcal{A}_3$ tries to impersonate S_j, so he must answer with a message encrypted with $K = (y_{i,j}^{u_1})^v$. Then the adversary of GE may easily check which of the keys is used: $K = (y_{i,j}^{u_1})^{v_0}$ or $K = (y_{i,j}^{u_1})^{v_1}$. If the equality holds for v_t, then the adversary from GE outputs $b = t$. □

Finally, we consider the core property, i.e., unlinkability between different sectors.

Definition 7 (Attack Model 4). *The adversary $\mathcal{A}_4$ controls all sectors S_j. $\mathcal{A}_4$ has access to whole communication between the sectors and the users and all white lists of the sectors. The goal of $\mathcal{A}_4$ is to decide if for two public keys $y_{i,j}$ and $y_{i',j'}$, from sectors S_j and $S_{j'}$, $j \neq j'$, it holds that $i = i'$.*

We may improve the chances of the adversary by indicating which users belong to which sectors, and given U_i and $U_{i'}$ both belonging to sectors S_j, $S_{j'}$ to indicate the public keys on the white lists of S_j, $S_{j'}$ that do not belong to U_i and $U_{i'}$. In this case we can model an advantaged adversary in the following way:

Definition 8 (Attack Model 4+). *Adversary $\mathcal{A}_4^+$ controls all sectors S_j. The only users are U_1 and U_2, both belonging to all sectors. $\mathcal{A}_4^+$ has access to whole communication between the sectors and the users, all white lists of the sectors, and the public keys y_1, y_2 of, respectively, U_1 and U_2. However, $\mathcal{A}_4^+$ has no control over the users, and their access pattern is random and cannot be influenced by $\mathcal{A}_4^+$. The goal of $\mathcal{A}_4^+$ is to link y_1 with the public key of U_1 on the white list of S_1.*

Proposition 5. *If adversary $\mathcal{A}_4^+$ has advantage p_4, then LDH Problem can be attacked with advantage p_4.*

Proof. An adversary attacking LDH Problem can easily transform its input to the input of $\mathcal{A}_4^+$. Indeed, given an input g, A, B, R, X, Y for LDH Problem, he assigns these values as follows: $Y_1 = R$, $y_1 = A$, $y_2 = B$, and $\{y_{1,1}, y_{2,1}\} = \{X, Y\}$ (so, the white list for S_1 is X, Y and it is not known which of the public keys is $y_{1,1}$ and which is $y_{2,1}$). The public key Y_j of sector S_j for $j \geq 2$ is chosen as g^{w_j}, where w_j is chosen at random. The public keys of, respectively, U_1 and U_2 in S_j are computed as $y_1^{w_j}, y_2^{w_j}$. Then the adversary generates access patterns for a holder of each public key in each sector and generates appropriate transcripts of the corresponding sessions. So generated input is fed into the algorithm run by adversary $\mathcal{A}_4^+$. The output of $\mathcal{A}_4^+$ links A, B with X, Y, as required. $\square$

If the adversary can link a user with a public key in *some* sector, then probability of breaking LDHP in the above proof has to be divided by the number of sectors.

5   Conclusions

The scheme presented in this paper is different from German restricted identification, however the reader may notice that both are built from the same basic primitives. This is advantageous from implementation point of view, since one can design a common platform for variety of application scenarios – reducing costs, enhancing flexibility and making standardization much easier. In particular, it would be useful to design anonymous credentials protocols based on exactly the same primitives.

In our opinion restricted identification might become one of the crucial tools for privacy protection and personal data protection in a near future. It moves the security mechanisms from organizational countermeasures to cryptographic mechanisms. Like elsewhere in the field of authentication techniques, there is not just a single application scenario, so many different mechanisms of this kind might be necessary.

Acknowledgment. We would like to thank Dennis Kügler and Jens Bender from BSI for many discussions and for proposing improvements concerning early drafts of this paper. In particular, we are thankful for discovering some flaws in the early versions of the protocol.

References

1. Camenisch, J., Groß, T., Heydt-Benjamin, T.S.: Rethinking accountable privacy supporting services: extended abstract. In: Bertino, E., Takahashi, K. (eds.) Digital Identity Management, pp. 1–8. ACM (2008)
2. Backes, M., Camenisch, J., Sommer, D.: Anonymous yet accountable access control. In: Atluri, V., di Vimercati, S.D.C., Dingledine, R. (eds.) WPES, pp. 40–46. ACM (2005)
3. Bundesamt für Sicherheit in der Informationstechnik: Advanced Security Mechanisms for Machine Readable Travel Documents 2.05. TR-03110 (2010)
4. Abdalla, M., Bellare, M., Rogaway, P.: The Oracle Diffie-Hellman Assumptions and an Analysis of DHIES. In: Naccache, D. (ed.) CT-RSA 2001. LNCS, vol. 2020, pp. 143–158. Springer, Heidelberg (2001)
5. Bresson, E., Chevassut, O., Pointcheval, D.: Group Diffie-Hellman Key Exchange Secure against Dictionary Attacks. In: Zheng, Y. (ed.) ASIACRYPT 2002. LNCS, vol. 2501, pp. 497–514. Springer, Heidelberg (2002)
6. Bao, F., Deng, R.H., Zhu, H.: Variations of Diffie-Hellman Problem. In: Qing, S., Gollmann, D., Zhou, J. (eds.) ICICS 2003. LNCS, vol. 2836, pp. 301–312. Springer, Heidelberg (2003)
7. Abdalla, M., Pointcheval, D.: Interactive Diffie-Hellman Assumptions with Applications to Password-Based Authentication. In: Patrick, A.S., Yung, M. (eds.) FC 2005. LNCS, vol. 3570, pp. 341–356. Springer, Heidelberg (2005)
8. Szydlo, M.: A Note on Chosen-Basis Decisional Diffie-Hellman Assumptions. In: Di Crescenzo, G., Rubin, A. (eds.) FC 2006. LNCS, vol. 4107, pp. 166–170. Springer, Heidelberg (2006)
9. Cheon, J.H.: Security Analysis of the Strong Diffie-Hellman Problem. In: Vaudenay, S. (ed.) EUROCRYPT 2006. LNCS, vol. 4004, pp. 1–11. Springer, Heidelberg (2006)
10. Cash, D., Kiltz, E., Shoup, V.: The twin Diffie-Hellman problem and applications. J. Cryptology 22(4), 470–504 (2009)
11. Shoup, V.: Sequences of games: a tool for taming complexity in security proofs (2006), http://www.shoup.net/papers/games.pdf

Mixed-Strategy Game Based Trust Management for Clustered Wireless Sensor Networks

Dong Hao[1], Avishek Adhikari[2], and Kouichi Sakurai[1]

[1] Graduate School of Informatics, Kyushu University, Japan
haodongpost@gmail.com, sakurai@csce.kyushu-u.ac.jp
[2] Department of Pure Mathematics, University of Calcutta, India
aamath@caluniv.ac.in

Abstract. Wireless sensor networks are vulnerable to a large number of security threats and malicious attacks. The traditional security approaches from encryption and authentication are insufficient to defend the insider attacks which are launched inside of the WSNs and bypass the crypto-based defence. Trust management has been recently suggested as one of the effective security mechanisms for distributed systems, and is a promising new approach to solve the security challenges in wireless sensor networks. However, to the best of our knowledge, it is still a challenge to establish an integrated trust management mechanism with comprehensive security analysis. In this paper, we consider the clustered wireless sensor network in which the cluster head is in charge of the trust management of other sensor nodes. We propose a novel, integrated trust management mechanism for the cluster wireless sensor networks, and analyze the optimal decision making policy by using game theory. First, the upstream/downstream joint monitoring scheme is implemented to securely and efficiently observe the behavior of the insider nodes. Then based on the monitoring results, the local trustworthiness and global trust worthiness are derived based on the trust exchange and the trust computation. Finally, by game theoretic analysis of the security interaction between the attacker and the network, the optimal trust policy can be made based on min-max rule, and the optimal utility of the WSNs can be guaranteed.

Keywords: Clustered Wireless Sensor Networks, Trust Management, Insider Threats, Mixed-Strategy Game, Quantal Response Equilibrium.

1 Introduction

1.1 Background and Related Works

Wireless sensors are small and inexpensive devices powered with low-energy batteries, equipped with radio transceivers, and capable of responding to physical radio signals. Wireless sensor networks (WSNs) are collections of wireless sensors that are autonomously distributed to gather data from their surrounding environments, to report the changes to data processing center[1]. Though the

L. Chen, M. Yung, and L. Zhu (Eds.): INTRUST 2011, LNCS 7222, pp. 239–257, 2012.
© Springer-Verlag Berlin Heidelberg 2012

development of wireless sensor networks was motivated by military applications such as battlefield surveillance, today such networks are used in many industrial and civilian applications[1, 20].

Although wireless sensor network is promising for various important applications, the security issues in wireless sensor networks have been a roadblock for their development[2, 20]. The critical goal of networks is to protect the network against various attacks which is especially putting more threat to wireless sensor networks due to their characteristics such as open medium, multi-hop, and dynamic topology[1, 20, 21]. The attacks against wireless sensor networks mainly fall into two categories: (1) Outsider attack: The adversary adopts the methods including eavesdropping on information, injecting fractional data to jam the networks traffics, and fabricating fake records to disturb the normal function of the network[20, 21]. For these kinds of outsider attacks, it is of no necessary for the adversary to compromise any insider sensor nodes thoroughly. (2) Insider attack: The adversary breaks through the safeguard (e.g. the cryptographic and authentication mechanisms), and consequently, the insider nodes are compromised by the adversary and are changed into malicious attackers[18–20, 30, 35]. Traditional security systems are mainly used to protect the WSNs from outsider attacks. However, since the insider attackers have access to the public and private keys and bypass the cryptography system, it is preferred to use cryptographic solutions as a first line of defence, and utilize non-cryptographic solutions as a second line to protect the network against the insider attackers[14].

In contrast to the conventional approaches, *trust management* is becoming a new methodology to solve the challenging issues for communication and networks security [2–13, 17, 22, 24, 28]. The notion trust management is first coined by M. Blaze et.al in 1996[3]. The original trust management is about making the policy for the authorization to strangers, by means of recommendations from third parties. Trust management is then embodied as a distributed authentication system. Several later access control systems such as SPKI (simple public key infrastructure)[15] and dRBAC(distributed role-based access control)[16] are also inspired by the idea of trust management. With the advancement of the research, the subsequential studies of trust management have approached to the extensive fields as evaluation, analysis, and quantification of the trust and trustworthiness of network entities over time. The key problem towards the studies of trust management is to obtain the precise, practicable trust values and correspondingly, how to make the optimal trust policies[6].

Similar to the implementation of trust management in wired networks[5], online service, and e-commerce systems[4], it is also of significance to introduce the trust management into the fields such as ad hoc networks, peer-to-peer networks, and also wireless sensor networks. Since the insiders are capable to launch attacks and break the crypto-based security systems, trust management is considered as one effective second line of defence for the wireless network security[7–12, 14, 17, 18, 32]. As a natural consequence of introducing trust management into wireless sensor network environments, trust has been put forward with quite different meanings and corresponding features. In wireless sensor networks, taking into consideration of trust management, each sensor node is assigned a trust value to reflect its trustworthiness according to its historical behavior and performance. And trustworthiness in WSNs is generally interpreted as belief, subjective probability and reputation which represent the quantified values of availability, realisability, or security property of the insider nodes. Obtaining the behavior record of the insider nodes of WSNs, the trust management scheme then calculate the trust value and carry out reward or punishment according to the specific trust policies[6].

In the literature, many authors address the issues of trust definition in different scenarios for wireless sensor networks[7–12]. Momani et al. propose the Data/Communication trust[9]. Lin et al. introduce Hybrid Trust base on Soft Trust and Hard Trust. These two works take into consideration of the veracity of data, connectivity of path, processing capability of node, and service level of network services. G. Saurabh et al. present a reputation based framework for data integrity for wireless sensor networks. Their scheme considers information which is collected by each insider node running the *Watchdog* mechanism to monitor the neighbors[7]. R.A. Shaikh et al. introduce peer evalutaion scheme based on direct observation of the monitor and recommendations from a third node. Therefore their work is based on group trust[8]. E. Aivaloglou et al. propose a hybrid trust and reputation management protocol by integrating certificate based trustworthiness and behavior based trustworthiness[11].

1.2 Challenging Issues

As discussed above, being an alternative solution to traditional security mechanisms, trust is gradually utilized in wireless sensor networks security[9], to maintain and manage the historical behavior of the insiders (generally known as *reputation*), and make policies for authorization or feedback (reward or punishment) to these insiders. In a word, trust for wireless sensor networks, is a mechanism that deals with the insider threats, based on historical behavior observations and decision policies[6]. A typical trust mechanism for WSNs should contain these important components.

– *Monitoring scheme*, which is preferred to be light weighted.
– *Trust information exchange*, which is required to be low cost.
– *Trust Policies* for authorization or reward/punishement decision.

Based on the special attributes of trust management for wireless sensor networks, and the previous works on this field, the unique challenging issues for establishing the trust management for wireless sensor networks mainly fall into the following categories:

(1) Low Cost Trust Observation and Exchange. Existing trust management mechanisms are mostly used in wired distributed systems, which differ from the WSNs trust management application, especially in the aspects of power-consumption and performance observation model. Therefore, it is of great significance to reconstruct these existing schemes to make them acclimate to the new

WSNs environments. Concretely, in WSNs, if the monitoring scheme is always running, the stringent power will be rapidly consumed[30]. Besides, if the trust information exchange scheme requires too much communication, it will become a burden to QoS[1, 20, 24]. Therefore, light weighted insider behavior monitoring scheme, and efficient insider information exchange scheme are essential for a more effective and low cost trust management mechanism.

(2) Trust Management against Insider Threats. The outsider attacks may be prevented by crypto-based solutions[20, 21]. However, as the insider attackers are inside the network, and have access to the pubilic/private key systems, they can bypass such secure systems[14]. Therefore, to design an effective detecting mechanism, we should implement methods other than cryptographic solutions as the alternative solution to cryptography. At the same time, we should also take into consideration the stringent power resource of each monitoring node.

(3) Policy and Decision Making for Trust Management. The final step of trust management is to make a decision about what kind of priority will be authorized to the insider nodes, according to certain decision-making policies. This kind of policy should guarantee that the network will maximize its potential utility, in other words, reduce the attacker's damage to minimum[6]. Thus, how to make these policies have always been a key problem for trust management, and it deserves a comprehensive theoretical and mathematical analysis.

1.3   Our Contribution

In view of the above related works and the challenging issues, in this paper, we propose an integrated trust management mechanism for the wireless sensor networks. We consider the clustered wireless sensor networks in which at least one cluster head exists among the insider nodes. The main objective of our trust management mechanism is to observe the historical behavior of insider nodes, exchange the observations from different routes, and make security decisions for classifying different insider nodes into different trustworthiness level, according to the trust policies.The main contributions of our work are summarized as:

(1) To observe the behavior of insider nodes, and to collect the evidence for trust management, we implement a light weight upstream/downstream joint monitoring scheme. By using this scheme, each insider will be observed by its upstream and downstream neighbors. By utilizing *Watchdog* and signed *Check Packets*, this joint monitoring scheme can be made cheat-proof. As well, the joint monitoring can reduce power consumption comparing to previous monitoring schemes which require either complex computation or need to be run in the *promiscuous mode*[20] consistently.

(2) An integrated trust computation and exchange mechanism is implemented. By using the check packet, each insider node will send its opinion on both its upstream and downstream neighbors to the destination node. Then destination node for each route will calculate the *local trust* of the insiders based on the information from the check packet, and then submit the local trust values to the

cluster head. The cluster head, which is capable of calculating the global trust, will finally make an authorization decision, and inform the decision to all the inside nodes in this network. Comparing with previous local reputation based schemes, our integrated trust computation will increase the accuracy and effectiveness of trust computing and exchanging. Moreover, since only the destination nodes need to submit the local trust to the cluster head, this protocol does not require hight communication cost.

(3) We analyze the interaction between the insider attacker and the cluster head as a repeated trust game with mixed-strategy. The final security policy is to classify the insiders into different trust levels. And this policy is defined according to the game equilibrium. This trust policy will bring the network system with optimized utility, by choosing the defence strategies that minimize the attack damages which the attacker wants to maximize. Without loss of generality, we consider two kinds of attackers: smart attacker and naive attacker, and we reveal the security decision making should be different for these two kinds of attackers.

2   Upstream and Downstream Joint Observation

One important issue to detect the misbehaving insiders in WSNs is how to identify the misbehavior, including packet dropping and packet tampering. In this section, we utilize the upstream/downstream monitor scheme[14] to maintain the history of packet loss and tamper at an arbitrary insider node.

2.1   Insider Threat Scenario

In WSNs, the insiders are the sensor nodes which have legitimately registered into the network and have legal identities and access to the public/private key system. The insider attacks in WSNs focus on the users which had internal access to information and network systems[18, 19, 34].

Following the reactive routing protocols[20], when a source node S wishes to send its data packets to the destination node D, it will first broadcast its ROUTE REQUEST message[1, 3, 20]. On receiving this message, the insiders which have the existing route to D will reply a ROUTE RESPONSE message, and sender will include the insiders which have good behavior history into its route to the destination D. After that, sender S will begin to transfer its data packets to destination D. On receiving the data packets from S, each insider can decide either to forward these packets or to drop them, or to tamper the packets. If the packets are dropped by the insiders, the packet receive ratio at D will decrease and the network performance will drop dramatically which reflects that the integrity is damaged. If the packets are tampered by the insiders, the confidentiality and availability will be damaged. Since packet tampering is more difficult to be detected, we consider that it causes more damage to the network than packet dropping.

2.2   Joint Monitoring in One Route

The whole network communication is divided into multiple *time windows*. In each segment of these time windows $TW(t)$[20], there are many routes responsible for data packet forwarding. To perceive the misbehavior of the WSN insiders, the most direct way is *traffic monitoring*[1, 20, 21]. Utilizing the upstream/downstream joint monitoring scheme[14], each node can be observed by its upstream and downstream neighbors in the route.

Consider in route x, the sender sends its data packets through the insider nodes $v_1, v_2, ..., v_m, ..., v_n$. Each time an insider v_m receives a data packet, it will update its local counter about how many packet it has received from its upstream neighbor v_{m-1}. We record this number as $n_r(v_{m-1}, v_m)$. Then the insider v_m will forward the data packet to its downstream neighbor v_{m+1}. Working under the *Promiscuous Mode*[20], sensor nodes are capable of observing the downstream nodes within its broadcast domain, about whether it tamper, drop or forward the packets, respectively. The node v_m will record the number of packets v_{m+1} dropped as $n_f(v_{m+1})$, the number of packets v_{m+1} tampered as $n_t(v_{m+1})$, and the number of packets v_{m+1} dropped as $n_d(v_{m+1})$.

Let $M_{S \to D}$ be an integral number. To obtain the trust of all the insider nodes along the route x, after every $M_{S \to D}$ data packets, the sender S will generate a *check packet*, and send it thought the route x to destination node D. When this check packet passes through route x, each insider in x will attach its opinions about its upstream and downstream neighbors to the variable field in the check packet. Noting that within one time window $TW(t)$, along one route x, there may be multiple check packets.

Consider a simple but representative case, when the insider m is included in a 5-hop route, described as $S \rightleftharpoons v_1 \rightleftharpoons v_2 \rightleftharpoons v_3 \rightleftharpoons D$, where S and D denote the sender and destination node, respectively. When the check packet passes each node, the node will attach their messages to the the empty fields in the check packet. The information in the check packets along the 5-hop route is:

$$S \xrightarrow{M_0} v_1 : M_0 = S \,\|M_{S \to D}\, \|C_F^{up}(S, v_1), C_T^{up}(v_1) \,\|Sign(S);$$
$$v_1 \xrightarrow{M_1} v_2 : M_1 = M_0 \,\|v_1\, \|n_r(S, v_1) \,\|C_F^{down}(v_1, S) \,\|C_F^{up}(v_1, v_2), C_T^{up}(v_2) \,\|Sign(v_1);$$
$$v_2 \xrightarrow{M_2} v_3 : M_2 = M_1 \,\|v_2\, \|n_r(v_1, v_2) \,\|C_F^{down}(v_2, v_1) \,\|C_F^{up}(v_2, v_3), C_T^{up}(v_3) \,\|Sign(v_2);$$
$$v_3 \xrightarrow{M_3} D : M_3 = M_2 \,\|v_3\, \|n_r(v_2, v_3) \,\|C_F^{down}(v_3, v_2) \,\|C_F^{up}(v_3, D) \,\|Sign(v_3).$$

The message attached to the check packet at each node are denoted as M_0, M_1, M_2 and M_3, respectively. The first field in M_0 and second field in M_1, M_2 and M_3 are the identities of each node. $M_{S \to D}$ is the total number of data packets S has sent to D during between every two check packet. C_F^{up} is the upstream neighbor's opinion on how the insider node behaves on packet dropping, based on the *Promiscuous mode* monitoring such as *Watchdog*. It describes the percentage of packets that an insider node drops, and observed by its upstream neighbor. For instance, $C_F^{up}(S, v_1)$ is S's opinion on insider v_1 about how v_1 behaves as packet dropping. On the other hand, C_F^{down} is downstream neighbor's opinion on how the insider node behaves as packet dropping, which also indicates the percentage of packets that an insider node m drops. C_T^{up} is the upstream neighbor's opinion on how one insider behaves as packet tampering. Finally, at each node, the message is attached with an Elliptic Curve Digital Signature $Sign(v_m)$[20]. The signature is generated based on the node's identity v_m, and can protect this message from being tampered.

On receiving the check packet, the destination node will retrieve the ID of each insider node, and verify the signatures. After that, the destination node will calculate the local trust of each insider node m in this route, based on the m' upstream/downstream neighbors' opinions. In the next section, we will introduce the local trust and global trust computation and exchange.

3   Trustworthiness Exchange Protocol

In the last section, the upstream/downstream joint monitoring scheme is implemented, and the insiders' historical behavior can be obtained by such monitoring scheme. Based on the observation records, in this section, we propose the local trust computation and global trust exchange protocol. The local trust means the trust values that are generated based on the monitoring information from a single route, while the global trust is the integrated trust value which collects the opinions on one insider node from all the routes.

3.1   Local Trust Computation

In the check packet, for each insider node v_m, there are two categories of opinions: the opinion about packet dropping, and about packet tampering. We first consider the packet dropping. As we illustrated in the last section, the upstream node v_{m-1}'s opinion on node v_m about its packet dropping is recorded as $C_F^{up}(v_{m-1}, v_m)$, which is located between interval $[0, 1]$. By using $Watchdog$[20] mechanism, the upstream node v_{m-1} can overhear whether node v_m forwards, drops, or tamper packets. Then $C_F^{up}(v_{m-1}, v_m)$ can be calculated as:

$$C_F^{up}(v_{m-1}, v_m) = \frac{n_d(v_m)}{n_f(v_m) + n_t(v_m) + n_d(v_m)} \tag{1}$$

where $n_f(v_m)$ denotes the number of packets that node v_m forwards to v_{m+1}, and monitored by v_{m-1} by using $Watchdog$; $n_t(v_m)$ denotes the number of packets being tampered by v_m and successfully observed by v_{m-1}. And $n_d(v_m)$ denotes the number of packets being dropped by v_m and observed by v_{m-1}.

We then investigate downstream node v_{m+1}'s opinion on v_m about packet dropping, which is denoted as $C_F^{down}(v_{m+1}, v_m)$. This opinion is generated according to the number of packets each node received, which is attached in the check packet, and it is also a real number located between interval $[0, 1]$. Recall that, in the check packet, the attached number of packets that v_m receives from v_{m-1} is $n_r(v_{m-1}, v_m)$, and the number of packets that v_{m+1} received from v_m is $n_r(v_{m-1}, v_m)$. Then node $C_F^{down}(v_{m+1}, v_m)$ can be recorded as:

$$C_F^{down}(v_{m+1}, v_m) = 1 - \frac{n_r(v_m, v_{m+1})}{n_r(v_{m-1}, v_m)} \tag{2}$$

On receiving the *Check Packet* which contains the opinions $C_F^{up}(v_{m-1}, v_m)$ and $C_F^{down}(v_{m+1}, v_m)$, the destination node D will calculate the route x's opinion on each insider node about how they behaves as packet dropping:

$$C_F(m) = \kappa \times C_F^{up}(v_{m-1}, v_m) + (1 - \kappa) \times C_F^{down}(v_{m+1}, v_m) \tag{3}$$

Since the accuracy of upstream monitoring and accuracy of downstream monitoring are different, we define κ and $1 - \kappa$ as the weights of upstream and downstream nodes' opinion about insider m, respectively. Larger $C_F(m)$ indicates v_m drops more data packets between every two check packets.

Besides the opinion about packet forwarding, another item observed is the ratio of packets that have been tampered by the insider v_m, which is denoted as $C_T^{up}(v_m)$. The upstream node v_{m-1} can observe the packet tempering behavior of node v_m by using *Watchdog*. $C_T^{up}(v_m)$ is defined as:

$$C_T^{up}(v_m) = \frac{n_t(v_m)}{n_f(v_m) + n_t(v_m) + n_d(v_m)} \tag{4}$$

where $n_f(v_m)$, $n_t(v_m)$ and $n_d(v_m)$ have the same meanings as in equation (1). After the destination node D receives the check packet, it will generate $C_T(m)$ to denote the route x's opinion on insider v_m about packet tampering. And $C_T(m) = C_T^{up}(v_m)$.

After the destination node D generates $C_F(m)$ and $C_T(m)$ for all the insiders in its route x, it will calculate the local trust value of the insiders in route x. The local trust value from route x for an insider node m is denoted as T_{xm}^{local}, which consists of two parts, one is trust for packet tampering and the other one is trust for packet dropping:

$$\begin{cases} T_{xm}^{local}(Packet\_Tamper) = \sum_{i}^{N_{cp}^x} RT_{xm}(i) \times \mu 1_{cp}/N_{cp}^x \\ T_{xm}^{local}(Packet\_Drop) = \sum_{i}^{N_{cp}^x} RD_{xm}(i) \times \mu 2_{cp}/N_{cp}^x \end{cases} \tag{5}$$

where $RD_{xm}(i)$ (or $RT_{xm}(i)$) is the value of $C_F(m)$ (or $C_T(m)$) corresponding to the i-th check packet. $\mu 1_{cp}$ and $\mu 2_{cp}$ are the discount factors of trustworthiness which mean the decaying of trust over time. N_{cp}^x denotes the total number of check packets generated along route x during time window $TW(t)$.

The metrics $T_{xm}^{local}(Packet\_Tamper)$ and $T_{xm}^{local}(Packet\_Drop)$ are called *local trust* for the reason that it indicates only the route x's opinion on insider node m. However, local trusts are insufficient to evaluate the insiders' trustworthiness. First, if only local trust is conducted, it will take a long time for a node to obtain enough observation records of all the other nodes in the network. Second, one insider may behave maliciously in one route, but legitimately in another route.

This may mislead those routes that have not been attacked before. Therefore, a comprehensive global trust value which is integrated from all the local routes is required.

3.2 Global Trust Computation

Assume within time window $TW(t)$, there are N routes along which the insider node m participates in. In other words, those N routes intersect at node m. At the end of $TW(t)$, the destination nodes of each route will submit the local trust value on the insiders to the cluster head. It is assumed that the cluster head is the trusted third party (TTP). Because if the cluster head is compromised by adversary, the entire network will also be besieged soon.

Let Ω denote the set of all the N routes which utilized insider m in the window $TW(t)$, and $x \in \Omega$ be one route. Let $H(x, m, t)$ be the number of times that route x has utilized the insider m during $TW(t)$. Therefore, the total number of times that insider m has been used in the past time window $TW(t)$ is recorded as $H(m, t) = \sum_{x \in \Omega} H(x, m, t)$. Let $T_{xm}^{local}(i) \in [0, 1]$ denote the local trustworthiness of insider m in the view of route x, where $i \in \{Packet\_Tamper, Packet\_Drop\}$. And let $Kr(x, t)$ be the balance factor of trust value from route x, during time window $TW(t)$. $Kr(x, t)$ is introduced to offset the risk of non-credible feedbacks from route x, such as bad-mouthing attack or whitewashing attack[20]. After these, the global trust value can be defined as a function of $T_{xm}^{local}(i)$, $H(x, m, t)$, and $Kr(x, t)$:

$$T_m(i) = \sum_{x \in \Omega} \left[\frac{H(x, m, t)}{\sum_{x \in \Omega} H(x, m, t)} \times T_{xm}^{local}(i) \times Kr(x, TW(t)) \right] \quad (6)$$

where $i \in \{Packet\_Tamper, Packet\_Drop\}$. The value of global trust measures a generalized trustworthiness that an insider m is held by all the routes, which utilized m as an insider node during the last time window $TW(t)$. Based on this global trust values during the past $TW(t)$, the cluster head will classify the insider nodes into different categories (e.g. *Legitimate*, *Suspicious* and *Malicious*). The legitimate insiders will be permitted to access more services of the network system. The malicious insiders will be isolated from the system immediately. And for the suspicious insiders, the cluster head will inform all the member nodes that such suspicious insider should be given more frequent observations. For example, each route x may reduce the value of $M_{S \rightarrow D}$ which will increase the frequency of generating the *check packet* to check the suspicious insider nodes.

It's worth noting that, the final format of the global trust value $T_m(i)$ where $i \in \{Packet\_Tamper, Packet\_Drop\}$, is a pair of real numbers locating in the interval $[0, 1]$, they can also be considered as probabilities. The global trust value thus can be indicated by the accumulative packet drop ratio and packet tamper ratio of the insider node m. The significance of calculating the global trust comparing to the local trust is that: in the global trust, the sample space which covers all the routes that utilized the insider node m, is much richer than the sample space for single route's local trust evaluation. According to the *Law of Large Numbers*[36], the average of the results obtained from a large number of trials should be close to the expected value, and will tend to become closer as more trials are performed. Therefore, the integrated global trust is more close to the real probability that each insider node drops (tampers) data packets.

4   Game-Based Analysis for Trust Policies

In this section, the proposed trust management mechanism is analyzed by game theory. The trust policy is made to distinguish the malicious, suspicious, and legitimate insider nodes based on the game equilibrium. The reason for utilizing game theory for the trust decision making is owing to the tradeoff existing in the communication phase. For instance, by dropping or tampering packets, the attacker may receive illegal utility, but may also take risk of being punished. For the cluster head, it can severely punish an insider node for its losing a little packet, but the usability of the network will decrease. Therefore, the interaction between the cluster head and the insider node is a multi-dimensional decision making problem which is often modeled and analyzed as a game[35].

4.1   Trust Game Model

In clustered WSNs, the game is between any one of the insider attackers who takes attack strategies, and cluster head who makes decision on how to classify the insiders based on the global trust values. The attacker wants to bring damage to the network, and the cluster head wants to prosecute the attacker out. The loss of the network system is the same as the gain of the attacker. Therefore, we model the game as zero-sum non-cooperative game[34]. The first step of game theory based analysis is to identify the players and their available actions (or strategy). The insider node is perfectly informed of the historical strategies of the cluster head, for the reason that the strategy of the cluster head, which is the global trust value, has been broadcasted to all the members in the network including the insider attacker. On the contrary, the insider's past strategies are not perfectly observed by the cluster head, because the observation mechanism is not perfectly accurate. Moreover, because the cluster head takes its strategy after the insider, we construct the game in an extensive form.

Fig.1 portrayed the one-shot trust game between the insider and the cluster head. This game is illustrated as a tree in which the attacker takes its attack strategy first and the cluster head takes the defence strategy in succession after the attacker. The red node at the root denotes the insider, and 1:1 means the first move of the first insider node. The insider node may take any one of the 3 strategies: *Behave Normally*(N), *Drop Packet*(D), and *Tamper Packet*(T), which are presented by red lines starting from the root. Similarly, the cluster head's moves start from a blue node, and 2:1 means the first move of the cluster head. The cluster head can make 3 kinds of decisions: Trust the insider, classify it as *Legitimate*(L), Semi-Trust the insider, consider it as *Suspicious*(S), and

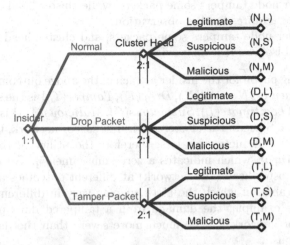

Fig. 1. Extensive Form of Trust Game

completely distrust the insider, classify it as *Malicious*(M). Since there is no observation mechanism with 100% detection rate[21], the cluster head is not totally certain that the insider chooses one of the strategies from its strategy space. Therefore, the cluster head's 3 sub-trees belong to the same information set, which is illustrated by a dash line linking the 3 blue nodes. After both the attacker and the cluster head choose their own strategies to fight against each other, the interaction between these two players will come to an outcome, which are denoted by different leave nodes in the end of the game tree. We can see that there are totally 9 leaf nodes at the end of the extensive game tree which identify all the possible outcomes (3 × 3) of the one-shot trust game. The following items describe the meanings of all the possible outcomes of this trust game.

- (N, L): Insider node behaves normally, and cluster head trusts the insider, classify it into legitimate member.
- (N, S): Insider node behaves normally, but cluster head mistakenly semi-trusts it, and classifies it as suspicious insider.
- (N, M): Insider node behaves normally, while cluster head makes an error, distrusts it, and classifies it as malicious attacker.
- (D, L): Insider node drops packets, but cluster head considers the drop as due to channel problems, classifies the insider as Legitimate Member.
- (D, S): Insider node drops packets, and cluster head correctly semi-trusts it, classifies it as suspicious and requires further observation.
- (D, M): Insider node drops packets, and cluster head distrusts it, severely classifies it as malicious and isolates it from service.
- (T, L): Insider node tampers some packets, but cluster head makes an error, wrongly trusts it, and regards it as legitimate.

- (T, S): Insider node tampers some packets, while cluster head classifies it as suspicious and requires further observation.
- (T, M): Insider node tampers some packets, and cluster head regards it as malicious and isolates it from service.

The corresponding payoff for the insider at each of the above outcomes is denoted as $U_m(u, v)$, where $u \in \{Normal(N), Drop(D), Tamper(T)\}$ is the strategy from insider, and $v \in \{Legitimate(L), Suspicious(S), Malicious(M)\}$ is the strategy of the cluster head. Since in the clustered wireless sensor network, the attacker's gain is the same as the network's loss, therefore the utility of the network is $U_n(u, v) = -U_m(u, v)$, which indicates a zero-sum game[35]. We illustrate the utilities for the cluster head (the network) at different outcomes as the matrix in the following table, in which the $U_n(u, v)$ may vary in different application scenarios[20]. For example, the damage from a tampered data packet in the battle field sensor network will be much more severe than the damage in the civilian applications.

Table 1. Different Payoffs for Network at Different Outcomes

Strategy	Trust(Legitimate)	Semi-Trust(Suspicious)	Distrust(Malicious)
Behave Normally	$U_n(N, L)$	$U_n(N, S)$	$U_n(N, M)$
Drop Packets	$U_n(D, L)$	$U_n(D, S)$	$U_n(D, M)$
Tamper Packets	$U_n(T, L)$	$U_n(T, S)$	$U_n(T, M)$

In Table 1, the first elements in each utility function are actions of the insiders, while the second elements are the actions of the cluster head. For example, $U_n(T, M)$ is the utility for the cluster head under the situation that the insider node tampers a packet, and the cluster head classify it as malicious and distrust it. It is worth noting that, $U_n(u, v)$ is the utility under *pure strategy*. In game theory, the notion of pure strategy means the players choose the strategies deterministically. That is to say, the players choose each strategy with probability 0 or 1. However, in the real case, the rational attacker will change its strategy over time, and sometimes just pretends to be legitimate and takes the malicious strategy with certain probability. This kind of rational attacker will choose each possible strategy with a certain probability. Thus, the trust game is a mixed-strategy game, in which the player's strategy is probability distribution over the action set.

Table 2 illustrates the mixed strategy for both the attacker and the cluster head. In this mixed strategy game, the attacker's strategy is a probability distribution $\{p, q, 1 - p - 1\}$ over all its possible action set $\{N, D, T\}$. Variables p, q, $1 - p - q$ are the probabilities for the attacker to adopt each of the actions *Behave Normally*$(u = N)$, *Drop Packet*$(u = D)$, and *Tamper Packet*$(u = T)$, respectively. On the contrary, for the cluster head, its strategy is a probability distribution $\{x, y, 1 - x - y\}$, over the cluster head action set $\{L, S, M\}$. Here x,

Table 2. Joint Distribution for Attacker and Cluster Head's Mixed Strategy

Strategy	Trust(Legitimate)	Semi-Trust(Suspicious)	Distrust(Malicious)
Behave Normally	px	py	$p(1-x-y)$
Drop Packets	qx	qy	$q(1-x-y)$
Tamper Packets	$(1-p-q)x$	$(1-p-q)y$	$(1-p-q)(1-x-y)$

y, $1-x-y$ are the probabilities for the cluster head to classify the insider node as
Legitimate($v = L$), Suspicious($v = S$) and Malicious($v = M$), respectively. The
mixed strategy of the insider attacker is denoted as $s_m(p,q)$ which is a probability distribution over action set $\{Normal, Drop, Tamper\}$, while m denotes this
potential attacker. And the mixed strategy for the cluster head is $s_n(x,y)$ which
is a probability distribution over $\{Legitimate, Suspicious, Malicious\}$, while n
indicates the cluster head. The combination in each grid in the Table.2 is the
joint probability for both the attacker and the defender to choose certain actions.
For example, the grid for $(1-p-q)(1-x-y)$ means the joint probability that
the attacker tamper the packet while the cluster head classify it as malicious at
the same time. The matrix in Table.2 is thus the joint probability distribution
for each possible outcome.

4.2 Trust Game Equilibrium

In the last subsection, we have construct the trust game model based on the
Attack-Defence interaction between the insider node and the cluster head. To
find the optimal defense strategy for the cluster head, we need to analyze this
trust game. The key point in the game analysis is to find the Nash equilibrium[31].
For this trust game, the Nash equilibrium points indicates the outcome in which
neither the insider nor the cluster head wants to unilaterally change its strategy.
Otherwise, the unilateral change of the strategy will only lead to its own utility
degradation[34, 35]. In the field of network security and trust management, a
security analysis deserving its name is a min-max method that the defender first
looks at the maximal damage that an attacker can cause for a specific defence,
and then searches for the defence that minimizes the maximal damages[6, 35].
This min-max decision rule, in zero-sum game theory, is well known as the necessary and sufficient condition for the Nash equilibrium[34].

We utilize the min-max rule to approach the Nash equilibrium. Taking into
consideration the payoff matrix in Table 1 and the Joint distribution of mixed-
strategy matrix in Table 2, the trust game's Nash equilibrium $(s_m^*(p,q), s_n^*(x,y))$
is restricted to the following function set:

$$\begin{cases} s_m^*(p,q) = \arg \min_{s_m(p,q)} \max_{s_n(x,y)} \mathbb{E}_m(s_n(x,y), s_m(p,q)); \\ s_n^*(x,y) = \arg \max_{s_n(x,y)} \min_{s_m(p,q)} \mathbb{E}_m(s_n(x,y), s_m(p,q)). \end{cases} \quad (7)$$

where $s_m(p,q)$ and $s_n(x,y)$ are the mixed strategy of attacker and cluster head, respectively. Furthermore, $s_n^*(x,y)$ denotes the dominant mixed strategy in which the value of x and y will bring the network with the optimal utility. $s_m^*(p,q)$ denotes the dominant mixed strategy of the attacker. $\mathbb{E}_m\left(s_n(x,y), s_m(p,q)\right)$ is the *overall utility expectation* in the status that attacker chooses the mixed strategy $s_m(p,q)$ while cluster head chooses the mixed strategy $s_n(x,y)$. This utility expectation is calculated by the mathematical expectation over the utility matrix from Table 1, taking into consideration of the mixed strategies in Table 2.

According to [34], every finite strategy game has at least one mixed strategy Nash equilibrium. Given the real numbers of the elements in Table 1, the above min-max function can be easily solved by nonlinear optimization method. Then the values of p, q, x and y can be derived. The values of p, q, and $1-p-q$ are the thresholds for the global trust values $T_m(i)$ according to equation (6). Comparing with the thresholds p, q and $1-p-q$, if $T_m(Packet\_Tamper)$ is higher than $(1-p-q)$, the insider m should be considered as malicious; if $T_m(Packet\_Drop)$ is higher than q, the insider m should be at least viewed as suspicious. As the time window $TW(t)$ changes, the strategies of both the attacker and the cluster head will also change, this is about the evolution of the trust game, which will be discuss in the next subsection.

4.3 Trust Game Evolution

In last section, we analyzed the trust game within single time window $TW(t)$. Since the communication of the network goes on, there are multiple time windows, the trust game is extended to multi-stage repeated game. We utilize the Quantal Response Equilibrium (QRE)[33] which is a generalization form of multi-round game Nash equilibrium to analyze the evolution of this trust game. The QRE is calculated by the following equation:

$$P_i^k = \frac{\exp(\lambda \times EU_i^k(P_{-i}))}{\sum_m \exp(\lambda \times EU_i^m(P_{-i}))} \tag{8}$$

where P_i^k is the probability for player choosing strategy k, which is the same as the p, q and $1-p-q$ (or x, y and $1-x-y$) in the one-shot trust game. $EU_i^k(P_{-i})$ is the expected utility to player i of choosing strategy k given other players are playing according to the probability distribution P_{-i}. In the trust game, $EU_i^k(P_{-i})$ is equal to $U_n(i,j)$. Larger λ indicates that the players become *more rational*, and are more eager to take Nash equilibrium strategies. Table 3 in Appendix shows the relationship between the strategies and the value of λ.

We consider the trust mechanism confronting two kinds of attackers: *1)Smart insider attackers* who are rational, prefer to protect itself, hide in the network and launch long-term attack; *2)Naive insider attackers*, who are irrational, and want to launch severe attacks even taking the risk of being detected. Following the utility preference ordering methord[37], the smart attacker's preference sequence of all the potential 9 outcomes is: $(T,L) > (D,L) > (T,S) > (D,S) \simeq (N,L) \simeq (T,M) > (N,S) > (D,M) > (N,M)$. On the contrary, the naive attacker will attach more importance on bring damage to the wireless network systems, than protect themselves. Therefore, its preference sequence for the potential outcomes is: $(T, L) > (T, S) > (D, L) > (D, S) \simeq (N, L) \simeq (T, M) > (D, M) > (N, S) > (N, M)$. Also following the method in[37], the example utilities $U_n(i, j)$ are defined. Then by using the tool GameBit[38], the QRE of the repeated trust game is derived.

Fig. 2. Comparison of Strategy Evolution of the Smart and Naive Attackers

Fig.2 illustrates the strategies' evolution of the smart and naive attackers. The red lines indicate the evolution of the strategies of naive attacker. The repeated trust game starts with equal probabilities (0.33) for each strategy. With the number of time window $TW(t)$ increases, the trust game repeats. In Fig.2(a), the naive attacker's probability for normal behavior(N) decreases faster than the smart attacker. In Fig.2(c), the smart attacker slowly increases its probability for tampering packet, to avoid being detected, while the naive attacker have less fear of taking risks, and is more eager to tamper packets. From this, we are aware of that the smart attacker are more tricky to avoid being detected. Based on this analysis, any insider whose strategy trajectories locate on the left of the red lines, should be classified as malicious immediately; Any nodes whose trajectories is on the right of the blue lines, can be considered as legitimate temporarily; And those nodes whose strategy evolution trajectory between the red and blue lines, should be at least viewed as suspicious.

Fig.3 illustrates the co-evolution of the strategies of smart attacker and cluster head while they play the trust game. From Fig.3(a) we can see: with the game repeats, the attacker prefers more to tamper packet, but gradually decreases the probability for dropping packets. This is because while time goes on, the risk of being detected also increases. Therefore the attacker does not want to take the risk of being considered as malicious for dropping packets. In Fig.3(b) we can see that, more repetitions of the trust game will give the cluster head more information to increase the detection accuracy. Therefore, the probability for wrongly classify the attacker as legitimate (green line) consecutively decreases. Noting that the blue line first increases to a peak value, but then decreases, finally even reaches to value 0. This interesting phenomena indicates significantly that: during the first period (before step 15), due to lack of observation, the cluster head can not make decision that the insider node is a smart attacker.

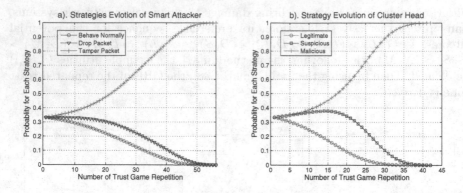

Fig. 3. Attacker and Cluster Head's Strategy Evolution

However, it becomes more suspicious of this insider attacker. With the trust game repeats, it obtains more and more information of the smart attacker's misbehavior. Therefore, it decidedly decreases the probability for the strategy for classifying the insider node as *Suspicious* and *Legitimate*, but increases the probability to identify it as a malicious attacker. More data about the trust game's co-evolution is illustrated in Table 3 in the appendix.

5   Conclusion

We proposed an integrated trust management mechanism for clustered wireless sensor network. The behavior of insider nodes are observed by a light weight upstream/downstream joint monitoring scheme. The opinions from the monitors are then calculated to get the local trust value. Local trust values are then submitted to the cluster head, and the global trust is generated according to our trust calculation and exchange algorithm. After that, the threshold for the global trust, is analyzed by a mixed-strategy repeated trust game. The analysis not only considers static case in which the trust game only runs one-shot, but also extends the attacker-defender trust game to a repeated scenario. The optimal trust policy is made based on the mixed strategy game analysis. By using this trust management mechanism, it is possible for the WSNs to reduce the potential damage from the malicious and suspicious insider attacker to minimum. The future work is to implement this trust management mechanism, design an effective intrusion detection system for WSNs by taking into consideration of false positive rate and false negative rate.

Acknowledgements. This work is partly supported by Grants-in-Aid for Scientific Research (B) (23300027), Japan Society for the Promotion of Science (JSPS). The first author Dong HAO is supported by the governmental scholarship from the China Scholarship Council (CSC). The second author Dr. Avishek

Adhikari's visit to Kyushu University is sponsored by the Strategic Japanese-Indian Cooperative Programme on Multidisciplinary Research Field, which combines Information and Communications Technology with Other Fields Supported by Japan Science and Technology Agency and Department of Science and Technology of the Government of India.

References

1. Yick, J., Mukherjee, B., Ghosal, D.: Wireless sensor network survey. Computer Networks 52(12), 2292–2330 (2008)
2. Perrig, A., Stankovich, J., Wagner, D.: Security in wireless sensor networks. Commun. ACM 47(6), 53–57 (2004)
3. Blaze, M., Feigenbaum, J., Lacy, J.: Decentralized Trust Management. In: Proceedings of the 17th IEEE Symp. on Security and Privacy, pp. 164–173. IEEE Computer Society (1996)
4. Josang, A., Ismail, R., Boyd, C.: A survey of trust and reputation systems for online service provision. Decis. Support Syst., 618–644 (March 2005)
5. Josang, A., Hayward, R., Pope, S.: Trust network analysis with subjective logic. In: Proceedings of the 29th Australasian Computer Science Conference (ACSC 2006), Darlinghurst, Australia, vol. 48, pp. 85–94 (2006)
6. Gollmann, D.: From Access Control to Trust Management, and Back – A Petition. In: Wakeman, I., Gudes, E., Jensen, C.D., Crampton, J. (eds.) IFIPTM 2011. IFIP AICT, vol. 358, pp. 1–8. Springer, Heidelberg (2011)
7. Ganeriwal, S., Srivastava, M.B.: Reputation-based framework for high integrity sensor networks. In: Proceedings of ACM Security for Ad-hoc and Sensor Networks, SASN (2004)
8. Shaikh, R.A., Jameel, H., Brian, J., Lee, H., Lee, S., Song, Y.J.: Group-Based Trust Management Scheme for Clustered Wireless Sensor Networks. IEEE Transactions on Parallel and Distributed Systems, 1698–1712 (November 2009)
9. Momani, M., Challa, S., Alhmouz, R.: Can we trust trusted nodes in wireless sensor networks? In: International Conference on Computer and Communication Engineering (ICCCE 2008) (May 2008)
10. Lin, C., Vijay, V.: A Hybrid Trust Model for Enhancing Security in Distributed Systems. In: The Second International Conference on Availability, Reliability and Security, pp. 35–42 (2007)
11. Aivaloglou, E., Gritzalis, S.: Hybrid trust and reputation management for sensor networks. Wirel. Netw. 16(5) (July 2010)
12. Spyropoulos, T., Psounis, K., Raghavendra, C.S.: Efficient Routing in Intermittently Connected Mobile Networks: The Single-Copy Case. IEEE/ACM Transactions on Networking 16(1), 63–76 (2008)
13. Gómez, F., Girao, J., Pérez, G.M.: TRIMS, a privacy-aware trust and reputation model for identity management systems. Comput. Netw. 54(16) (November 2010)
14. Shila, D.M., Cheng, Y.: Mitigating selective forwarding attacks with a Channel Aware Approach in WMNs. IEEE Transaction on Wireless Communications (May 2010)
15. Ellison, C.M., Franz, B., Rivest, R., Thomas, B.M., Ylonen, T.: Simple public key infrastructure certificate theory. IETF RFC 2693 (1999)
16. Freudenthal, E., Pesin, T., Port, L., Keenan, E., Karamcheti, V.: dRBAC: Distributed role-based access control for dynamic coalition environments. Technical Report, TR 2001-819, New York University (2001)

17. Velloso, B., Laufer, P., Duarte, O., Pujolle, G.: A Trust Model Robust to Slander Attacks in Ad Hoc Networks. In: Proceedings of 17th International Conference on Computer Communications and Networks (ICCCN 2008), pp. 1–6 (2008)
18. Lynch, D.M.: Securing against insider attacks. Information Security Systems 15(5), 39–47 (2006)
19. Kantzavelou, I., Katsikas, S.: A game-based intrusion detection mechanism to confront internal attackers. Computers Security 29(8), 859–874 (2010)
20. Anjum, F., Mouchtaris, P.: Security for Wireless Ad Hoc Networks. Wiley-Interscience (2007) ISBN:0471756881
21. Bace, R.G.: Intrusion detection. Macmillan Publishing Co., Inc., Indianapolis (2001)
22. Xue, X.Y., Leneutre, J., BenOthman, J.: A Trust-based Routing Prtocol for Ad Hoc Networks. In: Proceeding of Mobile and Wireless Communications Networks, pp. 251–262 (October 2004)
23. Royer, E.M., Toh, C.K.: A review of current routing protocols for ad hoc mobile wireless networks. IEEE Personal Communications, 46–55 (April 1999)
24. Bao, F., Chen, I.-R., Chang, M., Cho, J.: Hierarchical trust management for wireless sensor networks and its application to trust-based routing. In: Proceedings of the 2011 ACM Symposium on Applied Computing, pp. 1732–1738. New York (2011)
25. Scott, K., Bambos, N.: Routing and channel assignment for low power transmission in PCS. In: Proc. IEEE ICUPC 1996, vol. 2, pp. 498–502 (1996)
26. Singh, S., Woo, M., Raghavendra, C.S.: Power-aware routing in mobile ad hoc networks. In: Proc. ACM MobiCom 1998, pp. 181–190 (1998)
27. Toh, C.-K.: Maximum battery life routing to support ubiquitous mobile computing in wireless ad hoc networks. IEEE Communications Magazine, 138–147 (June 2001)
28. Li, H., Singhal, M.: Trust Management in Distributed Systems. Computer, 45–53 (February 2007)
29. Xiong, L., Liu, L.: Building Trust in Decentralized Peerto- Peer Electronic Communities. In: Proc. 5th Intl. Conf. Electronic Commerce Research (ICECR-5) (2002)
30. Hao, D., Ren, Y., Sakurai, K.: A Game Theory-Based Surveillance Mechanism against Suspicious Insiders in MANETs. In: Chen, L., Yung, M. (eds.) INTRUST 2010. LNCS, vol. 6802, pp. 237–252. Springer, Heidelberg (2011)
31. Liu, D., Wang, X.F., Camp, J.L.: 'Game Theoretic Modeling and Analysis of Insider Threats. International Journal of Critical Infrastructure Protection, 75–80 (2008)
32. Pirzada, A.A., Mcdonald, C., Datta, A.: Performance comparison of trust-based reactive routing protocols. IEEE Transactions on Mobile Computing 5(6), 695–710 (2006)
33. Richard, M.K., Thomas, P.: Quantal Response Equilibria for Extensive Form Games. Experimental Economics 1, 9–41 (1998)
34. Gibbons, R.: Game Theory for Applied Economics. Princeton University Press, Princeton (1992)
35. Alpcan, T., Basar, T.: Network Security: A Decision and Game Theoretic Approach, November 30. Cambridge University Press (2010)
36. Mitzenmacher, M., Upfal, E.: Probability and Computing: Randomized Algorithms and Probabilistic Analysis. Cambridge University Press, New York (2005)
37. Binmore, K.G.: Playing for real: a text on game theory. Oxford University Press (2007) ISBN 0195300572, 9780195300574
38. McKelvey, R.D., McLennan, A.M., Turocy, T.L.: Gambit: Software Tools for Game Theory, Version 0, September 01 (2010), http://www.gambit-project.org

Appendix: Quantal Response Equilibria of Trust Game

Table 3. Quantal Response Equilibria (QRE) Calculations

		Insider Attacker			Cluster Head		
Step	λ	Normal	Drop	Tamper	Legitimate	Suspicious	Malicious
1	0.000	0.333	0.333	0.333	0.333	0.333	0.333
2	0.008	0.330	0.333	0.337	0.327	0.337	0.337
3	0.016	0.326	0.333	0.340	0.319	0.340	0.341
4	0.025	0.322	0.333	0.344	0.311	0.344	0.345
5	0.035	0.318	0.333	0.349	0.302	0.348	0.350
...	...	...	...	...	...	...	...
12	0.126	0.281	0.328	0.391	0.218	0.374	0.408
13	0.143	0.274	0.326	0.399	0.203	0.376	0.421
14	0.161	0.268	0.324	0.408	0.188	0.377	0.436
15	0.180	0.261	0.322	0.418	0.172	0.377	0.452
16	0.200	0.253	0.319	0.428	0.156	0.375	0.470
17	0.221	0.246	0.316	0.439	0.140	0.371	0.490
18	0.242	0.238	0.312	0.450	0.124	0.364	0.512
19	0.265	0.229	0.308	0.463	0.109	0.355	0.536
20	0.289	0.221	0.303	0.476	0.094	0.343	0.563
...	...	...	...	...	...	...	...
36	0.802	0.070	0.157	0.772	0.000	0.014	0.085
37	0.852	0.062	0.145	0.793	0.000	0.009	0.991
38	0.907	0.054	0.133	0.813	0.000	0.005	0.995
39	0.967	0.046	0.121	0.833	0.000	0.003	0.997
40	1.033	0.039	0.108	0.853	0.000	0.002	0.998
41	1.105	0.032	0.096	0.872	0.000	0.001	0.999
42	1.184	0.026	0.083	0.891	0.000	0.000	1.000
...	...	...	...	...	...	...	...
47	1.732	0.005	0.030	0.964	0.000	0.000	1.000
...	...	...	...	...	...	...	...
54	3.216	0.000	0.002	0.998	0.000	0.000	1.000
55	3.529	0.000	0.001	0.999	0.000	0.000	1.000
56	3.874	0.000	0.000	1.000	0.000	0.000	1.000

Hash Chains at the Basis
of a Secure Reactive Routing Protocol

Thouraya Bouabana-Tebibel

National School of Computer Science
Laboratory of Communication in Informatics Systems
Algiers, Algeria
t_tebibel@esi.dz

Abstract. Presently, the main concern of ad hoc routing protocols is no longer to find an optimal route to a given destination but to find the safe route free from malicious attackers. Several secure ad hoc routing protocols proposed, in the literature, are based on public key cryptography which drawback is to consume much more resources and decrease consequently network performances. In this paper, we propose a secure routing scheme for the DSR protocol. The proposed scheme combines the hash chains and digital signatures to provide a high level of security while reducing the costs of hop-by-hop signature generation and verification. The proposed protocol is analyzed using the NS-2 simulator.

Keywords: DSR, routing protocols, mobile ad hoc networks, hash chains, digital signature.

1 Introduction

MANET or Mobile Ad hoc Network is a set of wireless mobile nodes, forming a temporary network without the use of any fixed infrastructure. Each node acts as a router (relay) and data packets are forwarded from node-to-node towards their destination in a multi-hop fashion. Ad hoc routing protocols have been designed to be more and more efficient without keeping security in mind. This makes them vulnerable to a variety of attacks which affect the reliability of data transmission. So, the present question is no longer to find an optimal route to a given destination but to provide a safe route free from malicious attackers.

In fact, most of ad hoc routing schemes provide no security system. All entities can participate in routing and there are no barriers for a malicious node to cause traffic disruptions. The attacker wants essentially to affect the routing process, in order to control the network and destroy routing operations [19,21]. He achieves his objectives by: message alteration, message fabrication, message replay and impersonation. In [22] a classification of insider attacks against mobile ad-hoc routing protocols is presented. It includes route disruption, route invasion, node isolation, and resource consumption.

L. Chen, M. Yung, and L. Zhu (Eds.): INTRUST 2011, LNCS 7222, pp. 258–270, 2012.
© Springer-Verlag Berlin Heidelberg 2012

Some solutions are proposed to secure the most important routing protocols against those attacks [4,6,7,11,13,17,18,28]. But they remain incomplete, blocking only a subset of attacks among all those well-known for the damage they cause to the networks. On the other hand, each secure scheme defines an appropriate environment of execution and presupposes a number of satisfied hypotheses to ensure its successful running. Indeed, protocols based on cryptography require a mechanism of key distribution and management [19]. Furthermore, when efficient, the used techniques are often too expensive in time calculation and memory space.

As a compromise, protocols based on reputation [9] integrate a new metric, the level of reliability of the route, to select the path towards destination. This reduces considerably the solution cost by diminishing calculation intensity.

As for intrusion detection systems, they can reduce the risks of intrusion but cannot completely eliminate them [23]. They also, sometimes fail with application of solutions as punishment of selfish nodes or location of malicious nodes which continuously change identity [29].

In terms of reliability, most of solutions rely on asymmetric cryptography and certificates delivered on line by authorities of certification. Message authentication and integrity are realized using digital signature [32]. When applied at each hop, they degrade the system performance.

DSR is a simple and efficient routing protocol designed specifically for use in multi-hop wireless ad hoc networks of mobile nodes. DSR allows the network to be completely self-organizing and self-configuring, without the need for any existing network infrastructure or administration. The protocol allows multiple routes to any destination and allows each sender to select and control the routes used in routing its packets. Another advantage of the DSR protocol is the very rapid recovery when routes change in the network. The DSR protocol is designed mainly for mobile ad hoc networks of up to about two hundred nodes and is designed to work well even with very high rates of mobility.

The aim of our work is to protect the DSR protocol routing messages by using strong cryptographic functions and keeping in mind as main objective, minimization of complex calculation burden. This will be achieved by means of two essential mechanisms. The first one relies on hash chains which consume a little time for their generation and require a minimal storage space. The second one is digital signature that reinforces authentication and ensures integrity, and non-repudiation of messages. The latter is only applied on the source and destination nodes to reduce the latency.

The remainder of the paper starts with a brief description of the reactive routing protocol DSR. Section 3 deals with the core of our secure routing scheme SRS_DSR. We simulate in section 4 the performance of the proposed protocol using NS-2 simulator. In Section 5, we discuss works related to ours. We conclude by motivating our work and showing its novelty and relevance versus related works.

2   DSR Protocol

DSR (Dynamic Source Routing) is a routing protocol based on Distance-Vector routing algorithm [14,15]. It is reactive involving route construction only when data are available for transmission. The protocol is composed of the two main mechanisms of "Route Discovery" and "Route Maintenance", which work together to allow nodes to discover and maintain routes to arbitrary destinations in the ad hoc network.

When a source node needs to determine a route to a destination node, it broadcasts a request message RREQ (Route REQuest). Intermediate nodes add their address to the packet and then broadcast it. When the request reaches the destination, or an intermediate node with an active route towards the destination, it generates a reply message RREP (Route REPly).The answer is sent unicast to the source following the reverse path, already built by the intermediate nodes.

RREQ packet format is shown in fig. 1. Option Type specifies that the packet is a RREQ. Opt Data len gives the packet length. Identification is a sequence number generated for each Route Request. It allows a receiving node to discard the RREQ in the case it has recently seen a copy of this Request. Target Address is the destination node address. Address[i] is the address of the i-th node recorded in the Route Request option. Each node propagating the Route Request adds its own address to this list, increasing the Opt Data Len value by 4 octets.

Option Type	Opt Data Len	Identification
Target Address		
Address [1]		
...		
Address [n]		

Fig. 1. RREQ packet format

RREP packet format is shown in fig. 2. It is composed of the same fields as RREQ excluding the Target Address and including a Reserved field and the Last hop external field which indicates that the last hop given by the Route Reply (the link from Address[n-1] to Address[n]) is actually an arbitrary path in a network external to the DSR network.

Option Type	Opt Data Len	Last hop ext	Reserved
Address [1]			
...			
Address [n]			

Fig. 2. RREP packet format

Link breaks are detected according to two ways. The first one occurs during the unicast reverse routing when a node reveals to be unreachable. The second way is based on information directly received from the MAC sub-layer. If a link breaks within an active route, the node involved before the link break may choose to repair locally the link or deliver an error message RERR (Route ERRor) listing the unreachable destinations. Thus, a new route discovery phase should be established by the source node [25].

As basic DSR scheme provides no security mechanism, malicious nodes can disturb the routing process. Table 1 summarizes the consequences of attacks affecting DSR control packets.

Table 1. Attacks against dsr

Target field	Attack
Target Address	The attacker creates routes to unavailable destinations in order to consume the network energy.
Identification	The attacker increments this field to invalidate any future requests from a legitimate node. He decrements it so as to the request will be considered as already processed.
Address [1..n]	The attacker modifies the addresses or alters their order.

3   SRS_DSR Solution

3.1   Basic Assumptions

The protocol is based on the following assumptions:

— a packet sent from node A is received by the latter one hop neighbor B before a third node C replays the packet to B.
— a trusted Certification Authority performs the pre-distribution of both private key and X509v3 certificate [8] to each member of the network through a physical contact. The conventional certificate X509v3 contains the public key, the identity of the certificate owner and other fields. All these fields are encrypted by means of a digital signature integrated to the certificate.

3.2   Proposed Scheme

The solution which we propose integrates security mechanisms that take into account the limited resources of nodes. These mechanisms are not based on unrealistic assumptions such as availability of an always-online security infrastructure (trusted third-party).

Our approach is inspired from Lamport authentication algorithm [16] used in remotely accessed computer systems. Authentication described by Lamport was designed for a client/server architecture where the management is centralized. In Lamport authentication, a server randomly chooses a password H_n. Afterwards, he applies to H_n, n times, a one-way function h to get n passwords $(H_{n-1}, H_{n-2}, ..., H_1, H_0)$ called One Time Password sequence or OTP, for short.

$$H_n \rightarrow h(H_n) = H_{n-1} \rightarrow h(H_{n-1}) = H_{n-2} \rightarrow h(H_{n-2}) = H_{n-3} \ldots \rightarrow h(H_1) = H_0$$

We were attracted by the effectiveness of hash functions because they reduce the high costs caused by traditional cryptographic mechanisms. Thus, we combined the use of hash chains authentication with digital signatures to achieve a satisfying security level. We adopt the notations of table 2.

Table 2. Notations

Symbol	Signification
SK_A, PK_A	Private key. Public key of node A
$[d]SK_A$	Signature of a message with the private key of A
$Cert_A$	A certificate belonging to node A
ID_A	Node A identifier
H_j^A	The jth element of the hash chain of node A

The security process we propose is divided into two phases: initialization phase and authentication phase.

3.2.1   Initialization Phase

As set in the basic assumptions, a trusted certification authority performs the pre-distribution of one certificate and one private key to each member of the network. Each entity A, identified by an ID_A, constructs its own OTP sequence and broadcasts the last value H_0^A to its one-hop neighbors. In order to ensure the provenance authenticity of H_0^A, we propose what follows. Node A first signs H_0^A using its private key and then transmits the clear H_0^A and signature $[H_0^A]SK_A$ as well as its identity ID_A and certificate $Cert_A$ to all one-hop neighbors, refer to (1). Each neighbor decrypts the encrypted H_0^A using the public key of node A transmitted within $Cert_A$. To ensure that the decrypted value is authentic and so, effectively transmitted by node A, the receiver compares it with the unencrypted value H_0^A. If the comparison matches, node A identity and H_0^A integrity are proved true. So, H_0^A value is saved in a new entry of the Neighbors table which keeps the H_0^A value of each neighbor. The comparison fails if either the sender authenticity or H_0^A integrity is compromised. In both cases, the message is ignored.

The one-hop neighbors also send the last values of their own hash chain and certificates to node A, see (2). At the end of this step, each node knows the H_0 value of its one-hop neighbors.

$$A \rightarrow Broadcast \quad PWD : \{ID_A, H_0^A, [H_0^A]SK_A, Cert_A\} \tag{1}$$

$$V \rightarrow A \quad PWDREP: \{IDv, H_0^V, [H_0^V]SK_V, Cert_V\} \tag{2}$$

3.2.2 Authentication Phase

Control packets RREQ, RREP and RERR are used to construct and maintain routes from source to destination nodes. For each phase of the routing, we will explain how the values of the hash chain and private keys are used.

Secure the route discovery. When a node S needs to know a route to some destination D, and such a route is not available, it broadcasts a route request RREQ, see (3).

$$S \rightarrow \text{Broadcast RREQ: } \{ \text{RREQ}^S, [\text{RREQ}^S]SK_S, \text{Cert}_S, H_i^S\} \tag{3}$$

This request contains the same basic DSR protocol fields excluding the Opt Data Len, see figure 1. We add the source node certificate Cert_s in case of large-scale networks where nodes have not necessarily the public keys of all the network members.

The RREQ fields transmitted by S are non-mutable. They are signed with the private key of S and accompanied by a hash value Hi ($1< i <n$). To not reuse a password already revealed, an index i is incremented within the node at every use.

The generated packet is then broadcasted on the channel. When a node receives it, it checks the H_i^S value to ensure that the packet comes from a legitimate node. To do so, it applies i times the hash function on H_i^S to obtain H_0^S, the password initially transmitted by the neighbor and stored in the Neighbors table. If the receiver does not reach H_0^S after i iterations, it infers that the message is fabricated by a malicious node. So, it rejects it without any process. Otherwise the message is accepted. The intermediate node adds its address to the packet. It signs this address and the previous one using its private key. Such a signature, applied to two successive node addresses, protects against any attempt to alter the addresses order. It is added with the node certificate to the packet. The node also replaces the received H_i by a new password of its own chain, and finally broadcasts the RREQ, see (4).

$$J \rightarrow \text{Broadcast RREQ: } \{\text{RREQ}^S, [\text{RREQ}^S]SK_S, \text{Cert}_S, ..., \text{Address}_j, [\text{Address}_{j-1}, \text{Address}_j]SK_j, \text{Cert}_j, H_i^J\} \tag{4}$$

Eventually, the message is received by the destination D which verifies the source signature, as well the intermediate node signatures, and then responds using a RREP. The source digital signature authenticates the source and destination nodes. This control is made on IDs and ID_d fields. The intermediate encryptions authenticate the intermediate nodes. This authentication is reinforced by the check of the addresses order. Once decrypted, the obtained value is compared with the two previous node addresses.

In (5) J denotes the last intermediate node of the path, connecting S to D. The destination node sends the response to J according to the following formula (5):

$$D \rightarrow J \text{ RREP:} \{\text{RREP}, [\text{RREP}]SK_D, \text{Cert}_D, H_i^D\} \tag{5}$$

RREP fields are signed by the destination node and value H_i^D is associated to the packet. Each node sending the response is authenticated along the path using H_i. The reverse route construction is exposed to the risk of a diversion launched by an attacker who responds instead of the destination node. This attack is detected thanks to the destination certificate which includes the destination identity. If the latter doesn't match with the destination identity invoked by the source node, one can deduce an intrusion attempt. As for the digital signature, it authenticates the source and destination nodes and controls the message replay. Finally, once the destination signature checked, the source node updates its cache with the new path.

In [30] an approach comparable to ours, called a Zero Common Knowledge authentication was proposed. It differs from ours in the use of $h(H_i)$. In this approach, the receiver checks the value H_i by calculating only $h(H_i)$ and testing the relationship $h(H_i) = H_i+1$. If checked then the node identity is proved true. This approach supposes the storage of the latest password which may put in check the control process in case of lost messages.

Secure Route Maintenance. When a link breaks within an active route, the precursor of the unreachable node does the following:

— Invalidates the routes including this node in its cache.
— Lists all receivers that are no longer reachable (Unreach_Address).
— Delivers an appropriate RERR to such receivers.

Let a node A discovering a link break, and a source node S using this path. A warns S about the topology changes by sending the following message RERR to it:

$$A \rightarrow S \quad RERR \quad : \{RERR_A, Cert_A, [RERR_A, Cert_A] SK_A\} \tag{6}$$

This packet is signed by A and verified by the intermediates nodes. Each node receiving the RERR message carries out the same operations and spreads it to different sources.

Update the Hash Chain. When the node depletes all its hash values, it should reset the passwords sequence to allow its authentication. The node chooses a new random value H_N_new, and then generates a new sequence, using the hash function and sends the final value H_0^A_new to the one-hop neighbors. To authenticate the update message, we use the last undisclosed hash value of the old sequence (instead of the certificate in PWD). Here is a simplified format of the update message:

$$A \rightarrow Broadcast \; UPDATE : \{ID_A, H_0^A\_new, (H_0^A\_new) SK_A, \; H_n\} \tag{7}$$

4   Simulation and Test

In order to evaluate the routing protocol performance, one often uses simulation. In fact, it would be very costly, or even impossible, to establish a network for testing purposes. An ad hoc network simulation does not take much time, and it keeps us closer to the real use of the routing protocol. These two major advantages help us to better see the behavior of the protocol in different scenarios and evaluate its performance.

We carry out simulations using the NS-2 simulator [20]. We choose NS-2 because of its popularity among academic researchers [26]. In addition, it already supports a verified version of DSR. Simulations are held considering a network of size 670 m x 670 m, composed of 20 nodes. We define simulations with parameters defined in table 3

Table 3. Simulation Parameters

Parameter	Value
Antenna	OmniAntinna
MAC layer type	IEEE 802.11
Radio propagation model	Two Ray Ground
Bandwidth	1Mb
CBR traffic	4 packets/s
Packet size	512 bit
Pause time	30 ms
Transmission range	250 m
Simulation time	200s

The nodes move according to the RWP mobility model (Random Waypoint Model). This model has become a standard in wireless networks research. It provides several scenarios where the mobile entities randomly move in the simulation area. For each experiment, we created several scenarios for traffic and mobility using the parameters set out above. Each time, we vary the speed between |0, 20m/s| and evaluate one of the following metrics:

1. *EED Average end to end delay:* it gives the average time required to transmit a data packet from the source to the destination node.
2. *APL Average path length:*   is calculated using the hop count field. It is often used as a metric for choosing the best path to route data.
3. *RL Routing load (the routing overhead):* it gives us information about the number of control packets generated by the protocol for the path establishment and route maintenance.

To evaluate the SRS_DSR performances, we carry out our experimentations on three protocols: ARAN (Authenticated Routing for Ad-hoc Networks) [26] that has been chosen for its robustness and its high level of security, DSR and SRS_DSR.

ARAN is a secure protocol, implementing asymmetric cryptography. It uses a trusted Certification Authority called CA to generate certificates. Before entering the Ad-hoc network, each node requests a certificate from the CA. In ARAN, each node signs the discovery packets and route reply messages before retransmitting them. Each node verifies the previous node digital signature and then replaces it with its own. The cryptographic operations cause additional delays at each hop thus increasing the route acquisition latency. Only the destination can answer the Request packet. When the source receives the RREP, it verifies the destination signature. This allows an end-to-end authentication between the source and destination. However, the latency increases especially for long paths.

Fig. 3 shows that the increase in the movement speed leads to a rather large increase of the end-to-end delay. Indeed, the nodes movement involves frequent link failure in the established paths. Nodes are forced to rebuild invalid routes. Thus, delivery of data packets is delayed. We note that the required delay for ARAN is much higher than that of DSR and SRS_DSR.

Indeed, SRS_DSR established routes faster than ARAN: the time spent to check the hash values in SRS_DSR is insignificant, compared to the time needed in a certificate checking or a digital signature. We can therefore say that the processing of digital signature using only the two path ends (source and destination) reduces the delay of packets transfer.

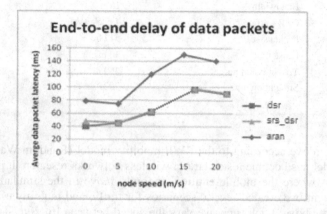

Fig. 3. End to End Delay (EED)

Fig. 4 shows the ratio of control packets relative to received packets. We note that the three protocols apply for the rule: the packets need increase with a higher speed. The space overhead caused by SRS_DSR is higher than the one of DSR and ARAN, because of the new control packets, namely PWD and UPDATE packets that we used to secure DSR.

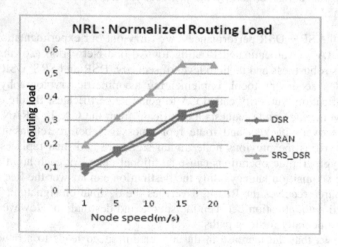

Fig. 4. Normalized routing Load

5   Related Work

The first works that deal with DSR security are those of Papadimitratos and Haas. They proposed SRP [24] in order to provide an end-to-end protection during the route discovery phase. They conducted tests on many known attacks and concluded that the proposed SRP proves to be secure in absence of grouped attacks. Their claim has never been formally proved.

Indeed, Buttyán and Vajda showed in [5] the weakness of the analysis presented in [24]. They presented an attack launched by a single hacker who succeeds to inject forged information during an SRP route construction.

Ariadne has been proposed by Hu et al. in [10,11] in order to improve the security mechanisms provided in SRP. It aims to secure all intermediate nodes by means of an appropriate authentication applied at each hop. They test their solution using different classes of attacks. But the solution was invalidated by Buttyán, Vajda and Ács in [5], [1] who succeed in launching several attacks.

To improve the weakness revealed in Ariadne, Buttyán and Vajda proposed a new version called enairA [5]. This solution remains insecure against an attack where two hackers encapsulate the control messages into data packets.

Other protocols have emerged as improvements to SRP, Ariadne, SAODV (Secure AODV) [33], FLSL (Adaptive Fuzzy Logic Based Security Level Routing Protocol) [12] and SAR (Security Aware Ad-hoc Routing) [21], for instance. In FLSL, a new attribute called security level is introduced in the format of the control messages to denote the reliability and dependability of certain mobile hosts or routes. The security level is used by source and destination nodes to determine the most secure and short-est route. As for SAR, it can discover a path with desired security attributes. The path found by the SAR protocol is not necessarily the shortest, but the safest of all the paths.

DSR and most of the on demand ad hoc routing protocols use single route reply along reverse path. Rapid change of topology causes that the route reply could not arrive to the source node. To avoid this, a new technique which tries multiple route replies is proposed in [27].

Latest researches in the area are conducted to secure ad hoc networks against grouped attacks. In [2] Awerbuch et al. propose ODSBR, the first on-demand routing protocol for ad hoc wireless networks that provides resilience to attacks caused by internal individual or colluding nodes. The protocol uses an adaptive probing technique that detects a malicious link after log n faults have occurred, where n is the length of the path. Problematic links are avoided by using a route discovery mechanism that relies on a new metric that captures adversarial behavior. Later, Awerbuch and Scheideler claim in [3] that the biggest threats appear to be join-leave attacks, used to isolate honest peers in the system, and against which no provably robust mechanisms are known so far. In this paper he showed that, on a high level, a scalable DHTcan be designed that is provably robust against adaptive adversarial join-leave attacks.

6   Conclusion

The purpose of this paper is to present a new scheme to secure the DSR protocol. We showed that the proposed scheme made of hash chains and end-to-end digital signature provides a high security level at a very low cost.

The initialization phase always raises the problem of secure distribution of keys and passwords, particularly on large scale systems when the by hand distribution becomes unrealizable. We proposed a remote pre-distribution carried out in an efficient and secure manner. We resorted afterwards to the use of one way hash chains to authenticate the control message senders during the route discovery. This authentication is principally useful while crossing the route from the source towards the destination. It guarantees the route drawing with legitimate nodes. Furthermore, the use of key-chain scheme is very well suited to pervasive computing devices since it requires nearly no computational power, very low bandwidth and memory storage.

At destination, the request message integrity is checked using a digital signature. This end-to-end checking ensures a fast source and destination authentication as well as a non message replay control.

The proposed solution can be extended to treat attacks. It will be also, interesting to validate this work by formalizing the specification and verification of the SRS_DSR protocol.

References

1. Ács, G., Buttyán, L., Vajda, I.: Provably secure on-demand source routing in mobile ad hoc networks. IEEE Transactions on Mobile Computing 5(11), 1533–1546 (2006)
2. Awerbuch, B., Curtmola, R., Holmer, D., Nita-Rotaru, C., Rubens, H.: ODSBR: An on-demand secure Byzantine resilient routing protocol for wireless ad hoc networks. ACM Trans. Inf. Syst. Secur. 10(3) (2007)
3. Awerbuch, B., Scheideler, C.: Robust random number generation for peer-to-peer systems. Theoretical Computer Science 410(6-7), 453–466 (2009)
4. Burmester, M., De Medeiros, B.: On the Security of Route Discovery in MANETs. IEEE Transactions on Mobile Computing 8(9), 1180–1188 (2009)
5. Buttyán, L., Vajda, I.: Towards provable security for ad hoc routing protocols. In: Setia, S., Swarup, V. (eds.) SASN, pp. 94–105. ACM (2004)
6. Cerri, D., Ghioni, A.: Securing AODV: The A-SAODV Secure Routing Prototype. IEEE Communications Magazine (February 2008)
7. Curtmola, R., Nita-Rotaru, C.: BSMR: Byzantine-Resilient Secure Multicast Routing in Multihop Wireless Networks. IEEE Transactions on Mobile Computing 8(4), 445–459 (2009)
8. Eichler, S., Roman, C.: Challenges of Secure Routing in MANETs: A Simulative Approach using AODV-SEC. Technical Report: LKN-TR-2. Technische Universität München, Germany (2006)
9. Galice, S., Minier, M., Ubéda, S.: A Trust Protocol for Community Collaboration. In: Etalle, S., Marsh, S. (eds.) IFIPTM. IFIP, vol. 238, pp. 169–184. Springer, Boston (2007)

10. Hu, Y.-C., Perrig, A., Johnson, D.B.: Ariadne: a secure on-demand routing protocol for ad hoc networks. In: Akyildiz, I.F., Lin, J.Y.-B., Jain, R., Bharghavan, V., Campbell, A.T. (eds.) MOBICOM, pp. 12–23. ACM (2002)

11. Hu, Y.-C., Perrig, A., Johnson, D.B.: A Secure On-Demand Routing Protocol for Ad Hoc Networks. Wireless Networks 11(1-2), 21–38 (2005)

12. Jin, L., Zhang, Z., Zhou, H.: Performance comparison of AODV, SAODV and FLSL routing protocols in mobile ad hoc network. In: 4th IEEE Consumer Communications and Networking Conference, CCNC 2007, pp. 479–483 (January 2007)

13. Jung, S., Lee, B., Talipov, E., Ahn, M.W., Kim, C.: Effects of Valid Source-Destination Edges for Node-Disjoint Multipaths on AD HOC Networks. In: MSV 2008, Las Vegas, USA, pp. 308–313 (2008)

14. Johnson, D.B., Maltz, D.A.: Dynamic source routing in ad hoc wireless networks. Mobile Computing, 153–181 (1996)

15. Johnson, D.B., Maltz, D.A., Hu, Y.C.: IETF RFC4728: The dynamic source routing protocol (DSR) for mobile ad hoc networks (February 2007)

16. Lamport, L.: Password Authentication with Insecure Communication. Communication of the ACM 24, 770–772 (1981)

17. Luo, H., Kong, J., Zerfos, P., Lu, S., Zhang, L.: URSA: Ubiquitous and robust access control for mobile ad hoc networks. IEEE/ACM Transactions on Networking 12(6), 1049–1063 (2004)

18. Mallouli, W., Wehbi, B., Cavalli, A.R.: Distributed Monitoring in Ad Hoc Networks: Conformance and Security Checking. In: The 7th International Conference on AD-HOC Networks & Wireless, Sophia Antipolis, France, September 10-12 (2008)

19. Mishra, A.: Security and quality of service in ad hoc wireless network, pp. 3–106. Cambridge University Press, New York (2008)

20. NS Manual. VINT Project (2008), http://www.isi.edu/nsnam/ns/doc/ns_doc.pdf

21. Naldurg, S., Yi, P., Kravets, R.: Security aware ad hoc routing for wireless networks. In: 2nd ACM Int. Symp. on Mobile Ad Hoc Networking & Computing, Long Beach, pp. 299–302. ACM Publisher, USA (2001)

22. Ning, P., Sun, K.: How to Misuse AODV: A Case Study of Insider Attacks against Mobile Ad-Hoc Routing Protocols. Ad Hoc Networks 3(6), 795–819 (2005)

23. Orset, J.-M., Alcalde, B., Cavalli, A.: An EFSM-Based Intrusion Detection System for Ad Hoc Networks. In: Peled, D.A., Tsay, Y.-K. (eds.) ATVA 2005. LNCS, vol. 3707, pp. 400–413. Springer, Heidelberg (2005)

24. Papadimitratos, P., Haas, Z.J.: Secure Routing for Mobile Ad hoc Networks. In: Proceedings of the SCS Commnication Networks and Distributed Systems Modeling and Simulation Conference (CNDS), San Antonio, TX, USA, pp. 193–204 (January 2002)

25. Pirzada, A., McDonald, C., Datta, A.: Performance Comparison of Trust-Based Reactive Routing Protocols. IEEE Transactions on Mobile Computing 5(6) (June 2006)

26. Sanzgiri, K., Dahill, B., Levine, B.N., Shields, C., Belding-Royer, E.M.: Authenticated routing for ad hoc networks. In: 10th IEEE International Conference on Network Protocols, Paris, France (2002)

27. Talipov, E., Jin, D., Jung, J., Ha, I., Choi, Y., Kim, C.: Path Hopping Based on Reverse AODV for Security. In: Kim, Y.-T., Takano, M. (eds.) APNOMS 2006. LNCS, vol. 4238, pp. 574–577. Springer, Heidelberg (2006)

28. Tsaur, W.-J., Pai, H.-T.: A New Security Scheme for On-Demand Source Routing in Mobile Ad Hoc Networks. In: IWCMC 2007, Honolulu, Hawaii, USA, August 12-16, pp. 577–582 (2007)

29. Tseng, C.-Y.H.: Distributed Intrusion Detection Models For Mobile Ad Hoc Networks. PhD Thesis, University of California (2006)
30. Weimerskirch, A., Westhoff, D.: Zero Common-Knowledge Authentication for Pervasive Networks. In: Matsui, M., Zuccherato, R. (eds.) SAC 2003. LNCS, vol. 3006, pp. 73–87. Springer, Heidelberg (2004)
31. Zapata, M.G.: Secure Ad hoc on Demand Distance Vector (SAODV) Routing. Mobile Ad Hoc Networking Working Group, Internet Draft (September 2005)
32. Zapata, M.G.: Key Management and Delayed Verification for Ad Hoc Networks. Journal of High Speed Networks 15(1), 93–109 (2006)

Evaluation of a PUF Device Authentication Scheme on a Discrete 0.13um SRAM

Patrick Koeberl[1], Jiangtao Li[1], Roel Maes[2],
Anand Rajan[1], Claire Vishik[1], and Marcin Wójcik[3]

[1] Intel Corporation
{patrickx.koeberl,jiangtao.li,anand.rajan,claire.vishik}@intel.com
[2] Catholic University of Leuven
roel.maes@esat.kuleuven.be
[3] University of Bristol
wojcik@cs.bris.ac.uk

Abstract. The contamination of electronic component supply chains by counterfeit hardware devices is a serious and growing risk in today's globalized marketplace. Current best practice for detecting counterfeit semiconductors includes visual checking, electrical testing, and reliability testing, all of which require significant investments in expertise, equipment, and time. In TRUST'11, Koeberl, Li, Rajan, Vishik, and Wu proposed a new device authentication scheme using SRAM Physically Unclonable Functions (PUFs) for semiconductor anti-counterfeiting. Their authentication scheme is simple, low cost, and practical. However, the method and corresponding parameters of their scheme are based on a theoretical SRAM PUF model without support from real experimental data. In this paper, we evaluate a real SRAM PUF on a discrete 0.13um SRAM, and use the PUF result to evaluate this device authentication scheme and show that this scheme indeed works well. We identify several gaps between the theoretical model and the experimental SRAM PUF result, and adjust the parameters of the scheme accordingly. In addition, we provide a new post-processing function that results in a smaller false rejection rate and false acceptance rate.

Keywords: physically unclonable functions, device authentication, hardware security, anti-counterfeiting, implementation and evaluation.

1 Introduction

Semiconductor counterfeiting is a growing problem in today's globalized marketplace. The majority of counterfeit semiconductors detected today are remarked devices where a device's markings are forged in order to misrepresent aspects of the device's performance, brand or some other key specification. Such devices, if embedded in an electronic system may fail in the field when subjected to a different operational environment than the part was designed for. The consequences of such failures might range from minor inconvenience to the end user to loss of life for devices which are embedded in safety-critical infrastructure.

L. Chen, M. Yung, and L. Zhu (Eds.): INTRUST 2011, LNCS 7222, pp. 271–288, 2012.

A number of high-profile instances of counterfeit product entering the semiconductor supply chain have been reported, in one instance involving the US Air Force, microprocessors for its F-15 flight control computer were procured from a broker and found to have been remarked [12].

Current approaches to detecting semiconductor counterfeits range from non-destructive optical and x-ray inspection of device samples to destructive testing. Such practices require significant investments in time and expertise and in many cases can only be applied to a sample of the device population. Device traceability and authentication standards which can support an anti-counterfeiting strategy are beginning to emerge. For example, SEMI T20-1109 [14] defines standardized device traceability and authentication mechanisms based on encrypted serial numbers applied at a variety of package levels ranging from the device package itself to higher levels such as product and shipping packaging. An authentication service provides for validation of the serial numbers. It is conceivable that such standards could be applied at the silicon level, for example by programming the serial number into non-volatile memory (NVM) such as EEPROM, flash, or fuses. However, secure serialization mechanisms have the shortcoming that they are clonable by any competent counterfeiter.

An alternative approach is to utilize the intrinsic properties of the silicon to enable a class of identification and authentication applications. Physically Uncloneable Functions (PUFs) are a promising security primitive that exploit the manufacturing variation inherent in any mass produced object to derive biometric-like fingerprints which are difficult to clone, even for the manufacturer. PUFs which exploit the process variation inherent in Integrated Circuit (IC) manufacturing are of particular interest due to the high levels of integration achievable in modern CMOS technologies.

Recently Koeberl, Li, Rajan, Vishik, and Wu proposed a new device authentication scheme using SRAM PUFs for semiconductor anti-counterfeiting [8]. In their scheme, each device is embedded with a small SRAM PUF which serves as an intrinsic unclonable fingerprint of the device. At manufacturing time, the manufacturer evaluates the PUF and extracts the m-bit PUF result into a short k-bit device ID. The manufacturer then creates a device certificate based on the device ID. Any verifier can authenticate the device by evaluating the SRAM PUF, re-computing the device ID, and verifying the device certificate. This scheme is simple and practical as it does not require any online databases or on-chip cryptographic operations. For hardware devices which already have SRAM and non-volatile storage embedded, this scheme takes almost no additional cost.

The security of the device authentication scheme [8] relies on the size of m, the size of the SRAM PUF. They assume that it is too expensive or uneconomical for an adversary to embed an m-bit PUF simulator into the non-volatile memory or circuit of a counterfeit device. This assumption is reasonable for economically motivated attackers and integrated circuits implemented in modern technology nodes. It is important to keep m reasonably large, while keeping k small to reduce the size of device certificate. The paper [8] provided a post-processing function to compress the m-bit PUF result into a k-bit device ID using a theoretical SRAM PUF model.

1.1   Our Contribution

Our paper can be seen as an improvement to [8] with the following contributions.

- We implement the device authentication scheme using a discrete $0.13\mu m$ SRAM chip as the SRAM PUF and show that the authentication scheme works well. We also show that the post-processing function in [8] is reasonably effective, compressing a 256-kb PUF into a 512-bit device ID with both False Reject Rate (FRR) and False Acceptance Rate (FAR) under 10^{-10}.
- Although the evaluated SRAM PUF exhibits low levels of bias ($< 1\%$) we discover that the PUF response is highly correlated with an estimated entropy of 63% or less. We consider this to be an important result since other work in the literature on SRAM PUFs assumes that the SRAM cell power-up states are independently distributed. This assumption may be incorrect for particular SRAM instantiations.
- We provide a couple of improvements of the device authentication scheme. One is that we modify the device certificate to address the device remarking issues. Second, we provide a new post-processing function which is more effective when the SRAM PUF result is biased or correlated. We show that our post-processing function can compress a 256-kb PUF into a 512-bit device ID with both FRR and FAR under 10^{-13}.

1.2   Related Work

Device authentication protocols typically rely on the secure storage of a cryptographic secret in non-volatile on-chip memory such as EEPROM, flash or fuses. Cloning of the device by extracting the secret and replicating it in another device instance is a possibility, unless explicit steps are taken to protect the secret. For example, the Trusted Platform Module (TPM) [16] uses a protected private key in non-volatile memory to enable remote device authentication and attestation applications. The approach taken in TPM may not be suitable for detecting semiconductor counterfeits.

In 2007, Suh and Devadas proposed a low cost authentication scheme based on silicon PUFs and using a challenge response protocol [15]. This authentication scheme places a number of constraints on the silicon PUF, which must posses a large number of challenge-response pairs, and the system since authentications must be on-line. In this paper, we choose to implement and evaluate the offline authentication scheme [8] instead, as we believe the offline authentication scheme has few limitations and is more appealing to the real applications.

An SRAM fingerprinting method is proposed in [6], where the power-up state of SRAM cells is used in a device identification scheme. Experiments show that a 64-bit SRAM fingerprint is sufficient to uniquely identify devices among a small population of 5,120 instances. A key difference between this work and the ideas in [8] is that the scheme's resistance to cloning attacks is not a design criterion.

Another related work is the authentication scheme in [3], which provides a strong binding between the paper medium and the data on it using a fingerprint extracted from the ultraviolet fibers. This scheme can be used to detect counterfeited tickets, banknotes, and prescriptions. The device authentication scheme in [8] shares some similarities between this scheme, however, it is different in that [8] is optimized for anti-counterfeiting of electronic devices and uses a silicon PUF from the hardware device.

1.3   Paper Outline

The rest of the paper is organized in the following way. We first review the concept and constructions of PUF in Section 2. We then review the device authentication scheme of [8] in Section 3 and provide our improvements. We outline our experimental setup and evaluation methodologies in Section 4. The results of the evaluations are analyzed in Section 5. We conclude our paper and discuss future work in Section 6.

2   Physically Unclonable Functions

Physically Unclonable Functions are physical challenge-response systems which when challenged respond with unique and unpredictable responses. PUFs are also *physically unclonable*, in other words it is extremely difficult to create a physical copy of a PUF with the same challenge-response behaviour as the original. Physical unclonability is achieved in all known PUFs by deriving the PUF response from the manufacturing variation inherent in any mass produced object. The PUF concept was introduced in [13] where the random arrangement of scattering particles in a transparent medium is the basis of an optical PUF. Silicon PUFs, introduced in [4], exploit the manufacturing variation inherent in the CMOS fabrication process. Variations in physical parameters such as transistor dopant concentrations and line widths result in measurable differences in circuit delays. Silicon PUFs are of considerable interest as they can leverage the high levels of integration possible in modern CMOS technology nodes.

A silicon PUF embodiment based on SRAM was introduced in [5]. Here, the power-up state of SRAM cells is used as the PUF response. A typical six-transistor SRAM cell is shown in Figure 1. The storage element in an SRAM cell consists of four cross-coupled transistors, denoted in the figure as M1, M2, M3 and M4. The cross-coupled structure is bistable i.e. it can assume one of two stable states. The power-up state for a particular cell is determined by the relative characteristics of the transistors forming the cross-coupled structure. Mismatches due to manufacturing variation of the transistors will cause the cell to have a preference to power-up in a particular state, a phenomenon that can be exploited as a PUF.

It is useful to consider SRAM PUFs as members of a larger grouping which we term cross-coupled PUFs due to the cross-coupled structure forming the bistable storage element. In fact, any digital storage element constructed from static logic will use a cross-coupled structure as its basis and one can envisage cross-coupled

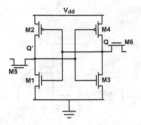

Fig. 1. Construction of an SRAM cell

PUFs based on the many flip-flop and latch variants available to the digital designer. An example of a cross-coupled PUF based on D-type flip-flops can be found in [9].

3 Device Authentication with SRAM PUFs

In this section, we first review the off-line device authentication scheme presented in [8] and then provide two improvements of this scheme.

3.1 Review of Off-Line Authentication Scheme

We now review the off-line device authentication scheme in [8] as follows. This scheme has two main building blocks: a digital signature scheme [11] and a family of SRAM PUFs. A digital signature scheme requires par of public key for device manufacturer's verification and private key for signing. For our applications we can divide this off-line authentication scheme on two phases: an enrolment phase Figure 2 and an evaluation phase Figure 3. In the former, the manufacturer certifies each device and ships them into the market; in the latter, the verifier accepts or rejects the hardware device after applying the verification procedure.

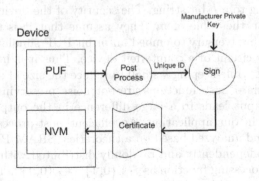

Fig. 2. Enrolment phase of the off-line device authentication scheme

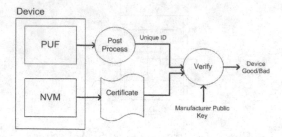

Fig. 3. Evaluation phase of the off-line device authentication scheme

Having those above-mentioned assumptions we can describe the off-line authentication scheme as follows:

Enrolment Phase. In this phase the manufacturer instantiates an SRAM PUF into the device D and runs the evaluation procedure to obtain the unique identity s. In the next step the manufacturer computes the device ID id_D using a post-processing function and creates a signature σ of the ID using private key. The last step of this procedure is to store previously generated signature and unique device ID as the device's certificate in the NVM of the device.

Evaluation Phase. In this phase the verifier who wants to verify the device runs the evaluation procedure of the SRAM PUF in the device and obtains s'. Having s', the verifier uses the post-processing function and obtains id'_D. The verifier then reads the certificate stored in the NVM of the device and uses the public key to verify the signature σ on id_D. If this step fails, the device is rejected otherwise the verifier checks the Hamming distance between id_D and id'_D. If it is greater than the previously set security parameter δ the device is rejected, otherwise verifier accepts the device.

Both the enrolment and evaluation phases use the post-processing functions to map an m-bit string to a k-bit string. The security of the device authentication scheme [8] relies on the value of m. They assume that it is too expensive or uneconomical for an adversary to embed an m-bit PUF simulator into the non-volatile memory or circuit of a counterfeit device. Thus it is important to keep m reasonably large, while keeping k small to reduce the size of device certificate. Observe that standard hash functions are not noise preserving, i.e., one small difference in the input leads to a large difference in the output, and thus we can not use them in our application. An efficient post-processing function is introduced in [8] and analyzed based on a theoretical SRAM PUF model where each PUF cell is independently and randomly distributed with small noise. We denote this post-processing function as $f_1 : \{0,1\}^m \to \{0,1\}^k$. This function can be computed in the following three steps:

1. Let ℓ be the largest odd number such that $k \cdot \ell \leq m$.
2. Divide the first $k \cdot \ell$ bits of string s into k groups $G_1, \ldots, G_k$, where each group has ℓ bits. The mapping from bits in s to k groups is random but fixed per function and is encoded in the algorithm.
3. For each group G_i, where $1 \leq i \leq k$, compute $t_i = \text{Voting}(G_i)$, the majority voting result of bits in G_i. More specifically, let $G = \{b_1, \ldots, b_\ell\}$ where $b_1, \ldots, b_\ell \in \{0, 1\}$. The majority voting function $\text{Voting}(G)$ is defined as follows: $\text{Voting}(G)$ outputs 1 if $b_1 + \cdots + b_\ell > \ell/2$ and outputs 0 otherwise.
4. The final output of f_1 is $t_1, t_2, \ldots, t_k$.

As in [8], we use the following terms to analyze the effectiveness of the post-processing functions.

Definition 1 (False Rejection Rate). *If the manufacturer certifies a legitimate device in the enrollment phase, the False Rejection Rate (FRR) is the probability that the device fails to be verified in the evaluation phase.*

Definition 2 (False Acceptance Rate). *The False Acceptance Rate (FAR) is the probability that an uncertified device with a random SRAM PUF embedded can be successfully verified in the evaluation phase, assuming the attacker can inject a valid device certificate into the counterfeit device.*

3.2 Our Improvements

We give two improvements to the device authentication scheme. The first is a new post-processing function which is more effective when the SRAM PUF result is biased. The second improvement is that we include additional data in the device certificate to address issues related to device remarking attacks.

In [8], the post-processing function f_1 is based on a theoretical model in which each SRAM PUF bit is randomly and independently distributed. In practice, a small bias in the SRAM PUF could exist. Some proposed SRAM architectures may exhibit larger biases due to specific features such as asymmetric designs intended to address leakage power and read stability in recent technology nodes [7,2]. As shown in Table 1, even a small bias in the raw PUF response will be significantly amplified in the device ID after the majority voting. As a result, the inter-distance and entropy of the device IDs may be significantly reduced. Small inter-distances will result in an increase in the FAR.

Table 1. Probability of '0' in Device ID after majority voting

Probability of '0' in PUF response	50%	50.5%	51%	52%	55%
Group size = 255	50%	56.35%	62.54%	73.88%	94.55%
Group size = 511	50%	58.95%	67.45%	81.73%	98.83%
Group size = 1023	50%	62.55%	73.89%	89.98%	99.93%

The motivation for a new post-processing function is to minimize the effect of a slight bias to '0' or '1' in the SRAM PUF response. Our method is straight-forward, we first apply XOR to the PUF response to remove bias, and then perform the majority voting. Note that, applying XOR to the PUF result will also increase the noise rate in the device ID. As shown in Table 2, assuming each bit in the PUF response is independently distributed, the bias in the device ID reduces significantly after we perform bit-wise XOR on the PUF response.

Table 2. Probability of '0' in Device ID after XOR and majority voting

Probability of '0' in PUF response	50%	50.5%	51%	52%	55%
Probability of '0' after bitwise XOR	50%	50%	50.02%	50.08%	50.5%
Group size = 255 after XOR	50%	50%	50.26%	51.02%	56.35%
Group size = 511 after XOR	50%	50%	50.36%	51.44%	58.95%
Group size = 1023 after XOR	50%	50%	50.51%	52.04%	62.55%

A new post-processing function. We now introduce a new post-processing function, denoted as f_2, as a generalization of the one in [8] but designed especially to remove any bias in the PUF data using an XOR operation. Function f_2 can be computed in the following five steps:

1. Let d be a small integer, a parameter to this function.
2. Let ℓ be the largest odd number such that $k \cdot \ell \cdot d \leq m$.
3. Divide the first $k \cdot \ell \cdot d$ bits of string s into k groups $G_1, \ldots, G_k$, where each group has $\ell \cdot d$ bits. The mapping from bits in s to k groups is random but fixed per function and is encoded in the algorithm.
4. For each group G_i, where $1 \leq i \leq k$, compress $\ell \cdot d$ bits into an ℓ-bit group G'_i using the XOR operation as follows. Let $G = \{b_0, b_1, \cdots, b_{\ell \cdot d - 1}\}$. $G' = \{c_0, c_1, \cdots, c_{\ell-1}\}$ is computed by setting $c_j = b_{d \cdot j} \oplus b_{d \cdot j + 1} \oplus \cdots \oplus b_{d \cdot j + d - 1}$, for $j = 0, \ldots, \ell - 1$.
5. For each group G'_i, where $1 \leq i \leq k$, $t_i = \text{Voting}(G'_i)$, the majority voting result of bits in G'_i. The final output of f_2 is $t_1, t_2, \ldots, t_k$.

Note that the function f_2 is similar to the function f_1, except that f_2 reduces any bias using the XOR operation [17]. The function f_1 is a special case of the function f_2 with parameter $d = 1$ and those functions can be treated as a family of post-processing functions. Nevertheless, we analyze them separately to stress that the first one will not reduce any bias. The XOR operation will also remove any correlations in the SRAM PUF response. In Section 4.2 we show that although the bias of the SRAM PUF response is small, it is found to be highly correlated. We shall show in Section 5 that the function f_2 is indeed better than f_1 for correlated, rather than biased SRAM PUF responses.

Configuration data in device certificate. The above device authentication scheme binds the device certificate with the device ID computed from the embedded PUF. Observe that this scheme only proves a hardware device is a legitimate device certified by the manufacturer but it does not address the device remarking attack, in which the attacker buys a legitimate low-end device from a device manufacturer and remarks it as a high-end device from the same manufacturer.

We can easily address this attack by adding configuration data in the data certificate signed by the manufacturer private key. The configuration data contains additional information about the device, such as model number, speed grade, size of NVM, size of SRAM, and device features. In the evaluation phase, the verifier validates not only the device ID and the signature, but also the configuration data in the certificate. This effectively addresses the remarking attack, unless that attacker can break the signature scheme or clone a PUF.

4   Experimental Methodology

In this section, we present the methodology used to evaluate the SRAM PUF performance and discuss the results in terms of PUF characteristics. The authentication scheme performance based on these results are given in Section 5.

4.1   PUF Performance

The following methodology was used to evaluate SRAM PUF performance. The experimental data is limited to a single 1MB Zero Bus Turnaround (ZBT) SRAM chip manufactured by ISSI on a $0.13\mu m$ CMOS process. Measurements were obtained at room temperature and nominal supply voltages. Note that SRAM PUF noise rates are influenced by the voltage and temperature operating conditions. In [5], temperature ranges of -20°C to 80°C are reported to result in maximum fractional hamming distances of 12% when compared to a reference measurement at 20°C. In the PUF based device authentication scheme in Section 3, the enrolment and evaluation processes both occur in production environments where temperature is controlled. Device supply voltages are typically controlled to within ± 5% or better either by the device tester or similar during enrolment and by the device power supply subsystem during evaluation. We therefore consider it reasonable to perform SRAM PUF measurements at room temperature and at nominal supply voltages. For further details on the experimental setup please consult the Appendix.

To emulate multiple PUFs on a single physical SRAM, the 1MB SRAM address space was divided into 32 logical PUFs of 32kB each. Inter- and intra-distance measures are used to evaluate the effectiveness of the 32 logical SRAM PUFs. The *inter-distance* metric measures the Hamming distance between two measurements (responses) collected from different (logical) PUF instances. Inter-distance assesses the uniqueness of a PUF response and ideally should be close to half the response length. The *intra-distance* metric measures the Hamming distance between responses collected from a single logical PUF instance at different moments. Intra-distance assesses the (un)reliability of a PUF response and ideally should be close to zero. The usability of a particular PUF implementation can be quickly evaluated by looking at the separation between its inter- and

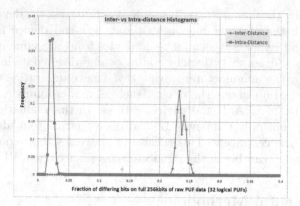

Fig. 4. Inter- vs intra-distance histograms

intra-distances. An implementation is said to show a good PUF behavior if on average its inter-distances are much larger than its intra-distances.

We evaluate the PUF behavior of the observed SRAM dumps. For every of the 32 logical PUFs, one of the 100 dumps is selected as a reference measurement. Intra-distances are calculated by comparing the remaining 99 dumps of every logical PUF to its respective reference measurement and counting the number of differing bits. Inter-distances are calculated by comparing the reference measurements of every possible pair of logical PUFs and counting the number of differing bits. The occurrence of inter- and intra-distances in our data set is summarized as a histogram in Figure 4, with inter- and intra-distances expressed as a fraction of the full logical PUF size of 32kB on the X-axis. This histogram shows that in our experiment the observed intra-distance is on average $\mu_{intra} = 2.2\%$ of the measured response length, which is in line with the results in [5] and is considered reasonable for measurements obtained at room temperature. The average inter-distance of our measured responses is around $\mu_{inter} = 23.6\%$ of the response length. This sub-optimal average inter-distance result is indicative of some level of bias in and/or correlation between (logical) PUF instances and will be further explored in Section 4.2. However, the observation that $\mu_{inter} \gg \mu_{intra}$ is a strong indication that the uninitialized power-up values of the considered SRAM memory show good PUF behavior.

4.2   Bias and Correlation

Ideally one would expect the average inter-distance to be 50% of the response length when all the response bits are unbiased and independent. Any statistically significant deviation from 50% indicates either a bias in the bit values, a dependence between different bit values, or both. Since we observe an average inter-distance of 23.6% < 50% we investigate the cause.

To evaluate a possible bias we consider the number of observed 1-values in the reference measurements of all 32 logical PUFs. The smallest number of observed 1-values is 128458 (49.00% of a 32kB PUF) and the largest number is 129737 (49.49% of a 32kB PUF). Although these values are very close to 50%, there is still a statistically significant deviation because the sample set is large. The respective observed p-values for an hypothesis of unbiased bits are $1.8 \cdot 10^{24}$ and $1.9 \cdot 10^{-7}$ which are a strong indication to reject this hypothesis and assume there is a bias. However, the observed bias is too small ($< 1\%$) to be the only cause for the small inter-distances.

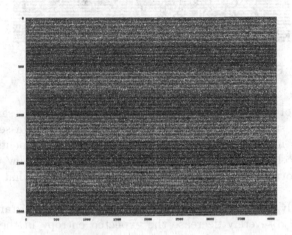

Fig. 5. Single dump of 1 MB SRAM

In order to investigate dependencies between different bits, we plot a single dump of the 1MB SRAM memory as a 2048x4096 bitmap, with a white pixel indicating a power-up value equal to 1 and a black pixel a power-up value of 0 for the considered bit. This bit map is shown in Figure 5 and an enlarged portion of this figure is shown in Figure 6. It is immediately clear from the observed patterns in these bitmaps that there exists a strong location-based correlation in the SRAM dump. From the enlarged plot, it is clear that consecutive lines have a strong tendency to power up with opposing values. From the full plot, additional large-scale patterns can be observed as darker and lighter bands in the bitmap. Similar patterns arise for any arrangement of the data where the number of lines and columns are a power of two. Since we defined logical PUFs as 32 ($= 2^5$) blocks of 262144 ($= 2^{18}$) consecutive bits from a single dump, strong correlations between different logical PUFs can be expected. This is the main cause for the observed small average inter-distance.

The underlying cause for these strong correlations is most likely to be found in the physical layout of the SRAM memory cells as a huge 2D array on the silicon die. In a typical SRAM architecture, cells in the same row and/or column

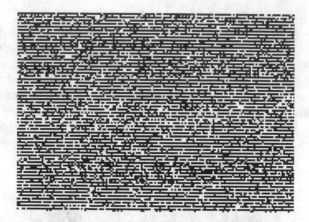

Fig. 6. Enlarged portion of a single SRAM dump

share a couple of elements. Cells in the same row are on the same word line, and cells in the same column share a couple of bitlines and a sense amplifier. A physical bias in the operation of any of these shared elements can cause a bias in all the cells connected to this element, which will show up as row- or column-based correlations in the PUF data, very similar to what we observe in our plots.

More generally, in addition to reducing the average inter-distance, these correlations will also severely decrease the expected entropy in the SRAM PUF response. Assessing entropy exactly is very hard, but an upper bound can be provided based on the compressibility of the data, since entropy is a lower bound for the smallest achievable compression. Using standard file compression techniques (zip), our 1MB SRAM dump files can be compressed to about 630kB, indicating an entropy level of 63% or less. We consider this an important result since such strong correlations leading to severely reduced entropy levels were never observed before for similar SRAM PUF constructions. In fact, many other works on SRAM PUFs or SRAM fingerprinting present very high estimated entropy levels of $> 90\%$ or assume an independent distribution of SRAM power-up states [1,10,6]. It is important to emphasize that although we observe correlations between different logical PUFs on the same device, the finding is of importance for the typical case where each device instantiates a single physical PUF. From our results it is clear that the actual entropy of an SRAM PUF will depend a lot on the physical instantiation of the SRAM memory and cannot be assumed to be very high without analysing its responses. Moreover, we show that merely looking at the bias in the responses is not sufficient, since strong dependencies between different bits can arise. For our data, the bias is very small ($< 1\%$) whilst we still observe severely reduced entropy levels ($< 63\%$).

5   Results and Analysis

The performance of our post-processing schemes is presented in this section. The key metric for our application is the FAR/FRR which we wish to maximise while keeping the storage cost of the device ID in bits as low as possible.

5.1   Result of the Function f_1

Figure 7 and Figure 8 show the results of applying the function f_1 for device IDs of 256- and 512-bits respectively. When compared to the raw PUF data of Figure 4, a degradation of the intra- and inter-distance results are observed, up around to a maximum of approximately 10% for the 512-bit device ID inter-distance result. The results show the first post-processing function to be largely noise preserving while also preserving the poor inter-distance results exhibited by the raw PUF data.

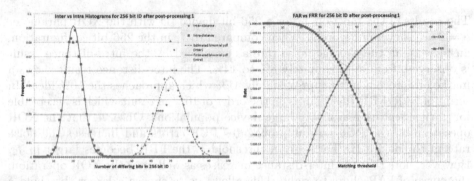

Fig. 7. Inter- vs intra-distance of 256-bit device IDs using f_1 and corresponding FAR/FRR rates

The FAR/FRR is estimated as follows. We model the inter-distance histogram as the probability density function for the bit difference between two device IDs; the FAR is the corresponding cumulative distribution function. Similarly, we model the intra-distance histogram as the probability density function for the number of error bits in the device ID; the FRR is the corresponding cumulative distribution function. The FAR/FRR for a 256-bit device ID is on the order of 10^{-5} which is unacceptable for most device authentication applications. Although the FAR/FRR performance of the 512-bit device ID is reasonable, at around 10^{-11}, the poor inter-distance result of the raw PUF data is preserved (there is a slight increase). In effect the low entropy of the raw PUF data is reflected in the resultant device ID. The efficiency of the 512-bit configuration is low as a result, although from the FAR/FRR perspective the performance is acceptable if the 512-bit device ID does not pose a storage issue.

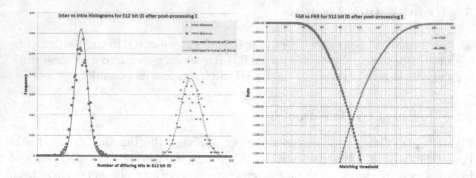

Fig. 8. Inter- vs intra-distance of 512-bit device IDs using f_1 and corresponding FAR/FRR rates

5.2 Results of the Function f_2

The results of the function f_2 for a 256-bit device ID with the XOR parameter $d = 2$ are shown in Figure 9. When compared to f_1 in the 256-bit configuration, an increase in the average noise rate as evidenced by the intra-distance result is observed, from approximately 8% to 14%. The inter-distance result shows a marked improvement to approximately 41% which approaches the 50% ideal. In terms of FAR/FRR the result is on the order of 10^{-7}, a result which is acceptable for authenticating reasonably large device populations. Observe that the XOR operation on the PUF output propagates PUF errors and increases the noise rate in the device ID. For a given threshold δ, the FRR becomes larger in f_2. However, note that the inter-distance increases as well after the XOR operation, the curve of FAR shifts to right. This allows us to choose a larger threshold δ for f_2 such that both FAR and FRR are smaller than using f_1.

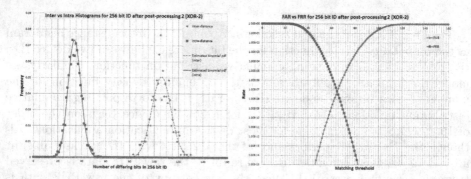

Fig. 9. Inter- vs intra-distance of 256-bit device IDs using f_2 with $d = 2$ and corresponding FAR/FRR rates

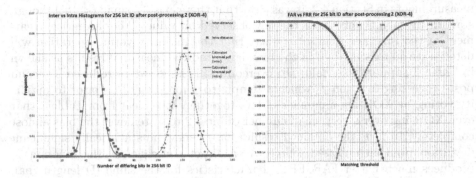

Fig. 10. Inter- vs intra-distance of 256-bit device IDs using f_2 with $d = 4$ and corresponding FAR/FRR rates

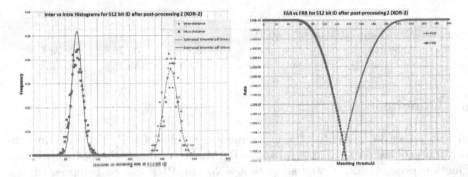

Fig. 11. Inter- vs intra-distance of 512-bit device IDs using f_2 with $d = 2$ and corresponding FAR/FRR rates

Figure 10 shows the results for a 256-bit device ID with $d = 4$. The intra-distance result indicates an average noise rate of more than double that of the first post-processing function. The inter-distance result is close to ideal at 47%. As for the $d = 2$ configuration above, the FAR/FRR of 10^{-7} may be acceptable for some applications.

In terms of FAR/FRR we see the best performance when using a 512-bit device ID with $d = 2$ as shown in Figure 11. In practice the rate of 10^{-13} can be considered negligible. As for the 256-bit, $d = 2$ case a similar increase in the average noise rate is observed as evidenced by the intra-distance result. Similarly, the inter-distance result approaches the 50% ideal.

5.3   Analysis

The considered post-processing functions affect the bias of the bit values in the output, and therefore also the average inter-distances. The effect of post-processing on the bias is shown in Table 3. From the analysis of SRAM PUF measurements in Section 4.2, it was clear that there exists a small ($<1\%$) though statistically significant bias on the raw observed bit values. The theoretical treatment of the function f_1 in [8] predicts that the majority voting operation will deteriorate an existing bias in the raw data, and the measured results as shown in Table 3 support this claim. To overcome this issue, we introduced a second post-processing function f_2 which attempts to remove any bias prior to majority voting by XOR-ing a number of bits together. It is clear from Table 3 that even XOR-ing over a very small number of bits (2 to 4) removes the bias almost completely. In fact, the obtained results for f_2 show no statistically significant deviation from an unbiased source. As a direct consequence, the function f_2 produces much better FAR/FRR characteristics for the same ID length than function f_1.

Table 3. Average bias in the output bits after the different post-processing functions

	Raw PUF data	f_1	$f_{2,d=2}$	$f_{2,d=4}$
Full PUF dump (32kB)	49.21%	-	-	-
256 bit ID	-	30.35%	49.78%	49.73%
512 bit ID	-	35.85%	49.46%	50.42%

6   Conclusions

In this paper we presented the experimental results of a PUF device authentication scheme on a discrete 0.13μm SRAM. We evaluate the post-processing function presented in [8] and show that a 256-kb PUF can be compressed into a 512-bit device ID while maintaining an FAR and FRR of better than 10^{-10}. During the analysis it is observed that the SRAM PUF is strongly correlated with a small bias of less than 1%. A upper bound on the entropy level of the complete 1MB SRAM is estimated at 63%. We consider this to be an important result, since it implies that SRAM PUF entropy levels can be severely reduced even when the observed bias is small. Our results show that the entropy of an SRAM PUF can depend strongly on the SRAM PUF architecture and physical implementation.

We introduce a new post-processing function which shows good performance when presented with strongly correlated PUF responses such as we encounter in this paper. We show that this new function exhibits a negligible FAR and FRR when compressing a 256-kb PUF into a 512-bit device ID.

Future work will include a more detailed analysis of the SRAM PUF correlations observed in order to determine the root cause, and experimental evaluation of the device authentication scheme presented here on multiple physical SRAM instances. The robustness of the scheme to expected environmental swings will also be evaluated.

Acknowledgement. This work has been supported in part by the European Commission through the FP7 programme UNIQUE. We thank the anonymous reviewers for their helpful reviews and comments.

References

1. Armknecht, F., Maes, R., Sadeghi, A.-R., Sunar, B., Tuyls, P.: PUF-PRFs: A new tamper-resilient cryptographic primitive. In: Advances in Cryptology – EURO-CRYPT 2009 Poster Session, pp. 96–102 (2000)
2. Azizi, N., Moshovos, A., Najm, F.N.: Low-leakage asymmetric-cell sram. In: Proceedings of the 2002 International Symposium on Low Power Electronics and Design, ISLPED 2002, pp. 48–51. ACM, New York (2002)
3. Bulens, P., Standaert, F.-X., Quisquater, J.-J.: How to strongly link data and its medium: the paper case. IET Information Security 4(3), 125–136 (2010)
4. Gassend, B., Clarke, D., van Dijk, M., Devadas, S.: Silicon physical random functions. In: ACM Conference on Computer and Communications Security, pp. 148–160. ACM Press, New York (2002)
5. Guajardo, J., Kumar, S.S., Schrijen, G.-J., Tuyls, P.: FPGA Intrinsic PUFs and Their Use for IP Protection. In: Paillier, P., Verbauwhede, I. (eds.) CHES 2007. LNCS, vol. 4727, pp. 63–80. Springer, Heidelberg (2007)
6. Holcomb, D.E., Burleson, W.P., Fu, K.: Initial SRAM state as a fingerprint and source of true random numbers for RFID tags. In: Conference on RFID Security 2007, Malaga, Spain, July 11-13 (2007)
7. Kim, J.-J., Rao, R., Kim, K.: Technology-circuit co-design of asymmetric sram cells for read stability improvement. In: 2010 IEEE Custom Integrated Circuits Conference (CICC), pp. 1–4 (September 2010)
8. Koeberl, P., Li, J., Rajan, A., Vishik, C., Wu, W.: A Practical Device Authentication Scheme Using SRAM PUFs. In: McCune, J.M., Balacheff, B., Perrig, A., Sadeghi, A.-R., Sasse, A., Beres, Y. (eds.) Trust 2011. LNCS, vol. 6740, pp. 63–77. Springer, Heidelberg (2011)
9. Maes, R., Tuyls, P., Verbauwhede, I.: Intrinsic pufs from flip-flops on reconfigurable devices. In: 3rd Benelux Workshop on Information and System Security (WISSec 2008), Eindhoven, NL, p. 17 (2008)
10. Maes, R., Tuyls, P., Verbauwhede, I.: Soft decision helper data algorithm for sram pufs. In: Proceedings of the 2009 IEEE International Conference on Symposium on Information Theory, ISIT 2009, vol. 3, pp. 2101–2105. IEEE Press, Piscataway (2009)
11. Menezes, A., van Oorschot, P.C., Vanstone, S.A.: Handbook of Applied Cryptography. CRC Press (1996)
12. U. S. G. A. Office. Defense supplier base: Dod should leverage ongoing initiatives in developing its program to mitigate risk of counterfeit parts. GAO-10-389 (March 2010)
13. Pappu, R.S.: Physical one-way functions. PhD thesis, Massachusetts Institute of Technology (March 2001)
14. SEMI T20-1109. Specification for authentication of semiconductors and related products (2009), http://www.semi.org/
15. Suh, G.E., Devadas, S.: Physical unclonable functions for device authentication and secret key generation. In: Design Automation Conference, pp. 9–14. ACM Press, New York (2007)

16. Trusted   Computing   Group.   TCG   TPM   specification   1.2   (2003),
    http://www.trustedcomputinggroup.org
17. von Neumann, J.: Various techniques used in connection with random digits. In:
    Householder, A.S., et al. (eds.) The Monte Carlo Method. National Bureau of
    Standards, Applied Mathematics Series, vol. 12, pp. 36–38 (1951)
18. Xilinx Inc. ML501 Evaluation Platform - User Guide, UG226 (v1.4), August 24
    (2009)

A   Experimental Setup

The experimental setup is based on the ML501 development platform from
Xilinx [18] housing a Virtex-5 XC5VLX50-1FFG676 FPGA chip. Collecting
SRAM PUF data directly from the FPGA chip is very difficult due to the automated initialisation procedure of the internal FPGA SRAM blocks, which
is hard to circumvent. Instead, we selected the Zero Bus Turnaround (ZBT),
high-speed, synchronous SRAM available on the board to collect experimental
SRAM PUF data. This SRAM chip (IS61NLP25636A-200TQL) is manufactured
using $0.13\mu m$ CMOS process technology by ISSI. The memory is organized as
256k x (32+4) bits (four parity bits, which are discarded in our case) which gives
1MB of total memory available for the analysis.

The development board is connected to the workstation via a serial null mo-
dem cable and the SRAM data is transmitted using the RS-232 standard. Python
scripts and the library for serial connections are used to control the transmission
on the workstation side. On the board side, the SRAM read-out is handled by
an FPGA design containing a ZBT memory controller, a UART interface and a
small data flow controller. A single complete readout of the 1MB SRAM memory
takes about two minutes with the RS-232 baudrate set to 115200kbps. To read
out a 32kB SRAM PUF, we estimate that it would take less than 4 seconds.
After a complete memory measurement, the board is powered off and on again
to collect the next SRAM dump. To assure a complete discharge of all on-board
capacitors, a delay of at least 10 seconds is kept between two consecutive power
cycles.

Using this measurement setup, 100 consecutive dumps of the 1MB uninitialized SRAM memory were collected and analyzed. All measurements were
obtained at an ambient temperature around 293K (room temperature). Measurements obtained when the chip was cold, i.e., after a prolonged ($> 10s$)
power-off time, were discarded. Further improvement of the measurement setup
might include automatic control of the power cycling as well as increasing the
data transmission speed.

A Performance Analysis of Identity-Based Encryption Schemes

Pengqi Cheng, Yan Gu, Zihong Lv, Jianfei Wang, Wenlei Zhu,
Zhen Chen, and Jiwei Huang

Tsinghua University, Beijing, 100084, China

Abstract. We implemented four of the most common IBE schemes: Cocks IBE, Boneh-Franklin IBE, Authenticated IBE, Hierarchical IBE. For each algorithm in an IBE scheme, we recorded the execution time and space cost with different lengths of key. Then, we made a comparison among these IBE schemes and analyzed their characteristics.

Keywords: Identity-Based Encryption (IBE), performance, time complexity, execution time, space cost.

1 Introduction and Our Main Work

In 1984, Shamir[6] first gave the concept of Identity-Based Encryption (IBE). In an IBE scheme, when Alice sends an email to Bob, Alice will use Bob's email address, bob@bob.com for example, to encrypt it, without needing to get Bob's public key certificate before sending it. When Bob receives an email, he first authenticates himself to the Private Key Generator (PKG) and gets his private key. Then he uses this private key to decrypt the email. This process is largely different from existing secure email infrastructure in the following aspects:

- Senders can send an email without a public key, which can reduce a lot of process for the certificate management.
- There is no need for an online lookup for a sender to obtain the recipient's certificate.
- Only the PKG holds the private key for recipients, and it is able to refresh the recipients' private keys in every short time period.

After the problem was posed, many implementations are presented by computer scientists to fulfill the idea given by Shamir. In this paper, we chose four of the most wide-used IBE schemes and compared their performance. These four IBE schemes are: Cocks IBE[3], Boneh-Franklin IBE[2], Authenticated IBE[5], and Hierarchical IBE[4]. Hierarchical IBE is a little special, because it is a cascade of IBE schemes to form a tree-style hierarchical PKG. These IBE schemes have different performance on server, clients and the need of bandwidth. So our work is to implement all these algorithms and make a comparison and analysis.

L. Chen, M. Yung, and L. Zhu (Eds.): INTRUST 2011, LNCS 7222, pp. 289–303, 2012.

2   Definitions

An identity-based encryption scheme is composed by the four following algorithms: Setup, Extract, Encrypt and Decrypt [2]:

1. **Setup**: gets a security parameter k, and then returns system parameters params and master-key. The system parameters are public, which include a finite message space $\mathcal{M}$ and a finite ciphertext space $\mathcal{C}$. The master-key is accessible only by the PKG.
2. **Extract**: based on params and master-key given by Setup, and an arbitrary ID $\in \{0, 1\}^*$, returns a private key d. Here ID will be used as a public key, and d is the corresponding private key.
3. **Encrypt**: gets params, ID and message $M \in \mathcal{M}$, and then outputs ciphertext $C \in \mathcal{C}$.
4. **Decrypt**: gets params, d and ciphertext $C \in \mathcal{C}$, and then outputs message $M \in \mathcal{M}$.

For correctness, these algorithms above must satisfy the standard consistency constraint, that is to say, if d is the private key generated by Extract corresponding to public key ID, then

$$\forall M \in \mathcal{M} : \mathsf{Decrypt}(\mathsf{params}, \mathsf{Encrypt}(\mathsf{params}, \mathsf{ID}, M), d) = M$$

3   Typical IBE Schemes

We will discuss four typical IBE schemes in this paper. First, we will introduce them in this section.

3.1   Cocks IBE[3]

- Setup
  The PKG gets following inputs to generate a private key:
  1. an RSA module $n = pq$, where p, q are two private prime numbers which satisfy $p \equiv q \equiv 3 \pmod 4$
  2. a message space $\mathcal{M} = \{-1, 1\}$ and a ciphertext space $\mathcal{C} = Z_n$
  3. a secure common hash function $f : \{0, 1\}^* \to Z_n$
- Extract
  - Input: parameters generated by Setup and an arbitrary ID
  - Output: the private key r
  1. Generate a which satisfies $(\frac{a}{p}) = 1$ with a deterministic procedure ID.
  2. Let $r = a^{\frac{n+5-p-q}{8}} \bmod n$ which satisfies $r^2 = \pm a \bmod n$.
- Encrypt
  - Input: parameters generated by Setup, ID of the sender and a message M
  - Output: corresponding ciphertext C

1. Select a random t which satisfies $m = (\frac{t}{n})$, where m is an arbitrary bit of M.
2. Let $c_1 = t + at^{-1} \bmod n$ and $c_2 = t - at^{-1} \bmod n$.
3. Send $s = \langle c_1, c_2 \rangle$ to the recipient.

– Decrypt
   - Input: ciphertext C and the private key and parameters generated by the PKG
   - Output: original message M
   1. Let $\alpha = c_1 + 2r$ if $r^2 = a$, otherwise $\alpha = c_2 + 2r$.
   2. Return $m = (\frac{\alpha}{n})$.

3.2 Boneh-Franklin IBE[2]

– Setup
   1. Get a security parameter k and two groups of order q (a generated prime number): G_1 and G_2, and an admissible bilinear map $\hat{e} : G_1 \times G_1 \to G_2$, and select a random generator $P \in G_1$.
   2. Generate a random number $s \in Z_q^*$. Let $P_{pub} = sP$.
   3. Select a hash function $H_1 : \{0,1\}^* \to G_1^*$. For any specified n, specify a hash function $H_2 : \{0,1\}^n \to G_2^n$.
   4. Return params $= \langle q, G_1, G_2, \hat{e}, n, P, P_{pub}, H_1, H_2 \rangle$ and master-key $= s$.

– Extract
   1. Get string ID $\in \{0,1\}^*$.
   2. Let $Q_{ID} = H_1(ID) \in G_1^*$.
   3. Return the private key $d_{ID} = sQ_{ID}$, where s is the master key.

– Encrypt
   1. Let $Q_{ID} = H_1(ID) \in G_1^*$.
   2. Select a random number $r \in Z_q^*$.
   3. Based on the message $M \in \mathcal{M}$, return the ciphertext C:

$$C = \langle rP, M \oplus H_2(g_{ID}^r) \rangle, g_{ID} = \hat{e}(Q_{ID}, P_{pub}) \in G_2^*$$

– Decrypt
Input the ciphertext $C = \langle U, V \rangle \in \mathcal{C}$ encrypted with ID. Return the message with the private key $d_{ID} \in G_1^*$:

$$M = V \oplus H_2(\hat{e}(d_{ID}, U))$$

3.3 Authenticated IBE[5]

– Setup
   1. Get a security parameter k and then generate a prime number q, two groups of order q: G_1 and G_2, and an admissible bilinear map $\hat{e} : G_1 \times G_1 \to G_2$. Select a random generator $P \in G_1$.
   2. Generate a random number $s \in Z_q^*$. Let $P_{pub} = sP$.

3. The PKG selects a random generator $g \in G_1$ and hash function $H_1 :$ $F_q \times G_2 \to \{0,1\}^n, H_2 : \{0,1\}^* \to G_1, H_3 : \{0,1\}^* \times \{0,1\}^* \to F_q, H_4 :$ $\{0,1\}^n \to \{0,1\}^n$.

4. Return params $= \langle q, G_1, G_2, g, g^s, \hat{e}, n, P, P_{pub}, H_1, H_2, H_3, H_4 \rangle$ and master-key $= s$.

– Extract
  The PKG calculates the private key of user ID_A: $d_A = H_2(\mathsf{ID}_A)^s$.

– Authenticated Encrypt
  User $A(\mathsf{ID}_A)$ uses another user $B(\mathsf{ID}_B)$'s private key d_A to encrypt the message $M \in \{0,1\}^*$:

1. Select a random number $r \in R\{0,1\}^n$.
2. Let $c_1 = H_3(r, M)$ and $c_2 = e(d_A, H_2(\mathsf{ID}_B))$.
3. Return the ciphertext $C = \langle r \oplus H_1(c_1, c_2), E_{H_4(r)}(M) \rangle$.

– Authenticated Decrypt
  User B uses A's ID ID_A, his private key d_B and params to decipher the ciphertext $\langle U, V, W \rangle$.

1. Let $c_2 = e(H_2(\mathsf{ID}_A), d_B)$.
2. Let $r = V \oplus H_1(U, c_2)$.
3. Let $M = D_{H_4(r)}(W)$.
4. Compare U and $H_3(r, M)$.
5. If $U \neq H_3(r, M)$, discard the ciphertext, otherwise return the message M.

3.4   Hierarchical IBE[4]

The Gentry-Silverberg hierarchical IBE scheme is composed by cascading Boneh-Franklin IBE schemes. In this scheme, every user has an n-tuple ID in the hierarchy tree. The n-tuple ID is composed by the IDs of the user itself and its ancestors. All users in the i-th level are denoted by $Level_i$. Thus, the root of the hierarchy tree, $Level_0$, is the PKG.

HIBE is composed by the five following algorithms:

– Root Setup
1. Based on a security parameter k, generate a big prime q using IG (BDH Parameter Generator).
2. Use q to generate two fields G_1 and G_2, which satisfy the bilinear map $\hat{e} : G_1 \times G_1 \to G_2$.
3. Pick an arbitrary element P_0 in G_1, and then pick a random number $S_0 \in Z/qZ$ as the master-key. Calculate the system parameter $Q_0 = S_0 P_0$.
4. Generate two hash functions $H_1 : \{0,1\}^* \to G_1, H_2 : G_2 \to \{0,1\}^n$.

– Lower-level Setup
  For each user $E_t \in Level_t$, specify a random number $s_t \in Z/qZ$.

– Extract

1. For each user E_t with $\mathsf{ID} = \langle \mathsf{ID}_1, \mathsf{ID}_2, \cdots, \mathsf{ID}_t \rangle$, its father calculates $P_t = H_1(\mathsf{ID}_1, \mathsf{ID}_2, \cdots, \mathsf{ID}_t) \in G_1$, where s_0 is the identity of G_1.
2. Return the private key $S_t = S_{t-1} + s_{t-1}P_t = \sum_{i=1}^{t} s_{i-1}P_i$ of E_t and parameter $Q_i = s_i P_0$.

- Encrypt
   1. For a message M and $\mathsf{ID} = \langle \mathsf{ID}_1, \mathsf{ID}_2, \cdots, \mathsf{ID}_t \rangle$, calculate:

$$P_i = H_1(\mathsf{ID}_1, \mathsf{ID}_2, \cdots, \mathsf{ID}_i) \in G_1$$

   2. For any $r \in Z/qZ$, return the ciphertext:

$$C = \langle rP_0, rP_2, \cdots, rP_t, M \oplus H_2(g^r) \rangle \,, g = e(Q_0, P_1) \in G_2$$

- Decrypt
   For ciphertext $C = \langle U_0, U_2, \cdots, U_t, V \rangle$ and $\mathsf{ID} = \langle \mathsf{ID}_1, \mathsf{ID}_2, \cdots, \mathsf{id}_t \rangle$, return the message:

$$M = V \oplus H_2 \left(\frac{\hat{e}(U_0, S_t)}{\prod_{i=2}^{t} \hat{e}(Q_{i-1}, U_i)} \right)$$

4 Performance Testing

4.1 Implementation

Based on the characters of these IBE schemes, we use the same framework for these different cases, except for Cocks IBE scheme. Therefore, we used Stanford IBE Secure Email[1] as the framework for those three schemes, and then modified some kernel functions. In this way, sources for different IBE schemes have the most amount of similar codes, which will decrease error caused by implementation. For Cocks IBE scheme, due to the reason that it is largely different from others, we directly finished its codes.

In summary, we have the final versions of four IBE schemes: Cocks IBE (Cocks), Boneh-Franklin IBE (BF), Authenticated IBE (AIBE), and Hierarchical IBE (HIBE).

4.2 Testing Method

Since an IBE scheme has four algorithms, we focus on the performance of each algorithm in order to guarantee that algorithms for different IBE schemes are running in the same condition. For the reason that the initializing process Setup is run only once for a certain IBE system, it is less valuable to test its performance so we just ignore it. Therefore, our goal is to test performance of the three algorithms Extract, Encrypt and Decrypt. For each algorithm of a certain IBE scheme, we record the execution time under different parameters. Obviously, different IBE schemes have different performance, and we will analyze the reasons that make such differences. In order to decrypt the ciphertext correctly, these schemes will add some additional information about parameters. The additional cost of space and bandwidth of such information will be discussed in Section 5.

4.3   Environment

Processor	Pentium Dual T2330 @ 1.60GHz
Memory	2GB RAM
OS	Arch Linux 2.6.38
Compiler	GCC 4.4.4
Timing	use command *time*, with accuracy of 1ms
File I/O	work in memory, so execution time can be ignored

5   Results and Analysis

5.1   Cocks IBE

Pbits	256	512
Extraction Time (1000 Keys)	0.870s	2.903s
Encryption Time	5.710s	12.636s
Decryption Time	2.497s	5.830s
Plain Text Length	2KB	2KB
ciphertext Length	4126KB	8224KB

Compared to other schemes in this paper, Cocks IBE is much easier. However, our test shows its performance is quite low. Even if the master key length is only 256 bits, the encryption/decryption speed is below 1KB/s, which cannot be acceptable in most cases. Moreover, the size of ciphertext is thousands times that of plain text. This conclusion is obvious, since for each bit of the message, the Encrypt algorithm returns two P-bit numbers. Therefore, considering both the time and space cost, Cocks IBE is not applicable for real environments.

5.2   Boneh-Franklin IBE

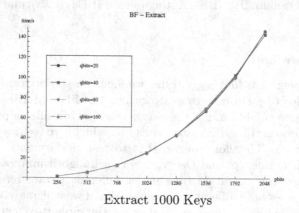

Extract 1000 Keys

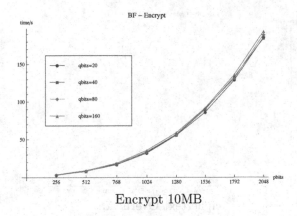

Encrypt 10MB

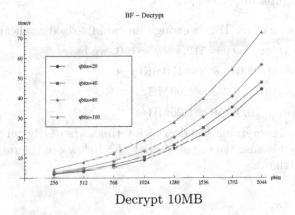

Decrypt 10MB

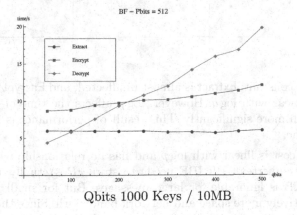

Qbits 1000 Keys / 10MB

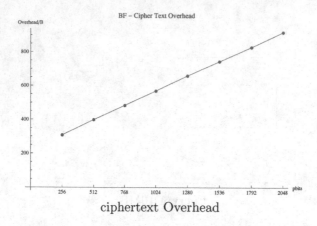

ciphertext Overhead

From these figures above, we get:

1. The performance of BF IBE is enough for middle-sized applications.

   Using typical values $\log p = 512, \log q = 160$, we have:

   Extraction speed: $1000/5.863 \approx 170.6\text{Key/s}$

   Encryption speed: $10/9.253 \approx 1.08\text{MB/s}$

   Decryption speed: $10/7.959 \approx 1.26\text{MB/s}$

2. The extraction, encryption and decryption times are nearly cubic with $\log p$, that is mainly because the calculation of H_1. Below are the results of cubic polynomial fitting:

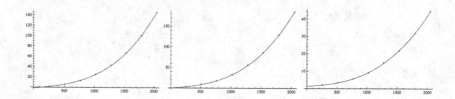

3. If $\log p$ holds constant, **Extract** is almost unaffected, and **Encrypt** and **Decrypt** are nearly linear with $\log q$. However, $\log p$ affects the time of **Encrypt** and **Decrypt** much more significantly. This result of performance is made by H_2 in this scheme.

4. Extra space cost is linear with $\log p$ and has no relationship with $\log q$, because in the ciphertext, BF IBE needs to store rP. Actually, added space less than 1KB is ignorable for large messages. But for small messages, it requires relatively more space and network bandwidth. Since the framework we used outputs base64 ciphertext, we can easily decrease the space cost by one fourth in practice.

5.3   Authenticated IBE

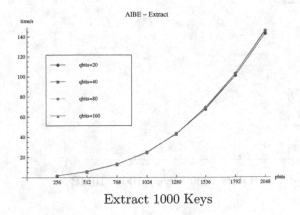

Extract 1000 Keys

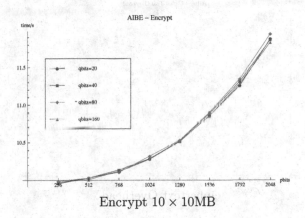

Encrypt 10 × 10MB

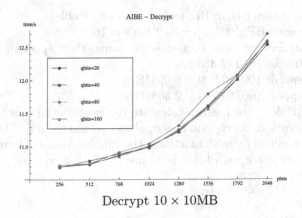

Decrypt 10 × 10MB

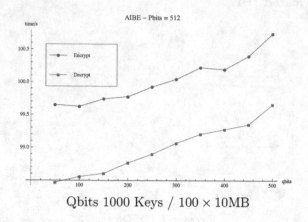

Qbits 1000 Keys / 100 × 10MB

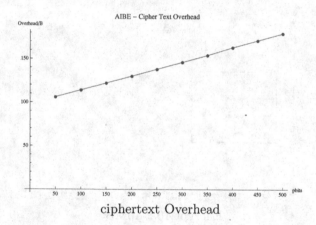

ciphertext Overhead

Here are our conclusions:

1. AIBE is a little faster than BF, so it is also applicable.
   As the same with BF, let $\log p = 512, \log q = 160$:
   Since the two Extract algorithms are the same, their speeds are not quite different: $1000/5.64 \approx 177.3\mathrm{Key/s}$
   Encryption speed: $100/10.009 \approx 9.99\mathrm{MB/s}$
   Decryption speed: $100/10.746 \approx 9.30\mathrm{MB/s}$
   Because AIBE does not need to calculate the exponential r as in BF, it has a higher encryption/decryption speed, about 10 times that of BF.
2. Like BF, determined by hash functions, the running times of Extract, Encrypt and Decrypt are cubic with $\log p$. Here are the fitting results:

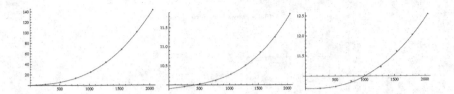

3. If $\log p$ remains unchanged, the relationship between running times and $\log q$ is just like that of BF.
4. Extra space cost is from $E_{H_4(r)}(M)$ in the ciphertext, which is determined by $\log q$ rather than $\log p$. It is also less than 1KB, which may only affect small files.

5.4 Hierarchical IBE

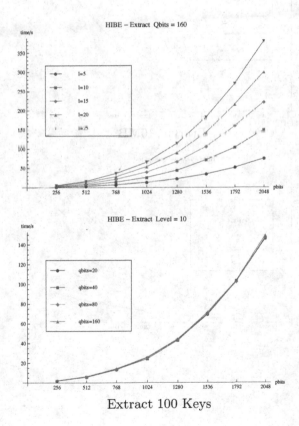

Extract 100 Keys

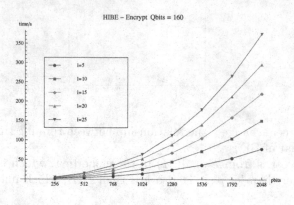

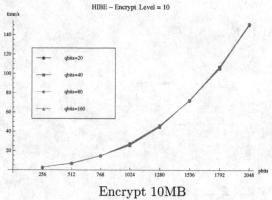

Encrypt 10MB

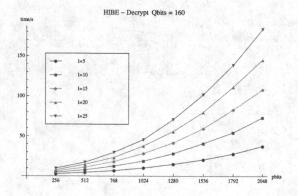

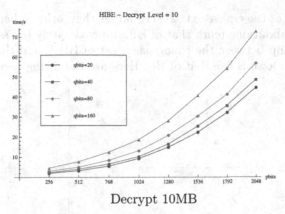

Decrypt 10MB

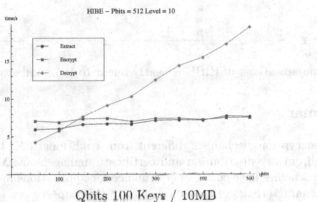

Qbits 100 Keys / 10MD

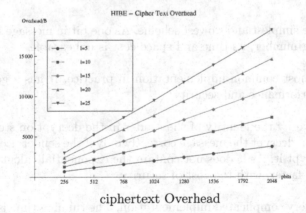

ciphertext Overhead

Here are our conclusions:

1. HIBE is slower than BF.
   Let $\log p = 512, \log q = 160, l = 10$, where l is the number of levels.
   Extraction speed: $100/6.37 \approx 15.7\text{Key/s}$
   Encryption speed: $10/7.21 \approx 1.38\text{MB/s}$
   Decryption speed: $10/7.769 \approx 1.28\text{MB/s}$

Added length of the ciphertext: 2187B, larger than other schemes
The speed is about one tenth that of BF, approximately the same as $1/l$.

2. The relationship between the time/space cost of HIBE and the two parameters $\log p$ and $\log q$ is like that of BF. Here are the fitting results:

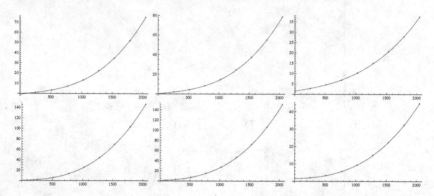

3. The time/space cost of HIBE is nearly linear to the number of levels.

6   Summary

As a new encryption mechanism different from traditional PKI-based schemes, IBE is free from key distribution and certificate management. Moreover, some typical IBE schemes have enough performance for applications in practice. Here we list the characteristics of all the schemes in this paper:

- **Cocks**
  Cocks is the simplest and slowest scheme. As one bit in message is translated into one big number, its time and space cost is unbearable.
- **BF**
  BF is the most common implementation in practice. It has a good balance between performance and security.
- **AIBE**
  AIBE can verify the identity of the sender in the decryption step, since the recipient can decrypt the message correctly only if the sender uses his private key to encrypt it. As it does not contain the exponential calculation in BF, it is a little faster, with the cost of security.
- **HIBE**
  HIBE is a very complicated implementation. The running time is linear with the number of levels. In practice, it is rare to use many levels.

In addition, all these schemes will store some extra information for decryption, which may add much cost while transferring a large amount of small files.

Currently, most IBE schemes take much use of elliptic curve encryption, so they cannot reach a very satisfying performance. Thus, it is critical to improve the performance in the future. Since the $O(\log^3 p)$ time cost of elliptic curve hash functions is the bottleneck of all the scheme, to make a breakthrough in the performance of IBE schemes, except optimizing such hash functions, the only way is to use totally different encryption/decryption algorithms in other transformation fields. We expect to see more creative improvement in this area.

References

1. http://crypto.stanford.edu/ibe/
2. Boneh, D., Franklin, M.: Identity-Based Encryption from the Weil Pairing. In: Kilian, J. (ed.) CRYPTO 2001. LNCS, vol. 2139, pp. 213–229. Springer, Heidelberg (2001)
3. Cocks, C.: An identity based encryption scheme based on quadratic residues. In: IMA International Conference, pp. 360–363. Springer (2001)
4. Gentry, C., Silverberg, A.: Hierarchical ID-Based Cryptography. In: Zheng, Y. (ed.) ASIACRYPT 2002. LNCS, vol. 2501, pp. 548–566. Springer, Heidelberg (2002)
5. Lynn, B.: Authenticated identity-based encryption. Cryptology ePrint Archive (2002)
6. Shamir, A.: Identity-Based Cryptosystems and Signature Schemes. In: Blakely, G.R., Chaum, D. (eds.) CRYPTO 1984. LNCS, vol. 196, pp. 47–53. Springer, Heidelberg (1985)

A (Corrected) DAA Scheme Using Batch Proof and Verification

Ernie Brickell[1], Liqun Chen[2], and Jiangtao Li[1]

[1] Intel Corporation, Hillsboro, Oregon, USA
{ernie.brickell,jiangtao.li}@intel.com
[2] Hewlett-Packard Laboratories, Bristol, UK
liqun.chen@hp.com

Abstract. Direct anonymous attestation (DAA) is a cryptographic primitive for providing anonymous signatures, and is a part of trusted computing technology from the Trusted Computing Group (TCG). DAA offers a nice balance between user authentication and privacy. One active research topic in trusted computing community is to develop DAA schemes that require minimum TPM resources. In 2010, Chen introduced a new DAA scheme using batch proof and verification. In this scheme, the TPM only needs to perform one or two exponentiations to create a DAA signature, depending on whether linkability is required. In this paper, we demonstrate an attack to this DAA scheme. The attack allows any malicious host to forge linkable DAA signatures without knowing the private key. We also present a patch to this DAA scheme to mitigate the attack. Our new DAA scheme has the same computational requirement for a TPM. We formally prove the new DAA scheme is secure in the random oracle model under the blind-4 bilinear LRSW assumption, the DDH assumption, and the gap-DL assumption.

Keywords: direct anonymous attestation, batch proof and verification, trusted platform module.

1 Introduction

Direct anonymous attestation (DAA) is a special digital signature primitive, providing a balance between user privacy and signer authentication in a reasonable way. A DAA scheme involves issuers, signers and verifiers. An issuer verifies legitimation of signers and issues a unique DAA credential to each legitimate signer. A signer proves possession of her credential to a verifier by providing a DAA signature without revealing her identity.

The concept and first concrete scheme of DAA were presented by Brickell, Camenisch, and Chen [12] for the purposes of remote anonymous attestation of a trusted computing platform. This DAA scheme was adopted by the Trusted Computing Group (TCG) and specified in the Trusted Platform Module (TPM) specification version 1.2 [46]. This specification has recently been adopted by ISO/IEC as an international standard [36]. Since the first introduction of DAA, it

L. Chen, M. Yung, and L. Zhu (Eds.): INTRUST 2011, LNCS 7222, pp. 304–337, 2012.
© Springer-Verlag Berlin Heidelberg 2012

has attracted lots of attention from both industry and cryptographic researchers, e.g. [4, 13, 16, 22, 38, 41, 43, 14, 26–29, 18].

One may view a DAA scheme as a modified group signature scheme. Unlike group signatures such as defined in [6, 8], DAA does not have the "open" feature where from a signature, the identity of its signer can be recovered by a trusted group manager. Signatures created by a DAA signer are anonymous even if a verifier and an issuer collude. Instead, DAA has user-controlled-traceability, where a DAA signer and verifier can jointly decide whether the verifier is allowed to link two signatures produced by this signer.

In DAA, the role of a signer is split between two parties, a principal signer with limited resource such as a trusted platform module (TPM), and an assistant signer with abundant computational power but less security tolerance such as an ordinary computer platform. We call the assistant signer the Host in our paper. The resource of TPM are very limited, thus, any technique to reduce the requirement on the TPM resources is useful. Note that the Host is just a helper to the TPM. It should not learn the DAA secret key or create a signature without involvement from the TPM.

Recently, Chen proposed a DAA scheme [23] based on a modification of the Chen, Page and Smart DAA scheme [30] and a modification of batch proof and verification technique developed by Peng, Boyd and Dawson [42]. Throughout the paper, we call this scheme Chen'10 DAA scheme. This DAA scheme claims to have the best efficiency in the TPM implementation. For the DAA signing operation, the TPM only performs one exponentiation, if linkability is not required; and two exponentiations, if linkability is required. The other existing pairing-based DAA schemes such as [14, 29, 28, 30, 18] require at least three exponentiations for the TPM.

In this paper, we present an attack to the Chen'10 DAA scheme [23] and then provide a correction of the DAA scheme. More specifically, our contributions of the paper are the following.

AN ATTACK TO CHEN'10 DAA SCHEME: We discover a flaw in this DAA scheme [23] such that an adversarial host can forge any linkable DAA signatures without knowing the private key and without any TPM involvement.

A CORRECTED DAA SCHEME WITH THE SAME TPM EFFICIENCY: We propose a corrected DAA scheme based on [23]. Our scheme has the same computational cost for TPM and slightly additional cost for the Host. We formally prove the security of this new DAA scheme under the DAA security model in [14, 22].

The rest of this paper is organized as follows. In Section 2, we review the batch proof and verification technique used in [23], describe the flaw in this technique, and present a new bath proof and verification technique for proving discrete log equality between two pairs of group elements. We then present an attack to the Chen'10 DAA scheme [23] in Section 3. After that, we describe our corrected DAA scheme in Section 4, and its security properties and rigorous security proofs in Section 5. We briefly discuss some implementation options in Section 6, and then provide a comparison between the proposed DAA scheme and seven other DAA schemes in Section 7. We conclude the paper in Section 8. For completeness, we recall definitions of DAA security model in Appendix A, and information of pairings and some relevant computational assumptions in Appendix B.

2   Batch Proof and Verification

In the rest of the paper, we use the following standard notation. Let S be a set of values, then $x \leftarrow S$ denote x is chosen uniformly at random from S. Let $\{0,1\}^*$ denote the set of binary strings with arbitrary length and $\{0,1\}^t$ denote the set of binary strings with t-bit length. Let $x\|y$ denote concatenation of two binary strings x and y. In a cyclic group $\mathbb{G}$, let g^x denote the exponentiation of a group element $g \in \mathbb{G}$ with an integer exponent x. In an elliptic curve base group $\mathbb{G}$, let $[x]P$ denote the point multiplication of point P by an integer x.

We make use of a batch proof and verification scheme, which is a modification of "strict verification of equality of logarithms with common exponent" by Peng, Boyd and Dawson [42], and call their scheme the PBD scheme. The target of the PBD scheme is given a security parameter L, a prime q, a cyclic group $\mathbb{G}$ of order q such that $|q| > L$, and $2n + 2$ group elements $g, y, g_i, y_i \in \mathbb{G}$ for $i = 1, 2, \ldots, n$, to prove $\log_g y = \log_{g_i} y_i$. For the purpose of our particular usage in the proposed DAA scheme, we focus on the simple case of discrete logarithm equality of two pairs of group elements. More specifically, given group elements $(g_0, g_1, y_0, y_1) \in \mathbb{G}^4$, the goal is to prove efficiently the discrete logarithm equality between two group elements y_0 and y_1 with regards to two bases g_0 and g_1 respectively, i.e., $\log_{g_0} y_0 = \log_{g_1} y_1$. Under the condition that the prover does not know the discrete logarithm relationship between the two bases g_0 and g_1, we reduce the double discrete-logarithm proof in the PBD scheme to a single discrete-logarithm proof.

2.1   Batch Proof and Verification Technique Used in [23]

In this subsection, we first review the batch proof and verification technique proposed in [23] and then show the flaw in this technique which leads to an attack to the Chen'10 DAA scheme. Let $(g_0, g_1, y_0, y_1) \in \mathbb{G}^4$ such that $\log_{g_0} y_0 = \log_{g_1} y_1$. Let $x = \log_{g_0} y_0$ be the discrete log value known to the prover. The prover proves the knowledge of x such that $g_0^x = y_0$ and $g_1^x = y_1$ with the following steps:

1. The prover randomly chooses $r \leftarrow \mathbb{Z}_q^*$ and sends the verifier $z \leftarrow (g_0 \cdot g_1)^r$.
2. The verifier randomly chooses and sends to the prover an integer $c \leftarrow \mathbb{Z}_q^*$ as a challenge.
3. The prover calculates and sends the verifier an integer $s \leftarrow r - c \cdot x \bmod q$.
4. The verifier verifies that $(g_0 \cdot g_1)^s \cdot (y_0 \cdot y_1)^c = z$. If this equation does not hold, the verifier outputs reject; otherwise outputs accept.

The above protocol is essentially a knowledge proof protocol which proves that the prover knows the discrete log between $g_0 \cdot g_1$ and $y_0 \cdot y_1$ without revealing the discrete log value. Obviously, if the prover knows the value of $\log_{g_0} g_1$, he can successfully run the above protocol to the verifier even if $\log_{g_0} y_0 \neq \log_{g_1} y_1$. It is required in [23], the prover does not know the value of $\log_{g_0} g_1$.

Observe that, if the prover has the flexibility to choose y_1 before the two party agree on (g_0, g_1, y_0, y_1), he can cheat even if he does not know $\log_{g_0} g_1$, $\log_{g_0} y_0$ or $\log_{g_1} y_1$. The attack is as follows. Let g_0, g_1, y_0 be the values agreed by both the prover and the verifier. The prover can successfully make the verifier believe that he has the knowledge of x such that $g_0^x = y_0$ and $g_1^x = y_1$ with the above protocol. The prover chooses a random value x and computes $y_1 \leftarrow (g_0 \cdot g_1)^x \cdot y_0^{-1}$. The prover then sends g_0, g_1, y_0, y_1 to the verifier and proves the knowledge of x such that $(g_0 \cdot g_1)^x = y_0 \cdot y_1$.

2.2   Newly Proposed Batch Proof and Verification Technique

To address the above attack, we propose a new batch proof and verification scheme that is a modification of the PBD scheme [42]. The scheme works as follows:

1. Given $(g_0, g_1, y_0, y_1) \in \mathbb{G}^4$, the verifier randomly chooses and sends to the prover two integers $t_0, t_1 \leftarrow \{0, 1, \ldots, 2^L - 1\}$.
2. The prover randomly chooses an integer $r \leftarrow \mathbb{Z}_q^*$ and sends the verifier $z \leftarrow (g_0^{t_0} \cdot g_1^{t_1})^r$.
3. The verifier randomly chooses and sends to the prover an integer $c \leftarrow \mathbb{Z}_q^*$ as a challenge.
4. The prover calculates and sends the verifier an integer $s \leftarrow r - c \cdot x \bmod q$, where $x = \log_{g_0} y_0 = \log_{g_1} y_1$.
5. The verifier verifies that $(g_0^{t_0} \cdot g_1^{t_1})^s \cdot (y_0^{t_0} \cdot y_1^{t_1})^c = z$. If this equation does not hold, the verifier outputs reject; otherwise outputs accept.

In this scheme, the values (g_0, g_1, y_0, y_1) are chosen by the prover under the condition that the verifier is able to verify that the prover does not know the discrete logarithm relationship between the values g_1 and g_0. Security of this proof and verification scheme is based on the discrete logarithm assumption.

Definition 1 (The discrete logarithm assumption). *Given two elements* $g_0, g_1 \in \mathbb{G}$, *computing* $\log_{g_0} g_1$ *is computationally infeasible.*

We now address security of the scheme with the following theorem.

Theorem 1. *Given a set of fixed values* $(g_0, g_1, y_0, y_1) \in \mathbb{G}^4$ *and two uniformly distributed random values* $t_0, t_1 \in \{0, 1, \ldots, 2^L - 1\}$, *a successful run of the above scheme convinces the verifier that the prover possesses the value* $x \in \mathbb{Z}_q^*$, *such that*

$$y_0 = g_0^x \wedge y_1 = g_1^x \tag{1}$$

is not satisfied with a probability no more than 2^{-L}, under the discrete logarithm assumption and the assumption that the prover does not know the discrete logarithm relationship between g_0 and g_1.

Proof. To prove this theorem, we first see that a successful run of the scheme convinces the verifier that the prover is in possession of the value $x \in \mathbb{Z}_q^*$, such that

$$(y_0^{t_0} \cdot y_1^{t_1}) = (g_0^{t_0} \cdot g_1^{t_1})^x \tag{2}$$

under the discrete logarithm assumption. This straightforwardly follows security of the Σ-protocol, i.e., a three-move random challenge-based knowledge proof protocol (also known as an identification scheme). Observe that the steps 2-5 of the scheme form such a Σ-protocol. By using a rewinding, the value x can be extracted from a successful adversary. This is true, except $t_0 = 0 \wedge t_1 = 0$. We omit the details of this well-known technique.

Our next step is to prove a lemma.

Lemma 1. *Successfully running the above scheme shows that*

$$y_0 = g_0^{a_0} \wedge y_1 = g_1^{b_1} \tag{3}$$

is satisfied for some values $a_0, b_1 \in \mathbb{Z}_q^*$, under the assumption that the discrete logarithm problem, i.e. given $g_0, g_1 \in \mathbb{G}$ computing $d = \log_{g_0} g_1$, is hard.

Proof. We use the following reduction to prove this lemma: if there is a polynomial adversary $\mathcal{A}$, who is able to persuade a verifier to output accept in a run of the scheme, then either $\mathcal{A}$ can be used by another algorithm $\mathcal{B}$ to solve the discrete logarithm problem (Case 1), or Equation 3 holds (Case 2). We prove these two cases separately.

Case 1. Suppose the algorithm $\mathcal{B}$ has the target that given two elements $g_0, g_1 \in \mathbb{G}$, computing $d = \log_{g_0} g_1$. $\mathcal{B}$ first randomly chooses four integers $a_0, a_1, b_0, b_1 \in \mathbb{Z}_q^*$ and computes $y_0 = g_0^{a_0} \cdot g_1^{b_0}$ and $y_1 = g_0^{a_1} \cdot g_1^{b_1}$. $\mathcal{B}$ runs the above batch proof and verification protocol with $\mathcal{A}$, in which $\mathcal{A}$, given the values $g_0, g_1, a_0, a_1, b_0, b_1$, plays the role of the prover and $\mathcal{B}$ plays the role of the verifier. If $\mathcal{A}$ successfully makes $\mathcal{B}$ accepting the proof, that means the two equations

$$(y_0^{t_0} \cdot y_1^{t_1}) = (g_0^{a_0} g_1^{b_0})^{t_0} \cdot (g_0^{a_1} g_1^{b_1})^{t_1} = (g_0^{t_0} \cdot g_1^{t_1})^x \tag{4}$$

and

$$a_0 \cdot t_0 + d \cdot b_0 \cdot t_0 + a_1 \cdot t_1 + d \cdot b_1 \cdot t_1 = (t_0 + d \cdot t_1) \cdot x \tag{5}$$

hold for some values $x, t_0, t_1 \in \mathbb{Z}_q^*$, where x is chosen by $\mathcal{A}$ and t_0 and t_1 are chosen by $\mathcal{B}$. $\mathcal{B}$ first rewinds $\mathcal{A}$ to extract the knowledge of the value x by forking on c, and then computes d by

$$d = (a_0 \cdot t_0 + a_1 \cdot t_1 - t_0 \cdot x)/(t_1 \cdot x - b_0 \cdot t_0 - b_1 \cdot t_1). \tag{6}$$

$\mathcal{B}$ outputs the value d as the result of the target.

Note that Case 1 is almost identical to the proof of Theorem 1 in [23] (assuming $t_0 = t_1 = 1$), but the proof with this case alone is not sound, because Case 2 is not covered; that causes vulnerability to the attack described in Subsection 2.1.

Case 2. This case shows that $\mathcal{B}$ may not be able to retrieve the discrete logarithm d if $\mathcal{A}$ is allowed to use $y_0 = g_0^{a_0} g_1^{b_0}$ and $y_1 = g_0^{a_1} g_1^{b_1}$ with the values a_0, a_1, b_0, b_1 in his own choice. The fact Equation 3 does not hold means either $b_0 \neq 0$ or $a_1 \neq 0$ is satisfied. In order to bypass the value d but still to make Equation 4 hold, the following two equations

$$a_0 \cdot t_0 + a_1 \cdot t_1 = x \cdot t_0, \tag{7}$$

$$b_0 \cdot t_0 + b_1 \cdot t_1 = x \cdot t_1 \tag{8}$$

must be satisfied simultaneously. Combining Equations 7 and 8, we have

$$a_0 \cdot t_0 \cdot t_1 + a_1 \cdot t_1^2 = b_0 \cdot t_0^2 + b_1 \cdot t_0 \cdot t_1. \tag{9}$$

Assume the verifier selects t_0 and t_1 uniformly at random from $\{0, 1, \ldots, 2^L - 1\}$, and these two values happen to satisfy either of the following two situations:

$$t_1 \neq 0 \wedge (t_0 = 0 \vee t_0 = (b_1 - a_0) \cdot t_1 / b_0); \tag{10}$$

$$t_0 \neq 0 \wedge (t_1 = 0 \vee t_1 = (a_0 - b_1) \cdot t_0 / a_1). \tag{11}$$

Note that we do not require the verifier knowing any value from (a_0, a_1, b_0, b_1). Obviously, the first situation (Equation 10) will make Equation 9 cannot hold, when $a_1 \neq 0$, and similarly the second situation (Equation 11) will make Equation 9 cannot hold, when $b_0 \neq 0$. Since the values t_0 and t_1 are randomly chosen from $\{0, 1, \ldots, 2^L - 1\}$, these two situations are valid. Therefore, we have found a contradiction to the assumption that either $a_1 \neq 0$ or $b_0 \neq 0$. Equation 3 must hold if $\mathcal{A}$ cannot be used by $\mathcal{B}$ to solve the discrete logarithm problem.

The lemma follows by combining these two cases.   □

By following Equations 2 and 3, we obtain

$$a_0 = b_1 = x. \tag{12}$$

Lemma 1 implies that among the 2^{2L} possible combinations of t_0 and t_1, at most 2^L of them can satisfy $(y_0^{t_0} \cdot y_1^{t_1}) = (g_0^{t_0} \cdot g_1^{t_1})^x$ and $\log_{g_0} y_0 \neq x$ (or $\log_{g_1} y_1 \neq x$). If $\log_{g_0} y_0 \neq x$ (or $\log_{g_1} y_1 \neq x$) and t_0 and t_1 are randomly chosen, $(y_0^{t_0} \cdot y_1^{t_1}) = (g_0^{t_0} \cdot g_1^{t_1})^x$ is satisfied with a probability no more than 2^{-L}. The theorem follows.   □

We further replace generation of random integer challenge with secure hash functions using the Fiat-Shamir transform [31], and therefore change the random challenge-based identification scheme to the Schnorr-type signature [44] of proof of knowledge. We make use of three collision-resistent hash functions, $H_\alpha : \mathbb{G}^4 \mapsto \{0,1\}^L$, $H_\beta : \mathbb{G}^4 \mapsto \{0,1\}^L$, and $H : \{0,1\}^* \mapsto \mathbb{Z}_q$, to generate the random integers t_0, t_1, and challenge c respectively. The modification, which will be used in our DAA scheme in Section 4, works as follows (both the prover and verifier take $(g_0, g_1, y_0, y_1) \in \mathbb{G}^4$ as input):

1. The prover computes $t_0 = H_\alpha(g_0, g_1, y_0, y_1)$ and $t_1 = H_\beta(g_0, g_1, y_0, y_1)$, randomly chooses $r \leftarrow \mathbb{Z}_q^*$ and computes $z \leftarrow (g_0^{t_0} \cdot g_1^{t_1})^r$, $c \leftarrow H(z)$, and $s \leftarrow r - c \cdot x \bmod q$, where $x = \log_{g_0} y_0 = \log_{g_1} y_1$, and sends the verifier the pair (c, s).
2. The verifier computes $t_0 = H_\alpha(g_0, g_1, y_0, y_1)$ and $t_1 = H_\beta(g_0, g_1, y_0, y_1)$, $z' \leftarrow (g_0^{t_0} \cdot g_1^{t_1})^s \cdot (y_0^{t_0} \cdot y_1^{t_1})^c$ and then verifies that $c = H(z')$. If this equation does not hold, the verifier outputs reject; otherwise outputs accept.

It is well-known that the signature scheme transferred based on the Fiat-Shamir transformation from an identification scheme is secure against chosen-message attacks in the random oracle model [7] if and only if the underlying identification scheme is secure [2]. Therefore, security of this scheme follows Theorem 1 under the discrete logarithm assumption and the random oracle model.

3   An Attack to the Chen'10 DAA Scheme

In this section, we first briefly review the batch-proof based DAA scheme in [23] with a focus on how the batch proof and verification protocol in Section 2.1 is used. We then present our attack.

3.1   Review of the Chen'10 DAA Scheme

The Chen'10 DAA scheme [23] is based on a modification of the Chen, Page, and Smart DAA scheme [30] and uses the batch proof and verification protocol described in Section 2.1. Let $\hat{t} : \mathbb{G}_1 \times \mathbb{G}_2 \to \mathbb{G}_T$ be a pairing function. Let P_1 and P_2 be the generators of $\mathbb{G}_1$ and $\mathbb{G}_2$ respectively, and both the groups are with the order of q. In this DAA scheme, the issuer has private key (x, y) and the corresponding public key (X, Y) such that $X = [x]P_2$ and $Y = [y]P_2$. Let f be a DAA private key known to a TPM. The DAA credential (A, B, C) is a Camenisch-Lysyanskaya signature [20] on f, such that $A \leftarrow G_1$, $B = [y]A$, and $C = [x + f \cdot x \cdot y]A$. The DAA credential can be verified with the following two equations

$$\hat{t}(A, Y) = \hat{t}(B, P_2)$$
$$\hat{t}(A + [f]B, X) = \hat{t}(C, P_2)$$

The DAA credential (A, B, C) can be randomly blinded. For any value $l \in \mathbb{Z}_q^*$, $([l]A, [l]B, [l]C)$ is a valid DAA credential on f as well.

Let $D = [f]B$ be a value computed by the TPM. The Host can store D along with the DAA credential (A, B, C) while the TPM keeps the secret key f. Let (R, S, T, W) be a blinded version of (A, B, C, D), i.e., $(R, S, T, W) = ([l]A, [l]B, [l]C, [l]D)$ for a random l. A DAA signature is essentially a proof of knowledge of f such that

$$W = [f]S, \quad \hat{t}(R, Y) = \hat{t}(S, P_2), \quad \hat{t}(R + W, X) = \hat{t}(T, P_2). \tag{13}$$

For the random base option, where DAA signatures are unlinkable, the above zero-knowledge proof is enough to convince to a verifier that the TPM is indeed certified by the issuer with a valid DAA credential. In the name base option, where the DAA signatures are linkable with regards to a particular basename, the following additional steps are needed in the signing process. Let $J \leftarrow H(\mathsf{bsn})$ where $H : \{0,1\}^* \to \mathbb{G}_1$ is a hash function that hashes strings into elements in $\mathbb{G}_1$, and bsn is the basename. Let $K \leftarrow [f]J$ be a value computed by the TPM, used for linking signatures computed under the basename. The TPM needs to perform a proof of knowledge of f such that

$$W = [f]S, \quad K = [f]J.$$

This is where the batch proof and verification in Section 2.1 is used. Let $V' \leftarrow S + J$ and $W' \leftarrow W + K$. The TPM proves the knowledge of f such that $W' = [f]V'$ instead of proving two equations $W = [f]S$ and $K = [f]J$. Let σ be the script of proof of knowledge of f such that $W' = [f]V'$. The DAA signature is (R, S, T, W, K, σ). A verifier can verify the signature by checking (R, S, T, W) values against the equations in (13), computing J from bsn, computing $V' \leftarrow S + J$ and $W' \leftarrow W + K$, and checking the proof of knowledge script σ on the (V', W') pair. The details of the DAA scheme are given in [23].

3.2   Details of Our Attack

We now describe an attack to the DAA scheme reviewed in the previous subsection. Our attack will allow any malicious host to forge any name base signatures without involvement from the TPM. Observe that the DAA scheme [23] assumes that both the signer (the TPM and Host) and the verifier agree on S, W, J, K before the prover performs the batch proof. However, in the actual DAA scheme, the signer does not need to commit S, W, J, K before the batch proof. In fact, the signer can choose K carefully in order to succeed in the batch proof. This leads to our attack.

Let the Host be the adversary. The Host already has (A, B, C, D) where (A, B, C) is a DAA credential on f and $D = [f]B$. We assume that f is unknown to the Host. We now show how the attacker creates a valid DAA signature without any help from the TPM. The attacker performs the following steps:

1. Chooses a random l and computes $(R, S, T, W) \leftarrow ([l]A, [l]B, [l]C, [l]D)$.
2. Computes $J \leftarrow H(\mathsf{bsn})$.
3. Chooses a random f' and computes $K \leftarrow [f'](J + S) - W$.
4. Computes $V' \leftarrow S + J$ and $W' \leftarrow W + K$.

5. Proves knowledge of f' such that $W' = [f']V'$ and produces a script σ.
6. Sets (R, S, T, W, K, σ) as the signature.

Observe that the attacker knows the discrete logarithm f' between V' and W', he can produce σ correctly with regards to (V', W'). The signature can be successfully verified by the verifier. Note that the attacker can forge the above signature without knowing the real secrete key f.

4   The Corrected DAA Scheme

In this section, we propose a corrected version of the Chen'10 DAA scheme using the improved batch proof and verification scheme described in Subsection 2.2. As mentioned early, a DAA scheme involves a set of issuers, signers, and verifiers. An Issuer is in charge of verifying the legitimacy of signers, and of issuing a DAA credential to each signer. A signer, which due to the split role is a pair of Host and associated TPM, can prove to a Verifier that the signer holds a valid DAA credential by providing a DAA signature. The Verifier can verify the DAA credential from the signature, but it cannot learn the identity of the signer. Linkability of signatures issued by a Host TPM pair is controlled by an input parameter bsn (standing for "base name") which is passed to the signing operation. There is assumed to be a list RogueList which contains a list of TPM secret keys which have been compromised. The scheme relies on the use of asymmetric pairings.

Throughout the constituent protocols and algorithms, the following notation is used. We let $\mathfrak{I}, \mathfrak{M}, \mathfrak{H}$ and $\mathfrak{V}$ denote the set of all Issuer, Host, TPM and Verifier entities. The value of bsn will be used by the signer/verifier to link signatures, if bsn $=\perp$ then this implies that signatures should be unlinkable.

Before proceeding with the description of our scheme, we recall a general issue that needs to be considered throughout. Specifically, every group element received by any entity needs to be checked for validity, i.e., that it is within the correct group; in particular, it is important that the element does not lie in some larger group which contains the group in question. This strict stipulation avoids numerous attacks such as those related to small subgroups. We implicitly assume that all transmitted group elements are elements of the specified groups: within our scheme, the use of Type-III pairings [32] allows efficient methods for checking subgroup membership as described by [24] and expanded upon in [30].

4.1   The Setup Algorithm

To initialise the system, one needs to select parameters for each protocol as well as the long term parameters for each Issuer and each TPM. On input of the security parameter 1^t, the Setup algorithm executes the following steps:

1. *Generate the Commitment Parameters* par_C. In this step, three groups $\mathbb{G}_1, \mathbb{G}_2$ and $\mathbb{G}_T$, of sufficiently large prime order q, are selected. Two random generators are then selected such that $\mathbb{G}_1 = \langle P_1 \rangle$ and $\mathbb{G}_2 = \langle P_2 \rangle$ along with a

pairing $\hat{t} : \mathbb{G}_1 \times \mathbb{G}_2 \mapsto \mathbb{G}_T$. Next, two hash functions $H_1 : \{0,1\}^* \mapsto \mathbb{Z}_q$ and $H_2 : \{0,1\}^* \mapsto \mathbb{Z}_q$ are selected and par_C is set to $(\mathbb{G}_1, \mathbb{G}_2, \mathbb{G}_T, \hat{t}, P_1, P_2, q, H_1, H_2)$.

Note that in our scheme, as the same as in [30], the TPM operations are strictly limited to $\mathbb{G}_1$. This allows a subset of par_C, namely par_T, to be set to $(\mathbb{G}_1, P_1, q)$ and installed on the TPM in preference to par_C.

2. *Generate Signature and Verification Parameters* par_S. Five additional hash functions are selected, namely $H_3 : \{0,1\}^* \mapsto \mathbb{G}_1$, $H_4 : \{0,1\}^* \mapsto \mathbb{Z}_q$, $H_5 : \{0,1\}^* \mapsto \mathbb{Z}_q$, $H_\alpha : \mathbb{G}_1^4 \mapsto \{0,1\}^L$ and $H_\beta : \mathbb{G}_1^4 \mapsto \{0,1\}^L$. par_S is set to $(H_3, H_4, H_5, L, H_\alpha, H_\beta)$.

3. *Generate the* Issuer *Parameters* par_I. For each $i \in \mathfrak{I}$, the following steps are performed. Two integers $x, y \leftarrow \mathbb{Z}_q$ are selected, and the Issuer private key isk is set to (x, y). Next, the values $X = [x]P_2 \in \mathbb{G}_2$ and $Y = [y]P_2 \in \mathbb{G}_2$ are computed; the Issuer public key ipk is set to (X, Y). Then an Issuer value K_I is derived from the Issuer public values. Finally, par_I is set to $(\{\mathsf{ipk}, K_I\})$ for each Issuer $i \in \mathfrak{I}$. In our scheme K_I is a representation of par_T[1].

4. *Generate TPM Parameters.* The TPM generates a public/private key pair $(\mathsf{PK}, \mathsf{SK})$, which can be authenticated based on the associated endorsement key. In addition, it generates the private secret value $\mathsf{DAAseed}$. We assume that the private key SK along with the secret $\mathsf{DAAseed}$ is embedded into the TPM (e.g., in non-volatile memory) and that each Issuer has access to the corresponding public endorsement key PK. We also assume either a public key IND-CCA encryption/decryption scheme (ENC/DEC) along with a MAC algorithm (MAC) or a digital signature/verification scheme (SIG/VER) has been selected for use with the keys in order to achieve an authentic channel between the TPM and Issuer.

5. *Publish Public Parameters.* Finally, the public system parameters par are set to $(\mathsf{par}_C, \mathsf{par}_S, \mathsf{par}_I, \mathsf{par}_T)$ and published.

Note that each TPM has a single $\mathsf{DAAseed}$, but can create multiple DAA secret keys, even associated with a single issuer. To allow this, a number cnt (standing for "counter value") is used as an additional input to DAA secret key generation: the TPM DAA secret key is generated by using $\mathsf{DAAseed}$, K_I and cnt as input, as described in the Join protocol of the next section.

4.2   The Join Protocol

This is a protocol between a given TPM $\mathfrak{m} \in \mathfrak{M}$, the corresponding Host $\mathfrak{h} \in \mathfrak{H}$ and an Issuer $i \in \mathfrak{I}$. The protocol proceeds as shown in Figure 1, and the TPM authentication is using an encryption-based authentic channel as used in [30]. The DAA credential is proved by Issuer without TPM's involvement. This approach was introduced in [9]. Here we give an overview of how a general Join protocol proceeds. There are 4 main stages to a Join protocol.

---

[1] If the same par_T is used by multiple issuers, in order to limit K_I to a single issuer, the issuer value K_I can be set by using both par_T and a unique issuer name.

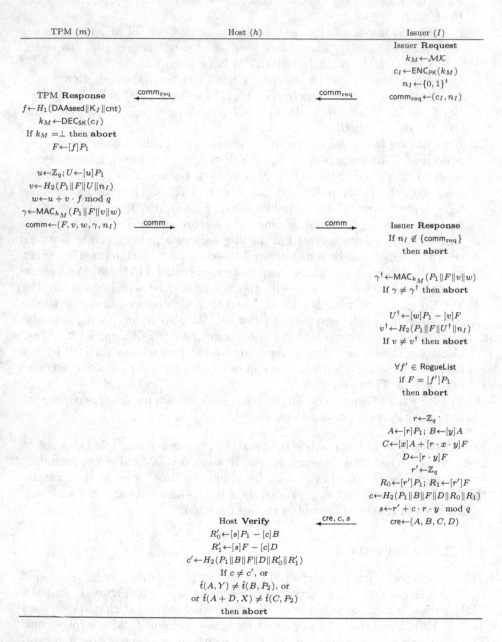

Fig. 1. The Join protocol

1. The TPM $\mathfrak{m}$ and Issuer $\mathfrak{i}$ first establish an authentic channel, which allows the Issuer to be sure that he only creates the DAA credential for a genuine TPM. The authentic channel is built by using either the ENC/DEC algorithm and MAC algorithm, or the SIG/VER algorithm under the key pair (SK, PK).

2. The TPM $\mathfrak{m}$ generates a DAA secret key, $f \leftarrow H_1(\mathsf{DAAseed} \| \mathsf{K}_I \| \mathsf{cnt}) \in \mathbb{Z}_q$, using the value K_I provided by the issuer, a counter value cnt provided by the host and its internal secret seed DAAseed. The TPM then computes a commitment on this value, i.e. $F = [f]P_1 \in \mathbb{G}_1$, along with a proof of possession of this value, i.e. (v, w). The commitment and proof are sent to the Issuer via the authentic channel.

3. The issuer performs some checks on the commitment and proof it receives and, if these correctly verify, computes a credential, $\mathsf{cre} = (A, B, C, D, c, s) \in \mathbb{G}_1^4 \times \mathbb{Z}_q^2$, which is a blindly signed CL signature [20] of f via F and a proof of this signature, and then sends it to the host.

4. The Host verifies the correctness of the credential.

4.3   The Sign/Verify Protocol

This is a protocol between a given TPM $\mathfrak{m} \in \mathfrak{M}$, Host $\mathfrak{h} \in \mathfrak{H}$ and Verifier $\mathfrak{v} \in \mathfrak{V}$ as described in Figure 2. We give an overview of the protocol with the following three steps:

1. The Host $\mathfrak{h}$ and Verifier $\mathfrak{v}$ first agree the content of the signed message msg and the base name bsn.

2. The TPM $\mathfrak{m}$ and Host $\mathfrak{h}$ then work together to produce a DAA signature on msg and associated with bsn. The signature should prove knowledge of a discrete logarithm f, knowledge of a valid credential cre and that this credential was computed for the same value f by a given Issuer $\mathfrak{i} \in \mathfrak{I}$. In the signing procedure between the two parts of the signer, the TPM uses the value of f and the Host uses the value of cre. We note that the Host will know a lot of the values needed in the computation and will be able to take on a lot of the computational workload. However, if the TPM has not had its secret f published (i.e. it is not a rogue module) then the Host $\mathfrak{h}$ will not know f and will be unable to compute the whole signature without the aid of the TPM. Therefore, we say that the TPM is the real signer and the Host is a helper. We also note that the four scalar multiplications in $\mathbb{G}_1$ by the Host are independent to the signed message msg or the base name bsn, so they can be precomputed.

3. Upon the receipt of the DAA signature, the Verifier $\mathfrak{v}$ checks the RogueList first, then checks whether the agreed bsn was used correctly. After these two checks pass successfully, $\mathfrak{v}$ verifies whether (R, S, T, W) is a valid CL signature on an unopened data string f and this data string is used as a private signing key to sign the agreed message msg and $\mathfrak{v}$'s fresh nonce n_V.

There are two major differences between this version and the protocol in [30]. At first, the values of J and K are omitted when bsn $= \perp$, and the function

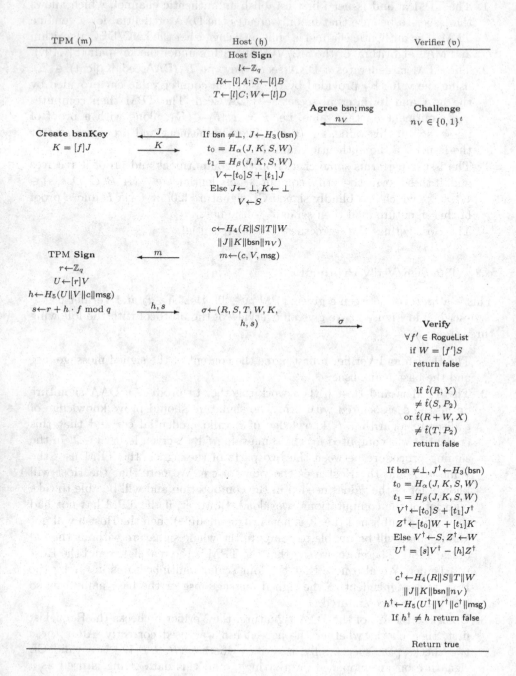

Fig. 2. The Sign/Verify protocol

of checking the RogueList is done with the pair of (S, W) rather than (J, K). Secondly, it makes use of a new process of batch proof and verification to compute the value $U = [r]V$, as opposed to the two values $R_1 = [r]J$ and $R_2 = [r]S$. This makes the total number of scalar multiplications in $\mathbb{G}_1$ by the TPM in the signing algorithm from 3 to 1 if bsn $= \perp$ or to 2 if bsn $\neq \perp$. This change comes at some modification in the host signing process and verification side. However, the total computational cost for the Host is not significantly increased and the total computational cost for the Verifier is reduced, from that of [30].

5   Security Properties of the Proposed DAA Scheme

In this section, we will state the security results for the new DAA scheme under the definitions of DAA security notions described in Section A.

As the same as the DAA scheme in [28], our DAA scheme requires the DDH problem for $\mathbb{G}_1$ to be hard. The formal definition of this problem is defined as follows:

Definition 2 ($\mathbb{G}_1$-DDH). *We define the* $\mathbf{Adv}_{\mathcal{A}}^{\mathrm{DDH}}(t)$ *of an* $\mathbb{G}_1$-*DDH adversary* $\mathcal{A}$ *against the set of parameters* $(\mathbb{G}_1, \mathbb{G}_2, \mathbb{G}_T, P, Q, q, \hat{t})$ *as*

$$\left| \Pr\left[x, y, z \leftarrow \mathbb{Z}_p; X \leftarrow xP, Y \leftarrow yP, Z \leftarrow zP; \mathcal{A}(\mathbb{G}_1, \mathbb{G}_2, \mathbb{G}_T, \hat{t}, P, Q, X, Y, Z, q) = 1 \right] \right.$$
$$\left. - \Pr\left[x, y \leftarrow \mathbb{Z}_p; X \leftarrow xP, Y \leftarrow yP; Z \leftarrow xyP; \mathcal{A}(\mathbb{G}_1, \mathbb{G}_2, \mathbb{G}_T, \hat{t}, P, Q, X, Y, Z, q) = 1 \right] \right|$$

We then say a tuple $(\mathbb{G}_1, \mathbb{G}_2, \mathbb{G}_T, P, Q, q, \hat{t})$ *satisfies the DDH assumption for* $\mathbb{G}_1$ *if for any p.p.t. adversary* $\mathcal{A}$ *its advantage* $\mathbf{Adv}_{\mathcal{A}}^{\mathrm{DDH}}(t)$ *is negligible in* t.

Our DAA scheme also requires a special representation of the LRSW problem, namely the blind-4 bilinear LRSW problem, to be hard. The formal definition of this problem, as introduced in [9], is defined as follows:

Definition 3 (Blind-4 Bilinear LRSW Advantage). *We define the blind-4 bilinear LRSW advantage* $\mathbf{Adv}_{\mathcal{A}}^{\mathrm{B-4-bLRSW}}(t)$ *of an adversary* $\mathcal{A}$ *against* $(\mathbb{G}_1, \mathbb{G}_2, P_1, P_2, q, \hat{t})$ *as*

$$\Pr\left[\begin{array}{c} x, y \leftarrow \mathbb{Z}_q; X \leftarrow [x]P_2, Y \leftarrow [y]P_2; \\ (f, A, B, C, D) \leftarrow \mathcal{A}^{\mathcal{O}_{X,Y}^B(\cdot)}(\mathbb{G}_1, \mathbb{G}_2, P_1, P_2, X, Y, q, \hat{t}) \\ \wedge \left(F = [f]P_1 \notin \mathcal{Q}, \ f \in \mathbb{Z}_q^\times, \ A \in \mathbb{G}_1, \ B = [y]A, \right. \\ \left. C = [x + f \cdot x \cdot y]A; D = [f]B \right) \end{array} \right]$$

where $\mathcal{Q}$ *is the set of queries that* $\mathcal{A}$ *made to* $\mathcal{O}_{X,Y}^B(\cdot)$, *which on input* $F = [f]P_1 \notin \mathcal{Q}$ *outputs a tuple* (A, B, C, D), *and* $q \approx 2^t$.

We then say a tuple $(\mathbb{G}_1, \mathbb{G}_2, P_1, P_2, q, \hat{t})$ satisfies the blind-4 bilinear LRSW assumption if for any p.p.t. adversary $\mathcal{A}$ its advantage $\mathbf{Adv}_{\mathcal{A}}^{\mathrm{B-4-bLRSW}}(t)$ is negligible in t.

As shown in [28], we shall require one other problem to be hard. Namely that the discrete logarithm problem in $\mathbb{G}_1$ is hard, even in the presence of an oracle which solves the *static* computational Diffie–Hellman problem for the underlying secret in the discrete logarithm problem. We call this problem Gap-DLP, since it is similar to the Gap-CDH problem, where one tries to solve the CDH problem with the presence of an oracle to solve DDH. Formally we define:

Definition 4 (Gap-DLP). *We define the Gap-DLP advantage* $\mathbf{Adv}_{\mathcal{A}}^{\text{Gap-DLP}}(t)$ *for* $\mathbb{G}_1$ *of an adversary* $\mathcal{A}$ *against* $(\mathbb{G}_1, \mathbb{G}_2, P_1, P_2, q, \hat{t})$ *as*

$$\Pr\left[x \leftarrow \mathbb{Z}_q; X \leftarrow [x]P_1; \mathcal{A}^{\mathcal{O}_x(\cdot)}(\mathbb{G}_1, \mathbb{G}_2, P_1, P_2, X, q, \hat{t}) = x\right]$$

where $\mathcal{O}_x$ *is the oracle which on input of* $Y \in \mathbb{G}_1$ *will return* $[x]Y$ *and* $q \approx 2^t$.

We then say a tuple $(\mathbb{G}_1, \mathbb{G}_2, P_1, P_2, q, \hat{t})$ satisfies the Gap-DLP assumption in $\mathbb{G}_1$ if for any p.p.t. adversary $\mathcal{A}$ its advantage $\mathbf{Adv}_{\mathcal{A}}^{\text{Gap-DLP}}(t)$ is negligible in t.

Some relevant but well-known preliminary information, such as definitions of pairings, and other computationally hard problems, is shown in Appendix B. The security analysis of the notions of user-controlled-anonymity and user-controlled-traceability is in the random oracle model [7], i.e., we will assume that the hash functions H_2 H_3 and H_5 in the DAA scheme are random oracles. Note that the hash function H_1 used to compute the value f, and H_4, H_α and H_β used in the Sign protocol are not simulated as random oracles. However, it is still required that outputs of these four hash functions are uniformly random distribution. In general, we will argue that our new DAA scheme is secure, i.e., correct, user-controlled-anonymous and user-controlled-traceable, as addressed in the following theorems.

Theorem 2. *The DAA scheme specified in Section 4 is correct.*

Proof. This theorem follows directly from the specification of the scheme. □

Theorem 3. *Under the* $\mathbb{G}_1$*-DDH assumption in Definition 2, the above DAA scheme is user-controlled-anonymous. More specifically, if there is an adversary* $\mathcal{A}$ *that succeeds with a non-negligible probability to break user-controlled-anonymity of the scheme, then there is a simulator* $\mathcal{S}$ *running in polynomial time that solves the* $\mathbb{G}_1$*-DDH problem with a non-negligible probability.*

Proof. We will show how an adversary $\mathcal{A}$ that succeeds with a non-negligible probability to break user-controlled-anonymity of the DAA scheme may be used to construct a simulator $\mathcal{S}$ that solves the $\mathbb{G}_1$-DDH problem. Let $(P, [\mathsf{a}]P, [\mathsf{b}]P, [\mathsf{c}]P) \in \mathbb{G}_1^4$ and $\mathsf{a}, \mathsf{b}, \mathsf{c} \in \mathbb{Z}_p^*$ be the instance of the $\mathbb{G}_1$-DDH problem that we wish to answer whether $[\mathsf{c}]P$ is equal to $[\mathsf{a} \cdot \mathsf{b}]P$ or not. We now describe the construction of the simulator $\mathcal{S}$, which performs the following game with $\mathcal{A}$, as defined in Section A.

In the initial of the game, $\mathcal{S}$ runs Setup (or takes $\mathcal{A}$'s input) to create an issuer, which is named by an identifier K_I and which is of two issuer public keys, say

i_0 and i_1. Each public key is presented as $(\mathbb{G}_1, \mathbb{G}_2, \mathbb{G}_T, p, \hat{t}, P_1, P_2, H_1, H_2, H_3,$
$H_4, H_5, H_\alpha, H_\beta, \mathsf{ipk} = (X, Y) = ([x]P_2, [y]P2)$ and its corresponding secret key
is presented as $\mathsf{isk} = (x, y)$. All the values of the public and secret keys are
known to $\mathcal{A}$. For the purpose of simplicity, we do not ask these two keys to be
completely different to each other. We only assume that these two public keys
have different P_1 values and their H_3 functions are each relevant to their P_1
values. Note that actually it does not matter if some other values between these
two keys are different from each other, although it is not required for the purpose
of our proof. Throughout the proof, except for some individual specification, we
do not use different notation to distinguish these two keys.

More specifically, in the first key for i_0, $P_1 = P$, and in the second one for i_1,
$P_1 = [\mathsf{b}]P$. In both of the public keys, $H_3(w) = [r_w]P_1 \in \mathbb{G}_1$, where r_w is chosen
uniformly at random in $\mathbb{Z}_p^*$. Note that since these two H_3 functions make use of
different P_1 as the base, so for the same input w value, their outputs of H_3 are
different to each other. Throughout the proof specification, $/i_b$, where $b = \{0, 1\}$,
indicates which issuer's public key is associated with.

$\mathcal{S}$ creates algorithms to respond to queries made by $\mathcal{A}$ during its attack, including
three random oracles denoted by H_2, H_3 and H_5 in the DAA scheme.

To maintain consistency between queries made by $\mathcal{A}$, $\mathcal{S}$ keeps the following
lists: L_i for $i = 2, 3, 5$ stores data for query and response pairs to random oracle
H_i. L_{jc} stores data for query and response records for Join queries and Corrupted
queries. Each item of L_{jc} is $\{ID/i_b, f, F, \mathsf{cre}, c\}$, where $c = 1$ means that the
corresponding signer is corrupted and $c = 0$ otherwise. L_s stores data for query
and response records for Sign queries. Each item of L_s is $\{ID/i_b, m, \mathsf{bsn}, \sigma, s\}$,
where $s = 1$ means that $\mathsf{bsn} = \perp$ and $s = 0$ means that $\mathsf{bsn} \neq \perp$ under the
Sign query. At the beginning of the simulation, $\mathcal{S}$ sets all the above lists empty.
An empty item is denoted by the symbol $*$. During the game, $\mathcal{A}$ will asks the
H_i queries up to q_i times, asks the Join query up to q_j times, asks the Corrupt
query up to q_c times, and asks the Sign query up to q_s times. All of these time
values are polynomial.

Simulator: $H_2(m)$. If $(m, h_2) \in L_2$, return h_2. Else choose h_2 uniformly at
random from $\mathbb{Z}_p^*$; add (m, h_2) to L_2 and return h_2.

Simulator: $H_3(m)/i_b$. If m has already been an entry of the H_3/i_b query, i.e. the
item $(m, w, h_3/i_b)$ for an arbitrary w and h_3/i_b exists in L_3, return h_3/i_b. Else
choose v from $\mathbb{Z}_p^*$ uniformly at random; compute $h_3/i_b \leftarrow [v]P_1$; add $(m, v, h_3/i_b)$
to L_3 and return h_3/i_b.

Simulator: $H_5(m)$. If $(m, h_5) \in L_5$, return h_5. Else choose h_5 uniformly at
random from $\mathbb{Z}_p^*$; add (m, h_5) to L_5 and return h_5.

Simulator: Join(ID). At the beginning of the simulation choose α, β uniformly
at random from $\{1, ..., q_j\}$. We show how to respond to the i-th query made by
$\mathcal{A}$ below. Note that we assume $\mathcal{A}$ does not make repeat queries, but we also
assume that for each query, the Join protocol could be run twice, one with i_0
and the other with i_1. Although it seems redundant for the query of every ID

to be run twice, it is necessary for $i = \alpha$ or β. We use ID_X/i_b, $b \in \{0,1\}$, to indicate the signer identity ID_X associated with i_b.

- If $i = \alpha$ and in the run associated with i_0, set $F_\alpha \leftarrow [a]P$ (i.e. $[a]P_1$); run $Join_t$ with $\mathcal{A}$ to get cre_α, and add $\{ID_\alpha/i_0, *, F_\alpha, cre_\alpha, 0\}$ to L_{jc}. Note that since $\mathcal{S}$ does not know the value $f_\alpha = a$ (which is indicated as $*$ in L_{jc}), it is not able to compute (v, w) by following the Schnorr signature scheme. However $\mathcal{S}$ can forge the signature by controlling the random oracle of H_2 as follows: randomly choose w and v and compute $U = [w]P_1 - [v]F_\alpha$. The only thing $\mathcal{S}$ has to take care of is checking the consistency of the L_2 entries. $\mathcal{S}$ verifies the validation of cre_α before accepting it. This is done by verifying (c, s) values in the Join protocol.
- If $i = \beta$ and in the run associated with i_1, set $F_\beta \leftarrow [c]P$ (i.e. $[c/b]P_1$); do the same thing as in the previous item to get cre_β.
- Else, including $i = \alpha$ with i_1 and $i = \beta$ with i_0, choose f uniformly at random from $\mathbb{Z}_p^*$; compute $F = [f]P_1$, if $F = [a]P_1$ or $[b]P_1$, abort outputting "**abortion 0**"; else run $Join_t$ with $\mathcal{A}$ to get cre; verify cre before accept it and then add $(ID/i_b, f, F, cre, 0)$ in L_{jc}.

Simulator: Corrupt(ID). We assume that $\mathcal{A}$ makes the queries $Join(ID)$ before it makes the Corrupt query using the identity. Otherwise, $\mathcal{S}$ answers the Join query first. Find the entry $(ID/i_b, f, F, cre, 0)$ in L_{jc}, return f and update the item to $(ID/i_b, f, F, cre, 1)$.

Simulator: Sign(ID, m, bsn). Let m' be the input message $\mathcal{A}$ wants to sign, and $n_V \in \{0,1\}^t$ be a nonce chosen by $\mathcal{A}$, so $m = (m', n_V)$. We assume that $\mathcal{A}$ makes the queries $Join(ID)$ before it makes the Sign query using the identity. Otherwise, $\mathcal{S}$ answers the Join query first. We have the following multiple cases to consider.

Case 1: $ID/i_b \neq ID_\alpha/i_0$ and $ID/i_b \neq ID_\beta/i_1$. Find the entry $(ID/i_b, f, F, cre, 0/1)$ in L_{jc}, compute $\sigma \leftarrow \text{Sign}$, add $(ID/i_b, m, \text{bsn}, \sigma, 0/1)$ to L_s and respond with σ.

Case 2: $ID/i_b = ID_\alpha/i_0$. $\mathcal{S}$ is not able to create such a signature since $\mathcal{S}$ does not know the corresponding secret key. But $\mathcal{S}$ is able to forge the signature by controlling the random oracles of H_3 and H_5. $\mathcal{S}$ finds the entry $(ID_\alpha/i_0, *, F_\alpha, cre_\alpha = (A_\alpha, B_\alpha, C_\alpha, D_\alpha), 0)$ in L_{jc}, and forges σ by performing the following steps:

1. When $\text{bsn} = \bot$, set $J = \bot$ and $K = \bot$.
2. When $\text{bsn} \neq \bot$, take the given bsn, search whether bsn is an entry of L_3; if yes, retrieve the corresponding v and $h_3 = [v]P_1$. With a new input of L_3, query H_3 to get v and h_3, and set $J \leftarrow h_3 = [v]P_1 = [v]P$ and $K \leftarrow [v]([a]P)$.
3. Choose random $l \leftarrow \mathbb{Z}_p^*$ and compute $R \leftarrow [l]A$, $S = [l]B$, $T = [l]C$ and $W = [l]D$.
4. Compute $\text{str} \leftarrow R\|S\|T\|W\|J\|K\|\text{bsn}\|n_v$.
5. Choose $s \in \mathbb{Z}_p^*$ at random.

6. Choose h at random; search whether h is an entry of L_5; if yes, go back to the beginning of this item.

7. Computer $t_0 = H_\alpha(J, K, S, W)$ and $t_1 = H_\beta(J, K, S, W)$.

8. Compute $V = [t_0]S + [t_1]J$ if bsn $\neq \perp$ or $V = S$ if bsn $= \perp$.

9. Compute $Z = [t_0]W + [t_1]K$ if bsn $\neq \perp$ or $V = S$ if bsn $= \perp$.

10. Compute $U \leftarrow [f]V - [c]Z$.

11. Set $w = U\|V\|H_4(\text{str})\|m$. Search whether w is an entry of L_5; if yes, go back to the beginning of the item of choosing s; otherwise, add (w, h) in L_5.

12. Output $\sigma = (R, S, T, W, K, h, s)$.

13. Add $(ID_\alpha/i_0, m, \text{bsn}, \sigma, 1/0)$ to L_s.

Case 3: $ID/i_b = ID_\beta/i_1$. Again, S cannot create this signature properly without the knowledge of f_β. S forges the signature in the same way as in Case 2 above, except when bsn $\neq \perp$, setting $J = h_3 = [v]P_1 = [v]([b]P)$ and $K = [v]([c]P)$. At the end of Phase 1, A outputs a message m, a basename bsn, two identities $\{ID_0, ID_1\}$. If $\{ID_0, ID_1\} \neq \{ID_\alpha, ID_\beta\}$, S aborts outputting "**abortion 1**". If bsn $= \perp$, S aborts outputting "**abortion 2**". We assume that Join has already been queried at ID_α and ID_β by A associated with both i_0 and i_1. If this is not the case we can define Join at these points as we wish i.e. as for ID_α/i_0, $F_\alpha = [a]P$ and for ID_β/i_1, $F_\beta = [c]P$. Neither ID_0 nor ID_1 should have been asked for the Corrupt query and the Sign query with the same bsn $\neq \perp$ by following the definition of the game defined in Section A.

S chooses a bit b at random, and generates the challenge in the same way as Case 2 or 3 of the Sign query simulation, by querying Sign(ID_α, m, bsn) with i_0 if $b = 0$ or Sign(ID_β, m, bsn) with i_1 otherwise. S returns the result v^* to A.

In Phase 2, S and A carry on the query and response process as in Phase 1. Again, A is not allowed to make any Corrupt query to either ID_0 or ID_1 and to make any Sign query to either ID_0 or ID_1 with the same bsn $\neq \perp$. At the end of Phase 2, A outputs b'. If $b' = b$, S outputs 0, which means $[c]P \neq [a \cdot b]P$; otherwise S outputs 1, which means $[c]P = [a \cdot b]P$.

Let ϵ be the probability that A succeeds in breaking the anonymity game. Suppose S does not abort during the above simulation. If $c \neq a \cdot b$, S emulates the anonymity game perfectly, i.e., $Pr[b = b'] = 1/2 + \epsilon$. If $c = a \cdot b$, then the private keys for ID_0/i_0 and ID_1/i_1 are identical and thus the signature σ^* is independent of b. It follows that $Pr[b = b'] = 1/2$. Therefore, assuming S does not abort, it has advantage at least $\epsilon/2$ in solving the $\mathbb{G}_1$-DDH problem.

We can argue that creating two issuer public keys in the game does not make the simulation distinguishable from the real DAA scheme. In the formal definition of DAA specified in Section A, a system can involves multiple issuers, signers and verifiers; each signer can obtain multiple DAA credentials associated with the same DAA secret. For the flexibility, the signer's DAA secret f is relevant to the issuer's identifier K_I, which could be the issuer's root public key as specified in [46] or the issuer's partial public parameters which is used by the TPM. In our proof, we only require that the two issuer public keys are associated with the same K_I value, and a single TPM DAA secret f could naturally be computed and then associated with the two different issuer pubic keys. Therefore the adversary $\mathcal{A}$ should not be able to notice any difference between the real DAA scheme and the simulation based on the double issuer public keys.

Let us now consider how our simulation could abort i.e. describe events that could cause $\mathcal{A}$'s view to differ when run by $\mathcal{S}$ from its view in a real attack.

It is clear that the simulations for H_2, H_3 and H_5 are indistinguishable from real random oracles.

If the event **abortion 0** happens, $\mathcal{S}$ gets the value a or b, $\mathcal{S}$ can compute $[a \cdot b]P$ and thus to solve the DDH problem (because the DDH problem is weaker than the CDH problem). Since $\mathcal{S}$ chooses its value uniformly at random from $\mathbb{Z}_p^*$, the chance of this event happening is negligible.

The event **abortion 1** happens only if $\{ID_0, ID_1\} \neq \{ID_\alpha, ID_\beta\}$. Since ID_α and ID_β are chosen at random, the probability of this case is at least $1/(q_j(q_j - 1))$.

The event **abortion 2** happens only if $\mathsf{bsn} = \bot$. We can see this case does not affect validation of the simulation. The reason is that a signature σ without (J, K) does not provide $\mathcal{A}$ any useful information to win the game, because every value in the signature is either a random distribution or being masked by a random l. Actually, this argument is required even in the case of $\mathsf{bsn} \neq \bot$.

Based on the above discussion, the probability that $\mathcal{S}$ does not abort the game at some stage and produces the correct output is non-negligible, since it follows the fact that $\mathcal{A}$ wins the game with a non-negligible probability. □

Theorem 4. *Under the blind-4 bilinear LRSW assumption and the Gap-DLP assumption in $\mathbb{G}_1$, the above DAA scheme is user-controlled-traceable. More specifically, if there is an adversary $\mathcal{A}$ that succeeds with a non-negligible probability to break user-controlled-traceability of the scheme, then there is a simulator $\mathcal{S}$ running in polynomial time that solves the blind-4 bilinear LRSW problem or the Gap-DLP problem with a non-negligible probability.*

Proof. We will show how an adversary $\mathcal{A}$ that succeeds with a non-negligible probability to break user-controlled-traceability of the DAA scheme may be used to construct a simulator $\mathcal{S}$ that solves the blind-4 bilinear LRSW problem or that solves the Gap-DLP problem in $\mathbb{G}_1$. Let $X, Y \in \mathbb{G}_2, X = [x]P_2, Y = [y]P_2 \in \mathbb{G}_2$ and $(A, B = [y]A, C = [x + x \cdot y \cdot m]A), D = [m]B \in \mathbb{G}_1^4 \leftarrow \mathcal{O}_{LRSW}([m]P_1, x, y)$ be the instance of the blind-4 bilinear LRSW problem that we wish to provide $(\tilde{m}, \tilde{A}, \tilde{B}, \tilde{C}, \tilde{D})$ such that $\tilde{m} \neq 0$, $\tilde{B} = [y]\tilde{A}$ and $\tilde{C} = [x + x \cdot y \cdot \tilde{m}]\tilde{A}, \tilde{D} = [\tilde{m}]\tilde{B}$ where $[\tilde{m}]P_1$ has not be queried to the oracle $\mathcal{O}$ before. Let $F^* = [f^*]P_1 \in \mathbb{G}_1$ and $[f^*]J \leftarrow \mathcal{O}_{Gap-DLP}(F^*, J)$ be the instance of the Gap-DLP problem, that we wish to provide $f^* \in \mathbb{Z}_q$.

We now describe the construction of the simulator $\mathcal{S}$. $\mathcal{S}$ performs the following game with $\mathcal{A}$, as defined in Section A. There are two cases for the initial process in the user-controlled-traceability game, each referring to one performance as follows.

The first performance covers the initial Case 1 of the game, where $\mathcal{S}$ sets $\mathcal{I}$'s public parameters, namely par, using the blind-4 bilinear LRSW challenge as $(\mathbb{G}_1, \mathbb{G}_2, \mathbb{G}_T, \hat{t}, q, P_1, P_2, H_1, H_2, H_3, H_4, H_5, H_\alpha, H_\beta, X, Y)$ and secret key, namely isk, as (x, y). S gives par to A. Note that S does not know isk. It also creates algorithms to respond to queries made by A during its attack.

S sets three random oracles H_2, H_3 and H_5 in the same way as in the proof of Theorem 3. The other hash functions are not random oracle, but still hold the properties of pre-image resistance, collision resistance and output uniform random distribution. To maintain consistency between queries made by A, S keeps the following lists: L_i for $i = 2, 3, 5$ stores data for query and response pairs to random oracle H_i. L_{jc} stores data for query and response records for Join queries and Corrupted queries. Each item of L_{jc} is $\{ID, f, F, \text{cre}, c\}$, where $c = 1$ means that the corresponding signer is corrupted (via either Case 2 of the Join query or the Corrupt query) and $c = 0$ otherwise. Note that the set of f values with $c = 1$ will be used as the RogueList list. L_s stores data for query/response records for Sign queries. Each item of L_s is $\{ID, m, \text{bsn}, \sigma, s\}$, where $s = 1$ means that bsn $= \bot$ under the Sign query and $s = 0$ means that bsn $\neq \bot$ under the Sign query. At the beginning of the simulation, S sets all the above lists empty. An empty item is denoted by the symbol $*$. During the game, A will asks the H_i queries up to q_i times, asks the Join query up to q_j times, asks the Corrupt query up to q_c times, and asks the Sign query up to q_s times. All of the time values are polynomial.

Simulator: $H_2(m)$. The same as in the proof of Theorem 3.

Simulator: $H_3(m)$. If m has already been an entry of the H_3 query, return h_3. Else choose j from $\mathbb{Z}_q^*$ uniformly at random, compute $h_3 = [j]P_1 \in \mathbb{G}_1$, add (m, j, h_3) to L_3, and return h_3.

Simulator: $H_5(m)$. The same as in the proof of Theorem 3.

Simulator: Join(ID). We assume A does not make repeat queries. Given a new ID from A (Case 1). If $ID \neq ID_m$, S chooses $f \in \mathbb{Z}_q^*$ uniformly at random, computes $F = [f]P_1$, asks O with the entry F to obtain cre $= (A, B, C, D)$, adds $\{ID, f, F, \text{cre}, 0\}$ to L_{jc}. Alternatively, S receives a new pair of ID and F from A (Case 2), S asks O with the entry F to provide cre $= (A, B, C, D)$, adds $\{ID, *, F, \text{cre}, 1\}$ to L_{jc}. Finally S responds with cre together with a proof c, s. In case S does not know the value f, he can forge (c, s) based on the random oracle H_2.

Simulator: Corrupt(ID). We assume that A makes the queries Join(ID) (Case 1) before it makes the Corrupt query using the identity. Otherwise, S answers the Join (Case 1) query first. Find the entry $(ID, f, F, \text{cre}, 0)$ in L_{jc}, return f and update the item to $(ID, f, F, \text{cre}, 1)$. We assume that A does not ask a Corrupt query on ID, which has been made for the Join (Case 2) query.

Simulator: Create-bsnKey(ID, J). We assume that A makes both the query Join(ID) and query $J = H_3(\text{bsn})$ for some input bsn value to obtain J as the answer before it makes the Create-bsnKey query using the identity and the value J. If the query Join(ID) has not been asked, S answers the Join query (Case 1) first. If the query $J = H_3(\text{bsn})$ has not been made, S queries it first. Find the entry $(., j, J)$ in L_3 where equation $J = [j]P_1$ holds and the entry $(ID, ., F, ., 0/1)$ in L_{jc}. Compute $K = [j]F$ and return it.

Simulator: Static-DH(ID, J). We assume that $\mathcal{A}$ makes the query Join(ID) (Case 1) before it makes this query; otherwise, $\mathcal{S}$ answers the Join (Case 1) query first. Find the entry $(ID, f, F, ., 0/1)$ in L_{jc} where equation $F = [f]P_1$ holds computes $K = [f]J$, and returns it. We assume that $\mathcal{A}$ does not ask a Static-DH query on ID, which has been made for the Join (Case 2) query.

Simulator: Sign(ID, m, bsn). Let m' be the input message $\mathcal{A}$ wants to sign, $n_V \in \{0, 1\}^{\ell_H}$ be a nonce chosen by $\mathcal{A}$, so $m = (m', n_V)$. We assume that $\mathcal{A}$ makes the queries Join(ID) (Case 1) before it makes the Sign query using the identity. If the query Join(ID) has not been asked before, $\mathcal{S}$ answers the Join query (Case 1) first. Find the entry $(ID, f, F, \mathsf{cre}, 0/1)$ in L_{jc}, compute $\sigma \leftarrow \mathsf{Sign}$. In the end, $\mathcal{S}$ adds $(ID, m, \mathsf{bsn}, \sigma, 1/0)$ to L_s and respond with σ. We assume that $\mathcal{A}$ does not ask a Sign query on ID, which has been made for the Join (Case 2) query.

Simulator: Semi-sign(ID, m, V, c). We assume that $\mathcal{A}$ makes the queries (Case 1) Join(ID) before it makes the Semi-sign query using the identity. Otherwise, $\mathcal{S}$ answers the Join query (Case 1) first. Find the entry $(ID, f, F, \mathsf{cre}, 0/1)$ in L_{jc}, compute (h, s) by following the TPM's action in Sign, add $(ID, m, ., \sigma = (*, *, *, *, *, h, s), .)$ to L_s and respond with (h, s). We assume that $\mathcal{A}$ does not ask a Semi-sign query on ID, which has been made for the Join (Case 2) query. Note that $\mathcal{A}$ can query Semi-sign with the same entry multiple times. $\mathcal{S}$ will respond with different (h, s) values.

At the end of the phase of probing above, $\mathcal{A}$ outputs an identity ID^*, a message m^*, a nonce n_V^*, a basename bsn^* and a signature $\sigma^* = (R^*, S^*, T^*, W^*, K^*, h^*, s^*)$. We consider the following two cases:

- Case 1. Suppose $\mathsf{Verify}(\sigma^*) = 1$, ID^* and $(ID^*, m^*, \mathsf{bsn}^*, \sigma^*, 1/0)$ (or $(ID^*, m^*, \mathsf{bsn}^*, \sigma^* = (*, *, *, *, *, h^*, s^*), *)$ is not in L_s. $\mathcal{S}$ rewinds $\mathcal{A}$ to extract the knowledge of f^*, satisfying $Z^* = [f^*]V$. There are two situations, dependent on whether $\mathsf{bsn} = \perp$ or not:

  1. When $\mathsf{bsn}^* = \perp$, $Z^* = W^*$ and $V^* = S^*$. The value $f^* \notin \mathsf{RogueList}$ (implied in $\mathsf{Verify}(\sigma^*) = 1$). The tuple $(f^*, R^*, S^*, T^*, W^*)$ are a valid blind-4 bilinear LRSW solution.
  2. When $\mathsf{bsn}^* \neq \perp$, $Z^* = [t_0^*]S^* + [t_1^*]K^*$, $t_0^* = H_\alpha(J^*, K^*, S^*, W^*)$, $t_1^* = H_\beta(J^*, K^*, S^*, W^*)$, $J^* = H_3(\mathsf{bsn}^*)$, $\hat{t}(R^*, Y) = \hat{t}(S^*, P_2)$, and $\hat{t}(T^*, P_2) = \hat{t}(R^* + W^*, X)$. Whether the tuple $(f^*, R^*, S^*, T^*, W^*)$ are a valid blind-4 bilinear LRSW solution or not depends on whether the equation $f^* = \log_{V^*} Z^* = \log_{S^*} W^* = \log_{J^*} K^*$ holds or not. The signature σ^* is a signature version of the batch proof and verification scheme described in Subsection 2.2. The security level is addressed using the length of two hash functions $H_\alpha : \mathbb{G}_1^4 \to \{0, 1\}^L$ and $H_\beta : \mathbb{G}_1^4 \to \{0, 1\}^L$. Theorem 1 shows that given t_0 and t_1 are random distribution (which is assumed to be held with the outputs of H_α and H_β), if $\log_{V^*} Z^* \neq \log_{S^*} W^*$ or

$\log_{V^*} Z^* \neq \log_{J^*} K^*$, $\log_V Z = \log_{[t_0]S + [t_1]J}[t_0]W + [t_1]K$ is satisfied with a probability no more than 2^{-L}. Therefore, if the value L is sufficiently large, the tuple $(f^*, R^*, S^*, T^*, W^*)$ are a valid blind-4 bilinear LRSW solution.

- Case 2. Suppose bsn $\neq \perp$. If there is no any entry $(ID, m', \text{bsn}, \sigma', 1/0)$ for the arbitrary pair of m' and σ' is found in L_s, $\mathcal{A}$ has not managed to break user-controlled-traceability. Otherwise, $\mathcal{S}$ runs $\text{Link}(\sigma, \sigma')$. If the output of Link is 1 or $\perp$, again, $\mathcal{A}$ has not managed to break user-controlled-traceability. Otherwise, there exist the following pair of data sets $\sigma^* = (R^*, S^*, T^*, W^*, K^*, h^*, s^*)$ and $\sigma' = (R', S', T', W', K', h', s')$. Both σ^* and σ' are associated with the same bsn and $\mathcal{S}$ has maintained the consistency of the random oracle H_3 outputs, therefore, they have $J^* = J'$. The only thing to make $K^* \neq K'$ happen is that $\mathcal{A}$ has managed to create a different f value for ID^*. Then $\mathcal{S}$ can use the same trick as in Case 1 to extract a right solution of the blind-4 bilinear LRSW problem from $\mathcal{A}$.

In either of the above two cases, $\mathcal{S}$ can solve the blind-4 bilinear LRSW problem with a non-negligible probability if $\mathcal{A}$ wins the game with a non-negligible probability. The theorem follows.

In the second performance, $\mathcal{S}$ performs the following game with $\mathcal{A}$, as defined in Initial Case 2 and Join Case 3 in Section A. In the initial of the game, $\mathcal{S}$ sets the system public parameters par as $(\mathbb{G}_1, \mathbb{G}_2, \mathbb{G}_T, p, \hat{t}, P_1, P_2, H_1, H_2, H_3, H_4, H_5, H_\alpha, H_\beta)$. $\mathcal{S}$ sends $\mathcal{A}$ the values of par and receives $\mathcal{J}$'s public key ipk $= (X, Y) = ([x]P_2, [y]P_2)$ from $\mathcal{A}$. Note that the values x, y, namely isk, are not known to $\mathcal{S}$, although $\mathcal{S}$ does verify that the value X, Y is in the right group $\mathbb{G}_2$.

$\mathcal{S}$ also creates algorithms to respond to queries made by $\mathcal{A}$ during its attack. $\mathcal{S}$ sets three random oracles H_2, H_3 and H_5, maintains consistency between queries made by $\mathcal{A}$, and keeps the lists of L_i (for $i = 2, 3, 5$), L_{jc} and L_s in the same way as in Performance 1. During the game, $\mathcal{A}$ will asks the H_i queries up to q_i times, asks the Join query up to q_j times, asks the Corrupt query up to q_c times, and asks the Sign query up to q_s times. All of the time values are polynomial.

Simulator: $H_2(m)$. The same as in the proof of Theorem 3.

Simulator: $H_3(m)$. If m has already been an entry of the H_3 query, i.e. the item (m, w, h_3) for an arbitrary w and h_3 exists in L_3, return h_3. Else choose v from $\mathbb{Z}_p^*$ uniformly at random; computer $h_3 \leftarrow [v]P_1$; add (m, v, h_3) to L_3 and return h_3.

Simulator: $H_5(m)$. The same as in the proof of Theorem 3.

Simulator: Join(ID). At the beginning of the performance, choose α uniformly at random from $\{1, ..., q_j\}$. We show how to respond to the i-th query made by $\mathcal{A}$ below. Note that we assume $\mathcal{A}$ does not make repeat queries.

- If $i = \alpha$, set $F_\alpha = F^*$ as in the Gap-DLP problem instance; run Join_t with $\mathcal{A}$ to get cre$_\alpha$, and add $\{ID_\alpha, *, F_\alpha, \text{cre}_\alpha, 0\}$ to L_{jc}. Note that since $\mathcal{S}$ does not know the value f_α (which is indicated as $*$ in L_{jc}), it is not able to compute (v, w) by following the Schnorr signature scheme. However $\mathcal{S}$ can forge the signature by controlling the random oracle of H_2 as the same as it did in the proof of Theorem 3. $\mathcal{S}$ verifies the validation of cre_α before accepting it.

– Else choose f uniformly at random from $\mathbb{Z}_p^*$; compute $F \leftarrow [f]P_1$, if $F = F_\alpha$, abort outputting "**abortion 0**"; else run Join_t with $\mathcal{A}$ to get cre; verify cre before accept it and then add $(ID, f, F, \mathsf{cre}, 0)$ into L_{jc}.

Simulator: Corrupt(ID). The same as in Performance 1.

Simulator: Create-bsnKey(ID, J). The same as in Performance 1.

Simulator: Static-DH(ID, J). We assume that $\mathcal{A}$ makes the query Join(ID) (Case 1) before it makes this query; otherwise, $\mathcal{S}$ answers the Join (Case 1) query first. Find the entry $(ID, f, F, ., 0/1)$ in L_{jc} where equation $F = [f]P_1$ holds and compute $K = [f]J$, If $ID = ID_\alpha$, $\mathcal{S}$ queries $\mathcal{O}_{Gap-DLP}(J)$ associated with F_α to obtain K. $\mathcal{S}$ returns K. We assume that $\mathcal{A}$ does not ask a Static-DH query on ID, which has been made for the Join (Case 2) query.

Simulator: Sign(ID, m, bsn). We assume that $\mathcal{A}$ makes the queries Join(ID) before it makes the Sign query using the identity. Otherwise, $\mathcal{S}$ first answers the Join query (as described before for this performance). Find the entry $(ID, f, F, \mathsf{cre}, 0/1)$ in L_{jc}. If $ID \neq ID_\alpha$, compute $\sigma \leftarrow$ Sign; otherwise, $\mathcal{S}$ does not know the value f, and it forges a σ using the same techniques as in the proof of Theorem 3. In the end, $\mathcal{S}$ adds $(ID, m, \mathsf{bsn}, \sigma, 1/0)$ to L_s and responds with σ.

Simulator: Semi-sign(ID, m, V, c). Again, we assume that $\mathcal{A}$ makes the queries Join(ID) before it makes the Semi-sign query using the identity. Otherwise, $\mathcal{S}$ answers the Join query first. Find the entry $(ID, f, F, \mathsf{cre}, 0/1)$ in L_{jc}. If $ID \neq ID_\alpha$, compute (h, s) by following TPM's action in Sign, otherwise, $\mathcal{S}$ does not know the value f, and it forges the triple (h, s) using the same techniques as it forges the signature σ. Add $(ID, m, \mathsf{bsn}, \sigma = (*, *, *, *, *, h, s), 1/0)$ to L_s and respond with (h, s).

At the end of the phase of probing above, $\mathcal{A}$ outputs an identity ID^*, a message m^*, a basename bsn^* and a signature σ^*. If $ID \neq ID_\alpha$, $\mathcal{S}$ aborts outputting "**abortion 1**". Otherwise, we consider the following situation:

If $\mathsf{Verify}(\sigma^*) = 1$ and $(ID^*, m^*, \mathsf{bsn}^*, \sigma^*, 1/0)$ (or $(ID^*, m^*, \mathsf{bsn}^*, \sigma^* = (*, *, *, *, *, h, s), 1/0)$ is not in L_s, $\mathcal{S}$ rewinds $\mathcal{A}$ to extract the knowledge of f^*. $\mathcal{S}$ outputs the value f^* as the Gap-DJP problem solution. This value along with the corresponding cre is a valid solution for the blind-4 bilinear LRSW problem.

By following the same discussion in the proof of Theorem 3, we can show how our simulation could only abort with reasonably small probabilities. **abortion 1** happens only if $ID^* \neq ID_\alpha$. Since ID_α is chosen at random, the probability of this case is at least $1/q_j$.

In either of the above two performances, $\mathcal{S}$ can solve the blind-4 bilinear LRSW problem with a non-negligible probability if $\mathcal{A}$ wins the game with a non-negligible probability. In the second performance, $\mathcal{S}$ can also solve the Gap-DLP problem with a non-negligible probability if $\mathcal{A}$ wins the game with a non-negligible probability. The theorem follows.

□

6   Implementation Consideration

There are multiple choices on implementing the hash functions H_α and H_β. Here are a couple of examples:

1. Use a solo hash function $H : \mathbb{G}4 \to \{0,1\}^{2L}$, and take the first half of the H output as H_α and the last half as H_β.
2. Use a solo hash function $H : \mathbb{G}_4 \to \{0,1\}^L$, and let $H_\alpha(J,K,S,W) = H(J,K,S,W)$ and $H_\beta(J,K,S,W) = H(S,W,J,K)$.
3. Use a solo hash function $H : \mathbb{G}_4 \times \{0,1\} \to \{0,1\}^L$, and let $H_\alpha(J,K,S,W) = H(0,J,K,S,W)$ and $H_\beta(J,K,S,W) = H(1,J,K,S,W)$.

As same as in the Chen'10 DAA scheme, the corrected DAA scheme follows the approach of [30], i.e. splitting the proof of equality of discrete logarithms from the credential verification step, we enable the use of batch pairing verification techniques as proposed in [30]. As surveyed in [34], computing a "product of pairings" is less expensive than computing the pairings independently; the methods improves verification of a blinded Camenisch-Lysyanskaya signature by around 40%.

7   Performance Comparison

In this section, we compare computational efficiency of the proposed DAA scheme with the seven existing DAA schemes, and show the result in Table 1. In the comparison, we do not include the scheme of [26], since it has a number of security problems as addressed in [25, 28]; we do not include the Chen'10 scheme [23] either for the same reason. We also do not include the schemes of [17, 33], since they do not split the signer role between the TPM and Host.

For the computational cost, we consider the Join protocol and the Sign/Verify protocol, with respect to each player. We do not specify the computational cost of the Setup algorithm and its verification, since this is only run once and the resulting parameters are only verified once by each part. We do not specify the cost for the linking algorithm either, as it is closely related to that of the verification algorithm. We also do not specify the cost for the RogueList check in the Join protocol, since it is an optional process. In the table, we let n denote the number of keys in the verifier's rogue secret key list.

For the RSA-DAA scheme, we let $\mathbb{G}_N$ denote the cost of an exponentiation modulo N, and $\mathbb{G}_N^m$ denote the cost of a multi-exponentiation of m values modulo N. Note, that a multi-exponentiation with m exponents can often be performed significantly faster than m separate exponentiations, which is why we separate

Table 1. Computational Cost of the Eight DAA Schemes

In	Protocol	TPM	Host	Issuer	Verifier
BCC [12]	Join	$3G_\rho + 2G_N^3$	$1G_\rho + 1G_N^2 + P_v$	$nG_\rho + 2G_N$ $+1G_N^4+$ $1G_\rho^2 + P_c$	
	Sig/Ver	$3G_\rho + 1G_N^3$	$1G_\rho + 1G_N + 1G_N^2$ $+2G_N^3 + 1G_N^4$		$1G_\rho^2 + 2G_N^4 + 1G_N^6 + nG_\rho$
BCL [14]	Join	$3G_1$	$6P$	$2G_1 + 2G_1^2$	
	Sig/Ver	$3G_T$	$3G_1 + 1G_T + 3P$		$1G_T^2 + 1G_T^3 + 5P + (n+1)G_T$
CMS [28]	Join	$3G_1$	$4P$	$2G_1 + 2G_1^2$	
	Sig/Ver	$2G_1 + 1G_T$	$3G_1 + 1P$		$1G_1^2 + 1G_T^2 + 5P + nG_1$
CF [29]	Join	$3G_1^2 + (2P)$	$(2P)$	$1G_1^2 + 1G_1^3$	
	Sig/Ver	$2G_1 + 1G_T^2$	$1G_1 + 2G_1^2 + 1G_1^3 + 1G_T^3$		$1G_1^2 + 2G_1^3 + 1G_T^5 + 3P + nG_T$
Chen [22]	Join	$2G_1$	$1G_1 + 2P$	$1G_1 + 1G_1^2$	
	Sig/Ver	$2G_1 + 1G_T$	$1G_1 + 1G_T^3$		$1G_1^2 + 1G_2^2 + 1G_T^4 + 1P + nG_1$
CPS [30]	Join	$3G_1$	$1P^4$	$2G_1 + 2G_1^2$	
	Sig/Ver	$3G_1$	$4G_1$		$2G_1^2 + 1P^4 + nG_1$
BL [18]	Join	$2G_1$	$1G_1 + 2P$	$1G_1 + 1G_1^2$	
	Sig/Ver	$3G_1$	$1G_1 + 1G_1^2 + 1G_T + 1P$		$1G_1^2 + 1G_2^2 + 1G_T^4 + 1P + nG_1$
this paper	Join	$2G_1$	$1P^4$	$2G_1^2 + G_1^3$	
	Sig/Ver	$1G_1/2G_1$	$4G_1 + 1G_{1(L)}^2$		$1G_1^2 + 1P^4 + nG_1$

this out. We let G_ρ denote the cost of an exponentiation modulo Γ (recall G_ρ is a subgroup of $\mathbb{F}_\Gamma^*$), and G_ρ^m denote the cost of a multi-exponentiation of m values modulo Γ. In addition we let P_c denote the cost of generating a prime number of the required size and P_v the cost of verifying that a given number of the required size is prime.

For the ECC-DAA schemes, we let G_i $(i = \{1, 2, T\})$ denote the cost of an exponentiation in the group G_i, and G_i^m denote the cost of a multi-exponentiation of m values in the group G_i. We also let P denote the cost of a pairing computation, and let P^m denote the cost of a batch pairing verification of m pairings, as described in Section 6. In additions, we let $G_{i(L)}$ denote the cost of an exponentiation in the group G_i with the size of the exponent being L instead of the size of the group order q. In the signing process of our proposed DAA scheme, if bsn $=\perp$, the TPM computes one scalar multiplication in G_1; if bsn $\neq\perp$, the TPM computes two. We let $1G_1/2G_1$ denote the cost of this computation.

We recall the following two observations made in [22]. In [29], the rogue ragging operation is not defined in the Verify algorithm, but it can be easily added in the same way as every existing DAA scheme does. So in Table 1, we add this computation $n \cdot G_T$. Again in this scheme, the pairing computation in the Join protocol can be done by the Host instead of the TPM, because it is expensive to implement the pairing operation in TPMs. As the same as in [22], we mark this change as $(2P)$ in Table 1.

When a DAA scheme is used in the trusted computing environment, as the original design in [12], the most significant performance is a TPM's computational cost, particularly the TPM's computational cost in the signing algorithm, since obviously the join algorithm is performed only for obtaining the DAA credential, so much less frequently than the signing algorithm is performed. As shown in the table, our proposed DAA scheme has the most efficient computational cost for the TPM in the Sign/Verify protocol. For each signing process, the TPM is only required to compute one exponentiation in $\mathbb{G}_1$ if linkability is not required and two exponentiations in $\mathbb{G}_1$ if linkability is required. But in the other DAA schemes in the table, this cost is at least three exponentiations. Based on this figure, our proposed scheme has the significant advantage compared with all the other DAA schemes in the table. Our scheme requires an extra computational cost of $1\mathbb{G}_{i(L)}^2$ for the Host in the signing process. When L is significantly smaller than $|q|$, which is true in most of applications, this extra cost is reasonably small. On the other hand, the Host has much more resources than the TPM anyway.

We do not discuss the communication and storage cost in details. The contribution made in this paper does not change the communication and storage cost from the original scheme in [30] significantly, except a minor improvement that we remove the value J from the signature, since it can be computed by the verifier from the agreed value of bsn.

8 Conclusions

In this paper, we have presented an attack to the Chen'10 DAA scheme which uses an efficient batch proof and verification protocol to prove discrete log equality between two pairs of group elements. The batch proof protocol in [23] assume that both the prover and verifier agree on the two pairs before the prover performs the batch proof. In the DAA scheme [23], however, the DAA signer does not need to commit the pairs. This leads to our attack. We provided a patch to this broken DAA scheme by proposing a new batch proof and verification protocol. The new batch proof protocol requires two additional hash computations by the prover. We integrated the new batch proof and verification protocol into the DAA scheme and proved our corrected DAA scheme is secure in the random oracle model under the blind-4 bilinear LRSW assumption, the DDH assumption, and the gap-DL assumption. Our new DAA scheme does not increase any computational cost of a TPM from the Chen'10 DAA scheme.

Acknowledgements. The second author would like to thank Colin Boyd and Kun Peng for their invaluable discussion on this work. All the authors would like to thank the anonymous reviewers of INTRUST 2011 for their thoughtful comments.

References

1. Au, M.H., Susilo, W., Mu, Y.: Constant-Size Dynamic k-TAA. In: De Prisco, R., Yung, M. (eds.) SCN 2006. LNCS, vol. 4116, pp. 111–125. Springer, Heidelberg (2006)
2. Abdalla, M., An, J.H., Bellare, M., Namprempre, C.: From Identification to Signatures via the Fiat-Shamir Transform: Minimizing Assumptions for Security and Forward-Security. In: Knudsen, L.R. (ed.) EUROCRYPT 2002. LNCS, vol. 2332, pp. 418–433. Springer, Heidelberg (2002)
3. Backes, M., Maffei, M., Unruh, D.: Zero knowledge in the applied Pi–calculus and automated verification of the direct anonymous attestation protocol. In: IEEE Symposium on Security and Privacy – SSP 2008, pp. 202–215 (2008)
4. Balfe, S., Lakhani, A.D., Paterson, K.G.: Securing peer-to-peer networks using trusted computing. In: Mitchell (ed.) Chapter 10 of Trusted Computing, pp. 271–298. IEEE, London (2005)
5. Bellare, M., Garay, J.A., Rabin, T.: Fast Batch Verification for Modular Exponentiation and Digital Signatures. In: Nyberg, K. (ed.) EUROCRYPT 1998. LNCS, vol. 1403, pp. 236–250. Springer, Heidelberg (1998)
6. Bellare, M., Micciancio, D., Warinschi, B.: Foundations of Group Signatures: Formal Definitions, Simplified Requirements, and a Construction Based on General Assumptions. In: Biham, E. (ed.) EUROCRYPT 2003. LNCS, vol. 2656, pp. 614–629. Springer, Heidelberg (2003)
7. Bellare, M., Rogaway, P.: Random oracles are practical: A paradigm for designing efficient protocols. In: The 1st ACM Conference on Computer and Communications Security, pp. 62–73. ACM Press (1993)
8. Bellare, M., Shi, H., Zhang, C.: Foundations of Group Signatures: The Case of Dynamic Groups. In: Menezes, A. (ed.) CT-RSA 2005. LNCS, vol. 3376, pp. 136–153. Springer, Heidelberg (2005)
9. Bernhard, D., Fuchsbauer, G., Ghadafi, E., Smart, N.P., Warinschi, B.: Anonymous attestation with user-controlled linkability (manuscript)
10. Boneh, D., Boyen, X.: Short Signatures Without Random Oracles. In: Cachin, C., Camenisch, J.L. (eds.) EUROCRYPT 2004. LNCS, vol. 3027, pp. 56–73. Springer, Heidelberg (2004)
11. Boyd, C., Pavlovski, C.: Attacking and Repairing Batch Verification Schemes. In: Okamoto, T. (ed.) ASIACRYPT 2000. LNCS, vol. 1976, pp. 58–71. Springer, Heidelberg (2000)
12. Brickell, E., Camenisch, J., Chen, L.: Direct anonymous attestation. In: The 11th ACM Conference on Computer and Communications Security, pp. 132–145. ACM Press (2004)
13. Brickell, E., Camenisch, J., Chen, L.: Direct anonymous attestation in context. In: Mitchell (ed.) Chapter 5 of Trusted Computing, pp. 143–174. IEEE, London (2005)
14. Brickell, E., Chen, L., Li, J.: Simplified security notions for direct anonymous attestation and a concrete scheme from pairings. Int. Journal of Information Security 8, 315–330 (2009)
15. Brickell, E., Chen, L., Li, J.: A New Direct Anonymous Attestation Scheme from Bilinear Maps. In: Lipp, P., Sadeghi, A.-R., Koch, K.-M. (eds.) Trust 2008. LNCS, vol. 4968, pp. 166–178. Springer, Heidelberg (2008)
16. Brickell, E., Li, J.: Enhanced privacy ID: A direct anonymous attestation scheme with enhanced revocation capabilities. In: The 6th ACM Workshop on Privacy in the Electronic Society – WPES 2007, pp. 21–30. ACM Press (2007)

17. Brickell, E., Li, J.: Enhanced privacy ID from bilinear pairing. Cryptology ePrint Archive. Report 2009/095 (2009), http://eprint.iacr.org/2009/095
18. Brickell, E., Li, J.: A pairing-based DAA scheme furhter reducing TPM resources. In: This proceedings
19. Camenisch, J., Groth, J.: Group Signatures: Better Efficiency and New Theoretical Aspects. In: Blundo, C., Cimato, S. (eds.) SCN 2004. LNCS, vol. 3352, pp. 120–133. Springer, Heidelberg (2005)
20. Camenisch, J., Lysyanskaya, A.: Signature Schemes and Anonymous Credentials from Bilinear Maps. In: Franklin, M. (ed.) CRYPTO 2004. LNCS, vol. 3152, pp. 56–72. Springer, Heidelberg (2004)
21. Canard, S., Traore, J.: List signature schemes and application to electronic voting. Presented in International Workshop on Coding and Cryptography (2003); see also the journal version of this paper by Canard, S., Schoenmakers, B., Stam, M., Traore, J.: List signature schemes. Discrete Applied Mathematics 154(2), 189–201 (2006)
22. Chen, L.: A DAA Scheme Requiring Less TPM Resources. In: Bao, F., Yung, M., Lin, D., Jing, J. (eds.) Inscrypt 2009. LNCS, vol. 6151, pp. 350–365. Springer, Heidelberg (2010); the full paper is in Cryptology ePrint Archive. Report 2010/008, http://eprint.iacr.org/2010/008
23. Chen, L.: A DAA Scheme Using Batch Proof and Verification. In: Acquisti, A., Smith, S.W., Sadeghi, A.-R. (eds.) TRUST 2010. LNCS, vol. 6101, pp. 166–180. Springer, Heidelberg (2010)
24. Chen, L., Cheng, Z., Smart, N.P.: Identity-based key agreement protocols from pairings. Int. Journal of Information Security 6, 213–242 (2007)
25. Chen, L., Li, J.: A note on the Chen-Morrissey-Smart DAA scheme (preprint)
26. Chen, L., Morrissey, P., Smart, N.P.: Pairings in Trusted Computing. In: Galbraith, S.D., Paterson, K.G. (eds.) Pairing 2008. LNCS, vol. 5209, pp. 1–17. Springer, Heidelberg (2008)
27. Chen, L., Morrissey, P., Smart, N.P.: On Proofs of Security for DAA Schemes. In: Baek, J., Bao, F., Chen, K., Lai, X. (eds.) ProvSec 2008. LNCS, vol. 5324, pp. 156–175. Springer, Heidelberg (2008)
28. Chen, L., Morrissey, P., Smart, N.P.: DAA: Fixing the pairing based protocols. Cryptology ePrint Archive. Report 2009/198 (2009), http://eprint.iacr.org/2009/198
29. Chen, X., Feng, D.: Direct anonymous attestation for next generation TPM. Journal of Computers 3(12), 43–50 (2008)
30. Chen, L., Page, D., Smart, N.P.: On the Design and Implementation of an Efficient DAA Scheme. In: Gollmann, D., Lanet, J.-L., Iguchi-Cartigny, J. (eds.) CARDIS 2010. LNCS, vol. 6035, pp. 223–237. Springer, Heidelberg (2010)
31. Fiat, A., Shamir, A.: How to Prove Yourself: Practical Solutions to Identification and Signature Problems. In: Odlyzko, A.M. (ed.) CRYPTO 1986. LNCS, vol. 263, pp. 186–194. Springer, Heidelberg (1987)
32. Galbraith, S., Paterson, K., Smart, N.P.: Pairings for cryptographers. Discrete Applied Mathematics 156, 3113–3121 (2008)
33. Ge, H., Tate, S.R.: A Direct Anonymous Attestation Scheme for Embedded Devices. In: Okamoto, T., Wang, X. (eds.) PKC 2007. LNCS, vol. 4450, pp. 16–30. Springer, Heidelberg (2007)
34. Granger, R., Smart, N.P.: On computing products of pairings. Cryptology ePrint Archive. Report 2006/172 (2006), http://eprint.iacr.org/2006/172

35. Hoshino, F., Abe, M., Kobayashi, T.: Lenient/Strict Batch Verification in Several Groups. In: Davida, G.I., Frankel, Y. (eds.) ISC 2001. LNCS, vol. 2200, pp. 81–94. Springer, Heidelberg (2001)
36. ISO/IEC 11889:2009 Information technology – Security techniques – Trusted Platform Module
37. ISO/IEC 14888-3 Information technology – Security techniques – Digital signatures with appendix – Part 3: Discrete logarithm based mechanisms
38. Leung, A., Chen, L., Mitchell, C.J.: On a Possible Privacy Flaw in Direct Anonymous Attestation (DAA). In: Lipp, P., Sadeghi, A.-R., Koch, K.-M. (eds.) Trust 2008. LNCS, vol. 4968, pp. 179–190. Springer, Heidelberg (2008)
39. Leung, A., Mitchell, C.J.: Ninja: Non Identity Based, Privacy Preserving Authentication for Ubiquitous Environments. In: Krumm, J., Abowd, G.D., Seneviratne, A., Strang, T. (eds.) UbiComp 2007. LNCS, vol. 4717, pp. 73–90. Springer, Heidelberg (2007)
40. Lysyanskaya, A., Rivest, R.L., Sahai, A., Wolf, S.: Pseudonym Systems (Extended Abstract). In: Heys, H.M., Adams, C.M. (eds.) SAC 1999. LNCS, vol. 1758, pp. 184–199. Springer, Heidelberg (2000)
41. Pashalidis, A., Mitchell, C.J.: Single sign-on using TCG-conformant platforms. In: Mitchell (ed.) Chapter 6 of Trusted Computing, pp. 175–193. IEEE, London (2005)
42. Peng, K., Boyd, C., Dawson, E.: Batch zero-knowledge proof and verification and its applications. ACM Trans. Inf. Syst. Secur. 10(2), article 6 (2007)
43. Rudolph, C.: Covert Identity Information in Direct Anonymous Attestation (DAA). In: Venter, H., Eloff, M., Labuschagne, L., Eloff, J., von Solms, R. (eds.) SEC 2007. IFIP, vol. 232, pp. 443–448. Springer, Boston (2007)
44. Schnorr, C.P.: Efficient Identification and Signatures for Smart Cards. In: Brassard, G. (ed.) CRYPTO 1989. LNCS, vol. 435, pp. 239–252. Springer, Heidelberg (1990)
45. Smyth, B., Ryan, M., Chen, L.: Direct Anonymous Attestation (DAA): Ensuring Privacy with Corrupt Administrators. In: Stajano, F., Meadows, C., Capkun, S., Moore, T. (eds.) ESAS 2007. LNCS, vol. 4572, pp. 218–231. Springer, Heidelberg (2007)
46. Trusted Computing Group. TCG TPM specification 1.2. (2003), http://www.trustedcomputinggroup.org

A   Formal Definition and Security Model of DAA

We recall the formal definition of DAA [22], which is a modification of the DAA security model described in [14] by adding the property of non-frameability (as described in [8]) or called exculpability (as described in [1]), i.e., the dishonest issuer and signers together are unable to create a judge-accepted proof that an honest signer produced a certain valid signature σ_0, e.g. it can be linked to some given signature σ_1 signed by the honest signer, unless this honest signer really did produce this signature σ_0.

A DAA scheme involves four types of players: a set of DAA issuers $i_k \in \mathfrak{I}$, TPM $\mathfrak{m}_i \in \mathfrak{M}$, host $\mathfrak{h}_i \in \mathfrak{H}$ and verifier $\mathfrak{v}_j \in \mathfrak{V}$. The index values, k, i, j, are polynomial. $\mathfrak{m}_i$ and $\mathfrak{h}_i$ form a computer platform in the trusted computing environment and share the role of a DAA signer. The following three cases are considered in the security model: (1) neither $\mathfrak{m}_i$ nor $\mathfrak{h}_i$ is corrupted by an adversary, (2) both of them are corrupted, and (3) $\mathfrak{h}_i$ is corrupted but not $\mathfrak{m}_i$. Like in other DAA papers, we do not consider the case that $\mathfrak{m}_i$ is corrupted but not $\mathfrak{h}_i$, because $\mathfrak{m}_i$ plays a principal role of the signer, i.e. holding the private signing key. Throughout the paper, for the purpose of simplicity, we may omit some of the index values if it does not occur any confusion; for example, we make use of i instead of i_k.

A DAA scheme $\mathcal{DAA}$ = (Setup, Join, Sign, Verify, Link) consists of the following five polynomial-time algorithms and protocols:

- Setup: On input of a security parameter 1^t, i uses this randomized algorithm to produce a pair (isk, par), where isk is the issuer's secret key, and par is the global public parameters for the system, including the issuer's public key ipk, a description of a DAA credential space C, a description of a finite message space M and a description of a finite signature space Σ. We will assume that par are publicly known so that we do not need to explicitly provide them as input to other algorithms.
- Join: This protocol, run between a signer ($\mathfrak{m}_i$, $\mathfrak{h}_i$) and an issuer i, consists of two randomized algorithms, namely Join$_t$ and Join$_i$. $\mathfrak{m}_i$ uses Join$_t$ to produce a pair (tsk$_i$, comm$_i$), where tsk$_i$ is the TPM's secret key and comm$_i$ is a commitment of tsk$_i$. On input of comm$_i$ and isk, i uses Join$_i$ to produce cre$_i$, which is a DAA credential associated with tsk$_i$. The value cre$_i$ is given to both $\mathfrak{m}_i$ and $\mathfrak{h}_i$, but the value tsk$_i$ is known to $\mathfrak{m}_i$ only.
- Sign: On input of tsk$_i$, cre$_i$, a basename bsn$_j$ (the name string of $\mathfrak{v}_j$ or a special symbol $\bot$), and a message m that includes the data to be signed and the verifier's nonce n_V for freshness, $\mathfrak{m}_i$ and $\mathfrak{h}_i$ run this protocol to produce a randomized signature σ on m under (tsk$_i$, cre$_i$) associated with bsn$_j$. The basename bsn$_j$ is used for controlling the linkability.
- Verify: On input of m, bsn$_j$, a candidate signature σ for m, and a set of rogue signers' secret keys RogueList, $\mathfrak{v}_j$ uses this deterministic algorithm to return either 1 (accept) or 0 (reject). Note that how to build the set of RogueList is out the scope of the DAA scheme.
- Link: On input of two signatures σ_0 and σ_1, $\mathfrak{v}_j$ uses this deterministic algorithm to return 1 (linked), 0 (unlinked) or $\bot$ (invalid signatures). Link will output $\bot$ if, by using an empty RogueList (which means to ignore the rogue TPM check), either Verify(σ_0) = 0 or Verify(σ_1) = 0 holds. Otherwise, Link will output 1 if signatures can be linked or 0 if the signatures cannot be linked. Note that, unlike Verify, the result of Link is not relied on whether the corresponding tsk $\in$ RogueList or not.

In this security model, a DAA scheme must hold the notions of *correctness*, *user-controlled-anonymity* and *user-controlled-traceability*. They are defined as follows.

Correctness. If both the signer and verifier are honest, that implies tsk$_i$ $\notin$ RogueList, the signatures and their links generated by the signer will be accepted by the verifier with overwhelming probability. This means that the above DAA algorithms must meet the following consistency requirement. If

$(\mathsf{isk}, \mathsf{par}) \leftarrow \mathsf{Setup}(1^t)$,
$(\mathsf{tsk}_i, \mathsf{cre}_i) \leftarrow \mathsf{Join}(\mathsf{isk}, \mathsf{par})$, and
$(m_b, \sigma_b) \leftarrow \mathsf{Sign}(m_b, \mathsf{bsn}_j, \mathsf{tsk}_i, \mathsf{cre}_i, \mathsf{par})|_{b=\{0,1\}}$,
then we must have

$1 \leftarrow \mathsf{Verify}(m_b, \mathsf{bsn}_j, \sigma_b, \mathsf{par}, \mathsf{RogueList})|_{b=\{0,1\}}$ and
$1 \leftarrow \mathsf{Link}(\sigma_0, \sigma_1, \mathsf{par})|_{\mathsf{bsn}_j \neq \perp}$.

User-Controlled-Anonymity. The notion of user-controlled-anonymity is defined via a game played by a challenger $\mathcal{C}$ and an adversary $\mathcal{A}$ as follows:

- *Initial:* $\mathcal{C}$ runs $\mathsf{Setup}(1^t)$ and gives the resulting isk and par to $\mathcal{A}$. Alternatively, $\mathcal{C}$ receives par from $\mathcal{A}$ with a request for initiating the game, and then verifies the validation of the par by checking whether each element of the par is in the right groups or not.
- *Phase 1:* $\mathcal{C}$ is probed by $\mathcal{A}$ who makes the following queries:
  - Sign. $\mathcal{A}$ submits a signer's identity ID, a basename bsn (either $\perp$ or a data string) and a message m of his choice to $\mathcal{C}$, who runs Sign to get a signature σ and responds with σ.
  - Join. $\mathcal{A}$ submits a signer's identity ID of his choice to $\mathcal{C}$, who runs Join_t with $\mathcal{A}$ to create tsk and to obtain cre from $\mathcal{A}$. $\mathcal{C}$ verifies the validation of cre and keeps tsk secret.
  - Corrupt. $\mathcal{A}$ submits a signer's identity ID of his choice to $\mathcal{C}$, who responds with the value tsk of the signer.
- *Challenge:* At the end of Phase 1, $\mathcal{A}$ chooses two signers' identities ID_0 and ID_1, a message m and a basename bsn of his choice to $\mathcal{C}$. $\mathcal{A}$ must not have made any Corrupt query on either ID_0 or ID_1, and not have made the Sign query with the same bsn if bsn $\neq \perp$ with either ID_0 or ID_1. To make the challenge, $\mathcal{C}$ chooses a bit b uniformly at random, signs m associated with bsn under $(\mathsf{tsk}_b, \mathsf{cre}_b)$ to get a signature σ and returns σ to $\mathcal{A}$.
- *Phase 2:* $\mathcal{A}$ continues to probe $\mathcal{C}$ with the same type of queries that it made in Phase 1. Again, it is not allowed to corrupt any signer with the identity either ID_0 or ID_1, and not allowed to make any Sign query with bsn if bsn $\neq \perp$ with either ID_0 or ID_1.
- *Response:* $\mathcal{A}$ returns a bit b'. We say that the adversary wins the game if $b = b'$.

Definition 5. *Let $\mathcal{A}$ denote an adversary that plays the game above. We denote by $\mathbf{Adv}[\mathcal{A}_{\mathcal{DAA}}^{anon}] = |\mathbf{Pr}[b' = b] - 1/2|$ the advantage of $\mathcal{A}$ in breaking the user-controlled-anonymity of $\mathcal{DAA}$. We say that a DAA scheme is user-controlled-anonymous if for any probabilistic polynomial-time adversary $\mathcal{A}$, the quantity $\mathbf{Adv}[\mathcal{A}_{\mathcal{DAA}}^{anon}]$ is negligible.*

Note that a value is *negligible* means this value is a function $\epsilon(t)$, which is said to be *negligible* in the parameter t if $\forall\, c \geq \mathbb{Z}_{>0}\ \exists\, t_c \in \mathbb{R}_{>0}$ such that $\forall\, t > t_c, \epsilon(t) < t^{-c}$.

User-Controlled-Traceability. The notion of User-Controlled-Traceability is defined via a game played by a challenger $\mathcal{C}$ and an adversary $\mathcal{A}$ as follows:

- *Initial:* There are two initial cases. In Initial Case 1. $\mathcal{C}$ executes $\mathsf{Setup}(1^t)$ and gives the resulting par to $\mathcal{A}$, and $\mathcal{C}$ keeps isk secret. In Initial Case 2. $\mathcal{C}$ receives par from $\mathcal{A}$ and does not know the value of isk.
- *Probing:* $\mathcal{C}$ is probed by $\mathcal{A}$ who makes the following queries:
  - Sign. The same as in the game of user-controlled-anonymity.
  - Semi-sign. $\mathcal{A}$ submits a signer's identity ID along with the data transmitted from $\mathfrak{h}_i$ to $\mathfrak{m}_i$ in Sign of his choice to $\mathcal{C}$, who acts as $\mathfrak{m}_i$ in Sign and responds with the data transmitted from $\mathfrak{m}_i$ to $\mathfrak{h}_i$ in Sign.
  - Join. There are three join cases of this query; the first two are used associated with the Initial Case 1, and the last one is used associated with the Initial Case 2. Suppose that $\mathcal{A}$ does not use a single ID for more than one join case or more than one time.
    * Join Case 1: $\mathcal{A}$ submits a signer's identity ID of his choice to $\mathcal{C}$, who runs Join to create tsk and cre for the signer, and finally $\mathcal{C}$ sends cre to $\mathcal{A}$ and keeps tsk secret.
    * Join Case 2: $\mathcal{A}$ submits a signer's identity ID with a tsk value of his choice to $\mathcal{C}$, who runs $\mathsf{Join_i}$ to create cre for the signer and puts the given tsk into the list of RogueList. $\mathcal{C}$ responds $\mathcal{A}$ with cre.
    * Join Case 3: $\mathcal{A}$ submits a signer's identity ID of his choice to $\mathcal{C}$, who runs $\mathsf{Join_t}$ with $\mathcal{A}$ to create tsk and to obtain cre from $\mathcal{A}$. $\mathcal{C}$ verifies the validation of cre and keeps tsk secret.
  - Corrupt. This is the same as in the game of user-controlled-anonymity, except that at the end $\mathcal{C}$ puts the revealed tsk into the list of RogueList.
- *Forge:* $\mathcal{A}$ returns a signer's identity ID, a signature σ, its signed message m and the associated basename bsn. We say that the adversary wins the game if either of the following two situations is true:

  1. With the Initial Case 1 ($\mathcal{A}$ does not have access to isk),
     (a) $\mathsf{Verify}(m, \mathsf{bsn}, \sigma, \mathsf{RogueList}) = 1$ (accepted), but σ is neither a response of the existing Sign queries nor a response of the existing Semi-sign queries (partially); and/or
     (b) In the case of bsn $\neq \perp$, there exists another signature σ' associated with the same identity and bsn, and the output of $\mathsf{Link}(\sigma, \sigma')$ is 0 (unlinked).
  2. With the Initial Case 2 ($\mathcal{A}$ knows isk), the same as the item (a), in the condition that the secret key tsk used to create σ was generated in the Join Case 3 (i.e., $\mathcal{A}$ does not have access to tsk).

Definition 6. *Let $\mathcal{A}$ be an adversary that plays the game above. We denote $\mathbf{Adv}[\mathcal{A}_{\mathcal{DAA}}^{trace}] = \mathbf{Pr}[\mathcal{A}\ wins]$ as the advantage that $\mathcal{A}$ breaks the user-controlled-traceability of $\mathcal{DAA}$. We say that a DAA scheme is user-controlled-traceable if for any probabilistic polynomial-time adversary $\mathcal{A}$, the quantity $\mathbf{Adv}[\mathcal{A}_{\mathcal{DAA}}^{trace}]$ is negligible.*

Note that in the above game of the user-controlled-traceability, we allow the adversary to corrupt the issuer. This is an important difference from the game in [14], since it covers the requirement of non-frameability or called exculpability.

Note also that following this game, if a malicious host without interacting with a valid TPM can make an honest verifier accept a forged DAA signature, the adversary (playing a role of the host) can win the game. This is simulated by using the Semi-sign query.

B   Preliminaries - Pairings and Relevant Hard Problems

Our new DAA scheme is based on asymmetric pairings. As discussed in [26], it will avoid the poor security level scaling problem in symmetric pairings and allow one to implement the DAA scheme efficiently at hight security levels. Throughout we let $\mathbb{G}_1 = \langle P \rangle$, $\mathbb{G}_2 = \langle Q \rangle$ and $\mathbb{G}_T$ be groups of large prime exponent $p \approx 2^t$ for security parameter t. All the three groups will be written multiplicatively. If $\mathbb{G}$ is some group then we use the notation $\mathbb{G}^\times$ to mean the non-identity elements of $\mathbb{G}$.

Definition 7 (Pairing). *A pairing (or bilinear map) is a map $\hat{t} : \mathbb{G}_1 \times \mathbb{G}_2 \to \mathbb{G}_T$ such that:*

1. *The map $\hat{t}$ is bilinear. This means that $\forall P, P' \in \mathbb{G}_1$ and $\forall Q, Q' \in \mathbb{G}_2$ that*
   - $\hat{t}(P \cdot P', Q) = \hat{t}(P, Q) \cdot \hat{t}(P', Q) \in \mathbb{G}_T$.
   - $\hat{t}(P, Q \cdot Q') = \hat{t}(P, Q) \cdot \hat{t}(P, Q') \in \mathbb{G}_T$.
2. *The map $\hat{t}$ is non-degenerate. This means that*
   - $\forall P \in \mathbb{G}_1^\times \exists Q \in \mathbb{G}_2$ *such that* $\hat{t}(P, Q) \neq 1_{\mathbb{G}_T} \in \mathbb{G}_T$.
   - $\forall Q \in \mathbb{G}_2^\times \exists P \in \mathbb{G}_1$ *such that* $\hat{t}(P, Q) \neq 1_{\mathbb{G}_T} \in \mathbb{G}_T$.
3. *The map $\hat{t}$ is computable i.e. there exist some polynomial time algorithm to compute $\hat{t}(P, Q) \in \mathbb{G}_T$ for all $(P, Q) \in \mathbb{G}_1 \times \mathbb{G}_2$.*

Our DAA scheme is based on the pairing based Camenisch-Lysyanskaya signature scheme [20]. This protocol is given by a triple of algorithms, as follows:

- **Key Generation:** The private key is a pair $(x, y) \in \mathbb{Z}_q \times \mathbb{Z}_q$, the public key is given by the pair $(X, Y) \in \mathbb{G}_2 \times \mathbb{G}_2$ where $X = [x]P_2$ and $Y = [y]P_2$.
- **Signing:** On input of a message $m \in \mathbb{Z}_q$ the signer generates $A \in \mathbb{G}_1$ at random and outputs the signature $(A, B, C) \in \mathbb{G}_1 \times \mathbb{G}_1 \times \mathbb{G}_1$, where $B = [y]A$ and $C = [x + m \cdot x \cdot y]A$.
- **Verification:** To verify a signature on a message the verifier checks whether $\hat{t}(A, Y) = \hat{t}(B, P_2)$ and $\hat{t}(A, X) \cdot \hat{t}([m]B, X) = \hat{t}(C, P_2)$.

The security of the above signature scheme is related to the hardness of a problem called the bilinear LRSW assumption [20, 40]. To describe this assumption we first define an oracle $\mathcal{O}_{X,Y}(\cdot)$ which on input $f \in \mathbb{Z}_q$ outputs a triple $(A, [y]A, [x + f \cdot x \cdot y]A)$ where $A \leftarrow \mathbb{G}_1, X = [x]P_2$ and $Y = [y]P_2$. We then have the following definition.

Definition 8 (bilinear LRSW Advantage). *We define the bilinear LRSW advantage of an adversary $\mathcal{A}$ against $(\mathbb{G}_1, \mathbb{G}_2, P_1, P_2, q, \hat{t})$ as*

$\mathbf{Adv}_{\mathcal{A}}^{\text{bLRSW}}(t) :=$

$$\Pr\left[\begin{array}{c} x, y \leftarrow \mathbb{Z}_q; X \leftarrow [x]P_2, Y \leftarrow [y]P_2; (f, A, B, C) \leftarrow \mathcal{A}^{\mathcal{O}_{X,Y}(\cdot)}(\mathbb{G}_1, \mathbb{G}_2, P_1, P_2, X, Y, q, \hat{t}) \\ \wedge \left(f \notin \mathcal{Q},\ f \in \mathbb{Z}_q^\times,\ A \in \mathbb{G}_1,\ B = [y]A,\ C = [x + f \cdot x \cdot y]A \right) \end{array} \right]$$

where $\mathcal{Q}$ is the set of queries that $\mathcal{A}$ made to $\mathcal{O}_{X,Y}(\cdot)$ and $q \approx 2^t$.

We then say that a tuple $(\mathbb{G}_1, \mathbb{G}_2, P_1, P_2, q, \hat{t})$ satisfies the bilinear LRSW assumption if for any p.p.t. adversary $\mathcal{A}$ its advantage $\mathbf{Adv}_{\mathcal{A}}^{\text{bLRSW}}(t)$ is negligible in t.

Definition 9 (Blind Bilinear LRSW Advantage). *We define the blind bilinear LRSW advantage $\mathcal{A}$ against $(\mathbb{G}_1, \mathbb{G}_2, P_1, P_2, q, \hat{t})$ as*

$\mathbf{Adv}_{\mathcal{A}}^{\text{B-bLRSW}}(t) :=$

$$\Pr\left[\begin{array}{c} x, y \leftarrow \mathbb{Z}_q; X \leftarrow [x]P_2, Y \leftarrow [y]P_2; (f, A, B, C) \leftarrow \mathcal{A}^{\mathcal{O}_{X,Y}^B(\cdot)}(\mathbb{G}_1, \mathbb{G}_2, P_1, P_2, X, Y, q, \hat{t}) \\ \wedge \left(F = [f]P_1 \notin \mathcal{Q},\ f \in \mathbb{Z}_q^\times,\ A \in \mathbb{G}_1,\ B = [y]A,\ C = [x + f \cdot x \cdot y]A \right) \end{array} \right]$$

where $\mathcal{Q}$ is the set of queries that $\mathcal{A}$ made to $\mathcal{O}_{X,Y}^B(\cdot)$ and $q \approx 2^t$.

We then say a tuple $(\mathbb{G}_1, \mathbb{G}_2, P_1, P_2, q, \hat{t})$ satisfies the blind bilinear LRSW assumption if for any p.p.t. adversary $\mathcal{A}$ its advantage $\mathbf{Adv}_{\mathcal{A}}^{\text{B-bLRSW}}(t)$ is negligible in t.

DAA Protocol Analysis and Verification[*]

Yu Qin[**], Xiaobo Chu, Dengguo Feng, and Wei Feng

State Key Laboratory of Information Security,
Institute of Software,
Chinese Academy of Science,
Beijing 100080, China
qin_yu@is.iscas.ac.cn

Abstract. Direct Anonymous Attestation (DAA) is a popular trusted computing protocol for the anonymous authentication designed for TPM or other embedding devices. Many DAA schemes give out detailed cryptographic proof, however, their security properties has not been yet automatically analyzed and verified particularly against the intruder's or the malicious participant's attack. It is proposed that a DAA analysis model focusing on the intruder's attacks in this paper. The analysis method is the good supplements to the DAA cryptographic proof, though the intruder's capability is not completely assumed. According to DAA protocol status analysis, we find out some attacks like rudolph attack, masquerading attack by using the Murphi tool. At last the paper gives out the reasons for these attacks, and also presents the recommendation solutions against these attacks. From our study, we propose that DAA protocol must be carefully analyzed from the intruder attacking point of view in the DAA system design and implementation.

Keywords: Trusted Computing, TPM, Direct Anonymous Attestation, Protocol Analysis, Security Verification.

1   Introduction

Trusted Computing is widely application technology in the security PC, notebook, mobile phone, embedded device and other peripherals. TCG composed of many IT enterprises has published a series of TPM specifications to guide the trusted computing industry by now. Trusted Computing aims to enhance system and network security at the level of the computer architecture, which is accepted by the computer industrial and academic institutions. With the rapid development of trusted computing, it is very important that the testing, evaluation and security analysis on the relevant functionality, interface, and protocol for trusted computing. If there is any

[*] This paper is supported by the National Natural Science Foundation of China under Grant No.91118006 and The Knowledge Innovation Project of Chinese Academy of Science (ISCAS2009-DR14).

[**] Corresponding author.

L. Chen, M. Yung, and L. Zhu (Eds.): INTRUST 2011, LNCS 7222, pp. 338–350, 2012.

potential vulnerability unable to reveal, it may cause bad consequence for trusted computing applications.

In the field of analysis and evaluation on trusted computing, some researchers have yet done the studies on trusted computing analysis including TPM commands, authorization protocol, application programming interface (API), and other application protocols. Danilo et al.[1] in Italy have exploited the known attack on OIAP (Object Independent Authorization Protocol) authorization protocol whereby an attacker intercepts a message, replaying the TPM legitimate command, and resulting in the message being processed twice by TPM. Chen et al. [2] in HP Laboratory, UK have studied the offline dictionary attack on TPM OIAP and OSAP (Object Specific Authorization Protocol) protocol, and further give some improvement method against the attack. An attacks with the same authdata be shared among users has been also studied by Chen [3], and they propose a new authorization protocol named SKAP (Session Key Authorization Protocol) for the purpose of substituting the original authorization protocol. The reference [4] has modeled and analyzed the Trusted Platform Module API version 1.2 specification, and it has found out some vulnerabilities that could arise from real TPM insecure implementations on TPM API. Stephanie et al. [5] in France have modeled the TPM commands, formalized the security properties, and have found out some attacks on TPM commands API using the tool ProVerif.

All above studies are analysis on simple TPM protocols or TPM application interfaces. There are only a few researches on Direct Anonymous Attestation (DAA) protocol so far, which only address the DAA formal description using process algebra without considering DAA attacks. Michael Backes et al. [6][7] in Saarland University, Germany have formalized the DAA protocol within the applied pi-calculus using a novel equational theory, and carried out the mechanized analysis for the security properties on secrecy, authentication, privacy . They have also developed a new type-checking tool to conduct the automated analysis for DAA protocol based on zero-knowledge proofs. These works are perfect to formalize proof exactly on DAA's properties. However it is not taken into consideration on some special behaviors of the intruder in the DAA analysis model, for example replaying DAA request, malicious Issuer and so on. In this paper we focus on the protocol status transformation and the intruder's model for analyzing the DAA protocol.

In this paper, we will model and analyze the security properties of the DAA protocol. From the protocol finite-state analysis point of view, we involve using verification tools to check the protocol execution sequences for desired properties. The main research idea is showed in the Figure 1. The current DAA protocol illustrated in the papers and TPM specification are all described in informal form, not suitable for protocol verifying. Throughout the protocol simplification, the formal DAA specification is derived from the informal description. Then we define the protocol participants' behaviors and the intruder's attacking capability, setting up the DAA verification model. At last we use Murphi[8] a common model checking tool to verify the DAA protocol for the desired security properties.

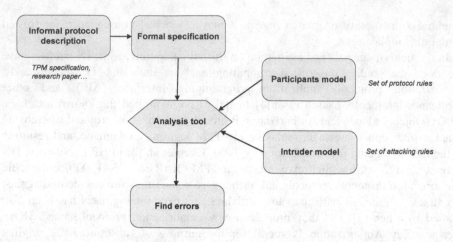

Fig. 1. The analysis flow chart for DAA protocol

2 DAA Protocol Verification

We will make the abstract summary on DAA protocol specification first, set up the finite state model, and then use the Murphi to verify the DAA protocol automatically in this section. Additionally we carefully analyze the causes of the attacks from the verification results; particularly logically reasoning about the masquerading attack.

2.1 Overview of DAA Protocol

Beginning with BCC DAA scheme [9] based on RSA cryptosystem in 2004, There are so many improvements and extensions on the DAA protocol [10][11][12]. The bilinear map on the elliptic curve is employed to build DAA protocol because of its high efficiencies. The representative examples are the first pairing DAA[13], EPID[14]. Although they have different cryptographic primitives, different protocol building method, the consistent protocol specification is derived from these DAA protocols. We take the representative schemes [9][13] fro example to summarize the high level abstract specification.

Table 1. The abstract specification for DAA protocol process

DAA Join	DAA Sign
$1. I \rightarrow P : nc = Enc\{n_I\}_{PK_{EK}}, bsn_I$	$1. V \rightarrow P : n_V, bsn_I$
$2. P \rightarrow M : nc, \varsigma_I = Hm(bsn_I)$	$2. P \rightarrow M : n_V, \varsigma_V = Hm(bsn_V)$
$3. M : n_I = Dec\{nc\}_{SK_{EK}}, comm = commit(f), N_I = \exp(\varsigma_I, f)$	$3. M \rightarrow P : N_V = \exp(\varsigma_V, f), n_t$
$4. M \rightarrow P : comm, N_I, n_t$	$4. P / M \rightarrow V : SPK\{N_V, DAA\_Certificate\}(m, n_V, n_t)$
$5. P / M \rightarrow I : SPK\{comm, N_I\}(n_I, n_t)$	
$6. I \rightarrow P : DAA\_Certificate\{N_I, comm, PK_I\}$	

The participants in DAA protocol include Issuer (I), Platform (P), Verifier (V), TPM (M). The main protocol processes are DAA Join and DAA Sign. The specific process for DAA protocol is introduced as the above table in arrow-and-message form.

The above DAA protocol abstraction is focused on communication messages and core functionality processing. Whatever algorithms and building blocks are used in the DAA protocol, the specification can describe the common DAA protocols as far as we know. The DAA specification is a little concrete in computation abstract, such that it can be simplified later for DAA verification model.

2.2 Modeling DAA Protocol

The cryptographic analysis and proof are beyond our scope, and the security for the protocol process is focused on in this paper. We attempt to model the DAA protocol in finite state machine, and verify the DAA security properties with the automatic verification tools. In order to reduce the difficulty of the protocol verification, some assumptions are considered in the DAA verification model.

(1) The TPM and Host are treated as one participant (the platform P) in DAA protocol analysis. The simple model ignores all the communication and interaction between TPM and Host. This assumption can significantly reduce the finite state size on the platform, and decrease the numbers of interacting messages.

(2) The honest participants behave as the correct protocol runs. The intruder or the malicious participant compromised by the intruder can make some specific attack detection, for example, we suppose that the Issuer maliciously distributes the special public key for conducting rudolph attack[15] in DAA Join.

(3) The algorithm and other cryptographic primitives are secure enough to resistant cryptgraphic forgeablity. The adversary can not forge the DAA signature without the DAA secret f. The adversary can intercept the messages from the network, replay the messages blindly, tamper the message without signature and construct new message with the known secret.

According to the above assumptions, we simplify standard process of the DAA protocol in Table 1, There are three major participants: the Issuer, Platform (each consists of the Host and TPM), and Verifier. The DAA protocol in our model is reduced to 4 messages: DAAJoinReq, DAAJoinRsp, DAASignReq, DAASignRsp (show in Figure 2). The DAA protocol usually has the two phases: Join and Sign/Verify. The goal of the DAA Join is to create the anonymous identity for the platform so it can prove its authenticity to verifiers. The DAA Join is started by the platform. The platform chooses and commits to a secret value f, authenticates it to the Issuer by its Endorsement Key EK (name as DAAJoinReq). The Issuer then certifies a DAA Certificate on the platforms commitment to f and its short-term public key (name as DAAJoinRsp). The platform stores its DAA Certificate internally after DAA Join. The DAA Sign/Verify is started by a verifier challenging with its basename and fresh nonce (name as DAASignReq). During the DAA Sign/Verify, the platform generates a message m and signs it using the DAA Certificate saved in DAA Join (name as DAASignRsp).

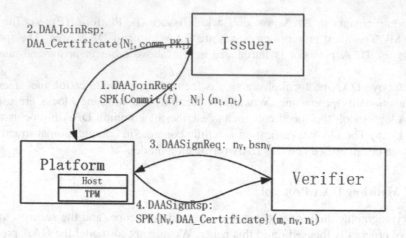

Fig. 2. The simplified message model for DAA protocol

The above simple DAA message model does not consider the interacting messages inside trust computing platform, treating TPM and Host as only one participant. We can formalize the DAA message in pi calculus, and it is oblivious to demonstrate the process behaviors for every participant in details.

$P\_Join \stackrel{\triangle}{=} v\, n1_t.cjoin(x).$

$let\; pk1_{spk} = pair(pair(commit(f), exp(hash(fst(x)), f)), pair(snd(x), n1_t))\; in$

$\overline{cjoin}\langle pair(spk(f, pk1_{spk}), pk1_{spk})\rangle.cjoin(z).\overline{csave}\langle z\rangle$

$P\_Sign \stackrel{\triangle}{=} v\, n2_t.csave(z).cjoin(v).$

$let\; pk2_{spk} = pair(pair(hash(z), exp(hash(fst(v)), f)), pair(snd(v), n2_t))\; in$

$\overline{csign}\langle pair(spk(f, pk2_{spk}), pk2_{spk})\rangle.csign(result)$

$Platform \stackrel{\triangle}{=} v\, f.(P\_Sign \mid P\_Join)$

$Issuer \stackrel{\triangle}{=} v\, n_i.\overline{cjoin}\langle pair(bsn_I, n_i)\rangle.cjoin(y).$

$if\; checkspk(snd(y), fst(y)) = true\; then\; \overline{cjoin}\langle cert(sk_I, commit(f))\rangle$

$Verifier \stackrel{\triangle}{=} v\, n_v.\overline{csign}\langle pair(bsn_V, n_v)\rangle.csign(u).$

$if\; checkspk(snd(u), fst(u)) = true\; then\; \overline{csign}\langle tag\_ok\rangle\; else\; \overline{csign}\langle tag\_failure\rangle$

$DAA \stackrel{\triangle}{=} v\, sk_I.v\, bsn_I.v\, bsn_V(!Issuer \mid !Platform \mid !Verifier)$

We set up the finite state machine model for DAA protocol based on the interacting messages process. The platform has the most states among the DAA protocol participants, and it is critical to check whether the platform state meets the DAA protocol requirements. We define the four finite states for the platform: P_INIT, P_WAIT, P_READY, P_DONE (illustrated in Figure 3). The platform is in P_INIT state after DAA system initializes. When the platform requests the DAA anonymous identity during the DAAJoinReq message, its state transforms to P_WAIT waiting to receive the response message. Then the platform transforms to P_READY after DAAJoinRsp message is received. Because the platform has the nothing changed between DAAJoinRsp and DAASignRsp even though it receives the DAASignReq message, we merge the two time spans into one P_READY state. Finally the platform finishes the DAA protocol arriving at P_DONE state.

Each participant besides the Intrude has its own states, and all states assemble together to form the DAA finite state space (showed in Figure 4). Each item has the four sub-states in the full state space, i.e. (P_WAIT, I_INIT, V_INIT, ADV_INIT). When the events on DAA message or Intruder's action occur, the state item shifts to another. Each state item must meet the DAA protocol's security property φ(Correctness, Anonymity, Unlinkability); Otherwise there is certainly an attacking path found from the transformation trace of the state item. The large state space is not convenient for the automatic verification tool to check the protocol; it must reduce the

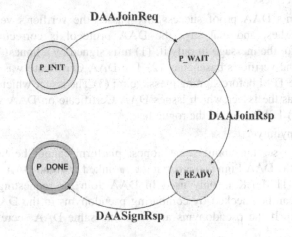

Fig. 3. The finite states of the platform

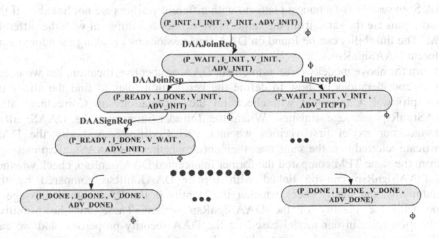

Fig. 4. The state space of the DAA protocol transition

state number by constraining the behaviors of Issuer and Intruder. We assume the Issuer is always honest except the rudolph attack, so the Issuer's states can be ignored in the usual case. The constraint on the attacking capability can also ignore the Intruder's state, and it does not affect the verification on security properties. These methods can reduce the state space size a little, and the verification tools can further reduce it.

The final goal of the DAA protocol is to provide a method for the verifier to ensure the authenticity of the platforms without disclosing their TPM identities. A platform is considered authentic if it embeds an authentic TPM inside the physical platform and has been correctly authenticated and authorized by the Issuer. We formalize three necessary properties in DAA protocol as the protocol verification targets. If the Intruder's actions lead to dissatisfy the security properties, we can find some attack path in the DAA model.

● Correctness

The platform's DAA proof successfully passes the verifier's verification after the protocol finishes, and that says the DAA protocol is correctness. The DAA is correctness for the message m only if: (1) m is signed by a honest TPM using a DAA Certificate and verifier's basename; (2) The DAA Certificate was issued by a honest Issuer for the TPM before signing message m; (3) The issuer which the verifier knows is the same as the issuer which issues DAA Certificate on DAA secret f used in the signature; (4) TPM is not on the rogue list.

● Anonymity

A DAA Sign session about some honest platform cannot be linked with its EK, namely that the DAA Sign session cannot be linked to some DAA Join session before because the TPM EK is only used in DAA Join for requesting DAA certificate. Anonymity can be checked by comparing pseudonyms in the DAASignRsp and the DAAJoinReq. If the pseudonyms are from the same DAA secret f, the anonymity breaks.

● Unlinkability

DAA Sign sessions of a honest platform with different verifiers are not linkable. If the pseudonyms are the same from the same TPM, or they are different with the different TPM, The linkability can be found on DAA sign sessions by checking pseudonyms in different DAASignRsp.

From the above model we can implement DAA protocol verification, but we needs further considerations on how to define the verification rules to find the attack on DAA protocol. Our model will check all the verifications on Correctness after DAASignRsp message finishes. When the Intruder intercepts the DAASignRsp message, our model first verifies whether PKI Certificate Authority the DAA certificate referred to is the same one, then check whether this DAASignRsp message is from the same TPM compared the former intercepted DAASignRsp, check whether the DAASignRsp can be linked with former DAAJoinRsp compared by the pseudonyms, and finally check whether the identity in the DAA signed message is same with the identity of the DAASignRsp sender. These are the primitive verification rules in our model based on the DAA security properties, and we can further improve our model and extend the rules for the higher security in future work.

2.3   Verification Results

We verify DAA protocol by using the Murphi, which is general-purpose model checking tool to analyze the cryptographic and security-related protocols. Murphi is able to find the rudolph attack described in reference [16] in 0.85 seconds, find link attack using issuer basename in 0.11 seconds, find masquerading attack in 0.10 seconds. After fixing these protocol vulnerabilities, Murphi failed to find any additional error in DAA protocol. The detailed number of reachable states and runtime on Lenovo Computer[1] is showed in Table 2 when varying the parameters of DAA model.

Table 2. The verification result using Murphi tool

	Issuer number	Platform number	Verifier number	Size of network	States	Times
Link attack	1	2	2	1	114	0.11s
Rudolph attack	2	2	2	1	19881	0.85s
Masquerading attack	1	2	2	1	404	0.10s
Fix above all	1	2	2	1	291850	9.14s

We find three attacks in DAA protocol by the finite status checking tool: Link attack using issuer basename in DAASignReq, Rudolph attack with malicious issuer using special short-term public key, Masquerading attack with the intruder forwarding the DAA request to a honest platform. From the attacking path of our verification results, we will discuss causes and precondition about these attacks in detail below.

1. Link attack using issuer basename

This attack is quit easy for the malicious verifier. The intruder (or malicious verifier) can know all pseudonyms used by TPM requesting DAA certificate with issuer basename. When requesting DAA sign, the intruder deliberately uses the issuer basename for linking the TPM, and then observes whether the pseudonym in DAASignRsp is equal to someone in DAAJoinReq at intruder's knowledge database. If equal, the attack is successful so that the intruder can link the TPM's identity. The formal attacking trace is summarized as follow:

Platform→Issuer: DAAJoinReq[SPK{Commit(f), N_I}(n_I, n_t)]
Intruder Intercept: DAAJoinReq
Issuer→Platform: DAAJoinRsp[DAA_Certificate{N_I, comm, PK_I}]
Verfier(Intruder) Constructs Message: DAASignReq[n_V, bsn_I]
Platform→Verfier(Intruder): DAASignRsp[SPK{N_V, DAA_Certificate}(m, n_V, n_t)]
Intruder Linked: $N_I = N_V$

2. Rudolph attack

It is usually assumed that the Issuer is honest in the attack on anonymity, but the issuer is compromised by the intruder in Rudolph attack. The malicious issuer can

---

[1] Intel 2.99GHz CPU, 4G Memory, Fedore Core 5 OS.

record the map relationship between Issuer short-term public key and TPM EK, and it can issue the DAA certificate to some TPM by the special short-term public key. When checking the DAASignRsp message, the verifier can collude with the issuer to distinguish this TPM's identity from what kind of short-term public key. The formal attacking trace is summarized as follow:

Platform P→Issuer: DAAJoinReq[SPK{Commit(f), NI}(nI, nt)]
Issuer→P: DAAJoinRsp[DAA_Certificate{NI, comm, PKI}]
Verfier→P: DAASignReq[nV, bsnV]
P→Verfier: DAASignRsp[SPK{NV, DAA_Certificate}(m, nV, nt)]
Intruder Intercept: DAASignRsp
Platform Q→Issuer: DAAJoinReq[SPK{Commit(f*), NI*}(nI*, nt*)]*
Issuer→Q: DAAJoinRsp[DAA_Certificate{NI*, comm*, PKI*}]*
Verfier→Q: DAASignReq[nV*, bsnV*]*
Q→Verfier: DAASignRsp[SPK{NV*, DAA_Certificate}(m*, nV*, nt*)]*
*Intruder Intercept: DAASignRsp**
Intruder Linked with help of Issuer: PKI in DAASignRsp ?= PKI in DAASignRsp**

3. Masquerading attack

Although DAA anonymity prevents exposure of the TPM identity, this results in cheating the verifier by another TPM anonymous identity. The verifier cannot tell that whether the attestation from the platform is the one directly interacting with it. It maybe forward the request to challenge another platform for DAA attestation (cf. Figure 5). Because the Murphi verification program can identity the source platform and message signing platform, the masquerading attack can been easily found out in our model. We omit formal attacking trace here which can be derived from the figure quickly.

Fig. 5. The diagram of masquerading attacking

2.4   Logic Analysis on Masquerading Attack

Owing to the anonymity of DAA, the malicious platform can easily masquerade a honest platform's identity for DAA. To analyze the masquerading attack more formally, we model the DAA procedure using predicate logic. Firstly, the initial state of DAA system particularly the participant's trust condition is defined as the following assumption. The assumptions 1,2,4,5 describe each participant's security or trust state in DAA system. The assumption 3 represents the DAA attestation action of honest platform P, and the assumption 6 defines the masquerading attack capability of malicious platform.

```
Assumptions:
1.TrustedVerifier(V)        V is default trust in DAA system.
2.PhysSecure(TPM)      TPM is physically secure in DAA attestation.
3.DAAPrv(TPM, P)      TPM attests the anonymous identity of the
platform P with DAA proof.
4.Honest(P)            The platform P is honest.
5.•Honest(Q)           The platform Q is not honest.
6.Masquerade(Q, P)    The platform Q forwards the DAA request to
the platform P for masquerading identity of P.
```

```
Predicates:
TrustedVerifier(v)    The verifier v is trust in DAA attestation
system
PhysSecure(t)          TPM t is physically secure
SaysTrust(v, t)       The verifier v asserts the TPM t is trust in
DAA attestation.
DAAPrv(t, p)          TPM t attests the anonymous identity of the
platform p.
ProvOn(t, p)          TPM t indicates it is installed on the
platform p with DAA attestation.
Honest(p)              The platform p is honest in DAA system.
ProvTrust(v, t)        The verifier v trusts TPM t after
attestation proof.
Masquerade(q, p)      The platform q forwards the DAA request to
the platform p and masquerades p for anonymous attestation.
```

Secondly we configure our assumptions about the concrete setting in a set of predicates (shown as above). The trust relationship and security condition are summarized in these predicates about the platform, verifier and TPM.

Thirdly the following axiom table summarizes our analysis rules for proving anonymous trust using TPM in DAA system. The first axiom illustrates the default trust that the verifier believes the TPM and its attestation in DAA system. The second axiom implies that TPM is physically resided on the platform from the DAA proof. The axiom 2 and 5 illustrate whether the DAA proof really shows the verifier's trust to TPM. The axiom 4 shows the logic description for masquerading attack.

```
Axiom:
1.  ∀v, t  TrustedVerifier(v) ∧ PhysSecure(t) → SaysTrust(v, t)
2.  ∀p, t  DAAPrv(t, p) → PrvOn(t, p)
3.  ∀p, v, t  PrvOn(t, p) ∧ Honest(p) → PrvTrust(v, t)
4.  ∀p, q, t DAAPrv(t, p) ∧ Masquerade(q, p) → DAAPrv(t, q)
5.  ∀p, v, t  PrvOn(t, p) ∧ ¬Honest(p) → ¬PrvTrust(v, t)
```

Finally, we can reason about the trustworthiness of the DAA participants by applying the set of axioms to the initial assumptions. Unfortunately, as shown in the following logic calculus, the reasoning leads to a logical contradiction, namely that the malicious platform Q proves the DAA identity to the verifier by pretending P's anonymous identity. This contradiction captures the essence of the masquerading attack, because it shows that the verifier cannot decide whether it should trust the platform Q.

Proof:

(1) TrustedVerifier(V)	Assumption 1
(2) PhysSecure(TPM)	Assumption 2
(3) SaysTrust(V, TPM)	Axiom 1: (1), (2)
(4) DAAPrv(TPM, P)	Assumption 3
(5) PrvOn(TPM, P)	Axiom 2: (4)
(6) Honest(P)	Assumption 4
(7) PrvTrust(V, TPM)	Axiom 3: (5), (6)
(8) Masquerade(Q, P)	Assumption 6
(9) DAAPrv(TPM, Q)	Axiom 4: (5), (6)
(10) PrvOn(TPM, Q)	Axiom 2: (9)
(11) ¬Honest(Q)	Assumption 5
(12) ¬PrvTrust(V, TPM)	Axiom 5: (10), (11)
(13) ⊥	(7), (12)

3   Solution

In this section, we will give the solutions respectively to ensure the anonymity, unlinkability. Aiming at the masquerading attack detected by the verification tool, we will analyze ways to prevent from cheating the verifier by forwarding request to another honest platform.

1) Solution to prevent link attack using issuer basename

It is very easy to avoid link attack using issuer basename. It results in the attack on the linkability that the platform's negligence of the verifier's basename checking. The platform will find this attack from the malicious verifier by the simple comparison of basename. If the verifier request with the issuer basename in DAA Sign request message, the platform can reject that directly.

2) Solution to prevent Rudolph attack

The Rudolph attack by the malicious issuer not only links the large number of the platforms, but also links small set of the platforms. It is a worse attack that there is no way for a platform to tell if the covert identity information is embedded into the short-term public key used to generate its DAA Certificate. The reference [16] gives out some solutions to overcome the problem. One is modification on the TCG DAA specification, and DAA issuer's public key numbers of uses are directly certified by a trust certificate authority (CA) ; Second is using n Trust Auditor to ensure that the Issuer's public key has being used more than a certain number of times; Third is that two or more platform could collaborate to compare the public key value that they have obtained from a particular Issuer, and prevent some platform is identified as the one with the DAA certificate issued by the special public key. This is an autonomic way with the self detection for the platform. Among all of the solutions, we recommend the trust auditor solution, because the trust third party is introduced in the DAA system to audit the Issuer's malicious behavior. It is an efficient solution to prevent the Rudolph attack without any modification on TCG DAA specification.

3) Solution to prevent masquerading attack

The platform's anonymity in DAA attestation leads to the masquerading attack by the intruder. The obvious way is to establish a mutually authenticated channel using other's authenticator such as username and password. But it is not perfect that the username authenticator breaks some anonymity to certain extent. We recommend Diffe-Hellman key exchange at the DAA Sign phase, and this prevents the intruder from cheating the verifier using masquerading attack. The Verifier can use the session key with key exchange to verify whether the interacting party is the DAA attestation participant. To protect DAA protocol against masquerading attacks, we enhance it with a key agreement. The enhanced DAA protocol is described as follow:

> Platform $P \rightarrow$ Issuer: DAAJoinReq[SPK{Commit(f), N_I}(n_I, n_t)]
> Issuer$\rightarrow$P: DAAJoinRsp[DAA_Certificate{N_I, comm, PK_I}]
> Verifier: GenrateKey(K^V, v), $K^V = g^v$ is public key, v is private key
> Verfier$\rightarrow$P: DAASignReq[n_V, bsn_V, K^V]
> P: GenrateKey(K^P, p), Compute $K = K^{PV} = g^{pv}$
> P$\rightarrow$Verfier: DAASignRsp[SPK{NV, DAA_Certificate}(m,   nV,   nt,   KP),
> c=EncK{nI}]
> Verifier: Verify SPK{NV, DAA_Certificate}(m, nV, nt, KP)
> Compute $K = K^{PV} = g^{pv}$, Verify DecK{c}

In the enhanced DAA protocol, the key agreement must be completed inside TPM chip with DAA_Sign interface, particularly the GenrateKey(KP, p) must run inside TPM. The TPM must bind the signature of knowledge proof and key agreement together, or the malicious software can bypass DAA attestation using the middle-man attack. The key agreement binds the TPM's DAA attestation with interacting participant's platform, otherwise the interaction between verifier and platform certainly fails in the verification on key agreement.

4   Conclusion

We set up the DAA finite state machine model to analyze its security properties in this paper. Firstly the paper summarizes the DAA protocol profile for DAA analysis and verification. Then we formalize the DAA analysis and verification model which is focused on the attacker's behaviors. In order to reduce verification complexity, our model simplifies the messages which have nothing to do with security. According to our model, we use Murphi tool to verify the DAA protocol, and find out some known attacks automatically on DAA. And the recommendation solutions are given out finally in this paper. From our study results, the DAA protocol has some potential security problems except the security strength on the cryptographic algorithm and cryptographic build blocks. These attacks must be carefully prevented in the DAA system design and implementation. In the future work, we will consider the inside messages between TPM and host, set up more complex model close to the real DAA system, and analyze internal attack in the platform especially the attack by the compromised host.

Acknowledgement. This paper is supported by the National Natural Science Foundation of China under Grant No.91118006 and The Knowledge Innovation Project of Chinese Academy of Science (ISCAS2009-DR14).

References

1. Bruschi, D., Cavallaro, L., Lanzi, A., Monga, M.: Replay attack in TCG specification and solution. In: Proceeding of 21st Annual Computer Security Applications Conference (ACSAC 2005), pp. 127–137. IEEE Computer Society (2005)
2. Chen, L., Ryan, M.D.: Offline dictionary attack on TCG TPM weak authorisation data, and solution. In: Future of Trust in Computing. Vieweg & Teubner (2008)
3. Chen, L., Ryan, M.: Attack, Solution and Verification for Shared Authorisation Data in TCG TPM. In: Degano, P., Guttman, J.D. (eds.) FAST 2009. LNCS, vol. 5983, pp. 201–216. Springer, Heidelberg (2010)
4. Amerson, H.L.: Automated Analysis of Security APIs. Massachusetts Institute of Technology, USA (2005)
5. Delaune, S., Kremer, S., Ryan, M.D., Steel, G.: A Formal Analysis of Authentication in the TPM. In: Degano, P., Etalle, S., Guttman, J. (eds.) FAST 2010. LNCS, vol. 6561, pp. 111–125. Springer, Heidelberg (2011)
6. Backes, M., Maffei, M., Unruh, D.: Zero-Knowledge in the Applied Pi-calculus and Automated Verification of the Direct Anonymous Attestation Protocol. In: Proceedings of the 2008 IEEE Symposium on Security and Privacy (SP 2008), pp. 202–215. IEEE Computer Society, Washington, DC (2008)
7. Backes, M., Hriţcu, C., Maffei, M.: Type-checking zero-knowledge. In: Proceedings of the 15th ACM Conference on Computer and Communications Security (CCS 2008), pp. 357–370. ACM, New York (2008)
8. Murphi, http://verify.stanford.edu/dill/murphi.html
9. Brickell, E., Camenisch, J., Chen, L.: Direct anonymous attestation. In: Proceedings of the 11th ACM Conference on Computer and Communications Security, pp. 132–145 (2004)
10. Brickell, E., Li, J.: Enhanced privacy id: a direct anonymous attestation scheme with enhanced revocation capabilities. In: Proceedings of the 2007 ACM Workshop on Privacy in the Electronic Society (WPES 2007), pp. 21–30 (2007)
11. Ge, H., Tate, S.R.: A Direct Anonymous Attestation Scheme for Embedded Devices. In: Okamoto, T., Wang, X. (eds.) PKC 2007. LNCS, vol. 4450, pp. 16–30. Springer, Heidelberg (2007)
12. Feng, D., Xu, J., Chen, X.: A Forward Secure Direct Anonymous Attestation Scheme. In: WSEAS ACC 2009 (2009)
13. Brickell, E., Chen, L., Li, J.: A New Direct Anonymous Attestation Scheme from Bilinear Maps. In: Lipp, P., Sadeghi, A.-R., Koch, K.-M. (eds.) Trust 2008. LNCS, vol. 4968, pp. 166–178. Springer, Heidelberg (2008)
14. Brickell E., Li, J.: Enhanced Privacy ID from Bilinear Pairing. Cryptology ePrint Archive, Report 2009/095 (2009), http://eprint.iacr.org/2009/095.pdf
15. Rudolph, C.: Covert Identity Information in Direct Anonymous Attestation (DAA). In: Venter, H., Eloff, M., Labuschagne, L., Eloff, J., von Solms, R. (eds.) SEC 2007. IFIP, vol. 232, pp. 443–448. Springer, Boston (2007)
16. Leung, A., Chen, L., Mitchell, C.J.: On a Possible Privacy Flaw in Direct Anonymous Attestation (DAA). In: Lipp, P., Sadeghi, A.-R., Koch, K.-M. (eds.) Trust 2008. LNCS, vol. 4968, pp. 179–190. Springer, Heidelberg (2008)

Author Index